P9-APY-453

Mary Ellen Guffey's

ESSENTIALS OF
BUSINESS
COMMUNICATION

7 EDITION

MARY ELLEN GUFFEY
Professor of Business Emerita
Los Angeles Pierce College

•

CAROLYN M. SEEFER, Contributing Editor
Professor of Business, Diablo Valley College

THOMSON
™
SOUTH-WESTERN

Australia · Brazil · Canada · Mexico · Singapore · Spain · United Kingdom · United States

THOMSON

SOUTH-WESTERN

Essentials of Business Communication, Seventh Edition
Mary Ellen Guffey

VP/Editorial Director:
Jack W. Calhoun

Sr. Publisher/Director of Development:
Melissa Acuña

Acquisitions Editor:
Erin Joyner

Developmental Editor:
Mary Draper

Sr. Marketing Manager:
Larry Qualls

Sr. Production Project Manager:
Deanna Quinn

Sr. Media Technology Editor:
Vicky True

Technology Project Editor:
Kelly Reid

Web Coordinator:
Scott Cook

Manufacturing Coordinator:
Diane Lohman

Production House:
GGS Book Services

Printer:
Quebecor World
Dubuque, IA

Sr. Marketing Communications Manager:
Shemika Britt

Art Director:
Stacy Shirley

Internal Designer:
Ann Small, a small design studio

Cover Designer:
Ann Small, a small design studio

Cover Images:
© Getty Images

Photography Manager:
John Hill

Photo Researcher:
Rose Alcorn

COPYRIGHT © 2007
Thomson South-Western, a part of The Thomson Corporation. Thomson, the Star logo, and South-Western are trademarks used herein under license.

Printed in the United States of America
1 2 3 4 5 09 08 07 06

Student Edition: ISBN 0-324-31392-6

ALL RIGHTS RESERVED.
No part of this work covered by the copyright hereon may be reproduced or used in any form or by any means—graphic, electronic, or mechanical, including photocopying, recording, taping, Web distribution or information storage and retrieval systems, or in any other manner—without the written permission of the publisher.

For permission to use material from this text or product, submit a request online at http://www.thomsonrights.com.

Library of Congress Control Number:
2005931270

For more information about our products, contact us at:

Thomson Learning Academic Resource Center

1-800-423-0563

Thomson Higher Education
5191 Natorp Boulevard
Mason, OH 45040

USA

Dr. Mary Ellen Guffey
Thomson South-Western

Dear Business Communication Students:

As we release the Seventh Edition of **Essentials of Business Communication,** I must confess that this is the best edition yet! **Essentials** continues to provide a cost-effective three-in-one learning package: (1) authoritative textbook, (2) practical workbook, and (3) self-teaching grammar/mechanics handbook.

I'm particularly excited about this edition because it brings you valuable workplace information. Let me describe a few of this edition's unparalleled features:

► **Increased Emphasis on Professionalism.** Content in every chapter helps you develop oral, written, and nonverbal skills that make you sound and look credible as well as promotable.

► **Enhanced Coverage of Communication Technologies.** The Seventh Edition demonstrates how the world of work is being changed by IP telephony, company intranets, wireless networks, Wi-Fi, voice recognition, videoconferencing, presence technology, and many other advances.

► **Strengthened Grammar/Mechanics Review Materials.** New Grammar/Mechanics Checkups in the textbook, as well as new digital Advanced Grammar/Mechanics Checkups and "Your Personal Language Trainer," help you revive rusty skills. No other textbook provides a better grammar/mechanics review program using both digital and print to build confidence and skills.

► **New Writing Coach Feature.** A step-by-step demonstration of the composition of e-mails, memos, and letters shows you how to compose and revise messages.

► **Expanded Coverage of Résumés.** New model documents emphasize a summary of qualifications and new cover letters. You also learn how to optimize your résumé for today's technologies.

Essentials provides even more support materials so that you leave this course confident and fully prepared with marketable skills. As one of the most accessible and responsive authors in the field, I am eager to learn whether you agree that this is the best edition yet!

Cordially,

Mary Ellen Guffey

Get Prepared. . .

Mary Ellen Guffey's **Essentials of Business Communication** has helped countless students prepare for success in today's technology-driven workplace. The Seventh Edition of this award-winning text contains the instruction you need for business communication success, with practice opportunities in every chapter to help you hone your skills.

Improve Your Writing and Grammar Skills...

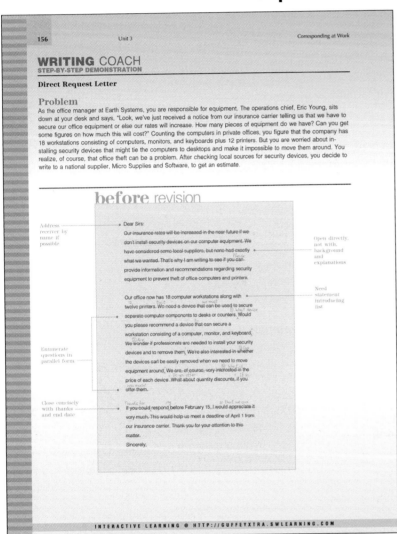

Guffey's textbook/workbook/handbook format teaches writing skills while reviewing and reinforcing your basic grammar and mechanics skills.

Writing Plans and Writing Improvement Exercises
Clear step-by-step writing plans structure the assignments so that novice writers can get started quickly and stay focused on the writing experience – without struggling to provide unknown details to unfamiliar, hypothetical cases.

◀ Writing Coach
This new step-by-step demonstration of the writing process shows you how to write and revise e-mails, memos, and letters using a brief case, writing instructions, and before-and-after documents.

◀ Emphasis on Grammar and Mechanics
Throughout the text, you will be encouraged to build on your basic grammar skills. Grammar/Mechanics Checkups, Grammar/Mechanics Challenges, and chapter discussions keep you in practice. Plus...**Your Personal Language Trainer,** a self-teaching grammar/mechanics review included in Guffey Xtra!, helps to further enhance language skills.

…with Time-tested Learning Tools

▶ **Model Documents**
Before-and-after sample documents and descriptive callouts are a road map to the writing process, demonstrating for you the effective use of the skills being taught, as well as the significance of the revision process in writing.

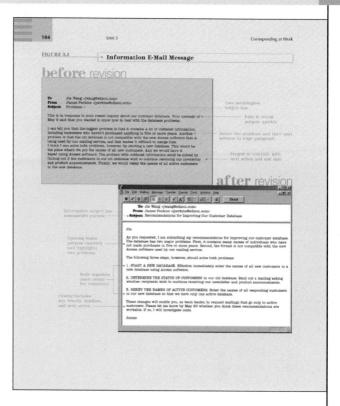

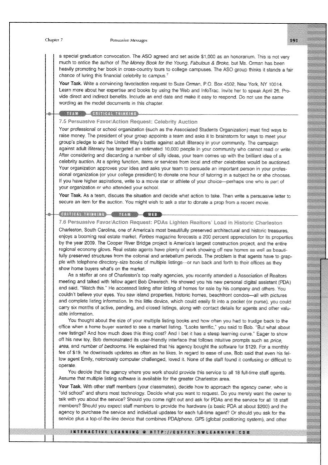

◀ **End-of-Chapter**
Concepts are translated into action, as you try out your skills in activities designed to mirror "real-world" experiences.

▶ **Communication Workshops**
Communication workshops develop critical thinking skills and provide insight into special business communication topics such as ethics, technology, career skills, and collaboration.

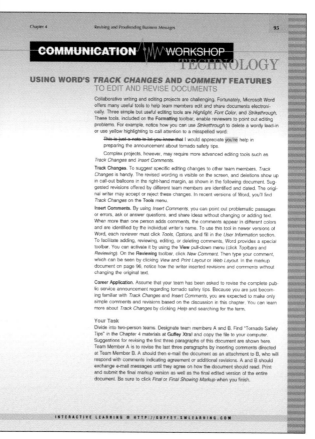

Videoconferencing, résumé scanning, IP telephony (VoIP), e-mail strategies, Web researching, and blogging... they're all covered here. *Essentials of Business Communication* explores how technology has changed the world of work. Discussions of these technologies are integrated into relevant chapters and become part of end-of-chapter activities so you can hit the ground running when you enter today's digital workplace. Technology discussions encompass the latest information on:

► Voice, Web, and videoconferencing
► Electronic presentations
► Instant messaging and other wireless technologies
► E-mail techniques, etiquette, risks, and tips
► Electronic networking, job boards, and job-searching advice

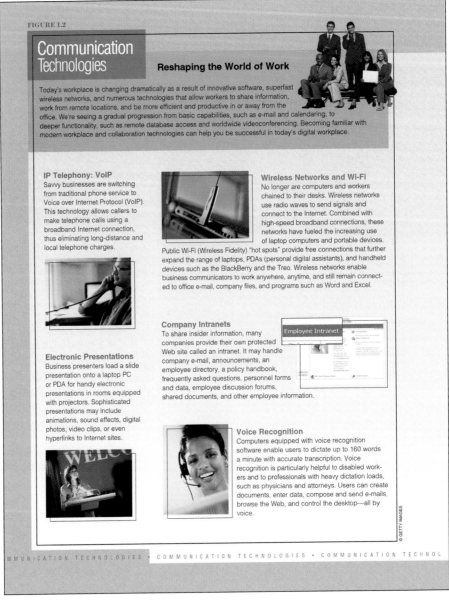

See this two-page figure in Chapter 1.

"Guffey seems to have her hands on the pulse of not only what is currently needed by students and instructors, but is looking toward what might be needed in the future. I think this is what has always made her textbooks seem more current than some of the other texts out there."

**Sheryl E. C. Joshua,
University of North Carolina, Greensboro**

Real Advice for Succeeding in the Job Market

You will use these skills in the real world. *Essentials of Business Communication* offers practical advice and models that you can understand and adapt to your needs. More emphasis is placed on job-search technology and résumé preparation, including a discussion of online job boards and the reality that few candidates actually find jobs online.

Inside you'll find:

► **Résumés in three forms:** traditional print-based résumés, scannable résumés, and embedded résumés for today's technologies.

► **New "Summary of Qualifications" for a résumé** immediately reveals a candidate's fit for a position.

► **E-portfolios and digitized materials** provide a snapshot of a candidate's performance, talents, and accomplishments.

► **Social online networking with specific Web sites to visit** to aid in networking and the job search.

► **Updated section about hiring and placement interviews** with discussion of group interviews and panel, sequential, and stress interviews.

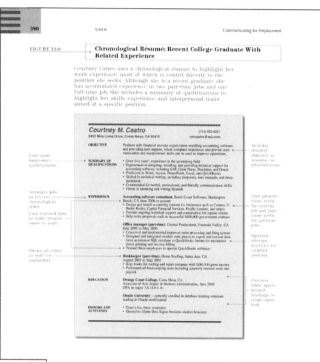

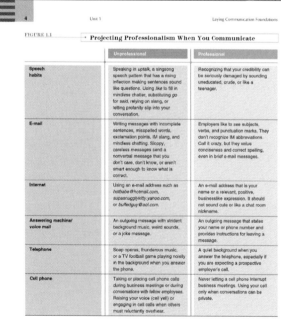

Guffey demonstrates how significant professionalism is to overall business communication endeavors. Coverage of professional workplace behavior has been enhanced in this edition with cues on how to act in business social situations. In this edition:

► **Etiquette tips for leaders and participants** to help them act appropriately and professionally in meetings.

► **Telephone etiquette tips** including how to handle calls professionally, courteously, and effectively.

► **Enhanced coverage of the importance of professionalism** when giving oral presentations, with added information about dressing professionally.

► **A section on creating professional visual aids** that add value to a presentation so that you will learn how to highlight main ideas, ensure visibility, enhance comprehension, and exemplify professionalism when designing and using visual aids.

Technology Tools That Inform, Educate, and Entertain

The book is just the beginning. Make the grade and improve your tech knowledge with Guffey's online resources and technology support.

Guffey Xtra!

Guffey Xtra! is an online study assistant that includes the following features:

▶ *Your Personal Language Trainer* is a cutting-edge self-teaching online tool that enables you to review an entire business English course, including grammar, punctuation, capitalization, and number style. Instead of using valuable class time to teach grammar, instructors can rely on Dr. Guffey to act as a personal trainer in helping students pump up their language muscles. *Your Personal Language Trainer* provides hundreds of sentence reinforcement exercises with immediate feedback and explanations for the best comprehension and retention.

▶ Student version PowerPoint slides
▶ Bonus chapters
▶ Speak Right! and Spell Right! practice activities
▶ Sentence Competency exercises
▶ Grammar/Mechanics Challenge exercises
▶ Advanced Grammar/Mechanics Challenge exercises
▶ Business Report topics

Companion Web Site
http://guffey.swlearning.com

▶ **Chapter Review Quizzes** reinforce chapter concepts, testing your knowledge and preparing you for exams.
▶ **Flash Cards and Key Terms** build vocabulary skills while reviewing text material.
▶ **Business Etiquette Guide** teaches basic business etiquette and workplace manners.
▶ **Listening Quiz** pinpoints listening strengths and weaknesses in interactive exercises.
▶ **APA and MLA Citation Formats** help you correctly cite business references.
▶ **Writing Help** links to the best college and university online writing labs.

InfoTrac® College Edition
With InfoTrac College Edition, you can receive complete, 24-hour-a-day access to over 18 million full-text articles from thousands of journals, popular periodicals, and newspapers such as *Newsweek, Time, The New York Times,* and *USA Today.*

Note: Access to *Guffey Xtra!* and *InfoTrac® College Edition* may come packaged with your new text if your instructor has ordered it. If not, you may purchase these online resources through 1Pass access at http://www.thomsonedu.com.

"This book is great! It will be going to work with me as a reference book. The interactive quizzes are wonderful. What a great way to review for tests! My instructor recommended your site, and I'm very glad she did."

Deanna Jokinen, student,
Dakota County Technical College

Brief Contents

Contents

UNIT 3
CORRESPONDING AT WORK 97

UNIT 4
REPORTING WORKPLACE DATA 237

UNIT 5
DEVELOPING SPEAKING AND TECHNOLOGY SKILLS 315

UNIT 6
COMMUNICATING FOR EMPLOYMENT 375

About the Author

A dedicated professional, Mary Ellen Guffey has taught business communication and business English topics for over thirty years. She received a bachelor's degree, *summa cum laude*, from Bowling Green State University; a master's degree from the University of Illinois, and a doctorate in business and economic education from the University of California, Los Angeles (UCLA). She has taught at the University of Illinois, Santa Monica College, and Los Angeles Pierce College.

Now recognized as the world's leading business communication author, Dr. Guffey corresponds with instructors around the globe who are using her books. She is the author of the award-winning *Business Communication: Process and Product*, the leading business communication textbook in this country and abroad. She has also written *Business English*, which serves more students than any other book in its field; *Essentials of College English*, (with Carolyn M. Seefer), and *Essentials of Business Communication*, the leading text/workbook in its market. *Essentials of Business Communication* recently received an award of excellence from the Text and Academic Authors Association. The Canadian editions of her books are bestsellers in that country; one was named Book of the Year by Nelson Canada.

Dr. Guffey is active professionally, serving on the review board of the *Business Communication Quarterly* of the Association for Business Communication, participating in all national meetings, and sponsoring business communication awards.

A teacher's teacher and leader in the field, Dr. Guffey acts as a partner and mentor to hundreds of business communication instructors nationally and internationally. Her workshops, seminars, teleconferences, newsletters, articles, teaching materials, and Web sites help novice and veteran business communication instructors achieve effective results in their courses. She maintains comprehensive Web sites for students and instructors. Her print and online newsletters are used by thousands of instructors in this country and around the world.

UNIT **1**

LAYING COMMUNICATION FOUNDATIONS

PHOTOS: © ROYALTY-FREE/CORBIS; © ROYALTY-FREE/CORBIS; © ROYALTY-FREE/CORBIS

CHAPTER 1

Building Your Career Success
With Communication Skills

BUILDING YOUR CAREER SUCCESS WITH COMMUNICATION SKILLS

> *If I went back to college again, I'd concentrate on two areas: learning to write and to speak before an audience. Nothing in life is more important than the ability to communicate effectively.*
>
> **Gerald R. Ford**, 38th President of the United States

OBJECTIVES

- Understand the importance of becoming an effective and professional communicator in today's changing workplace.
- Examine the process of communication.
- Discuss how to become an effective listener.
- Analyze nonverbal communication and explain techniques for improving nonverbal communication skills.
- Explain how culture affects communication, and describe methods for improving cross-cultural communication.
- Identify specific techniques that improve effective communication among diverse workplace audiences.

PHOTOS: © ROYALTY-FREE/CORBIS; © ROYALTY-FREE/CORBIS; © ROYALTY-FREE/CORBIS

THE IMPORTANCE OF COMMUNICATION SKILLS TO YOUR CAREER

Three decades ago when he was president, Gerald Ford spoke about the importance of communication skills. If he had a second chance at college, he said, he'd concentrate on learning to write and learning to speak. Today, communication is even more important and more challenging than in President Ford's time. We live in an information age that revolves around communication.

Communication skills are critical to your job placement, performance, career advancement, and organizational success.

Developing excellent communication skills is extremely important to your future career. Surveys of employers often show that communication skills are critical to effective job placement, performance, career advancement, and organizational success.[1] In making hiring decisions, employers often rank communication skills among the most requested competencies. Many job advertisements specifically ask for excellent oral and written communication skills. In a poll of recruiters, oral and written communication skills were by a large margin the top skill set sought in applicants.[2] Another survey of managers and executives ranked the skills most lacking in job candidates, and writing skills topped that list.[3]

© PHOTODISC COLLECTION/GETTY IMAGES

Communication skills consistently rank near the top of competencies sought by recruiters. Because more and more messages are being sent, writing skills are particularly important to succeed in first jobs and to be promoted into management.

Writing Skills and Professionalism Lead to Success

Advancements in technology mean that writing skills are increasingly important because more messages are being exchanged.

Writing skills are particularly important today because technological advances enable us to transmit messages more rapidly, more often, and to greater numbers of people than ever before. Writing skills, which were always a career advantage, are now a necessity.[4] They can be your ticket to work—or your ticket out the door, according to a business executive responding to a recent survey. This survey of 120 American corporations, by the National Commission on Writing, a panel established by the College Board, found that two thirds of salaried employees have some writing responsibility. Yet, about one third of them do not meet the writing requirements for their positions.[5]

"Businesses are crying out—they need to have people who write better," said Gaston Caperton, executive and College Board president. The ability to write opens doors to professional employment. People who cannot write and communicate clearly will not be hired. If already working, they are unlikely to last long enough to be considered for promotion.

Writing is a marker of high-skill, high-wage, professional work, according to Bob Kerrey, president of New School University in New York and chair of the National Commission on Writing. If you can't express yourself clearly, he says, you limit your opportunities for salaried positions.[6] But writing skills are also important for non-salaried workers such as electricians, engineers, technicians, and supervisors, who must create reports for government agencies and regulatory bodies. Even hourly workers must be able to communicate to exchange messages.

Businesses don't want spellbinding storytellers; they want people who can write clearly and concisely.

Lamenting the sorry state of business writing skills, a front-page article in *The New York Times* announced, "What Corporate America Can't Build: A Sentence." Quoted in the article, Susan Traiman, a director of the Business Roundtable, an association of leading chief executives, said, "It's not that companies want to hire Tolstoy."[7] They aren't seeking spellbinding authors; they just want people who can write clearly and concisely. Because so many lack these skills, businesses are spending as much as $3.1 billion annually on remedial training.

In addition to expecting employees to write clearly, businesses expect employees to act in a businesslike and professional manner on the job. Some new-hires have no idea that excessive absenteeism or tardiness are grounds for termination. Others are surprised to learn that they are expected to devote their full attention to their duties when on the job. One young man wanted to read Harry Potter novels when things got slow. Even more employees don't realize that they are sabotaging their careers when they sprinkle their conversation with *like*, *you know*, and uptalk (making declarative statements sound like questions). Companies are reluctant to promote people into management who do not look or sound credible. Figure 1.1 reviews six areas you will want to check to be sure you are not sending the wrong message with unwitting or unprofessional behavior.

FIGURE 1.1

Projecting Professionalism When You Communicate

	Unprofessional	Professional
Speech habits	Speaking in *uptalk*, a singsong speech pattern that has a rising inflection making sentences sound like questions. Using *like* to fill in mindless chatter, substituting *go* for *said*, relying on slang, or letting profanity slip into your conversation.	Recognizing that your credibility can be seriously damaged by sounding uneducated, crude, or like a teenager.
E-mail	Writing messages with incomplete sentences, misspelled words, exclamation points, IM slang, and mindless chatting. Sloppy, careless messages send a nonverbal message that you don't care, don't know, or aren't smart enough to know what is correct.	Employers like to see subjects, verbs, and punctuation marks. They don't recognize IM abbreviations. Call it crazy, but they value conciseness and correct spelling, even in brief e-mail messages.
Internet	Using an e-mail address such as *hotbabe@hotmail.com*, *supasnugglykitty.yahoo.com*, or *buffedguy@aol.com*.	An e-mail address that is your name or a relevant, positive, businesslike expression. It should not sound cute or like a chat room nickname.
Answering machine/ voice mail	An outgoing message with strident background music, weird sounds, or a joke message.	An outgoing message that states your name or phone number and provides instructions for leaving a message.
Telephone	Soap operas, thunderous music, or a TV football game playing noisily in the background when you answer the phone.	A quiet background when you answer the telephone, especially if you are expecting a prospective employer's call.
Cell phone	Taking or placing cell phone calls during business meetings or during conversations with fellow employees. Raising your voice (cell yell) or engaging in cell calls when others must reluctantly overhear.	Never letting a cell phone interrupt business meetings. Using your cell only when conversations can be private.

Using This Book to Build Career Communication Skills

Because communication skills are learned, you control how well you communicate.

This book focuses on developing basic writing skills. You will, however, also learn to improve your listening, nonverbal, and speaking skills. The abilities to read, listen, speak, and write effectively, of course, are not inborn. When it comes to communication, it's more *nurture* than *nature*. Good communicators are not born; they are made. Thriving in the dynamic and demanding new world of work will depend on many factors, some of which you cannot control. One factor that you *do* control, however, is how well you communicate.

Developing career-boosting communication skills requires instruction, practice, and feedback from a specialist.

The goal of this book is to teach you basic business communication skills. These include learning how to write an e-mail, letter, or report and how to make a presentation. Anyone can learn these skills with the help of instructional materials and good model documents, all of which you'll find in this book. You also need practice—with meaningful feedback. You need someone such as your instructor to tell you how to modify your responses so that you can improve.

We've designed this book, its supplements, and two Web sites (*http://guffeyxtra .swlearning.com* and *http://guffey.swlearning.com*) to provide you and your instructor with everything necessary to make you a successful business communicator in today's dynamic but demanding workplace. Given the increasing emphasis on communication, many businesses are paying huge sums to communication coaches and trainers to teach employees the very skills that you are learning in this course. Your coach is your instructor. So, get your money's worth! Pick your instructor's brains.

This book and this course might well be the most important in your entire college career.

With this book as your guide and your instructor as your coach, you may find this course to be the most important in your entire college curriculum. To get started, this first chapter presents an overview. You'll take a quick look at the changing workplace, the communication process, listening, nonverbal communication, culture and communication, and workplace diversity. The remainder of the book is devoted to developing specific writing and speaking skills.

Succeeding in the Changing World of Work

Trends in the new world of work emphasize the importance of communication skills.

The world of work is changing dramatically. The kind of work you'll do, the tools you'll use, the form of management you'll work under, the environment in which you'll work, the people with whom you'll interact—all are undergoing a pronounced transformation. Many of the changes in this dynamic workplace revolve around processing and communicating information. As a result, the most successful players in this new world of work will be those with highly developed communication skills. The following business trends illustrate the importance of excellent communication skills.

- **Flattened management hierarchies.** To better compete and to reduce expenses, businesses have for years been trimming layers of management. This means that as a frontline employee, you will have fewer managers. You will be making decisions and communicating them to customers, to fellow employees, and to executives.

Today's employees must contribute to improving productivity and profitability.

- **More participatory management.** Gone are the days of command-and-control management. Now, even new employees like you will be expected to understand and contribute to the big picture. Improving productivity and profitability will be everyone's job, not just management's.

- **Increased emphasis on self-directed work groups and virtual teams.** Businesses today are often run by cross-functional teams of peers. You can expect to work with a team in gathering information, finding and sharing solutions, implementing decisions, and managing conflict. You may even become part of a virtual team whose members are in remote locations and who communicate almost exclusively electronically. Good communication skills are extremely important in working together successfully in all team environments, especially if members do not meet face-to-face.

FIGURE 1.2

Communication
Technologies

Reshaping the World of Work

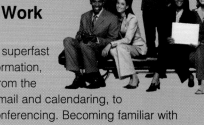

Today's workplace is changing dramatically as a result of innovative software, superfast wireless networks, and numerous technologies that allow workers to share information, work from remote locations, and be more efficient and productive in or away from the office. We're seeing a gradual progression from basic capabilities, such as e-mail and calendaring, to deeper functionality, such as remote database access and worldwide videoconferencing. Becoming familiar with modern workplace and collaboration technologies can help you be successful in today's digital workplace.

IP Telephony: VoIP

Savvy businesses are switching from traditional phone service to Voice over Internet Protocol (VoIP). This technology allows callers to make telephone calls using a broadband Internet connection, thus eliminating long-distance and local telephone charges.

Electronic Presentations

Business presenters load a slide presentation onto a laptop PC or PDA for handy electronic presentations in rooms equipped with projectors. Sophisticated presentations may include animations, sound effects, digital photos, video clips, or even hyperlinks to Internet sites.

Wireless Networks and Wi-Fi

No longer are computers and workers chained to their desks. Wireless networks use radio waves to send signals and connect to the Internet. Combined with high-speed broadband connections, these networks have fueled the increasing use of laptop computers and portable devices. Public Wi-Fi (Wireless Fidelity) "hot spots" provide free connections that further expand the range of laptops, PDAs (personal digital assistants), and handheld devices such as the BlackBerry and the Treo. Wireless networks enable business communicators to work anywhere, anytime, and still remain connected to office e-mail, company files, and programs such as Word and Excel.

Company Intranets

To share insider information, many companies provide their own protected Web site called an intranet. It may handle company e-mail, announcements, an employee directory, a policy handbook, frequently asked questions, personnel forms and data, employee discussion forums, shared documents, and other employee information.

Voice Recognition

Computers equipped with voice recognition software enable users to dictate up to 160 words a minute with accurate transcription. Voice recognition is particularly helpful to disabled workers and to professionals with heavy dictation loads, such as physicians and attorneys. Users can create documents, enter data, compose and send e-mails, browse the Web, and control the desktop—all by voice.

© GETTY IMAGES

Global competition, expanding markets, and the ever-increasing pace of business accelerate the development of exciting collaboration tools. Employees working together may be down the hall, across the country, or around the world. With today's tools, workers exchange ideas, solve problems, develop products, forecast future performance, and complete team projects any time of the day or night and anywhere in the world.

Voice Conferencing

Telephone "bridges" join two or more callers from any location to share the same call. Voice conferencing (also called audioconferencing, teleconferencing, or just plain conference calling) enables people to collaborate by telephone. Communicators at both ends use an enhanced speakerphone to talk and be heard simultaneously.

Web Conferencing

With services such as WebEx and Live Meeting, all you need are a PC and an Internet connection to hold a meeting. Although the functions of Web conferencing (also called desktop or media conferencing) are constantly evolving, it currently incorporates screen sharing, voice communication, slide presentations, text messaging, and application sharing (e.g., participants can work on a spreadsheet together).

Videoconferencing

Videoconferencing allows participants to meet in special conference rooms equipped with cameras and television screens. Groups see each other and interact in real time although they may be worlds apart. Faster computers, rapid Internet connections, and better cameras now enable 2 to 200 participants to sit at their own PCs and share applications, spreadsheets, presentations, and photos.

Video Phones

Using advanced video compression technology, video phones transmit real-time audio and video so that communicators can see  each other as they collaborate. With a video phone, you can videoconference without a computer or a television screen.

One-Number Dialing

Smart phones switch seamlessly between cellular networks and corporate Wi-Fi connections allowing employees to take their phones around corporate campuses, into their homes, or on the road. One-number dialing reduces frustration and wasted time.

Presence Technology

Responding to the demand for immediate communication, "presence awareness" builds on instant messaging. In a presence-enabled workplace, you would know whether to contact someone via voice, e-mail, or instant messaging. This awareness avoids time wasted in voice mailboxes and waiting for e-mail responses. A light on your telephone might indicate when key people on your team are present on your internal phone network. Still being developed, presence technology is built on Session Initiation Protocol (SIP).

Increasing global competition and revolutionary technologies demand cultural and communication skills.

- **Heightened global competition.** Because American companies are moving beyond local markets, you may be interacting with people from many different cultures. As a successful business communicator, you will want to learn about other cultures. You'll also need to develop multicultural skills including sensitivity, flexibility, patience, and tolerance.
- **Innovative communication technologies.** E-mail, fax, instant messaging, text messaging, the Web, mobile technologies, audio- and videoconferencing, company intranets, and voice recognition—all these innovative technologies are reshaping the way we communicate at work, as summarized in Figure 1.2. You can expect to be communicating more often and more rapidly than ever before. Your writing and speaking skills will be showcased as never before.
- **New work environments.** Mobile technologies and the desire for a better balance between work and family have resulted in flexible working arrangements. You may become part of an increasing number of workers who are telecommuters or virtual team members. Working as a telecommuter or virtual team member requires even more communication, because staying connected with the office or with one another means exchanging many messages. Another work environment trend is the movement toward open offices divided into small work cubicles. Working in a cubicle requires new rules of office etiquette and civility.
- **Focus on information and knowledge as corporate assets.** Corporate America is increasingly aware that information is the key to better products and increased profitability. You will be expected to gather, sort, store, and disseminate data in a timely and accurate fashion. This is the new way of business life.

EXAMINING THE COMMUNICATION PROCESS

As you can see, you can expect to be communicating more rapidly, more often, and with greater numbers of people than ever before. The most successful players in this new world of work will be those with highly developed communication skills. Because good communication skills are essential to your success, we need to take a closer look at the communication process.

Communication is the transmission of information and meaning from one individual or group to another.

Just what is communication? For our purposes *communication is the transmission of information and meaning from one individual or group to another*. The crucial element in this definition is *meaning*. Communication has as its central objective the transmission of meaning. The process of communication is successful only when the receiver understands an idea as the sender intended it. This process generally involves five steps, discussed here and shown in Figure 1.3.

1. **Sender has an idea.** The form of the idea may be influenced by the sender's mood, frame of reference, background, culture, and physical makeup, as well as the context of the situation.

2. **Sender encodes the idea in a message.** *Encoding* means converting the idea into words or gestures that will convey meaning. A major problem in communicating any message verbally is that words have different meanings for different people. That's why skilled communicators try to choose familiar words with concrete meanings on which both senders and receivers agree.

The communication process has five steps: idea formation, message encoding, message transmission, message decoding, and feedback.

3. **Message travels over a channel.** The medium over which the message is transmitted is the *channel*. Messages may be sent by computer, telephone, letter, or memorandum. They may also be sent by means of a report, announcement, picture, spoken word, fax, or other channel. Because both verbal and nonverbal messages are carried, senders must choose channels carefully. Anything that disrupts the transmission of a message in the communication process is called *noise*.

© C SQUARED STUDIOS/PHOTODISC/GETTY IMAGES

FIGURE 1.3 • **Communication Process**

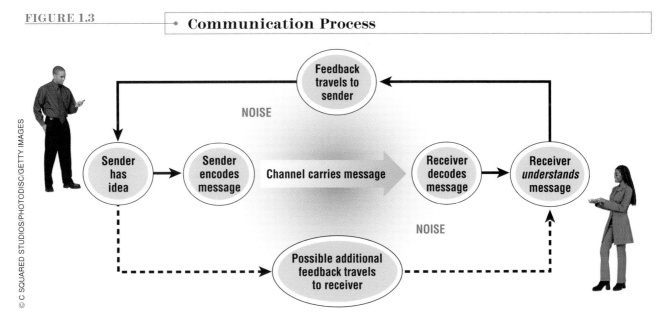

Communication barriers and noise may cause the communication process to break down.

Channel noise ranges from static that disrupts a telephone conversation to spelling errors in an e-mail message. Such errors damage the credibility of the sender.

4. **Receiver decodes message.** The person for whom a message is intended is the *receiver.* Translating the message from its symbol form into meaning involves *decoding.* Successful communication takes place only when a receiver understands the meaning intended by the sender. Such success is often hard to achieve because no two people share the same background. Success is further limited because barriers and noise may disrupt the process.

5. **Feedback travels to sender.** The verbal and nonverbal responses of the receiver create *feedback,* a vital part of the entire communication process. Feedback helps the sender know that the message was received and understood. Senders can encourage feedback by asking questions such as *Am I making myself clear?* and *Is there anything you don't understand?* Senders can further improve feedback by delivering the message at a time when receivers can respond. Senders should provide only as much information as a receiver can handle. Receivers can improve the process by paraphrasing the sender's message. They might say, *Let me try to explain that in my own words,* or *My understanding of your comment is . . .*

DEVELOPING BETTER LISTENING SKILLS

An important part of the communication process is listening. By all accounts, however, most of us are not very good listeners. Do you ever pretend to be listening when you're not? Do you know how to look attentive in class when your mind wanders far away? How about "tuning out" people when their ideas are boring or complex? Do you find it hard to focus on ideas when a speaker's clothing or mannerisms are unusual?

You probably answered *yes* to one or more of these questions because many of us have developed poor listening habits. In fact, some researchers suggest that we listen at only 25 percent efficiency. Such poor listening habits are costly in business. Letters must be rewritten, shipments reshipped, appointments rescheduled, contracts renegotiated, and directions restated.

Most individuals listen at only 25 percent efficiency.

© Ted Goff (www.tedgoff.com)

COMMUNICATION TOOLS

Observers have suggested that the best communication tools are ears.

Most North Americans speak at about 125 words per minute. The human brain can process information at least three times as fast.

To improve listening skills, we must first recognize barriers that prevent effective listening. Then we need to focus on specific techniques that are effective in improving listening skills.

Barriers to Effective Listening

As you learned earlier, barriers and noise can interfere with the communication process. Have any of the following barriers and distractions prevented you from hearing what's said?

- **Physical barriers.** You cannot listen if you cannot hear what is being said. Physical impediments include hearing disabilities, poor acoustics, and noisy surroundings. It's also difficult to listen if you're ill, tired, uncomfortable, or worried.
- **Psychological barriers.** Everyone brings to the communication process a different set of cultural, ethical, and personal values. Each of us has an idea of what is right and what is important. If other ideas run counter to our preconceived thoughts, we tend to "tune out" the speaker and thus fail to hear.
- **Language problems.** Unfamiliar words can destroy the communication process because they lack meaning for the receiver. In addition, emotion-laden or "charged" words can adversely affect listening. If the mention of words such as *abortion* or *overdose* has an intense emotional impact, a listener may be unable to think about the words that follow.
- **Nonverbal distractions.** Many of us find it hard to listen if a speaker is different from what we view as normal. Unusual clothing, speech mannerisms, body twitches, or a radical hairstyle can cause enough distraction to prevent us from hearing what the speaker has to say.
- **Thought speed.** Because we can process thoughts more than three times faster than speakers can say them, we can become bored and allow our minds to wander.

The better a business-person listens to a customer, the better she or he will be at fulfilling expectations, resolving disputes, reducing uncertainty, and projecting goodwill. Any employee listening to a customer should learn to defer judgment, pay attention to content rather than surface issues, focus on main ideas, and avoid replying to sidetracking issues.

© PHOTODISC COLLECTION/GETTY IMAGES

- **Faking attention.** Most of us have learned to look as if we are listening even when we're not. Such behavior was perhaps necessary as part of our socialization. Faked attention, however, seriously threatens effective listening because it encourages the mind to engage in flights of unchecked fancy. Those who practice faked attention often find it hard to concentrate even when they want to.
- **Grandstanding.** Would you rather talk or listen? Naturally, most of us would rather talk. Because our own experiences and thoughts are most important to us, we grab the limelight in conversations. We sometimes fail to listen carefully because we're just waiting politely for the next pause so that we can have our turn to speak.

Tips for Becoming an Active Listener

You can reverse the harmful effects of poor habits by making a conscious effort to become an active listener. This means becoming involved. You can't sit back and hear whatever a lazy mind happens to receive. The following techniques will help you become an active and effective listener.

> To become an active listener, stop talking, control your surroundings, develop a positive mind-set, listen for main points, and capitalize on lag time.

- **Stop talking.** The first step to becoming a good listener is to stop talking. Let others explain their views. Learn to concentrate on what the speaker is saying, not on what your next comment will be.
- **Control your surroundings.** Whenever possible, remove competing sounds. Close windows or doors, turn off TVs, unplug your iPod, and move away from loud people, noisy appliances, or engines. Choose a quiet time and place for listening.

© Ted Goff (www.tedgoff.com)

"How can I listen to you if you don't say the things I want to hear?"

- **Establish a receptive mind-set.** Expect to learn something by listening. Strive for a positive and receptive frame of mind. If the message is complex, think of it as mental gymnastics. It's hard work but good exercise to stretch and expand the limits of your mind.
- **Keep an open mind.** We all sift and filter information through our own biases and values. For improved listening, discipline yourself to listen objectively. Be fair to the speaker. Hear what is really being said, not what you want to hear.
- **Listen for main points.** Heighten your concentration and satisfaction by looking for the speaker's central themes. Congratulate yourself when you find them!
- **Capitalize on lag time.** Make use of the quickness of your mind by reviewing the speaker's points. Anticipate what's coming next. Evaluate evidence the speaker has presented. Don't allow yourself to daydream. Try to guess what the speaker's next point will be.
- **Listen between the lines.** Focus both on what is spoken as well as what is unspoken. Listen for feelings as well as for facts.
- **Judge ideas, not appearances.** Concentrate on the content of the message, not on its delivery. Avoid being distracted by the speaker's looks, voice, or mannerisms.
- **Hold your fire.** Force yourself to listen to the speaker's entire argument or message before reacting. Such restraint may enable you to understand the speaker's reasons and logic before you jump to false conclusions.
- **Take selective notes.** In some situations thoughtful notetaking may be necessary to record important facts that must be recalled later. Select only the most important points so that the notetaking process does not interfere with your concentration on the speaker's total message.

> Listening actively may mean taking notes and providing feedback.

- **Provide feedback.** Let the speaker know that you are listening. Nod your head and maintain eye contact. Ask relevant questions at appropriate times. Getting involved improves the communication process for both the speaker and the listener.

IMPROVING YOUR NONVERBAL COMMUNICATION SKILLS

Understanding messages often involves more than merely listening to spoken words. Nonverbal cues, in fact, can speak louder than words. These cues include eye contact, facial expression, body movements, space, time, territory, and appearance. All these nonverbal cues affect how a message is interpreted, or decoded, by the receiver.

Nonverbal communication includes all unwritten and unspoken messages, intended or not.

Just what is nonverbal communication? It includes all unwritten and unspoken messages, whether intended or not. These silent signals have a strong effect on receivers. But understanding them is not simple. Does a downward glance indicate modesty? Fatigue? Does a constant stare reflect coldness? Dullness? Do crossed arms mean defensiveness? Withdrawal? Or do crossed arms just mean that a person is shivering?

Messages are even harder to decipher when the verbal codes and nonverbal cues do not agree. What will you think if Scott says he's not angry, but he slams the door when he leaves? What if Alicia assures the hostess that the meal is excellent, but she eats very little? The nonverbal messages in these situations speak more loudly than the words.

When verbal and nonverbal messages clash, listeners tend to believe the nonverbal message.

When verbal and nonverbal messages conflict, receivers put more faith in nonverbal cues. In one study speakers sent a positive message but averted their eyes as they spoke. Listeners perceived the total message to be negative. Moreover, they thought that averted eyes suggested lack of affection, superficiality, lack of trust, and nonreceptivity.[8]

Successful communicators recognize the power of nonverbal messages. Although it's unwise to attach specific meanings to gestures or actions, some cues broadcast by body language are helpful in understanding the feelings and attitudes of senders.

How the Eyes, Face, and Body Send Silent Messages

Words seldom tell the whole story. Indeed, some messages are sent with no words at all. The eyes, face, and body can convey a world of meaning without a single syllable being spoken.

EYE CONTACT

The eyes are thought to be the best predictor of a speaker's true feelings.

The eyes have been called the *windows to the soul*. Even if they don't reveal the soul, the eyes are often the best predictor of a speaker's true feelings. Most of us cannot look another person straight in the eyes and lie. As a result, in American culture we tend to believe people who look directly at us. Sustained eye contact suggests trust and admiration; brief eye contact signals fear or stress. Good eye contact enables the message sender to see whether a receiver is paying attention, showing respect, responding favorably, or feeling distress. From the receiver's viewpoint, good eye contact, in North American culture, reveals the speaker's sincerity, confidence, and truthfulness.

© Ted Goff (www.tedgoff.com)

"I know you're saying no, but I think your body language is saying maybe."

FACIAL EXPRESSION

The expression on a person's face can be almost as revealing of emotion as the eyes. Experts estimate that the human face can display over 250,000 expressions.[9] To hide their feelings, some people can control these expressions and maintain "poker faces." Most of us, however, display our emotions openly. Raising or lowering the eyebrows, squinting the eyes, swallowing nervously, clenching the jaw, smiling broadly—these voluntary and involuntary facial expressions can add to or entirely replace verbal messages.

POSTURE AND GESTURES

A person's posture can convey anything from high status and self-confidence to shyness and submissiveness. Leaning toward a speaker suggests attraction and interest; pulling away or shrinking back denotes fear, distrust, anxiety, or disgust. Similarly, gestures can communicate entire thoughts via simple movements. However, the meanings of some of these movements differ in other cultures. Unless you know local customs, they can get you into trouble. In the United States and Canada, for example, forming the thumb and forefinger in a circle means everything's OK. But in Germany and parts of South America, the OK sign is obscene.

What does your own body language say about you? To take stock of the kinds of messages being sent by your body, ask a classmate to critique your use of eye contact, facial expression, and body movements. Another way to analyze your nonverbal style is to videotape yourself making a presentation. Then study your performance. This way you can make sure your nonverbal cues send the same message as your words.

> Nonverbal messages often have different meanings in different cultures.

How Time, Space, and Territory Send Silent Messages

In addition to nonverbal messages transmitted by your body, three external elements convey information in the communication process: time, space, and territory.

TIME

How we structure and use time tells observers about our personality and attitudes. For example, when Donald Trump, multimillionaire real estate developer, gives a visitor a prolonged interview, he signals his respect for, interest in, and approval of the visitor or the topic to be discussed.

SPACE

How we order the space around us tells something about ourselves and our objectives. Whether the space is a bedroom, a dorm room, an office, or a department, people reveal themselves in the design and grouping of their furniture. Generally, the more formal the arrangement, the more formal and closed the communication. The way office furniture is arranged sends cues on how communication is to take place. Former FBI director J. Edgar Hoover used to make his visitors sit at a small table below his large, elevated desk. Clearly, he did not want office visitors to feel equal to him.[10]

TERRITORY

Each of us has a certain area that we feel is our own territory, whether it's a specific spot or just the space around us. Your father may have a favorite chair in which he is most comfortable, a cook might not tolerate intruders in his or her kitchen, and veteran employees may feel that certain work areas and tools belong to them. We all maintain zones of privacy in which we feel comfortable. Figure 1.4 illustrates the four zones of social interaction among Americans, as formulated by anthropologist Edward T. Hall.[11] Notice that Americans are a bit standoffish; only intimate friends and family may stand closer than about 1½ feet. If someone violates that territory, Americans feel uncomfortable and defensive and may step back to reestablish their space.

© ScienceCartoonsPlus.com

"Sorry, Ridgely, but this area is my personal space."

> People convey meaning in how they structure and organize time and how they order the space around themselves.

How Appearance Sends Silent Messages

The physical appearance of a business document, as well as the personal appearance of an individual, transmits immediate and important nonverbal messages.

PHOTOS: LEFT TO RIGHT: © PHOTODISC BLUE/GETTY IMAGES; PHOTODISC RED/GETTY IMAGES; PHOTODISC RED/GETTY IMAGES; PHOTODISC RED/GETTY IMAGES

FIGURE 1.4

> **Four Space Zones for Social Interaction**

| **Intimate Zone** (1 to 1½ feet) | **Personal Zone** (1½ to 4 feet) | **Social Zone** (4 to 12 feet) | **Public Zone** (12 or more feet) |

APPEARANCE OF BUSINESS DOCUMENTS

The appearance of a message and of an individual can convey positive or negative nonverbal messages.

The way a letter, memo, or report looks can have either a positive or a negative effect on the receiver. Sloppy e-mail messages send a nonverbal message that says you are in a terrific hurry or that the receiver is not important enough for you to care. Envelopes—through their postage, stationery, and printing—can suggest routine, important, or junk mail. Letters and reports can look neat, professional, well organized, and attractive—or just the opposite. In succeeding chapters you'll learn how to create documents that send positive nonverbal messages through their appearance, format, organization, readability, and correctness.

PERSONAL APPEARANCE

The way you look—your clothing, grooming, and posture—telegraphs an instant nonverbal message about you. Based on what they see, viewers make quick judgments about your status, credibility, personality, and potential. If you want to be considered professional, think about how you present yourself. One marketing manager said, "I'm young and pretty. It's hard enough to be taken seriously, and if I show up in jeans and a T-shirt, I don't stand a chance."[12] As a businessperson, you'll want to think about what your appearance says about you. Although the rules of business attire have loosened up, some workers show poor judgment. You'll learn more about professional attire and behavior in later chapters.

Tips for Improving Your Nonverbal Skills

Because nonverbal cues can mean more than spoken words, learn to use nonverbal communication positively.

Nonverbal communication can outweigh words in the way it influences how others perceive us. You can harness the power of silent messages by reviewing the following tips for improving nonverbal communication skills:

- **Establish and maintain eye contact.** Remember that in the United States and Canada, appropriate eye contact signals interest, attentiveness, strength, and credibility.
- **Use posture to show interest.** Encourage communication interaction by leaning forward, sitting or standing erect, and looking alert.
- **Improve your decoding skills.** Watch facial expressions and body language to understand the complete verbal and nonverbal messages being communicated.
- **Probe for more information.** When you perceive nonverbal cues that contradict verbal meanings, politely seek additional cues (*I'm not sure I understand, Please tell me more about . . . ,* or *Do you mean that . . . *).
- **Avoid assigning nonverbal meanings out of context.** Don't interpret nonverbal behavior unless you understand a situation or a culture.
- **Associate with people from diverse cultures.** Learn about other cultures to widen your knowledge and tolerance of intercultural nonverbal messages.

- **Appreciate the power of appearance.** Keep in mind that the appearance of your business documents, your business space, and yourself sends immediate positive or negative messages to receivers.
- **Observe yourself on videotape.** Ensure that your verbal and nonverbal messages are in sync by taping and evaluating yourself making a presentation.
- **Enlist friends and family.** Ask them to monitor your conscious and unconscious body movements and gestures to help you become a more effective communicator.

UNDERSTANDING HOW CULTURE AFFECTS COMMUNICATION

Verbal and nonverbal meanings are even more difficult to interpret when people are from different cultures.

Comprehending the verbal and nonverbal meanings of a message is difficult even when communicators are from the same culture. But when they are from different cultures, special sensitivity and skills are necessary.

Negotiators for a North American company learned this lesson when they were in Japan looking for a trading partner. The North Americans were pleased after their first meeting with representatives of a major Japanese firm. The Japanese had nodded assent throughout the meeting and had not objected to a single proposal. The next day, however, the North Americans were stunned to learn that the Japanese had rejected the entire plan. In interpreting the nonverbal behavioral messages, the North Americans made a typical mistake. They assumed the Japanese were nodding in agreement as fellow North Americans would. In this case, however, the nods of assent indicated comprehension—not approval.

Every country has a unique culture or common heritage, joint experience, and shared learning that produce its culture. Their common experience gives members of that culture a complex system of shared values and customs. It teaches them how to behave; it conditions their reactions. Global business, new communication technologies, the Internet, and even Hollywood are spreading Western values throughout the world. Yet, cultural differences can still cause significant misunderstandings.

Comparing traditional North American values with those in other cultures will broaden your worldview. This comparison should also help you recognize some of the values that influence your actions and affect your opinions of others.

Comparing Key Cultural Values

Until relatively recently, typical North Americans shared the same broad cultural values. Some experts identified them as "Anglo" or "mainstream" values.[13] These values largely represented white, male, Northern European views. Women and many minorities now entering the workforce may eventually modify these values. However, a majority of North Americans are still governed by these mainstream values.

Although North American culture is complex, we'll focus on four dimensions to help you better understand some of the values that shape your actions and judgments of others. These four dimensions are individualism, formality, communication style, and time orientation.

INDIVIDUALISM

While North Americans value individualism and personal responsibility, other cultures emphasize group- and team-oriented values.

One of the most identifiable characteristics of North Americans is their *individualism*. This is an attitude of independence and freedom from control. They think that initiative and self-assertion result in personal achievement. They believe in individual action, self-reliance, and personal responsibility; and they desire a large degree of freedom in their personal lives. Other cultures emphasize membership in organizations, groups, and teams; they encourage acceptance of group values, duties, and decisions. Members of these cultures typically resist independence because it fosters competition and confrontation instead of consensus.

FORMALITY

Although North Americans value informality and directness, other cultures may value tradition and indirectness.

A second significant dimension of North American culture is our attitude toward *formality*. Americans place less emphasis on tradition, ceremony, and social rules than do people in some other cultures. They dress casually and are soon on a first-name basis with others. Their lack of formality is often characterized by directness. In business dealings North Americans tend to come to the point immediately; indirectness, they feel, wastes time, a valuable commodity.

COMMUNICATION STYLE

North Americans tend to be direct and to understand words literally.

A third important dimension of our culture relates to *communication style*. North Americans value straightforwardness, are suspicious of evasiveness, and distrust people who might have a "hidden agenda" or who "play their cards too close to the chest."[14] North Americans also tend to be uncomfortable with silence and impatient with delays. What's more, they tend to use and understand words literally. Latins, on the other hand, enjoy plays on words; Arabs and South Americans sometimes speak with extravagant or poetic figures of speech (such as "the Mother of all battles").

TIME ORIENTATION

North Americans correlate time with productivity, efficiency, and money.

A fourth dimension of our culture relates to *time orientation*. North Americans consider time a precious commodity to be conserved. They correlate time with productivity, efficiency, and money. Keeping people waiting for business appointments wastes time and is also rude. In other cultures, time may be perceived as an unlimited and never-ending resource to be enjoyed. Being late for an appointment is not a grievous sin.

Figure 1.5 compares a number of cultural values for U.S. Americans, Japanese, and Arabs. Notice that belonging, group harmony, and collectiveness are very important to Japanese people, while family matters rank highest with Arabs. As we become aware of the vast differences in cultural values illustrated in Figure 1.5, we can better understand why communication barriers develop and how misunderstandings occur in cross-cultural interactions.

Controlling Ethnocentrism and Stereotyping

The process of understanding and accepting people from other cultures is often hampered by two barriers: ethnocentrism and stereotyping. These two barriers,

FIGURE 1.5   **Comparison of Cultural Values Ranked by Priority***

U.S. Americans	Japanese	Arabs
1. Freedom	1. Belonging	1. Family security
2. Independence	2. Group harmony	2. Family harmony
3. Self-reliance	3. Collectiveness	3. Parental guidance
4. Equality	4. Age/Seniority	4. Age
5. Individualism	5. Group consensus	5. Authority
6. Competition	6. Cooperation	6. Compromise
7. Efficiency	7. Quality	7. Devotion
8. Time	8. Patience	8. Patience
9. Directness	9. Indirectness	9. Indirectness
10. Openness	10. Go-between	10. Hospitality

*1 represents the most important value.
Source: Reprinted from *Multicultural Management*, F. Elashmawi and P. R. Harris, p. 72, © 2000 with permission of Elsevier Science.

however, can be overcome by developing tolerance, a powerful and effective aid to communication.

ETHNOCENTRISM

Ethnocentrism is the belief in the superiority of one's own culture and group.

The belief in the superiority of one's own culture is known as *ethnocentrism*. This natural attitude is found in all cultures. Ethnocentrism causes us to judge others by our own values. If you were raised in North America, the values just described probably seem "right" to you, and you may wonder why the rest of the world doesn't function in the same sensible fashion. A North American businessperson in an Arab or Asian country might be upset at time spent over coffee or other social rituals before any "real" business is transacted. In these cultures, however, personal relationships must be established and nurtured before earnest talks may proceed.

STEREOTYPES

A *stereotype* is an oversimplified behavioral pattern applied to entire groups.

Our perceptions of other cultures sometimes cause us to form stereotypes about groups of people. A *stereotype* is an oversimplified perception of a behavioral pattern or characteristic applied to entire groups. For example, the Swiss are hardworking, efficient, and neat; Germans are formal, reserved, and blunt; Americans are loud, friendly, and impatient; Canadians are polite, trusting, and tolerant; Asians are gracious, humble, and inscrutable. These attitudes may or may not accurately describe cultural norms. When applied to individual business communicators, such stereotypes may create misconceptions and misunderstandings. Look beneath surface stereotypes and labels to discover individual personal qualities.

TOLERANCE

Developing intercultural tolerance means practicing empathy, being nonjudgmental, and being patient.

Working among people from other cultures demands tolerance and flexible attitudes. As global markets expand and as our society becomes increasingly multiethnic, tolerance becomes critical. *Tolerance*, here, does not mean "putting up with" or "enduring," which is one part of its definition. Instead, we use *tolerance* in a broader sense. It means having sympathy for and appreciating beliefs and practices different from our own.

One of the best ways to develop tolerance is by practicing *empathy*. This means trying to see the world through another's eyes. It means being nonjudgmental, recognizing things as they are rather than as they "should be." It includes the ability to accept others' contributions in solving problems in a culturally appropriate manner. When Kal Kan Foods began courting the pet owners of Japan, for example, an Asian advisor suggested that the meat chunks in its Pedigree dog food be cut into perfect little squares. Why? Japanese pet owners feed their dogs piece by piece with chopsticks. Instead of insisting on what "should be" (feeding dogs chunky meat morsels), Kal Kan solved the problem by looking at it from another cultural point of view (providing neat small squares).[15]

The following tips provide specific suggestions for preventing miscommunication in oral and written transactions across cultures.

Tips for Minimizing Oral Miscommunication Among Cross-Cultural Audiences

When you have a conversation with someone from another culture, you can reduce misunderstandings by following these suggestions:

- **Use simple English.** Speak in short sentences (under 20 words) with familiar, short words. Eliminate puns, sports and military references, slang, and jargon (special business terms). Be especially alert to idiomatic expressions that can't be translated, such as *burn the midnight oil* and *under the weather.*
- **Speak slowly and enunciate clearly.** Avoid fast speech, but don't raise your voice. Overpunctuate with pauses and full stops. Always write numbers for all to see.

"He doesn't understand you. Try shouting a little louder."

© 1989 by NEA, Inc.

© BERRY'S WORLD reprinted by permission of Newspaper Enterprise Association, Inc.

- **Encourage accurate feedback.** Ask probing questions, and encourage the listener to paraphrase what you say. Don't assume that a *yes*, a nod, or a smile indicates comprehension or assent.
- **Check frequently for comprehension.** Avoid waiting until you finish a long explanation to request feedback. Instead, make one point at a time, pausing to check for comprehension. Don't proceed to B until A has been grasped.
- **Observe eye messages.** Be alert to a glazed expression or wandering eyes. These tell you the listener is lost.
- **Accept blame.** If a misunderstanding results, graciously accept the blame for not making your meaning clear.
- **Listen without interrupting.** Curb your desire to finish sentences or to fill out ideas for the speaker. Keep in mind that North Americans abroad are often accused of listening too little and talking too much.
- **Remember to smile!** Roger Axtell, international behavior expert, calls the smile the single most understood and most useful form of communication in either personal or business transactions.
- **Follow up in writing.** After conversations or oral negotiations, confirm the results and agreements with follow-up letters. For proposals and contracts, engage a translator to prepare copies in the local language.

Tips for Minimizing Written Miscommunication Among Cross-Cultural Audiences

When you write to someone from a different culture, you can improve your chances of being understood by following these suggestions:

You can improve cross-cultural written communication by adopting local styles, using short sentences and short paragraphs, avoiding ambiguous wording, and citing numbers carefully.

- **Consider local styles.** Learn how documents are formatted and how letters are addressed and developed in the intended reader's country. Decide whether to use your organization's preferred format or adjust to local styles.
- **Consider hiring a translator.** Engage a translator if (1) your document is important, (2) your document will be distributed to many readers, or (3) you must be persuasive.
- **Use short sentences and short paragraphs.** Sentences with fewer than 20 words and paragraphs with fewer than 8 lines are most readable.
- **Avoid ambiguous wording.** Include relative pronouns (*that, which, who*) for clarity in introducing clauses. Stay away from contractions (especially ones like *Here's the problem*). Avoid idioms (*once in a blue moon*), slang (*my presentation really bombed*), acronyms (*ASAP* for *as soon as possible*), abbreviations (*DBA* for *doing business as*), and jargon (*input, output, clickstream*). Use action-specific verbs (*purchase a printer* rather than *get a printer*).
- **Cite numbers carefully.** For international trade it's a good idea to learn and use the metric system. In citing numbers, use figures (*15*) instead of spelling them out (*fifteen*). Always convert dollar figures into local currency. Avoid using figures to express the month of the year. In North America, for example, March 5, 2006, might be written as 3/5/06, while in Europe the same date might appear as 5.3.06. For clarity, always spell out the month.

CAPITALIZING ON WORKFORCE DIVERSITY

As global competition opens world markets, North American businesspeople will increasingly interact with customers and colleagues from around the world. At the same time, the North American workforce is also becoming more diverse—in race, ethnicity, age, gender, national origin, physical ability, and countless other characteristics.

You can expect to be interacting with customers and colleagues who may differ from you in race, ethnicity, age, gender, national origin, physical ability, and many other characteristics.

No longer, say the experts, will the workplace be predominantly male or Anglo-oriented. Nearly 85 percent of the new entrants to the workforce will be women, minorities, and immigrants, according to estimates from the U.S. Bureau of Labor Statistics. By 2012 groups now considered minorities (African Americans, Hispanics, Asians, Native Americans, and others) will make up 34 percent of the workforce. Nearly half (48 percent) of all workers will be women, and more than 19 percent will be fifty-five years or older.[16]

While the workforce is becoming more diverse, the structure of many businesses in North America is also changing. As you learned earlier, many workers are now organized by teams. Organizations are flatter, and rank-and-file workers are increasingly making decisions among themselves. What does all this mean for you as a future business communicator? Simply put, your job may require you to interact with colleagues and customers from around the world. Your work environment will probably demand that you cooperate effectively with small groups of coworkers. What's more, these coworkers may differ from you in race, ethnicity, gender, age, and other ways.

Flatter organizations and emphasis on teamwork increase interactivity within small groups.

A diverse work environment, however, has many benefits. Consumers want to deal with companies that respect their values and create products and services tailored to their needs. Organizations that hire employees with different experiences and backgrounds are better able to create the different products that these consumers desire. In addition, businesses with diverse workforces suffer fewer discrimination lawsuits, fewer union clashes, and less government regulatory action. That's why a growing number of companies view today's diversity movement as a critical bottom-line business strategy. Organizations such as PepsiCo, UPS, Nike, Reebok, and Enterprise Rent-a-Car want employees who speak the same language, literally and figuratively, as their customers.[17] These organizations are convinced that it improves employee relationships and increases business.

Tips for Effective Communication With Diverse Workplace Audiences

Capitalizing on workplace diversity is an enormous challenge for most organizations and individuals. Harmony and acceptance do not follow automatically when people who are dissimilar work together. The following suggestions can help you become a more effective communicator as you enter a rapidly evolving workplace with ethnically diverse colleagues and clients.

Successful communicators understand the value of differences, don't expect conformity, create zero tolerance for bias and stereotypes, and practice open-minded listening.

- **Understand the value of differences.** Diversity makes an organization innovative and creative. Sameness fosters *groupthink*, an absence of critical thinking sometimes found in homogeneous groups. Case studies, for example, of the Kennedy administration's decision to invade Cuba and of the *Challenger*

© Grantland Enterprises; www.grantland.net

Copyright 1992, Grantland Enterprises, Inc. All rights reserved

GRANTLAND®

I DON'T UNDERSTAND WHY PEOPLE DISCRIMINATE AGAINST WOMEN OR MINORITIES OR THE DISABLED.

IT DOESN'T MAKE ANY SENSE!

IT'S LIKE THROWING AWAY A PRESENT BEFORE YOU'VE OPENED IT—

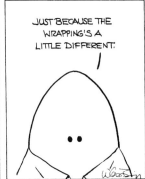
JUST BECAUSE THE WRAPPING'S A LITTLE DIFFERENT.

missile disaster suggest that groupthink prevented alternatives from being considered.[18] Diversity in problem-solving groups encourages independent and creative thinking.

- **Don't expect conformity.** Gone are the days when businesses could say, "This is our culture. Conform or leave." The CEO of athletic shoemaker Reebok stressed seeking people who have new and different stories to tell. "It accomplishes next to nothing to employ those who are different from us if the condition of their employment is that they become the same as us. For it is their differences that enrich us, expand us, provide us the competitive edge."[19]

- **Create zero tolerance for bias and stereotypes.** Cultural patterns exist in every identity group, but applying these patterns to individuals results in stereotyping. Assuming that African Americans are good athletes, that women are poor at math, that French Canadians excel at hockey, or that European American men are insensitive fails to admit the immense differences in people in each group. Check your own use of stereotypes and labels. Don't tell sexist or ethnic jokes at meetings. Avoid slang, abbreviations, and jargon that imply stereotypes. Challenge others' stereotypes politely but firmly.

- **Practice focused, thoughtful, and open-minded listening.** Much misunderstanding can be avoided by attentive listening. Listen for main points; take notes if necessary to remember important details. The most important part of listening, especially among diverse communicators, is judging ideas, not appearances or accents.

- **Invite, use, and give feedback.** As you learned earlier, a critical element in successful communication is feedback. You can encourage it by asking questions such as *Is there anything you don't understand?* When a listener or receiver responds, use that feedback to adjust your delivery of information. Does the receiver need more details? A different example? Slower delivery? As a good listener, you should also be prepared to give feedback. For example, summarize your understanding of what was said or agreed on.

- **Make fewer assumptions.** Be careful of seemingly insignificant, innocent workplace assumptions. For example, don't assume that everyone wants to observe the holidays with a Christmas party and a decorated tree. Celebrating only Christian holidays in December and January excludes those who honor Hanukkah, Kwanzaa, and the Chinese New Year. Moreover, in workplace discussions don't assume that everyone is married or wants to be or is even heterosexual, for that matter. For invitations, avoid phrases such as "managers and their *wives*." *Spouses* or *partners* is more inclusive. Valuing diversity means making fewer assumptions that everyone is like you or wants to be like you.

- **Learn about your cultural self.** Knowing your own cultural biases helps you become more objective and adaptable. Begin to recognize the stock reactions and thought patterns that are automatic to you as a result of your upbringing. Become more aware of your own values and beliefs so that you will recognize them when you are confronted by differing values.

- **Learn about other cultures and identity groups.** People are naturally threatened by the unknown. Consider the following proverb: "I saw in the distance what I took to be a beast, but when I came close, I saw it was my brother and my sister." The same error occurs in communities and work groups. From a distance an unknown person may appear to be threatening. But when the person is recognized or better known, our reactions change. Learning more about diverse groups and individuals helps you reduce the threat of the unknown.

- **Seek common ground.** Look for areas where you and others not like you can agree or share opinions. Be prepared to consider issues from many perspectives, all of which may be valid. Accept that there is room for different points of view to coexist peacefully. Although you can always find differences, it's much harder to find similarities. Look for common ground in shared experiences, mutual goals, and similar values. Concentrate on your objective even when you may disagree on how to reach it.

Successful communicators invite, use, and give feedback; make few assumptions; learn about their own cultures and other cultures; and seek common ground.

Learning about other cultures and seeking common ground help people work together to achieve common goals.

SUMMING UP AND LOOKING FORWARD

This chapter described the importance of becoming an effective business communicator in this information economy. Many of the changes in today's dynamic workplace revolve around processing and communicating information. Flattened management hierarchies, participatory management, increased emphasis on work teams, heightened global competition, and innovative communication technologies are all trends that increase the need for good communication skills. To improve your skills, you should understand the communication process. Communication doesn't take place unless senders encode meaningful messages that can be decoded and understood by receivers.

One important part of the communication process is listening. You can become a more active listener by keeping an open mind, listening for main points, capitalizing on lag time, judging ideas and not appearances, taking selective notes, and providing feedback. The chapter also described ways to help you improve your nonverbal communication skills.

You learned the powerful effect that culture has on communication, and you became more aware of key cultural values for North Americans. Finally, the chapter discussed ways that businesses and individuals can capitalize on workforce diversity.

The following chapters present the writing process. You will learn specific techniques to help you improve your written and oral expression. Remember, communication skills are not inherited. They are learned. John Bryan, the highly respected former CEO of Sara Lee, recognized this when he said that communication skills are "about 99 percent developed." Bryan contended that "the ability to construct a succinct memo, one that concentrates on the right issues, and the ability to make a presentation to an audience—these are skills that can be taught to almost anyone."[20] Remember that writing skills function as a gatekeeper. Poor skills keep you in low-wage, dead-end work. Good skills open the door to high wages and career advancement.[21]

CRITICAL THINKING

1. Why is it important for business and professional students to develop good communication skills, and why is it difficult or impossible to do without help?

2. Recall a time when you experienced a problem as a result of poor communication. What were the causes of and possible remedies for the problem?

3. How are listening skills important to employees, supervisors, and executives? Who should have the best listening skills?

4. What arguments could you give for or against the idea that body language is a science with principles that can be interpreted accurately by specialists?

5. Because English is becoming the world's language and because the United States is a dominant military and trading force, why should Americans bother to learn about other cultures?

CHAPTER REVIEW

6. Are communication skills acquired by *nature* or by *nurture*? Explain.

7. List seven trends in the workplace that affect business communicators. Be prepared to discuss how they might affect you in your future career.

8. Give a brief definition of the following words:
   a. Encode
   b. Channel
   c. Decode

9. List 11 techniques for improving your listening skills. Be prepared to discuss each.

10. What is nonverbal communication? Give several examples.

11. Name five unprofessional communication techniques that can sabotage a career.

12. Describe the concept of North American individualism. How does this concept set North Americans apart from people in some other cultures?

13. What is ethnocentrism, and how can it be reduced?

14. List seven suggestions for enhancing comprehension when you are talking with people for whom English is a second language. Be prepared to discuss each.

15. List at least eight suggestions for becoming a more effective communicator in a diverse workplace. Be prepared to discuss each.

EXPAND YOUR LEARNING WITH THESE BONUS RESOURCES!

Guffey Companion Web Site

http://guffey.swlearning.com

Your companion Web site offers review quizzes, a glossary of key terms, and flash cards to build your knowledge of chapter concepts. Additional career tools include *Dr. Guffey's Guide to Business Etiquette and Workplace Manners*, *Listening Quiz*, and electronic citation formats (MLA and APA) for business writers. You'll also find updated links to all chapter URLs.

Guffey Xtra!

http://guffeyxtra.swlearning.com

This online study assistant illustrates chapter concepts in PowerPoint. It strengthens your language skills with *Your Personal Language Trainer* (a grammar/mechanics review), *Speak Right!*, *Spell Right!*, and *Sentence Competency Exercises*. In addition, **Guffey Xtra!** brings you bonus online chapters: *Employment and Other Interviewing* and *How to Write Instructions*. You'll also find the Grammar/Mechanics Challenge exercises so that you can revise without rekeying.

INFOTRAC COLLEGE EDITION

Building Knowledge and Research Skills

To excel as a knowledge worker in today's digital workplace, you must know how to find and evaluate information on the Internet. As a student purchasing a new copy of Guffey's *Essentials of Business Communication*, 7e, you have an extraordinary opportunity to develop these research skills. For four months you have special access to InfoTrac College Edition, a comprehensive Web-based collection of millions of journal, magazine, encyclopedia, and newspaper articles. You'll find many activities and study questions in this text that help you build knowledge and develop research skills using InfoTrac. Watch for the InfoTrac icons. InfoTrac is available only with NEW copies of your textbook.

How to Use InfoTrac

With your Web browser on your computer screen, key the following URL: www.infotrac-college.com. Click *Register New Account*. Establish your logon name and password. (You may wish to read Thomson's Privacy Policy). When you feel confident, go to the *Keyword Search* page and enter your search term. If you need a little help, click *InfoTrac Demo*.

ACTIVITIES AND CASES

1.1 Pumping Up Your Basic Language Muscles With Xtra!

You can enlist the aid of your author to help you pump up your basic language skills. As your personal trainer, Dr. Guffey provides a three-step workout plan and hundreds of interactive questions to help you brush up on your grammar and mechanics skills. You receive immediate feedback in the warm-up sessions, and when you finish a complete workout you can take a short test to assess what you learned. These workouts are completely self-teaching, which means you can review at your own pace and repeat as often as you need. *Your Personal Language Trainer* is available to you at http://guffeyxtra.swlearning.com. In addition to pumping up your basic language muscles, you can also use *Spell Right!* and *Speak Right!* to improve your spelling and pronunciation skills.

Your Task. Begin using *Your Personal Language Trainer* to brush up your basic grammar and mechanics skills by completing one to three workouts per week or as many as your instructor advises. Be prepared to submit a printout of your "fitness" (completion) certificate when you finish a workout module. If your instructor directs, complete the spelling exercises in *Spell Right!* and submit a certificate of completion for the spelling final exam.

1.2 Getting To Know You

Because today's work and class environments often involve cooperating in teams or small groups, getting to know your fellow classmates is important. To learn something about the people in this class and to give you practice in developing your communication skills, your instructor may choose one of the following activities:

Your Task

a. For larger classes, divide into groups of four or five. Take one minute to introduce yourself briefly (name, major interest, hobbies, goals) within your group. Spend five minutes in the first group session. Record the first name of each individual you meet. Then informally regroup. In new groups again spend five minutes on introductions. After three or four sessions, study your name list. How many names can you associate with faces?

b. For smaller classes, introduce yourself in a two-minute oral presentation while standing before the class at the rostrum. Where are you from? What are your educational goals? What are your interests? What do you expect from this class? This informal presentation may serve as the first of two or three oral presentations correlated with Chapter 12.

c. For online classes, write a letter of introduction about yourself answering the questions in (b). Post your letter to your discussion board. Read and comment on the letters of other students. Think about how people in virtual teams must learn about each other through online messages.

1.3 Class Listening

Have you ever consciously observed the listening habits of others?

Your Task. In one of your classes, study student listening habits for a week. What barriers to effective listening did you observe? How many of the suggestions described in this chapter are being implemented by listeners in the class? Write a memo or an e-mail message to your instructor briefly describing your observations. (See Chapter 5 to learn more about memos.)

1.4 How Good Are Your Listening Skills? Self-Checked Rating Quiz

You can learn whether your listening skills are excellent or deficient by completing a brief quiz.

Your Task. Take Dr. Guffey's Listening Quiz at *http://guffey.swlearning.com*. What two listening behaviors do you think you need to work on the most?

INFOTRAC

1.5 Finding Relevant Listening Advice

Your manager, Rasheed Love, has been asked to be part of a panel discussion at a management conference. The topic is "Workplace Communication Challenges," and his area of expertise is listening. He asks you to help him prepare for the discussion by doing some research.

Your Task. Using an InfoTrac subject search, locate at least three articles with suggestions for improving workplace listening skills. Use full-text articles, not abstracts. In a memo to Rasheed Love, present a two- to three-sentence summary explaining why each article is helpful. Include the author's name, publication, date of publication, and page number. Then list at least ten listening suggestions. See Chapter 5 for memo format. Begin your memo with a sentence such as, "As you requested, I found three articles on listening techniques. After discussing the articles, I will present a list with the most helpful suggestions."

1.6 Silent Messages

Becoming more aware of the silent messages you send helps you make them more accurate.

Your Task. Analyze the kinds of silent messages you send your instructor, your classmates, and your employer. How do you send these messages? Group them into categories, as suggested by what you learned in this chapter. What do these messages mean? Be prepared to discuss them in small groups or in a memo to your instructor.

1.7 Body Language

Can body language be accurately interpreted?

Your Task. What attitudes do the following body movements suggest to you? Do these movements always mean the same thing? What part does context play in your interpretations?

a.   Whistling, wringing hands

b.   Bowed posture, twiddling thumbs

c.   Steepled hands, sprawling sitting position

d.   Rubbing hand through hair

e.   Open hands, unbuttoned coat

f.   Wringing hands, tugging ears

1.8 Universal Sign For "I Goofed"

In an effort to promote peace and tranquillity on the highways, motorists submitted the following suggestions to a newspaper columnist.[22]

Your Task. In small groups consider the pros and cons for each of the following gestures intended as an apology when a driver makes a mistake. Why would some fail?

a.   Lower your head slightly and bonk yourself on the forehead with the side of your closed fist. The message is clear: "I'm stupid. I shouldn't have done that."

b.   Make a temple with your hands, as if you were praying.

c.   Move the index finger of your right hand back and forth across your neck—as if you were cutting your throat.

d.   Flash the well-known peace sign. Hold up the index and middle fingers of one hand, making a *V*, as in Victory.

e.   Place the flat of your hands against your cheeks, as children do when they've made a mistake.

f.   Clasp your hand over your mouth, raise your brows, and shrug your shoulders.

g.   Use your knuckles to knock on the side of your head. Translation: "Oops! Engage brain."

h.   Place your right hand high on your chest and pat a few times, like a basketball player who drops a pass or a football player who makes a bad throw. This says, "I'll take the blame."

i.   Place your right fist over the middle of your chest and move it in a circular motion. This is universal sign language for "I'm sorry."

j.   Open your window and tap the top of your car roof with your hand.

k.   Smile and raise both arms, palms outward, which is a universal gesture for surrender or forgiveness.

l.   Use the military salute, which is simple and shows respect.

m.   Flash your biggest smile, point at yourself with your right thumb and move your head from left to right, as if to say, "I can't believe I did that."

1.9 Alice In Wonderland Travels to Tokyo

Jeff Davis is the leader of a creative team representing a large American theme park company. The owners of a Japanese park rely on the American company to develop new attractions for their Tokyo park. But the Japanese own their park and must approve any new addition. Jeff and his team recently traveled to Japan to make an important presentation to the owners. His team had worked for the past year developing the concept of an outdoor garden maze with a network of hedge passageways for children to wander through. The concept was based on *Alice in Wonderland*.

The jobs of Jeff's entire team depended on selling the idea of this new attraction (including restaurants and gift shops) to the owners of the Tokyo park. Because the Japanese smiled and nodded throughout the presentation, Jeff assumed they liked the idea. When he pushed for final approval, the Japanese smiled and said that an outdoor garden attraction might be difficult in their climate. Jeff explained away that argument. Then, he asked for a straightforward *yes* or *no*, but the Japanese answered, "We will have to study it very carefully." Thinking he had not made himself clear, Jeff began to review the strong points of the presentation.

Your Task. Analyze the preceding cross-cultural incident. What cultural elements may be interfering with communication in this exchange?

TEAM — CRITICAL THINKING

1.10 Cross-Cultural Gap At Resort Hotel In Thailand

The Laguna Beach Resort Hotel in Phuket, Thailand, nestled between a tropical lagoon and the sparkling Andaman Sea, is one of the most beautiful resorts in the world. Fortunately, it was spared serious damage from the region's tidal waves. (You can take a virtual tour by using Google and searching for "Laguna Beach Resort Phuket.") When Brett Peel arrived as the director of the hotel's kitchen, he thought he had landed in paradise. Only on the job six weeks, he began wondering why his Thai staff would answer *yes* even when they didn't understand what he had said. Other foreign managers discovered that junior staff managers rarely spoke up and never expressed an opinion contrary to those of senior executives. What's more, guests with a complaint thought that Thai employees were not taking them seriously because the Thais smiled at even the worst complaints. Thais also did not seem to understand deadlines or urgent requests.[23]

Your Task. In teams decide how you would respond to the following. If you were the director of this hotel, would you implement a training program for employees? If so, would you train only foreign managers, or would you include local Thai employees as well? What topics should a training program include? Would your goal be to introduce Western ways to the Thais? At least 90 percent of the hotel guests are non-Thai.

1.11 Translating Idioms

Many languages have idiomatic expressions that do not always make sense to outsiders.

Your Task. Explain in simple English what the following idiomatic expressions mean. Assume that you are explaining them to people for whom English is a second language.

a.   class act

b.   grey area

c.   cold shoulder

d.   eager beaver

e.   early bird

f.   get your act together

g.   go ape

h.   go behind someone's back

i.   the bottom of the barrel

1.12 Analyzing Diversity At Reebok

Reebok grew from a $12 million a year sport shoe company into a $3 billion footwear and apparel powerhouse without giving much thought to the hiring of employees. "When we were growing very, very fast, all we did was bring another friend into work the next day," recalled Sharon Cohen, Reebok vice president. "Everybody hired nine of their friends. Well, it happened that nine white people hired nine of their friends, so guess what? They were white, all about the same age. And then we looked up and said, 'Wait a minute. We don't like the way it looks here.' That's the kind of thing that can happen when you are growing very fast and thoughtlessly."[24]

Your Task. In what ways would Reebok benefit by diversifying its staff? What competitive advantages might it gain? Outline your reasoning in an e-mail message to your instructor.

VIDEO RESOURCES

Two special sets of videos accompany Guffey's *Essentials of Business Communication*, 7e. These videos take you beyond the classroom to build the communication skills you will need to succeed in today's rapidly changing workplace.

Video Library 1, *Building Workplace Communication Skills*, presents five videos that introduce and reinforce concepts in selected chapters. These excellent tools ease the learning load by demonstrating chapter-specific material to strengthen your comprehension and retention of key ideas.

Video Library 2, *Bridging the Gap*, presents six videos transporting you inside high-profile companies such as Yahoo, Ben & Jerry's, and Zubi Advertising. You'll be able to apply your new skills in structured applications aimed at bridging the gap between the classroom and the real world of work.

We recommend two videos for this chapter:

Career Success Starts With Communication Foundations. This film, made especially for Guffey books, illustrates the changing business world, flattened management hierarchies, the communication process, communication flow, ethics, listening, nonverbal communication, and other topics to prepare you for today's workplace. The film is unique in that many concepts

are demonstrated through role-playing. B to discuss critical-thinking questions at the fil conclusion.

Erasing Stereotypes: Zubi Advertising. This film features a successful businessperson who used her knowledge of Hispanic culture to build an advertising company that creates ads appealing to the Hispanic American market. Despite the obstacles of being a female and a Cuban in Miami, Teresa Zubizarreta created a hugely successful advertising agency. With headquarters in Miami and satellite offices in Los Angeles, Chicago, Houston, Detroit, and New York, Teresa Zubizarreta and her 70-person team work to craft precise messages aimed at Hispanic audiences. Your instructor may ask you to watch for specific information as you view this film.

● GRAMMAR/MECHANICS CHECKUP—1

These checkups are designed to improve your control of grammar and mechanics. They systematically review all sections of the Grammar/Mechanics Handbook. Answers are provided near the end of the book. You will find Advanced Grammar/Mechanics Checkups with immediate feedback at **Guffey Xtra!** (*http://guffeyxtra.swlearning.com*).

Nouns

Review Sections 1.02–1.06 in the Grammar/Mechanics Handbook. Then study each of the following statements. Underscore any inappropriate form, and write a correction in the space provided. Also record the appropriate G/M section and letter to illustrate the principle involved. If a sentence is correct, write *C*. When you finish, compare your responses with those provided. If your answers differ, study carefully the principles shown in parentheses.

attorneys   (1.05d)   **Example**   <u>Attornies</u> seem to be the only ones who benefit from class action suits.

_____   1. Some companys are giving up land lines and using cell phones exclusively.

_____   2. Business is better on Saturday's than on Sundays.

_____   3. Some of the citys in Craig's report offer excellent opportunities.

_____   4. Frozen chickens and turkies are kept in the company's lockers.

_____   5. All secretaries were asked to check supplies and other inventorys.

_____   6. Only the Bushs and the Sanchezes brought their entire families.

_____   7. In the 1990s profits grew rapidly; in the late 2000's investments soared.

_____   8. Both editor in chiefs instituted strict proofreading policies.

_____   9. Luxury residential complexs are part of the architect's plan.

_____   10. Voters in three countys are likely to approve new gas taxes.

_____   11. The instructor was surprised to find two Cassidy's in one class.

_____   12. André sent digital photos of two valleys in France before we planned our trip.

_____   13. Most companies have copies of statements showing their assets and liabilitys.

_____   14. My flat-screen monitor makes it difficult to distinguish between o's and a's.

_____   15. Both runner-ups complained about the winner's behavior.

MECHANICS CHALLENGE—1

The following memo has many faults in grammar, spelling, punctuation, capitalization, word use, and number form. Correct the errors with standard proofreading marks (see Appendix B) or revise the message online at **Guffey Xtra!** Study the guidelines in the Grammar/Mechanics Handbook to sharpen your skills. When you finish, your instructor can show you the revised version of this memo.

TO: Jocelyn Smith-Garcia

FROM: Kevin West, Manager

DATE: November 4, 200x

SUBJECT: SUGGESTION FOR TELECOMMUTING SUCCESSFULLY

To help you become an effective telecommuter, Jocelyn, we have a few suggestions to share with you. I understand you will be working at home for the next 9 months. The following guidelines should help you stay in touch with us, and compleate your work satisfactory.

- Be sure to check your message bored daily, and respond immediate to those who are trying to reach you.

- Check your e-mail at least 3 times a day, answer all messages promply, make sure that you sent copys of relevent message's to the appropriate officestaff.

- Transmit all spread sheet work to Zachary Jacksen in our computer services department, he will analyze each week's activitys, and update all inventorys.

- Provide me with end-of-week reports indicating the major accounts you serviced.

In prepareing your work area you should make sure you have adequate space for your computer, printer, fax and storage. For Security reasons you're workingarea should be off limits to your family and friends.

We will continue to hold once-a-week staff meetings on Friday's at 10 a.m. in the morning. Do you think it would be possible for you to attend 1 or 2 of these meetings? The next one is Friday, November 17th.

I know you will enjoy working at home Joclyn. Following these basic guidelines should help you accomplish your work, and provide the office with adequate contact with you.

Communication Workshops (such as the one on the next page) provide insight into special business communication topics and skills not discussed in the chapters. These topics cover ethics, technology, career skills, and collaboration. Each workshop includes a career application with a case study or problem to help you develop skills relevant to the workshop topic.

COMMUNICATION WORKSHOP
TECHNOLOGY

USING JOB BOARDS TO LEARN ABOUT
EMPLOYMENT POSSIBILITIES IN YOUR FIELD

Nearly everyone looking for a job today starts with the Web. This communication workshop will help you use the Web to study job openings in your field. Locating jobs or internships on the Web has distinct advantages. For a few job seekers, the Web leads to bigger salaries, wider opportunities, and faster hiring. The Web, however, can devour huge chunks of time and produce slim results.

In terms of actually finding a job, using the Web does not always result in success. Web searching seems to work best for professionals looking for similar work in their current fields and for those who are totally flexible about location. Yet, the Web is an excellent place for any job seeker to learn what's available, what qualifications are necessary, and what salaries are being offered. Thousands of job boards with many job listings for employers across the United States and abroad are available on the Web.

Career Application. Assume that you are about to finish your degree or certification program, and you are now looking for a job. At the direction of your instructor, conduct a survey of electronic job advertisements in your field. What's available? How much is the salary? What are the requirements?

Your Task

- Visit Monster.com *<www.monster.com>*, one of the most popular job boards.

- **Study the opening page.** Remember that most job boards are supported by advertisements. As a result, you might get a pop-up ad, which you should ignore. Close any pop-up boxes. From the opening page, click *Find Jobs*.

- Read *More Search Tips*. Before entering any keywords, it's wise to spend a few moments learning how to search. Click *More Search Tips* for many helpful hints on precise searching. Browsing this information may take a few minutes, but it's well worth the effort. Scroll down to learn about safe job searching, keyword searching, location and company searching, and sorting and viewing your results. Close this box by clicking the *X* in the top right corner.

- **Conduct a practice search.** Back on the search page, enter a search term in the *Enter Key Word(s)* box. Skip the *Enter Company Name* box and then click a geographical area in the *Select Location* box. Just for fun, try "Honolulu, Hawaii." In the *Select Job Category* box, select an appropriate term, such as Advertising or Accounting. Then press click *Get Results*. You should see many current job ads.

- **Conduct a real search.** Now conduct a job search in your career area and in geographical areas of your choice. Select three ads and print them. If you cannot print, make notes on what you find.

- **Visit another site.** Try *www.CollegeRecruiter.com*, which claims to be the highest-traffic entry-level job site for students and graduates, or *www.careerbuilder.com*, which says it is the nation's largest employment network. Become familiar with the site's searching tools, and look for jobs in your field. Select and print three ads.

- **Analyze the skills required.** From the ads you printed, how often do they mention communication, teamwork, computer skills, or professionalism? What tasks do the ads mention? What is the salary range identified in these ads for this position? Your instructor may ask you to submit your findings and/or report to the class.

PHOTOS: © ROYALTY-FREE/CORBIS; © PHOTODISC COLLECTION/GETTY IMAGES; © PHOTODISC COLLECTION/GETTY IMAGES

UNIT 2

THE WRITING PROCESS

CHAPTER 2

CREATING BUSINESS MESSAGES

> *I wanted to know where they came from, what their interests were, and what I could talk to them about.*
>
> **John H. Johnson**, founder of *Ebony* and *Jet* magazines and Fashion Fair cosmetics, talking about customers[1]

OBJECTIVES

- Understand that business writing should be audience oriented, purposeful, and economical.
- Identify and implement the three phases of the writing process.
- Appreciate the importance of analyzing the task and profiling the audience for business messages.
- Create messages that spotlight audience benefits and cultivate a "you" view.
- Develop a conversational tone and use positive language.
- Explain the need for inclusive language, plain expression, and familiar words.
- List seven ways technology helps improve business writing.

THE BASICS OF BUSINESS WRITING

Excellent communicators, like John H. Johnson, focus on the audience for their messages.

In communicating with others, newspaper founder and businessman John H. Johnson always concentrated on what they wanted rather than what he wanted. An exceedingly successful entrepreneur, Johnson was born in a tin-roof shack in Arkansas. Despite the odds, he became the first African-American on the *Forbes* magazine list of the 400 richest people in America. "Being poor made me run scared," he confessed. It also motivated him to find ways to succeed in publishing and in life. What is his greatest success secret? Focusing totally on his audience. With prospective advertisers, he always talked about what he could do for them. How could he help them improve their bottom line? How could he help them increase their sales? How could he make their lives easier?[2]

Audience awareness is one of the basics of business communication. This chapter focuses on writing for business audiences. Business writing may be different from other writing you have done. High school or college essays and term papers may have required you to describe your feelings, display your knowledge, and meet a

PHOTOS: © ROYALTY-FREE/CORBIS; © PHOTODISC COLLECTION/GETTY IMAGES; © PHOTODISC COLLECTION/GETTY IMAGES

minimum word count. Business writing, however, has different goals. In preparing business messages and oral presentations, you'll find that your writing needs to be:

Business writing is audience oriented, purposeful, and economical.

- **Audience oriented.** Like publisher John Johnson, you will concentrate on looking at a problem from the receiver's perspective instead of seeing it from your own.
- **Purposeful.** You will be writing to solve problems and convey information. You will have a definite purpose to fulfill in each message.
- **Economical.** You will try to present ideas clearly but concisely. Length is not rewarded.

These distinctions actually ease the writer's task. You won't be searching your imagination for creative topic ideas. You won't be stretching your ideas to make them appear longer. One writing consultant complained that "most college graduates entering industry have at least a subliminal perception that in technical and business writing, quantity enhances quality."[3] Wrong! Get over the notion that longer is better. Conciseness is what counts in business.

Following a systematic process helps beginning writers create effective messages and presentations.

The ability to prepare concise, audience-centered, and purposeful messages does not come naturally. Very few people, especially beginners, can sit down and compose a terrific letter or report without training. However, following a systematic process, studying model messages, and practicing the craft can make nearly anyone a successful business writer or speaker.

THE WRITING PROCESS FOR BUSINESS MESSAGES AND ORAL PRESENTATIONS

The writing process has three parts: prewriting, writing, and revising.

Whether you are preparing an e-mail message, memo, letter, or oral presentation, the process will be easier if you follow a systematic plan. Our plan breaks the entire task into three separate phases: prewriting, writing, and revising. As you can see in Figure 2.1, however, the process is not always linear. It does not always proceed from Step 1 to Step 2; often the writer must circle back and repeat an earlier step.

To illustrate the writing process, let's say that you own a popular local McDonald's franchise. At rush times, you face a problem. Customers complain about the chaotic multiple waiting lines to approach the service counter. You once saw two customers nearly get into a fistfight over cutting into a line. What's more, customers often are so intent on looking for ways to improve their positions in line that they fail to examine the menu. Then they are undecided when their turn arrives. You want to convince other franchise owners that a single-line (serpentine) system would work better. You could telephone the other owners. But you want to present a serious argument with good points that they will remember and be willing to act on when they gather for their next district meeting. You decide to write a letter that you hope will win their support.

FIGURE 2.1 ·——• **The Writing Process**

Spending adequate time on the first phase of the writing process results in less pain in the writing and revising stages. The first phase of the writing process involves analyzing information currently available, deciding what the purpose of your message is, anticipating the reaction of the receiver, and thinking of ways to adapt your message for the best reception.

© JACK HOLLINGSWORTH/PHOTODISC/GETTY IMAGES

Prewriting

The first phase of the writing process involves analyzing and anticipating the audience and then adapting to that audience.

The first phase of the writing process prepares you to write. It involves *analyzing* the audience and your purpose for writing. The audience for your letter will be other franchise owners, some highly educated and others not. Your purpose in writing is to convince them that a change in policy would improve customer service. You are convinced that a single-line system, such as that used in banks, would reduce chaos and make customers happier because they would not have to worry about where they are in line.

Prewriting also involves *anticipating* how your audience will react to your message. You're sure that some of the other owners will agree with you, but others might fear that customers seeing a long single line might go elsewhere. In *adapting* your message to the audience, you try to think of the right words and the right tone that will win approval.

Writing

The second phase of the writing process includes researching, organizing the message, and actually writing it.

The second phase involves researching, organizing, and then composing the message. In *researching* information for this letter, you would probably investigate other kinds of businesses that use single lines for customers. You might check out your competitors. What are Wendy's and Burger King doing? You might do some calling to see whether other franchise owners are concerned about chaotic lines. Before writing to the entire group, you might brainstorm with a few owners to see what ideas they have for solving the problem.

Once you have collected enough information, you would focus on *organizing* your letter. Should you start out by offering your solution? Or should you work up to it slowly, describing the problem, presenting your evidence, and then ending with the solution? The final step in the second phase of the writing process is actually *composing* the letter. Naturally, you'll do it at your computer so that you can make revisions easily.

Revising

The third phase of the writing process includes revising for clarity and readability, proofreading for errors, and evaluating for effectiveness.

The third phase of the process involves revising, proofreading, and evaluating your letter. After writing the first draft, you'll spend a lot of time *revising* the message for clarity, conciseness, tone, and readability. Could parts of it be rearranged to make your point more effectively? This is the time when you look for ways to improve the organization and sound of your message. Next, you'll spend time *proofreading* carefully to ensure correct spelling, grammar, punctuation, and format. The final phase involves *evaluating* your message to decide whether it accomplishes your goal.

Scheduling the Writing Process

Although Figure 2.1 shows the three phases of the writing process equally, the time you spend on each varies depending on the complexity of the problem, the purpose, the audience, and your schedule. One expert gives these rough estimates for scheduling a project:

- Prewriting—25 percent (planning and worrying)
- Writing—25 percent (organizing and composing)
- Revising—50 percent (45 percent revising and 5 percent proofreading)

Because revising is the most important part of the writing process, it takes the most time.

These are rough guides, yet you can see that good writers spend most of their time on the final phase of revising and proofreading. Much depends, of course, on your project, its importance, and your familiarity with it. What's critical to remember, though, is that revising is a major component of the writing process.

It may appear that you perform one step and progress to the next, always following the same order. Most business writing, however, is not that rigid. Although writers perform the tasks described, the steps may be rearranged, abbreviated, or repeated. Some writers revise every sentence and paragraph as they go. Many find that new ideas occur after they've begun to write, causing them to back up, alter the organization, and rethink their plan.

ANALYZING THE PURPOSE AND THE AUDIENCE

We've just taken a look at the total writing process. As you begin to develop your business writing skills, you should expect to follow this process closely. With experience, though, you'll become like other good writers and presenters who alter, compress, and rearrange the steps as needed. At first, however, following a plan is very helpful. The remainder of this chapter covers the first phase of the writing process. You'll learn to analyze the purpose for writing, anticipate how your audience will react, and adapt your message to the audience.

Identifying Your Purpose

As you begin to compose a message, ask yourself two important questions: (1) Why am I sending this message? (2) What do I hope to achieve? Your responses will determine how you organize and present your information.

The primary purpose of most business messages is to inform or to persuade; the secondary purpose is to promote goodwill.

Your message may have primary and secondary purposes. For college work your primary purpose may be merely to complete the assignment; secondary purposes might be to make yourself look good and to get a good grade. The primary purposes for sending business messages are typically to inform and to persuade. A secondary purpose is to promote goodwill: you and your organization want to look good in the eyes of your audience.

Selecting the Best Channel

After identifying the purpose of your message, you need to select the most appropriate communication channel. Some information is most efficiently and effectively delivered orally. Other messages should be written, and still others are best delivered electronically. Whether to set up a meeting, send a message by e-mail, or write a report depends on some of the following factors:

Choosing an appropriate channel depends on the importance of the message, the feedback required, the need for a permanent record, the cost, and the degree of formality needed.

- Importance of the message
- Amount and speed of feedback and interactivity required
- Necessity of a permanent record
- Cost of the channel
- Degree of formality desired

FIGURE 2.2

Choosing Communication Channels

Channel	Best Use
Face-to-face conversation	When you need a rich, interactive medium to be persuasive, deliver bad news, share a personal message, or seek an immediate response.
Telephone call	When you need to deliver or gather information quickly, when nonverbal cues are unimportant, and when you cannot meet in person.
Voice mail message	When you wish to leave important or routine information that the receiver can respond to when convenient.
Fax	When your message must cross time zones or international boundaries, when a written record is significant, or when speed is important.
E-mail	When you need feedback but not immediately. Insecurity makes it problematic for personal, emotional, or private messages. Effective for communicating with a large, dispersed audience.
Face-to-face group meeting	When group decisions and consensus are important. Inefficient for merely distributing information.
Video- or teleconference	When group consensus and interaction are important but members are geographically dispersed.
Memo	When you want a written record to explain policies clearly, discuss procedures, or collect information within an organization.
Letter	When you need a written record of correspondence with customers, the government, suppliers, or others outside an organization.
Report or proposal	When you are delivering considerable data internally or externally.

An interesting theory, called media richness, describes the extent to which a channel or medium recreates or represents all the information available in the original message. A richer medium, such as face-to-face conversation, permits more interactivity and feedback. A leaner medium, such as a report or proposal, presents a flat, one-dimensional message. Richer media enable the sender to provide more verbal and visual cues, as well as allow the sender to tailor the message to the audience.

Many factors help you decide which of the channels shown in Figure 2.2 is most appropriate for delivering a workplace message.

Switching to Faster Channels

Technology and competition continue to accelerate the pace of business today. As a result, communicators are switching to ever-faster means of exchanging information. In the past business messages within organizations were delivered largely by hard-copy memos. Responses would typically take a couple of days. However, that's too slow for today's communicators. They want answers and action now! Cell phones, instant messaging, faxes, Web sites, and especially e-mail can deliver that information much faster than can traditional channels of communication.

Channels of choice today must be fast, cheap, and easy.

Within many organizations, hard-copy memos are still written, especially for messages that require persuasion, permanence, or formality. However, the channel of choice for corporate communicators today is clearly e-mail. It's fast, cheap, and easy. Thus, fewer hard-copy memos are being written. Fewer letters to customers are also being written. That's because many customer service functions can now be served through Web sites or by e-mail.

Whether your channel choice is e-mail, a hard-copy memo, or a report, you'll be a more effective writer if you spend sufficient time in the prewriting phase.

© STOCKBYTE PLATINUM/GETTY IMAGES

Wireless channels increase the speed of communication and enable business-people to be productive away from the office. But too much toggling back and forth on wireless gadgets dilutes performance, increases irritability, and causes managers to become disorganized underachievers, says Harvard psychiatrist Dr. E. M. Hallowell. (Michelle Conlin, "Take A Vacation From Your BlackBerry," *BusinessWeek*, 20 December 2004, 56.)

ANTICIPATING THE AUDIENCE

A good writer anticipates the audience for a message: What is the reader like? How will that reader react to the message? Although you can't always know exactly who the reader is, you can imagine some of the reader's characteristics. Even writers of direct-mail sales letters have a general idea of the audience they wish to target. Picturing a typical reader is important in guiding what you write. One copywriter at Lands' End, the catalog company, pictures his sister-in-law whenever he writes product descriptions for the catalog. By profiling your audience and shaping a message to respond to that profile, you are more likely to achieve your communication goals.

Profiling the Audience

By profiling your audience before you write, you can identify the appropriate tone, language, and channel.

Visualizing your audience is a pivotal step in the writing process. The questions in Figure 2.3 will help you profile your audience. How much time you devote to answering these questions depends greatly on your message and its context. An analytical report that you compose for management or an oral presentation before a big group would, of course, demand considerable audience anticipation. On the other hand, an e-mail message to a coworker or a letter to a familiar supplier might require only a few moments of planning. No matter how short your message, though, spend some time thinking about the audience so that you can tailor your words to your readers or listeners. Remember that most readers or listeners will be thinking, *What's in it for me?* or *What am I supposed to do with this information?*

Responding to the Profile

Profiling your audience helps you make decisions about shaping the message. You'll discover what kind of language is appropriate, whether you're free to use specialized

FIGURE 2.3 ————— • **Asking the Right Questions to Profile Your Audience**

Primary Audience

Who is my primary reader or listener?

What are my personal and professional relationships with that person?

What position does the individual hold in the organization?

How much does that person know about the subject?

What do I know about that person's education, beliefs, culture, and attitudes?

Should I expect a neutral, positive, or negative response to my message?

Secondary Audience

Who might see or hear this message in addition to the primary audience?

How do these people differ from the primary audience?

Do I need to include more background information?

How must I reshape my message to make it understandable and acceptable to others to whom it might be forwarded?

After profiling the audience, you can decide whether the receiver will be neutral, positive, or hostile toward your message.

technical terms, whether you should explain everything, and so on. You'll decide whether your tone should be formal or informal, and you'll select the most desirable channel. Imagining whether the receiver is likely to be neutral, positive, or negative will help you determine how to organize your message.

Another advantage of profiling your audience is considering the possibility of a secondary audience. For example, let's say you start to write an e-mail message to your supervisor, Sheila, describing a problem you're having. Halfway through the message you realize that Sheila will probably forward this message to her boss, the vice president. Sheila will not want to summarize what you said; instead she will take the easy route and merely forward your e-mail. When you realize that the vice president will probably see this message, you decide to back up and use a more formal tone. You remove your inquiry about Sheila's family, you reduce your complaints, and you tone down your language about why things went wrong. Instead, you provide more background information, and you are more specific in identifying items that the vice president might not recognize. Analyzing the task and anticipating the audience help you adapt your message so that you can create an efficient and effective message.

ADAPTING TO THE TASK AND AUDIENCE

After analyzing your purpose and anticipating your audience, you must convey your purpose to that audience. Adaptation is the process of creating a message that suits your audience.

Writers improve the tone of a message by emphasizing reader benefits, cultivating a "you" attitude, and using a conversational tone and inclusive language.

One important aspect of adaptation is *tone*. Conveyed largely by the words in a message, tone reflects how a receiver feels upon reading or hearing a message. Skilled communicators create a positive tone in their messages by using a number of adaptive techniques, some of which are unconscious. These include spotlighting audience benefits, cultivating a "you" attitude, sounding conversational, and using positive expression. Additional adaptive techniques include using inclusive language and preferring plain language with familiar words.

© Ted Goff (www.tedgoff.com)

"You haven't been listening. I keep telling you that I don't want a product fit for a king."

Audience Benefits

Focusing on the audience sounds like a modern idea, but actually one of America's early statesmen and authors recognized this fundamental writing principle over 200 years ago. In describing effective writing, Ben Franklin observed, "To be good, it ought to have a tendency to benefit the reader."[4] These wise words have become a fundamental guideline for today's business communicators. Expanding on Franklin's counsel, a contemporary communication consultant gives this solid advice to his business clients: "Always stress the benefit to the readers of whatever it is you're trying to get them to do. If you can show them how you're going to save them frustration or help them meet their goals, you have the makings of a powerful message."[5]

Adapting your message to the receiver's needs means putting yourself in that person's shoes. It's called *empathy*. Empathic senders think about how a receiver will decode a message. They try to give something to the receiver, solve

> Empathy involves shaping a message that appeals to the receiver.

the receiver's problems, save the receiver's money, or just understand the feelings and position of that person. Which of the following messages is more appealing to the audience?

Sender focus	To enable us to update our stockholder records, we ask that the enclosed card be returned.
Audience focus	So that you may promptly receive dividend checks and information related to your shares, please return the enclosed card.
Sender focus	Our warranty becomes effective only when we receive an owner's registration.
Audience focus	Your warranty begins working for you as soon as you return your owner's registration.
Sender focus	We offer a CD language course that we are convinced will be rewarding if ordered immediately.
Audience focus	The sooner you order your CD language program, the sooner the rewards will be yours.
Sender focus	The Human Resources Department requires that the enclosed questionnaire be completed immediately so that we can allocate our training resource funds.
Audience focus	By filling out the enclosed questionnaire, you can be one of the first employees to sign up for the new career development program.

"You" View

> Because receivers are most interested in themselves, emphasize the word *you* whenever possible.

Notice how many of the previous audience-focused messages included the word *you*. In concentrating on receiver benefits, skilled communicators naturally develop the "you" view. They emphasize second-person pronouns (*you, your*) instead of first-person pronouns (*I/we, us, our*). Whether your goal is to inform, persuade, or promote goodwill, the catchiest words you can use are *you* and *your*. Compare the following examples.

"I/we" view	I have granted you permission to attend the communication seminar.
"You" view	You may attend the seminar to improve your communication skills.

"I/we" view	We have shipped your order by UPS, and we are sure it will arrive in time for the sales promotion December 1.
"You" view	Your order will be delivered by UPS in time for your sales promotion December 1.
"I/we" view	I'm asking all employees to respond to the attached survey about working conditions.
"You" view	Because your ideas count, please complete the attached survey about working conditions.

Your goal is to focus on the reader. But second-person pronouns can be overused and misused. Readers appreciate genuine interest; on the other hand, they resent obvious attempts at manipulation. Some sales messages, for example, are guilty of overkill when they include *you* dozens of times in a direct-mail promotion. Furthermore, the word can sometimes create the wrong impression. Consider this statement: *You cannot return merchandise until you receive written approval.* The word *you* appears twice, but the reader feels singled out for criticism. In the following version the message is less personal and more positive: *Customers may return merchandise with written approval.* Another difficulty in emphasizing the "you" view and de-emphasizing *we/I* is that it may result in overuse of the passive voice. For example, to avoid *We will give you* (active voice), you might write *You will be given* (passive voice). The active voice in writing is generally preferred because it identifies who is doing the acting. You'll learn more about active and passive voice in Chapter 3.

Emphasize *you* but don't eliminate all *I* and *we* statements.

In recognizing the value of the "you" attitude, writers do not have to sterilize their writing and totally avoid any first-person pronouns or words that show their feelings. Skilled communicators are able to convey sincerity, warmth, and enthusiasm by the words they choose. Don't be afraid to use phrases such as *I'm happy* or *We're delighted*, if you truly are. When speaking face-to-face, communicators show sincerity and warmth with nonverbal cues such as a smile and a pleasant voice tone. In letters, memos, and e-mail messages, however, only expressive words and phrases can show these feelings. These phrases suggest hidden messages that say to readers and customers *You are important, I hear you*, and *I'm honestly trying to please you.*

Conversational but Professional

Most instant messages, e-mail messages, business letters, memos, and reports replace conversation. Thus, they are most effective when they convey an informal, conversational tone instead of a formal, pretentious tone. Workplace messages should not, however, become so casual that they sound low-level and unprofessional.

Strive for conversational expression, but also remember to be professional.

Instant messaging (IM) enables coworkers to have informal, spontaneous conversations. Some companies have accepted IM as a serious workplace tool. With the increasing use of instant messaging and e-mail, however, a major problem has developed. Sloppy, unprofessional expression appears in many workplace messages. You'll learn more about the dangers of e-mail in Chapter 5. At this point, though, we focus on the tone of the language.

To project a professional image, you must sound educated and mature. Overuse of expressions such as *totally awesome, you know*, and *like*, as well as reliance on needless abbreviations (*BTW* for *by the way*), make a businessperson sound like a teenager. Professional messages do not include IM abbreviations, slang, sentence fragments, and chitchat. We urge you to strive for a warm, conversational tone that avoids low-level diction. Levels of diction, as shown in Figure 2.4, range from unprofessional through formal.

Your goal is a warm, friendly tone that sounds professional. Although some writers are too casual, others are overly formal. To impress readers, they use big words,

FIGURE 2.4

Levels of Diction

Unprofessional (low-level diction)	Conversational (mid-level diction)	Formal (high-level diction)
badmouth	criticize	denigrate
guts	nerve	courage
pecking order	line of command	dominance hierarchy
ticked off	upset	provoked
rat on	inform	betray
rip off	steal	expropriate
Sentence Example If we just hang in there, we can snag the contract.	**Sentence Example** If we don't get discouraged, we can win the contract.	**Sentence Example** If the principals persevere, they can secure the contract.

long sentences, legal terminology, and third-person constructions. Stay away from expressions such as *the undersigned, the writer*, and *the affected party*. You'll sound more friendly with familiar pronouns such as *I, we*, and *you*. Study the following examples to see how to achieve a professional, yet conversational tone:

Unprofessional	Hey, boss, GR8 news! Firewall now installed!! BTW, check with me b4 announcing it.
Improved	Mr. Smith, our new firewall software is now installed. Please check with me before announcing it.
Unprofessional	Look, dude, this report is totally bogus. And the figures don't look kosher. Show me some real stats. Got sources?
Improved	Because the figures in this report seem inaccurate, please submit the source statistics.
Overly formal	All employees are herewith instructed to return the appropriately designated contracts to the undersigned.
Conversational	Please return your contracts to me.
Overly formal	Pertaining to your order, we must verify the sizes that your organization requires prior to consignment of your order to our shipper.
Conversational	We'll send your order as soon as we confirm the sizes you need.

Positive Language

Positive language creates goodwill and gives more options to receivers.

The clarity and tone of a message are considerably improved if you use positive rather than negative language. Positive language generally conveys more information than negative language does. Moreover, positive messages are uplifting and pleasant to read. Positive wording tells what *is* and what *can be done* rather than what *isn't* and what *can't be done*. For example, *Your order cannot be shipped by January 10*, is not nearly as informative as *Your order will be shipped January 20*.

Notice in the following examples how you can revise the negative tone to reflect a more positive impression.

Negative	We are unable to complete your order until we receive proof of your payment.
Positive	We look forward to completing your order as soon as we receive your payment.
Negative	We are sorry that we must reject your application for credit at this point in time.
Positive	At present we can serve you on a cash basis only.
Negative	If you fail to pass the exam, you will not qualify.
Positive	You'll qualify if you pass the exam.
Negative	Although I've never had a paid position before, I have worked as an intern in an attorney's office while completing my degree requirements.
Positive	My experience in an attorney's office and my recent training in legal procedures and computer applications can be assets to your organization.

Inclusive Language

Sensitive communicators avoid language that excludes people.

A business writer who is alert and empathic will strive to use words that include rather than exclude people. Some words have been called *sexist* because they seem to exclude females. Notice the use of the masculine pronouns *he* and *his* in the following sentences:

If a physician is needed, *he* will be called.
Every renter must read *his* rental agreement carefully.

These sentences illustrate an age-old grammatical rule called "common gender." When a speaker or writer did not know the gender (sex) of an individual, masculine pronouns (such as *he* or *his*) were used. Masculine pronouns were understood to indicate both men and women. Today, however, sensitive writers and speakers replace common-gender pronouns with alternate inclusive constructions. You can use any of four alternatives.

Sexist	Every attorney has ten minutes for *his* summation.
Alternative 1	*All attorneys* have ten minutes for *their* summations. (Use a plural noun and plural pronoun.)
Alternative 2	Attorneys have ten minutes for summations. (Omit the pronoun entirely.)
Alternative 3	Every attorney has ten minutes for *a* summation. (Use an article instead of a pronoun.)
Alternative 4	Every attorney has ten minutes for *his* or *her* summation. (Use both a masculine and a feminine pronoun.)

Note that the last alternative, which includes a masculine and a feminine pronoun, is wordy and awkward. Don't use it too frequently.

Other words are considered sexist because they suggest stereotypes. For example, the nouns *fireman* and *mailman* suggest that only men hold these positions. You can avoid offending your listener or reader by using neutral job titles.

Instead of This	Try This	Instead of This	Try This
chairman	department head	stewardess	flight attendant
fireman	firefighter	waiter, waitress	server
mailman	letter carrier	workman	worker
policeman	police officer		

Plain English

Inflated, unnatural writing that is intended to impress readers often confuses them.

Business communicators who are conscious of their audience try to use plain language that expresses clear meaning. They avoid showy words, long sentences, and confusing expressions. Some business, legal, and government documents, however, are written in an inflated style that obscures meaning. This style of writing has been given various terms such as *legalese, federalese, bureaucratese,* and *doublespeak.*

Over the past 30 years, consumer groups and the government have joined forces in the Plain English movement. It encourages businesses, professional organizations, and government bodies to write any official document—such as a contract, warranty, insurance policy, or lease—in clear, concise language.[6] As a result of the Plain English movement, numerous states have passed laws requiring that business contracts and public documents be written in plain language. One branch of the government, the Securities and Exchange Commission, has even written "A Plain English Handbook." This booklet illustrates many of the principles of good writing, some of which are shown in Figure 2.5. Throughout this textbook we will be practicing these principles to help you improve your writing skills. Don't be impressed by high-sounding language and legalese, such as *herein, thereafter, hereinafter, whereas,* and similar expressions. Your writing will be better if you use plain English.

Familiar Words

Familiar words are more meaningful to readers and listeners.

Clear messages contain words that are familiar and meaningful to the receiver. How can we know what is meaningful to a given receiver? Although we can't know with certainty, we can avoid long or unfamiliar words that have simpler synonyms. Whenever possible in business communication, substitute short, common, simple words. Don't, however, give up a precise word if it says exactly what you mean.

FIGURE 2.5 ⟶ • **Selected Principles of Plain English**

- Use the active voice with strong verbs.
- Don't be afraid of personal pronouns (e.g., *I, we,* and *you*).
- Bring abstractions down to earth (instead of *asset,* write *one share of IBM common stock*).
- Omit superfluous words (instead of *in the event that,* write *if*).
- Use positive expression (instead of *it is not unlike,* write *it is similar*).
- Prefer short sentences and keep sentences parallel.
- Remove jargon and legalese.
- Keep the subject, verb, and object close together.

Source: U.S. Securities and Exchange Commission, "A Plain English Handbook" (http://www.sec.gov/pdf/handbook.pdf).

DILBERT   By Scott Adams

Although you yourself may not use some of the words in the following list of unfamiliar words, you may see them in business documents. Remember that the simple alternatives shown here will make messages more readable for most people.

Less Familiar Words	Simple Alternatives	Less Familiar Words	Simple Alternatives
ascertain	learn	perpetuate	continue
compensate	pay	perplexing	troubling
conceptualize	see	reciprocate	return
encompass	include	remuneration	salary
hypothesize	guess	stipulate	require
monitor	check	terminate	end
operational	working	utilize	use

As you revise a message, you have a chance to correct any writing problems. Notice in Figures 2.6 and 2.7 what a difference revision makes. Before revision,

FIGURE 2.6

Improving a Faulty E-Mail Message

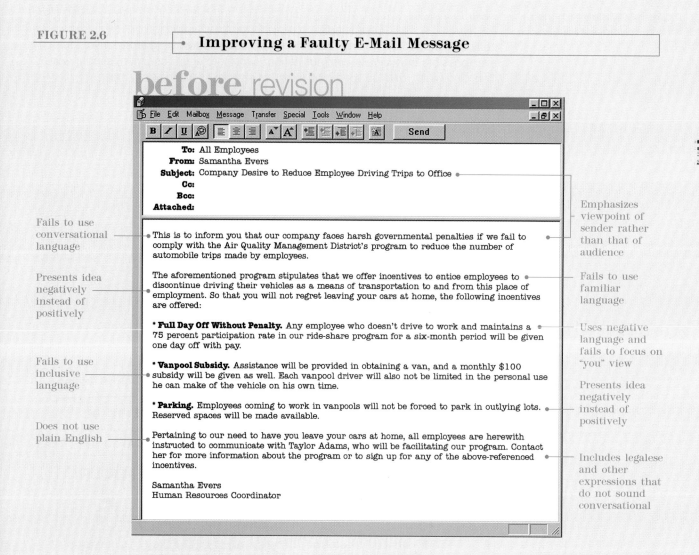

before revision

Fails to use conversational language

Presents idea negatively instead of positively

Fails to use inclusive language

Does not use plain English

Emphasizes viewpoint of sender rather than that of audience

Fails to use familiar language

Uses negative language and fails to focus on "you" view

Presents idea negatively instead of positively

Includes legalese and other expressions that do not sound conversational

To: All Employees
From: Samantha Evers
Subject: Company Desire to Reduce Employee Driving Trips to Office
Cc:
Bcc:
Attached:

This is to inform you that our company faces harsh governmental penalties if we fail to comply with the Air Quality Management District's program to reduce the number of automobile trips made by employees.

The aforementioned program stipulates that we offer incentives to entice employees to discontinue driving their vehicles as a means of transportation to and from this place of employment. So that you will not regret leaving your cars at home, the following incentives are offered:

* **Full Day Off Without Penalty.** Any employee who doesn't drive to work and maintains a 75 percent participation rate in our ride-share program for a six-month period will be given one day off with pay.

* **Vanpool Subsidy.** Assistance will be provided in obtaining a van, and a monthly $100 subsidy will be given as well. Each vanpool driver will also not be limited in the personal use he can make of the vehicle on his own time.

* **Parking.** Employees coming to work in vanpools will not be forced to park in outlying lots. Reserved spaces will be made available.

Pertaining to our need to have you leave your cars at home, all employees are herewith instructed to communicate with Taylor Adams, who will be facilitating our program. Contact her for more information about the program or to sign up for any of the above-referenced incentives.

Samantha Evers
Human Resources Coordinator

the message failed to use familiar language. Many negative ideas could have been expressed positively. After revision the message is shorter, more conversational, and emphasizes the viewpoint of the reader rather than that of the sender. Which message do you think will be more likely to achieve its goal?

DILBERT   **By Scott Adams**

FIGURE 2.7   • **Revised E-Mail Message**

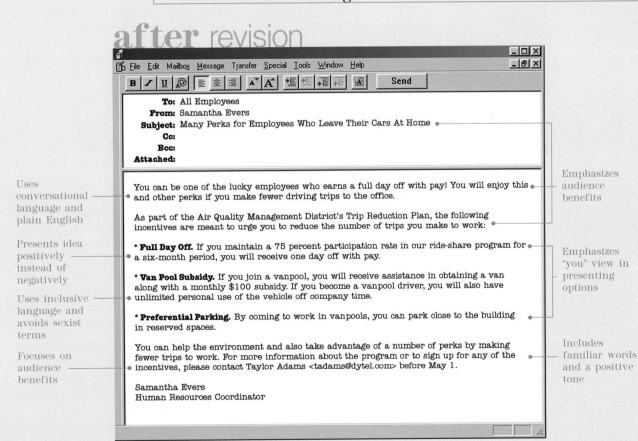

after revision

Uses conversational language and plain English

Presents idea positively instead of negatively

Uses inclusive language and avoids sexist terms

Focuses on audience benefits

To: All Employees
From: Samantha Evers
Subject: Many Perks for Employees Who Leave Their Cars At Home
Cc:
Bcc:
Attached:

You can be one of the lucky employees who earns a full day off with pay! You will enjoy this and other perks if you make fewer driving trips to the office.

As part of the Air Quality Management District's Trip Reduction Plan, the following incentives are meant to urge you to reduce the number of trips you make to work:

* **Full Day Off.** If you maintain a 75 percent participation rate in our ride-share program for a six-month period, you will receive one day off with pay.

* **Van Pool Subsidy.** If you join a vanpool, you will receive assistance in obtaining a van along with a monthly $100 subsidy. If you become a vanpool driver, you will also have unlimited personal use of the vehicle off company time.

* **Preferential Parking.** By coming to work in vanpools, you can park close to the building in reserved spaces.

You can help the environment and also take advantage of a number of perks by making fewer trips to work. For more information about the program or to sign up for any of the incentives, please contact Taylor Adams <tadams@dytel.com> before May 1.

Samantha Evers
Human Resources Coordinator

Emphasizes audience benefits

Emphasizes "you" view in presenting options

Includes familiar words and a positive tone

TECHNOLOGY IMPROVES YOUR BUSINESS WRITING

Thus far, we've concentrated on the basics of business writing, especially the prewriting phase of analyzing, anticipating, and adapting to the intended audience. Another basic for beginning business communicators is learning to use technology to enhance their writing efforts. Although computers and software programs cannot actually do the writing for you, they provide powerful tools that make the process easier and the results more professional. Here are seven ways your computer can help you improve written documents, oral presentations, and even Web pages.

Fighting Writer's Block. Because word processors enable ideas to flow almost effortlessly from your brain to a screen, you can expect fewer delays resulting from writer's block. You can compose rapidly, and you can experiment with structure and phrasing, later retaining and polishing your most promising thoughts. Many authors "sprint write," recording unedited ideas quickly, to start the composition process and also to brainstorm for ideas on a project. Then, they tag important ideas and use computer outlining programs to organize those ideas into logical sequences.

Collecting Information Electronically. As a knowledge worker in an information economy, you will need to find information quickly. Much of the world's information is now accessible by computer. You can locate the titles of books, as well as full-text articles from magazines, newspapers, and government publications. Massive amounts of information are available from the Internet, CD-ROMs, and online services. Through specialized information-retrieval services (such as EBSCO Business Source Premier, or LexisNexis), you can have at your fingertips up-to-the-minute legal, scientific, scholarly, and business information. The most amazing source of electronic information is the Web, with its links to sites around the world—some incredibly helpful and others worthless.

Outlining and Organizing Ideas. Many word processors include some form of "outliner," a feature that enables you to divide a topic into a hierarchical order with main points and subpoints. Your computer keeps track of the levels of ideas automatically so that you can easily add, cut, or rearrange points in the outline. This feature is particularly handy when you're preparing a report or organizing a presentation. Some programs even enable you to transfer your outline directly to slide frames to be used as visual aids in a talk.

Improving Correctness and Precision. Nearly all word processing programs today provide features that catch and correct spelling and typographical errors. Poor spellers and weak typists universally bless their spell checkers for repeatedly saving them from humiliation. Many word processing programs today also provide grammar checkers that can detect errors in capitalization, word use (such as *it's, its*), double negatives, verb use, subject–verb agreement, sentence structure, number agreement, number style, and other writing faults. However, most grammar programs don't actually correct the errors they detect. You must know how to do that. Still, grammar checkers can be very helpful. In addition to spelling and grammar programs, thesaurus programs help you choose precise words that say exactly what you intend.

Adding Graphics for Emphasis. Your letters, memos, and reports may be improved by the addition of graphs and artwork to clarify and illustrate data. You can import charts, diagrams, and illustrations created in database, spreadsheet, graphics, or draw-and-paint programs. Moreover, ready-made pictures, called clip art, can be used to symbolize or illustrate ideas.

Designing and Producing Professional-looking Documents, Presentations, and Web Pages. Many word processing programs today include a large selection of scalable fonts (for different character sizes and styles), italics, boldface, symbols, and styling techniques to aid you in producing consistent formatting and professional-looking results. Moreover, today's presentation software enables you to incorporate showy slide effects, color, sound, pictures, and even movies into your talks for management or

---

Powerful writing tools can help you fight writer's block, collect information, outline and organize ideas, improve correctness and precision, add graphics, design professional-looking documents, and collaborate.

The most valuable employees are able to find accurate information quickly and cheaply by using commercial databases (such as EBSCO, Lexis, or InfoTrac) or by searching the Web.

Savvy business communicators rely heavily on their word processing programs to correct spelling, typographical, and even grammatical errors.

customers. Web document builders such as FrontPage and Dreamweaver also help you design and construct Web pages.

Using Collaborative Software for Team Writing. Assume you are part of a group preparing a lengthy proposal to secure a government contract. You expect to write one segment of the proposal yourself and help revise parts written by others. Special word processing programs with commenting, strikeout, and revision features allow you to revise easily and to identify each team member's editing. Some collaborative programs, called *groupware*, also include decision-support tools to help groups generate, organize, and analyze ideas more efficiently than they could in traditional meetings.

SUMMING UP AND LOOKING FORWARD

In this chapter you learned that good business writing is audience centered, purposeful, and economical. To achieve these results, business communicators typically follow a systematic writing process. This process includes three phases: prewriting, writing, and revising. In the prewriting phase, communicators analyze the task and the audience. They select an appropriate channel to deliver the message, and they consider ways to adapt their message to the task and the audience. Effective techniques include spotlighting audience benefits, cultivating the "you" view, striving to use conversational language, and expressing ideas positively. Good communicators also use inclusive language, plain English, and familiar words. Today's computer software provides wonderful assistance for business communicators. Technological tools help you fight writer's block, collect information, outline and organize ideas, improve correctness and precision, add graphics, design professional-looking documents and presentations, and collaborate on team writing projects.

The next chapter continues to examine the writing process. It presents additional techniques to help you become a better writer. You'll learn how to eliminate repetitious and redundant wording, as well as how to avoid wordy prepositional phrases, long lead-ins, needless adverbs, and misplaced modifiers.

CRITICAL THINKING

1. How can the three-phase writing process help the writer of a business report as well as the writer of an oral presentation?

2. If adapting your tone to the receiving audience and developing reader benefits are so important, why do we see so much writing that fails to reflect these suggestions?

3. Discuss the following statement: *The English language is a land mine—it is filled with terms that are easily misinterpreted as derogatory and others that are blatantly insulting. . . . Being fair and objective is not enough; employers must also appear to be so.*

4. Why is writing in a natural, conversational tone difficult for many people?

5. If computer software is increasingly able to detect writing errors, can business communicators stop studying writing techniques? Why?

CHAPTER REVIEW

6. How is business writing different from academic and other writing?

7. List the three phases of the writing process and summarize what happens in each phase. Which phase requires the most time?

8. What five factors are important in selecting an appropriate channel to deliver a message? What makes one channel richer than another?

9. How does profiling the audience help a business communicator prepare a message?

10. What is meant by *audience benefit*? Give an original example.

11. List three specific techniques for developing a warm, friendly, and conversational tone in business messages.

12. Why does positive language usually tell more than negative language? Give an original example.

13. List five examples of sexist pronouns and nouns.

14. List at least five principles of the Plain English movement.

15. Name seven ways your computer can help you improve written documents.

EXPAND YOUR LEARNING WITH THESE BONUS RESOURCES!

Guffey Companion Web Site

http://guffey.swlearning.com

Your companion Web site offers review quizzes, a glossary of key terms, and flash cards to build your knowledge of chapter concepts. Additional career tools include *Dr. Guffey's Guide to Business Etiquette and Workplace Manners*, *Listening Quiz*, and electronic citation formats (MLA and APA) for business writers. You'll also find updated links to all chapter URLs.

Guffey Xtra!

http://guffeyxtra.swlearning.com

This online study assistant illustrates chapter concepts in PowerPoint. It strengthens your language skills with *Your Personal Language Trainer* (a grammar/mechanics review), *Speak Right!*, *Spell Right!*, and *Sentence Competency Exercises*. In addition, **Guffey Xtra!** brings you bonus online chapters: *Employment and Other Interviewing* and *How to Write Instructions*. You'll also find the Grammar/Mechanics Challenge exercises so that you can revise without rekeying.

WRITING IMPROVEMENT EXERCISES

Selecting Communication Channels

Using Figure 2.2, suggest the best communication channels for the following messages. Assume that all channels shown are available. Be prepared to explain your choices.

16. You need to know whether Elizabeth in Reprographics can produce a special brochure for your department within two days.

17. A prospective client in Italy wants price quotes for a number of your products—pronto!

18. As assistant to the vice president, you are to investigate the possibility of developing internship programs with several nearby colleges and universities.

19. You must respond to a notice from the Internal Revenue Service insisting that you did not pay the correct amount for last quarter's employer's taxes.

20. As a manager, you must inform an employee that continued tardiness is jeopardizing her job.

21. Members of your task force must meet to discuss ways to improve communication among 5,000 employees at 32 branches of your large company. Task force members are from Los Angeles, Orlando, San Antonio, White Plains, and Columbus (Ohio).

22. As department manager, you need to inform nine staff members of a safety training session scheduled for the following month.

Audience Benefits and the "You" View

Revise the following sentences to emphasize the perspective of the audience and the "you" view.

23. Our safety policy forbids us from renting power equipment to anyone who cannot demonstrate proficiency in its use.

24. To prevent us from possibly losing large sums of money in stolen identity schemes, our bank now requires verification of any large check presented for immediate payment.

25. So that we may bring our customer records up-to-date and eliminate the expense of duplicate mailings, we are asking you to complete and return the enclosed card.

26. For just $139 per person, we have arranged a two-night getaway package to Orlando that includes hotel accommodations, Pleasure Island tickets, and complimentary breakfasts.

27. We find it necessary to request all employees to complete the enclosed questionnaire so that we may develop a master schedule for summer vacations.

28. We are offering an in-house training program for employees who want to improve their writing skills.

29. To enable us to continue our policy of selling name brands at discount prices, we can give store credit but we cannot give cash refunds on returned merchandise.

30. We regret to announce that the bookstore will distribute free iPods only to students in classes in which the instructor has requested these devices as learning tools.

Conversational, Professional Tone

Revise the following sentences to make the tone conversational yet professional.

31. As per your recent request, the undersigned is happy to inform you that we are sending you forthwith the brochures you requested.

32. Pursuant to your letter of the 12th, please be advised that your shipment was sent June 9.

33. BTW, Amy was pretty ticked off because the manager accused her of ripping off office supplies.

34. Hey, Sam! Look, I need you to pound on Lisa so we can drop this budget thingy in her lap.

35. Kindly be informed that your vehicle has been determined to require corrective work.

36. He didn't have the guts to badmouth her 2 her face.

37. The undersigned respectfully reminds affected individuals that employees desirous of changing their health plans must do so before December 30.

Positive Expression
Revise the following statements to make them more positive.

38. It is impossible for the contractor to complete the footings until the soil is no longer soggy.

39. We must withhold authorizing payment of your consultant's fees because the Legal Committee claims your work is not completed.

40. In the complaint that you sent in your July 2 letter, you claim that our representative was hostile and refused to help you.

41. Plans for the new health center cannot move forward without full community support.

42. If you do not fill in all blanks in the application form, we cannot issue a password.

43. You won't be disappointed with your new smart phone.

Inclusive Language
Revise the following sentences to eliminate terms that are considered sexist or that suggest stereotypes.

44. Every employee must wear his ID badge on the job.

45. A policeman is responsible for covering his territory.

46. The conference will include special excursions for the wives of executives.

47. Does each salesman have his own PDA loaded with his special sales information?

48. Serving on the panel are a lady veterinarian, a female doctor, two businessmen, and an Indian CPA.

Plain English and Familiar Words
Revise the following sentences to use plain expression and more familiar words.

49. The proposal stipulates that all other agreements be terminated before the plan begins to be operational.

50. Our attorney ascertained that we must compensate the consultants despite perplexing results.

51. We appear to have some slippage in the development schedule, which may have an adverse reaction vis-à-vis the revenue picture.

52. Although our CPA monitored most transactions, she didn't know that our business encompassed so many client services.

ACTIVITY

INFOTRAC

2.1 Understanding Plain English

You work in a small financial services organization. Your boss is new to her job, and she wants to learn more about plain English in relation to investments and prospectus information. She doesn't have the time or expertise to do much Internet research. She asks you to help her.

Your Task. Using InfoTrac, find an article that explains how the Securities and Exchange Commission (SEC) wants writers to use plain English. (**Hint:** Use this search term: "Plain English AND SEC." One good article is by Rick Lowry, published in the *Sacramento Business Journal.* You might find other good InfoTrac articles with the search term "Plain English.") In a memo to Eileen Fowler, summarize your findings, listing at least five rules for text and five for graphics. See Chapter 5 for format suggestions. You could begin your memo with, *As you suggested, I am submitting the following information about. . . .* Be sure to identify the authors and articles you summarize.

VIDEO RESOURCE

Video Library 1, *Building Workplace Communication Skills.* Your instructor may show you a video titled *Guffey's 3-x-3 Writing Process Develops Fluent Workplace Skills.* It shows all three phases of the writing process so that you can see how it guides the development of a complete message in a workplace environment. This video illustrates concepts in Chapters 2, 3, and 4.

GRAMMAR/MECHANICS CHECKUP—2

Pronouns

Review Sections 1.07–1.09 in the Grammar Review section of the Grammar/Mechanics Handbook. Then study each of the following statements. In the space provided, write the word that completes the statement correctly and the number of the G/M principle illustrated. When you finish, compare your responses with those provided near the end of the book. If your responses differ, study carefully the principles in parentheses.

<u>its</u>   (1.09d)   **Example**   The Personnel Resources Committee must submit (its, their) findings soon.

1. We expected Mrs. Johnson to call. Was it (she, her) who left the message?
2. Someone on the men's basketball team left (his, their) car lights on.
3. A serious disagreement between management and (he, him) caused his resignation.
4. Does anyone in the office know for (who, whom) these CDs were ordered?
5. It looks as if (her's, hers) is the only report that cites electronic sources.
6. Sloan asked my friend and (I, me, myself) to help her complete the report.
7. My friend and (I, me, myself) were also asked to work on Saturday.
8. Both printers were sent for repairs, but (yours, your's) will be returned shortly.
9. Give the budget figures to (whoever, whomever) asked for them.
10. Everyone except the broker and (I, me, myself) claimed a share of the commission.
11. No one knows that problem better than (he, him, himself).
12. Investment brochures and information were sent to (we, us) shareholders.
13. If any one of the women tourists has lost (their, her) scarf, she should see the driver.
14. Neither the glamour nor the excitement of the position had lost (its, it's, their) appeal.
15. Any new subscriber may cancel (their, his or her) subscription within the first month.

GRAMMAR/MECHANICS CHALLENGE—2

Revise the following interoffice memo that has faults in grammar, spelling, punctuation, capitalization, word use, and number form. Also pay attention to developing a conversational but professional tone, using familiar words, and striving for positive expression. Use standard proofreading marks (see Appendix B) to correct the errors or revise this document at your computer using the file at the **Guffey Xtra!** Web site. When you finish, your instructor may show a possible revision of this memo.

MADISON FINANCIAL SERVICES
Interoffice Memo

DATE: July 20, 200x

TO: Jeannine Horn, Manager, Human Resources

FROM: Douglas Waterson, CEO

SUBJECT: Losing Payroll Data Because of Hacking

It has come to the attention of the writer that on July 18th the software database maintained by Quantum data services for the purpose of preparing payroll for our employees was accessed illegally. We did not learn about the "hacking" of the system until yesterday when Quantum made a examination of their system.

Our employees payroll records include social security #s, employees addresses and payroll information such as various deductions. A review of the five hundred sixty-six names in the database shows no damage to the data or modification of the data. We don't think their was any malicious intention to destroy or annihilate the data. Individual bank account information and such like for employees are not part of the file. It appears that names may have been copied however no other information was lost.

The computers holding the database were immediatley taken off-line, and meticulously examined to ascertain whether any data were found to be corrupted. New more extensive firewalls have been added, to provide better Security. However, because of these changes, payroll records will not be available before July 24th.

A letter from myself to all employees as well as the same message on the company Intranet, will henceforth go out this p.m.. Pertaining to this matter, please do what you can to minimize concern among employees. Ensure them that there personal data have not been harvested, and that we have took appropriate steps to prevent and avoid future hacking. I appreciate your help.

Communication Workshops, such as the one provided here, offer insight into special business communication topics and skills not discussed in the chapters. These workshops cover ethics, technology, career skills, collaboration, and other workplace topics. Each workshop includes a career application with a case study or problem to help you develop skills relevant to the workshop topic.

COMMUNICATION WORKSHOP
CAREER SKILLS

SHARPENING YOUR SKILLS
FOR CRITICAL THINKING, PROBLEM SOLVING, AND DECISION MAKING

Gone are the days when management expected workers to check their brains at the door and do only as they were told. Today, you'll be expected to use your brains in thinking critically. You'll be solving problems and making decisions. Much of this book is devoted to helping you solve problems and communicate those decisions to management, fellow workers, clients, the government, and the public. Faced with a problem or an issue, most of us do a lot of worrying before separating the issues or making a decision. You can change all that worrying to directed thinking by channeling it into the following procedure:

- **Identify and clarify the problem.** Your first task is to recognize that a problem exists. Some problems are big and unmistakable, such as failure of an air-freight delivery service to get packages to customers on time. Other problems may be continuing annoyances, such as regularly running out of toner for an office copy machine. The first step in reaching a solution is pinpointing the problem area.

- **Gather information.** Learn more about the problem situation. Look for possible causes and solutions. This step may mean checking files, calling suppliers, or brainstorming with fellow workers. For example, the air-freight delivery service would investigate the tracking systems of the commercial airlines carrying its packages to determine what is going wrong.

- **Evaluate the evidence.** Where did the information come from? Does it represent various points of view? What biases could be expected from each source? How accurate is the information gathered? Is it fact or opinion? For example, it is a fact that packages are missing; it is an opinion that they are merely lost and will turn up eventually.

- **Consider alternatives and implications.** Draw conclusions from the gathered evidence and pose solutions. Then weigh the advantages and disadvantages of each alternative. What are the costs, benefits, and consequences? What are the obstacles, and how can they be handled? Most important, what solution best serves your goals and those of your organization? Here's where your creativity is especially important.

- **Choose and implement the best alternative.** Select an alternative and put it into action. Then, follow through on your decision by monitoring the results of implementing your plan. The freight company decided to give its unhappy customers free delivery service to make up for the lost packages and downtime. Be sure to continue monitoring and adjusting the solution to ensure its effectiveness over time.

Career Application. Let's return to the McDonald's problem (discussed on page 33) in which some franchise owners are unhappy with the multiple lines for service. Customers don't seem to know where to stand to be the next served. Tempers flare when aggressive customers cut in line, and other customers spend so much time protecting their places in line that they fail to study the menu. Then they don't know what to order when they approach the counter. As a franchise owner, you would like to find a solution to this problem. Any changes in procedures, however, must be approved by all the McDonald's owners in a district. That means you'll have to get a majority to agree. You know that McDonald's management feels that the multiline system accommodates higher volumes of customers more quickly than a single-line system. Moreover, the problem of perception is important. What happens when customers open the door to a restaurant and see a long single line? Do they stick around to learn how fast the line is moving?

Your Task

- Individually or with a team, use the critical thinking steps outlined here. Begin by clarifying the problem.

- Where could you gather information to help you solve this problem? Would it be wise to see what your competitors are doing? How do banks handle customer lines? Airlines? Sports arenas?

- Evaluate your findings and consider alternatives. What are the pros and cons of each alternative?

- Within your team choose the best alternative. Present your recommendation to your class and give your reasons for choosing it.

CHAPTER 3

IMPROVING WRITING TECHNIQUES

As technological advances such as e-mail allow us to communicate more rapidly, more often, and with greater numbers of people, writing is becoming a larger part of everyone's job.

Max Messmer, if chairman and CEO of Robert Half International[1]

OBJECTIVES

- Contrast formal and informal methods of researching data and generating ideas for messages.
- Specify how to organize information into outlines.
- Compare direct and indirect patterns for organizing ideas.
- Distinguish components of complete and effective sentences.
- Emphasize important ideas and de-emphasize unimportant ones.
- Use active voice, passive voice, and parallelism effectively in messages.
- Develop sentence unity by avoiding zigzag writing, mixed constructions, and misplaced modifiers.
- Identify strategies for achieving paragraph coherence and composing the first draft of a message.

Even in an age filled with technological advances, says author and CEO Max Messmer, proficiency in written communication is highly valued. Developing that proficiency takes instruction and practice. You've already learned some techniques for writing effectively, such as using a conversational tone, positive language, plain expression, and familiar words. This chapter presents additional writing tips that help you gather information, organize it into outlines, and compose sentences.

In Chapter 2 we focused on the prewriting stage of the writing process. Figure 3.1 reviews the entire process. This chapter addresses the second stage, which includes researching, organizing, and composing.

RESEARCHING TO COLLECT NEEDED INFORMATION

The second stage of the writing process involves research, which means collecting the necessary information to prepare a message.

No smart businessperson would begin writing a message before collecting the needed information. We call this collection process *research*, a rather formal-sounding term. For simple documents, though, the process can be quite informal. Research is necessary before beginning to write because the information you collect helps shape the message. Discovering significant data after a message is completed often means

PHOTOS: © ROYALTY-FREE/CORBIS; © PHOTODISC COLLECTION/GETTY IMAGES; © PHOTODISC COLLECTION/GETTY IMAGES

FIGURE 3.1

The Writing Process

1 PREWRITING

Analyzing
Anticipating
Adapting

2 WRITING

Researching
Organizing
Composing

3 REVISING

Revising
Proofreading
Evaluating

starting over and reorganizing. To avoid frustration and inaccurate messages, collect information that answers this primary question:

- What does the receiver need to know about this topic?

When the message involves action, search for answers to secondary questions:

- What is the receiver to do?
- How is the receiver to do it?
- When must the receiver do it?
- What will happen if the receiver doesn't do it?

Whenever your communication problem requires more information than you have in your head or at your fingertips, you must conduct research. This research may be formal or informal.

Formal Research Methods

Formal research may include searching libraries and electronic databases or investigating primary sources (interviews, surveys, and experimentation).

Long reports and complex business problems generally require some use of formal research methods. Let's say you are a market specialist for Coca-Cola, and your boss asks you to evaluate the impact on Coke sales of private-label or generic soft drinks (the bargain-basement-brand knockoffs sold at Kmart and other outlets). Or, let's assume you must write a term paper for a college class. Both tasks require more data than you have in your head or at your fingertips. To conduct formal research, you could:

- **Search manually.** You'll find helpful background and supplementary information through manual searching of resources in public and college libraries. These

© MANCHAN/GETTY IMAGES

As you begin any writing project, you will probably want to conduct formal or informal research by gathering necessary background information. You can look in the files, talk to your boss, interview the target audience, or brainstorm with colleagues for ideas.

traditional sources include books and newspaper, magazine, and journal articles. Other sources are encyclopedias, reference books, handbooks, dictionaries, directories, and almanacs.

- **Access electronically.** Much of the printed material just described is now available from the Internet, databases, or CDs that can be accessed by computer. College and public libraries subscribe to retrieval services that permit you to access most periodic literature. You can also find extraordinary amounts of information by searching the Web. You'll learn more about using electronic sources in Chapters 9 and 10.

Good sources of primary information are interviews, surveys, questionnaires, and focus groups.

- **Go to the source.** For firsthand information, go directly to the source. For the Coca-Cola report, for example, you could find out what consumers really think by conducting interviews or surveys, by putting together questionnaires, or by organizing focus groups. Formal research includes structured sampling and controls that enable investigators to make accurate judgments and valid predictions.
- **Conduct scientific experiments.** Instead of merely asking for the target audience's opinion, scientific researchers present choices with controlled variables. Let's say, for example, that Coca-Cola wants to determine at what price and under what circumstances consumers would switch from Coca-Cola to a generic brand. The results of such experimentation would provide valuable data for managerial decision making.

Because formal research techniques are particularly necessary for reports, you'll study resources and techniques more extensively in Chapters 9 and 10.

Informal Research and Idea Generation

Most routine tasks—such as composing e-mail messages, memos, letters, informational reports, and oral presentations—require data that you can collect informally. Here are some techniques for collecting informal data and for generating ideas:

Informal research may include looking in the files, talking with your boss, interviewing the target audience, conducting an informal survey, and brainstorming.

- **Look in the files.** If you are responding to an inquiry, you often can find the answer to the inquiry by investigating the company files or by consulting colleagues.
- **Talk with your boss.** Get information from the individual making the assignment. What does that person know about the topic? What slant should be taken? What other sources would he or she suggest?
- **Interview the target audience.** Consider talking with individuals at whom the message is aimed. They can provide clarifying information that tells you what they want to know and how you should shape your remarks.
- **Conduct an informal survey.** Gather unscientific but helpful information via questionnaires or surveys. In preparing a memo report predicting the success of a proposed fitness center, for example, circulate a questionnaire asking for employee reactions.
- **Brainstorm for ideas.** Alone or with others, discuss ideas for the writing task at hand, and record at least a dozen ideas without judging them. Small groups are especially fruitful in brainstorming because people spin ideas off one another.

ORGANIZING TO SHOW RELATIONSHIPS

Writers of well-organized messages group similar ideas so that readers can see relationships and follow arguments.

Once you've collected data, you must find some way to organize it. Organizing includes two processes: grouping and patterning. Well-organized messages group similar items; ideas follow a sequence that helps the reader understand relationships and accept the writer's views. Unorganized messages proceed free-form, jumping from one thought to another. Such messages fail to emphasize important points. Puzzled readers can't see how the pieces fit together, and they become frustrated and irritated. Many communication experts regard poor organization as the greatest failing of business writers. Two simple techniques can help you organize data: the scratch list and the outline.

FIGURE 3.2

Format for an Outline

TITLE: MAJOR IDEA OR PURPOSE
I. FIRST MAJOR COMPONENT
   A. FIRST SUBPOINT
      1. DETAIL, ILLUSTRATION, EVIDENCE
      2. DETAIL, ILLUSTRATION, EVIDENCE
   B. SECOND SUBPOINT
      1.
      2.
II. SECOND MAJOR COMPONENT
   A. FIRST SUBPOINT
      1.
      2.
   B. SECOND SUBPOINT
      1.
      2.

Tips for Making Outlines
- Define the main topic in the title.
- Divide the topic into main points, preferably three to five.
- Break the components into subpoints.
- Don't put a single item under a major component if you have only one subpoint; integrate it with the main item above it or reorganize.
- Strive to make each component exclusive (no overlapping).
- Use details, illustrations, and evidence to support subpoints.

Outlining

Two simple ways to organize data are the scratch list and the outline.

In developing simple messages, some writers make a quick scratch list of the topics they wish to cover. They then compose a message at their computers directly from the scratch list. Most writers, though, need to organize their ideas—especially if the project is complex—into a hierarchy, such as an outline. The beauty of preparing an outline is that it gives you a chance to organize your thinking before you get bogged down in word choice and sentence structure. Figure 3.2 shows a format for an outline.

The Direct Pattern

Business messages typically follow either (1) the direct pattern, with the main idea first, or (2) the indirect pattern, with the main idea following an explanation and evidence.

After developing an outline, you will need to decide where in the message you will place the main idea. Placing the main idea at the beginning of the message is called the *direct pattern*. In the direct pattern the main idea comes first, followed by details, an explanation, or evidence. Placing the main idea later in the message (after the details, explanation, or evidence) is called the *indirect pattern*. The pattern you select is determined by how you expect the audience to react to the message, as shown in Figure 3.3.

In preparing to write any message, you need to anticipate the audience's reaction to your ideas and frame your message accordingly. When you expect the reader to be pleased, mildly interested, or, at worst, neutral—use the direct pattern. That is, put your main point—the purpose of your message—in the first or second sentence. Compare the direct and indirect patterns in the following memo openings. Notice how long it takes to get to the main idea in the indirect opening.

Indirect Opening

For the past several years, we have had a continuing problem scheduling vacations, personal days, and sick time. Our Human Resources people struggle with unscheduled absences. After considerable investigation, the Management Council has decided to try a centralized paid time-off program starting January 1. This memo will describe its benefits and procedures.

Direct Opening

This memo describes the benefits and procedures of a new paid time-off program to begin January 1.

FIGURE 3.3

Audience Response Determines Pattern of Organization

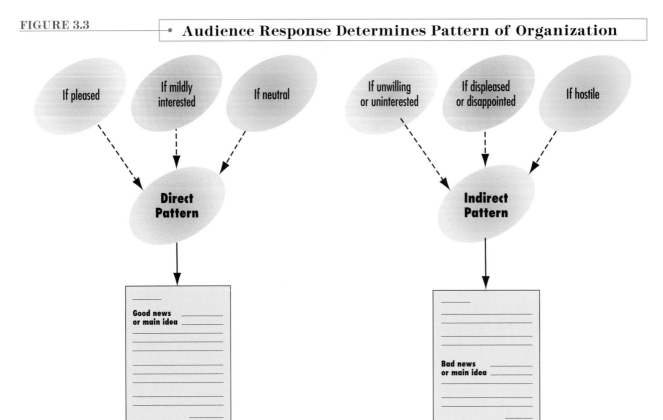

Frontloading saves the reader's time, establishes the proper frame of mind, and prevents frustration.

Explanations, background, and details should follow the direct opening. What's important is getting to the main idea quickly. This direct method, also called *frontloading*, has at least three advantages:

- **Saves the reader's time.** Many of today's businesspeople can devote only a few moments to each message. Messages that take too long to get to the point may lose their readers along the way.
- **Sets a proper frame of mind.** Learning the purpose up front helps the reader put the subsequent details and explanations in perspective. Without a clear opening, the reader may be thinking, *Why am I being told this?*
- **Prevents frustration.** Readers forced to struggle through excessive verbiage before reaching the main idea become frustrated. They resent the writer. Poorly organized messages create a negative impression of the writer.

This frontloading technique works best with audiences who are likely to be receptive to or at least not likely to disagree with what you have to say. Typical business messages that follow the direct pattern include routine requests and responses, orders and acknowledgments, nonsensitive memos, e-mail messages, informational reports, and informational oral presentations. All these tasks have one element in common: none has a sensitive subject that will upset the reader.

The Indirect Pattern

The indirect pattern works best when the audience may be uninterested, unwilling, displeased, or even hostile.

When you expect the audience to be uninterested, unwilling, displeased, or perhaps even hostile, the indirect pattern is more appropriate. In this pattern you don't reveal the main idea until after you have offered an explanation and evidence. This approach works well with three kinds of messages: (1) bad news, (2) ideas that require persuasion, and (3) sensitive news, especially when being transmitted to superiors. The indirect pattern has these benefits:

- **Respects the feelings of the audience.** Bad news is always painful, but the trauma can be lessened when the receiver is prepared for it.

- **Encourages a fair hearing.** Messages that may upset the reader are more likely to be read when the main idea is delayed. Beginning immediately with a piece of bad news or a persuasive request, for example, may cause the receiver to stop reading or listening.
- **Minimizes a negative reaction.** A reader's overall reaction to a negative message is generally improved if the news is delivered gently.

Typical business messages that could be developed indirectly include letters and memos that refuse requests, deny claims, and deny credit. Persuasive requests, sales letters, sensitive messages, and some reports and oral presentations also benefit from the indirect strategy. You'll learn more about how to use the indirect pattern in Chapters 7 and 8.

In summary, business messages may be organized directly, with the main idea first, or indirectly, with the main idea delayed. Although these two patterns cover many communication problems, they should be considered neither universal nor inviolate. Every business transaction is distinct. Some messages are mixed: part good news, part bad; part goodwill, part persuasion. In upcoming chapters you'll practice applying the direct and indirect patterns in typical situations. Then, you'll have the skills and confidence to evaluate communication problems and vary these patterns depending on the goals you wish to achieve.

WRITING EFFECTIVE SENTENCES

After deciding how to organize your message, you are ready to begin composing it. As you create your first draft, you'll be working at the sentence level of composition. Although you've used sentences all your life, you may be unaware of how they can be shaped and arranged to express your ideas most effectively. First, let's review some basic sentence elements.

Sentences must have subjects and verbs and must make sense.

Complete sentences have subjects and verbs and make sense.

SUBJECT   VERB   SUBJECT   VERB

Employees expect vacations. Our company has a paid time-off plan.

Clauses have subjects and verbs, but phrases do not.

Clauses and phrases, the key building blocks of sentences, are related groups of words. Clauses have subjects and verbs; phrases do not.

PHRASE   PHRASE

The CEO of our company sent an e-mail to all staff members.

PHRASE   PHRASE

After reading the message, we learned about the paid time-off plan.

CLAUSE   CLAUSE

Because the plan sounds good, most employees accepted it immediately.

CLAUSE   CLAUSE

When companies use a paid time-off plan, they have a stable workforce.

Independent clauses may stand alone; dependent clauses may not.

Clauses may be divided into two groups: independent and dependent. Independent clauses are grammatically complete. Dependent clauses depend for their meaning on independent clauses. In the two preceding examples, the clauses beginning with *Because* and *When* are dependent. Dependent clauses are often introduced by words such as *if, when, because,* and *as.*

INDEPENDENT CLAUSE

They have a stable workforce.

DEPENDENT CLAUSE   INDEPENDENT CLAUSE

When companies use a paid time-off plan, they have a stable workforce.

By learning to distinguish phrases, independent clauses, and dependent clauses, you'll be able to punctuate sentences correctly and avoid three basic sentence faults: the fragment, the run-on sentence, and the comma splice.

Avoiding Sentence Fragments

Fragments are broken-off parts of sentences and should not be punctuated as sentences.

One of the most serious errors a writer can make is punctuating a fragment as if it were a complete sentence. A fragment is a broken-off part of a sentence.

Fragment	Because most transactions require a permanent record. Good writing skills are critical.
Revision	Because most transactions require a permanent record, good writing skills are critical.
Fragment	The recruiter requested a writing sample. Even though the candidate seemed to communicate well.
Revision	The recruiter requested a writing sample, even though the candidate seemed to communicate well.

When two independent clauses are run together without punctuation or a coordinating conjunction, a run-on (fused) sentence results.

Fragments often can be identified by the words that introduce them—words such as *although, as, because, even, except, for example, if, instead of, since, such as, that, which,* and *when.* These words introduce dependent clauses. Make sure such clauses always connect to independent clauses.

Avoiding Run-On (Fused) Sentences

A sentence with two independent clauses must be joined by a coordinating conjunction (*and, or, nor, but*) or by a semicolon (;). Without a conjunction or a semicolon, a run-on sentence results.

© Randy Glasbergen.
www.glasbergen.com

"Sentence fragments, comma splices, run-ons — who cares?
I know what I meant!"

Run-on	Most job seekers present a printed résumé some are also using Web sites as electronic portfolios.
Revision 1	Most job seekers present a printed résumé, but some are also using Web sites as electronic portfolios.
Revision 2	Most job seekers present a printed résumé; some are also using Web sites as electronic portfolios.

Avoiding Comma-Splice Sentences

When two independent clauses are joined by a comma without a conjunction, a comma splice results.

A comma splice results when a writer joins (splices together) two independent clauses with a comma. Independent clauses may be joined with a coordinating conjunction (*and, or, nor, but*) or a conjunctive adverb (*however, consequently, therefore,* and others). Notice that clauses joined by coordinating conjunctions require only a comma. Clauses joined by a coordinating adverb require a semicolon. Here are three ways to rectify a comma splice:

Comma splice	Some employees responded by e-mail, others picked up the telephone.
Revision 1	Some employees responded by e-mail, and others picked up the telephone.
Revision 2	Some employees responded by e-mail; however, others picked up the telephone.
Revision 3	Some employees responded by e-mail; others picked up the telephone.

Controlling Sentence Length

Sentences of 20 or fewer words have the most impact.

Because your goal is to communicate clearly, you're better off limiting your sentences to about 20 or fewer words. The American Press Institute reports that reader comprehension drops off markedly as sentences become longer.[2] Thus, in crafting your sentences, think about the relationship between sentence length and comprehension:

Sentence Length	Comprehension Rate
8 words	100%
15 words	90%
19 words	80%
28 words	50%

Instead of stringing together clauses with *and, but*, and *however*, break some of those complex sentences into separate segments. Business readers want to grasp ideas immediately. They can do that best when thoughts are separated into short sentences. On the other hand, too many monotonous short sentences will sound "grammar schoolish" and may bore or even annoy the reader. Strive for a balance between longer sentences and shorter ones.

IMPROVING WRITING TECHNIQUES

Writers can significantly improve their messages by focusing on a few writing techniques. In this section we'll focus on emphasizing and de-emphasizing ideas, using active and passive voice strategically, developing parallelism, and achieving sentence unity. You'll also learn to avoid zigzag writing, mixed constructions, and dangling and misplaced modifiers.

Developing Emphasis

When you are talking with someone, you can emphasize your main ideas by saying them loudly or by repeating them slowly. You could even pound the table if you want to show real emphasis! Another way you could signal the relative importance of an idea is by raising your eyebrows or by shaking your head or whispering in a low voice. But when you write, you must rely on other means to tell your readers which ideas are more important than others. Emphasis in writing can be achieved primarily in two ways: mechanically or stylistically.

ACHIEVING EMPHASIS THROUGH MECHANICS

You can emphasize an idea mechanically by using underlining, italics, boldface, font changes, all caps, dashes, and tabulation.

To emphasize an idea in print, a writer may use any of the following devices:

Underlining	Underlining draws the eye to a word.
Italics and boldface	Using *italics* or **boldface** can convey special meaning and provide emphasis.
Font changes	Changing from a large font to a small font or to a different font adds interest and emphasis.
All caps	Printing words in ALL CAPS is like shouting them.
Dashes	Dashes—if used sparingly—can be effective in capturing attention.
Tabulation	Listing items vertically makes them stand out: 1. First item 2. Second item 3. Third item

Other means of achieving mechanical emphasis include the arrangement of space, color, lines, boxes, columns, titles, headings, and subheadings. Today's software and color printers provide a wonderful array of capabilities for setting off ideas.

Speakers can emphasize their words nonverbally with voice and gestures, but writers do not have these options. Instead, writers emphasize important parts of a message (1) mechanically, such as using underlining, boldface, or all caps, or (2) stylistically, such as using vivid words or placing ideas strategically.

© PHOTODISC COLLECTION/GETTY IMAGES

ACHIEVING EMPHASIS THROUGH STYLE

Although mechanical means are occasionally appropriate, more often a writer achieves emphasis stylistically. That is, the writer chooses words carefully and constructs sentences skillfully to emphasize main ideas and de-emphasize minor or negative ideas. Here are four suggestions for emphasizing ideas stylistically:

You can emphasize ideas stylistically by using vivid words, labeling the main idea, and positioning the main idea strategically.

- **Use vivid words.** Vivid words are emphatic because the reader can picture ideas clearly.

  | General | *One business* uses *personal* selling techniques. |
  | Vivid | *Avon* uses *face-to-face* selling techniques. |

  | General | *Someone* will *contact* you *as soon as possible.* |
  | Vivid | *Ms. Stevens* will *telephone* you *before 5 p.m. tomorrow, May 3.* |

- **Label the main idea.** If an idea is significant, tell the reader.

  | Unlabeled | Consider looking for a job online, but also focus on networking. |
  | Labeled | Consider looking for a job online; but, *most important*, focus on networking. |

- **Place the important idea first or last in the sentence.** Ideas have less competition from surrounding words when they appear first or last in a sentence. Observe how the concept of *productivity* is emphasized in the first and second examples:

Emphatic	*Productivity* is more likely to be increased when profit-sharing plans are linked to individual performance rather than to group performance.
Emphatic	Profit-sharing plans linked to individual performance rather than to group performance are more effective in increasing *productivity*.
Unemphatic	Profit-sharing plans are more effective in increasing *productivity* when they are linked to individual performance rather than to group performance.

- **Place the important idea in a simple sentence or in an independent clause.** Don't dilute the effect of the idea by making it share the spotlight with other words and clauses.

Emphatic	You are the first trainee that we have hired for this program. (Use a simple sentence for emphasis.)
Emphatic	Although we considered many candidates, you are the first trainee that we have hired for this program. (Independent clause contains main idea.)
Unemphatic	Although you are the first trainee that we have hired for this program, we had many candidates and expect to expand the program in the future. (Main idea is lost in a dependent clause.)

DE-EMPHASIZING WHEN NECESSARY

To de-emphasize an idea, such as bad news, try one of the following stylistic devices:

- Use general words.

You can de-emphasize ideas by using general words and placing the ideas in dependent clauses.

Vivid	Our records indicate that *you were recently fired*.
General	Our records indicate that *your employment status has changed recently*.

- **Place the bad news in a dependent clause connected to an independent clause with something positive.** In sentences with dependent clauses, the main emphasis is always on the independent clause.

Emphasizes bad news	We cannot issue you credit at this time, but we have a special plan that will allow you to fill your immediate needs on a cash basis.
De-emphasizes bad news	Although credit cannot be issued at this time, you can fill your immediate needs on a cash basis with our special plan.

Using Active and Passive Voice

Active-voice sentences are preferred because the subject is the doer of the action.

In sentences with active-voice verbs, the subject is the doer of the action. In passive-voice sentences, the subject is acted upon.

Active verb	The manager *completed* performance reviews for all employees. (The subject, *manager*, is the doer of the action.)
Passive verb	Performance reviews *were completed* for all employees. (The subject, *reviews*, is acted upon.)

Although active-voice verbs are preferred in business writing, passive-voice verbs perform useful functions.

In the first sentence, the active-voice verb emphasizes the manager. In the second sentence, the passive-voice verb emphasizes the performance review. In sentences with passive-voice verbs, the doer of the action may be revealed or left unknown. In business writing, as well as in personal interactions, some situations demand tact and sensitivity. Instead of using a direct approach with active verbs, we may prefer the indirectness that passive verbs allow. Rather than making a blunt announcement with an active verb (*Tyler made a major error in the estimate*), we can soften the sentence with a passive construction (*A major error was made in the estimate*).

Here's a summary of the best use of active- and passive-voice verbs:

- **Use the active voice for most business writing.** It clearly tells what the action is and who is performing that action. *Congress passed new laws.*
- **Use the passive voice to emphasize an action or the recipient of the action.** *New laws were passed by Congress.*
- **Use the passive voice to de-emphasize negative news.** *Credit cannot be granted.*
- **Use the passive voice to conceal the doer of an action.** *An error was made in projecting profits.*

© Ted Goff (www.tedgoff.com)

"To make this easy to read,
I have divided it into three
parts: A, B, and 3."

How can you tell if a verb is active or passive? Identify the subject of the sentence and decide whether the subject is doing the acting or it is being acted upon. For example, in the sentence *An appointment was made for January 1*, the subject is *appointment*. The subject is being acted upon; therefore, the verb (*was made*) is passive. Another clue in identifying passive-voice verbs is that they generally include a *to be* helping verb, such as *is, are, was, were, be, being,* or *been*.

Achieving Parallelism

Parallelism is a skillful writing technique that involves balanced writing. Sentences written so that their parts are balanced or parallel are easy to read and understand. To achieve parallel construction, use similar structures to express similar ideas. For example, the words *computing, coding, recording,* and *storing* are parallel because the words all end in *-ing*. To express the list as *computing, coding, recording,* and *storage* is disturbing because the last item is not what the reader expects. Try to match nouns with nouns, verbs with verbs, and clauses with clauses. Avoid mixing active-voice verbs with passive-voice verbs. Your goal is to keep the wording balanced in expressing similar ideas.

Balanced wording helps the reader anticipate and comprehend your meaning.

Lacks parallelism	The policy affected all vendors, suppliers, and *those involved with consulting*.
Matches nouns	The policy affected all vendors, suppliers, and *consultants*.
Lacks parallelism	Our primary goals are to increase productivity, reduce costs, and *the improvement of product quality*.
Matches verbs	Our primary goals are to increase productivity, reduce costs, and *improve product quality*.
Lacks parallelism	We are scheduled to meet in Dallas on January 5, *we are meeting in Montreal on the 15th of March*, and in Chicago on June 3.
Matches phrases	We are scheduled to meet in Dallas on January 5, *in Montreal on March 15*, and in Chicago on June 3. (Parallel construction matches phrases.)
Lacks parallelism	Mrs. Horne audits all accounts lettered A through L; accounts lettered M through Z are audited by Mr. Shapiro.
Matches clauses	Mrs. Horne audits all accounts lettered A through L; Mr. Shapiro audits accounts lettered M through Z.

All items in a list should be expressed in balanced constructions.

In presenting lists of data, whether shown horizontally or tabulated vertically, be certain to express all the items in parallel form.

Parallelism in vertical list	Our advertising program has three primary objectives: 1. Increase the frequency of product use 2. Introduce complementary products 3. Enhance the corporate image

Developing Unity

Unified sentences contain only related ideas.

Unified sentences contain thoughts that are related to only one main idea. The following sentence lacks unity because the first clause has little or no relationship to the second clause:

Lacks unity	Our insurance plan is available in all the states and provinces, and you may name anyone as a beneficiary for your coverage.

| Revision | Our insurance plan is available in all the states and provinces. What's more, you may name anyone as a beneficiary for your coverage. |

The ideas are better expressed by separating the two dissimilar clauses and by adding a connecting phrase, as shown above. Other writing faults that destroy sentence unity are (1) zigzag writing, (2) mixed constructions, and (3) misplaced modifiers.

AVOIDING ZIGZAG WRITING

Zigzag sentences often should be broken into two sentences.

Sentences that twist or turn unexpectedly away from the main thought are examples of zigzag writing. Such confusing writing may result when too many thoughts are included in one sentence or when one thought does not relate to another. To rectify a zigzag sentence, revise it so that the reader understands the relationship between the thoughts. If that is impossible, move the unrelated thoughts to a new sentence or add explanatory information.

| Zigzag writing | I appreciate the time you spent with me in our interview last week, and I have enrolled in a PhotoShop course. |
| Revision | I appreciate the time you spent with me in our interview last week. As a result of your advice, I have enrolled in a PhotoShop course. |

| Zigzag writing | GAP coverage protects car buyers who put little or no money down, but later they find they are "upside down" on an auto loan because the car was totaled. |
| Revision | GAP coverage protects car buyers who put little or no money down. If the car is totaled, this protection avoids being "upside down" on the loan, that is, owing more than the car is worth. |

AVOIDING CONFUSING MIXED CONSTRUCTIONS

Mixed grammatical constructions confuse readers.

Writers who fuse two different grammatical constructions destroy sentence unity and meaning.

| Mixed construction | The reason she was hired is *because* she is qualified. |
| Revision | The reason she was hired is *that* she is qualified. (The construction introduced by *the reason is* should be a noun clause beginning with *that*, not an adverbial clause beginning with *because*.) |

| Mixed construction | When the stock market index rose five points was our signal to sell. |
| Revision | When the stock market index rose five points, we were prepared to sell. *OR:* Our signal to sell was an increase of five points in the stock market index. |

AVOIDING DANGLING AND MISPLACED MODIFIERS

Modifiers must be close to the words they describe or limit.

For clarity, modifiers must be close to the words they describe or limit. A modifier dangles when the word or phrase it describes is missing from its sentence. A modifier is misplaced when the word or phrase it describes is not close enough to be clear. In both instances, the solution is to position the modifier closer to the word(s) it describes or limits. Introductory verbal phrases are particularly dangerous; be sure to follow them immediately with the words they logically describe or modify.

| Dangling modifier | To win the lottery, a ticket must be purchased. (The introductory verbal phrase must be followed by a logical subject.) |
| Revision | To win the lottery, you must purchase a ticket. |

| Dangling modifier | Driving through Malibu Canyon, the ocean suddenly came into view. (Is the ocean driving through Malibu Canyon?) |
| Revision | Driving through Malibu Canyon, we saw the ocean suddenly come into view. |

Try this trick for detecting and remedying these dangling modifiers. Ask the question *Who?* or *What?* after any introductory phrase. The words immediately following should tell the reader who or what is performing the action. Try the *who?* test on the previous danglers.

Misplaced modifier	Seeing his error too late, the envelope was immediately resealed by Matt. (Did the envelope see the error?)
Revision	Seeing his error too late, Matt immediately resealed the envelope.
Misplaced modifier	A wart appeared on my left hand that I want removed. (Is the left hand to be removed?)
Revision	A wart that I want removed appeared on my left hand.
Misplaced modifier	The busy personnel director interviewed only candidates who had excellent computer skills in the morning. (Were the candidates skilled only in the morning?)
Revision	In the morning the busy personnel director interviewed only candidates who had excellent computer skills.

• STRIVING FOR PARAGRAPH COHERENCE

Three ways to create paragraph coherence are (1) repetition of key ideas, (2) use of pronouns, and (3) use of transitional expressions.

A paragraph is a group of sentences with a controlling idea, usually stated first. Paragraphs package similar ideas into meaningful groups for readers. Effective paragraphs are coherent; that is, they hold together. But coherence does not happen accidentally. It is achieved through effective organization and (1) repetition of key ideas, (2) use of pronouns, and (3) use of transitional expressions.

- **Repetition of key ideas or key words.** Repeating a word or key thought from a preceding sentence helps guide a reader from one thought to the next. This redundancy is necessary to build cohesiveness into writing.

| Effective repetition | Our philosophy holds that every customer is really a *guest*. All new employees to our theme parks are trained to treat visitors as special *guests*. These *guests* are never told what they can or cannot do. |

Notice that the repetition of the word *guest* creates coherence between sentences. Good writers find similar words to describe the same idea, thus using repetition to clarify a topic for the reader.

- **Use of pronouns.** Pronouns such as *this, that, they, these*, and *those* promote coherence by connecting the thoughts in one sentence to the thoughts in a previous sentence. To make sure that the pronoun reference is clear, consider joining the pronoun with the word to which it refers, thus making the pronoun into an adjective.

| Pronoun repetition | All new park employees receive a two-week orientation. *They* learn that every staffer has a vital role in preparing for the show. *This* training includes how to maintain enthusiasm. |

Be very careful, though, in using pronouns. A pronoun without a clear antecedent can be most annoying. In the last example notice how confusing *this* becomes if the word *training* is omitted.

> **Faulty**   When company profits increased, employees were given either a cash payment or company stock. *This* became a real incentive to employees.
>
> **Revision**   When company profits increased, employees were given either a cash payment or company stock. *This profit-sharing plan* became a real incentive to employees.

<table>
<tr><td>Used wisely, transitional expressions guide readers smoothly from idea to idea.</td><td>

• **Use of transitional expressions.** One of the most effective ways to achieve paragraph coherence is through the use of transitional expressions. These expressions act as road signs: they indicate where the message is headed, and they help the reader anticipate what is coming. Here are some of the most effective transitional expressions. They are grouped according to uses.

</td></tr>
</table>

Time Association	Contrast	Illustration
before, after	although	for example
first, second	but	in this way
meanwhile	however	
next	instead	
until	nevertheless	
when, whenever	on the other hand	

Cause, Effect	Additional Idea
consequently	furthermore
for this reason	in addition
hence	likewise
therefore	moreover

Controlling Paragraph Length

<table>
<tr><td>The most readable paragraphs contain eight or fewer printed lines.</td><td>

Although no rule regulates the length of paragraphs, business writers recognize the value of short paragraphs. Paragraphs with eight or fewer printed lines look inviting and readable. Long, solid chunks of print appear formidable. If a topic can't be covered in eight or fewer printed lines (not sentences), consider breaking it into smaller segments.

</td></tr>
</table>

COMPOSING THE FIRST DRAFT

Once you've researched your topic, organized the data, and selected a pattern of organization, you're ready to begin composing. Communicators who haven't completed the preparatory work often suffer from "writer's block" and sit staring at a piece of paper or at the computer screen. It's easier to get started if you have organized your ideas and established a plan. Composition is also easier if you have a quiet environment in which to concentrate. Businesspeople with messages to compose set aside a given time and allow no calls, visitors, or other interruptions. This is a good technique for students as well.

<table>
<tr><td>Create a quiet place in which to write. Experts recommend "sprint writing" for first drafts.</td><td>

As you begin composing, keep in mind that you are writing the first draft, not the final copy. Some experts suggest that you write quickly (*sprint writing*). If you get your thoughts down quickly, you can refine them in later versions. Other writers, such as your author, prefer to polish sentences as they go. Different writers have different styles. Whether you are a sprint writer or a polisher, be sure you compose at your computer. Learn to compose your thoughts at your keyboard. Don't write a first draft by hand and then transfer it to the computer. This wastes time and develops poor habits. Businesspeople must be able to compose at their keyboards, and now is the time to develop that confidence and skill.

</td></tr>
</table>

SUMMING UP AND LOOKING FORWARD

This chapter explained the second phase of the writing process, including researching, organizing, and composing. Before beginning a message, every writer collects data, either formally or informally. For most simple messages, you would look in the files, talk with your boss, interview the target audience, or possibly conduct an informal survey. Information for a message is then organized into a list or an outline. Depending on the expected reaction of the receiver, the message can be organized directly (for positive reactions) or indirectly (for negative reactions or when persuasion is necessary).

In composing the first draft, writers must be sure that sentences are complete. Emphasis can be achieved through mechanics (underlining, italics, font changes, all caps, and so forth) or through style (using vivid words, labeling the main idea, and positioning the important ideas). Important writing techniques include the skillful use of active- and passive-voice verbs, developing parallelism, and achieving unity while avoiding zigzag writing, mixed constructions, and misplaced modifiers. Coherent paragraphs result from planned repetition of key ideas, proper use of pronouns, and inclusion of transitional expressions.

In the next chapter you'll learn helpful techniques for the third phase of the writing process, which includes revising and proofreading.

CRITICAL THINKING

1. Many critics think that writing skills have declined in recent years. What do you think are the reasons for deteriorating writing skills, and what can be done to improve skills?

2. Why is audience analysis so important in choosing the direct or indirect pattern of organization for a business message?

3. How are speakers different from writers in the way they emphasize ideas?

4. Why are short sentences and short paragraphs appropriate for business communication?

5. When might it be unethical to use the indirect method of organizing a message?

CHAPTER REVIEW

6. How is the first phase of the writing process different from the second phase?

7. Distinguish between formal and informal methods of researching data for a business message.

8. What is the difference between a list and an outline?

9. What is frontloading and what are its advantages?

10. When is the indirect method appropriate, and what are the benefits of using it?

11. List five techniques for achieving emphasis through mechanics.

12. List four techniques for achieving emphasis through style.

13. What is parallelism? Give an original example.

14. List three techniques for developing paragraph coherence.

15. What environment should you establish if you have something to write?

EXPAND YOUR LEARNING WITH THESE BONUS RESOURCES!

Guffey Companion Web Site

http://guffey.swlearning.com

Your companion Web site offers review quizzes, a glossary of key terms, and flash cards to build your knowledge of chapter concepts. Additional career tools include *Dr. Guffey's Guide to Business Etiquette and Workplace Manners*, *Listening Quiz*, and electronic citation formats (MLA and APA) for business writers. You'll also find updated links to all chapter URLs.

Guffey Xtra!

http://guffeyxtra.swlearning.com

This online study assistant illustrates chapter concepts in PowerPoint. It strengthens your language skills with *Your Personal Language Trainer* (a grammar/mechanics review), *Speak Right!, Spell Right!*, and *Sentence Competency Exercises*. In addition, **Guffey Xtra!** brings you bonus online chapters: *Employment and Other Interviewing* and *How to Write Instructions*. You'll also find the Grammar/Mechanics Challenge exercises so that you can revise without rekeying.

WRITING IMPROVEMENT EXERCISES

Revising Sentences

In the following, identify the sentence fault (fragment, run-on, comma splice). Then revise to remedy the fault.

16. Although they began as a side business for Disney. Destination weddings now represent a major income source.

17. About 2,000 weddings are held yearly. Which is twice the number just ten years ago.

18. Weddings may take place in less than one hour, however the cost may be as much as $5,000.

19. Limousines line up outside Disney's wedding pavilion, ceremonies are scheduled in two-hour intervals.

20. Many couples prefer a traditional wedding others request a fantasy experience.

Emphasis

For each of the following sentences, circle (a) or (b). Be prepared to justify your choice.

21. Which is more emphatic?
    a. They offer a lot of products.
    b. CyberGuys offers computer, travel, and office accessories.

22. Which is more emphatic?
    a. Increased advertising would improve sales.
    b. Adding $50,000 in advertising would double our sales.

23. Which is more emphatic?
    a. We must consider several factors.
    b. We must consider cost, staff, and safety.

24. Which sentence places more emphasis on *product loyalty?*
    a. Product loyalty is the primary motivation for advertising.
    b. The primary motivation for advertising is loyalty to the product, although other purposes are also served.

25. Which sentence places more emphasis on the seminar?
    a. An executive training seminar that starts June 1 will include four candidates.
    b. Four candidates will be able to participate in an executive training seminar that we feel will provide a valuable learning experience.

26. Which sentence places more emphasis on the date?
    a. The deadline is April 1 for summer vacation reservations.
    b. April 1 is the deadline for summer vacation reservations.

27. Which is *less* emphatic?
   a. One division's profits decreased last quarter.
   b. Profits in consumer electronics dropped 15 percent last quarter.

28. Which sentence *de-emphasizes* the credit refusal?
   a. We are unable to grant you credit at this time, but we welcome your cash business and encourage you to reapply in the future.
   b. Although credit cannot be granted at this time, we welcome your cash business and encourage you to reapply in the future.

29. Which sentence gives more emphasis to *leadership*?
   a. She has many admirable qualities, but most important is her leadership skill.
   b. She has many admirable qualities, including leadership skill, good judgment, and patience.

30. Which is more emphatic?
   a. We notified three departments: (1) Marketing, (2) Accounting, and (3) Distribution.
   b. We notified three departments:
      1. Marketing
      2. Accounting
      3. Distribution

Active-Voice Verbs

Business writing is more forceful if it uses active-voice verbs. Revise the following sentences so that verbs are in the active voice. Put the emphasis on the doer of the action. Add subjects if necessary.

     Example   Firewall software was installed on his computer.
     Revision   Craig installed firewall software on his computer.

31. A company credit card was used by the manager to purchase office supplies.

32. To protect students, laws were passed in many states that prohibited the use of social security numbers as identification.

33. Checks are processed more quickly by banks because of new regulations.

34. Millions of packages are scanned by FedEx every night as packages stream through its Memphis hub.

Passive-Voice Verbs

When indirectness or tact is required, use passive-voice verbs. Revise the following sentences so that they are in the passive voice.

     Example   Travis did not submit the proposal before the deadline.
     Revision   The proposal was not submitted before the deadline.

35. Accounting seems to have made a serious error in this report.

36. We cannot ship your order for smart surge protectors until May 5.

37. The government first issued a warning regarding the use of this pesticide more than 15 months ago.

38. Your insurance policy does not automatically cover damage to rental cars.

39. We cannot provide patient care unless patients show proof of insurance.

Parallelism

Revise the following sentences so that their parts are balanced.

40. (**Hint:** Match verbs.) To improve your listening skills, you should stop talking, your surroundings should be controlled, be listening for main points, and an open mind must be kept.

41. (**Hint:** Match active voice of verbs.) Paula Day, director of the Okefenokee branch, will now supervise all Eastern Division operations; the Western Division will be supervised by our Oroville branch director, Reggie Kostiz.

42. (**Hint:** Match verb phrases.) Our newly hired employee has started using the computer and to learn her coworkers' names.

43. (**Hint:** Match adjectives.) Training seminars must be stimulating and a challenge.

44. Our new telecommunications software allows you to meet with customers over the Internet for training, Web-based meetings can be held, and other online collaboration within virtual teams is also facilitated.

45. We need more trained staff members, office space is limited, and the budget for overtime is much too small.

46. The application for a grant asks for this information: funds required for employee salaries, how much we expect to spend on equipment, and what is the length of the project.

47. Sending an e-mail establishes a more permanent record than to make a telephone call.

Sentence Unity

The following sentences lack unity. Rewrite, correcting the identified fault.

Example   (Dangling modifier) When collecting information for new equipment, the Web proved to be my best resource.

Revision   When collecting information for new equipment, I found the Web to be my best resource.

48. (Dangling modifier) To win the lottery, a ticket must be purchased.

49. (Mixed construction) The reason why our boss is such a good manager is because he genuinely listens to employees.

50. (Misplaced modifier) The exciting Mandalay Bay is just one of the fabulous hotels you see strolling along the Las Vegas strip.

51. (Dangling modifier) Angered by slow computer service, complaints were called in by hundreds of unhappy users.

52. (Zigzag sentence) Fishermen pump money into the local economy when salmon make their annual spawning runs, renting rooms, filling restaurants, and buying supplies from stores and shops in the region.

Coherence

Revise the following paragraphs to improve coherence. Study the example and review the chapter. Be aware that the transitional expressions and keywords selected depend largely on the emphasis desired. Many possible revisions exist.

Example	Computer style checkers rank somewhere between artificial intelligence and artificial ignorance. Style checkers are like clever children: smart but not wise. Business writers should be cautious. They should be aware of the usefulness of style checkers. They should know their limitations.
Revision	Computer style checkers rank somewhere between artificial intelligence and artificial ignorance. *For example*, they are like clever children: smart but not wise. *For this reason*, business writers should be cautious. *Although* they should be aware of the usefulness of these software programs, business writers should *also* know their limitations.

53. Managers can avoid costly hiring mistakes with two techniques. They should write a solid job description. They should explain special job expectations during the hiring interview. Will the applicant be expected to travel? Are tight deadlines common? The manager should not frighten away applicants.

54. No one likes to turn out poor products. We began highlighting recurring problems. Employees make a special effort to be more careful in doing their work right the first time. It doesn't have to be returned to them for corrections.

55. Service was less than perfect for many months. We lacked certain intangibles. We didn't have the customer-specific data that we needed. We made the mistake of removing all localized, person-to-person coverage. We are returning to decentralized customer contacts.

ACTIVITY

INFOTRAC

3.1 How Do Supervisors Improve Their Writing?

Nearly everyone who goes to college will eventually be promoted into some kind of supervisory position. In that role you will be writing memos, letters, instructions, reports, and other business documents.

Your Task. Using InfoTrac, find an article that describes how supervisors can improve their writing skills. We recommend "Writing Clearly and Forcefully" by W. H. Weiss, which appeared in the December 2001 issue of *Supervision*. However, you may find a more recent article that is equally helpful. Read the article carefully, and make a list of eight to ten suggestions that you think would be most helpful to you in improving your own writing. Discuss your list in small groups or submit it to your instructor.

GRAMMAR/MECHANICS CHECKUP—3

Verbs

Review Sections 1.10–1.15 in the Grammar Review section of the Grammar/Mechanics Handbook. Then study each of the following statements. Underline any verbs that are used incorrectly. In the space provided write the correct form (or *C* if correct) and the number of the G/M principle illustrated. When you finish, compare your responses with those provided near the end of the book. If your responses differ, study carefully the principles in parentheses.

is for *are*   (1.10e)   **Example**   Are you certain that the database of our customers' names and addresses <u>are</u> secure?

_____   1. Posted at our company's intranet is all personnel forms and information about benefits.

_____   2. If even one of my e-mail messages are blocked by spam controls, I am unhappy.

_____   3. Verizon, together with many other large ISPs, were singled out for using overzealous spam blockers.

_____   4. Neither the sender nor the receiver of blocked messages know what has happened.

_____   5. A typical e-mail user might loose anywhere from one message a month to as many as five a week.

_____   6. The time and energy that is required to follow up on e-mail messages reduce efficiency.

_____   7. Either the message or its attachment has triggered the spam-blocking software.

_____   8. After many of its customers had began to complain about lost messages, one company sued.

_____   9. If you could have saw the number of nondelivery error messages, you would have been upset also.

_____   10. Although Sloan acts as if she was the manager, she can't solve the e-mail disruption dilemma.

_____   11. Ramon discovered that a lot of his legitimate e-mail had went to junk folders that he never checked.

In the space provided write the letter of the sentence that illustrates consistency in subject, voice, and mood.

_____   12. a. When Trevor sent an e-mail message, its delivery was expected.
                            b. When Trevor sent an e-mail message, he expected it to be delivered.

_____   13. a. All employees must wear photo identification; only then will you be admitted.
                            b. All employees must wear photo identification; only then will they be admitted.

14. a. First, check all computers for viruses; then, install a firewall.
    b. First, check all computers for viruses; then, a firewall must be installed.

15. a. When Scott examined the computers, the spyware was discovered.
    b. When Scott examined the computers, he discovered the spyware.

GRAMMAR/MECHANICS CHALLENGE—3

The following business letter has faults in grammar, spelling, punctuation, capitalization, word use, wordiness, parallelism, dangling modifiers, and number form. Correct the errors with standard proofreading marks (see Appendix B), or revise the message online at **Guffey Xtra!**

GARTH I. PETERSON
CERTIFIED FINANCIAL PLANNER

3392 Econlockhatchee Trail
Orlando, FL 32822-6588
(407) 551-8791
garth.peterson@flor.com

Current date

Mrs. Julie Noriega
392 Blue Lagoon Way
Orlando, FL 32814

Dear Julie:

This is to inform you that, as your Financial Planner, I'm happy to respond to your request for clarification on the Tax status of eBay profits.

As you in all probability are all ready aware of, you can use eBay to clean out your closets. It can also be used to run a small business. Your smart to enquire about your tax liability. Although there is no clear line that separates fun from profit or a hobby from a business. One thing is certin, the IRS taxs all income.

There are a number of factors that help determine whether or not your hobby should or should not be considered a business. To use eBay safely the following questions should be considered:

1. Do you run the operation in a businesslike manner? Do you keep records, is your profit and loss tracked, or do you keep a seperate checking account?

2. Do you devote alot of time and effort to eBay? If you spend eighteen hours a day selling on eBay the IRS would tend to think your in a business.

3. Some people depend on the income from their eBay activities for their livelihood.

Are you selling items for more then they cost you? If you spend four dollars for a Garage Sale vase and sell it for fifty dollars the IRS would probably consider this a business transaction. All profits is taxable. Even for eBay sellers who are just playing around. If you wish to discuss this faarther please call me at 551-8791.

Sincerely,

Garth Peterson

COMMUNICATION WORKSHOP ETHICS

USING ETHICAL TOOLS
TO HELP YOU DO THE RIGHT THING

In your career you will no doubt face times when you are torn by conflicting loyalties. Should you tell the truth and risk your job? Should you be loyal to your friends even if it means bending the rules? Should you be tactful or totally honest? Is it your duty to help your company make a profit, or should you be socially responsible?

Being ethical, according to the experts, means doing the right thing *given the circumstances.* Each set of circumstances requires analyzing issues, evaluating choices, and acting responsibly. Resolving ethical issues is never easy, but the task can be made less difficult if you know how to identify key issues. The following questions may be helpful.

- **Is the action you are considering legal?** No matter who asks you to do it or how important you feel the result will be, avoid anything that is prohibited by law. Giving a kickback to a buyer for a large order is illegal, even if you suspect that others in your field do it and you know that without the kickback you will lose the sale.

- **How would you see the problem if you were on the opposite side?** Looking at all sides of an issue helps you gain perspective. Consider the issue of mandatory drug testing among employees. From management's viewpoint such testing could stop drug abuse, improve job performance, and lower health insurance premiums. From the employees' viewpoint mandatory testing reflects a lack of trust of employees and constitutes an invasion of privacy. By weighing both sides of an issue, you can arrive at a more equitable solution.

- **What are the alternate solutions?** Consider all dimensions of other options. Would the alternative be more ethical? Under the circumstances, is the alternative feasible? Can an alternate solution be implemented with a minimum of disruption and with a high degree of probable success?

- **Can you discuss the problem with someone whose opinion you value?** Suppose you feel ethically bound to report accurate information to a client—even though your boss has ordered you not to do so. Talking about your dilemma with a coworker or with a colleague in your field might give you helpful insights and lead to possible alternatives.

- **How would you feel if your family, friends, employer, or coworkers learned of your action?** If the thought of revealing your action publicly produces cold sweats, your choice is probably not a wise one. Losing the faith of your friends or the confidence of your customers is not worth whatever short-term gains might be realized.

Career Application. One of the biggest accounting firms uses an ethical awareness survey that includes some of the following situations. You may face similar situations with ethical issues on the job or in employment testing.

Your Task

In teams or individually, decide whether each of the following ethical issues is (a) very important, (b) moderately important, or (c) unimportant. Then decide whether you (a) strongly approve, (b) are undecided, or (c) strongly disapprove of the action taken.[3] Apply the ethical tools presented here in determining whether the course of action is ethical. What alternatives might you suggest?

- **Recruiting.** You are a recruiter for your company. Although you know company morale is low, the turnover rate is high, and the work environment in many departments is deplorable, you tell job candidates that it's "a great place to work."

- **Training Program.** Your company is offering an exciting training program in Hawaii. Although you haven't told anyone, you plan to get another job shortly. You decide to participate in the program anyway because you've never been to Hawaii. One of the program requirements is that participants must have "long-term career potential" with the firm.

- **Thievery.** As a supervisor, you suspect that one of your employees is stealing. You check with a company attorney and find that a lie detector test cannot be legally used. Then you decide to scrutinize the employee's records. Finally, you find an inconsistency in the employee's records. You decide to fire the employee, although this inconsistency would not normally have been discovered.

- **Downsizing.** As part of the management team of a company that makes potato chips, you are faced with the rising price of potatoes. Rather than increase the cost of your chips, you decide to decrease slightly the size of the bag. Consumers are less likely to notice a smaller bag than a higher price.

CHAPTER 4

REVISING AND PROOFREADING BUSINESS MESSAGES

Vigorous writing is concise. A sentence should contain no unnecessary words . . . for the same reason that a drawing should have no unnecessary lines and a machine no unnecessary parts.

Strunk and White, *The Elements of Style*

OBJECTIVES

- Understand the third phase of the writing process: revision.
- Revise messages to achieve concise wording by eliminating wordy prepositional phrases, long lead-ins, outdated expressions, and needless adverbs.
- Revise messages to eliminate fillers, repetitious words, and redundancies.
- Revise messages to use jargon sparingly and avoid slang and clichés.
- Revise messages to include precise verbs, concrete nouns, and vivid adjectives.
- Describe effective techniques for proofreading routine and complex documents.

UNDERSTANDING THE PROCESS OF REVISION

Revision involves improving content and sentence structure; proofreading involves correcting grammar, spelling, punctuation, format, and mechanics.

To be successful in the business world, you must be able to turn out business messages and presentations that are concise, clear, and vigorous. In this chapter you'll concentrate on techniques to achieve those qualities. These techniques are part of the third phase of the writing process, which centers on revising and proofreading. Revising means improving the content and sentence structure of your message. It may include adding, cutting, and recasting what you've written. Proofreading involves correcting the grammar, spelling, punctuation, format, and mechanics of your messages.

Both revising and proofreading require a little practice to develop your skills. That's what you will be learning in this chapter. Take a look at Figure 4.1. Notice how the revised version of this memo is clearer, more concise, and more vigorous because we removed much deadwood. Major ideas stand out when they are not lost in a forest of words.

Rarely is the first or even the second version of a message satisfactory. Experts say that only amateurs expect writing perfection on the first try. The revision stage is your chance to make sure your message is clear, forceful, and says what you mean. This is "where your message gets hammered out, where the real work takes place" as you struggle to clarify your thoughts.[1]

FIGURE 4.1

Memo Revised for Conciseness

NorthStar Telecommunication Services
Interoffice Memo

DATE: November 12, 200x

TO: Rodney Hawkins

FROM: Sierra McKinney

SUBJECT: Investigation of Web Sites ~~of Some of Our Competitors~~ *Competitors'*

~~This is just a short note to inform you that~~ as you requested, I have ~~made an investigation of~~ *investigated*
several of our competitors' Web sites. Attached ~~hereto~~ is a summary of my findings.
~~of my investigation.~~ I was ~~really~~ most interested in ~~making a comparison of the employment of~~ *comparing* *marketing*
strategies ~~for marketing~~ as well as ~~the use of~~ navigational graphics ~~used~~ to guide visitors
through the sites. ~~In view of the fact that~~ *Because* we will be revising our own Web site ~~in the near future~~ *soon*,
I was ~~extremely~~ intrigued by the organization, ~~kind of~~ marketing tactics, and navigation at
each ~~and every~~ site I visited.
~~In the event that~~ *If* you would like to discuss this information with me, ~~feel free to~~ *please* call me at
Extension 219.

Attachment

Some communicators write the
first draft quickly; others revise
and polish as they go.

Many professional writers compose the first draft quickly without worrying about language, precision, or correctness. Then they revise and polish extensively. Other writers, however, prefer to revise as they go—particularly for shorter business documents. Whether you revise as you go or do it when you finish a document, you'll want to focus on concise wording. This includes eliminating wordy prepositional phrases, long lead-ins, outdated expressions, needless adverbs, fillers, and repetitious and redundant words. You will decide whether to include jargon, slang, and clichés. You will also be looking for precise words that say exactly what you mean.

CONCISE WORDING

Main points are easier to understand in concise messages.

In business, time is indeed money. Translated into writing, this means that concise messages save reading time and, thus, money. In addition, messages that are written directly and efficiently are easier to read and comprehend. In the revision process look for shorter ways to say what you mean. Examine every sentence that you write. Could the thought be conveyed in fewer words? Notice how the following flabby expressions could be said more concisely.

Flabby phrases can often be reduced to a single word.

Flabby	Concise	Flabby	Concise
at a later date	later	fully cognizant of	aware of
at this point in time	now	in addition to the above	also
afford an opportunity	allow	in spite of the fact that	even though
are of the opinion that	believe, think that	in the event that	if
at the present time	now, presently	in the amount of	for
despite the fact that	although	in the near future	soon
due to the fact that	because	in view of the fact that	because
during the time	while	inasmuch as	since
feel free to	please	more or less	about
for the period of	for	until such time as	until

Wordy Prepositional Phrases

Replace wordy prepositional phrases with adverbs whenever possible.

Some wordy prepositional phrases may be replaced by single adverbs. For example, *in the normal course of events* becomes *normally* and *as a general rule* becomes *generally.*

Wordy	Wal-Mart approached the union issue *in a careful manner.*
Concise	Wal-Mart approached the union issue *carefully.*
Wordy	Our office will *in all probability* be relocated.
Concise	Our office will *probably* be relocated.
Wordy	We have taken this action *in very few cases.*
Concise	We have *seldom* taken this action.

Long Lead-Ins

Avoid long lead-ins that delay the reader from reaching the meaning of the sentence.

Delete unnecessary introductory words. The meat of the sentence often follows the words *that* or *because.*

Wordy	*This e-mail message is being sent to all of you to let you know that* new parking permits will be issued January 1.
Concise	New parking permits will be issued January 1.
Wordy	*You will be interested to learn that* you can now be served at our Web site.
Concise	You can now be served at our Web site.
Wordy	*I am writing this letter because* Dr. Steven Hunt suggested that your organization was hiring trainees.
Concise	Dr. Steven Hunt suggested that your organization was hiring trainees.

Outdated Expressions

Don't try to sound businesslike by using outdated expressions.

The world of business has changed greatly in the past century or two. Yet, some business writers continue to use antiquated phrases and expressions left over from the past. They are trapped by the notion that these familiar phrases are necessary to sound "businesslike." Forget that idea! Replace oudated expressions such as those shown here with more modern phrasing:

Outdated Expressions	Modern Phrasing
are in receipt of	have received
as per your request	at your request
attached hereto	attached
enclosed please find	enclosed is/are
pursuant to your request	at your request
thanking you in advance	thank you
I trust that	I think, I believe
under separate cover	separately

Needless Adverbs

Avoid excessive use of adverb intensifiers.

Eliminating adverbs such as *very, definitely, quite, completely, extremely, really, actually, somewhat,* and *rather* streamlines your writing. Omitting these intensifiers generally makes you sound more credible and businesslike. Writers who wish to sound sincere and conversational often include some intensifiers, but they guard against excessive use.

Wordy	We *actually* did not *really* give his proposal a *very* fair trial.
Concise	We did not give his proposal a fair trial.

Smart communicators make sure their vocabularies are as contemporary as the offices in which they work. They avoid outdated expressions, clichés, and wordiness.

© MANCHAN/PHOTODISC/GETTY IMAGES

Wordy	Hewlett-Packard officials were *extremely* upset to learn that its printers were *definitely* being counterfeited.
Concise	Hewlett-Packard officials were upset to learn that its printers were being counterfeited.

Fillers

Avoid fillers that fatten sentences with excess words. Beginning an idea with *There is* usually indicates that writers are spinning their wheels until they decide where the sentence is going. Used correctly, *there* indicates a specific place (*I placed the box there*). Used as fillers, *there* and occasionally *it* merely take up space. Most, but not all, sentences can be revised so that these fillers are unnecessary.

Wordy	*There is* only one candidate who passed the writing test.
Concise	Only one candidate passed the writing test.

Wordy	*It was* our auditor *who made a discovery* of the theft.
Concise	Our auditor discovered the theft.

Repetitious Words

Avoid the monotony of unintentionally repeated words.

Good communicators vary their words to avoid unintentional repetition. Not only does this shorten a message, but it also improves vigor and readability. Variety of expression can be achieved by searching for appropriate synonyms and by substituting pronouns. Compare the following wordy paragraph with the more concise version. Notice in the concise version that synonyms (*representatives, members*) replace the overused *employee.*

Wordy	Concise
Employees will be able to elect an additional six employees to serve with the four previously elected employees who currently comprise the employees' board of directors.	Employees may vote for six additional representatives to serve with the previously elected members of their board of directors.

Good writers are also alert to the overuse of the articles *a, an,* and particularly *the.* Often the word *the* can simply be omitted, particularly with plural nouns.

Wordy	The committee members agreed on many of the rule changes.
Improved	Committee members agreed on many rule changes.

Redundant Words

Redundancies convey a meaning more than once.

Repetition of words to achieve emphasis or effective transition is an important writing technique discussed in the previous chapter. The needless repetition, however, of words whose meanings are clearly implied by other words is a writing fault called *redundancy.* For example, in the expression *final outcome,* the word *final* is redundant and should be omitted, since *outcome* implies finality. Learn to avoid redundant expressions such as the following:

Don't use words that repeat meaning. Which words could be omitted?

absolutely essential	*grateful* thanks
adequate *enough*	*mutual* cooperation
advance warning	*necessary* prerequisite
basic fundamentals	*new* beginning
big *in size*	*passing* fad
combined *together*	*past* history
consensus *of opinion*	reason *why*
continue *on*	red *in color*
each *and every*	refer *back*
exactly identical	repeat *again*
few *in number*	*true* facts

Jargon

Jargon, which is terminology unique to a certain profession, should be reserved for individuals who understand it.

Except in certain specialized contexts, you should avoid jargon and unnecessary technical terms. Jargon is special terminology that is peculiar to a particular activity or profession. For example, geologists speak knowingly of *exfoliation, calcareous ooze,* and *siliceous particles.* Engineers are familiar with phrases such as *infrared processing flags, output latches,* and *movable symbology.* Telecommunication experts use such words and phrases as *protocols, clickstream, neural networks,* and *asynchronous transmission.*

Every field has its own special vocabulary. Using that vocabulary within the field is acceptable and even necessary for accurate, efficient communication. Don't use specialized terms, however, if you have reason to believe that your reader may misunderstand them.

Slang

Slang sounds fashionable, but it lacks precise meaning and should be avoided in business writing.

Slang is composed of informal words with arbitrary and extravagantly changed meanings. Slang words quickly go out of fashion because they are no longer appealing when everyone begins to understand them. Consider the following statement of a government official who had been asked why his department was dropping a proposal to lease offshore oil lands: "The Administration has an awful lot of other things in the pipeline, and this has more wiggle room so they just moved it down the totem pole." He added, however, that the proposal might be offered again since "there is no pulling back because of hot-potato factors."

The meaning here, if the speaker really intended to impart any, is considerably obscured by the use of slang. Good communicators, of course, aim at clarity and avoid unintelligible slang.

If you want to sound professional, avoid expressions such as *snarky, lousy, blowing the budget, bombed,* and *getting burned.* Good communicators aim at clarity and avoid unintelligible slang.

Clichés

Clichés are dull and sometimes ambiguous.

Clichés are expressions that have become exhausted by overuse. These expressions lack not only freshness but also clarity. Some have no meaning for people who are new to our culture. The following partial list contains clichés you should avoid in business writing.

below the belt	last but not least
better than new	make a bundle
beyond a shadow of a doubt	pass with flying colors
easier said than done	quick as a flash
exception to the rule	shoot from the hip
fill the bill	stand your ground
first and foremost	think outside the box
good to go	true to form

Precise Verbs

Precise verbs make your writing forceful, clear, and lively.

Effective writing creates meaningful images in the mind of the reader. Such writing is sparked by robust, concrete, and descriptive words. Ineffective writing is often dulled by insipid, abstract, and generalized words. The most direct way to improve lifeless writing is through effective use of verbs. Verbs not only indicate the action of the subject but also deliver the force of the sentence. Select verbs carefully so that the reader can visualize precisely what is happening.

General	A representative will *contact* you next week.
Precise	A representative will (*telephone, fax, e-mail, visit*) you next week.
General	Our manager *asked* everyone to volunteer.
Precise	Our manager (*urged, begged, coaxed*) everyone to volunteer.
General	We must *consider* this problem.
Precise	We must (*clarify, remedy, rectify*) this problem.
General	The newspaper was *affected* by the strike.
Precise	The newspaper was (*crippled, silenced, demoralized*) by the strike.

Buried Verbs

Converting verbs into wordy noun expressions weakens business writing.

Buried verbs are those that are needlessly converted to wordy noun expressions. This happens when verbs such as *acquire, establish*, and *develop* are made into nouns such as *acquisition, establishment*, and *development*. Such nouns often end in *tion, ment*, and *ance*. In the following sentences, see how you can make your writing more concise and more powerful by avoiding wordy verb/noun conversions:

examined
Our auditor ~~made an examination of~~ the books.

agreed
Unions and management ~~reached an agreement~~ to continue talking.

appear
Celebrities promised to ~~make an appearance~~ at the charity event.

discussed
The webmaster and the designer ~~had a discussion about~~ graphics.

approve
Both companies must ~~grant approval of~~ the merger.

Concrete Nouns

Concrete nouns help readers visualize the meanings of words.

Nouns name persons, places, and things. Abstract nouns name concepts that are difficult to visualize, such as *automation, function, justice, institution, integrity, form, judgment*, and *environment*. Concrete nouns name objects that are more easily imagined, such as *desk, car*, and *laptop*. Nouns describing a given object can range from the very abstract to the very concrete—for example, *object, motor vehicle, car, convertible, Mustang*. All of these words or phrases can be used to describe a Mustang convertible. However, a reader would have difficulty envisioning a Mustang convertible when given just the word *object* or even *motor vehicle* or *car*.

In business writing, help your reader "see" what you mean by using concrete language.

General	we received *numerous* inquiries
Concrete	we received *78* inquiries
General	*that company's* new *gadget*
Concrete	*Sony Ericsson's S710 camera that includes an MP3 player*
General	*a person* called
Concrete	*James Grover, the senior marketing manager*, called
General	we have to move *a lot of stuff*
Concrete	we have to move *three rooms of furniture*
General	Negotiators use many skills
Concrete	Negotiators use *tact, diplomacy, empathy*, and *business savvy*

Vivid Adjectives

A thesaurus (computer or printed) helps you select precise words and increase your vocabulary.

Including highly descriptive, dynamic adjectives makes writing more vivid and concrete. Be careful, though, neither to overuse them nor to lose objectivity in selecting them.

General	Amanda submitted her report on time.
Vivid	Amanda submitted her *detailed 12-page* report on time.
General	We must hire a good employee.
Vivid	We must hire a *productive, efficient* employee.
General	Rick needs a better truck.
Vivid	Rick needs a *rugged, four-wheel-drive Dodge* truck.
General	We enjoyed the movie.
Vivid	We enjoyed the *entertaining and absorbing* movie.
Overkill	We enjoyed the *gutsy, exciting, captivating*, and *thoroughly marvelous* movie.

When your message is in final form, you may proofread at the screen or from a printed copy. If the document is complex, always print a copy and allow enough time to proofread it two or three times.

UNDERSTANDING THE PROCESS OF PROOFREADING

Proofreading before a document is completed is generally a waste of time.

Once you have the message in its final form, it's time to proofread. Don't proofread earlier because you may waste time checking items that eventually are changed or omitted.

What to Watch for in Proofreading

Careful proofreaders check for problems in these areas:

- **Spelling.** Now's the time to consult the dictionary. Is *recommend* spelled with one or two *c*'s? Do you mean *affect* or *effect*? Use your computer spell checker, but don't rely on it totally.
- **Grammar.** Locate sentence subjects; do their verbs agree with them? Do pronouns agree with their antecedents? Review the principles in the Grammar/Mechanics Handbook if necessary. Use your computer's grammar checker, but don't let it replace careful manual proofreading.
- **Punctuation.** Make sure that introductory clauses are followed by commas. In compound sentences put commas before coordinating conjunctions (*and, or, but, nor*). Double-check your use of semicolons and colons.
- **Names and numbers.** Compare all names and numbers with their sources because inaccuracies are not immediately visible. Especially verify the spelling of the names of individuals receiving the message. Most of us are offended when someone misspells our name.
- **Format.** Be sure that letters, printed memos, and reports are balanced on the page. Compare their parts and format with those of standard documents shown in Appendix A. If you indent paragraphs, be certain that all are indented.

How to Proofread Routine Documents

Routine documents need a light proofreading.

Most routine messages, including e-mails, require a light proofreading. Use the down arrow to reveal one line at a time, thus focusing your attention at the bottom of the screen. Read carefully for faults such as omitted or doubled words. Be sure to use your spell checker.

For routine messages such as printed letters or memos, a safer proofreading method is reading from a printed copy. You're more likely to find errors and to observe the tone.

© REZA ESTAKHRIAN/STONE/GETTY IMAGES

"Things really look different on paper," observed veteran writer Louise Lague at *People* magazine. "Don't just pull a letter out of the printer and stick it in an envelope. Read every sentence again. You'll catch bad line endings, strange page breaks, and weird spacing. You can also get a totally different feeling about what you've said when you see it in print. Sometimes you can say something with a smile on your face; but if you put the same thing in print, it won't work."[2] Use standard proofreading marks, shown in Figure 4.2, to indicate changes.

How to Proofread Complex Documents

Long, complex, or important documents demand more careful proofreading using the following techniques:

For both routine and complex documents, it's best to proofread from a printed copy, not on a computer screen.

- Print a copy, preferably double-spaced, and set it aside for at least a day. You'll be more alert after a breather.
- Allow adequate time to proofread carefully. A common excuse for sloppy proofreading is lack of time.
- Be prepared to find errors. One student confessed, "I can find other people's errors, but I can't seem to locate my own." Psychologically, we don't expect to find errors, and we don't want to find them. You can overcome this obstacle by anticipating errors and congratulating, not criticizing, yourself each time you find one.
- Read the message at least twice—once for word meanings and once for grammar/mechanics. For very long documents (book chapters and long articles or reports), read a third time to verify consistency in formatting.
- Reduce your reading speed. Concentrate on individual words rather than ideas.
- For documents that must be perfect, have someone read the message aloud. The reader should spell names and difficult words, note capitalization, and read punctuation.
- Use standard proofreading marks, shown in Figure 4.2, to indicate changes.

FIGURE 4.2

• Proofreading Marks

Most proofreaders use these standard marks to indicate revisions.

	Delete		Insert
	Capitalize		Insert space
	Lowercase (don't capitalize)		Insert punctuation
	Transpose		Insert period
	Close up		Start paragraph

Marked Copy

~~This is to inform you that~~ beginning september 1, the doors leading to the West side of the building will have alarms. Because ~~of the fact that~~ these exits (doors) also function as fire exits, they can not ~~actually~~ be locked consequently, we are installing alarms. Please ~~utilize~~ (use) the east side exists to avoid setting off the ear-piercing alarms.

© Randy Glasbergen
www.glasbergen.com

GLASBERGEN

"But there can't be any errors. My grammar
and spell checkers found nothing wrong!"

Your computer word processing program may include a style or grammar checker. These programs generally analyze aspects of your writing style, including readability level and use of passive voice, trite expressions, split infinitives, and wordy expressions. To do so, they use sophisticated algorithms (step-by-step procedures) to identify significant errors. In addition to finding spelling and typographical errors, grammar checkers can find subject–verb lack of agreement, word misuse, spacing irregularities, punctuation problems, and many other faults. However, they won't find everything. While grammar and spell checkers can help you a great deal, you are the final proofreader.

SUMMING UP AND LOOKING FORWARD

Revision is the most important part of the writing process. To revise for clarity and conciseness, look for flabby phrases that can be shortened (such as *more or less*). Eliminate wordy prepositional phrases (*in all probability*), long lead-ins (*This is to inform you that*), outdated expressions (*pursuant to your request*), needless adverbs (*definitely, very*), and fillers (*There are*). Also watch for repetitious words and redundancies (*combined together*). Use jargon only when it is clear to receivers, and avoid slang and clichés altogether.

The best writing includes precise verbs, concrete nouns, and vivid adjectives. After revising a message, you're ready for the last step in the writing process: proofreading. Watch for irregularities in spelling,

grammar, punctuation, names and numbers, and format. Although routine messages may be proofread on the screen, you will have better results if you proofread from a printed copy. Complex documents should be printed, put away for a day or so, and then proofread several times.

In these opening chapters you've studied the writing process. You've also learned many practical techniques for becoming an effective business communicator. Now it's time for you to put these techniques to work. Chapter 5 introduces you to writing e-mail messages and memorandums, the most frequently used forms of communication for most businesspeople. Later chapters present letters and reports.

CRITICAL THINKING

1. *A real writer can sit down at a computer and create a perfect document the first time.* Do you agree or disagree with this statement? Why?

2. *Carefully written short messages often take longer to write than longer messages.* Do you agree or disagree with this statement? Why?

3. Because clichés are familiar and have stood the test of time, do they help clarify writing?

4. If your boss writes in a flowery, formal tone and relies on outdated expressions, should you follow that style also?

5. Is it unethical to help a friend revise a report when you know that the friend will be turning that report in for a grade?

CHAPTER REVIEW

6. How is revising different from proofreading?

7. Why is conciseness especially important in business?

8. What is a long lead-in? Give an original example.

9. What's wrong with using adverbs such as *very, really*, and *actually*?

10. What is a redundancy? Give an example.

11. What is jargon? When can it be used? What are examples in your field?

12. What happens when a verb (such as *describe*) is converted to a noun expression (*to make a description*)? Give an original example.

13. Should you proofread when you are writing or after you finish? Why?

14. What five areas should you especially pay attention to when you proofread?

15. How does the proofreading of routine documents differ from that of complex documents?

WRITING IMPROVEMENT EXERCISES

Wordiness

Revise the following sentences to eliminate flabby phrases, wordy prepositional phrases, outdated expressions, and long lead-ins.

| Example | This is to inform you that in view of the fact that Monday is a holiday, we will be closed. |
| Revision | Because Monday is a holiday, we will be closed. |

16. This memo is to notify staff members that meetings held on a weekly basis are the manager's preference.

The manger prefr weeky meeting

17. We cannot send an apology at this point in time in spite of the fact that we were in all probability wrong.

[handwritten: Even tho   we were probability wrong]

18. Pursuant to your request, you will find attached hereto your January invoice.

19. There have been some complaints on the part of customers who made the statements that their orders were sent to wrong addresses.

20. You will be interested to learn that you may feel free to use this debit card for the purpose of purchasing items for a period of 30 days.

Buried Verbs

Revise these sentences, centering the action in the verbs and eliminating wordiness.

> **Example**   Enrique wanted to make application to the program.
> **Revision**   Enrique wanted to apply to the program.

21. The homeowner came to the realization that her asking price was too high.

22. Customers show a preference for rich colors.

[handwritten: Customer prefer rich colors.]

23. Employees conducted an investigation into efforts at staff reduction.

24. Insurance representatives placed the damage assessment at $1,000.

[handwritten: Change the assessment at 1000.]

25. Mr. James made a recommendation that an e-mail policy be developed in the immediate future.

[handwritten: A recommendation]

26. The CEO must give his approval to the plan before we meet tomorrow at 10 a.m. in the morning.

Needless Adverbs, Fillers, Repetitious Words, Buried Verbs

Revise the following sentences to eliminate needless adverbs, fillers (such as *there is* and *it is*), buried verbs, unintentional repetition, and other wordiness.

27. There is an extremely high number of businesses that are giving consideration to bringing an end to customer service that involves personal service.

28. It is certainly clear that our CPA must perform an analysis of profits before we can make a decision regarding bonuses for this year.

29. There is one manager who said it was absolutely essential that we find a solution to the problem in production at the present time.

30. In spite of the fact that it's a longer commute, I made the decision to take them up on the job they offered me.

31. Inasmuch as you are fully cognizant of our very real budget problems, there is no reason why we should repeat the discussion of the problem over again.

Redundancies, Jargon, Slang, Clichés

Revise the following sentences to eliminate redundancies, jargon, slang, clichés, and any other wordiness.

Example   Once we collect all the true facts, we are good to go on the government contract.
Revision   Once we collect the facts, we can proceed with the government contract.

32. First and foremost, we plan to emphasize an instructional training program.

33. There was a consensus of opinion among managers that they had to collect together as much data as possible to pump up profits or face the fact that their bonuses would go down the tubes.

34. If at all possible, Ryan did not intend to repeat again his lengthy presentation that really bombed and lasted until 5 p.m. in the afternoon.

35. Despite the fact that the parking lot is extremely small in size, we are at a loss to explain the reason why management pulled the plug on a plan to enlarge it in size.

Vivid Words

Revise the following sentences to include vivid, concrete, and precise language. Use your imagination to add appropriate words.

Example   They said it was a long way off.
Revision   Management officials announced that the merger would not take place for two years.

36. Please contact our representative soon.

37. A manager from that company notified me a few days ago about the meeting change.

38. The new cell phone comes in a variety of colors.

39. They said her report was good.   *who are they* Corporate officials said Sallie Maes 06-07
what report? report was well researched   *fiscal budget*
who is her?
what does good mean?

40. Profits increased when workers saw the big picture.

ACTIVITY

INFOTRAC

4.1 Being Conversational but Concise

Like business writers, newspaper journalists strive to be conversational but concise. They must be watchful to avoid the same problems of wordiness addressed in this chapter.

Your Task. Using InfoTrac, locate Paula LaRocque's article, "It's a True Fact Writing Can Repeat Again What's Been Said Before" (Article No. A54175089). After reading the article, answer the following questions in a written memo or in class discussion:

a. According to LaRocque, what are the two worst enemies of clarity, precision, and brevity?

b. How can a writer be both conversational and concise?

c. List ten wordy expressions found in LaRocque's article that are not in this chapter. Include their shorter forms.

GRAMMAR/MECHANICS CHECKUP—4

Adjectives and Adverbs

Review Sections 1.16 and 1.17 of the Grammar/Mechanics Handbook. Then study each of the following statements. Underscore any inappropriate forms. In the space provided write the correct form (or *C* if correct) and the number of the G/M principle illustrated. You may need to consult your dictionary for current practice regarding some compound adjectives. When you finish, compare your responses with those provided at the end of the book. If your answers differ, carefully study the principles in parentheses.

cost-effective   (1.17e)   **Example**   We need a cost-effective solution for this continuing problem.

1. The newly opened restaurant offered many tried and true menu items.

2. Most of the seven year old equipment was still working.

3. Although purchased seven years ago, the equipment still looked brightly.

4. E-mail messages are exchanged so quick that business moves more rapidly than ever.

5. The CEO assured employees that they only had to cut back expenses by 5 percent.

6. You may submit work related expenses to be reimbursed.

7. Ann and Jim said that they're planning to start there own business next year.

8. Have you ever made a spur of the moment decision?

9. Not all decisions that are made on the spur of the moment turn out badly.

10. The committee offered a well thought out plan to revamp online registration.

11. You must complete a change of address form when you move.

12. Each decision will be made on a case by case basis.

13. I could be more efficient if my printer were more nearer my computer.

14. If you reject his offer to help, Kurt will feel badly.

15. The truck's engine is running smooth after its tune-up.

● GRAMMAR/MECHANICS CHALLENGE—4

The following letter has faults in grammar, punctuation, conversational language, outdated expressions, sexist language, concise wording, long lead-ins, and other problems. Correct the errors with standard proofreading marks or revise the message online at **Guffey Xtra!** When you finish, your instructor may show you a possible revision of this letter.

FOREST FINANCIAL SERVICES
3410 Willow Grove Boulevard
Philadelphia, PA 19137
215.593.4400
www.forestfinancial.com

June 9, 200x

Ms. Bonnie Jeffers
First Trust Guaranty, Inc.
1359 North Grand Avenue
Walnut, CA 91790

Dear Ms. Jeffer:

We are in appreciation of the fact that you have shown patience with us during the time of our merger with Capital One.

Pursuant to our telephone conversation this morning, this is to advise that two (2) agent's packages will be delivered to you next week. Due to the fact that new forms had to be printed; we do not have them immediately available.

Although we cannot offer a 50/50 commission split, we are able to offer new agents a 60/40 commission split. There are two new agreement forms that show this commission ratio. When you get ready to sign up a new agent have her fill in these up to date forms.

When you send me an executed agency agreement please make every effort to tell me what agency package was assigned to the agent. On the last form that you sent you overlooked this information. We need this information to distribute commissions in an expeditious manner.

If you have any questions, don't hesitate to call on me.

Yours very sincerely,

Brian Simpson
Senior Sales Manager

USING WORD'S *TRACK CHANGES* AND *COMMENT* FEATURES
TO EDIT AND REVISE DOCUMENTS

Collaborative writing and editing projects are challenging. Fortunately, Microsoft Word offers many useful tools to help team members edit and share documents electronically. Three simple but useful editing tools are *Highlight, Font Color*, and *Strikethrough*. These tools, included on the **Formatting** toolbar, enable reviewers to point out editing problems. For example, notice how you can use *Strikethrough* to delete a wordy lead-in or use yellow highlighting to call attention to a misspelled word:

> ~~This is just a note to let you know that~~ I would appreciate you're help in preparing the announcement about tornado safety tips.

Complex projects, however, may require more advanced editing tools such as *Track Changes* and *Insert Comments*.

Track Changes. To suggest specific editing changes to other team members, *Track Changes* is handy. The revised wording is visible on the screen, and deletions show up in call-out balloons in the right-hand margin, as shown in the following document. Suggested revisions offered by different team members are identified and dated. The original writer may accept or reject these changes. In recent versions of Word, you'll find *Track Changes* on the **Tools** menu.

Insert Comments. By using *Insert Comments*, you can point out problematic passages or errors, ask or answer questions, and share ideas without changing or adding text. When more than one person adds comments, the comments appear in different colors and are identified by the individual writer's name. To use this tool in newer versions of Word, each reviewer must click *Tools, Options*, and fill in the *User Information* section. To facilitate adding, reviewing, editing, or deleting comments, Word provides a special toolbar. You can activate it by using the **View** pull-down menu (click *Toolbars* and *Reviewing*). On the **Reviewing** toolbar, click *New Comment*. Then type your comment, which can be seen by clicking *View* and *Print Layout* or *Web Layout*. In the markup document on page 96, notice how the writer inserted revisions and comments without changing the original text.

Career Application. Assume that your team has been asked to revise the complete public service announcement regarding tornado safety tips. Because you are just becoming familiar with *Track Changes* and *Insert Comments*, you are expected to make only simple comments and revisions based on the discussion in this chapter. You can learn more about *Track Changes* by clicking *Help* and searching for the term.

Your Task

Divide into two-person teams. Designate team members A and B. Find "Tornado Safety Tips" in the Chapter 4 materials at **Guffey Xtra!** and copy the file to your computer. Suggestions for revising the first three paragraphs of this document are shown here. Team Member A is to revise the last three paragraphs by inserting comments directed at Team Member B. A should then e-mail the document as an attachment to B, who will respond with comments indicating agreement or additional revisions. A and B should exchange e-mail messages until they agree on how the document should read. Print and submit the final markup version as well as the final edited version of the entire document. Be sure to click *Final* or *Final Showing Markup* when you finish.

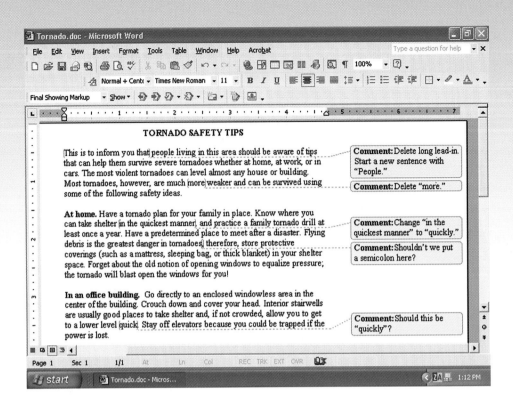

CORRESPONDING AT WORK

CHAPTER 5

E-MAIL AND MEMORANDUMS

"E-mail is changing our behavior, our way of inter-acting with people, our institutions. And it is hap-pening incredibly fast.... Because it's spread so fast, it has raced ahead of our abilities to fully adapt to this new form of commu-nication."

Michael D. Eisner, former CEO, Walt Disney Company[1]

OBJECTIVES

- Analyze the writing process and how it helps you produce effective e-mail mes-sages and memos.
- Discuss the structure and formatting of e-mail messages and memos.
- Describe smart e-mail practices, including getting started; content, tone, and cor-rectness; netiquette; reading and replying to e-mail; personal use; and other practices.
- Write information and procedure e-mail messages and memos.
- Write request and reply e-mail messages and memos.

APPLYING THE WRITING PROCESS TO PRODUCE EFFECTIVE E-MAIL MESSAGES AND MEMOS

E-mail is increasingly the channel of choice for internal messages and even for many external messages.

As former Disney CEO Michael Eisner recognized, e-mail has transformed many aspects of our lives, especially the way business is conducted. Written communica-tion to anyone within the office or almost anywhere in the world can now be com-pleted nearly instantaneously. In the past, internal communication (written messages within organizations) generally took the form of hard-copy memorandums. In today's workplace e-mail is increasingly the communication channel of choice for most in-ternal and many external messages. Business leaders such as Michael Eisner rec-ognize the functions and benefits but also the potential dangers of e-mail.

A primary function of e-mail is exchanging messages within organizations. Such internal communication has taken on increasing importance today. Organizations are downsizing, flattening chains of command, forming work teams, and empowering rank-and-file employees. Given more power in making decisions, employees find that they need more information. They must collect, exchange, and evaluate information about the products and services they offer. Management also needs input from

PHOTOS: © IMAGESOURCE/GETTY IMAGES; © JULES FRAZIER/PHOTODISC/

Former Disney CEO Michael Eisner thinks long and hard before dashing off e-mail messages, especially when he's angry. "I learned early in the hard paper world of the '70s that when I was annoyed with someone, I should write it down in a memo. I would then put the memo in my desk drawer and leave it there until the next day." By the next morning, his anger had passed; and he realized that telephoning or seeing the other person was a better way to respond.

© SCOTT AUDETTE/AP WIDE WORLD PHOTOS

employees to respond rapidly to local and global market changes. This growing demand for information means an increasing use of e-mail, although hard-copy memos are still written.

Skillful documents get the job done and make you look professional.

Developing skill in writing e-mail messages and memos brings you two important benefits. First, well-written documents are likely to achieve their goals. They create goodwill by being cautious, caring, and clear. They do not intentionally or unintentionally create ill feelings. Second, well-written internal messages enhance your image within the organization. Individuals identified as competent, professional writers are noticed and rewarded; most often, they are the ones promoted into management positions.

This chapter concentrates on direct e-mail messages and memos. These straightforward messages open with the main idea because their topics are not sensitive and require little persuasion. You'll study the writing process as well as the structure and format of e-mail messages and memos. Because e-mail is such a powerful channel of communication, we'll devote special attention to composing smart e-mail messages and reading and responding to e-mail professionally. Finally, you'll learn to write procedure, information, request, and reply messages.

Careful writing takes time—especially at first. By following a systematic plan and practicing your skill, however, you can speed up your efforts and greatly improve the product. Let's review the three-phase writing process to see how it applies to e-mail messages and memos.

Phase 1: Analysis, Anticipation, and Adaptation

Before writing, ask questions that help you analyze, anticipate, and adapt your message.

In Phase 1, prewriting, you'll need to spend some time analyzing your task. It's amazing how many of us are ready to put our pens or computers into gear before engaging our minds. Before writing, ask yourself these important questions:

- **Do I really need to write this e-mail or memo?** A phone call or a quick visit to a nearby coworker might solve the problem—and save the time and expense of a written message. On the other hand, some written messages are needed to provide a permanent record.
- **Should I send an e-mail or a hard-copy memo?** It's tempting to use e-mail for all your correspondence. But a phone call or face-to-face visit is a better channel choice if you need to (1) convey enthusiasm, warmth, or other emotion; (2) supply a context; or (3) smooth over disagreements.

Randy Glasbergen.
www.glasbergen.com

"Be careful what you write. My wonderful, charming, brilliant boss reads everyone's e-mail."

- **Why am I writing?** Know why you are writing and what you hope to achieve. This will help you recognize what the important points are and where to place them.
- **How will the reader react?** Visualize the reader and the effect your message will have. In writing e-mail messages and memos, imagine that you are sitting and talking with your reader. Avoid speaking bluntly, failing to explain, or ignoring your reader's needs. Consider ways to shape the message to benefit the reader. Also be careful about what you say because your message may very well be forwarded to someone else—or may be read by your boss.
- **How can I save my reader's time?** Think of ways that you can make your message easier to comprehend at a glance. Use bullets, asterisks, lists, headings, and white space to improve readability.

Phase 2: Research, Organization, and Composition

Gather background information; organize it into an outline; compose your message; and revise for clarity, correctness, and feedback.

Phase 2, writing, involves gathering documentation, organizing, and actually composing the first draft. Although some of your e-mail messages and memos will be short, you'll want to follow these steps in the process to ensure an effective message:

- **Conduct research.** Check the files, talk with your boss, and possibly consult the target audience to collect information before you begin to write. Gather any documentation necessary to support your message.
- **Organize your information.** Make a brief outline of the points you want to cover in your message. For short messages jot down notes on the document you are answering or make a scratch list at your computer.
- **Compose your first draft.** At your computer compose the message from your outline. As you compose, avoid amassing huge blocks of text. No one wants to read endless lines of type. Instead, group related information into paragraphs, preferably short ones. Paragraphs separated by white space look inviting. Be sure each paragraph begins with the main point and is backed up by details. If you bury your main point in the middle of a paragraph, it may be missed.

Phase 3: Revision, Proofreading, and Evaluation

Phase 3, revising, involves putting the final touches on your message. Careful and caring writers will ask a number of questions as they do the following:

- **Revise for clarity and conciseness.** Viewed from the receiver's perspective, are the ideas clear? Do they need more explanation? If the message is passed on to others, will they need further explanation? Consider having a colleague critique your message if it is an important one.
- **Proofread for correctness.** Are the sentences complete and punctuated properly? Did you overlook any typos or misspelled words? Remember to use your spell checker and grammar checker to proofread your message before sending it.
- **Plan for feedback.** How will you know whether this message is successful? You can improve feedback by asking questions (such as *Are you comfortable with these suggestions?* or *What do you think?*). Remember to make it easy for the receiver to respond.

ANALYZING THE STRUCTURE AND FORMAT OF E-MAIL MESSAGES AND MEMOS

E-mail messages and memos inform employees, request data, give responses, confirm decisions, and provide directions.

Whether electronic or hard copy, direct e-mail messages and memos generally contain four parts: (1) an informative subject line that summarizes the message, (2) an opening that reveals the main idea immediately, (3) a body that explains and justifies the main idea, and (4) an appropriate closing.

Writing the Subject Line

Subject lines summarize the purpose of the message in abbreviated form.

In e-mails and memos an informative subject line is mandatory. It summarizes the central idea, thus providing quick identification for reading and for filing. In e-mail messages, subject lines are essential. Busy readers glance at a subject line and decide whether and when to read the message. Those without subject lines are often automatically deleted.

What does it take to get your message read? For one thing, stay away from meaningless or dangerous words. A sure way to get your message deleted or ignored is to use a one-word heading such as *Issue, Problem, Important*, or *Help*. Including a word such as *Free* is dangerous because it may trigger spam filters. Try to make your subject line "talk" by including a verb. Explain the purpose of the message and how it relates to the reader (*Need You to Showcase Two Items at Our Next Trade Show* rather than *Trade Show*). Finally, update your subject line to reflect the current message (*Staff Meeting Rescheduled for May 12* rather than *Re: Re: Staff Meeting*). A subject line is usually written in an abbreviated style, often without articles (*a, an, the*). It need not be a complete sentence, and it does not end with a period.

Opening With the Main Idea

Direct e-mails and memos open by revealing the main idea immediately.

Most e-mails and memos cover nonsensitive information that can be handled in a straightforward manner. Begin by frontloading; that is, reveal the main idea immediately. Even though the purpose of the memo or e-mail is summarized in the subject line, that purpose should be restated—and amplified—in the first sentence. Busy readers want to know immediately why they are reading a message. As you learned in Chapter 3, most messages should begin directly. Notice how the following indirect opener can be improved by frontloading.

Indirect Opening	Direct Opening
For the past six months the Human Resources Development Department has been considering changes in our employee benefit plan.	Please review the following proposal regarding employee benefits, and let me know by May 20 if you approve these changes.

Explaining in the Body

Designed for easy comprehension, the body explains one topic.

The body provides more information about the reason for writing. It explains and discusses the subject logically. Good e-mail messages and memos generally discuss only one topic. Limiting the topic helps the receiver act on the subject and file it appropriately. A writer who, for example, describes a computer printer problem and also requests permission to attend a conference runs a 50 percent failure risk. The reader may respond to the printer problem but forget about the conference request.

The body of e-mail messages and memos should have high *skim value*. This means that information should be easy to read and comprehend. Three techniques for improving readability include lists, headings, and graphics techniques.

Because business communicators often juggle many tasks and projects at the same time, they appreciate e-mail messages that are well-organized with listed items and headings that provide high "skim value."

© ROYALTY-FREE/COMSTOCK/GETTY IMAGES

USING NUMBERED AND BULLETED LISTS FOR QUICK COMPREHENSION

One of the best ways to ensure rapid comprehension of ideas is through the use of numbered or bulleted lists. Ideas formerly buried within sentences or paragraphs stand out when listed. Readers not only understand your message more rapidly and easily but also consider you efficient and well organized. Lists provide high "skim value." This means that readers use lists to read quickly and grasp main ideas. By breaking up complex information into smaller chunks, lists improve readability, comprehension, and retention. They also force the writer to organize ideas and write efficiently. Use numbered lists for items that represent a sequence or reflect a numbering system. Use bulleted lists to highlight items that don't necessarily show a chronology.

Numbered lists represent sequences; bulleted lists highlight items that may not show a sequence.

Numbered List
Our recruiters follow these steps in hiring applicants:
1. Examine the application.
2. Interview the applicant.
3. Check the applicant's references.

Bulleted List
To attract upscale customers, we feature the following:
• Quality fashions
• Personalized service
• A generous return policy

In listing items vertically, capitalize the word at the beginning of each line. Add end punctuation only if the statements are complete sentences. Be sure to use parallel construction. Notice in the numbered list that each item begins with a verb. In the bulleted list each item follows an adjective/noun sequence. Be careful, however, not to overuse the list format. One writing expert warns that too many lists make messages look like grocery lists.[2]

ADDING HEADINGS FOR VISUAL IMPACT

Headings that summarize ideas enable readers to preview and review quickly.

Headings are another important tool for highlighting information and improving readability. They encourage the writer to organize carefully so that similar material is grouped together. This helps the reader separate major ideas from details. Moreover, headings enable a busy reader to skim familiar or less important information. They also provide a quick preview or review. Headings appear most often in reports, which you'll study in greater detail in Unit 4. However, main headings, subheadings,

Effective category headings
summarize topics in parallel form
to help readers grasp ideas
quickly.

and category headings can also improve readability in e-mail messages, memos, and letters. Here, they are used with bullets to summarize categories:

Category Headings

Our company focuses on the following areas in the employment process:
- **Attracting applicants.** We advertise for qualified applicants, and we also encourage current employees to recommend good people.
- **Interviewing applicants.** Our specialized interviews include simulated customer encounters as well as scrutiny by supervisors.
- **Checking references.** We investigate every applicant thoroughly, including conversations with former employers and all listed references.

IMPROVING READABILITY WITH OTHER GRAPHICS TECHNIQUES

Vertical lists and headings are favorite tools for improving readability, but other graphics techniques can also focus attention.

To highlight individual words, use CAPITAL letters, underlining, **bold** type, or *italics*. Be careful with these techniques, though, because readers may feel they are being shouted at.

One final technique to enhance comprehension is blank space. Space is especially important in e-mail messages when formatting techniques don't always work. Grouping ideas under capitalized headings with blank space preceding the heading can greatly improve readability.

Closing With a Purpose

Messages should close with
(1) action information including
dates and deadlines, (2) a summary, or (3) a closing thought.

Generally close an e-mail message or a memo with (1) action information, dates, or deadlines; (2) a summary of the message; or (3) a closing thought. Here again the value of thinking through the message before actually writing it becomes apparent. The closing is where readers look for deadlines and action language. An effective memo or e-mail closing might be, *Please submit your report by June 15 so that we can have your data before our July planning session.*

In more complex messages a summary of main points may be an appropriate closing. If no action request is made and a closing summary is unnecessary, you might end with a simple concluding thought (*I'm glad to answer your questions* or *This sounds like a useful project*). You needn't close messages to coworkers with goodwill statements such as those found in letters to customers or clients. However, some closing thought is often necessary to prevent a feeling of abruptness. Closings can show gratitude or encourage feedback with remarks such as *I sincerely appreciate your help* or *What are your ideas on this proposal?* Other closings look forward to what's next, such as *How would you like to proceed?* Avoid closing with overused expressions such as *Please let me know if I may be of further assistance.* This ending sounds mechanical and insincere.

Putting It All Together

Now let's follow the development of a routine information e-mail message to see how we can apply the ideas just discussed. Figure 5.1 shows the first draft of an e-mail message James Perkins, marketing manager, wrote to his boss, Jie Wang. Although it contained solid information, the message was so wordy and dense that the main points were submerged.

After writing the first draft, James realized that he needed to reorganize his message into an opening, body, and closing. He also desperately needed to improve the readability. In studying what he had written, he realized that he was talking about two main problems. He also discovered that he could present a three-part solution. These ideas didn't occur to him until he had written the first draft. Only in the revision stage was he able to see in his own mind that he was talking about two separate problems

FIGURE 5.1   • **Information E-Mail Message**

before revision

To   Jie Wang <jwang@edison.com>
From   James Perkins <jperkins@edison.com>
Subject: Problems •———————————————————————————— Uses meaningless
                                                          subject line

This is in response to your recent inquiry about our customer database. Your message of •——— Fails to reveal
May 9 said that you wanted to know how to deal with the database problems.   purpose quickly

I can tell you that the biggest problem is that it contains a lot of outdated information,
including customers who haven't purchased anything in five or more years. Another •——— Buries two problems and three-part
problem is that the old database is not compatible with the new Access software that is   solution in huge paragraph
being used by our mailing service, and this makes it difficult to merge files.

I think I can solve both problems, however, by starting a new database. This would be
the place where we put the names of all new customers. And we would have it   Forgets to conclude with
keyed using Access software. The problem with outdated information could be solved by •——— next action and end date
finding out if the customers in our old database wish to continue receiving our newsletter
and product announcements. Finally, we would rekey the names of all active customers
in the new database.

after revision

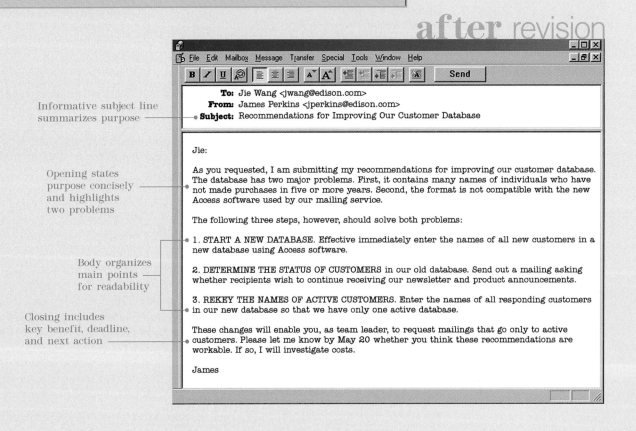

Informative subject line
summarizes purpose

Opening states
purpose concisely
and highlights
two problems

Body organizes
main points
for readability

Closing includes
key benefit, deadline,
and next action

Revision helps you think through a problem, clarify a solution, and express it clearly.

as well as a three-part solution. The revision process can help you think through a problem and clarify a solution.

In the revised version, James was more aware of the subject line, opening, body, and closing. He used an informative subject line and opened directly by explaining why he was writing. His opening also outlined the two main problems so that his reader understood the background of the following recommendations. In the body of his message, James identified three corrective actions, and he highlighted them for improved readability. Notice that he listed his three recommendations using numbers (bullets don't always transmit well in e-mail messages) with capitalized headings. Numbers, asterisks, white space, and capitalized letters work well in e-mail messages to highlight important points. Notice, too, that James closed his message with a deadline and a reference to the next action to be taken.

Formatting E-Mail Messages

Because e-mail is a developing communication channel, its formatting and usage conventions are still fluid. Users and authorities, for instance, do not always agree on what's appropriate for salutations and closings. The following suggestions, however, can guide you in formatting most e-mail messages, but always check with your organization to observe its practices.

GUIDE WORDS

E-mails contain guide words, optional salutations, and a concise and easy-to-read message.

Following the guide word *To*, some writers insert just the recipient's electronic address, such as *mphilly@accountpro.com*. Other writers prefer to include the receiver's full name plus the electronic address, as shown in Figure 5.2. By including full names in the *To* and *From* slots, both receivers and senders are better able to identify the message. By the way, the order of *Date, To, From, Subject*, and other guide words varies depending on your e-mail program and whether you are sending or receiving the message.

Most e-mail programs automatically add the current date after *Date*. On the *Cc* line (which stands for *carbon* or *courtesy copy*) you can type the address of anyone who is to receive a copy of the message. Remember, though, to send copies only to those people directly involved with the message. Most e-mail programs also include a line for *Bcc* (*blind carbon copy*). This sends a copy without the addressee's knowledge. Many savvy writers today use *Bcc* for the names and addresses of a list of receivers, a technique that avoids revealing the addresses to the entire group. On the subject line, identify the subject of the memo. Be sure to include enough information to be clear and compelling.

SALUTATION

On messages to outsiders, salutations are important to show friendliness and to indicate the beginning of the message.

How to treat the salutation is a problem. Many writers omit a salutation because they consider the message a memo. In the past, hard-copy memos were sent only to company insiders, and salutations were omitted. However, when e-mail messages travel to outsiders, omitting a salutation seems curt and unfriendly. Because the message is more like a letter, a salutation is appropriate (such as *Dear Jake; Hi, Jake; Greetings*; or just *Jake*). Including a salutation is also a visual cue to where the message begins. Many messages are transmitted or forwarded with such long headers that finding the beginning of the message can be difficult. A salutation helps, as shown in Figure 5.2. Other writers do not use a salutation; instead, they use the name of the recipient in the first sentence.

BODY

When typing the body of an e-mail message, use standard caps and lowercase characters—never all uppercase or all lowercase characters. Cover just one topic, and try to keep the total message under three screens in length. To assist you, many e-mail programs have basic text-editing features, such as cut, copy, paste, and word-wrap. However, avoid graphics, font changes, boldface, and italics unless your reader's system can handle them. Some e-mail writers use _Book Title_ to show

FIGURE 5.2

Formatting an E-Mail Request

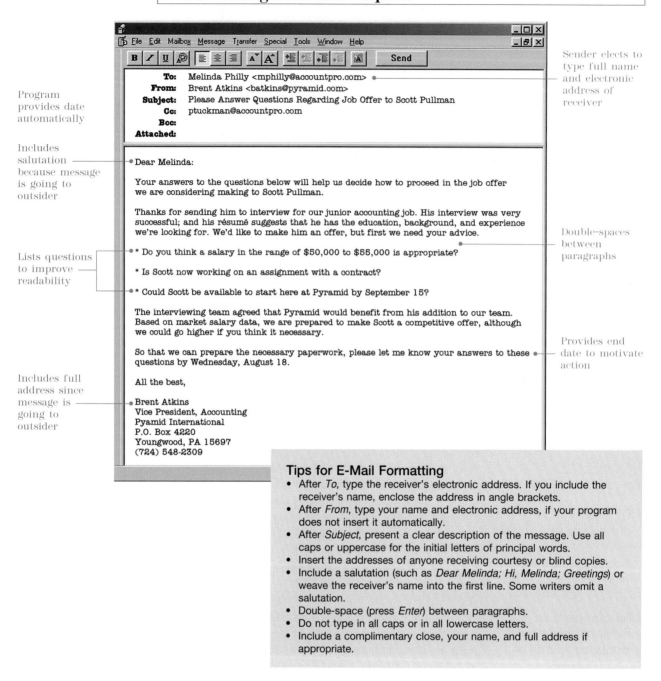

Program provides date automatically

Includes salutation because message is going to outsider

Lists questions to improve readability

Includes full address since message is going to outsider

Sender elects to type full name and electronic address of receiver

Double-spaces between paragraphs

Provides end date to motivate action

Tips for E-Mail Formatting
- After *To*, type the receiver's electronic address. If you include the receiver's name, enclose the address in angle brackets.
- After *From*, type your name and electronic address, if your program does not insert it automatically.
- After *Subject*, present a clear description of the message. Use all caps or uppercase for the initial letters of principal words.
- Insert the addresses of anyone receiving courtesy or blind copies.
- Include a salutation (such as *Dear Melinda; Hi, Melinda; Greetings*) or weave the receiver's name into the first line. Some writers omit a salutation.
- Double-space (press *Enter*) between paragraphs.
- Do not type in all caps or in all lowercase letters.
- Include a complimentary close, your name, and full address if appropriate.

underlining and *emphasized word* to show italics. However, as more and more programs offer HTML formatting options, writers are able to use all the graphics, colors, and fonts available in their word processing program.

CLOSING LINES

E-mail messages to outsiders should include the writer's name and identification.

Writers of e-mail messages sent within organizations may omit closings and even skip their names at the end of messages. To be safe, however, always type your name. It identifies you and helps readers sort out your message within a string (thread) of messages. It also personalizes your message. For messages going to outsiders, include a closing such as *Cheers* or *All the best* followed by the writer's name and e-mail address (because some systems do not transmit your address automatically). If the recipient is unlikely to know you, it's wise to include your title, organization, full address, and telephone. Some veteran e-mail users include a *signature file* with identifying information embellished with keyboard art.

Formatting Hard-Copy Memos

Hard-copy memos are useful for internal messages that require a permanent record or formality.

Hard-copy memorandums deliver information within organizations. Although e-mail is more often used, hard-copy memos are still useful for important internal messages that require a permanent record or formality. For example, changes in procedures, official instructions, and organization reports are often prepared as hard-copy memos. Because e-mail is new and still evolving, we examined its formatting carefully in the previous paragraphs.

Hard-copy memos require less instruction because formatting is fairly standardized. Some offices use memo forms imprinted with the organization name and, optionally, the department or division names. Although the design and arrangement of memo forms vary, they usually include the basic elements of *Date, To, From*, and *Subject*. Large organizations may include other identifying headings, such as *File Number, Floor, Extension, Location*, and *Distribution*. Because of the difficulty of aligning computer printers with preprinted forms, many business writers store memo formats in their computers and call them up when preparing memos. The guide words are then printed with the message, thus eliminating alignment problems.

If no printed or stored computer forms are available, memos may be typed on company letterhead, as shown in Figure 5.3, or typed on plain paper. On a full sheet of paper, start the guide words 2 inches from the top; on a half sheet, start 1 inch from the top. Double-space and type in all caps the guide words. Align all the fill-in information 2 spaces after the longest guide word (usually *Subject*). Leave 2 blank lines between the last line of the heading and the first line of the memo. Single-space within paragraphs and double-space between paragraphs. Memos are generally formatted with side margins of 1 to 1.25 inches, or they may conform to the printed memo form. Do not justify the right margins. Research has shown that "ragged-right" margins in printed messages are easier to read.

USING E-MAIL SMARTLY AND SAFELY

Escalation in the popularity and use of e-mail staggers the imagination. Worldwide e-mail traffic is expected to triple between 2005 and 2009, from 100 million to over 300 million messages.[3] E-mail is now twice as likely as the telephone to be used to communicate at work. One survey revealed that the average employee spends about 25 percent of the workday on e-mail.[4] We have become so dependent on e-mail that 53 percent of people using it at work say that their productivity drops when they are away from it.[5]

E-mail messages may be dangerous because they travel long distances and are difficult to erase.

Most of us admit that we can't get along without e-mail. But wise communicators recognize its dangers as well as its benefits. Disney's Michael Eisner gave a speech to University of Southern California students telling them of his experience and warning that thoughtless messages could cause irreparable harm.[6] Wise communicators know that their messages can travel (intentionally or unintentionally) long distances. A quickly drafted note may end up in the boss's mailbox or be forwarded to an adversary's box. Making matters worse, computers—like elephants and spurned lovers—never forget. Even erased messages can remain on network servers. Increasingly, e-mail has turned into the "smoking gun" uncovered by prosecutors to prove indelicate or even illegal intentions.[7]

E-mail has become the corporate equivalent of DNA evidence. Like forgotten land mines, damaging e-mails have been dug up to prove a prosecutor's case. For example, in the antitrust suit against Microsoft, Bill Gates squirmed when the court heard his e-mail in which he asked, "How much do we need to pay you to screw

FIGURE 5.3

• Hard-Copy Memo—Reply to Request

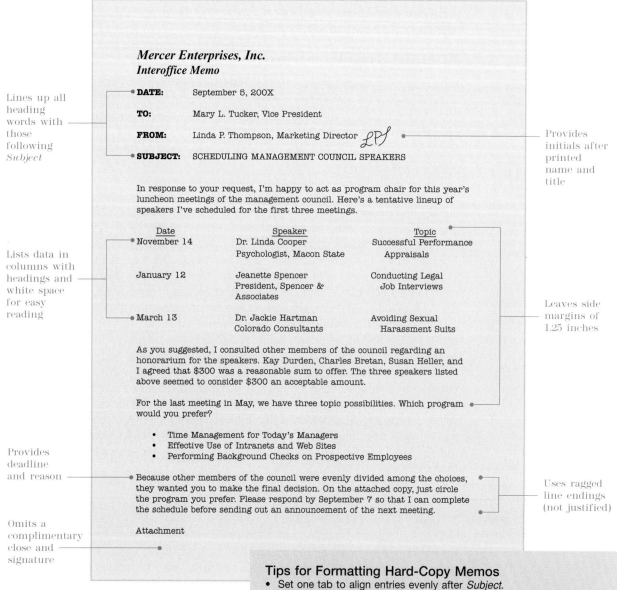

Lines up all heading words with those following *Subject*

Lists data in columns with headings and white space for easy reading

Provides deadline and reason

Omits a complimentary close and signature

Provides initials after printed name and title

Leaves side margins of 1.25 inches

Uses ragged line endings (not justified)

Mercer Enterprises, Inc.
Interoffice Memo

DATE: September 5, 200X

TO: Mary L. Tucker, Vice President

FROM: Linda P. Thompson, Marketing Director *LPT*

SUBJECT: SCHEDULING MANAGEMENT COUNCIL SPEAKERS

In response to your request, I'm happy to act as program chair for this year's luncheon meetings of the management council. Here's a tentative lineup of speakers I've scheduled for the first three meetings.

Date	Speaker	Topic
November 14	Dr. Linda Cooper Psychologist, Macon State	Successful Performance Appraisals
January 12	Jeanette Spencer President, Spencer & Associates	Conducting Legal Job Interviews
March 13	Dr. Jackie Hartman Colorado Consultants	Avoiding Sexual Harassment Suits

As you suggested, I consulted other members of the council regarding an honorarium for the speakers. Kay Durden, Charles Bretan, Susan Heller, and I agreed that $300 was a reasonable sum to offer. The three speakers listed above seemed to consider $300 an acceptable amount.

For the last meeting in May, we have three topic possibilities. Which program would you prefer?

• Time Management for Today's Managers
• Effective Use of Intranets and Web Sites
• Performing Background Checks on Prospective Employees

Because other members of the council were evenly divided among the choices, they wanted you to make the final decision. On the attached copy, just circle the program you prefer. Please respond by September 7 so that I can complete the schedule before sending out an announcement of the next meeting.

Attachment

Tips for Formatting Hard-Copy Memos
• Set one tab to align entries evenly after *Subject*.
• Type the subject line in all caps or capitalize the initial letters of principal words.
• Leave 1 or 2 blank lines after the subject line.
• Single-space all but the shortest memos. Double-space between paragraphs.
• For full-page memos on plain paper, leave a 2-inch top margin.
• For half-page memos, leave a 1-inch top margin.
• Use 1.25-inch side margins.
• For a two-page memo, use a second-page heading with the addressee's name, page number, and date.
• Hardwrite your initials after your typed name.
• Place bulleted or numbered lists flush left or indent them 0.5 inches.

Netscape?" In another case banker Frank Quattrone was found guilty of obstructing justice based on an e-mail message in which he instructed employees to "clean up" their e-mail files after he learned that he was being investigated for securities irregularities.[8] More often, e-mail writers simply forget that their message is a permanent record. "It's as if people put their brains on hold when they write e-mail," said one expert. "They think that e-mail is a substitute for a phone call, and that's the danger."[9] Another observer noted that e-mail is like an electronic truth serum.[10] Writers seem to blurt out thoughts without reflecting.

Early e-mail users were encouraged to ignore stylistic and grammatical considerations. They thought that "words on the fly" required little editing or proofing. Correspondents used emoticons (such as sideways happy faces) to express their emotions. Some e-mail today is still quick and dirty. As this communication channel continues to mature, however, messages are becoming more proper, more professional, and more careful.

Getting Started

Because e-mail is now a mainstream communication channel, messages should be well organized, carefully composed, and grammatically correct.

Despite its dangers and limitations, e-mail is a mainstream channel of communication. That's why it's important to take the time to organize your thoughts, compose carefully, and be concerned with correct grammar and punctuation. The following pointers will help you get off to a good start in using e-mail smartly and safely.

- **Consider composing offline.** Especially for important messages, think about using your word processing program to write offline. Then upload your message to the e-mail network. This avoids "self-destructing" (losing all your writing through some glitch or pressing the wrong key) when working online.
- **Get the address right.** E-mail addresses are sometimes complex, often illogical, and always unforgiving. Omit one character or misread the letter *l* for the number *1*, and your message bounces. Solution: Use your electronic address book for people you write to frequently. Double-check every address that you key in manually. Also be sure that you don't reply to a group of receivers when you intend to answer only one.
- **Avoid misleading subject lines.** As discussed earlier, make sure your subject line is relevant and helpful. Generic tags such as *Hi!* and *Important!* may cause your message to be deleted before it is opened.
- **Apply the top-of-screen test.** When readers open your message and look at the first screen, will they see what is most significant? Your subject line and first paragraph should convey your purpose.

Content, Tone, and Correctness

Although e-mail seems as casual as a telephone call, it's not. Because it produces a permanent record, think carefully about what you say and how you say it.

- **Be concise.** Don't burden readers with unnecessary information. Remember that monitors are small and typefaces are often difficult to read. Organize your ideas tightly.

Avoid sending sensitive, confidential, inflammatory, or potentially embarrassing messages because e-mail is not private.

- **Don't send anything you wouldn't want published.** Because e-mail seems like a telephone call or a person-to-person conversation, writers sometimes send sensitive, confidential, inflammatory, or potentially embarrassing messages. Beware! E-mail creates a permanent record that does not go away even when deleted. Every message is a corporate communication that can be used against you or your employer. Don't write anything that you wouldn't want your boss, your family, or a judge to read!
- **Don't use e-mail to avoid contact.** E-mail is inappropriate for breaking bad news or for resolving arguments. For example, it's improper to fire a person by e-mail. It's also not a good channel for dealing with conflict with supervisors, subordinates, or others. If there is any possibility of hurt feelings, pick up the telephone or pay the person a visit.

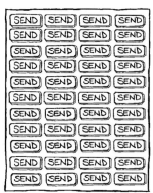

- **Care about correctness.** People are still judged by their writing, whether electronic or paper-based. Sloppy e-mail messages (with missing apostrophes, haphazard spelling, and stream-of-consciousness writing) make readers work too hard. They resent not only the information but also the writer.
- **Care about tone.** Your words and writing style affect the reader. Avoid sounding curt, negative, or domineering.
- **Resist humor and tongue-in-cheek comments.** Without the nonverbal cues conveyed by your face and your voice, humor can easily be misunderstood.

Netiquette

Although e-mail is a relatively new communication channel, a number of rules of polite online interaction are emerging.

- **Limit any tendency to send blanket copies.** Send copies only to people who really need to see a message. It is unnecessary to document every business decision and action with an electronic paper trail.
- **Never send "spam."** Sending unsolicited advertisements ("spam") either by fax or e-mail is illegal in the United States.
- **Consider using identifying labels.** When appropriate, add one of the following labels to the subject line: *Action* (action required, please respond); *FYI* (for your information, no response needed); *Re* (this is a reply to another message); *Urgent* (please respond immediately).
- **Use capital letters only for emphasis or for titles.** Avoid writing entire messages in all caps, which is like SHOUTING.
- **Don't forward without permission.** Obtain approval before forwarding a message.
- **Reduce attachments.** Because attachments may carry viruses, some receivers won't open them. Consider including short attachments within an e-mail message. If you must send a longer attachment, explain it.

Don't send blanket copies or spam, reduce attachments, and use identifying labels if appropriate.

Reading and Replying to E-Mail

The following tips can save you time and frustration when reading and answering messages:

- **Scan all messages in your inbox before replying to each individually.** Because subsequent messages often affect the way you respond, skim all messages first (especially all those from the same individual).
- **Print only when necessary.** Generally, read and answer most messages online without saving or printing. Use folders to archive messages on special topics. Print only those messages that are complex, controversial, or involve significant decisions and follow-up.

Cathy

Cathy © Cathy Guisewite. Reprinted with permission of Universal Press Syndicate. All Rights Reserved.

Skim all messages before responding, paste in relevant sections, revise the subject if the topic changes, provide a clear first sentence, and never respond when angry.

- **Acknowledge receipt.** If you can't reply immediately, tell when you can (*Will respond Friday*).
- **Don't automatically return the sender's message.** When replying, cut and paste the relevant parts. Avoid irritating your recipients by returning the entire "thread" (sequence of messages) on a topic.
- **Revise the subject line if the topic changes.** When replying or continuing an e-mail exchange, revise the subject line as the topic changes.
- **Provide a clear, complete first sentence.** Avoid fragments such as *That's fine with me* or *Sounds good!* Busy respondents forget what was said in earlier messages, so be sure to fill in the context and your perspective when responding.
- **Never respond when you're angry.** Always allow some time to cool off before shooting off a response to an upsetting message. You often come up with different and better alternatives after thinking about what was said. If possible, iron out differences in person.

Personal Use

Remember that office computers are meant for work-related communication.
- **Don't use company computers for personal matters.** Unless your company specifically allows it, never use your employer's computers for personal messages, personal shopping, or entertainment.
- **Assume that all e-mail is monitored.** Employers legally have the right to monitor e-mail, and many do.

Other Smart E-Mail Practices

Depending on your messages and audience, the following tips promote effective electronic communication.

Design your messages to enhance readability, and double-check before sending.

- **Use design to improve the readability of longer messages.** When a message requires several screens, help the reader with headings, bulleted listings, side headings, and perhaps an introductory summary that describes what will follow. Although these techniques lengthen a message, they shorten reading time.
- **Consider cultural differences.** When using this borderless tool, be especially clear and precise in your language. Remember that figurative clichés (*pull up stakes, playing second fiddle*), sports references (*hit a home run, play by the rules*), and slang (*cool, stoked*) cause confusion abroad.
- **Double-check before hitting the *Send* button.** Have you included everything? Avoid the necessity of sending a second message, which makes you look careless. Use spell-check and reread for fluency before sending. It's also a good idea to check your incoming messages before sending, especially if several people are involved in a rapid-fire exchange. This helps avoid "passing"—sending out a message that might be altered depending on an incoming note.

WRITING INFORMATION AND PROCEDURE E-MAIL MESSAGES AND MEMOS

Thus far in this chapter we've reviewed the writing process, analyzed the structure and format of e-mail messages and memos, and presented a number of techniques for using e-mail smartly and safely. Now we're going to apply those techniques to two categories of messages that you can expect to be writing as a business communicator: (1) information and procedure messages and (2) request and reply messages.

Writing plans help beginners get started by providing an outline of what to include.

In this book you will be shown a number of writing plans appropriate for different messages. These plans provide a skeleton; they are the bones of a message. Writers provide the flesh. Simply plugging in phrases or someone else's words won't work. Good writers provide details and link their ideas with transitions to create fluent and meaningful messages. However, a writing plan helps you get started and gives you ideas about what to include. At first, you will probably rely on these plans considerably. As you progress, they will become less important. Later in the book, no plans are provided.

Writing Plan for Information and Procedure E-Mail Messages and Memos

- *Subject line:* Summarize the content of the message.
- *Opening:* Expand the subject line by stating the main idea concisely in a full sentence.
- *Body:* Provide background data and explain the main idea. In describing a procedure or giving instructions, use command language (*do this, don't do that*).
- *Closing:* Request action, summarize the message, or present a closing thought.

Information and procedure messages generally flow downward from management to employees.

Information and procedure messages distribute routine information, describe procedures, and deliver instructions. They typically flow downward from management to employees and relate to the daily operation of an organization. In writing these messages, you have one primary function: conveying your idea so clearly that no further explanation (return message, telephone call, or personal visit) is necessary.

You've already seen the development of a routine information message in Figure 5.1. It follows the writing plan with an informative subject line, an opening that states the purpose directly, and a body that organizes the information for maximum readability. The closing in an information message depends on what was discussed. If the message involves an action request, it should appear in the closing—not in the opening or in the body. If no action is required, the closing can summarize the message or offer some kind of closing thought.

Procedure messages must be especially clear and readable. Figure 5.4 shows the first draft of a hard-copy memo written by Troy Bell. His memo was meant to announce a new procedure for employees to follow in advertising open positions. However, the tone was negative, the explanation of the problem rambled, and the new procedure was unclear. Notice, too, that Troy's first draft told readers what they *shouldn't* do (*Do not submit advertisements for new employees directly to an Internet job bank or a newspaper*). It's more helpful to tell readers what they *should* do. Finally, Troy's memos closed with a threat instead of showing readers how this new procedure will help them.

In the revision Troy improved the tone considerably. The subject line contains a *please*, which is always pleasant to see even if one is giving an order. The subject line also includes a verb and specifies the purpose of the memo. Instead of expressing his ideas with negative words and threats, Troy revised his message to explain objectively and concisely what went wrong.

Procedures and instructions are often written in numbered steps using command language (Do this, don't do that).

Troy realized that his original explanation of the new procedure was vague. Messages explaining procedures are most readable when the instructions are broken down into numbered steps listed chronologically. Each step should begin with an action verb in the command mode. Notice in Troy's revision in Figure 5.4 that

FIGURE 5.4   • **Procedure Memo**

before revision

TO: Ruth DiSilvestro, Manager
FROM: Troy Bell, Human Resources
SUBJECT: Job Advertisement Misunderstanding •———

Vague, negative subject line

We had no idea last month when we implemented new hiring procedures that major •——— problems would result. Due to the fact that every department is now placing Internet advertisements for new-hires individually, the difficulties occurred. This cannot continue. Perhaps we did not make it clear at that time, but all newly hired employees who are hired for a position should be requested through this office.

Fails to pinpoint main idea in opening

Do not submit your advertisements for new employees directly to an Internet job bank or a •——— newspaper. After writing them, they should be brought to Human Resources, where they will be centralized. You should discuss each ad with one of our counselors. Then we will place the ad at an appropriate Internet site or other publication. If you do not follow these guidelines, chaos will result. You may pick up applicant folders from us the day after the •——— closing date in an ad.

New procedure is hard to follow

Uses threats instead of showing benefits to reader

after revision

DATE: January 5, 200x

TO: Ruth DiSilvestro, Manager

FROM: Troy Bell, Human Resources. TB

SUBJECT: Please Follow New Job Advertisement Procedure •———

Informative, courteous, upbeat subject line

Combines "you" view with main idea in opening

•To find the right candidates for your open positions as fast as possible, we're implementing a new routine. Effective today, all advertisements for departmental job openings should be routed through the Human Resources Department.

A major problem resulted from the change in hiring procedures implemented last month. Each department is placing job advertisements for new hires •——— individually, when all such requests should be centralized in this office. To process applications more efficiently, please follow this procedure:

Explains why change in procedures is necessary

•1. Write an advertisement for a position in your department.

2. Bring the ad to Human Resources and discuss it with one of our counselors.

Lists easy-to-follow steps; starts each with a verb

3. Let Human Resources place the ad at an appropriate Internet job bank or submit it to a newspaper.

•4. Pick up applicant folders from Human Resources the day following the closing date provided in the ad.

Following these guidelines will save you work and will also enable Human •——— Resources to help you fill your openings more quickly. Call Ann Edmonds at Ext. 2505 if you have questions about this procedure.

Closes by reinforcing benefits to reader

numbered items begin with *Write, Bring, Let,* and *Pick up.* It's sometimes difficult to force all the steps in a procedure into this kind of command language. Troy struggled, but by trying out different wording, he finally found verbs that worked.

Why should you go to so much trouble to make lists and achieve parallelism? Because readers can comprehend what you have said much more quickly. Parallel language also makes you look professional and efficient.

In writing information and procedure messages, be careful of tone. Today's managers and team leaders seek employee participation and cooperation. These goals can't be achieved, though, if the writer sounds like a dictator or an autocrat. Avoid making accusations and fixing blame. Rather, explain changes, give reasons, and suggest benefits to the reader. Assume that employees want to contribute to the success of the organization and to their own achievement. Notice in the Figure 5.4 revision that Troy tells readers that they will save time and have their open positions filled more quickly if they follow the new procedures.

The writing of instructions and procedures is so important that we have developed a special bonus online supplement providing you with more examples and information. This online supplement extends your textbook with in-depth material including links to real businesses to show you examples of well-written procedures and instructions. To use this free supplement, go to **Guffey Xtra!** (*http://guffeyxtra .swlearning.com*) and locate *How to Write Instructions.*

> Parallel language (balanced construction) improves readability and makes the writer look professional.

WRITING REQUEST AND REPLY E-MAIL MESSAGES AND MEMOS

Business organizations require information as their fuel. To make operations run smoothly, managers and employees request information from each other and then respond to those requests. Knowing how to write those requests and responses efficiently and effectively can save you time and make you look good.

Writing Plan for Request Messages

- *Subject line:* Summarize the request and note the action desired.
- *Opening:* Begin with the request or a brief statement introducing it.
- *Body:* Provide background, justification, and details. If asking questions, list them in parallel form.
- *Closing:* Request action by a specific date. If possible, provide a reason. Express appreciation, if appropriate.

Making Requests

> Use the direct approach in routine requests for information or action, opening with the most important question, a polite command, or a brief introductory statement.

If you are requesting routine information or action within an organization, the direct approach works best. Generally, this means asking for information or making the request without first providing elaborate explanations and justifications. Remember that readers are usually thinking, "Why me? Why am I receiving this?" Readers can understand the explanation better once they know what you are requesting.

If you are seeking answers to questions, you have three options for opening the message: (1) ask the most important question first, followed by an explanation and then the other questions; (2) use a polite command (*Please answer the following questions regarding . . .*); or (3) introduce the questions with a brief statement (*Your answers to the following questions will help us . . .*).

In the body of the memo, explain and justify your request. When you must ask many questions, list them, being careful to phrase them similarly. Be courteous and friendly. In the closing include an end date (with a reason, if possible) to promote a quick response.

The e-mail message shown in Figure 5.5 requests information. The functional subject line uses a verb in noting the action desired (*Need Your Reactions to Our Casual-Dress Policy*). The reader knows immediately what is being requested. The message opens with a polite command followed by a brief explanation. Notice that the questions are highlighted with asterisks to provide the high "skim value" that is important in

FIGURE 5.5   **Request E-Mail Message**

Provides functional subject line noting desired action

Includes the receiver's name in the first sentence

Lists questions in parallel form and uses asterisks to produce high "skim value"

Opens directly by immediately describing the request

Explains reasoning behind request and gives details

Closes with end date and reason

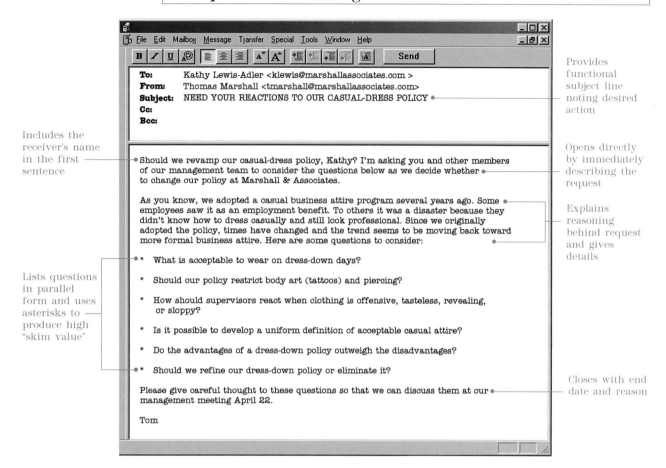

business messages. The reader can quickly see what is being asked. The message concludes with an end date and a reason. Providing an end date helps the reader know how to plan a response so that action is completed by the date given. Expressions such as *do it whenever you can* or *complete it as soon as possible* make little impression on procrastinators or very busy people. It's always wise to provide a specific date for completion. Dates can be entered on calendars to serve as reminders.

Replying to Requests

Much business correspondence reacts or responds to previous messages. When replying to an e-mail, memo, or other document, be sure to follow the three-phase writing process. Analyze your purpose and audience, collect whatever information is necessary, and organize your thoughts. Make a brief outline of the points you plan to cover following this writing plan:

Writing Plan for Replies

- *Subject line:* Summarize the main information from your reply.
- *Opening:* Start directly by responding to the request with a summary statement.
- *Body:* Provide additional information and details in a readable format.
- *Closing:* Add a concluding remark, summary, or offer of further assistance.

Overused and long-winded openers bore readers and waste their time.

Writers sometimes fall into bad habits in replying to messages. Here are some trite and long-winded openers that are best avoided:

In response to your message of the 15th . . . *(States the obvious)*
Thank you for your memo of the 15th in which you . . . *(Suggests the writer can think of nothing more original)*
I have before me your memo of the 15th in which you . . . *(Unnecessarily identifies the location of the previous message)*

Direct opening statements can also be cheerful and empathic.

Pursuant to your request of the 15th . . . *(Sounds old-fashioned)*
This is to inform you that . . . *(Delays getting to the point)*

Instead of falling into the trap of using one of the preceding shopworn openings, start directly by responding to the writer's request. If you agree to the request, show your cheerful compliance immediately. Consider these good-news openers:

Yes, we will be glad to . . . *(Sends message of approval by opening with "Yes.")*
Here are answers to the questions you asked about . . . *(Sounds straightforward, businesslike, and professional.)*
You're right in seeking advice about . . . *(Opens with two words that every reader enjoys seeing and hearing.)*
We are happy to assist you in . . . *(Shows writer's helpful nature and goodwill.)*
As you requested, I am submitting . . . *(Gets right to the point.)*

After a direct and empathic opener, provide the information requested in a logical and coherent order. If you are answering a number of questions, arrange your answers in the order of the questions. In the hard-copy memo response shown in Figure 5.3, information describing dates, speakers, and topics was listed in columns with headings. Although listing format requires more space than paragraph format, listing vastly improves readability and comprehension.

In providing additional data, use familiar words, short sentences, short paragraphs, and active-voice verbs. When alternatives exist, make them clear. Consider using graphic highlighting techniques, as shown in Figure 5.3, for both the speakers' schedules and the three program choices offered further along in the message. Imagine how much more effort would be required to read and understand the memo without the speaker list or the bulleted choices.

If further action is required, be specific in spelling it out. What may be crystal clear to you (because you have been thinking about the problem) is not always immediately apparent to a reader with limited time and interest.

SUMMING UP AND LOOKING FORWARD

E-mail messages and memorandums serve as vital channels of information for business communicators today. They use a standardized format to request and deliver information. Because e-mail is increasingly a preferred channel choice, this chapter presented many techniques for sending and receiving safe and effective e-mail messages. You learned to apply the direct strategy in writing messages that inform, request, and respond. You also learned to use bullets, numbers, and parallel form for listing information so that your messages have high "skim value." In the next chapter you will extend the direct strategy to writing direct letters and goodwill messages.

CRITICAL THINKING

1. How can the writer of a business memo or an e-mail message develop a conversational tone and still be professional? Why do e-mail writers sometimes forget to be professional?

2. What factors help you decide whether to write a memo, send an e-mail, make a telephone call, leave a voice mail message, or deliver a message in person?

3. Why are lawyers and technology experts warning companies to store, organize, and manage computer data, including e-mail and instant messages, with sharper diligence?

4. Discuss the ramifications of the following statement: *Once a memo or any other document leaves your hands, you have essentially published it.*

5. Ethical Issue: Should managers have the right to monitor the e-mail messages and instant messages of employees? Why or why not? What if employees are warned that e-mail could be monitored? If a company sets up an e-mail policy, should only in-house transmissions be monitored? Only outside transmissions?

CHAPTER REVIEW

6. List five questions you should ask yourself before writing an e-mail or memo.

7. What four parts are standard in most e-mail message and memos?

8. What techniques can writers use to improve the readability and comprehension in the body of e-mails and memos?

9. How are the structure and formatting of e-mail messages and memos similar and different?

10. Suggest at least ten pointers that you could give to a first-time e-mail user.

11. Name at least five rules of e-mail etiquette that show respect for others.

12. What are three possibilities in handling the salutation for an e-mail message?

13. What is the writing plan for an information or procedure message?
    Subject line:
    Opening:
    Body:

    Closing:

14. What is the writing plan for a request message?
    Subject line:
    Opening:
    Body:
    Closing:

15. What is the writing plan for a reply message?
    Subject line:
    Opening:
    Body:
    Closing:

WRITING IMPROVEMENT EXERCISES

Message Openers

Compare the following sets of message openers. Circle the opener that illustrates a direct opening. Be prepared to discuss the weaknesses and strengths of each.

16. A memo announcing a new procedure:
    a. It has come to our attention that increasing numbers of staff members are using instant messaging (IM) in sending business messages. We realize that IM often saves time and gets you fast responses, and we are prepared to continue to allow its use, but we have developed some specific procedures that we want you to use to make sure it is safe as well as efficient.
    b. The following new procedures for using instant messaging (IM) will enable staff members to continue to use it safely and efficiently.

17. An e-mail message inquiring about software:
    a. We are interested in your voice-recognition software that we understand allows you to dictate and copy text without touching a keyboard. We are interested in answers to a number of questions, such as the cost for a single-user license and perhaps the availability of a free trial version.
    b. Please answer the following questions about your voice-recognition software.

18. An e-mail message announcing a training program:
    a. If you would like to join our in-house leadership training program, please attend an orientation meeting June 1.
    b. For some time we have been investigating the possibility of conducting in-house leadership training courses for interested staff members.

19. An e-mail message introducing a new manager:
    a. This is a message to bring you good news. You will be pleased to learn that our long wait is over. After going without a chief for many weeks, we are finally able to welcome our new manager, Kristi Bostock, who comes to us from our Atlanta office. Please welcome her.
    b. Please welcome our new manager, Kristi Bostock, who comes from our Atlanta office.

Opening Paragraphs

The following opening paragraphs are wordy and indirect. After reading each paragraph, identify the main idea. Then, write an opening sentence that illustrates a more direct opening.

20. Our management team would like to find additional ways to improve employee motivation through recognition and reward programs. The current programs do not seem to generate an appropriate level of motivation. Because we need input from employees, we will be conducting an extensive study of all employees. But we will begin with focus groups of selected employees, and you have been selected to be part of the first focus group.

21. Customer service is an integral part of our business. That's why I was impressed when three of you came to me to ask if you might attend a seminar called "Customer Satisfaction Strategies." I understand the seminar will take place March 15 and will require you to miss a full day of work. This memo is to inform the staff that Ellen Tucker, Ryan Ho, and Sal Avila will be gone March 15 to attend the conference on customer service and satisfaction.

Bulleted and Numbered Lists

22. Use the following information to compose a list that includes an introductory statement and a numbered vertical list.
    In purchasing software, be sure to follow these steps. You should tie payments to the achievement of milestones. You should also include a detailed description of all required testing. Finally, you should spell out what type of ongoing support the contract covers.

23. Use the following wordy instructions to compose a concise bulleted vertical list with an introductory statement:
    To write information for a Web site, there are three important tips to follow. For one thing, you should make the formatting as simple as possible. Another thing you must do is ensure the use of strong visual prompts. Last but not least, you should limit directions that are not needed.

24. Revise the following wordy paragraph into an introduction with a list. Should you use bullets or numbers?
    In writing to customers granting approval for loans, you should follow four steps that include announcing that loan approval has been granted. You should then specify the terms and limits. Next, you should remind the reader of the importance of making payments that are timely. Finally, a phone number should be provided for assistance.

25. Revise the following wordy information into a concise bulleted list with category headings:
    Our attorney made a recommendation that we consider several things to avoid litigation in regard to sexual harassment. The first thing he suggested was that we take steps regarding the establishment of an unequivocal written policy prohibiting sexual harassment within our organization. The second thing we should do is make sure training sessions are held for supervisors regarding a proper work environment. Finally, some kind of official procedure for employees to lodge complaints is necessary. This procedure should include investigation of complaints.

WRITING COACH
STEP-BY-STEP DEMONSTRATION

Request E-Mail   *To help you master the entire writing process, the* Writing Coach *takes you through the problem, the writing plan, the first draft, and the final product.*

Problem

Like many office workers who sit in front of a computer all day, Trevor Williams noticed that he was spending more and more time on e-mail. As vice president of marketing at a big Midwest company, however, he was in a position to do something about it. He calls you, his assistant, into his office and says, "Some days I receive 300 or 400 messages. All this e-mail is just taking too much time! People can't get any work done around here. So I want to come up with a plan for reducing our reliance on e-mail. I think we should discuss this problem at the next supervisory committee meeting on May 10. Before the meeting, though, we need information from our people. I'd like to know how much time our employees are actually spending on e-mail. We will want to know about how many messages they are sending and receiving each day. Maybe we ought to have one day a week—let's say, Friday—that is totally e-mail free. Would that work?" Mr. Williams continues to brainstorm with you. You think you should send messages to three key supervisors asking them questions that might help solve the problem. Despite Mr. Williams' distaste for e-mail, he asks you to draft an e-mail message for him to send.

before revision

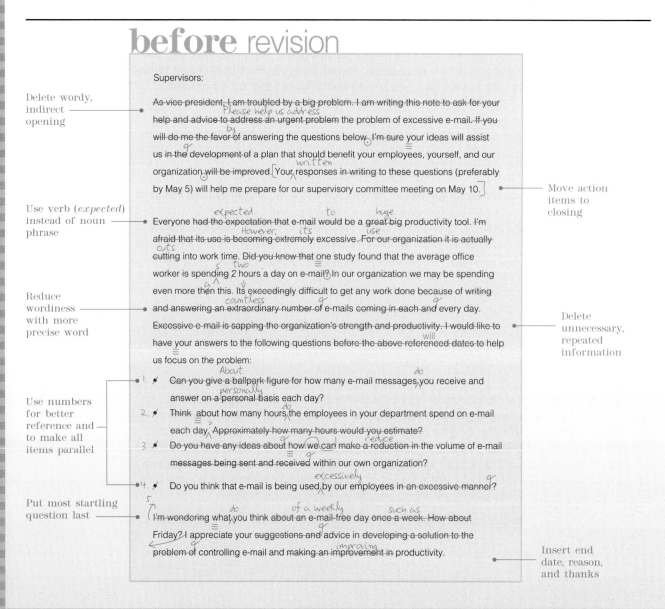

Delete wordy, indirect opening

Use verb (*expected*) instead of noun phrase

Reduce wordiness with more precise word

Use numbers for better reference and to make all items parallel

Put most startling question last

Move action items to closing

Delete unnecessary, repeated information

Insert end date, reason, and thanks

Supervisors:

As vice president, I am troubled by a big problem. I am writing this note to ask for your *Please help us address* help and advice to address an urgent problem the problem of excessive e-mail. If you *by* will do me the favor of answering the questions below. I'm sure your ideas will assist us in the development of a plan that should benefit your employees, yourself, and our organization will be improved. *written* Your responses in writing to these questions (preferably by May 5) will help me prepare for our supervisory committee meeting on May 10.

expected   *to*   *huge* Everyone had the expectation that e-mail would be a great big productivity tool. I'm *However,   its   use* afraid that its use is becoming extremely excessive. For our organization it is actually *cuts* cutting into work time. Did you know that one study found that the average office *s two* worker is spending 2 hours a day on e-mail? In our organization we may be spending *a* even more then this. Its exceedingly difficult to get any work done because of writing *countless* and answering an extraordinary number of e-mails coming in each and every day. Excessive e-mail is sapping the organization's strength and productivity. I would like to *will* have your answers to the following questions before the above referenced dates to help us focus on the problem:

About 1. Can you give a ballpark figure for how many e-mail messages you receive and *do* *personally* answer on a personal basis each day?

2. Think about how many hours the employees in your department spend on e-mail *do* each day. Approximately how many hours would you estimate?

3. Do you have any ideas about how we can make a reduction in the volume of e-mail *reduce* messages being sent and received within our own organization?

excessively 4. Do you think that e-mail is being used by our employees in an excessive manner?

5. *do*   *of a weekly*   *such as* I'm wondering what you think about an e-mail-free day once a week. How about Friday? I appreciate your suggestions and advice in developing a solution to the *improving* problem of controlling e-mail and making an improvement in productivity.

Writing Plan

SUBJECT LINE

Summarize the request and note the action desired.

Write the subject line after you finish the body of the message.

OPENING

Begin with the request or a brief statement introducing it.

The purpose of this messages is to gather information to solve the problem of excessive reliance on e-mail. The primary audience will be key supervisors who are busy but probably willing to help solve a problem. A secondary audience might be their employees. Strive to develop a "you" view. How can this request benefit the receivers?

BODY

Provide background, justification, and details. If asking questions, list them in parallel form.

Explain concisely the problem of excessive use of e-mail. For high "skim value," organize the body into a list of numbered questions. Write them in parallel form, and arrange them so that the most difficult or most startling questions are last.

CLOSING

Request action by a specific date. Provide a reason. Express appreciation.

Explain that you want responses to your questions by May 5 so that you can prepare for a supervisory committee meeting May 10.

after revision

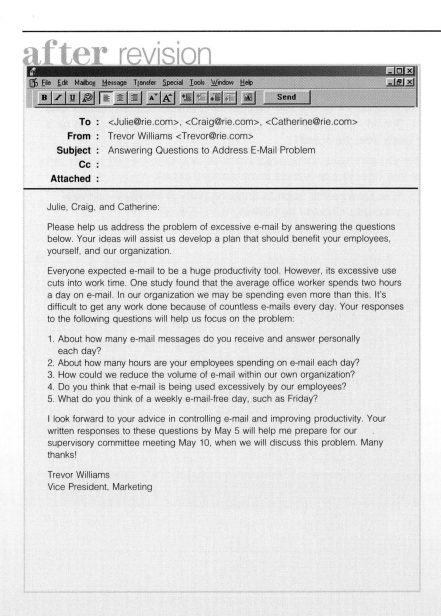

E-mail window:

To : <Julie@rie.com>, <Craig@rie.com>, <Catherine@rie.com>
From : Trevor Williams <Trevor@rie.com>
Subject : Answering Questions to Address E-Mail Problem
Cc :
Attached :

Julie, Craig, and Catherine:

Please help us address the problem of excessive e-mail by answering the questions below. Your ideas will assist us develop a plan that should benefit your employees, yourself, and our organization.

Everyone expected e-mail to be a huge productivity tool. However, its excessive use cuts into work time. One study found that the average office worker spends two hours a day on e-mail. In our organization we may be spending even more than this. It's difficult to get any work done because of countless e-mails every day. Your responses to the following questions will help us focus on the problem:

1. About how many e-mail messages do you receive and answer personally each day?
2. About how many hours are your employees spending on e-mail each day?
3. How could we reduce the volume of e-mail within our own organization?
4. Do you think that e-mail is being used excessively by our employees?
5. What do you think of a weekly e-mail-free day, such as Friday?

I look forward to your advice in controlling e-mail and improving productivity. Your written responses to these questions by May 5 will help me prepare for our supervisory committee meeting May 10, when we will discuss this problem. Many thanks!

Trevor Williams
Vice President, Marketing

WRITING IMPROVEMENT CASES

5.1 Request E-Mail: Planning a Charity Golf Event

The following e-mail from Brad O'Bannon requests information about planning a charity golf tournament. His first draft must be revised.

Your Task. Analyze Brad's message. It suffers from many writing faults that you have studied. List its weaknesses and then outline an appropriate writing plan. If your instructor directs, revise it. Could this message benefit from category headings?

Date:	Current
To:	Gail Lobanoff <globanoff@monarch.net>
From:	Brad O'Bannon <bobannon@cox.net>
Subject:	Need Help!

The Family Outreach Center badly needs funds. We've tried other things, but now we want to try a charity golf event. In view of the fact that you have expertise in this area and since you volunteered to offer your assistance, I am writing this e-mail to pick your brain, so to speak, in regard to questions that have to do with five basic fundamentals in the process of preparation. I'm going to need your answers these areas before February 15. Is that possible? Maybe you would rather talk to me. Should I contact you?

In regard to the budget, I have no idea how to estimate costs. For example, what about administrative costs. How about marketing? And there are salaries, cell-phone rentals, copiers, and a lot of other things.

I also need help in choosing a golf course. Should it be a public course? Or a private course? Resort? One big area that I worry about is sponsors. Should I go after one big sponsor? But let's say I get Pepsi to be a sponsor. Then do I have to ban Coke totally from the scene?

Another big headache is scoring. I'll bet you can make some suggestions for tabulating the golf results. And posting them. By the way, did you see that Tiger Woods is back in the winner's circle?

I've noticed that other golf tournaments have extra events, such as a pairing party to introduce partners. Many also have an awards dinner to award prizes. Should I be planning extra events?

Brad O'Bannon
Philanthropy and Gifts Coordinator
Family Outreach Center of Miami

1. List at least five weaknesses in the preceding request e-mail.

2. Outline a writing plan for this message.
   Subject line:

   Opening:
   Body:

   Closing:

5.2 Information E-Mail: Workplace Issues

In the following e-mail message, Paul Rouse intends to inform his boss, Ceresa Rothery, about a conference he attended on the topic of workplace violence. This first draft of his information message is poorly written.

Your Task. Analyze Paul's first draft. It suffers from wordiness, poor organization, and other faults. List its weaknesses and outline an appropriate writing plan. If your instructor directs, revise it.

Date:	Current
To:	Ceresa Rothery <crothery@rancho.com>
From:	Paul Rouse <prouse@rancho.com>
Subject:	REPORT
Cc:	

Ceresa:

I went to the Workplace Issues conference on November 3, as you suggested. The topic was how to prevent workplace violence, and I found it extremely fascinating. Although we have been fortunate to avoid serious incidents at our company, it's better to be safe than sorry. Because of the fact that I was the representative from our company and you asked for a report, here it is. Susan Sloan was the presenter, and she made suggestions in three categories, which I will make a summary of here.

Ms. Sloan cautioned organizations to prescreen job applicants. As a matter of fact, wise companies do not offer employment until after a candidate's background has been checked. Just the mention of a background check is sufficient and motivational enough to make some candidates head for the hills. These candidates, of course, are the ones with something to hide.

A second suggestion was that companies should become involved in the preparation of a good employee handbook that outlines what employees should do when they are suspicious of potential workplace violence. This handbook should include a way for informers to be anonymous.

A third recommendation had to do with recognizing red-flag behavior. This involves having companies train managers in the recognition of signs of potential workplace violence. What are some of the red flags? One sign is an increasing number of arguments (most of them petty) with coworkers. Another sign is extreme changes in behavior or statements that indicate the existence of depression over family or financial problems. Another sign is bullying or harassing behavior. Bringing a firearm to work or displaying an extreme fascination with firearms is another sign.

It seems to me that the best recommendation is prescreening job candidates. This is because it is most feasible. If you want me to do more research on prescreening techniques, do not hesitate to let me know. Let me know before the date of November 18 if you want me to make a report at our management meeting. Scheduled for December 3.

Did you know, by the way, that the next Workplace Issues conference is in January, and the topic is employee e-mail monitoring? That should be juicy!

Paul

1. List at least five weaknesses in the preceding information e-mail.

2. Outline a writing plan for this memo:
    Subject line:
    Opening:
    Body:
    Closing:

5.3 Request Memo: Choosing Your Holiday

The following memo requests a response from staff members. However, it is so poorly written that they may not know what to do.

Your Task. Analyze the message. List its weaknesses and outline an appropriate writing plan. If your instructor directs, revise it.

Date: Current
To: All Employees
From: Kimberly Jackson, Human Resources
Subject: Changing Holiday Plan

As you all know, in the past we've offered all employees 11 holidays (starting with New Year's Day in January and proceeding through Christmas Day the following December). Other companies offer similar holiday schedules.

In addition, we've given all employees one floating holiday. As you may remember, we determined that day by a companywide vote. As a result, all employees had the same day off. Now, however, we're giving consideration to a new plan that we feel would be better. This new plan involves a floating holiday that each individual employee may decide for theirself. We've given it considerable thought and decided that such a plan could definitely work. We would allow each employee to choose a day that they want. Of course, we would have to issue certain restrictions. Selections would have to be subject to our staffing needs within individual departments. For example, if everyone wanted the same day, we could not allow everyone to take it. In that case, we would allow the employee with the most seniority to have the day off.

Before we institute the new plan, though, we wanted to see what employees thought about this. Is it better to continue our current companywide uniform floating holiday? Or should we try an individual floating holiday? Please let us know what you think as soon as possible.

1. List at least five faults in this message.

2. Outline a general writing plan for this message.
   Subject line:
   Opening:
   Body:
   Closing:

ACTIVITIES AND CASES

CRITICAL THINKING — E-MAIL

5.4 Information E-Mail or Memo: What I Do on the Job

Some employees have remarked to the boss that they are working more than other employees. Your boss has decided to study the matter by asking all employees to describe exactly what they are doing. If some jobs are found to be overly demanding, your boss may redistribute job tasks or hire additional employees.

Your Task. Write a well-organized memo describing your duties, the time you spend on each task, and the skills needed for what you do. Provide enough details to make a clear record of your job. Use actual names and describe actual tasks. Describe a current or previous job. If you have not worked, report to the head of an organization to which you belong. Describe the duties of an officer or of a committee. Your boss or organization head appreciates brevity. Keep your memo under one page.

CRITICAL THINKING   E-MAIL

5.5 Information E-Mail or Memo: Party Time!

Staff members in your office were disappointed that no holiday party was given last year. They don't care what kind of party it is, but they do want some kind of celebration this year.

Your Task. You have been asked to draft a memo to the office staff about a December holiday party. Decide what kind of party you would like. Include information about where the party will be held, when it is, what the cost will be, a description of the food to be served, whether guests are allowed, and whom to make reservations with.

E-MAIL

5.6 Information/Procedure E-Mail or Memo: Parking Guidelines With a Smile

As Adelle Justice, director of Human Resources, you must remind both day-shift and swing-shift employees of the company's parking guidelines. Day-shift employees must park in Lots A and B in their assigned spaces. If they have not registered their cars and received their white stickers, the cars will be ticketed.

Day-shift employees are forbidden to park at the curb. Swing-shift employees may park at the curb before 3:30 p.m. Moreover, after 3:30 p.m., swing-shift employees may park in any empty space—except those marked Tandem, Handicapped, Vanpool, Carpool, or Management. Day-shift employees may loan their spaces to other employees if they know they will not be using them.

One serious problem is lack of registration (as evidenced by white stickers). Registration is done by Employee Relations. Any car without a sticker will be ticketed. To encourage registration, Employee Relations will be in the cafeteria May 12 and 13 from 11:30 a.m. to 1:30 p.m. and from 3 p.m. to 5 p.m. to take applications and issue white parking stickers.

Your Task. Write an information/procedure e-mail or memo to employees that reviews the parking guidelines and encourages them to get their cars registered. Use listing techniques, and strive for a tone that fosters a sense of cooperation rather than resentment.

E-MAIL   WEB

5.7 Information/Procedure E-Mail or Memo: Countdown to Performance Appraisal Deadline

It's time to remind all supervisory personnel that they must complete employee performance appraisals by April 15. Your boss, James Robinson, director, Human Resources, asks you to draft a procedure memo or e-mail announcing the deadline. In talking with Jim, you learn that he wants you to summarize some of the main steps in writing these appraisals. Jim says that the appraisals are really important this year because of changes in work and jobs. Many offices are installing new technologies, and some offices are undergoing reorganization. It's been a hectic year.

Jim also mentions that some supervisors will want to attend a training workshop on February 20 where they can update their skills. Supervisors who want to reserve a space at the training workshop should contact Lynn Jeffers at *ljeffers@rainco.com*. When you ask him what procedures you should include in the memo, he tells you to consult the employee handbook and pick out the most important steps.

In the handbook you find suggestions that say each employee should have a performance plan with three or four main objectives. In the appraisal the supervisor should mention three strengths the employee has, as well as three areas for improvement. One interesting comment in the handbook indicated that improvements should focus on skills, such as time management, rather than on things like being late frequently. Supervisors are supposed to use a scale of 1 to 5 to assess employees: 1 = consistently exceeds requirements; 5 = does not meet requirements at all. You think to yourself that this scale is screwy; it's certainly not like grades in school. But you can't change the scale. Finally, supervisors should meet with employees to discuss the appraisal. The completed appraisal should be sent to your office.

Your Task. Draft a memo or e-mail from James Robinson, Director, Human Resources, to all department heads, managers, and supervisors. Announce the April 15 deadline for performance appraisals. List five or six steps to be taken by supervisors in completing performance appraisals. If you need more information about writing performance appraisals, search that term on the Web. You'll find many sites with helpful advice.

E-MAIL   **TEAM**

5.8 Information E-Mail or Memo: Planning for Important Milestone

Your company hired a writing consultant to help employees improve their communication skills.

Your Task. The following poorly written message was assigned as an exercise to train your team in recognizing good and bad writing. In small groups discuss its weaknesses and then compose, either individually or as a team, an improved version.

Date: Current

To: All Employees

From: Margaret Tilly, Coordinator, Employee Resources

Subject: An Important Milestone in Your Life

We know that retirement is an important milestone in anyone's life, and we are aware that many employees do not have sufficient information that relates to the prospect of their retirement. Many employees who are approaching retirement age have come to this office wanting to talk about health, financial needs, family responsibilities, and income from outside sources and how these all relate to their retirement. It would be much easier for us to answer all these questions at once, and that is what we will try to do.

We would like to answer your questions at a series of retirement planning sessions in the company cafeteria. The first meeting is November 17. We will start at 4 p.m., which means that the company is giving you one hour of released time to attend this important session. We will meet from 4 to 6 p.m. when we will stop for dinner. We will begin again at 7 p.m. and finish at 8 p.m.

We have arranged for three speakers. They are: our company benefits supervisor, a financial planner, and a psychologist who treats retirees who have mental problems. The three sessions are planned for: November 17, November 30, and December 7.

CRITICAL THINKING   **E-MAIL**   **INFOTRAC**   **TEAM**   **WEB**

5.9 Procedure E-Mail or Memo: Should Sales Reps Use Company Cell Phones While Driving?

You saw a recent article that sent chills straight through you. A stockbroker for Smith Barney was making cold calls on his cell phone while driving. His car hit and killed a motorcyclist. The brokerage firm was sued and accused of contributing to an accident by encouraging employees to use cell phones while driving. To avoid the risk of paying huge damages awarded by an emotional jury, the brokerage firm offered the victim's family a $500,000 settlement.

As operations manager of D'anza, a hair care and skin products company, you begin to worry. You know that your company has already provided its 75 sales representatives with cell phones to help them keep in touch with home base while they are in the field.

Your Task. In teams discuss the problem. Should sales reps use their phones while driving? Is this practice allowed in your state? What happens when sales reps work in other states? Consider the possibility of ordering inexpensive hands-free devices for all sales reps. Use the Web and InfoTrac to research cell phone use, laws, and safety tips. As a team, decide on a company plan. Provide hands-free devices? Forbid calls while driving? Assume you are free to make any decision. Individually or as a team, write an e-mail or memo to sales reps explaining your decision and suggesting safety ideas. How will your decision benefit the receivers?

E-MAIL

5.10 Request E-Mail: Learning About Team Retreats

Tiptoeing gingerly across a wobbling jerrybuilt bridge of slender planks stretched between two boxes, the chief financial officer of Wells Fargo completed his task. Cheers greeted Howard Atkins as he reached the other side with a final lunge. His team of senior financial executives applauded their leader who made it across the bridge without falling off.

Atkins had pulled together a group of 73 financial executives, risk managers, accountants, and group presidents for team-building exercises on the sun-drenched lawns of a luxury hotel in Sonoma, California. The three-day retreat also provided conventional business meetings with reports and presentations. Atkins described the attendees as "very high-powered, very capable, very technically skilled, very competitive people." Yet, he was striving for an even higher level of performance. "They are very individualistic in their approach to their work," he said. "What I have been trying to do is get them to see the power of acting more like a team." And by the end of the day, he was clearly pleased with what he saw. He credits double-digit gains in Wells Fargo income and earnings in large part to the bank's people programs. "Success is more often than not a function of execution, and execution is really about people, so we invest pretty heavily in our people."

For his company's team-building exercises, Atkins chose low-stress challenges such as balancing on planks, building tents blindfolded, and stepping through complex webs of ropes. But other companies use whitewater rafting, rock walls, treetop rope bridges, and even fire pits as metaphors for the business world.

Your boss at BancFirst saw the news about Wells Fargo and is intrigued. He is understandably dubious about the value of team building that could result from a retreat. Yet, he is interested because he believes that the widespread use of electronic technology is reducing personal contact. He asks you to have the Human Resources Department investigate.[11]

Your Task. As assistant to the president, draft an e-mail to Charlotte Evers, Manager, Human Resources. Ask her to investigate the possibility of a retreat for BancFirst. Your message should include many questions for her to answer. Include an end date and a reason.

CRITICAL THINKING — **INFOTRAC** — **E-MAIL** — **TEAM**

5.11 Reply Memo or E-Mail: Office Romances Off Limits?

Where can you find the hottest singles scene today? Some would say in your workplace. Because people are working long hours and have little time for outside contacts, relationships often develop at work. Estimates suggest that one third to one half of all romances start at work. Your boss is concerned about possible problems resulting from relationships at work. What happens if a relationship between a superior and subordinate results in perceived favoritism? What happens if a relationship results in a nasty breakup? Your boss would like to simply ban all relationships among employees. But that's not likely to work. He asks you, his assistant, to learn what guidelines could be established regarding office romances.

Your Task. Using InfoTrac, read Timothy Bland's "Romance in the Workplace: Good Thing or Bad?" (Article No. A66460590). From this article select four or five suggestions that you could make to your boss in regard to protecting an employer. Why is it necessary for a company to protect itself? Discuss your findings and reactions with your team. Individually or as a group, submit your findings and reactions in a well-organized, easy-to-read e-mail or memo to your boss (your instructor). You may list main points from the article, but use your own words to write the message.

CRITICAL THINKING — **E-MAIL** — **TEAM**

5.12 Reply Memo or E-Mail: One Sick Day Too Many

As director of Human Resources at a midsized insurance company, you received an inquiry from Suzette Chase, who is supervisor of Legal Support. It seems that one of Suzette's veteran employees recently implemented a four-day workweek for herself. On the fifth morning, the employee calls in with some crisis or sickness that makes it impossible for her to get to work. Suzette asks for your advice in how to handle this situation.

In the past you've told supervisors to keep a written record (a log) of each absence. This record should include the financial and productive impact of the absence. It should include a space where the employee can include her comments and signature. You've found that a written document always increases the significance of the event. You've also told supervisors that they must be objective and professional. It's difficult, but they should not personalize the situation.

Occasionally, of course, an absence is legitimate. Supervisors must know what is unavoidable and what is a lame excuse. In other words, they must know how to separate reasons from excuses. Another thing to consider is how the employee reacts when approached. Is her attitude sincere, or does she automatically become defensive?

You also tell supervisors that "if they talk the talk, they must walk the walk." In other words, they must follow the same policies that are enforced. The best plan, of course, is to clearly define what is and is not acceptable attendance policy and make sure every new-hire is informed.

Your Task. In teams discuss what advice to give to Suzette Chase regarding her habitually absent worker. Why is a log important? What other suggestions can you make? How should you conclude this message? Individually or in teams, write a well-organized reply memo or e-mail message to Suzette Chase, Supervisor, Legal Support. Remember that bulleted items improve readability.

INFOTRAC — **E-MAIL** — **TEAM**

5.13 Reply E-Mail: Managing the Mountains of E-Mail

E-mail has become an essential part of our business lives. Yet workers throughout the country may be losing hours from each business day because of it. Some are distracted from work and waste valuable time on meaningless communications, says Dr. Mark Langemo, records management author and expert. In an article titled "11 Practical Strategies for Managing E-Mail" (InfoTrac Article No. A111112220), Dr. Langemo tells how companies can manage e-mail more efficiently and reduce their legal vulnerability. The vice president of your company has been complaining that e-mail is out of control. He asks you to be on the lookout for any ideas he should present to management for dealing with the problem.

Your Task: Using InfoTrac, study the article. You believe that some of the suggestions would certainly work for your company. You decide to discuss them with your team. Decide which of the suggestions are most appropriate, and organize them into a set of procedures. What should be done first? Some of the suggestions could be combined with others. Once your team agrees on a set of procedures, write an e-mail to Vice President Stanton Childress (or your instructor). In your own words, list the most significant strategies and explain each briefly.

E-MAIL — **TEAM** — **WEB**

5.14 Reply E-Mail or Memo: Cross-Cultural Dilemma

The Air Force's highest-ranking female fighter pilot, Lt. Col. Martha McSally, was unhappy about being required to wear neck-to-toe robes in Saudi Arabia when she's off base. She filed a federal lawsuit seeking to overturn the policy that requires female servicewomen to wear such conservative clothing even when they are off base.

After seeing an article about this in the newspaper, your boss was concerned about sending female engineers to Saudi Arabia. Your company has been asked to submit a proposal to develop telecommunications within that country, and some of the company's best staff members are female. If your company wins the contract, it will undoubtedly need women to be in Saudi Arabia to complete the project. Because your boss knows little about the country, he asks you, his assistant, to do some research to find out what is appropriate business dress.

Your Task. Visit two or three Web sites and learn about dress expectations in Saudi Arabia. Is Western-style clothing acceptable for men? For women? Are there any clothing taboos? Should guest workers be expected to dress like natives? In teams discuss your findings. Individually or collectively, prepare a memo or e-mail addressed to J. E. Rivers, your boss. Summarize your most significant findings.

E-MAIL

5.15 Reply Memo or E-Mail: Scheduling Appointments to Interview a New Project Manager

You're frustrated! Your boss, Paul Rosenberg, has scheduled three appointments to interview applicants for the position of project manager. All of these appointments are for Thursday, May 5. However, he now must travel to Atlanta on that weekend. He asks you to reschedule all the appointments for one week later. He also wants a brief summary of the background of each candidate.

Despite your frustration, you call each person and are lucky to arrange these times. Carol Chastain, who has been a project manager for nine years with Piedmont Corporation, agrees to come at 10:30 a.m. Richard Emanuel, who is a systems analyst and a consultant to many companies, will come at 11:30. Lara Lee, who has an M.A. degree and six years of experience as senior project coordinator at High Point Industries, will come at 9:30 a.m. You're wondering whether Mr. Rosenberg forgot to include Hilary Iwu, operations personnel officer, in these interviews. Ms. Iwu usually is part of the selection process.

Your Task. Write an e-mail or memo to Mr. Rosenberg including all the vital information he needs.

CRITICAL THINKING — **E-MAIL** — **INFOTRAC** — **TEAM**

5.16 Reply E-Mail: Reaching Consensus Regarding Casual-Dress Policy

Casual dress in professional offices has been coming under attack. Your boss, Kathy Lewis-Adler, received the e-mail shown in Figure 5.5. She thinks it would be a good assignment for her group of management trainees to help her respond to that message. She asks your team to research answers to the first five questions in CEO Thomas Marshall's message. She doesn't expect you to answer the final question, but any information you can supply to the first questions would help her shape a response.

Marshall & Associates is a public CPA firm with a staff of 120 CPAs, bookkeepers, managers, and support personnel. Located in downtown Pittsburgh, the plush offices in One Oxford Center overlook the Allegheny River and the North Shore. The firm performs general accounting and audit services as well as tax planning and preparation. Accountants visit clients in the field and also entertain them in the downtown office.

Your Task. Decide whether the entire team will research each question in Figure 5.5 or whether team members will be assigned certain questions. Collect information, discuss it, and reach consensus on what you will report to Ms. Lewis-Adler. Write a concise, one-page response from your team. Your goal is to inform, not persuade. Remember that you represent management, not students or employees.

`INFOTRAC`   `TEAM`   `WEB`

5.17 Reply Memo: Squawking About a Company E-Mail Policy

At first, he couldn't figure it out. The IS (Information Systems) network manager at Lionel Trains in Chesterfield, Michigan, fretted that his company would have to upgrade its Internet connection because operations were noticeably slower than in the past. Upon checking, however, he discovered that extensive recreational Web surfing among employees was the real reason for the slowdown. Since the company needed a good policy regulating the use of e-mail and the Internet, he assigned your team the task of investigating existing policies. Your team leader, Rick Rodriquez, who has quite a sense of humor, said, "Adopting an Internet policy is a lot like hosting a convention of pigeons. Both will result in a lot of squawking, ruffled feathers, and someone getting dumped on." Right! No one is going to like having e-mail and Internet use restricted. It is, indeed, a dirty job, but someone has to do it.

Your Task. Working individually, locate examples or models of company e-mail and Internet policies. Use InfoTrac and the Web trying variations of the search term "Company E-Mail Policy." Print any helpful material. Then meet as a group and select six to eight major topics that you think should be covered in a company policy. Your investigation will act as a starting point in the long process of developing a policy that provides safeguards but is not overly restrictive. You are not expected to write the policy at this time. But you could attach copies of anything interesting. Your boss would especially like to know where he could see or purchase model company policies. Send a reply memo to Rick Rodriquez, your team leader.

VIDEO RESOURCES

This important chapter offers two learning videos.

Video Library 1, *Building Workplace Communication Skills: Smart E-Mail Messages and Memos Advance Your Career.* Watch this chapter-specific video for a demonstration of how to use e-mail skillfully and safely. You'll better understand the writing process in relation to composing messages. You'll also see tips for writing messages that advance your career instead of sinking it.

Video Library 2, *Bridging the Gap: Innovation, Learning, and Communication: A Study of Yahoo.* This video familiarizes you with managers and inside operating strategies at the Internet company Yahoo. After watching the film, assume the role of assistant to John Briggs, senior producer, who appeared in the video. John has just received a letter asking for permission from another film company to use Yahoo offices and personnel in an educational video, similar to the one you just saw.

John wants you to draft a message for him to send to the operations manager, Ceci Lang, asking for permission for VX Studios to film. VX says it needs about 15 hours of filming time and would like to interview four or five managers as well as founders David Filo and Jerry Yang. VX would need to set up its mobile studio van in the parking lot and would need permission to use advertising film clips. Although VX hopes to film in May, it is flexible about the date. John Briggs reminds you that Yahoo has participated in a number of films in the past two years, and some managers are complaining that they can't get their work done.

Your Task. After watching the video, write a memo or e-mail request message to Ceci Lang, operations manager, asking her to allow VX Studios to film at Yahoo. Your message should probably emphasize the value of these projects in enhancing Yahoo's image among future users. Supply any other details you think are necessary to create a convincing request memo that will win authorization from Ceci Lang to schedule this filming.

GRAMMAR/MECHANICS CHECKUP—5

Prepositions and Conjunctions

Review Sections 1.18 and 1.19 in the Grammar Review section of the Grammar/ Mechanics Handbook. Then study each of the following statements. Write *a* or *b* to indicate the sentence in which the idea is expressed more effectively. Also record the number of the G/M principle illustrated. When you finish, compare your responses with those provided. If your answers differ, study carefully the principles shown in parentheses.

b _____ (1.18a)   **Example**   a. When did you graduate high school?
                                          b. When did you graduate from high school?

_____   1. a. Your iPod was more expensive than mine.
                      b. Your iPod was more expensive then mine.

_____   2. a. Don't you hate when your inbox is filled with spam?
                      b. Don't you hate it when your inbox is filled with spam?

_____   3. a. If the company called you, than it must be looking at your résumé.
                      b. If the company called you, then it must be looking at your résumé.

_____   4. a. Ethnocentrism is when you believe your culture is best.
                      b. Ethnocentrism involves the belief that your culture is best.

_____   5. a. Business messages should be clear, correct, and written with conciseness.
                      b. Business messages should be clear, correct, and concise.

_____   6. a. What type computer monitor do you prefer?
                      b. What type of computer monitor do you prefer?

_____   7. a. Do you know where the meeting is at?
                      b. Do you know where the meeting is?

_____   8. a. Did you send an application to the headquarters in Cincinnati or to the branch in St. Louis?
                      b. Did you apply to the Cincinnati headquarters or the St. Louis branch?

_____   9. a. That Hollywood actor appeared in movies, plays, and television.
                      b. That Hollywood actor appeared in movies, in plays, and on television.

_____   10. a. She had a great interest, as well as a profound respect for, historical homes.
                      b. She had a great interest in, as well as a profound respect for, historical homes.

_____   11. a. Volunteers should wear long pants, bring gloves, and sunscreen should be applied.
                      b. Volunteers should wear long pants, bring gloves, and apply sunscreen.

_____   12. a. His PowerPoint presentation was short like we hoped it would be.
                      b. His PowerPoint presentation was short as we hoped it would be.

_____   13. a. An ethics code is where a set of rules spells out appropriate behavior standards.
                      b. An ethics code is a set of rules spelling out appropriate behavior standards.

_____   14. a. Please keep the paper near the printer.
                      b. Please keep the paper near to the printer.

_____   15. a. A behavioral interview question is when the recruiter says, "Tell me about a time. . . ."
                      b. A behavioral interview question is one in which the recruiter says, "Tell me about a time. . . ."

GRAMMAR/MECHANICS CHALLENGE—5

The following memo has faults in grammar, punctuation, spelling, capitalization, number form, repetition, wordiness, and other problems. Correct the errors with standard proofreading marks (see Appendix B) or revise the message online at **Guffey Xtra!**

DATE: March 2, 200x

TO: Department Heads, Managers, and Supervisors

FROM: James Robbins, Director, Human Resources   *JR*

SUBJECT: Submitting Appraisals of Performance by April 15th

Please be informed that performance appraisals for all you're employees' are due, before April 15th. These appraisal are esspecially important and essential this year. Because of job changes, new technologys and because of office re-organization.

To complete your performance appraisals in the most effective way, you should follow the procedures described in our employee handbook, let me briefly make a review of those procedures;

1. Be sure each and every employee has a performance plan with 3 or 4 main objective.

2. For each objective make an assessment of the employee on a scale of 5 (consistently excedes requirements) to 0 (does not meet requirements at all.

3. You should identify 3 strengths that he brings to the job.

4. Name 3 skills that he can improve. These should pertain to skills such as Time Management rather then to behaviors such as habitual lateness.

5. The employee should be met with to discuss his appraisal.

6. Finish the appraisal and send the completed appraisal to this office.

We look upon appraisals like a tool for helping each worker assess his performance. And enhance his output. If you would like to discuss this farther, please do not hessitate to call me.

COMMUNICATION WORKSHOP
ETHICS

WHOSE COMPUTER
IS IT ANYWAY?

Many companies provide their employees with computers and Internet access. Should employees be able to use those computers for online shopping, personal messages, and personal work, as well as to listen to music and play games?

But It's Harmless

The Wall Street Journal reports that many office workers have discovered that it's far easier to shop online than to race to malls and wait in line. To justify her Web shopping at work, one employee, a recent graduate, says, "Instead of standing at the water cooler gossiping, I shop online." She went on to say, "I'm not sapping company resources by doing this."

Some online office shoppers say that what they're doing is similar to making personal phone calls. So long as they don't abuse the practice, they see no harm. Besides, shopping at the office is far faster than shopping from slow dial-up connections at home. Marketing director David Krane justifies his online shopping by explaining that his employer benefits because he is more productive when he takes minibreaks. "When I need a break, I just pull up a Web page and just browse," he says. "Ten minutes later, I'm all refreshed, and I can go back to business-plan writing."

Companies Cracking Down

Employers, however, do not approve of the increasing use of company networks for personal online activities. A study of business organizations found that one in five companies has terminated an employee for e-mail infractions.[12] UPS discovered an employee running a personal business from his office computer. Lockheed Martin fired an employee who disabled its entire company network for six hours because of an e-mail message heralding a holiday event that the worker sent to 60,000 employees. Employees who use company Internet connections to download large documents—especially MP3 music—gobble up a huge amount of bandwidth.[13]

Attorney Carole O'Blenes thinks that companies should begin cracking down. Online shopping generates junk e-mail that could cause the company's server to crash. And what about productivity? "Whether they're checking their stocks, shopping, or doing research for their upcoming trip to Spain," she says, "that's time diverted from doing business."[14]

What's Reasonable?

Some companies try to enforce a "zero tolerance" policy, prohibiting any personal use of company equipment. Ameritech Corporation specifically tells employees that "computers and other company equipment are to be used only to provide service to customers and for other business purposes." Companies such as Boeing, however, allow employees to use faxes, e-mail, and the Internet for personal reasons. But Boeing sets guidelines. Use has to be of "reasonable duration and frequency" and can't cause "embarrassment to the company."[15] Strictly prohibited are chain letters, obscenity, and political and religious solicitation.

Career Application. As an administrative assistant at Texas Technologies in Fort Worth, you have just received an e-mail from your boss asking for your opinion. It seems that many employees have been shopping online; one person actually received four personal packages from UPS in one morning. Although reluctant to do so, management is considering installing monitoring software that not only tracks Internet use but also blocks pornography, hate, and game sites.

Your Task

- In teams or as a class, discuss the problem of workplace abuse of e-mail and the Internet. Should full personal use be allowed?

- Are computers and their links to the Internet similar to other equipment such as telephones?

- Should employees be allowed to access the Internet for personal use if they use their own private e-mail accounts?

- Should management be allowed to monitor all Internet use?

- Should employees be warned if e-mail is to be monitored?

- What specific reasons can you give to support an Internet crackdown by management?

- What specific reasons can you give to oppose a crackdown?

Decide whether you support or oppose the crackdown. Explain your views in an e-mail or a memo to your boss, Arthur W. Rose, *awrose@txtech.com*.

PHOTOS: © ROYALTY-FREE/CORBIS; © RYAN McVAY/PHOTODISC/GETTY IMAGES;

6

DIRECT LETTERS AND GOODWILL MESSAGES

A good business letter can get you a job interview, get you off the hook, or get you money. It's totally asinine to blow your chances of getting whatever you want—with a business letter that turns people off instead of turning them on.[1]

Malcolm Forbes,
Publisher and Founder,
Forbes Magazine

OBJECTIVES

- Write direct requests for information and action.
- Write direct claims.
- Write direct responses to information requests.
- Write adjustment letters.
- Write letters of recommendation.
- Write goodwill messages.

WRITING EFFECTIVE DIRECT BUSINESS LETTERS

Publisher Malcolm Forbes understood the power of business letters. They can get you anything you want if you can write letters that turn people on instead of off. This chapter teaches you how to turn readers on with effective business letters and goodwill messages. Most of these messages travel outside an organization.

Letters communicate with outsiders and produce a formal record.

Although e-mail is incredibly successful for both internal and external communication, many important messages still call for letters. Business letters are important when a permanent record is required, when formality is necessary, and when a message is sensitive and requires an organized, well-considered presentation. In this book we'll divide messages into three groups: (1) direct letters communicating straightforward requests, replies, and goodwill messages in Chapter 6; (2) persuasive messages including sales pitches in Chapter 7; and (3) negative messages delivering refusals and bad news in Chapter 8.

This chapter concentrates on direct letters through which we conduct everyday business and convey goodwill to outsiders. Such letters go to suppliers, government agencies, other businesses, and most important, customers. Customer letters receive a high priority because these messages encourage product feedback, project a favorable image of the company, and promote future business. You'll learn to write direct requests for information and action, direct claims, direct responses to information requests, adjustment letters, letters of recommendation, and goodwill messages.

DIRECT REQUESTS FOR INFORMATION AND ACTION

The content of a message and its anticipated effect on the reader determine the strategy you choose.

Like memos, letters are easiest to write when you have a plan to follow. The plan for letters, just as for memos, is fixed by the content of the message and its expected effect on the receiver. Many of your messages will request information or action. Although the specific subject of each inquiry may differ, the similarity of purpose in direct requests enables writers to use the following writing plan:

Writing Plan for Direct Requests for Information or Action

- *Opening:* Ask the most important question first or express a polite command.
- *Body:* Explain the request logically and courteously. Ask other questions if necessary.
- *Closing:* Request a specific action with an end date, if appropriate, and show appreciation.

Opening Directly

Readers find the openings and closings of letters most interesting and often read them first.

The most emphatic positions in a letter are the openings and closings. Readers tend to look at them first. The writer, then, should capitalize on this tendency by putting the most significant statement first. The first sentence of a direct request is usually a question or a polite command. It should not be an explanation or justification, unless resistance to the request is expected. When the information requested is likely to be forthcoming, immediately tell the reader what you want. This saves the reader's time and may ensure that the message is read. A busy executive skims the mail, quickly reading subject lines and first sentences only. That reader may grasp your request rapidly and act on it. A request that follows a lengthy explanation, on the other hand, may never be found.

A letter inquiring about hotel accommodations, shown in Figure 6.1, begins immediately with the most important idea. Can the hotel provide meeting rooms and accommodations for 250 people? Instead of opening with an explanation of who the writer is or how the writer happens to be writing this letter, the letter begins more directly.

Begin an information request letter with the most important question or a summarizing statement.

If your request involves several questions, you could open with a polite request, such as *Will you please answer the following questions about . . . .* Note that although this request sounds like a question, it's actually a disguised command. Because you expect an action rather than a reply, punctuate this polite command with a period instead of a question mark. If you use a period, however, some readers will think you have made a punctuation error. To avoid this punctuation problem, just omit *Will you* and start with *Please answer*, as the writer did in Figure 6.1.

Providing Details in the Body

The body of a request letter may contain an explanation or a list of questions.

The body of a letter that requests information should provide necessary details. Remember that the quality of the information obtained from a request letter depends on the clarity of the inquiry. If you analyze your needs, organize your ideas, and frame your request logically, you are likely to receive a meaningful answer that doesn't require a follow-up message. Whenever possible, itemize the information to improve readability. Notice that the questions in Figure 6.1 are bulleted, and they are parallel. That is, they use the same balanced construction.

FIGURE 6.1 ——— Direct Request Letter

Letterhead ———

DCC 958 Alum Creek Drive Columbus, OH 43208   PHONE: (614) 455-3201
                                                    FAX: (614) 455-6621 WEB: www.dcc.com
Digital Communication Corporation

Dateline ———

October 14, 200x

Inside address ———

Mr. Dennis Purdy, Manager
MGM Grand Hotel and Casino
3799 Las Vegas Boulevard South
Las Vegas, NV 89109

Salutation ———

Dear Mr. Purdy:

Can the MGM Grand Hotel provide meeting rooms and accommodations for
about 250 DCC sales representatives from May 25 through May 29?

Your hotel received strong recommendations because of its excellent resort and
conference facilities. Our spring sales conference is scheduled for next May, and
I am collecting information for our planning committee. Please answer these
additional questions regarding the MGM Grand:

Body ———

- Does the hotel have a banquet room that can seat 250?

- Do you have at least four smaller meeting rooms, each to accommodate a
  maximum of 75?

- What kinds of computer facilities are available for electronic presentations?

- What is the nearest airport, and do you provide transportation to and from it?

Answers to these questions and any other information you can provide will help
us decide which conference facility to choose. Your response before November 15
would be most appreciated since our planning committee meets November 19.

Complimentary close ———

Sincerely yours,

Carol A. Allen

Author's name and
identification ———

Carol A. Allen
Corporate Travel Department

Reference initials ———

CAA:gdr

Tips for Formatting Letters
- Start the date 2 inches from the top or 1 blank line below the
  letterhead.
- For block style, begin all lines at the left margin.
- Leave side margins of 1 to 1½ inches depending on the length of the
  letter.
- Single-space the body and double-space between paragraphs.
- Bulleted items may appear flush left or indented.

Closing With Appreciation and an Action Request

The ending of a request letter should tell the reader what you want done and when.

Use the final paragraph to ask for specific action, to set an end date if appropriate, and to express appreciation. As you learned in working with memos, a request for action is most effective when you supply an end date and reason for that date, as shown in Figure 6.1.

It's always appropriate to end a request letter with appreciation for the action taken, but try to do so in a fresh and efficient manner. For example, you could hook your thanks to the end date (*Thanks for responding before November 15 when we must make a decision*). You might connect your appreciation to a statement developing reader benefits (*We are grateful for the information you will provide because it will help us improve our service to you*). You could also describe briefly how the information will help you (*I appreciate this information that will enable me to . . .*). When possible make it easy for the reader to comply with your request (*Note your answers on this sheet and return it in the postage-paid envelope* or *Here's my e-mail address so that you can reach me quickly*). Avoid cliché endings such as *Thank you for your cooperation.* Your appreciation will sound most sincere if you avoid mechanical, tired expressions.

● DIRECT CLAIMS

Direct claims are written by customers to identify and correct a wrong.

In business many things can go wrong—promised shipments are late, warranted goods fail, or service is disappointing. When you as a customer must write to identify or correct a wrong, the letter is called a *claim.* Straightforward claims are those to which you expect the receiver to agree readily. But even these claims often require a letter. While your first action may be a telephone call or a visit to submit your claim, you may not get the results you seek. Written claims are often taken more seriously, and they also establish a record of what happened. Claims that require persuasion are presented in Chapter 7. In this chapter you'll learn to apply the following writing plan for a straightforward claim that uses a direct approach.

Writing Plan for Direct Claims

- *Opening:* Describe clearly the desired action.
- *Body:* Explain the nature of the claim, tell why the claim is justified, and provide details regarding the action requested.
- *Closing:* End courteously with a goodwill statement that summarizes your action request.

Customers who call to complain may not reach the right person at the best time. To register a serious claim, always write a letter. A letter creates a paper trail and is taken more seriously than a telephone call. Use the direct strategy for straightforward claims.

© KEITH BROFSKY/PHOTODISC/GETTY IMAGES

Opening With a Clear Statement

Claim letters open with a clear problem statement or with an explanation of the action necessary to solve the problem.

When you, as a customer, have a legitimate claim, you can expect a positive response from a company. Smart businesses want to hear from their customers. They know that retaining a customer is far less costly than recruiting a new customer. That's why you should open a claim letter with a clear statement of the problem or with the action you want the receiver to take. You might expect a replacement, a refund, a new order, credit to your account, correction of a billing error, free repairs, free inspection, or cancellation of an order. When the remedy is obvious, state it immediately (*Please send us 25 Sanyo digital travel alarm clocks to replace the Sanyo analog travel alarm clocks sent in error with our order shipped January 4*). When the remedy is less obvious, you might ask for a change in policy or procedure or simply for an explanation (*Because three of our employees with confirmed reservations were refused rooms September 16 in your hotel, please clarify your policy regarding reservations and late arrivals*).

Explaining and Justifying in the Body

Providing details without getting angry improves the effectiveness of a claim letter.

In the body of a claim letter, explain the problem and justify your request. Provide the necessary details so that the difficulty can be corrected without further correspondence. Avoid becoming angry or trying to fix blame. Bear in mind that the person reading your letter is seldom responsible for the problem. Instead, state the facts logically, objectively, and unemotionally. Let the reader decide on the causes. Include copies of all pertinent documents such as invoices, sales slips, catalog descriptions, and repair records. (By the way, be sure to send copies and NOT your originals, which could be lost.) When service is involved, cite names of individuals spoken to and dates of calls. Assume that a company honestly wants to satisfy its customers—because most do. When an alternative remedy exists, spell it out (*If you are unable to send 25 Sanyo digital travel alarm clocks immediately, please credit our account now and notify us when they become available*).

Concluding With an Action Request

Close a claim letter with a summary of the action requested and a courteous goodwill statement.

End a claim letter with a courteous statement that promotes goodwill and summarizes your action request. If appropriate, include an end date (*We realize that mistakes in ordering and shipping sometimes occur. Because we've enjoyed your prompt service in the past, we hope that you will be able to send us the Sanyo digital travel alarm clocks by January 15*). Finally, in making claims, act promptly. Delaying claims makes them appear less important. Delayed claims are also more difficult to verify. By taking the time to put your claim in writing, you indicate your seriousness. A written claim starts a record of the problem, should later action be necessary. Be sure to keep a copy of your letter.

When Keith Krahnke received a statement showing a charge for a three-year service warranty that he did not purchase, he was furious. He called the store but failed to get satisfaction to his complaint. Then he decided to write. You can see the first draft of his direct claim letter in Figure 6.2. This draft gave him a chance to vent his anger, but it accomplished little else. The tone was belligerent, and it assumed that the company intentionally mischarged him. Furthermore, it failed to tell the reader how to remedy the problem. The revision, also shown in Figure 6.2, tempered the tone, described the problem objectively, and provided facts and figures. Most important, it specified exactly what Keith wanted to be done.

Notice in Figure 6.2 that Keith used the personal business letter style, which is appropriate for you to use in writing personal messages. Your return address, but not your name, appears above the date. Keith used modified block style, in which the return address, date, and closing lines start at the center. Full block style, however, is also appropriate for personal business letters.

FIGURE 6.2   • **Direct Claim Letter**

before revision

Dear Good Vibes:

You call yourselves Good Vibes, but all I'm getting from your service are bad ●——— Sounds angry; jumps
vibes! I'm furious that you have your salespeople slip in unwanted service   to conclusions
warranties to boost your sales.

When I bought my Panatronic DVR from Good Vibes, Inc., in August, I
specifically told the salesperson that I did NOT want a three-year service
warranty. But there it is on my Visa statement this month! You people have ●——— Forgets that mistakes
obviously billed me for a service I did not authorize. I refuse to pay this   happen
charge.

How can you hope to stay in business with such fraudulent practices? I was
expecting to return this month and look at MP3 players, but you can be sure ●——— Fails to suggest
I'll find an honest dealer this time.   solution

                              Sincerely,

after revision

                                        1201 Lantana Court   Personal
                                        Lake Worth, FL 33461 ●—————— business letter
                                        September 3, 200x   style

                    Mr. Sam Lee, Customer Service
                    Good Vibes, Inc.
                    2003 53rd Street
                    West Palm Beach, FL 33407

                    Dear Mr. Lee:

                    Please credit my Visa account to correct an erroneous charge of $299. ●——— States simply
                                                                                           and clearly
Explains   On August 1 I purchased a Panatronic DVR from Good Vibes, Inc. Although   what to do
objectively   the salesperson discussed a three-year extended warranty with me, I
what went   decided against purchasing that service for $299. However, when my credit
wrong   card statement arrived this month, I noticed an extra $299 charge from ●——— Doesn't blame
                    Good Vibes, Inc. I suspect that this charge represents the warranty I   or accuse
                    declined. Enclosed is a copy of my sales invoice along with my Visa
Documents   statement on which I circled the charge.
facts
                    Please authorize a credit immediately and send a copy of the transaction to
                    me at the above address. I'm enjoying all the features of my Panatronic   Summarizes
                    DVR and would like to be shopping at Good Vibes for an MP3 player shortly. ●——— request and
                                                                                               courteously
                              Sincerely,   suggests
                                                                                               continued
                              Keith Krahnke   business once
                                                                                               problem is
                              Keith Krahnke   resolved

                    Enclosure

REPLIES TO INFORMATION REQUESTS

Before responding to requests, gather facts, check figures, and seek approval if necessary.

Often, your messages will respond favorably to requests for information or action. A customer wants information about a product. A supplier asks to arrange a meeting. Another business inquires about one of your procedures. But before responding to any inquiry, be sure to check your facts and figures carefully. Any letter written on company stationery is considered a legally binding contract. If a policy or procedure needs authorization, seek approval from a supervisor or executive before writing the letter. In complying with requests, you'll want to apply the same direct pattern you used in making requests.

Writing Plan for Information Replies

- *Subject line:* Identify previous correspondence and/or refer to the main idea.
- *Opening:* Deliver the most important information first.
- *Body:* Arrange information logically, explain and clarify it, provide additional information if appropriate, and build goodwill.
- *Closing:* End pleasantly.

Summarizing in the Subject Line

Use the subject line to identify previous correspondence and the main idea.

An information response letter might contain a subject line, which helps the reader recognize the topic immediately. Knowledgeable business communicators use a subject line to refer to earlier correspondence or to summarize the main idea. Notice in Figure 6.3 that the subject line identifies the subject completely (*Your July 12 Inquiry About WorkZone Software*). A subject line helps the reader recognize the topic immediately.

Opening Directly

In the first sentence of an information response, deliver the information the reader wants. Avoid wordy, drawn-out openings (*I have before me your letter of July 12, in which you request information about . . .*). More forceful and more efficient is an opener that answers the inquiry (*Here is the information you wanted about . . .*). When agreeing to a request for action, announce the good news promptly (*Yes, I will be happy to speak to your business communication class on the topic of . . .*).

Arranging Information Logically

A good way to answer questions is to number or bullet each one.

When answering a group of questions or providing considerable data, arrange the information logically and make it readable by using lists, tables, headings, boldface, italics, or other graphic devices. When customers or prospective customers inquire about products or services, your response should do more than merely supply answers. You'll also want to promote your organization and products. Be sure to present the promotional material with attention to the "you" view and to reader benefits (*You can use our standardized tests to free you from time-consuming employment screening*). You'll learn more about special techniques for developing sales and persuasive messages in Chapter 7.

Closing Pleasantly

To avoid abruptness, include a pleasant closing remark that shows your willingness to help the reader. Provide extra information if appropriate. Tailor your remarks to fit this letter and this reader. Refer to the information provided or to its use (*The enclosed list summarizes our recommendations. We wish you all the best in redesigning your Web site*). Since everyone appreciates being recognized as an individual, avoid form-letter closings such as *If we may be of further assistance, ...*

FIGURE 6.3 ──────── • **Direct Reply Letter**

SONOMA SOFTWARE, INC.
520 Sonoma Parkway
Petaluma, CA 94539
(707) 784-2219
www.sonomasoft.com

July 15, 200x •

Mr. Jeffrey M. White
White-Rather Enterprises
1349 Century Boulevard
Wichita Falls, TX 76308

Dear Mr. White:

Subject: Your July 12 Inquiry About WorkZone Software •

• Yes, we do offer personnel record-keeping software specially designed
for small businesses like yours. Here are answers to your three
questions about this software:

• 1. Our WorkZone software provides standard employee forms so that •
you are always in compliance with current government regulations.

2. You receive an interviewer's guide for structured employee interviews,
as well as a scripted format for checking references by telephone.

• 3. Yes, you can update your employees' records easily without the •
need for additional software, hardware, or training.

Our WorkZone software was specially designed to provide you with
expert forms for interviewing, verifying references, recording
attendance, evaluating performance, and tracking the status of your
employees. We even provide you with step-by-step instructions and
suggested procedures. You can treat your employees as if you had a
professional human resources specialist on your staff.

• On page 6 of the enclosed pamphlet, you can read about our WorkZone •
software. To receive a preview copy or to ask questions about its use,
just call 1-800-354-5500. Our specialists are eager to help you
weekdays from 8 to 5 PST. If you prefer, visit our Web site to receive
more information or to place an order.

Sincerely,

Linda DeLorme

Linda DeLorme
Senior Marketing Representative

Enclosure

Side annotations:

Chooses modified block style with date and closing lines started at the center

Identifies previous correspondence and subject

Puts most important information first

Lists answers to sender's questions in order asked

Emphasizes "you" view

Helps reader find information by citing pages

Links sales promotion to reader benefits

Makes it easy to respond

ADJUSTMENT LETTERS

When a company responds favorably to a customer's claim, the response is called an adjustment.

Even the best-run and best-loved businesses occasionally receive claims or complaints from consumers. When a company receives a claim and decides to respond favorably, the letter is called an *adjustment letter*. Most businesses make adjustments promptly—they replace merchandise, refund money, extend discounts, send coupons, and repair goods. Businesses make favorable adjustments to legitimate claims for two reasons. First, consumers are protected by contractual and tort law for recovery of damages. If, for example, you find an insect in a package of frozen peas, the food processor of that package is bound by contractual law to replace it. If you suffer injury, the processor may be liable for damages. Second, and more obviously, most organizations genuinely want to satisfy their customers and retain their business.

Whether selling carpets, computers, or cars, businesses want happy customers. When something goes wrong, most companies try their best to satisfy their customers. Research shows that seven out of ten customers who complain will do business with the company again so long as their concern is handled properly. Adjustment letters respond to customer complaints.

To compete globally and to pump up local markets, most businesses recognize the value of retaining current customers. A survey of financial services companies revealed that the average cost to retain a customer was $57. To recruit a new customer cost a whopping $279. One way to retain customers is to listen to what they have to say—even when it's a complaint. For many reasons, businesses are eager to respond to customer claims and retain the customer's goodwill.

In responding to customer claims, you must first decide whether to grant the claim. Unless the claim is obviously fraudulent or represents an excessive sum, you'll probably grant it. When you say *yes*, your adjustment letter will be good news to the reader, so you'll want to use the direct pattern. When your response is *no*, the indirect pattern might be more appropriate. Chapter 8 discusses the indirect pattern for conveying negative news.

Favorable responses to customer claims follow the direct pattern; unfavorable responses follow the indirect pattern.

In responding to a claim, you have three goals:
- To rectify the wrong, if one exists
- To regain the confidence of the customer
- To promote future business and goodwill

In responding favorably to a claim, use the direct strategy described in the following writing plan:

Writing Plan for Adjustment Letters

- *Subject line:* (optional) Identify the previous correspondence and make a general reference to the main topic.
- *Opening:* Grant the request or announce the adjustment immediately. Include sales promotion if appropriate.
- *Body:* Provide details about how you are complying with the request. Try to regain the customer's confidence; include sales promotion if appropriate.
- *Closing:* End positively with a forward-looking thought; express confidence in future business relations. Avoid referring to unpleasantness.

© COMSTOCK ROYALTY-FREE/COMSTOCK

Revealing Good News in the Opening

Readers want to learn the good news immediately.

Instead of beginning with a review of what went wrong, present the good news immediately. When Amy Hopkins responded to the claim of customer Sound Systems, Inc., about a missing shipment, her first draft, shown at the top of Figure 6.4, was angry. No wonder. Sound Systems had apparently provided the wrong shipping address, and the goods were returned. But once Amy and her company decided to send a second shipment and comply with the customer's claim, she had to give up the anger and strive to retain the goodwill and the business of this customer. The improved version of her letter announces that a new shipment will arrive shortly.

© Ted Goff (www.tedgoff.com)

If you decide to comply with a customer's claim, let the receiver know immediately. Don't begin your letter with a negative statement (*We are very sorry to hear that you are having trouble with your dishwasher*). This approach reminds the reader of the problem and may rekindle the heated emotions or unhappy feelings experienced when the claim was written. Instead, focus on the good news. The following openings for various letters illustrate how to begin a message with good news:

> You're right! We agree that the warranty on your American Standard Model UC600 dishwasher should be extended for six months.

> You will be receiving shortly a new slim Nokia 8860 cell phone to replace the one that shattered when dropped recently.

> Please take your portable Admiral microwave oven to A-1 Appliance Service, 200 Orange Street, Pasadena, where it will be repaired at no cost to you.

> The enclosed check for $325 demonstrates our desire to satisfy our customers and earn their confidence.

Be enthusiastic, not grudging, when making an adjustment.

In announcing that you will make an adjustment, be sure to do so without a grudging tone—even if you have reservations about whether the claim is legitimate. Once you decide to comply with the customer's request, do so happily. Avoid halfhearted or reluctant responses (*Although the American Standard dishwasher works well when used properly, we have decided to allow you to take yours to A-1 Appliance Service for repair at our expense*).

CATHY

Cathy © Cathy Guisewite. Reprinted with permission of Universal Press Syndicate. All rights reserved.

FIGURE 6.4 • **Customer Adjustment Letter**

before revision

Gentlemen:

Fails to reveal good
news immediately and
blames customer

In response to your recent complaint about a missing shipment, it's
very difficult to deliver merchandise when we have been given an
erroneous address.

Creates ugly tone with
negative words and
sarcasm

Our investigators looked into your problem shipment and determined
that it was sent immediately after we received the order. According to
the shipper's records, it was delivered to the warehouse address given
on your stationery: 3590 University Avenue, St. Paul, Minnesota
55114. Unfortunately, no one at that address would accept delivery, so
the shipment was returned to us. I see from your current stationery
that your company has a new address. With the proper address, we
probably could have delivered this shipment.

Sounds grudging and
reluctant in granting
claim

Although we feel that it is entirely appropriate to charge you shipping
and restocking fees, as is our standard practice on returned goods, in
this instance we will waive those fees. We hope this second shipment
finally catches up with you at your current address.

Sincerely,

Amy Hopkins

after revision

E~W~ **ELECTRONIC WAREHOUSE**

930 Abbott Park Place
Providence, RI 02903-5309

Phone: (401) 876-8201
Fax: (401) 876-8345
Web: www.ewarehouse.com

February 21, 200x

Mr. Jeremy Garber
Sound Systems, Inc.
2293 Second Avenue
St. Paul, MN 55120

Dear Mr. Garber:

Uses customer's name
in salutation

Subject: Your February 14 Letter About Your Purchase Order

You should receive by February 25 a second shipment of the speakers, DVDs,
headphones, and other electronic equipment that you ordered January 20.

Announces good news
immediately

The first shipment of this order was delivered January 28 to 3590 University
Avenue, St. Paul, Minnesota 55114. When no one at that address would accept
the shipment, it was returned to us. Now that I have your letter, I see that the
order should have been sent to 2293 Second Avenue, St. Paul, Minnesota 55120.
When an order is undeliverable, we usually try to verify the shipping address
by telephoning the customer. Somehow the return of this shipment was not
caught by our normally painstaking shipping clerks. You can be sure that I will
investigate shipping and return procedures with our clerks immediately to see
whether we can improve existing methods.

Regains confidence of
customer by
explaining what
happened and by
suggesting plans for
improvement

Your respect is important to us, Mr. Garber. Although our rock-bottom
discount prices have enabled us to build a volume business, we don't want to
be so large that we lose touch with valued customers like you. Over the years
our customers' respect has made us successful, and we hope that the prompt
delivery of this shipment will retain yours.

Closes confidently
with genuine appeal
for customer's respect

Sincerely,

Amy Hopkins

Amy Hopkins
Distribution Manager

c: David Cole
    Shipping Department

Explaining Compliance in the Body

Most businesses comply with claims because they want to promote customer goodwill.

In responding to claims, most organizations sincerely want to correct a wrong. They want to do more than just make the customer happy. They want to stand behind their products and services; they want to do what's right.

In the body of the letter, explain how you are complying with the claim. In all but the most routine claims, you should also seek to regain the confidence of the customer. You might reasonably expect that a customer who has experienced difficulty with a product, with delivery, with billing, or with service has lost faith in your organization. Rebuilding that faith is important for future business.

How to rebuild lost confidence depends on the situation and the claim. If procedures need to be revised, explain what changes will be made. If a product has defective parts, tell how the product is being improved. If service is faulty, describe genuine efforts to improve it. Notice in Figure 6.4 that the writer promises to investigate shipping procedures to see whether improvements might prevent future mishaps.

Sometimes the problem is not with the product but with the way it's being used. In other instances customers misunderstand warranties or inadvertently cause delivery and billing mix-ups by supplying incorrect information. Remember that rational and sincere explanations will do much to regain the confidence of unhappy customers.

Because negative words suggest blame and fault, avoid them in letters that attempt to build customer goodwill.

In your explanation avoid emphasizing negative words such as *trouble, regret, misunderstanding, fault, defective, error, inconvenience*, and *unfortunately*. Keep your message positive and upbeat.

Deciding Whether to Apologize

Whether to apologize is a debatable issue. Studies of adjustment letters received by consumers show that a majority do contain apologies, either in the opening or in the closing.[2] Attorneys generally discourage apologies fearing that they admit responsibility and will trigger lawsuits. But an analysis of case outcomes indicates that both judges and juries tend to look on apologies favorably. A few states are even passing laws that protect those who apologize.[3] Some business writing experts advise against apologies, contending that they are counterproductive and merely remind the customer of unpleasantness related to the claim. If, however, it seems natural to you to apologize, do so. People like to hear apologies. It raises their self-esteem, shows the humility of the writer, and acts as a form of "psychological compensation."[4] Don't, however, fall back on the familiar phrase, *I'm sorry for any inconvenience we may have caused*. It sounds mechanical and insincere. Instead, try something like this: *We understand the frustration our delay has caused you, We're sorry you didn't receive better service*, or *You're right to be disappointed*. If you feel that an apology is appropriate, do it early and briefly. Remember, however, that the primary focus of your letter is on (1) how you are complying with the request, (2) how the problem occurred, and (3) how you are working to prevent its recurrence.

Apologize if it seems natural and appropriate.

Using Sensitive Language

The language of adjustment letters must be particularly sensitive, since customers are already upset. Here are some don'ts:

Avoiding negative language retains customer goodwill, and resale information rebuilds customer confidence.

- Don't use negative words (*trouble, regret, misunderstanding, fault, error, inconvenience, you claim*).
- Don't blame customers—even when they may be at fault.
- Don't blame individuals or departments within your organization; it's unprofessional.
- Don't make unrealistic promises; you can't guarantee that the situation will never recur.

To regain the confidence of your reader, consider including resale information. Describe a product's features and any special applications that might appeal to the reader. Promote a new product if it seems appropriate.

Showing Confidence in the Closing

Close an adjustment letter with appreciation, thanks for past business, a desire to be of service, or the promotion of a new product.

End positively by expressing confidence that the problem has been resolved and that continued business relations will result. You might mention the product in a favorable light, suggest a new product, express your appreciation for the customer's business, or anticipate future business. It's often appropriate to refer to the desire to be of service and to satisfy customers. Notice how the following closings illustrate a positive, confident tone:

> You were most helpful in informing us of this situation and permitting us to correct it. We appreciate your thoughtfulness in writing to us.

> Thanks for writing. Your satisfaction is important to us. We hope that this refund check convinces you that service to our customers is our No. 1 priority. Our goals are to earn your confidence and continue to justify that confidence with quality products and excellent service.

> Your flat panel Inspiron 1200 Notebook will come in handy whether you're working at home or on the road. And you can upgrade to a 17-inch display for only $100. Take a look at the enclosed booklet detailing the big savings for essential technology on a budget. We value your business and look forward to your future orders.

LETTERS OF RECOMMENDATION

Letters of recommendation present honest, objective evaluations of individuals and help match candidates to jobs.

Letters of recommendation may be written to nominate people for awards and for membership in organizations. More frequently, though, they are written to evaluate present or former employees. The central concern in these messages is honesty. Thus, you should avoid exaggerating or distorting a candidate's qualifications to cover up weaknesses or to destroy the person's chances. Ethically and legally, you have a duty to the candidate as well as to other employers to describe that person truthfully and objectively. You don't, however, have to endorse everyone who asks. Since recommendations are generally voluntary, you can—and should—resist writing letters for individuals you can't truthfully support. Ask these people to find other recommenders who know them better.

Some businesspeople today refuse to write recommendations for former employees because they fear lawsuits. Other businesspeople argue that recommendations are useless because they're always positive. Despite the general avoidance of

Letters of recommendation make a big difference to employment candidates. Well-written letters help match candidates with jobs. To be safe, writers should focus on information necessary to evaluate job performance.

© COMSTOCK ROYALTY FREE/COMSTOCK

negatives, well-written recommendations do help match candidates with jobs. Hiring companies learn more about a candidate's skills and potential. As a result, they are able to place a candidate properly. Therefore, you should learn to write such letters because you will surely be expected to do so in your future career.

For letters of recommendation, use the direct strategy as described in the following writing plan:

Writing Plan for a Letter of Recommendation

- *Opening:* Identify the applicant, the position, and the reason for writing. State that the message is confidential. Establish your relationship with the applicant. Describe the length of employment or relationship.
- *Body:* Describe job duties. Provide specific examples of the applicant's professional and personal skills and attributes. Compare the applicant with others in his or her field.
- *Closing:* Summarize the significant attributes of the applicant. Offer an overall rating. Draw a conclusion regarding the recommendation.

Identifying the Purpose in the Opening

The opening names the candidate, identifies the purpose, and describes the relationship of the writer.

Begin an employment recommendation by identifying the candidate and the position sought, if you know it. State that your remarks are confidential, and suggest that you are writing at the request of the applicant. Describe your relationship with the candidate, as shown in the first paragraph of the employment recommendation letter in Figure 6.5. Letters that recommend individuals for awards may open with more supportive statements, such as, *I'm very pleased to nominate Robert Walsh for the Employee-of-the-Month award. For the past 16 months, Mr. Walsh served as staff accountant in my division. During that time he distinguished himself by . . . .*

Providing Evidence in the Body

The body of an employment recommendation should describe the candidate's job performance and potential in specific terms.

The body of an employment recommendation should describe the applicant's job performance and potential. Employers are particularly interested in such traits as communication skills, organizational skills, people skills, the ability to work with a team, the ability to work independently, honesty, dependability, ambition, loyalty, and initiative. In describing these traits, be sure to back them up with evidence. One of the biggest weaknesses in letters of recommendation is that writers tend to make global, nonspecific statements (*He was careful and accurate* versus *He completed eight financial statements monthly with about 99 percent accuracy*). Employers prefer definite, task-related descriptions, as shown in the second and third paragraphs of Figure 6.5.

Be especially careful to support any negative comments with verification (not *He was slower than other customer service reps* but *He answered 18 calls an hour, whereas most service reps average 30 calls an hour*). In reporting deficiencies, be sure to describe behavior (*her last two reports were late and had to be rewritten by her supervisor*) rather than evaluate it (*she is unreliable and her reports are careless*).

Evaluating in the Closing

The closing presents an overall evaluation and may encourage a telephone call.

In the final paragraph of a recommendation, you should offer an overall evaluation. Indicate how you would rank this person in relation to others in similar positions. Many managers add a statement indicating whether they would rehire the applicant, given the chance. If you are strongly supportive, summarize the candidate's best qualities. In the closing you might also offer to answer questions by telephone. Such a statement, though, could suggest that the candidate has weak skills and that you will make damaging statements orally but not in print.

General letters of recommendation, written when the candidate has no specific position in mind, often begin with the salutation TO PROSPECTIVE EMPLOYERS. More

FIGURE 6.5 ──────── • **Employment Recommendation Letter**

ST. ELIZABETH'S HOSPITAL

2404 Euclid Avenue
Cleveland, OH 44414-2900
216-439-8700
ww.stelizabeth.com

February 21, 200x

Vice President, Human Resources
Healthcare Enterprises
3529 Springfield Street
Cincinnati, OH 45890

Illustrates
simplified letter
style ──────── • RECOMMENDATION OF LANCE W. OLIVER

Identifies ──────── • At the request of Lance W. Oliver, I submit this confidential information in   •──────── Mentions
applicant and   support of his application for the position of assistant director in your Human   confidentiality
position   Resources Department. Mr. Oliver served under my supervision as assistant   of message
                        director of Guest Relations at St. Elizabeth's Hospital for the past three years.   •──────── Tells
                                                                                                              relationship to
                                                                                                              writer
                        • Mr. Oliver was in charge of many customer service programs for our 770-bed
                        hospital. A large part of his job involved monitoring and improving patient
                        satisfaction. Because of his personable nature and superior people skills, he got
Supports general   along well with fellow employees, patients, and physicians. His personnel record
qualities with ────   includes a number of "Gotcha" citations, given to employees caught in the act of
specific details   performing exemplary service.

                        • Mr. Oliver works well with a team, as evidenced by his participation on the
                        steering committee to develop our "Service First Every Day" program. His most
                        significant contributions to our hospital, though, came as a result of his own   Describes and
                        creativity and initiative. He developed and implemented a patient hotline to   interprets
                        hear complaints and resolve problems immediately. This enormously successful •─────── accomplish-
                        telephone service helped us improve our patient satisfaction rating from 7.2   ments
                        last year to 8.4 this year. That's the highest rating in our history, and
                        Mr. Oliver deserves a great deal of the credit.

Summarizes ────   • We're sorry to lose Mr. Oliver, but we recognize his desire to advance his
main points and   career. I am confident that his resourcefulness, intelligence, and enthusiasm
offers evaluation   will make him successful in your organization. I recommend him without
                        reservation.

                        Mary E. O'Rourke

                        MARY E. O'ROURKE, DIRECTOR, GUEST RELATIONS

                        MEO:rtd

Tips for Writing Letters of Recommendation
- Identify the purpose and confidentiality of the message.
- Establish your relationship with the applicant.
- Describe the length of employment and job duties, if relevant.
- Provide specific examples of the applicant's professional and personal skills.
- Compare the applicant with others in the same field.
- Offer an overall rating of the applicant.
- Summarize the significant attributes of the applicant.
- Draw a conclusion regarding the recommendation.

specific recommendations, to support applications to known positions, adc̲
individual. When the addressee's name is unknown, consider using the simplified letter format, shown in Figure 6.5, which avoids a salutation.

WRITING WINNING GOODWILL MESSAGES

Written goodwill messages carry more meaning than ready-made cards.

Goodwill messages, which include thanks, recognition, and sympathy, seem to intim-
idate many communicators. Finding the right words to express feelings is sometimes
more difficult than writing ordinary business documents. Writers tend to procrastinate
when it comes to goodwill messages, or else they send a ready-made card or pick up
the telephone. Remember, though, that the personal sentiments of the sender are always more expressive and more meaningful to readers than are printed cards or oral
messages. Taking the time to write gives more importance to our well-wishing. Personal notes also provide a record that can be reread, savored, and treasured.

Messages that express thanks, recognition, and sympathy should be written promptly.

In expressing thanks, recognition, or sympathy, you should always do so
promptly. These messages are easier to write when the situation is fresh in your mind.
They also mean more to the recipient. What's more, a prompt thank-you note carries
the hidden message that you care and that you consider the event to be important.
You will learn to write four kinds of goodwill messages—thanks, congratulations, praise,
and sympathy. Instead of writing plans for each of them, we recommend that you concentrate on the five Ss. Goodwill messages should be:

- **Selfless.** Be sure to focus the message solely on the receiver, not the sender.
  Don't talk about yourself; avoid such comments as *I remember when I . . . .*
- **Specific.** Personalize the message by mentioning specific incidents or characteristics of the receiver. Telling a colleague *Great speech* is much less effective
  than *Great story about McDonald's marketing in Moscow.* Take care to verify
  names and other facts.
- **Sincere.** Let your words show genuine feelings. Rehearse in your mind how you
  would express the message to the receiver orally. Then transform that conversational language to your written message. Avoid pretentious, formal, or flowery
  language (*It gives me great pleasure to extend felicitations on the occasion of
  your firm's twentieth anniversary*).
- **Spontaneous.** Keep the message fresh and enthusiastic. Avoid canned phrases
  (*Congratulations on your promotion, Good luck in the future*). Strive for directness and naturalness, not creative brilliance.
- **Short.** Although goodwill messages can be as long as needed, try to accomplish your purpose in only a few sentences. What is most important is remembering an individual. Such caring does not require documentation or
  wordiness. Individuals and business organizations often use special note
  cards or stationery for brief messages.

Thanks

When someone has done you a favor or when an action merits praise, you need to extend thanks or show appreciation. Letters of appreciation may be written to customers
for their orders, to hosts and hostesses for their hospitality, to individuals for kindnesses
performed, and especially to customers who complain. After all, complainers are actually providing you with free consulting reports from the field. Complainers who feel
that they were listened to often become the greatest promoters of an organization.[5]

Send letters of thanks to customers, hosts, and individuals who have performed kind acts.

Because the receiver will be pleased to hear from you, you can open directly
with the purpose of your message. The letter in Figure 6.6 thanks a speaker who addressed a group of marketing professionals. Although such thank-you notes can be
quite short, this one is a little longer because the writer wants to lend importance to
the receiver's efforts. Notice that every sentence relates to the receiver and offers

FIGURE 6.6   • **Favor Thank-you**

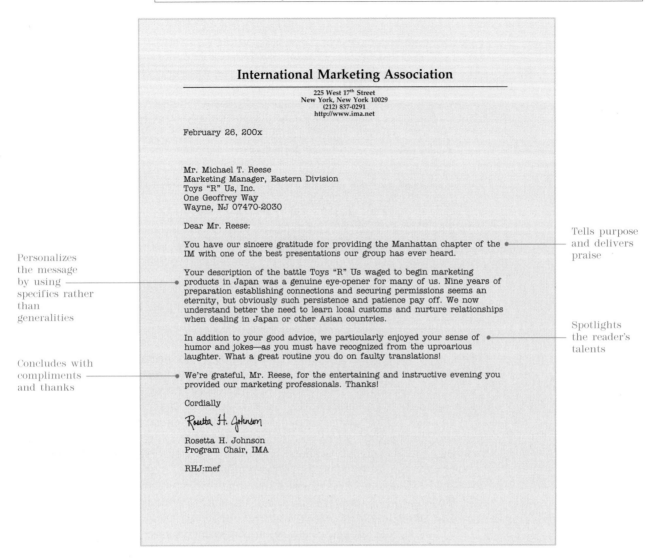

International Marketing Association

225 West 17th Street
New York, New York 10029
(212) 837-0291
http://www.ima.net

February 26, 200x

Mr. Michael T. Reese
Marketing Manager, Eastern Division
Toys "R" Us, Inc.
One Geoffrey Way
Wayne, NJ 07470-2030

Dear Mr. Reese:

You have our sincere gratitude for providing the Manhattan chapter of the
IM with one of the best presentations our group has ever heard.

Your description of the battle Toys "R" Us waged to begin marketing
products in Japan was a genuine eye-opener for many of us. Nine years of
preparation establishing connections and securing permissions seems an
eternity, but obviously such persistence and patience pay off. We now
understand better the need to learn local customs and nurture relationships
when dealing in Japan or other Asian countries.

In addition to your good advice, we particularly enjoyed your sense of
humor and jokes—as you must have recognized from the uproarious
laughter. What a great routine you do on faulty translations!

We're grateful, Mr. Reese, for the entertaining and instructive evening you
provided our marketing professionals. Thanks!

Cordially

Rosetta H. Johnson

Rosetta H. Johnson
Program Chair, IMA

RHJ:mef

Personalizes the message by using specifics rather than generalities

Concludes with compliments and thanks

Tells purpose and delivers praise

Spotlights the reader's talents

---

enthusiastic praise. By using the receiver's name along with contractions and positive words, the writer makes the letter sound warm and conversational.

Should you use e-mail or e-cards to send goodwill messages? Although electronic messages may be acceptable for close friends or in isolated instances, goodwill messages sent by land mail are much better. Recently an employee wrote to etiquette maven Miss Manners. He said that he had been invited to the home of his boss for a formal dinner. He thanked his boss by sending him an e-card. Later he noticed that his boss seemed remote. Miss Manners asked whether the boss had served him dinner out of a can. If not, then why send him a canned thank-you?

Personally written notes that show appreciation and express thanks are significant to their receivers. In expressing thanks, you generally write a short note on special notepaper or heavy card stock. It's acceptable to print the message on a computer, perhaps in a script font, but use special paper. The following messages provide models for expressing thanks for a gift, for a favor, and for hospitality.

E-mail and e-cards are inappropriate for serious thank-you and other goodwill messages.

To Express Thanks for a Gift

Thanks, Laura, to you and the other members of the department for honoring me with the elegant Waterford crystal vase at the party celebrating my twentieth anniversary with the company.

Identify the gift, tell why you appreciate it, and explain how you will use it.

The height and shape of the vase are perfect to hold roses and other bouquets from my garden. Each time I fill it, I'll remember your thoughtfulness in choosing this lovely gift for me.

To Send Thanks for a Favor

Tell what the favor means using sincere, simple statements.

I sincerely appreciate your filling in for me last week when I was too ill to attend the planning committee meeting for the spring exhibition.

Without your participation much of my preparatory work would have been lost. It's comforting to know that competent and generous individuals like you are part of our team, Mark. Moreover, it's my very good fortune to be able to count you as a friend. I'm grateful to you.

To Extend Thanks for Hospitality

Compliment the fine food, charming surroundings, warm hospitality, excellent host and hostess, and good company.

Jeffrey and I want you to know how much we enjoyed the dinner party for our department that you hosted Saturday evening. Your charming home and warm hospitality, along with the lovely dinner and sinfully delicious chocolate dessert, combined to create a truly memorable evening.

Most of all, though, we appreciate your kindness in cultivating togetherness in our department. Thanks, Jennifer, for being such a special person.

Goodwill Response

Take the time to respond to any goodwill message you may receive.

Should you respond when you receive a congratulatory note or a written pat on the back? By all means! These messages are attempts to connect personally; they are efforts to reach out, to form professional and/or personal bonds. Failing to respond to notes of congratulations and most other goodwill messages is like failing to say "You're welcome" when someone says "Thank you." Responding to such messages is simply the right thing to do. Do avoid, though, minimizing your achievements with comments that suggest that you don't really deserve the praise or that the sender is exaggerating your good qualities.

To Answer a Congratulatory Note

Thanks for your kind words regarding my award, and thanks, too, for sending me the newspaper clipping. I truly appreciate your thoughtfulness and warm wishes.

To Respond to a Pat on the Back

Your note about my work made me feel good. I'm grateful for your thoughtfulness.

Sympathy

Sympathy notes should refer to the misfortune sensitively and offer assistance.

Most of us can bear misfortune and grief more easily when we know that others care. Notes expressing sympathy, though, are probably more difficult to write than any other kind of message. Commercial "In sympathy" cards make the task easier—but they are far less meaningful. Grieving friends want to know what you think—not what Hallmark's card writers think. To help you get started, you can always glance through cards expressing sympathy. They will supply ideas about the kinds of thoughts you might wish to convey in your own words. In writing a sympathy note, (1) refer to the death or misfortune sensitively, using words that show you understand what a crushing blow it is; (2) in the case of a death, praise the deceased in a personal way; (3) offer assistance without going into excessive detail; and (4) end on a reassuring, forward-looking note. Sympathy messages may be typed, although handwriting seems more personal. In either case, use notepaper or personal stationery.

In condolence notes mention the loss tactfully and recognize the good qualities of the deceased.

Assure the receiver of your concern. Offer assistance.

Conclude on a positive, reassuring note.

To Express Condolences

We are deeply saddened, Gayle, to learn of the death of your husband. Warren's kind nature and friendly spirit endeared him to all who knew him. He will be missed.

Although words seem empty in expressing our grief, we want you to know that your friends at QuadCom extend their profound sympathy to you. If we may help you or lighten your load in any way, you have but to call.

We know that the treasured memories of your many happy years together, along with the support of your family and many friends, will provide strength and comfort in the months ahead.

SUMMING UP AND LOOKING FORWARD

In this chapter you learned to write letters that request information, make direct claims, respond favorably to information requests, and make adjustments. You also learned to write letters of recommendation and a variety of goodwill messages. All of these everyday business messages use the direct strategy. They open immediately with the main idea followed by details and explanations. Not all messages, however, are straightforward. In the next chapter you'll learn to use the indirect pattern when you must be persuasive.

CRITICAL THINKING

1. A recent article in a professional magazine carried this headline: "Is Letter Writing Dead?"[6] How would you respond to such a question?

2. Which is more effective in claim letters—anger or objectivity? Why?

3. Is it insensitive to include resale or sales promotion information in an adjustment letter?

4. Why is it important to regain the confidence of a customer when you respond to a claim letter?

5. Is it appropriate for businesspeople to write goodwill messages expressing thanks, recognition, and sympathy to business acquaintances? Why or why not?

CHAPTER REVIEW

6. Under what conditions is it important to send business letters rather than e-mail messages?

7. What determines whether you write a letter directly or indirectly?

8. What are the two most important positions in a letter?

9. List two ways that you could begin a direct inquiry letter that asks many questions.

10. What three elements are appropriate in the closing of a request for information?

11. What is a claim letter? Give an original example.

12. What are the three goals of a writer of an adjustment letter?

13. Why do some companies comply with nearly all claims?

14. What information should the opening in a letter of recommendation include?

15. The best goodwill messages include what five characteristics?

WRITING IMPROVEMENT EXERCISES

Letter-Opening Choices
Your Task. Indicate which of the following entries represents an effective direct opening.

16. a. Will you please allow me to introduce myself. I am Daryl Davidson, and I am assistant to the director of Human Resources at MicroSynergy. Our company has an intranet, which we would like to use more efficiently to elicit feedback on employee issues and concerns. I understand that you have a software product called "Opinionware" that might do this, and I need to ask you some questions about it.
    b. Please answer the following questions about your software product "Opinionware," which we are considering for our intranet.   _____

17. a. Thank you for your e-mail of March 22 in which you inquired about the availability of a CD burner and DVD combo drive.   _____
    b. We have on hand an ample supply of CD burner/DVD combo drives.

18. a. Yes, the next Michigan Computer Show featuring the latest computer hardware and software will be held in the Gibraltar Trade Center from April 15–18.   _____
    b. This will acknowledge receipt of your inquiry of December 2 in which you ask about the next Michigan Computer Show.

19. a. Your letter of July 26 requesting a refund has been referred to me because Mr. Avila is away from the office.
    b. Your refund check for $175 is enclosed.

Direct Openings

Your Task. Revise the following openings so that they are more direct. Add information if necessary.

20. My name is Brandon Brockway, and I am assistant to the manager of Information Services & Technology at HealthCentral, Inc. Our company needs to do a better job of integrating human resources and payroll functions. I understand that you have a software product called "HRFocus" that might do this, and I need to ask you some questions about it.

21. Anderson Associates has undertaken a management initiative to pursue an internship program. I have been appointed as the liaison person to conduct research regarding our proposed program. We are fully aware of the benefits of a strong internship program, and our management team is eager to take advantage of some of these benefits. We would be deeply appreciative if you would be kind enough to help me out with answers to a number of specific questions.

22. Your letter of March 4 has been referred to me. Pursuant to your inquiry, I have researched your question in regard to whether or not we offer our European-style patio umbrella in colors. This unique umbrella is one of our most popular items. Its 10-foot canopy protects you when the sun is directly overhead, but it also swivels and tilts to virtually any angle for continuous sun protection all day long. It comes in two colors: cream and forest green.

23. Pursuant to your inquiry of June 14, which was originally sent to *Classic Motorcycle Magazine*, I am happy to respond to you. In your letter you ask about the tire choices for the Superbike and Superstock teams competing at the Honda Superbike Classic in Alabama. As you noted, the track temperatures reached above 125 degrees and the new asphalt surface had an abrasive effect on tires. With the added heat and reduced grip, nearly all of the riders in the competition selected Dunlop Blue Groove hard compound front and rear tires.

24. I am pleased to receive your inquiry regarding the possibility of my acting as a speaker at the final semester meeting of your business management club meeting on May 2. The topic of online résumés interests me and is one on which I think I could impart helpful information to your members. Therefore, I am responding in the affirmative to your kind invitation.

25. Thank you for your recent order of February 4. We are sure your customers and employees will love the high-quality Color-Block Sweatshirts with an 80/20 cotton/polyester blend that you ordered from our spring catalog. Your order is currently being processed and should leave our warehouse in Iowa in mid-February. We use UPS for all deliveries in southern California. Because you ordered sweatshirts with your logo embroidered in a two-tone combination, your order cannot be shipped until February 18. You should not expect it until about February 20.

26. We have just received your letter of October 3 regarding the unfortunate troubles you are having with your Premier DVD player. In your letter you ask if you may send the flawed DVD player to us for inspection. It is our normal practice to handle all service requests through our local dealers. However, in your circumstance we are willing to take a look at your unit here at our Columbus plant. Therefore, please send it to us so that we may determine what's wrong.

Closing Paragraph
Your Task. The following concluding paragraph to a claim letter response suffers from faults in strategy, tone, and emphasis. Revise and improve.

27. As a result of your complaint of November 3, we are sending a replacement shipment of PC power packs by BigDog Express. Unfortunately, this shipment will not reach you until November 10. We hope that you will not allow this troubling incident and the resulting inconvenience and lost sales you suffered to jeopardize our future business relations. In the past we have been able to provide you with quality products and prompt service.

WRITING COACH
STEP-BY-STEP DEMONSTRATION

Direct Request Letter

Problem

As the office manager at Earth Systems, you are responsible for equipment. The operations chief, Eric Young, sits down at your desk and says, "Look, we've just received a notice from our insurance carrier telling us that we have to secure our office equipment or else our rates will increase. How many pieces of equipment do we have? Can you get some figures on how much this will cost?" Counting the computers in private offices, you figure that the company has 18 workstations consisting of computers, monitors, and keyboards plus 12 printers. But you are worried about installing security devices that might tie the computers to desktops and make it impossible to move them around. You realize, of course, that office theft can be a problem. After checking local sources for security devices, you decide to write to a national supplier, Micro Supplies and Software, to get an estimate.

before revision

Address receiver by name if possible

Dear Sirs:

~~Our insurance rates will be increased in the near future if we don't install security devices on our computer equipment. We have considered some local suppliers, but none had exactly what we wanted. That's why I am writing to see if you can~~ Please provide information and recommendations regarding security equipment to prevent theft of office computers and printers.

Open directly, not with, background and explanations

Our office now has 18 computer workstations along with
12
twelve printers. ~~We need a device~~ that ~~can be used~~ to secure we must
~~separate computer components~~ to desks or counters. Would ① What device
you ~~please~~ recommend a ~~device that can~~ secure a to
workstation consisting of a computer, monitor, and keyboard?
② Are
~~We wonder if~~ professionals ~~are~~ needed to install your security
devices and to remove them? ~~We're also interested in whether~~ ③ Can
the devices ~~can~~ be easily removed when we need to move
④ What is
equipment around? ~~We are, of course, very interested in~~ the
? Do you offer   ? If so,
price of each device? ~~What about~~ quantity discounts? ~~if you~~
how much?
~~offer them.~~

Need statement introducing list

Enumerate questions in parallel form

Thanks for   ing   so that we can
~~If you could~~ respond before February 15? ~~I would appreciate it
very much. This would help us~~ meet a deadline of April 1 from
our insurance carrier. ~~Thank you for your attention to this
matter.~~

Close concisely with thanks and end date

Sincerely,

Writing Plan

OPENING

Ask the most important question first or express a polite command.

The purpose of this letter is to request information about security devices. The primary audience will be staff members at a company that wants to sell such devices, so a direct approach is appropriate.

BODY

Explain the request logically and courteously. Ask other questions if necessary.

Before writing the letter, you need to inventory the current equipment and decide what questions to ask. The questions should be organized into a logical sequence.

CLOSING

Request a specific action with an end date, if appropriate, and show appreciation.

Decide how soon the information is needed to meet the insurance deadline.

---

after revision

EARTH SYSTEMS

Geotechnical Engineers	www.earthsystems.com	(805) 558-8791
4439 Hitchcock Way	Ventura, CA 93105	

January 28, 200x

Mr. Jeff Lee, Customer Service
Micro Supplies and Software
P.O. Box 6418
Fort Atkinson, WI 53538

Dear Mr. Lee:

Please provide information and recommendations regarding security equipment to prevent theft of office computers and printers.

Our office now has 18 computer workstations and 12 printers that we must secure to desks or counters. Answers to the following questions will help us select the best devices for our purposes:

1. What device would you recommend to secure a workstation consisting of a computer, monitor, and keyboard?

2. Are professionals needed to install your security devices and remove them?

3. Can the devices be easily removed when we need to move equipment around?

4. What is the price of each device? Do you offer quantity discounts? If so, how much?

Thanks for responding before February 15 so that we can meet an April 1 deadline from our insurance carrier.

Sincerely,

Deanna Gomez

Deanna Gomez
Office Manager

WRITING IMPROVEMENT CASES

6.1 Direct Request: Las Vegas Conference

The following letter from Brianna Phelps inquires about conference facilities in Las Vegas. Her first draft must be revised.

Your Task. Analyze Brianna's letter. It suffers from many writing faults that you have studied. List its weaknesses and then outline an appropriate writing plan. If your instructor directs, revise the letter.

Current date

Meeting Manager
The Venetian
3355 Las Vegas Boulevard
Las Vegas, NV 89109

Dear Sir:

My name is Brianna Phelps, and I am a recently hired member of the Marketing and Special Events Division of my company, Cynergy. I have been given the assignment of making initial inquiries for the purpose of arranging our next marketing meeting. Pursuant to this assignment, I am writing to you. We would like to find a resort hotel with conference facilities, and we have heard excellent things about The Venetian.

Our marketing meeting will require banquet facilities where we can all be together, but we will also need at least four meeting rooms that are small in size. Each of these rooms should accommodate in the neighborhood of 75. We hope to arrange our conference October 23–27, and we expect about 250 sales associates. Most of our associates will be flying in, so I'm interested in transportation to and from the airport.

Does The Venetian have public address systems in the meeting rooms? Due to the fact that we will be making electronic presentations, how about audio-visual equipment and computer facilities for presentations?
I am also interested in learning whether the Sands Convention Center is part of The Venetian. Thank you for your cooperation.

Sincerely,

1.   List at least five specific weaknesses in Brianna's letter.

2.   Outline a writing plan for an information request.
     Opening:
     Body:
     Closing:

6.2 Direct Reply: McDonald's Goes Green

Fast-food giant McDonald's is often accused of generating excessive litter and abusing the environment with its packaging and products. It receives letters from consumers asking what it is doing to reduce waste and improve the environment.

Your Task. As part of a group of interns at McDonald's, you are to revise the following rough draft of an information response letter to be sent to people inquiring about the company's environmental policies and practices. Analyze the letter and list at least five weaknesses. What writing plan should this letter follow? If your instructor agrees, revise it. Add an appropriate subject line and any additional information you know about McDonald's environmental practices.

Current date

Ms. Julie Kahn
176 Prospect Avenue
Elmhurst, IL 60126

Dear Ms. Kahn:

This is in response to your inquiry about McDonald's environmental policies. As a leader in the fast-food industry, reducing waste and conserving the environment are extremely important to those of us here at McDonald's. Since it began working with the Environmental Defense Fund 80 percent of its restaurant waste stream has been eliminated by McDonald's. McDonald's is reducing it's impact on landfills and world resources. McDonald's have introduced a number of practices that are environmentally-friendly.

For one thing, we are developing new packaging. In fact, we have reduced our polystyrene use by 90 percent. Another thing we are doing is increasing recycling. Our suppliers are using corrugated boxes with at least 35 percent recycled content. Reusable salad lids and shipping pallets, bulk condiment dispensers, and refillable coffee mugs are being tested. Another thing we are doing has to do with composting. More of our restaurants are experimenting with compositing egg shells, coffee grounds, and food scraps. Another thing we are doing has to do with reduced waste. All of our suppliers must meet new waste-reduction goals. And restaurant crews have been retrained to give waste reduction equal priority with quality quickness and cleanliness.

As you can see, McDonald's cares about preserving the earths resources for today. And for the future. We think we are doing a great job in our commitment to conservation. But you can see for yourself by visiting your local McDonald's We hope you will use the enclosed sandwich coupons and experience first hand the changes we're making at McDonald's.

Sincerely,

1.   List at least five weaknesses in the preceding letter.

2.   Outline a writing plan for an information response.
     Subject line:
     Opening:
     Body:

     Closing:

6.3 Claim Letter: Disturbed by Rental Car Charges

Your Task. Analyze the following poorly written letter. List its weaknesses, and outline a writing plan. If your instructor directs, revise the letter.

Current date

Mr. Sergio Harris, Manager
Customer Service
Avon Car Rentals
6501 King Lawrence Road
Raleigh, NC 27607

Dear Customer Service Manager Sergio Harris,

This is to inform you that you can't have it both ways. Either you provide customers with cars with full gas tanks or you don't. And if you don't, you shouldn't charge them when they return with empty tanks!

In view of the fact that I picked up a car in Raleigh August 22 with an empty tank, I had to fill it immediately. Then I drove it until August 25. When I returned to Charlotte, I naturally let the tank go nearly empty, since that is the way I received the car in Raleigh.

But your attendant in Charlotte charged me to fill the tank—$46.50 (premium gasoline at premium prices)! Although I explained to him that I had received it with an empty tank, he kept telling me that company policy required that he charge for a fill-up. My total bill came to $466.50, which, you must agree, is a lot of money for a rental period of only three days. I have the signed rental agreement and a receipt showing that I paid the full amount and that it included $46.50 for a gas fill-up when I returned the car.

Inasmuch as my company is a new customer and inasmuch as we had hoped to use your agency for our future car rentals because of your competitive rates, I trust that you will give this matter your prompt attention.

Disappointedly yours,

1. List at least five weaknesses.

2. Outline a writing plan for a claim.
    Opening:
    Body:

    Closing:

ACTIVITIES AND CASES

6.4 Direct Request: Conference at the Fabulous Paris Las Vegas

Your company, Vortex Enterprises, has just had an enormously successful two-year sales period. CEO Kenneth Richardson has asked you, as marketing manager, to arrange a fabulous conference/retreat. "This will be a giant thank-you gift for all 75 of our engineers, product managers, and salespeople," he says. Warming up to the idea, he says, "I want the company to host a four-day combination sales conference/vacation/ retreat at some spectacular location. Let's begin by inquiring at Paris Las Vegas. I hear it's awesome!" You check its Web site and find some general information. However, you decide to write a letter so that you can have a permanent, formal record of all the resorts you investigate. You estimate that your company will require about 75 rooms—preferably with a view of the Strip. You'll also need about three conference rooms for

one and a half days. You want to know room rates, conference facilities, and entertainment possibilities for families. The CEO gave you two possible times: July 8–12 or August 18–22. You know that these are off-peak times, and you wonder whether you can get a good room rate. What entertainment will be showing at Paris Las Vegas during these times? One evening the CEO will want to host a banquet for about 140 people. Oh yes, he wants a report from you by March 1.

Your Task: Write a well-organized information request to Ms. Nancy Mercado, Manager, Convention Services, Paris Las Vegas, 281 Paris Drive, Las Vegas, NV 87551. Spell out your needs and conclude with a logical end date.

6.5 Direct Request: Informational Interview

You want to learn more about careers in your field, and you've found someone who is willing to talk to you. The manager you selected is a busy person, and he will try to work a personal interview into his schedule. However, in case he can't meet you in person, he would like to have your questions in letter form so that he could answer them in a telephone conversation if necessary.

Your Task. Write an information request to a real or hypothetical person in a company where you would like to work. If you want to start your own business, write to someone who has done it. Assume that the person has agreed to talk with you, but you haven't set a date. To learn more about informational interviews and how to write questions, look at the "Checklist for Conducting Informational and Other Interviews." It can be found at **Guffey Xtra!** in the online chapter, "Employment and Other Interviewing." Use your imagination in creating five to eight interview questions. Be sure to show appreciation.

TEAM

6.6 Direct Request: Beach Bike Rentals Seeks Web Exposure

As the successful co-owners of Beach Bike Rentals, you and your partner decide that you need a Web site to attract even more business to your resort location. Primarily you rent bicycles and surreys to tourists visiting hotels along the beach. In addition, you carry tandems, pedal go-carts, mountain bikes, slingshot and chopper trikes, and other unique bikes, as well as inline skates.

Business is good at your sunny beachside location, but a Web site would provide 24-hour information and attract a wider audience. The trouble is that you don't know anything about creating, hosting, or maintaining a Web site. Your partner has heard of a local company called Spiderside Web Production, and you decide to inquire about creating a Web site. You and he prefer to write a letter so that you can work on your questions together and create a unified, orderly presentation.

Your Task. In teams of two or three, prepare an information request with logical questions about designing, hosting, and maintaining a Web site for a small business. You are not expected to create the content of the site. That will come later. Instead you want to ask questions about how a Web site is developed. You know for sure that you want a page that invites resort and hotel operators to feature your fun-filled facilities at their sites, but you don't know how to go about it. Address your letter to Richard Wolziac, Spiderside Web Production, 927 El Fuerte Boulevard, Carlsbad, CA 92008. Be sure to include an end date and a reason.

6.7 Direct Request: Krispy Kreme Bake Sale

You've always loved Krispy Kreme doughnuts, so you were delighted to learn that they are now being sold in a nearby shopping center. You also heard that they can be used in fund-raising events. As chair of the spring fund-raising committee for Noah's Ark Children's Center, you need to find out more about how Krispy Kreme's fund-raising partnership works. Do you hold a traditional bake sale or what? How do you make any money if you sell the doughnuts at their regular retail price? You looked at the company's Web site and got basic information. You're still unclear about how certificates work in fund-raising. And what about Krispy Kreme partnership cards? You left a brief note at the Krispy Kreme Web site, but you didn't get a response. Now you decide to write.

Your Task. Compose a letter asking specific questions about how you can partner with Krispy Kreme in raising funds. Use your return address in a personal business letter style (see Figure 6.2). Send your letter to Customer Relations, Krispy Kreme Doughnut Corporation, P.O. Box 83, Winston-Salem, NC 27103. You need feedback by March 1 if you are to use Krispy Kreme in your spring fund-raising event. How do you want Krispy Kreme to respond?

WEB

6.8 Direct Request: Computer Code of Conduct

As an assistant in the campus computer laboratory, you have been asked by your boss to help write a code of conduct for use of the laboratory facilities. This code will spell out what behavior and activities are allowed in your lab. The first thing you are to do is conduct a search of the Internet to see what other college or university computing labs have written as conduct codes.

Your Task. Using at least two search engines, search the Web employing variations of the keywords "Computer Code of Conduct." Print two or three codes that seem appropriate. Write a letter (or an e-mail message, if your instructor agrees) to the director of an educational computer laboratory asking for further information about its code and its effectiveness. Include at least five significant questions. Attach your printouts to your letter.

6.9 Direct Claim: Headaches From "No Surprise" Offer

As vice president of Breakaway Travel Service, you are angry with Virtuoso Enterprises. Virtuoso is a catalog company that provides imprinted promotional products for companies. Your travel service was looking for something special to offer in promoting its cruise ship travel packages. Virtuoso offered free samples of its promotional merchandise, under its "No Surprise" policy.

You figured, what could you lose? So on February 5 you placed a telephone order for a number of samples. These included an insulated lunch sack, an AM-FM travel radio, a square-ended barrel bag with fanny pack, as well as a deluxe canvas attaché case and two colors of garment-dyed sweatshirts. All items were supposed to be free. You did think it odd that you were asked for your company's MasterCard credit number, but Virtuoso promised to bill you only if you kept the samples.

When the items arrived, you were not pleased, and you returned them all on February 11 (you have a postal receipt showing the return). But your March credit statement showed a charge of $229.13 for the sample items. You called Virtuoso in March and spoke to Rachel, who assured you that a credit would be made on your next statement. However, your April statement showed no credit. You called again and received a similar promise. It's now May and no credit has been made. You decide to write and demand action.

Your Task. Write a claim letter that documents the problem and states the action that you want taken. Add any information you feel is necessary. Address your letter to Ms. Paula Loveday, Customer Services, Virtuoso Enterprises, 420 Ninth Street South, LaCrosse, WI 54602.

6.10 Direct Claim: This Desk Is Going Back

As the founder and president of a successful consulting firm, you decided to splurge and purchase a fine executive desk for your own office. You ordered an expensive desk described as "North American white oak embellished with hand-inlaid walnut cross-banding." Although you would not ordinarily purchase large, expensive items by mail, you were impressed by the description of this desk and by the money-back guarantee promised in the catalog.

When the desk arrived, you knew that you had made a mistake. The wood finish was rough, the grain looked splotchy, and many of the drawers would not pull out easily. The advertisement had promised "full suspension, silent ball-bearing drawer slides."

Your Task. Because you are disappointed with the desk, you decide to send it back, taking advantage of the money-back guarantee. Write a claim letter to Patrick Dwiggens, Operations Manager, Premier Wood Products, P.O. Box 528, High Point, NC 27261, asking for your money back. You're not sure whether the freight charges can be refunded, but it's worth a try. Supply any details needed.

6.11 Direct Claim: Backing Out of Project Management Seminar

Ace Executive Training Institute offered a seminar titled "Enterprise Project Management Protocol" that sounded terrific. It promised to teach project managers how to estimate work, report status, write work packages, and cope with project conflicts. Because your company often is engaged in large cross-functional projects, it decided to send four key managers to the seminar to be held June 1–2 at the Ace headquarters in Pittsburgh. The fee was $2,200 each, and it was paid in advance. About six weeks before the seminar, you learned that three of the managers would be tied up in projects that would not be completed in time for them to attend.

Your Task. On your company letterhead, write a claim letter to Addison O'Neill, Registrar, Ace Executive Training Institute, 5000 Forbes Avenue, Pittsburgh, PA 15244. Ask that the seminar fees for three employees be returned because they cannot attend. Give yourself a title and supply any details necessary.

6.12 Direct Claim: A Matter of Mismeasurement

As the owner of Custom Designs, you recently completed a living room remodel that required double-glazed, made-to-order oak French doors. You ordered them, by telephone, on April 14 from Capitol Lumber and Hardware. When they arrived on May 18, your carpenter gave you the bad news: the doors were cut too small. Instead of measuring a total of 11 feet 8 inches, the doors measured 11 feet 4 inches. In your carpenter's words, "No way can I stretch those doors to fit these openings!" You waited nearly five weeks for these doors, and your clients wanted them installed immediately. Your carpenter said, "I can rebuild this opening for you, but I'm going to have to charge you for my time." His extra charge came to $376.

You feel that the people at Capitol Lumber should reimburse you for this amount because it was their error. In fact, you actually saved them a bundle of money by not returning the doors. You decide to write to Capitol Lumber and enclose a copy of your carpenter's bill. You wonder whether you should also include a copy of Capitol Lumber's invoice, even though it does not show the exact door measurements. You are a good customer of Capitol Lumber and Hardware, having used their quality doors, windows, and hardware on many other remodeling jobs. You're confident that it will grant this claim.

Your Task. Write a claim letter to Sal Rodriguez, Sales Manager, Capitol Lumber and Hardware, 3568 East Washington Avenue, Indianapolis, IN 46204.

6.13 Direct Claim: The Real Thing

Let's face it. Like most consumers, you've probably occasionally been unhappy with service or with products you have used.

Your Task. Select a product or service that has disappointed you. Write a claim letter requesting a refund, replacement, explanation, or whatever seems reasonable. Generally, such letters are addressed to customer service departments. For claims about food products, be sure to include bar-code identification from the package, if possible. Your instructor may ask you to actually mail this letter. Remember that smart companies want to know what their customers think, especially if a product could be improved. Give your ideas for improvement. When you receive a response, share it with your class.

WEB

6.14 Direct Reply: So You Want an Internship at the Gap?

The Gap Inc. headquarters in the San Francisco Bay area is a popular place to work. Many students inquire about summer internships. Although it supplies oodles of information about internships at its Web site, Gap Inc. still receives letters requesting this information. As one of its current summer interns, you have been given a task by your supervisor. She wants you to write a general letter that she can use to reply to requests from college students seeking summer internships. She doesn't have time to answer each one individually, and she doesn't want to tell them all to just go to the Web site. She feels responsible to reply in a way that builds goodwill for Gap, which also operates Old Navy and Banana Republic.

Your Task. Draft a reply to students seeking summer intern information. Go to the Gap Web site and study its offerings. Prepare a letter that describes the summer intern program, its requirements, and how to apply. Summarize some of the lengthy descriptions from the Web site. Use bulleted lists where appropriate. Since the letter may involve two pages, group similar information under side headings that improve its readability. Although your letter may become a form letter, address your draft to Lisa M. Hernandez, 493 Cesar Court, Walnut Creek, CA 94598.

WEB

6.15 Direct Reply: River Rafting on the Web

As the program chair for the campus Ski Club, you have been asked by the president to investigate river rafting. The Ski Club is an active organization, and its members want to schedule a summer activity. A majority favored rafting. Use a browser to search the Web for relevant information. Select five of the most promising Web sites offering rafting. If possible, print a copy of your findings.

Your Task. Summarize your findings in a letter to Brian Krauss, Ski Club president. The next meeting of the Ski Club is May 8, but you think it would be a good idea if you could discuss your findings with Brian before the meeting. Write to Brian Krauss, SIU Ski Club, 303 Founders Hall, Carbondale, IL 62901.

WEB

6.16 Direct Reply: Krispy Kreme Helps Raise Funds

Despite low-carb and low-fat diet fads, people still crave yummy doughnuts—especially the oh-so-light yet rich and scrumptious Krispy Kreme creations. As a customer service representative at Krispy Kreme in Winston-Salem, you have received a letter from a customer interested in using your doughnuts as a fund-raising activity for Noah's Ark Children's Center (see Activity 6.7). Although much of the information is at the Web site, you must answer this customer's letter personally.

Your Task. Respond to Mrs. Tiffany Lane, Noah's Ark Children's Center, 4359 Blue Creek Road, Austin, TX 78746. You need to explain the three ways that Krispy Kreme helps organizations raise funds. Use the Krispy Kreme Web site to gather information, but summarize and paraphrase what you find. Compose a letter that not only provides information but also promotes your product. Consider using bullet points and paragraph headings to set off the major points.

WEB

6.17 Direct Reply: What Is a FICO Credit Rating Score?

You were delighted to be selected as one of three interns for the prestigious architectural firm of Studio 1030. On the job you soon discovered that many of the firm's architects worked independently and relied on the office staff for clerical and technical support. One of the firm's retired architects, Harold M. Zimmerman, who lived in Benton Harbor, Michigan, was recently called back to the office because of the increasing demand for custom-designed homes. He was reluctant to return, saying that he's been out of touch. But Studio 1030 owner Lars Pedersen said, "Look, Hal, we really need you to help out for six months or so. We've got a support staff that will pitch in to assist you, if necessary."

Almost immediately, Mr. Zimmerman realized that the entire world of mortgage finance had changed in the past decade. He heard about two clients who were eager to have plans drawn for new homes, but they could not qualify for building loans because of low FICO scores. Mr. Zimmerman confessed to the owner that he knew very little about FICO at all. What's more, Mr. Zimmerman admitted that he was not comfortable doing Internet research.

The owner decides that this would be a good internship project for you. He asks you to prepare a letter to Mr. Zimmerman, who prefers to work at home, replying to his request for information about FICO. Although you've vaguely heard of it, you could not immediately define what the term means. However, you recognize a good opportunity when you see it! Here's a chance to learn something about credit ratings, and it's also a good chance to show off your research and communication skills.

Your Task. Go to *http://www.myfico.com* and study its information. (Use a search engine with the term "My Fico" if this URL fails.) What does "FICO" stand for? Who uses this term and why? What factors affect a FICO score? How can individuals improve their FICO scores? Summarize your findings in your own words in a well-organized, concise letter addressed to Mr. Harold Zimmerman, 2938 East Lakeview Avenue, Benton Harbor, MI 49022. Use bulleted lists for some of the information. Assume you are writing on Studio 1030 stationery.

INFOTRAC

6.18 Direct Reply: Restricting Internet Use on the Job

As an intern at a large accounting firm, you are surprised at the broad range of expertise expected of the CPAs. In fact, you think they may go too far in trying to please their clients. One client recently asked Greg Moltiere, your boss, to help her out with an Internet use policy for her small company. Although Mr. Moltiere is not an expert in this area, he wants to assist this client, who is not at all computer savvy. She has a growing company, and many of her employees are using the Internet. She called Mr. Moltiere and asked him to help her out with general information about Internet use policies. The client asked these questions: Why does a company need an Internet use policy? What does an Internet policy generally cover? Where can I see a sample Internet policy? Do I really need such a policy for my company?

Your Task. Mr. Moltiere asks you to use the Web to learn more about Internet use policies. For Greg Moltiere's signature, draft a direct reply letter answering the client's questions. His goal is to provide common information that encourages the client to develop an Internet policy for her company. Offer any additional material that you think will be useful. An InfoTrac search using the keywords "Internet Use Policy" will produce current information. Address the letter to Ms. Sherry Stratton, Stratton Convalescent Services, 2389 Three Rivers Boulevard, Poplar Bluff, MO 63901.

WEB

6.19 Direct Reply: Describing Your Major

A friend in a distant city is considering moving to your area for more education and training in your field. This individual wants to know about your program of study.

Your Task. Write a letter describing a program in your field (or any field you wish to describe). What courses must be taken? Toward what degree, certificate, or employment position does this program lead? Why did you choose it? Would you recommend this program to your friend? How long does it take? Add any information you feel would be helpful.

CRITICAL THINKING

6.20 Adjustment: A Matter of Mismeasurement

As Sal Rodriguez, sales manager of Capitol Lumber and Hardware, you must respond to a problem. Your firm manufactures quality precut and custom-built doors and frames. You have received a letter dated May 25 from Candace Olmstead (described in Activity 6.12). Ms. Olmstead is an interior designer, and she complains that the oak French doors she recently ordered for a client were made to the wrong dimensions.

Although they were the wrong size, she kept the doors and had them installed because her clients were without outside doors. However, her carpenter charged an extra $376 to install them. She claims that you should reimburse her for this amount, because your company was responsible for the error. You check her June 9 order and find that the order was filled correctly. In a telephone order, Ms. Olmstead requested doors that measured 11 feet 4 inches, and that's what you sent. Now she says that the doors should have been 11 feet 8 inches. Your policy forbids refunds or returns on custom orders. Yet, you remember that in the early part of June, you had two new people working the phones taking orders. It's possible that they did not hear or record the measurements correctly. You don't know whether to grant this claim or refuse it. But you do know that you must look into the training of telephone order takers and be sure that they verify all custom order measurements. It might also be a good idea to have your craftsmen call a second time to confirm custom measurements.

Ms. Olmstead is a successful interior designer and has provided Capitol Lumber and Hardware with a number of orders. You value her business but aren't sure how to respond.

Your Task. Decide how to treat this claim and then write to Candace Olmstead, Custom Designs, 903 Hazel Dell Parkway, Carmel, IN 46033. In your letter remind her that Capitol Lumber and Hardware has earned a reputation as the manufacturer of the finest wood doors and frames on the market. Your doors feature prime woods, and the craftsmanship is meticulous. The designs of your doors have won awards, and the engineering is ingenious. You have a new line of greenhouse windows that are available in three sizes. Include a brochure describing these windows.

*6.21 Adjustment: Unhappy Customer Returns Desk

As Patrick Dwiggens, operations manager, Premier Wood Products, it is your job to reply to customer claims; and today you must respond to Valerie Vickers (described in Activity 6.10). You are disturbed that she is returning the executive desk (Invoice No. 3499), but your policy is to comply with customer wishes. If she doesn't want to keep the desk, you will certainly return the purchase price plus shipping charges. Desks are occasionally damaged in shipping, and this may explain the marred finish and the sticking drawers.

You will try to persuade Ms. Vickers to give Premier Wood Products another chance. After all, your office furniture and other wood products are made from the finest hand-selected woods by master artisans. Since she is apparently furnishing her office, send her another catalog and invite her to look at the traditional conference desk on page 10-E. This is available with a matching credenza, file cabinets, and accessories. She might be interested in your furniture-leasing plan, which can produce substantial savings.

Your Task. Write to Valerie Vickers, President, Financial Advisors, Inc., 203 Elm Street, Youngwood, PA 15697. In granting her claim, promise that you will personally examine any furniture she may order in the future.

6.22 Adjustment: No Birds Will Be Harmed

You didn't want to do it. But guests were complaining about the pigeons that roost on the Scottsdale Hilton's upper floors and tower. Pigeon droppings splattered sidewalks, furniture, and people. As the hotel manager, you had to take action. You called an exterminator, who recommended Avitrol. This drug, he promised, would disorient the birds, preventing them from finding their way back to the Hilton. The drugging, however, produced a result you didn't expect: pigeons began dying.

After a story hit the local newspapers, you began to receive complaints. The most vocal came from the Avian Affairs Coalition, a local bird-advocacy group. It said that the pigeons are really Mediterranean rock doves, the original "Dove of Peace" in European history and the same species the Bible said Noah originally released from his ark during the great flood. Activists claimed that Avitrol is a lethal drug causing birds, animals, and even people who ingest as little as 1/600th of a teaspoon to convulse and die lingering deaths of up to two hours.

Repulsed at the pigeon deaths and the bad publicity, you stopped the use of Avitrol immediately. You are now considering installing wires that offer a mild, nonlethal electrical shock. These wires, installed at the Maricopa County Jail in downtown Phoenix for $50,000, keep thousands of pigeons from alighting and could save $1 million in extermination and cleanup costs over the life of the building. You are also considering installing netting that forms a transparent barrier, sealing areas against entry by birds.

Your Task. Respond to Mrs. Deborah Leverette, 24 Canyon Lake Shore Drive, Spring Branch, TX 52319, a recent Scottsdale Hilton guest. She sent a letter condemning the pigeon poisoning and threatening to never return to the hotel unless it changed its policy. Try to regain the confidence of Mrs. Leverette and promote further business.[8]

6.23 Employment Recommendation: Recommending Yourself

You are about to leave your present job. When you ask your boss for a letter of recommendation, to your surprise he tells you to write it yourself and then have him sign it. Actually, this is not an unusual practice today. Many businesspeople find that employees are very perceptive and accurate when they evaluate themselves.

Your Task. Use specifics from a current or previous job. Describe your duties and skills. Be sure to support general characteristics with specific examples. In writing, speak of yourself in the third person (*Lisa worked under my supervision during the summer of . . . . Lisa was in charge of . . . . I consider her to be reliable . . .*).

6.24 Thanks for a Favor: Got the Job!

Congratulations! You completed your degree and got a terrific job in your field. One of your instructors was especially helpful to you when you were a student. This instructor also wrote an effective letter of recommendation that was instrumental in helping you obtain your job.

Your Task. Write a letter thanking your instructor.

TEAM

6.25 Thanks for a Favor: Emerging World of Online Networking

Your business communication class recently enjoyed a guest speaker, Diane Domeyer. She is executive director of OfficeTeam, the nation's leading staff service specializing in the temporary placement of highly skilled administrative and office support professionals. Her topic was "The Emerging World of Online Networking." At first, the class didn't know what online networking involved. Ms. Domeyer discussed special networks that allow individuals to network with others in their career fields at Web sites such as Ryze.com and ContactSpan.com. The International Association of Administrative Professionals even has a bulletin board in the Member's Place section of its Web site that allows members from around the world to connect. Your class learned about how to network online, including where to go, do's and don'ts, etiquette, and having realistic expectations.

Your Task. Individually or in groups, draft a thank-you letter to Ms. Diane Domeyer, Executive Director, Office Team, P.O. Box 310, Palo Alto, CA 94063. Use your imagination to fill in details.

6.26 Thanks for the Hospitality: Holiday Entertaining

You and other members of your staff or organization were entertained at an elegant dinner during the winter holiday season.

Your Task. Write a thank-you letter to your boss (supervisor, manager, vice president, president, or chief executive officer) or to the head of an organization to which you belong. Include specific details that will make your letter personal and sincere.

(TEAM)----(WEB)

6.27 Sending Good Wishes: Personalizing Group Greeting Cards

When a work colleague has a birthday, gets promoted, or retires, someone generally circulates a group greeting card. In the past it wasn't a big deal. Office colleagues just signed their names and passed the store-bought card along to others. But the current trend is toward personalization with witty, oh-so-clever quips. And that presents a problem. What should you say—or not say?

You know that people value special handwritten quips, but you realize that you're not particularly original and you don't have a store of "bon mots" (clever sayings, witticisms). You're tired of the old standbys, such as *This place won't be the same without you* and *You're only as old as you feel.*

Your Task. To be prepared for the next greeting card that lands on your desk at work, you decide to work with some friends to make a list of remarks appropriate for business occasions. Use the Web to research witty sayings appropriate for promotions, birthdays, births, weddings, illnesses, or personal losses. Use a search term such as "Birthday Sayings," "Retirement Quotes," or "Cool Sayings." You may decide to assign each category (birthday, retirement, promotion, and so forth) to a separate team. Submit the best sayings in a memo to your instructor.

6.28 Responding to Good Wishes: Saying Thank You

Your Task. Write a short note thanking a friend who sent you good wishes when you recently completed your degree.

6.29 Extending Sympathy: To a Spouse

Your Task. Imagine that a coworker was killed in an automobile accident. Write a letter of sympathy to his or her spouse.

VIDEO RESOURCES

Video Library 2, *Bridging the Gap*
Social Responsibility and Communication: Ben & Jerry's.
In an exciting inside look, you see managers discussing six factors that determine Ben & Jerry's continuing success. Toward the end of the video, you'll listen in on a discussion of a new packaging material made with unbleached paper. As a socially responsible company, Ben & Jerry's wanted to move away from ice cream packages made from bleached papers. Bleaching requires chlorine, a substance that contains dioxin, which is known to cause cancer, genetic and reproductive defects, and learning disabilities. In producing paper, pulp mills using chlorine are also adding to dioxin contamination of waterways. After much research, Ben & Jerry's found a chlorine-free, unbleached paperboard for its packages. That was the good news. The bad news is that the inside of the package is now brown.

Assume you've been hired at Ben & Jerry's to help answer incoming letters. Although you're fairly new, your boss gives you a letter from an unhappy customer. This customer opened a pint of Ben & Jerry's "World's Best

Vanilla" and then threw it out. After seeing the brown inner lid, he decided that his pint must have been used for chocolate before it was used for vanilla. Or, he said, "the entire pint has gone bad and somehow turned the sides brown." Whatever the reason, he wasn't taking any chances. He wants his money back.

Your Task. Write a letter that explains the brown carton, justifies the reason for using it, and retains the customer's business. Address the letter to Mr. Cecil Hamm, 1608 South McKenna, Poteau, OK 74954.

Video Library 2, *Bridging the Gap*
MeetingsAmerica. In Salt Lake City, MeetingsAmerica arranges conferences and conventions for visitors to the city. Businesses planning big conferences often outsource arrangements such as registration, ground transportation, special events, and other details. In this video you'll learn how MeetingsAmerica operates as a destination meeting organization. Your instructor may provide a special writing activity after you see this video.

GRAMMAR/MECHANICS CHECKUP—6

Commas 1

Review the Grammar Review section of the Grammar/Mechanics Handbook Sections 2.01–2.04. Then study each of the following statements and insert necessary commas. In the space provided write the number of commas that you add; write *0* if no commas are needed. Also record the number of the G/M principle illustrated. When you finish, compare your responses with those shown at the end of the book. If your answers differ, study carefully the principles shown in parentheses.

2   (2.01)   **Example**   Sometimes we are so engrossed in our job our family or a relationship that we forget about ourselves.

1. We think on the other hand that camera phones are not a good idea in offices.

2. We are certain Mr. Nosrati that your UPS delivery will arrive before 11 a.m.

3. Our software helps your employees be more creative collaborative and productive in team projects.

4. The spring leadership conference will take place April 3 at the South Beach Marriott Hotel beginning at 2 p.m.

5. Needless to say we were depressed at the stock market drop.

6. Amazon closed distribution centers in McDonough Georgia and Grand Forks North Dakota to save money.

7. By the way the best things in life aren't things.

8. The last council meeting that was recorded in the minutes was held on March 23 2005 in Phoenix.

9. Mr. Maslow Mrs. Kim and Ms. Garcia were all promoted.

10. The shipment addressed to McMahon Industries 6920 Main Street Detroit MI 48201 arrived two weeks late.

11. The manager feels nevertheless that the support of all employees is critical.

12. Successful teams encourage open communication resolve conflict fairly and promote interaction among members.

13. Our team works hard to retain your business Mr. Sherman.

14. President Carson however thinks that all staff members need training.

15. Rachel moved from Hartford Connecticut to San Diego California because she was offered a better job.

GRAMMAR/MECHANICS CHALLENGE—6

The following letter has faults in grammar, punctuation, spelling, capitalization, number form, repetition, wordiness, and other problems. Correct the errors with standard proofreading marks (see Appendix B) or revise the message online at **Guffey Xtra!**

January 20, 200x

Mr. Jason R. Weingartner
3201 Rose Avenue
Mar Vista, CA 90066

Dear Mr. Weingartner:

SUBJECT: Your February 5th Letter Requesting Information About New All Natural
             Products

We have received your letter of February 5 in which you inquire about our all-natural products. Needless to say, we are pleased to be able to answer in the affirmative. Yes, our new line of freeze dried back packing foods meet the needs of older adults and young people as well. You asked a number of questions, and here are answers to you're questions about our products.

- Our all natural foods contains no preservatives, sugars or additives. The inclosed list of dinner items tell what foods are cholesterol-, fat-, and salt-free.

- Large orders recieve a five percent discount when they're placed direct with Outfitters, Inc. You can also purchase our products at Malibu Sports Center, 19605 Pacific Coast Highway Malibu CA, 90265.

- Outfitters, Inc., food products are made in our sanitary kitchens which I personally supervise. The foods are flash froze in a patented vacum process that retain freshness, texture and taste.

- Outfitters, Inc., food products are made from choice ingredients that combines good taste and healful quality.

- Our foods stay fresh, and tasty for up to 18 months.

Mr. Weingartner I started Outfitters, Inc., five years ago because of the fact that discerning back packers rejected typical camping fare. Its a great pleasure to be able at this point in time to share my custom meals with back packers like you.

I hope you'll enjoy the enclosed sample meal, "Saturday Night on the Trail" is a four-coarse meal complete with fruit candys and elegant appetizers. Please call me personally at (213) 459-3342 to place an order, or to ask other questions about my backpacking food products.

Sincerely,

COMMUNICATION WORKSHOP
CAREER SKILLS

DR. GUFFEY'S GUIDE TO BUSINESS ETIQUETTE
AND WORKPLACE MANNERS

Etiquette, civility, and goodwill efforts may seem out of place in today's fast-paced, high-tech offices. Yet, etiquette and courtesy are more important than ever if diverse employees are to be able to work cooperatively and maximize productivity and work-flow. Many organizations recognize that good manners are good for business. Some colleges and universities offer management programs that include a short course in manners. Companies are also conducting manners seminars for trainee and veteran managers. Why is politeness regaining legitimacy as a leadership tool? Primarily because courtesy works.

Good manners convey a positive image of an organization. People like to do business with people who show respect and treat others civilly. People also like to work in a pleasant environment. Considering how much time is spent at work, doesn't it make sense to prefer an agreeable environment to one that is rude and uncivil?

Etiquette is more about attitude than about formal rules of behavior. That attitude is a desire to show others consideration and respect. It includes a desire to make others feel comfortable. You don't have to become an etiquette nut, but you might need to polish your social competencies a little to be an effective businessperson today.

You can brush up your workplace etiquette skills online at your companion Web site *http://guffey.swlearning.com*. Look for "Dr. Guffey's Guide to Business Etiquette and Workplace Manners." Of interest to both workplace newcomers and veterans, this guide covers the following topics:

Professional Image
Introductions and Greetings
Networking Manners
General Workplace Manners
Coping With Cubicles
Interacting With Superiors
Managers' Manners
Business Meetings
Business Gifts

Business Cards
Dealing With Angry Customers
Telephone Manners
Cell Phone Etiquette
E-Mail Etiquette
Gender-Free Etiquette
Business Dining
Avoiding Social Blunders When Abroad

To gauge your current level of knowledge of business etiquette, take the preview quiz at the student Web site. Then, study all 17 business etiquette topics. These easy-to-read topics are arranged in bulleted lists of Dos and Don'ts. After you complete this etiquette module, your instructor may test your comprehension by giving a series of posttests.

Career Application. You've been a manager at OfficeTemps, a company specializing in employment placement and human resources information, for a long time. But you've never received a letter like this before. A reporter preparing an article for a national news organization writes to you requesting information about how workplace etiquette is changing in today's high-tech environment. Her letter lists the following questions:

- Are etiquette and workplace manners still important in today's fast-paced Information Age work environment? Why or why not?
- Do today's workers need help in developing good business manners? Why or why not?
- Are the rules of office conduct changing? If so, how?
- What advice can you give about gender-free etiquette?

- What special manners do people working in shared workspaces need to observe?

The reporter asks for any other information you can share with her regarding her topic, "Information Age Etiquette."

Your Task

In teams or individually, prepare an information response letter addressed to Ms. Lindsey Ann Evans, National Press Association, 443 Riverside Drive, New York, NY 10024. Use the data you learned in this workshop. Conduct additional Web research if you wish. Remember that you will be quoted in her newspaper article, so make it interesting!

CHAPTER 7

PERSUASIVE MESSAGES

> *Facts and figures alone will never convince anyone. If you can't connect your facts to the dreams of the client, then all the statistics and charts in the world won't make any impression.[1]*
>
> **René Nourse**, Vice President, Investments, Prudential Securities Incorporated

OBJECTIVES

- Outline the components of a writing plan for persuasive requests including the opening, body, and closing.
- Write effective persuasive messages that request favors and action.
- Write effective persuasive messages within organizations.
- Write effective persuasive messages that make claims and request adjustments.
- Outline the components of a writing plan for sales letters including gaining attention, building interest, reducing resistance, and motivating action.
- Implement special techniques in writing online sales messages.

The ability to persuade is a primary factor in personal and business success.

The ability to persuade is a key factor in the success you achieve in your business messages, in your career, and in your interpersonal relations. Persuasive individuals, such as René Nourse at Prudential Securities Incorporated, are those who present convincing arguments that influence or win over others.

René Nourse persuades people to invest in stocks and bonds. She knows that facts and figures alone are not convincing; they must be connected to people's desires and needs. Applying this persuasive technique and many others can help you become a persuasive communicator. Because their ideas generally prevail, persuasive individuals become decision makers—managers, executives, and entrepreneurs. This chapter will examine techniques for presenting ideas persuasively, whether in your career or in your personal life.

PERSUASIVE REQUESTS

Use persuasion when you must change attitudes or produce action.

Persuasion is necessary when resistance is anticipated or when ideas require preparation before they can be presented effectively. For example, let's say you bought a new car and the transmission repeatedly required servicing. When you finally got tired of taking it in for repair, you decided to write to the car manufacturer's district

PHOTOS: © PHOTODISC COLLECTION/GETTY IMAGES; © DIGITAL VISION/ GETTY IMAGES; © ROYALTY-FREE/CORBIS

office asking that the company install a new transmission in your car. You knew that your request would be resisted. You had to convince the manufacturer that replacement, not repair, is needed. Direct claim letters, such as those you wrote in Chapter 6, are straightforward. Persuasive requests, on the other hand, are generally more effective when they are indirect. Reasons and explanations should precede the main idea. To overcome possible resistance, the writer lays a logical foundation before delivering the request. A writing plan for a persuasive request requires deliberate development.

Writing Plan for a Persuasive Request

- *Opening:* **Obtain the reader's attention and interest.** Describe a problem, state something unexpected, suggest reader benefits, offer praise or compliments, or ask a stimulating question.
- *Body:* **Build interest.** Explain logically and concisely the purpose of the request. Prove its merit. Use facts, statistics, expert opinion, examples, specific details, and direct and indirect benefits. **Reduce resistance.** Anticipate objections, offer counterarguments, establish credibility, demonstrate competence, and show the value of your proposal.
- *Closing:* **Motivate action.** Ask for a particular action. Make the action easy to take. Show courtesy, respect, and gratitude.

> The indirect pattern is appropriate when requesting favors and action, persuading within organizations, and making claims or requesting adjustments.

In this chapter you'll learn to apply the preceding writing plan to messages that (1) request favors and action, (2) persuade within organizations, and (3) make claims and request adjustments.

Requesting Favors and Action

Persuading someone to do something that largely benefits you is not easy. Fortunately, many individuals and companies are willing to grant requests for time, money, information, special privileges, and cooperation. They grant these favors for a variety of reasons. They may just happen to be interested in your project, or they may see goodwill potential for themselves. Often, though, they comply because they see that others will benefit from the request. Professionals sometimes feel obligated to contribute their time or expertise to "pay their dues."

> People are more likely to grant requests if they see direct or indirect benefits to themselves.

You may find that you have few direct benefits to offer in your persuasion. Instead, you'll be focusing on indirect benefits, as the writer does in Figure 7.1. In asking an individual to speak before a restaurant industry meeting, the writer has little to offer as a direct benefit other than a $200 honorarium. But indirectly, the writer offers

Whether you are asking for favors or action, the ability to persuade is critical in personal and business success. Nancy Loome, representing a Clinton, Mississippi, PTA, used all her persuasive skills to convince lawmakers to maintain current funding levels for K–12 schools.

© AP WIDE WORLD PHOTOS

FIGURE 7.1   **Persuasive Favor Request**

before revision

Dear Ms. Daugherty:

Would you be willing to speak to the members of the DC chapter of the National Restaurant Alliance? We hate to ask such a busy person, but we hoped you might be free on June 10 and would be able to come down from Philadelphia to join us in Washington.

→ Fails to pique interest; provides easy excuse

You would address our members on the topic of avoiding the seven cardinal sins in food service. This is a topic we understand you presented at your local chapter with some success. Although we can offer you only a $200 honorarium, we will also include dinner.

→ Does not promote direct and indirect benefits

Our group is informal, but I'm sure they would be interested in a 45-minute speech. Please let me know if you can join us at 7 p.m. at the Red Sage restaurant in Washington.

→ Does not anticipate objections; fails to make it easy to respond

after revision

NATIONAL RESTAURANT ALLIANCE

1250 17th Street, Washington, DC 20034   www.restaurant.com   (202) 351-4300

February 23, 200x

Ms. Nancy J. Daugherty
Operations Manager
Roxbury Hotels and Restaurants, Inc.
303 Lombard Plaza
Philadelphia, PA 19146

Dear Ms. Daugherty:

Piques reader's interest with praise →

News of the excellent presentation you made at your local chapter of the National Restaurant Alliance has reached us here in Washington, and we are very impressed.

← Gains attention

Running a successful restaurant operation, as we all know, is tough even on a good day. The intense pace is frenzied, from scrubbing the vegetables early in the morning to latching the front door at day's end. In all this haste, it's easy to lapse into food service faults that can land an operation in big trouble. Your presentation focusing on seven cardinal sins in the food service industry certainly captured our attention.

← Builds interest

Notes indirect benefit →

Notes direct benefit →

The DC chapter of the National Restaurant Alliance asked me to invite you to be the featured speaker at our June 10 dinner on the topic of "Avoiding the Seven Cardinal Sins in Food Service." By sharing your expertise, you can help other restaurant operators recognize and prevent potential problems involving discrimination, workplace safety, hiring practices, and so forth. Although we can offer you only a small honorarium of $200 plus your travel expenses, we can promise you a big audience of enthusiastic restaurateurs eager to hear your presentation.

Offsets reluctance by making the talk informal and easy to organize →

Our relaxed group doesn't expect a formal address; they are most interested in hearing about best practices and solutions to prospective problems. To make your talk easy to organize, I've enclosed a list of questions our members submitted. Most talks are about 45 minutes long.

← Reduces resistance

Makes it easy to accept →

Can we count on you to join us for dinner at 7 p.m. June 10 at the Red Sage restaurant in Washington? Just call me at (202) 351-1220 before March 15 to make arrangements.

← Motivates action

Sincerely,

Bronna McNeeley

Bronna McNeeley
Program Chair, NRA

BMN:grw
Enclosure

enticements such as an enthusiastic audience and a chance to help other restaurant owners prevent food service problems.

The hurriedly written first version of the request suffers from many faults. It fails to pique the interest of the reader in the opening. It also provides an easy excuse for Ms. Daugherty to refuse (*hate to ask such a busy person*). The body fails to give her any incentive to accept the invitation. The letter also does not anticipate objections and fails to suggest counterarguments. Finally, the closing doesn't supply a telephone number or e-mail address for an easy response.

In the revised version, the writer gains attention with praise for a presentation Ms. Daugherty made. The letter builds interest with a number of appeals. The primary appeal is to the reader's desire to serve the restaurant industry, although a receptive audience and an opportunity to serve as an expert have a certain ego appeal as well. Together, these appeals—professional, egoistic, and monetary—make a persuasive argument rich and effective. The writer also anticipates objections and counters them by telling Ms. Daugherty that the talk is informal. The writer provides a list of questions so that the speaker can organize her talk more easily. The closing motivates action and makes acceptance as simple as a telephone call.

> A combination of appeals—professional, egoistic, and monetary—can be effective in persuasive requests.

Persuading Within Organizations

Instructions or directives moving downward from superiors to subordinates usually require little persuasion. Employees expect to be directed in how to perform their jobs. These messages (such as information about procedures, equipment, or customer service) follow the direct pattern, with the purpose immediately stated. However, employees are sometimes asked to perform in a capacity outside their work roles or to accept changes that are not in their best interests (such as pay cuts, job transfers, or reduced benefits). In these instances, a persuasive memo using the indirect pattern may be most effective.

> Internal persuasive memos present honest arguments detailing specific reader benefits.

The goal is not to manipulate employees or to seduce them with trickery. Rather, the goal is to present a strong but honest argument, emphasizing points that are important to the receiver. In business, honesty is not just the best policy—it's the *only* policy. People see right through puffery and misrepresentation. For this reason, the indirect pattern is effective only when supported by accurate, honest evidence.

Another form of persuasion within organizations centers on suggestions made by subordinates. Convincing management to adopt a procedure or invest in a product or new equipment generally requires skillful communication. Managers are just as resistant to change as others are. Providing evidence is critical when subordinates submit recommendations to their bosses. "The key to making a request of a superior," advised communication consultant Patricia Buhler, "is to know your needs and have documentation [facts, figures, evidence]." Another important factor is moderation. "Going in and asking for the world [right] off the cuff is most likely going to elicit a negative response," she added.[2] Equally important is focusing on the receiver's needs. How can you make your suggestion appealing to the receiver?

> Persuasive memos sent internally are often effective if they show how costs are saved.

In Figure 7.2 you see the draft copy of a persuasive memo that needs revision. Marketing Manager Mona Massey wants her boss to authorize the purchase of a second copy machine. She was so excited about a good deal that she wrote her memo quickly and didn't spend much time organizing it. Before sending it, though, she reconsidered. Although she thought that her request was totally reasonable, she realized that her memo failed to present a well-organized "dollars-and-cents" case. She also recognized that if she spent a little more time developing her persuasive argument, she had a better chance of gaining approval.

Notice that Mona's revision is longer. But it's far more effective. A successful persuasive message will typically take more space than a direct message because proving a case requires evidence. Mona's revised memo includes a subject line that tells the purpose of the memo without disclosing the actual request. By delaying the request until she's had a chance to describe the problem and discuss a solution, Mona prevents the reader's premature rejection.

FIGURE 7.2 ● **Persuasive Memo**

before revision

TO: Kenneth Richardson, Vice President

Although you've opposed the purchase of additional copiers in the past, I think I've found a great deal on a copier that's just too good to pass up, but we must act before May 1. Copy City has reconditioned copiers that are practically being given away. If we move fast, they will provide many free incentives—like a free copier stand, free starter supplies, free delivery, and free installation.

We must find a way to reduce copier costs in my department. Our current copier can't keep up with our demand. We're sending secretaries or sales reps to Copy Quick for an average of 10,000 copies a month. These copies cost 7 cents a page and waste a lot of time. We're making at least eight trips a week, adding up to a considerable expense in travel time and copy costs.

Please give this matter your immediate attention and get back to me as soon as possible. We don't want to miss this great deal.

Begins poorly with reminder of past negative feelings

Sounds high-pressured

Fails to compare costs and emphasize savings in logical, coherent presentation

Does not request or motivate specific action

after revision

DATE: April 18, 200x

TO: Kenneth Richardson, Vice President

FROM: Mona Massey, Marketing   MM

SUBJECT: Saving Time and Money on Copying

Describes topic without revealing request

Summarizes problem

We're losing money on our current copy services and wasting the time of employees as well. Because our Canon copier is in use constantly, we find it increasingly necessary to send major jobs out to Copy Quick. Just take a look at how much we spend each month for outside copy service:

Copy Costs: Outside Service

10,000 copies/month made at Copy Quick	$700.00
Salary costs for assistants to make 32 trips to drop off originals and pick up copies	384.00
Total	$1,084.00

Uses headings and columns for easy comparison

When sales reps make the trips, the costs are even greater. Because this expense must be reduced, I've been considering alternatives. New copiers with collating capability and automatic multidrawer paper feeding are very expensive. But reconditioned copiers with all the features we need are available—and at attractive prices and terms. From Copy City we can get a fully remanufactured copier that is guaranteed to work like new. After we make an initial payment of $219, our monthly costs would look like this:

Proves credibility of request with facts and figures

Copy Costs: Remanufactured Copier

Paper supplies for 10,000 copies	$130.00
Toner and copy supplies	95.00
Labor of assistants to make copies	130.00
Monthly financing charge for copier (purchase price of $1,105 amortized at 10% with 29 payments)	34.52
Total	$389.52

As you can see, **a remanufactured copier saves us nearly $700 per month.**

Highlights most important benefit

Provides more benefits

For a limited time Copy City is offering a free 15-day trial offer, a free copier stand (worth $165), free starter supplies, and free delivery and installation. We have office space available, and my staff is eager to add a second machine.

Counters possible resistance

Makes it easy to grant approval

Call me at Ext. 630 if you have questions. This copier is such a good opportunity that I've attached a purchase requisition authorizing the agreement with Copy City. With your approval before May 1, we can have our machine by May 10 and start saving time and nearly $700 every month. Fast action will also take advantage of Copy City's free start-up incentives.

Repeats main benefit with motivation to act quickly

Attachment

When selling an idea to
management, writers often are
successful if they make a strong
case for saving money.

The strength of this revision, though, is in the clear presentation of comparison figures showing how much money can be saved by purchasing a remanufactured copier. Although the organization pattern is not obvious, the revised memo begins with an attention-getter (frank description of problem), builds interest (with easy-to-read facts and figures), provides benefits, and reduces resistance. Notice that the conclusion tells what action is to be taken, makes it easy to respond, and repeats the main benefit to motivate action.

Making Claims and Requesting Adjustments (Complaint Letters)

Persuasive claim and adjustment letters generally focus on damaged products, mistaken billing, inaccurate shipments, warranty problems, return policies, insurance snafus, faulty merchandise, and so on. The direct pattern is usually best for requesting straightforward adjustments (see Chapter 6). When you feel your request is justified and will be granted, the direct strategy is most efficient. But if a past request has been refused or ignored or if you anticipate reluctance, then the indirect pattern is appropriate.

Effective claim/complaint letters
make reasonable requests backed
by solid evidence.

In a sense, a claim is a complaint letter. Someone is complaining about something that went wrong. Some complaint letters just vent anger; the writers are mad, and they want to tell someone about it. If the goal, however, is to change something (and why bother to write except to motivate change?), then persuasion is necessary. Effective claim letters make a reasonable claim, present a logical case with clear facts, and adopt a moderate tone. Anger and emotion are not effective persuaders.

LOGICAL DEVELOPMENT

Strive for logical development in a claim letter. You might open with sincere praise, an objective statement of the problem, a point of agreement, or a quick review of what you have done to resolve the problem. Then you can explain precisely what happened or why your claim is legitimate. Don't provide a blow-by-blow chronology of details; just hit the highlights. Be sure to enclose copies of relevant invoices, shipping orders, warranties, and payments. Close with a clear statement of what you want done: refund, replacement, credit to your account, or other action. Be sure to think through the possibilities and make your request reasonable.

MODERATE TONE

Claim letters should adopt a
moderate tone, appeal to the
receiver's sense of responsibility,
and specify needed actions.

The tone of the letter is important. Don't suggest that the receiver intentionally deceived you or intentionally created the problem. Rather, appeal to the receiver's sense of responsibility and pride in its good name. Calmly express your disappointment in view of your high expectations of the product and of the company. Communicating your feelings, without rancor, is often your strongest appeal.

If at all possible, address your complaint letter to a specific person. If you truly want a problem addressed, take the time to call the organization or search its Web site. Find out who should be addressed. Who should be informed about your issue? Who has the authority to act? Addressing a specific person is more likely to generate action than addressing a generic customer service department. Whether you address an individual or a department, the tone of your message should, of course, be moderate.

Merilee Knapp's letter, shown in Figure 7.3, follows the persuasive pattern. She wants to return three answering machines. Notice that she addressed her letter to the marketing manager, whose name she learned by calling the company. Notice, too, her positive opening; her calm, well-documented claims; and her request for specific action.

• **Claim Request (Complaint Letter)**

CHAMPION AUTOMOTIVES
309 Porterville Plaza, Lansing, Michigan 48914 (517) 690-3500
www.championauto.com

November 29, 200x

Mr. Jeffrey Thomas
Vice President
Marketing and Product Development
Raytronic Electronics
594 Stanton Street
Mobile, AL 36617

Addresses an individual

Dear Mr. Thomas:

Subject: Code-A-Phone Model 100S

Begins with compliment

Your Code-A-Phone Model 100S answering unit came well recommended. We liked our neighbor's unit so well we purchased three for different departments in our business.

Describes problem calmly

After the three units were unpacked and installed, we discovered a problem. Apparently our office fluorescent lighting interferes with the electronics in these units. When the lights are on, heavy static interrupts every telephone call. When the lights are off, the static disappears.

We can't replace the fluorescent lights; thus we tried to return the Code-A-Phones to the place of purchase (Office Mart, 2560 Haslett Avenue, Lansing, MI 48901). A salesperson inspected the units and said they could not be returned since they were not defective and they had been used.

Suggests responsibility

Stresses disappointment

Because the descriptive literature and instructions for the Code-A-Phones say nothing about avoiding use in rooms with fluorescent lighting, we expected no trouble. We were quite disappointed that this well-engineered unit—with its time/date stamp, room monitor, and auto-dial features—failed to perform as we hoped it would.

Appeals to company's desire to preserve good reputation

Tells what action to take

If you have a model with similar features that would work in our offices, give me a call. Otherwise, please authorize the return of these units and refund the purchase price of $519.45 (see enclosed invoice). We're confident that a manufacturer with your reputation for excellent products and service will want to resolve this matter quickly.

Sincerely,

Merilee Knapp

Merilee Knapp, President

MK:ett
Enclosure

Tips for Making Claims and Complaints

• Begin with a compliment, point of agreement, statement of the problem, or brief review of action you have taken to resolve the problem.
• Provide identifying data.
• Prove that your claim is valid; explain why the receiver is responsible.
• Enclose document copies supporting your claim.
• Appeal to the receiver's fairness, ethical and legal responsibilities, and desire for customer satisfaction.
• Describe your feelings and your disappointment.
• Avoid sounding angry, emotional, or irrational.
• Close by telling exactly what you want done.

CRAFTING WINNING SALES LETTERS

Traditional direct-mail marketing uses land mail; electronic marketing uses e-mail, Web sites, and fax.

Sales messages use persuasion to promote specific products and services. In our coverage we will be most concerned with sales messages delivered by mail. Many of the concepts you will learn about sales persuasion, however, can be applied to radio and TV advertising, as well as print, online, and wireless media. Smart companies strive to develop a balanced approach to their overall marketing strategy, including both online e-marketing and direct mail when appropriate.

Traditional hard-copy sales letters are still the most personal and powerful form of advertising.

Toward the end of this chapter, you will learn about preparing online sales messages. However, we'll give most emphasis to traditional direct-mail campaigns featuring letters. Sellers feel that "even with all the new media we have available today, a letter remains one of the most powerful ways to make sales, generate leads, boost retail traffic, and solicit donations."[3] Hard-copy sales letters are still recognized as the most "personal, one-to-one form of advertising there is."[4] Sales letters are generally part of a package that may contain a brochure, price list, illustrations, testimonials, and other persuasive appeals. Professionals who specialize in traditional direct-mail services have made a science of analyzing a market, developing an effective mailing list, studying the product, preparing a sophisticated campaign aimed at a target audience, and motivating the reader to act. You've probably received many direct-mail packages, often called "junk mail."

Learning to write sales letters helps you sell yourself as well as become a smarter consumer.

We're most concerned here with the sales letter: its strategy, organization, and evidence. Because sales letters are usually written by specialists, you may never write one on the job. Why, then, learn how to write a sales letter? In many ways, every letter we create is a form of sales letter. We sell our ideas, our organizations, and ourselves. Learning the techniques of sales writing will help you be more successful in any communication that requires persuasion and promotion. Furthermore, you'll recognize sales strategies, thus enabling you to become a more perceptive consumer of ideas, products, and services.

Planning Sales Messages

Your primary goal in writing a sales message is to get someone to devote a few moments of attention to it.[5] You may be promoting a product, a service, an idea, or yourself. In each case the most effective messages will follow a writing plan. This is the same recipe we studied earlier, but the ingredients are different.

Writing Plan for a Sales Letter

- *Opening:* **Gain attention.** Offer something valuable; promise a benefit to the reader; ask a question; or provide a quotation, fact, product feature, testimonial, startling statement, or personalized action setting.
- *Body:* **Build interest.** Describe central selling points and make rational and emotional appeals. **Reduce resistance.** Use testimonials, money-back guarantees, free samples, performance tests, or other techniques.
- *Closing:* **Motivate action.** Offer a gift, promise an incentive, limit the offer, set a deadline, or guarantee satisfaction.

GAINING ATTENTION

Openers for sales messages should be brief, honest, relevant, and provocative.

One of the most critical elements of a sales letter is its opening paragraph. This opener should be short (one to five lines), honest, relevant, and stimulating. Marketing pros have found that eye-catching typographical arrangements or provocative messages, such as the following, can hook a reader's attention:

- **Offer:** *A free trip to Hawaii is just the beginning!*
- **Promise a benefit:** *Now you can raise your sales income by 50 percent or even more with the proven techniques found in . . . .*
- **Question:** *Do you yearn for an honest, fulfilling relationship?*
- **Quotation or proverb:** *Necessity is the mother of invention.*

© KNIGHT-RIDDER/TRIBUNE PHOTOS

When Subway began promoting its low-fat sandwiches as healthier options for takeout-eating Americans, it gained attention by showing Lanette Kovach, its chief nutritionist, with a platter of mouth-watering menu options. The first step in developing a sales or persuasive message is gaining attention and shaping the message to the reader's interests.

- **Fact:** *The Greenland Eskimos ate more fat than anyone in the world. And yet . . . they had virtually no heart disease.*
- **Product feature:** *Volvo's snazzy new convertible ensures your safety with a roll bar that pops out when the car tips 40 degrees to the side.*
- **Testimonial:** *"The Journal surprises, amuses, investigates, and most of all educates."* (*The New Republic* commenting on *The Wall Street Journal*)
- **Startling statement:** *Let the poor and hungry feed themselves! For just $100 they can.*
- **Personalized action setting:** *It's 4:30 p.m. and you've got to make a decision. You need everybody's opinion, no matter where they are. Before you pick up your phone to call them one at a time, pick up this card: AT&T Teleconference Services.*

Other openings calculated to capture attention might include a solution to a problem, an anecdote, a personalized statement using the receiver's name, or a relevant current event.

BUILDING INTEREST

Build interest by describing the product or service and making rational or emotional appeals.

In this phase of your sales message, you should describe clearly the product or service. In simple language emphasize the central selling points that you identified during your prewriting analysis. Those selling points can be developed using rational or emotional appeals.

Rational appeals are associated with reason and intellect. They translate selling points into references to making or saving money, increasing efficiency, or making the best use of resources. In general, rational appeals are appropriate when a product is expensive; long-lasting; or important to health, security, and financial success. Emotional appeals relate to status, ego, and sensual feelings. Appealing to the emotions is sometimes effective when a product is inexpensive, short-lived, or nonessential. Many clever sales messages, however, combine emotional and rational strategies for a dual appeal. Consider these examples:

Rational appeals focus on making or saving money, increasing efficiency, or making good use of resources.

Rational Appeal
You can buy the things you need and want, pay household bills, pay off higher-cost loans and credit cards—as soon as you're approved and your Credit-Line account is opened.

Emotional appeals focus on status, ego, and sensual feelings.

Emotional Appeal
Leave the urban bustle behind and escape to sun-soaked Bermuda! To recharge your batteries with an injection of sun and surf, all you need is your bathing suit, a little suntan lotion, and your Credit-Line card.

© TOM MERTON/PHOTODISC/GETTY IMAGES

To capture attention in its sales messages for Pampers diapers, Procter & Gamble may show appealing babies. But the copy develops an emotional yet rational appeal when it talks about the development of babies when they get a good night's sleep from having a drier diaper than that sold by the competition. "This is probably the biggest challenge for our advertising—how you move beyond functional advertising to emotional resonance," reports manager Austin Lally.

Dual Appeal

New Credit-Line cardholders are immediately eligible for a $100 travel certificate and additional discounts at fun-filled resorts. Save up to 40 percent while lying on a beach in picturesque, sun-soaked Bermuda, the year-round resort island.

A physical description of your product is not enough, however. Zig Ziglar, thought by some to be America's greatest salesperson, pointed out that no matter how well you know your product, no one is persuaded by cold, hard facts alone. In the end, he contended, "People buy because of the product benefits."[6] Your job is to translate those cold facts into warm feelings and reader benefits. Let's say a sales letter promotes a hand cream made with aloe and cocoa butter extracts, along with Vitamin A. Those facts become, "Nature's hand helpers—including soothing aloe and cocoa extracts, along with firming Vitamin A—form invisible gloves that protect your sensitive skin against the hardships of work, harsh detergents, and constant environmental assaults."

REDUCING RESISTANCE

Marketing pros use a number of techniques to overcome resistance and build desire.

- **Testimonials:** *"I learned so much in your language courses that I began to dream in French."*—Holly Franker, Beaumont, Texas
- **Names of satisfied users (with permission, of course):** *Enclosed is a partial list of private pilots who enthusiastically subscribe to our service.*
- **Money-back guarantee or warranty:** *We offer the longest warranties in the business—all parts and service on-site for two years!*
- **Free trial or sample:** *We're so confident that you'll like our new accounting program that we want you to try it absolutely free.*
- **Performance tests, polls, or awards:** *Our TP-3000 was named Best Web Phone, and Etown.com voted it Cell Phone of the Year.*

© by Randy Glasbergen.
www.glasbergen.com

"Resistance to our men's fragrance? Nothing that a testimonial from Shaq wouldn't overcome!"

In addition, you need to anticipate objections and questions the receiver may have. When possible, translate these objections into selling points (*If you're worried about training your staff members on the new software, remember that our offer includes $1,000 of on-site one-on-one instruction*). Be sure, of course that your claims are accurate and do not stretch the truth. To learn more about what is legal in sales messages, see the Communication Workshop at the end of this chapter.

When price is an obstacle, consider these suggestions:

- Delay mentioning price until after you've created a desire for the product.
- Show the price in small units, such as the price per issue of a magazine.
- Demonstrate how the reader saves money by, for instance, subscribing for two or three years.
- Compare your prices with those of a competitor.

MOTIVATING ACTION

Techniques for motivating action include offering a gift or incentive, limiting an offer, and guaranteeing satisfaction.

All the effort put into a sales message is wasted if the reader fails to act. To make it easy for readers to act, you can provide a reply card, a stamped and preaddressed envelope, a toll-free telephone number, an easy Web site, or a promise of a follow-up call. Because readers often need an extra push, consider including additional motivators, such as the following:

- **Offer a gift:** *You'll receive a free cell phone with the purchase of any new car.*
- **Promise an incentive:** *With every new, paid subscription, we'll plant a tree in one of America's Heritage Forests.*
- **Limit the offer:** *Only the first 100 customers receive free checks.*
- **Set a deadline:** *You must act before June 1 to get these low prices.*
- **Guarantee satisfaction:** *We'll return your full payment if you're not entirely satisfied—no questions asked.*

"I find it hard to believe that we've actually won 20 million dollars when they send the letter bulk mail."

From *The Wall Street Journal*–permission, Cartoon Features Syndicate.

The final paragraph of the sales letter carries the punch line. This is where you tell readers what you want done and give them reasons for doing it. Most sales letters also include postscripts because they make irresistible reading. Even readers who might skim over or bypass paragraphs are drawn to a P.S. Therefore, use a postscript to reveal your strongest motivator, to add a special inducement for a quick response, or to reemphasize a central selling point.

PUTTING IT ALL TOGETHER

Because direct mail is an expensive way to advertise, messages should present complete information with a personalized tone for specific audiences.

Sales letters are a preferred marketing medium because they can be personalized, directed to target audiences, and filled with a more complete message than other advertising media. But direct mail is expensive. That's why the total sales message is crafted so painstakingly.

Let's examine a sales letter, shown in Figure 7.4, addressed to a target group of small-business owners. To sell the new magazine *Small Business Monthly*, the letter incorporates all four components of an effective persuasive message. Notice that the personalized action-setting opener places the reader in a familiar situation (getting into an elevator) and draws an analogy between failing to reach the top floor and failing to achieve a business goal.

The writer develops a rational central selling point (a magazine that provides valuable information for a growing small business) and repeats this selling point in all the components of the letter. Notice, too, how a testimonial from a small-business executive lends support to the sales message, and how the closing pushes for action. Since the price of the magazine is not a selling feature, it's mentioned only on

FIGURE 7.4   • **Sales Letter**

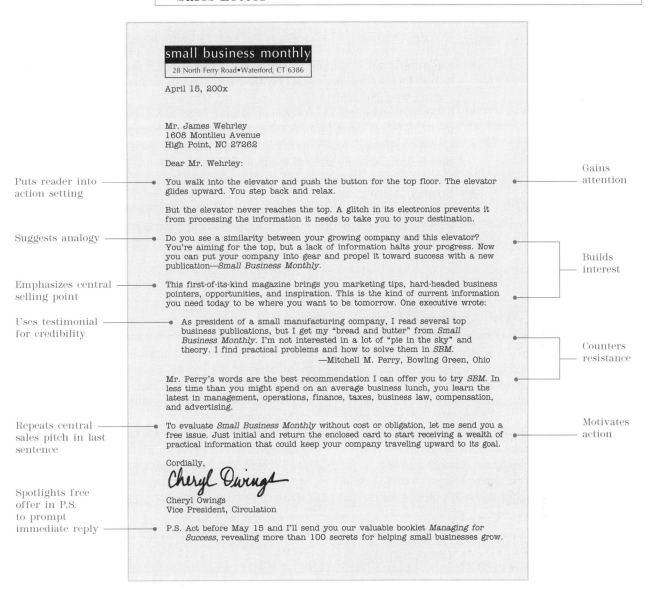

the reply card. This sales letter saves its strongest motivator—a free booklet—for the high-impact P.S. line.

In developing effective sales messages, some writers may be tempted to cross the line that separates legal from illegal sales tactics. Be sure to check out the Communication Workshop for this chapter to see specific examples of what is legal and what is not.

Writing Successful Online Sales Messages

E-mail messages can be used to upsell, cross-sell, cut costs, and attract customers.

To make the best use of limited advertising dollars, many businesses are turning to e-mail marketing campaigns instead of traditional direct mailings. E-mail marketing can attract new customers, keep existing ones, upsell, cross-sell, and cut costs. As consumers feel more comfortable and secure with online advertising, they will be receiving more e-mail sales messages. If your organization requires an online sales message, try using the following techniques gleaned from the best-performing e-mails:

- **Communicate only with those who have given permission!** By sending messages only to "opt-in" folks, you greatly increase your "open rate"—those e-mail messages that will be opened. E-mail users detest spam. However, receivers are

Send only targeted, not "blanket," mailings. Include something special for a select group.

surprisingly receptive to offers specifically for them. Remember that today's customer is *somebody*—not *anybody*.

- **Craft a catchy subject line.** Offer discounts or premiums. Promise solutions to everyday work-related problems. Highlight hot new industry topics. Invite readers to scan a top-ten list, such as issues, trends, or people.
- **Keep the main information "above the fold."** E-mail messages should be top heavy. Primary points should appear early in the message so that they capture the reader's attention.
- **Make the message short, conversational, and focused.** Because on-screen text is taxing to read, be brief. Focus on one or two central selling points only.
- **Convey urgency.** Top-performing e-mail messages state an offer deadline or demonstrate why the state of the industry demands action on the reader's part. Good messages also tie the product to relevant current events.
- **Sprinkle testimonials throughout the copy.** Consumers' own words are the best sales copy. These comments can serve as callouts or be integrated into the copy.
- **Provide a means for opting out.** It's polite and a good business tactic to include a statement that tells receivers how to be removed from the sender's mailing database.

SUMMING UP AND LOOKING FORWARD

The ability to persuade is a powerful and versatile communication tool. In this chapter you learned to apply the indirect strategy in making favor and action requests, writing persuasive messages within organizations, making claims and requesting adjustments, and writing sales letters. You also learned techniques for developing successful online sales messages. In the Communication Workshop following this chapter, you can examine examples of what is legal and what is not in sales letters.

The techniques suggested in this chapter will be useful in many other contexts beyond the writing of these business documents. You will find that logical organization of arguments is also extremely effective in expressing ideas orally or any time you must overcome resistance to change.

In coming chapters you will learn how to modify and generalize the techniques of direct and indirect strategies in preparing and writing informal and formal reports and proposals. Nearly all businesspeople today find that they must write an occasional report.

CRITICAL THINKING

1. Why is the ability to persuade a significant trait in both business and personal relations?

2. What are some of the underlying motivations that prompt individuals to agree to requests that do not directly benefit themselves or their organizations?

3. Because of the burden that "junk mail" places on society (depleted landfills, declining timber sup-

plies, overburdened postal system), how can it be justified?

4. Why is it important to know your needs and have documentation when you make requests of superiors?

5. Some individuals will never write an actual sales letter. Why is it nevertheless important for them to learn the techniques for doing so?

CHAPTER REVIEW

6. List and discuss the four key elements in a persuasive request.

7. How can a subordinate be effective in persuading a superior to adopt a new procedure or purchase new equipment?

8. Generally, the direct pattern is best for requesting straightforward claims. When is the indirect pattern appropriate?

9. Name eight tips for making claims and complaints.

10. List at least ten ways to gain a reader's attention in the opening of a sales letter.

11. In selling a product, when are rational appeals most effective? When are emotional appeals most effective?

12. Name six writing techniques that reduce resistance in a sales message.

(continued on page 188)

WRITING COACH
STEP-BY-STEP DEMONSTRATION

Favor Request

Problem

As program chair of the Southern Florida University Management Society, you must invite a well-known business writer to speak at your organization's banquet on February 2. The author, Joyce Lain Kennedy, has written many columns and books on careers, focusing recently on Internet job searching. Unfortunately, the SFU Management Society has no budget for speakers. But you saw a recent newspaper item saying that Ms. Kennedy has a winter home in St. Petersburg, so she might consider coming since she is a neighbor and since she has a track record of speaking to student audiences.

before revision

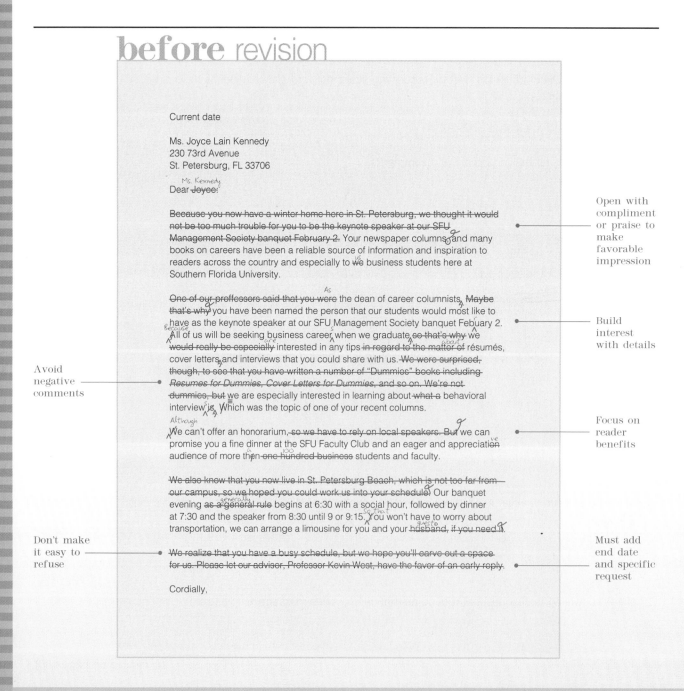

Current date

Ms. Joyce Lain Kennedy
230 73rd Avenue
St. Petersburg, FL 33706

Dear ~~Joyce:~~ Ms. Kennedy

~~Because you now have a winter home here in St. Petersburg, we thought it would not be too much trouble for you to be the keynote speaker at our SFU Management Society banquet February 2.~~ Your newspaper columns and many books on careers have been a reliable source of information and inspiration to readers across the country and especially to ~~we~~ us business students here at Southern Florida University.

~~One of our proffessors said that you were~~ As the dean of career columnists, ~~Maybe that's why~~ you have been named the person that our students would most like to have as the keynote speaker at our SFU Management Society banquet February 2. Because All of us will be seeking business careers when we graduate, ~~so that's why we~~ would really be ~~especially~~ interested in any tips ~~in regard to the matter of~~ about résumés, cover letters, and interviews that you could share with us. ~~We were surprised, though, to see that you have written a number of "Dummies" books including *Resumes for Dummies, Cover Letters for Dummies*, and so on. We're not dummies, but~~ we are especially interested in learning about ~~what a~~ behavioral interview ~~is~~ which was the topic of one of your recent columns.

Although ~~W~~we can't offer an honorarium, ~~so we have to rely on local speakers. But~~ we can promise you a fine dinner at the SFU Faculty Club and an eager and appreciative audience of more than ~~one hundred~~ 100 business students and faculty.

~~We also know that you now live in St. Petersburg Beach, which is not too far from our campus, so we hoped you could work us into your schedule.~~ Our banquet evening ~~as a general rule~~ generally begins at 6:30 with a social hour, followed by dinner at 7:30 and the speaker from 8:30 until 9 or 9:15. So that ~~Y~~you won't have to worry about transportation, we can arrange a limousine for you and your ~~husband, if you need it.~~ guests

~~We realize that you have a busy schedule, but we hope you'll carve out a space for us. Please let our advisor, Professor Kevin West, have the favor of an early reply.~~

Cordially,

Margin annotations (left):
Avoid negative comments

Don't make it easy to refuse

Margin annotations (right):
Open with compliment or praise to make favorable impression

Build interest with details

Focus on reader benefits

Must add end date and specific request

Writing Plan

OPENING

Obtain the reader's attention and interest

Describe a problem, state something unexpected, suggest reader benefits, offer praise or compliments, or ask a stimulating question.

BODY

Build interest

Explain logically and concisely the purpose of the request. Prove its merit. Use facts, statistics, expert opinion, examples, specific details, and direct and indirect benefits.

Reduce resistance

Anticipate objections, offer counterarguments, establish credibility, demonstrate competence, and show the value of your proposal.

CLOSING

Motivate action

Ask for a particular action. Make the action easy to take. Show courtesy, respect, and gratitude.

---

after revision

SOUTHERN FLORIDA UNIVERSITY

Management Society
Box 2997 A
Sarasota FL 34230

November 1, 200x

Ms. Joyce Lain Kennedy
230 73rd Avenue
St. Petersburg, FL 33706

Dear Ms. Kennedy:

Your newspaper columns and many books on careers have been a reliable source of information and inspiration to readers across the country and especially to us business students here at Southern Florida University.

As the dean of career columnists, you have been named the person that our students would most like to have as the keynote speaker at our SFU Management Society banquet February 2. Because all of us will be seeking business careers when we graduate, we are interested in any tips about résumés, cover letters, and interviews that you could share with us. We are especially interested in learning about behavioral interviews, which was the topic of one of your recent columns. Although we can't offer an honorarium, we can promise you a fine dinner at the SFU Faculty Club and an eager and appreciative audience of more than 100 students and faculty.

Our banquet evening generally begins at 6:30 with a social hour, followed by dinner at 7:30, and the speaker's remarks from 8:30 until 9 or 9:15. So that you won't have to worry about transportation, we can arrange a limousine for you and your guest.

Please make this our most memorable banquet yet! Just call our advisor, Professor Kevin West, at (813) 886-2449 before November 15 to accept this invitation.

Cordially,

Gina Caracas

Gina Caracas
Secretary

13. Name five techniques for motivating action in the closing of a sales message.

14. What are some advantages and disadvantages to advertisers in using e-mail marketing?

15. What techniques do writers of successful online sales messages use?

WRITING IMPROVEMENT EXERCISES

Strategies

For each of the following situations, check the appropriate writing strategy.

Direct Strategy	Indirect Strategy	
_____	_____	16. An appeal for a contribution to Direct Relief, an international charity
_____	_____	17. An announcement that henceforth all dental, health, and life insurance benefits for employees will be reduced
_____	_____	18. A request to another company for verification of employment regarding a job applicant
_____	_____	19. A letter to a painting contractor demanding payment for replacing office floor tiles damaged by sloppy painters
_____	_____	20. A request for information about a wireless office network
_____	_____	21. A letter to a grocery store requesting permission to display posters advertising a school fund-raising car wash
_____	_____	22. A request for a refund of the cost of a computer program that does not perform the functions it was expected to perform
_____	_____	23. A request for correction of a routine billing error on your company credit card
_____	_____	24. An invitation to a prominent financial expert to address the annual stockholders' meeting
_____	_____	25. A memo to employees describing the schedule and menu selections of a new mobile catering service

WRITING IMPROVEMENT CASES

7.1 Persuasive Memo: Importing T-Shirts From China

Your Task. Analyze the following memo. List its weaknesses. If your instructor directs, revise it.

Date:	Current
To:	Alexandra Schwab, VP, Media Relations
From:	Norman Porticella, Product Manager
Subject:	T-Shirts From China

Trade shows are a great way for us to meet customers and sell our Life Fitness equipment. But instead of expanding our visits to these trade shows, we continue to cut back the number that we attend. Lately we've been sending fewer staff members. I know that you've been asking us to find ways to reduce costs, but perhaps we're not going about it right.

With increased air fares and hotel charges, my staff has tried to find ways to live within our very tight budget. Yet, we're being asked to find additional ways to reduce our costs. I'm currently thinking ahead to the big Las Vegas trade show coming up in September.

One area where we could make a change is in the gift that we give away. In the past we have presented booth visitors with a nine-color T-shirt that is silk screened and gorgeous. But it comes at a cost of $15 for each and every one of these beauties from a top-name designer. To save money, I suggest that we try a $4 T-shirt made in China, which is reasonably presentable. It's got our name on it, and, after all, folks just use these shirts for workouts. Who cares if it is a fancy silk-screened T-shirt or a functional Chinese one that has "Life Fitness" plastered on the chest? Since we give away 2,000 T-shirts at our largest show, we could save big bucks by dumping the designer shirt. But we have to act quickly. I've enclosed a cheap one for you to see.

Let me know what you think.

1. List at least five weaknesses.

7.2 Claim Request: Copier Ripoff!

The following letter makes a claim, but the message is not as effective as it could be.

Your Task. Analyze the letter and list its weaknesses. If your instructor directs, revise the letter.

Current date
Mr. Kurt Littleton
Lawson Business Products
291 Bostwick Northeast
Grand Rapids, MI 49503

Dear Sir:

Three months ago we purchased four of your E-Studio 120 photocopiers, and we've had nothing but trouble ever since.

Your salesperson, Julia Franks, assured us that the E-Studio 120 could easily handle our volume of 3,000 copies a day. This seemed strange since the sales brochure said that the E-Studio 120 was meant for 500 copies a day. But we believed Ms. Franks. Big mistake! Our four E-Studio 120 copiers are down constantly; we can't go on like this. Because they're still under warranty, they eventually get repaired. But we're losing considerable business in downtime.

Your Ms. Franks has been less than helpful, so I telephoned the district manager, Ron Rivera. I suggested that we trade in our E-Studio 120 copiers (which we got for $2,500 each) on two E-Studio 600 models (at $13,500 each). However, Mr. Rivera said he would have to charge 50 percent depreciation on our E-Studio 120 copiers. What a ripoff! I think that 20 percent depreciation is more reasonable since we've had the machines only three months. Mr. Rivera said he would get back to me, and I haven't heard from him since.

I'm writing to your headquarters because I have no faith in either Ms. Franks or Mr. Rivera, and I need action on these machines. If you understood anything about business, you would see what a sweet deal I'm offering you. I'm willing to stick with your company and purchase your most expensive model—but I can't take such a steep loss on the E-Studio 120 copiers. The E-Studio 120 copiers are relatively new; you should be able to sell them with no trouble. And think of all the money you'll save by not having your repair technicians making constant trips to service our 120 copiers! Please let me hear from you immediately.

Sincerely yours,

1. List at least five weaknesses.

7.3 Sales Letter Analysis

Your Task. Select a one- or two-page sales letter received by you or a friend. (If you are unable to find a sales letter, your instructor may have a collection.) Study the letter and then answer these questions:

a. What techniques capture the reader's attention?

b. Is the opening effective? Explain.

c. What are the central selling points?

d. Does the letter use rational, emotional, or a combination of appeals? Explain.

e. What reader benefits are suggested?

f. How does the letter build interest in the product or service?

g. How is price handled?

h. How does the letter anticipate reader resistance and offer counterarguments?

i. What action is the reader to take? How is the action made easy?

j. What motivators spur the reader to act quickly?

ACTIVITIES AND CASES

INFOTRAC   WEB

7.4 Persuasive Favor/Action Request: Financial Advice for the Young, Fabulous, and Broke

Despite spending countless hours in the classroom and writing stacks of meticulous research papers, many graduates who are about to enter the real world are clueless when it comes to basic personal finance, according to the experts. As program chair for the Associated Student Organization at Arizona International University, Tempe, you suggest that the group invite financial celebrity Suze Orman to be its keynote speaker at a special graduation convocation. The ASO agreed and set aside $1,000 as an honorarium. This is not very much to entice the author of *The Money Book for the Young, Fabulous & Broke*, but Ms. Orman has been heavily promoting her book in cross-country tours to college campuses. The ASO group thinks it stands a fair chance of luring this financial celebrity to campus.[7]

Your Task. Write a convincing favor/action request to Suze Orman, P.O. Box 4502, New York, NY 10014. Learn more about her expertise and books by using the Web and InfoTrac. Invite her to speak April 26. Provide direct and indirect benefits. Include an end date and make it easy to respond. Do not use the same wording as the model documents in this chapter.

TEAM   **CRITICAL THINKING**

7.5 Persuasive Favor/Action Request: Celebrity Auction

Your professional or school organization (such as the Associated Students Organization) must find ways to raise money. The president of your group appoints a team and asks it to brainstorm for ways to meet your group's pledge to aid the United Way's battle against adult illiteracy in your community. The campaign against adult illiteracy has targeted an estimated 10,000 people in your community who cannot read or write. After considering and discarding a number of silly ideas, your team comes up with the brilliant idea of a celebrity auction. At a spring function, items or services from local and other celebrities would be auctioned. Your organization approves your idea and asks your team to persuade an important person in your professional organization (or your college president) to donate one hour of tutoring in a subject he or she chooses. If you have higher aspirations, write to a movie star or athlete of your choice—perhaps one who is part of your organization or who attended your school.

Your Task. As a team, discuss the situation and decide what action to take. Then write a persuasive letter to secure an item for the auction. You might wish to ask a star to donate a prop from a recent movie.

CRITICAL THINKING   **TEAM**   **WEB**

7.6 Persuasive Favor/Action Request: PDAs Lighten Realtors' Load in Historic Charleston

Charleston, South Carolina, one of America's most beautifully preserved architectural and historic treasures, enjoys a booming real estate market. *Forbes* magazine forecasts a 200 percent appreciation for its properties by the year 2009. The Cooper River Bridge project is America's largest construction project, and the entire regional economy glows. Real estate agents have plenty of work showing off new homes as well as beautifully preserved structures from the colonial and antebellum periods. The problem is that agents have to grapple with telephone directory–size books of multiple listings—or run back and forth to their offices as they show home buyers what's on the market.

As a staffer at one of Charleston's top realty agencies, you recently attended a Association of Realtors meeting and talked with fellow agent Bob Drewisch. He showed you his new personal digital assistant (PDA) and said, "Watch this." He accessed listing after listing of homes for sale by his company and others. You couldn't believe your eyes. You saw island properties, historic homes, beachfront condos—all with pictures and complete listing information. In this little device, which could easily fit into a pocket (or purse), you could carry six months of active, pending, and closed listings, along with contact details for agents and other valuable information.

You thought about the size of your multiple listing books and how often you had to trudge back to the office when a home buyer wanted to see a market listing. "Looks terrific," you said to Bob. "But what about new listings? And how much does this thing cost? And I bet it has a steep learning curve." Eager to show off his new toy, Bob demonstrated its user-friendly interface that follows intuitive prompts such as *price, area,* and *number of bedrooms*. He explained that his agency bought the software for $129. For a monthly fee of $19, he downloads updates as often as he likes. In regard to ease of use, Bob said that even his fellow agent Emily, notoriously computer challenged, loved it. None of the staff found it confusing or difficult to operate.

You decide that the agency where you work should provide this service to all 18 full-time staff agents. Assume that multiple listing software is available for the greater Charleston area.

Your Task. With other staff members (your classmates), decide how to approach the agency owner, who is "old school" and shuns most technology. Decide what you want to request. Do you merely want the owner to talk with you about the service? Should you come right out and ask for PDAs and the service for all 18 staff members? Should you expect staff members to provide the hardware (a basic PDA at about $200) and the agency to purchase the service and individual updates for each full-time agent? Or should you ask for the service plus a top-of-the-line device that combines PDA/phone, GPS (global positioning system), and other capabilities? Learn more about PDA possibilities on the Web. Explore this information with your team. Once you decide on a course of action, what appeals would be most persuasive? Discuss how to handle price in your persuasive argument. Individually or as a group, prepare a persuasive message to George R. Hollings, President, Hollings Carolina Realty. Decide whether you should deliver your persuasive message as a printed memo or an e-mail.[8]

TEAM

7.7 Persuasive Favor/Action Request: Servers Want Recourse From Stingy Customers

Centered in the heart of a 2,400-acre Florida paradise, the Bayside Inn Golf and Beach Resort offers gracious hospitality and beautiful accommodations. Its restaurant, Dolphin Watch, overlooks the scenic Choctawhatchee Bay, a perfect place to spy dolphins. As a server in the Dolphin Watch, you enjoy working in this resort setting—except for one thing. You have occasionally been "stiffed" by a patron who left no tip. You know your service is excellent, but some customers just don't get it. They seem to think that tips are optional, a sign of appreciation. For servers, however, tips are 80 percent of their income.

In a recent *New York Times* article, you learned that some restaurants—like the famous Coach House Restaurant in New York—automatically add a 15 percent tip to the bill. In Santa Monica the Lula restaurant prints "gratuity guidelines" on checks, showing customers what a 15 or 20 percent tip would be. You also know that American Express recently developed a gratuity calculation feature on its terminals. This means that diners don't even have to do the math!

Your Task. Because they know you are studying business communication, your fellow servers have asked you to write a serious letter to Nicholas Ruiz, General Manager, Bayside Inn Golf and Beach Resort, 9300 Emerald Coast Parkway West, Sandestin FL 32550-7268. Persuade him to adopt mandatory tipping guidelines in the restaurant. Talk with fellow servers (your classmates) to develop logical persuasive arguments.

CRITICAL THINKING

7.8 Persuasive Favor/Action Request: Dictionary Definition of *McJobs* Angers McDonald's

The folks at McDonald's fumed when they heard about the latest edition of a highly regarded dictionary, *Merriam-Webster's Collegiate Dictionary*, defined the word *McJob* as "a low-paying job that requires little skill and provides little opportunity for advancement." Naturally, McDonald's was outraged. One executive said, "It's a slap in the face to the 12 million men and women who work hard every day in America's 900,000 restaurants."

The term *McJob* was coined by Canadian novelist Douglas Coupland in his 1991 novel *Generation X*. In this novel the term described a low-prestige, low-dignity, low-benefit, no-future job in the service sector. But McDonald's strongly objects to this corruption of its name. For one thing, the company rejects the notion that its jobs are dead ends. Significant members of top management—including the president, chief operating officer, and CEO—began their McDonald's careers behind the counter. Moreover, when it comes to training, McDonald's trains more young people than the U.S. armed forces.

What's more, McDonald's is especially proud of its "MCJOBS" program for mentally and physically challenged people. Some officers even wonder if the dictionary term *McJob* doesn't come dangerously close to the trademarked name for its special program. Another point that rankles McDonald's is that, according to its records, over 1,000 people who now own McDonald's restaurants received their training while serving customers. Who says that its jobs have no future?

The CEO is burned up about Merriam-Webster's dictionary definition, and he wants to send a complaint letter. But he is busy and asks you, a member of the communication staff, to draft a first version. He's so steamed that he's thinking of sending a copy of the letter to news agencies.

Your Task. Before writing this letter, decide what action, if any, to request. Think about an appropriate tone and also about the two possible audiences. Then write a persuasive letter for the signature of the CEO. Include the "a slap in the face" statement, which he insists on inserting. Address your letter to Frederick C. Mish, editor in chief, Merriam-Webster. Look for a street address on the Web.

WEB   **CRITICAL THINKING**

7.9 Persuasive Favor/Action Request: Appealing to Your Congressional Representative to Listen and Act

Assume you are upset about an issue, and you want your representative or senator to know your position. Choose a national issue about which you feel strongly: student loans, social security depletion, human rights in other countries, federal safety regulations for employees, environmental protection, affirmative action, gun control, taxation of married couples, finding a cure for obesity, the federal deficit, or some other area regulated by Congress.

Your Task. Use your favorite Web search engine (such as *www.google.com*) to obtain your congressional representative's address. Try the search term "Contacting Congress." You should be able to find e-mail and land addresses, along with fax and telephone numbers. Remember that although e-mail and fax messages are fast, they don't carry as much influence as personal letters. What's more, congressional representatives are having trouble responding to the overload of e-mail messages they receive. Decide whether it's better to send an e-mail message or a letter. For best results, consider these tips: (1) Use the proper form of address (*The Honorable John Smith, Dear Senator Smith* or *The Honorable Joan Doe, Dear Representative Doe*). (2) Identify yourself as a member of his or her state or district. (3) Immediately state your position (*I urge you to support/oppose . . . because . . .*). (4) Present facts and illustrations and how they affect you personally. If legislation were enacted, how would you or your organization be better off or worse off? Avoid generalities. (5) Offer to provide further information. (6) Keep the message polite, constructive, and brief (one page tops).

CRITICAL THINKING   **INFOTRAC**   **TEAM**

7.10 Persuasive Favor/Action Request: Vending Machines Are Cash Cows to Schools

"If I start to get huge, then, yeah, I'll cut out the chips and Coke," says seventeen-year-old Nicole O'Neill, as she munches sour-cream-and-onion potato chips and downs a cold can of soda fresh from the snack machine. Most days her lunch comes from a vending machine. The trim high school junior, however, isn't too concerned about how junk food affects her weight or overall health. Although she admits she would prefer a granola bar or fruit, few healthful selections are available from school vending machines.

Vending machines loaded with soft drinks and snacks are increasingly under attack in schools and lunchrooms. Some school boards, however, see them as cash cows. In Gresham, Oregon, the school district is considering a lucrative soft drink contract. If it signs an exclusive 12-year agreement with Coca-Cola to allow vending machines at Gresham High School, the school district will receive $75,000 up front. Then it will receive an additional $75,000 three years later. Commission sales on the 75-cent drinks will bring in an additional $322,000 over the 12-year contract, provided the school sells 67,000 cans and bottles every year. In the past the vending machine payments supported student body activities such as sending students to choir concerts and paying athletic participation fees. Vending machine funds also paid for an electronic reader board in front of the school and a sound system for the gym. The latest contract would bring in $150,000, which is already earmarked for new artificial turf on the school athletic field.

Coca-Cola's vending machines would dispense soft drinks, Fruitopia, Minute Maid juices, Powerade, and Dasani water. The hands-down student favorite, of course, is calorie-laden Coke. Because increasing childhood and adolescent obesity across the nation is a major health concern, the Gresham Parent–Teacher Association (PTA) decided to oppose the contract. The PTA realizes that the school board is heavily influenced by the income generated from the Coca-Cola contract. It wonders what other school districts are doing about their vending machine contracts.

Your Task. As part of a PTA committee, you have been given the task of researching and composing a persuasive but concise (no more than one page) letter addressed to the school board. Use InfoTrac or the Web to locate articles that might help you develop arguments, alternatives, and counterarguments. Meet with your team to discuss your findings. Then individually or as a group, write a letter to the Board of Directors, Gresham-Barlow School District, P.O. Box 310, Gresham, OR 97033.

✳ 7.11 Personal Persuasive Memo: Dear Boss

In your own work or organization experience, identify a problem for which you have a solution. Should a procedure be altered to improve performance? Would a new or different piece of equipment help you perform your work better? Could some tasks be scheduled more efficiently? Are employees being used most effectively? Could customers be better served by changing something? Do you want to work other hours or perform other tasks?

Your Task. Once you have identified a situation requiring persuasion, write a memo to your boss or organization head. Use actual names and facts. Employ the concepts and techniques in this chapter to help you convince your boss that your idea should prevail. Include concrete examples, anticipate objections, emphasize reader benefits, and end with a specific action to be taken.

7.12 Persuasive Memo: Scheduling Meetings More Strategically

The following memo, with names changed, was actually sent.

Your Task. Based on what you have learned in this chapter, improve this memo. Expect the staff to be somewhat resistant because they've never before had meeting restrictions.

Date: Current
To: All Managers and Employees
From: Lynn Wasson, CEO
Subject: SCHEDULING MEETINGS

Please be reminded that travel in the greater Los Angeles area is time consuming. In the future we're asking that you set up meetings that

1. Are of critical importance

2. Consider travel time for the participants

3. Consider phone conferences (or video or e-mail) in lieu of face-to-face meetings

4. Meetings should be at the location where most of the participants work and at the most opportune travel times

5. Traveling together is another way to save time and resources.

We all have our traffic stories. A recent one is that a certain manager was asked to attend a one-hour meeting in Burbank. This required one hour of travel in advance of the meeting, one hour for the meeting, and two and a half hours of travel through Los Angeles afterward. This meeting was scheduled for 4 p.m. Total time consumed by the manager for the one-hour meeting was four and a half hours.

Thank you for your consideration.

CRITICAL THINKING — **E-MAIL** — **INFOTRAC**

7.13 Persuasive Internal Request: Curbing Profanity on the Job

As sales manager for a large irrigation parts manufacturer, you are concerned about the use of profanity by your sales associates. Some defend profanity, claiming that it helps them fit in. Your female sales reps have said that it helps relax listeners and drive home a point as well as makes them "one of the boys." You have done some research, however, and learned that courts have ruled that profanity can constitute sexual harassment—whether in person or in print. In addition to causing legal problems, profanity on the job projects a negative image of the individual and of the company. Although foul language is heard increasingly on TV and in the movies, you think it's a bad habit and you want to see it curbed on the job.

Your Task. Use InfoTrac and the Web to locate articles related to the use of profanity and strategies employed by organizations for dealing with it. One good resource is *www.cusscontrol.com*. In small groups or in class, discuss the place of formal and informal language in communication. Prepare a list of reasons people curse and reasons not to do so. Your instructor may ask you to interview employers to learn their reactions to the issue of workplace profanity. As sales manager at Rain City, compose a persuasive e-mail or memo to your sales staff that will encourage them to curb their use of profanity.[9]

7.14 Persuasive Claim: Legal Costs for Sharing a Slice of Heaven

Originally a shipbuilding village, the town of Mystic, Connecticut, captures the spirit of the nineteenth-century seafaring era. But it is best known for Mystic Pizza, a bustling local pizzeria featured in a movie that launched the film career of Julia Roberts. Today, customers line the sidewalk waiting to taste its pizza, called by some "a slice of Heaven."

Assume that you are the business manager for Mystic Pizza's owners. They were approached by an independent vendor who wants to use the Mystic Pizza name and secret recipes to distribute frozen pizza through grocery and convenience stores. As business manager, you worked with a law firm, Giordano, Murphy, and Associates. This firm was to draw up contracts regarding the use of Mystic Pizza's name and quality standards for the product. When you received the bill from Henry Giordano, you were flabbergasted.

It itemized 38 hours of attorney preparation, at $400 per hour, and 55 hours of paralegal assistance, at $100 per hour. The bill also showed $415 for telephone calls, which might be accurate because Mr. Giordano had to talk with the owners, who were vacationing in Italy at the time. You seriously doubt, however, that an experienced attorney would require 38 hours to draw up the contracts in question. When you began checking, you discovered that excellent legal advice could be obtained for $200 an hour.

Your Task. Decide what you want to request, and then write a persuasive request to Henry Giordano, Attorney at Law, Giordano, Murphy, and Associates, 254 Sherborn Street, Boston, MA 02215. Include an end date and a reason for it.

7.15 Persuasive Claim: Champagne Breakfast Appears Only on Credit Card

As regional manager for an electronics parts manufacturer, you and two other employees attended a conference in Washington, D.C. You stayed at the Harvard House Hotel because your company recommends that employees use this hotel chain. Generally, your employees have liked their accommodations, and the rates have been within your company's budget. The hotel's service has been excellent.

Now, however, you're unhappy with the charges you see on your company's credit statement from Harvard House. When your department's administrative assistant made the reservations, she was assured that you would receive the weekend rates and that a hot breakfast—in the hotel restaurant, the Atrium—would be included in the rate. You hate those cold sweet rolls and instant coffee "continental" breakfasts, especially when you have to leave early and won't get another meal until afternoon. So you and the other two employees went to the restaurant and ordered a hot meal from the menu.

When you received the credit statement, though, you see a charge for $81 for three champagne buffet breakfasts in the Atrium. You hit the ceiling! For one thing, you didn't have a buffet breakfast and certainly no champagne. The three of you got there so early that no buffet had been set up. You ordered pancakes and sausage, and for this you were billed $25 each. You're outraged! What's worse, your company may charge you personally for exceeding the expected rates.

In looking back at this event, you remembered that other guests on your floor were having a "continental" breakfast in a lounge on your floor. Perhaps that's where the hotel expected all guests on the weekend rate to eat. However, your administrative assistant had specifically asked about this matter when she made the reservations, and she was told that you could order breakfast from the menu at the hotel's restaurant.

Your Task. You want to straighten out this matter, and you can't do it by telephone because you suspect that you will need a written record of this entire mess. Write a claim request to Customer Service, Washington Harvard House Hotel, 1221 22nd Street, N.W., Washington, DC 20037. Should you include a copy of the credit statement showing the charge?

INFOTRAC　　**WEB**

7.16 Sales Letter: Getting in Shape at General Foods

Obesity in this country is swelling to unprecedented levels with nearly 60 percent of adults overweight. In addition to the risks to individuals, businesses estimate a loss of $5.5 billion in lowered productivity resulting from absenteeism and weight-related chronic disease. Companies from Wall Street to the Rust Belt are launching or improving programs to help employees lose weight. Union Pacific Railroad is considering giving out pedometers to track workers around the office, as well as dispensing weight-loss drugs. Merrill Lynch sponsors Weight Watchers meetings. Caterpillar instituted the Healthy Balance Program. It promotes long-term behavioral change and healthier lifestyles for Caterpillar workers. Estimates suggest that employers and employees could save $1,200 a year for each person's medical costs if overweight employees shed their excess weight.

As a sales representative for Vector Lifetime Fitness, one of the country's leading fitness operators, you are convinced that your fitness equipment and programs are instrumental in helping people lose weight. With regular exercise at an on-site fitness center, employees lose weight and improve overall health. As employee health improves, absenteeism is reduced and overall productivity increases. Moreover, employees love working out before or after work. They make the routine part of their workday, and they often have work buddies who share their fitness regimen.

Although many companies resist spending money to save money, fitness centers need not be large or expensive to be effective. Studies show that moderately sized centers coupled with motivational and training programs yield the greatest success. For just $30,000, Vector Lifetime Fitness will provide exercise equipment including treadmills, elliptical trainers, exercise bikes, multigyms, and weight machines. Their fitness experts will design a fitness room, set up the equipment, and create appropriate programs. Best of all, the one-time cost is usually offset by cost savings within one year of center installation. For additional fees Vector can provide fitness consultants for employee fitness assessments. Vector specialists will also train employees on the proper use of the equipment and clean and manage the facility—for an extra charge, of course.

Your Task. Use InfoTrac or the Web to update your obesity statistics. Then prepare a sales letter addressed to Cheryl O'Berry, Vice President, Human Resources, General Foods, Inc., 2300 Thousand Lakes Blvd., Eagan, MN 65123. Ask for an appointment to meet with her. Send a brochure detailing the products and services that Vector Lifetime Fitness provides. As an incentive, offer a free fitness assessment for all employees if General Foods installs a fitness facility by December 1.

7.17 Sales Letter: Promoting Your Product or Service

Identify a situation in your current job or a previous one in which a sales letter is/was needed. Using suggestions from this chapter, write an appropriate sales letter that promotes a product or service. Use actual names, information, and examples. If you have no work experience, imagine a business you'd like to start: word processing, pet grooming, car detailing, tutoring, specialty knitting, balloon decorating, delivery service, child care, gardening, lawn care, or something else. Write a letter selling your product or service to be distributed to your prospective customers. Be sure to tell them how to respond.

VIDEO RESOURCE

Video Library 2, *Bridging the Gap*

Persuasion and Profitability: World Gym. World Gym Showplace Square has been rated the best gym in the Bay Area. The physical plant has over 35,000 square feet stocked with free weights, treadmills, lifecycles, Stairmasters, recumbent bikes, and rowing machines. Although business is good, World Gym finds that most of its traffic comes from 4 p.m. to 8 p.m. If it could persuade members to come later and stay until 10 or 11 p.m., it could increase profitability and improve service. The owners, Joe and Robin Talmudge, are thinking of adding video cameras inside and outside to improve security.

This might encourage members to stay later. After watching the film, you'll see some of the problems facing the Talmudges.

Your Task. As an assistant to the owners, you have been asked to draft a letter to members that persuades them to fill out a simple questionnaire regarding the addition of security cameras. In the prewriting phase, decide the purpose of your message. Consider the best channel, along with direct and indirect benefits you can suggest. Write a message addressed to "Valued World Gym Members." Your instructor may help you think through this case with specific questions.

GRAMMAR/MECHANICS CHECKUP—7

Commas 2

Review the Grammar/Mechanics Handbook Sections 2.05–2.09. Then study each of the following statements and insert necessary commas. In the space provided write the number of commas that you add; write *0* if no commas are needed. Also record the number of the G/M principle(s) illustrated. When you finish, compare your responses with those provided at the end of the book. If your answers differ, study carefully the principles shown in parentheses.

1 _____ (2.06a)   **Example**   When U.S. organizations engage in overseas business, they must train their staffs accordingly.

_____   1. If you are based in New York City and working with a sales office in Australia you will be dealing with a 16-hour time difference.

_____   2. One international support person works with time zones around the world and she keeps several clocks set to different zones.

3. Dealing with the unfamiliar is less challenging if you are patient and if you are able to avoid becoming irritated at misunderstandings.

4. Michelle Sanchez who was recently transferred to the parent company in France quickly became fluent in French.

5. The imaginative promising software company opened its offices April 22 in Paris.

6. Any sales associate who earns at least 1,000 recognition points this year will be honored with a bonus vacation trip to Tahiti.

7. James Manning the marketing manager for Chevron's Global Power Generation frequently engages in videoconferences that span time zones.

8. In a period of less than six weeks Mr. Manning made several trips to the West Coast and to Asia.

9. When you are working with foreign clients for whom English is a second language you may have to speak slowly and repeat yourself.

10. To be most successful you must read between the lines and learn to pick up on different cultural vibes.

Review of Commas 1 and 2

11. Michelle's new job involved setting up meetings arranging travel plans and communicating with people who did not speak her language.

12. After she was hired she was told to report for work on Monday June 2 in Paris.

13. In the fall we expect to open a new branch in Sunnyvale which is an area of considerable growth.

14. As we discussed on the telephone the ceremony is scheduled for Thursday March 4 at 3 p.m.

15. Michelle had to ask a foreign executive with a thick accent to repeat himself several times and she was uncomfortable in this situation.

● GRAMMAR/MECHANICS CHALLENGE—7

The following letter has faults in grammar, punctuation, spelling, proofreading, and number form. **Hint:** Look for commas to remove as well as add. Correct the errors with standard proofreading marks (see Appendix B) or revise the message online at **Guffey Xtra!**

ConEx
Consolidated Express

Current date

Mr. Robert T. Hesser
111349 Pinestone Court
San Diego, CA 92128

Dear Mr. Hessur:

Beginning Febrary 15 your rates for ConEx domestic services will change to those in the inclosed rate agreement. These new rates reflect an increase on the average of between 3% and 4%, however, rates for ConEx standard overnight service is decreasing for heavier weights and ConEx express saver rates are staying the same for heavier weights.

ConEx express saver gives you ConEx value for your less urgent shipments. It affords you an opportunity for delivery in 3 business days at some of our most affordable rates ever yet it offer such ConEx extra's as commited delivery 24 hour access to shipment information and our money back guarantee.

Because we recognize the growing number of business who's work extends right through the week end ConEx announces a welcome innovation Sunday delivery. Starting March 10th shipments dropped off or picked up on Friday or Saterday can be delivered to fifty U.S. metropolitan areas on Sunday via ConEx priority overnight service—for a twenty dollar special handling fee.

Enhancements to our Web site (www.conex.com) makes using ConEx easy and fast. In addition ConEx gives you alot of ways to satisfy your customers expectations which range from reliable on time delivery to consistent dependable handling. We appreciate you chosing ConEx, and strive to all ways meet your express shipping needs.

Sincerely,

Donald M. Humphries

Donald M. Humphries

MAKING SURE YOUR SALES
LETTERS ARE LEGAL

In promoting products and writing sales letters, you must be careful with the words you choose and the claims you make. Information contained in sales letters has gotten some writers into trouble. Let's look at what is legal and what is not in six areas:

- **Puffery.** In a sales letter, you can write, *Hey, we've got something fantastic! It's the very best product on the market!* Called *puffery*, such promotional claims are not taken literally by reasonable consumers.

- **Substantiation of claims.** If you write that *three out of four dentists recommend* your toothpaste, you'd better have competent and reliable scientific evidence to support the claim. Such a claim goes beyond puffery and requires proof.

- **Forward-looking statements.** *We estimate that we'll open 50 new stores, increasing our market share substantially.* Companies are allowed to make forward-looking statements to investors if the companies use "safe harbor" language. This language includes words such as *estimate, anticipate, believe, expect, intend, potential,* and *predict.* Courts, however, are increasingly requiring companies to provide more specific information about risks and uncertainties related to their forward-looking statements.

- **Right of publicity.** The unauthorized use of a celebrity's name, likeness, or nickname is not permitted in sales messages. For example, late-night talk-show host Johnny Carson won a case against a portable toilet firm that promoted a "Here's Johnny" toilet. Similarly, film star Dustin Hoffman won millions of dollars for the unauthorized use of a digitally altered photo showing him in an evening gown and Ralph Lauren heels. Even a commercial showing the image of a celebrity such as Tiger Woods on a camera phone is risky.

- **Deceptive advertising.** You cannot tell people that they are *winners* or *finalists* in a sweepstake unless they actually are. American Family Publishers was found guilty of sending letters tricking people into buying magazine subscription in the belief that they had won $1.1 million. Companies may not misrepresent the nature, characteristics, qualities, or geographic origin of goods or services being promoted.

- **Unsolicited merchandise.** If you enclose unsolicited merchandise with a letter, don't expect the receiver to be required to pay for it or return it. Express Publishing, for example, sent a copy of its *Food & Wine Magazine's Cookbook* with a letter inviting recipients to preview the book. "If you don't want to preview the book, simply return the advance notice card within 14 days." Courts, however, have ruled that recipients are allowed to retain, use, or discard any unsolicited merchandise without paying for it or returning it.

Career Application. Consumers today accept advertisers' tendencies to stretch the truth in promoting their products. Most of us realize that polar bears don't enjoy sipping Pepsi and that the Energizer battery will not go on and on forever no matter what its bunny does. A reasonable person would not really expect a miracle cream to perform "a facelift without surgery." But the line between legitimate puffery and misleading statements can be hard to distinguish. The *Uniform Commercial Code* obligates companies to stand behind any specific or quantifiable statement about product quality. Quantifiable statements must be supported with evidence.

Your Task

Collect three sales letters or advertisements. In teams or in class, analyze the sales messages in terms of the six problem areas presented here. Specifically, discuss the following questions:

- What are some examples of puffery that you can identify?

- What claims are made in the letters or advertisements? Are the claims substantiated by reliable scientific evidence? What proof is offered?

- Do any of your examples include names, images, or nicknames of celebrities? How likely is it that the celebrity authorized this use?

- Did free merchandise accompany a sales letter? What does the letter tell the receiver to do with it?

- Does the sales letter or advertisement contain deceptive or unethical statements?

CHAPTER 8

NEGATIVE MESSAGES

OBJECTIVES

- Describe the goals and strategies of business communicators in delivering bad news, including knowing when to use the direct and indirect patterns.

- Explain the writing process and how to avoid legal problems related to bad-news messages.

- Discuss and illustrate techniques for delivering bad news sensitively.

- Outline a plan for refusing routine requests and claims.

- Describe techniques for breaking bad news to customers.

- Outline a plan for breaking bad news to employees.

- Distinguish between ethical and unethical use of the indirect strategy.

More thought goes into bad news messages. That's because we need to explain the whys and try to offer alternatives.

Cathy Dial, former manager, Consumer Affairs, Frito-Lay, a division of PepsiCo[1]

© RYAN McVAY/PHOTODISC/GETTY IMAGES

STRATEGIES FOR DELIVERING BAD NEWS

Breaking bad news was a fact of business life for Cathy Dial at PepsiCo, as it is for nearly every business communicator. In all businesses, things occasionally go wrong. Goods are not delivered, a product fails to perform as expected, service is poor, billing gets fouled up, or customers are misunderstood. Because bad news disappoints, irritates, and sometimes angers the receiver, such messages must be written carefully. The bad feelings associated with disappointing news can generally be reduced if (1) the reader knows the reasons for the rejection and (2) the bad news is revealed with sensitivity. You've probably heard people say, *It wasn't so much the bad news that I resented. It was the way I was told!*

The direct strategy, which you learned to apply in earlier chapters, frontloads the main idea, even when it's bad news. This direct strategy appeals to efficiency-oriented writers who don't want to waste time with efforts to soften the effects of bad news.[2] Many business writers, however, prefer to use the indirect pattern in delivering negative messages. The indirect strategy is especially appealing to relationship-oriented writers. They care about how a message will affect its receiver.

The sting of bad news can be reduced by giving reasons and communicating sensitively.

In this chapter you'll learn when to use the direct pattern and when to use the indirect pattern to deliver bad news. You'll study the goals of business communicators in working with bad news. The major focus of this chapter, however, is on developing techniques for breaking bad news sensitively. You'll apply those techniques to refusing routine requests and claims, breaking bad news to customers, and delivering bad organizational news to employees.

Establishing Goals in Communicating Bad News

Delivering bad news is not the happiest writing task you may have, but it can be gratifying if you do it effectively. As a business communicator working with bad news, you will have many goals, the most important of which are these:

In communicating bad news, key goals include getting the receiver to accept it, maintaining goodwill, and avoiding legal liability.

- **Acceptance.** Make sure the reader understands and *accepts* the bad news. The indirect pattern helps in achieving this objective.
- **Positive image.** Promote and maintain a good image of yourself and your organization. Realizing this goal assumes that you will act ethically.
- **Message clarity.** Make the message so clear that additional correspondence is unnecessary.
- **Protection.** Avoid creating legal liability or responsibility for you or your organization.

These are ambitious goals, and we're not always successful in achieving them all. The patterns and writing plans you're about to learn, however, provide the beginning communicator with strategies and tactics that many writers have found successful in conveying disappointing news sensitively and safely. With experience, you'll be able to vary these patterns and adapt them to your organization's specific writing tasks.

Using the Indirect Pattern to Prepare the Reader

Whereas good news can be revealed quickly, bad news is generally easier to accept when broken gradually. Revealing bad news slowly and indirectly shows sensitivity to your reader. By preparing the reader, you tend to soften the impact. A blunt announcement of disappointing news might cause the receiver to stop reading and toss the message aside. The indirect strategy enables you to keep the reader's attention until you have been able to explain the reasons for the bad news. In fact, the most important part of a bad-news letter is the explanation, which you'll learn about shortly. The indirect plan consists of four parts, as shown in Figure 8.1:

The indirect pattern softens the impact of bad news by giving reasons and explanations first.

- **Buffer.** Offer a neutral but meaningful statement that does not mention the bad news.
- **Reasons.** Give an explanation of the causes for the bad news before disclosing it.
- **Bad news.** Provide a clear but understated announcement of the bad news that may include an alternative or compromise.
- **Closing.** Include a personalized, forward-looking, pleasant statement.

FIGURE 8.1 • **Four-Part Indirect Pattern for Bad News**

Buffer	Reasons	Bad News	Closing
Open with a neutral but meaningful statement that does not mention the bad news.	Explain the causes of the bad news before disclosing it.	Reveal the bad news without emphasizing it. Provide an alternative or compromise, if possible.	End with a personalized, forward-looking, pleasant statement. Avoid referring to the bad news.

© GIRAUD PHILLIPPE/CORBIS SYGMA/CORBIS

Hotel giant Starwood accidentally listed exclusive bungalows at a Bora Bora resort in the South Pacific for $85 instead of $850 a night over the Internet. The deal was pounced on by 136 people who booked thousands of nights. Honoring the rate, however, would have cost the company $2 million in lost revenue. When companies are forced to deliver bad news, they generally prefer to use the indirect pattern beginning with a buffer and reasons before announcing the bad news.

Using the Direct Pattern in Specific Instances

Many bad-news letters are best organized indirectly, beginning with a buffer and reasons. The direct pattern, with the bad news first, may be more effective, though, in situations such as the following:

The direct pattern is appropriate when the receiver might overlook the bad news, when directness is preferred, when firmness is necessary, when the bad news is not damaging, or when the goodwill of the receiver is unimportant.

- **When the receiver may overlook the bad news.** With the crush of mail today, many readers skim messages, looking only at the opening. If they don't find substantive material, they may discard the message. Rate increases, changes in service, new policy requirements—these critical messages may require boldness to ensure attention.
- **When organization policy suggests directness.** Some companies expect all internal messages and announcements—even bad news—to be straightforward and presented without frills.
- **When the receiver prefers directness.** Busy managers may prefer directness. Such shorter messages enable the reader to get in the proper frame of mind immediately. If you suspect that the reader prefers that the facts be presented straightaway, use the direct pattern.
- **When firmness is necessary.** Messages that must demonstrate determination and strength should not use delaying techniques. For example, the last in a series of collection letters that seek payment of overdue accounts may require a direct opener.
- **When the bad news is not damaging.** If the bad news is insignificant (such as a small increase in cost) and doesn't personally affect the receiver, then the direct strategy certainly makes sense.
- **When the receiver's goodwill is not an issue.** Rarely, a business may have to send a message rejecting a customer's business. For instance, Filene's Basement, a chain of bargain retail stores, sent letters to two sisters announcing that their business was no longer welcome. The sisters had a history of returning items and making complaints about service.[3]

Applying the Writing Process

The writing process is especially important in crafting bad-news messages because of the potential consequences of poorly written messages.

Thinking through the entire writing process is especially important in bad-news letters. Not only do you want the receiver to understand and accept the message, but you want to be careful that your words say only what you intend.

ANALYSIS, ANTICIPATION, AND ADAPTATION

In Phase 1 (prewriting) you need to analyze the bad news so that you can anticipate its effect on the receiver. If the disappointment will be mild, announce it directly. If the bad news is serious or personal, consider techniques to reduce the pain. Adapt your words to protect the receiver's ego. Instead of *You neglected to change the oil, causing severe damage to the engine*, switch to the passive voice: *The oil wasn't changed, causing severe damage to the engine.* Choose words that show you respect the reader as a responsible, valuable person.

RESEARCH, ORGANIZATION, AND COMPOSITION

In Phase 2 (writing) you can gather information and brainstorm for ideas. Jot down all the reasons you have that explain the bad news. If four or five reasons prompted your negative decision, concentrate on the strongest and safest ones. Avoid presenting any weak reasons; readers may seize on them to reject the entire message. After selecting your best reasons, outline the four parts of the indirect pattern: buffer, reasons, bad news, closing. Flesh out each section as you compose your first draft.

REVISION, PROOFREADING, AND EVALUATION

In Phase 3 (revising) you're ready to switch positions and put yourself into the receiver's shoes. Have you looked at the problem from the receiver's perspective? Is your message too blunt? Too subtle? Does the message make the refusal, denial, or bad-news announcement clear? Prepare the final version, and proofread for format, punctuation, and correctness.

Preventing Legal Problems

Before we examine the components of a bad-news message, let's look more closely at how you can avoid exposing yourself and your employer to legal liability in writing negative messages. Although we can't always anticipate the consequences of our words, we should avoid libel and defamation, careless language, and misrepresenting our organization.

DON'T BE GUILTY OF LIBEL OR DEFAMATION

Defamation involves any published statement that is false and harms a person's reputation. Libel is written defamation; slander is spoken.

Calling people names (such as *deadbeat, crook*, or *quack*) can get you into trouble. *Defamation* is the legal term for any false statement that harms an individual's reputation. When the abusive language is written, it's called *libel*; when spoken, it's *slander*.

To be actionable (likely to result in a lawsuit), abusive language must be (1) false, (2) damaging to one's good name, and (3) "published"—that is, spoken within the presence of others or written. Thus, if you were alone with Jane Doe and accused her of accepting bribes and selling company secrets to competitors, she couldn't sue because the defamation wasn't published. Her reputation was not damaged. But if anyone heard the words or if they were written, you might be legally liable.

In a new wrinkle, you may now be prosecuted and lose your job if you transmit a harassing or libelous message by e-mail or post messages in a chat group, on a message board, or on your own weblog (blog). Such electronic transmission is considered to be "published." Moreover, a company may incur liability for messages sent through its computer system by employees. That's why many companies are increasing their monitoring of both outgoing and internal messages. "Off-the-cuff, casual e-mail conversations among employees are exactly the type of messages that tend to trigger lawsuits and arm litigators with damaging evidence," says e-mail guru Nancy Flynn.[4] Instant messaging adds another danger for companies. Its use in U.S. companies doubled in just two years. What's worse, it's a largely unmonitored channel.[5] Whether they use print or electronic media, competent communicators avoid making unproven charges and letting their emotions prompt abusive language.

AVOID CARELESS LANGUAGE

As the marketplace becomes increasingly litigious, we must be certain that our words communicate only what we intend. Take the case of a factory worker injured on the job. His attorney subpoenaed company documents and discovered a seemingly harmless letter sent to a group regarding a plant tour. These words appeared in the letter: "Although we are honored at your interest in our company, we cannot give your group a tour of the plant operations as it would be too noisy and dangerous." The court found in favor of the worker, inferring from the letter that working conditions were indeed hazardous.[6] The letter writer did not intend to convey the impression of dangerous working conditions, but the court accepted that interpretation.

Careless language includes statements that could be damaging or misinterpreted.

This case emphasizes an important caution. Be careful in making statements that are potentially damaging or that could be misinterpreted. Be wary of explanations that convey more information than you intend. Remember, too, that e-mail and instant messages are especially risky. You may think that a mere tap of the delete key makes a file disappear. No way! Messages continue to exist on backup storage devices in the files of the sender and the recipient. Today attorneys may demand all company files pertaining to a case, including long-forgotten e-mail and even instant messaging files.

DON'T MISREPRESENT YOUR ORGANIZATION

Avoid statements that may make you feel good but misrepresent your organization.

Most of us hate to have to reveal bad news—that is, to be the bad guy. To make ourselves look better, to make the receiver feel better, and to maintain good relations, we are tempted to make statements that are legally dangerous. Consider the case of a law firm interviewing job candidates. One of the firm's partners was asked to inform a candidate that she was not selected. The partner's letter said, "Although you were by far the most qualified candidate we interviewed, unfortunately, we have decided we do not have a position for a person of your talents at this time." To show that he personally had no reservations about this candidate and to bolster the candidate, the partner offered his own opinion. But he differed from the majority of the recruiting committee. When the rejected interviewee learned later that the law firm had hired two male attorneys, she sued, charging sexual discrimination. The court found in favor of the rejected candidate. It agreed that a reasonable inference could be made from the partner's letter that she was the "most qualified candidate."[7]

Use organizational stationery for official business only, and beware of making promises that can't be fulfilled.

Two important lessons emerge. First, business communicators act as agents of their organizations. Their words, decisions, and opinions are assumed to represent those of the organization. If you want to communicate your personal feelings or opinions, use your personal e-mail address or write on plain paper (rather than company letterhead) and sign your name without title or affiliation. Second, volunteering extra information can lead to trouble. Thus, avoid supplying data that could be misused, and avoid making promises that can't be fulfilled. Don't admit or imply responsibility for conditions that caused damage or injury. Even apologies (*We're sorry that a faulty bottle cap caused damage to your carpet*) may suggest liability.

TECHNIQUES FOR DELIVERING BAD NEWS SENSITIVELY

Legal matters aside, let's now study specific techniques for using the indirect pattern in sending bad-news messages. In this pattern the bad news is delayed until after explanations have been given. The four components of the indirect pattern, shown in Figure 8.2, include buffer, reasons, bad news, and closing.

Buffering the Opening

A buffer is a device to reduce shock or pain. To buffer the pain of bad news, begin with a neutral but meaningful statement that makes the reader continue reading. The buffer should be relevant and concise and provide a natural transition to

FIGURE 8.2   • Delivering Bad News Sensitively

Buffer	Reasons	Bad News	Closing
Best news	Cautious explanation	Embedded placement	Forward look
Compliment	Reader or other benefits	Passive voice	Information about
Appreciation	Company policy	Implied refusal	alternative
Agreement	explanation	Compromise	Good wishes
Facts	Positive words	Alternative	Freebies
Understanding	Evidence that matter		Resale
Apology	was considered fairly		Sales promotion
	and seriously		

the explanation that follows. The individual situation, of course, will help determine what you should put in the buffer. Avoid trite buffers such as *Thank you for your letter.* Here are some possibilities for opening bad-news messages.

BEST NEWS

Start with the part of the message that represents the best news. For example, a message to workers announced new health plan rules limiting prescriptions to a 34-day supply and increasing co-payments. With home delivery, however, employees could save up to $24 on each prescription. To emphasize the good news, you might write, *You can now achieve significant savings and avoid trips to the drugstore by having your prescription drugs delivered to your home.*[8]

COMPLIMENT

Openings can buffer the bad news with compliments, appreciation, agreement, relevant facts, and understanding.

Praise the receiver's accomplishments, organization, or efforts. But do so with honesty and sincerity. For instance, in a letter declining an invitation to speak, you could write, *The Thalians have my sincere admiration for their fund-raising projects on behalf of hungry children. I am honored that you asked me to speak Friday, November 5.*

APPRECIATION

Convey thanks to the reader for doing business, for sending something, for conveying confidence in your organization, for expressing feelings, or simply for providing feedback. Suppose you had to draft a letter that refuses employment. You could say, *I appreciated learning about the hospitality management program at Cornell and about your qualifications in our interview last Friday.* Avoid thanking the reader, however, for something you are about to refuse.

AGREEMENT

Make a relevant statement with which both reader and receiver can agree. A letter that rejects a loan application might read, *We both realize how much the export business has been affected by the relative weakness of the dollar in the past two years.*

FACTS

Provide objective information that introduces the bad news. For example, in a memo announcing cutbacks in the hours of the employees' cafeteria, you might say, *During the past five years the number of employees eating breakfast in our cafeteria has dropped from 32 percent to 12 percent.*

UNDERSTANDING

Show that you care about the reader. Notice how in this letter to customers announcing a product defect, the writer expresses concern: *We know that you expect superior performance from all the products you purchase from OfficeCity. That's why we're writing personally about the Exell printer cartridges you recently ordered.*

APOLOGY

As you learned in Chapter 6, a carefully worded apology may be appropriate. If you do apologize, do it early, briefly, and sincerely. For example, a manufacturer of super premium ice cream might respond to a customer's complaint with, *We're genuinely sorry that you were disappointed in the price of the ice cream you recently purchased at one of our scoop shops. Your opinion is important to us, and we appreciate your giving us the opportunity to look into the problem you describe.* In responding to a complaint about poor service, a company might write, *I appreciate the frustration our delay has caused you. I'm sorry you didn't receive better service.* Or, *You're right to be concerned.*

Good buffers avoid revealing the bad news immediately. Moreover, they do not convey a false impression that good news follows. Additionally, they provide a natural transition to the next bad-news letter component—the reasons.

Presenting the Reasons

Bad-news messages should explain reasons before stating the negative news.

The most important part of a bad-news letter is the section that explains why a negative decision is necessary. Without sound reasons for denying a request or refusing a claim, a letter will fail, no matter how cleverly it is organized or written. One study found that if managers offered coworkers good reasons for bad news, employees were 43 percent less likely to experience anger, to blame, or to feel stress.[9] As part of your planning before writing, you must analyze the problem. If you decide to refuse a request, you should have specific reasons. Before disclosing the bad news, try to explain those reasons. Providing an explanation reduces feelings of ill will and improves the chances that the reader will accept the bad news.

BEING CAUTIOUS IN EXPLAINING

If the reasons are not confidential and if they will not create legal liability, you can be specific: *Growers supplied us with a limited number of patio roses, and our demand this year was twice that of last year.* In refusing a speaking engagement, tell why the date is impossible: *On January 17 we have a board of directors meeting that I must attend.* Don't, however, make unrealistic or dangerous statements in an effort to look good.

CITING READER OR OTHER BENEFITS IF PLAUSIBLE

Readers accept bad news more readily if they see that someone benefits.

Readers are more open to bad news if in some way, even indirectly, it may help them. In refusing a customer's request for free hemming of skirts and slacks, Lands' End wrote: "We tested our ability to hem skirts a few months ago. This process proved to be very time-consuming. We have decided not to offer this service because the additional cost would have increased the selling price of our skirts substantially, and we did not want to impose that cost on all our customers."[10] Readers also accept bad news better if they recognize that someone or something else benefits, such as other workers or the environment: *Although we would like to consider your application, we prefer to fill managerial positions from within.* Avoid trying to show reader benefits, though, if they appear insincere: *To improve our service to you, we're increasing our brokerage fees.*

EXPLAINING COMPANY POLICY

Readers resent blanket policy statements prohibiting something: *Company policy prevents us from making cash refunds* or *Contract bids may be accepted from local companies only* or *Company policy requires us to promote from within.* Instead of hiding behind company policy, gently explain why the policy makes sense: *We prefer*

© Ted Goff (www.tedgoff.com)

"Dear Valued Customer: We're
sorry, but company policy forbids
apologies. Sincerely yours..."

to promote from within because it rewards the loyalty of our employees. In addition, we've found that people familiar with our organization make the quickest contribution to our team effort. By offering explanations, you demonstrate that you care about readers and are treating them as important individuals.

CHOOSING POSITIVE WORDS

Because the words you use can affect a reader's response, choose carefully. Remember that the objective of the indirect pattern is holding the reader's attention until you've had a chance to explain the reasons justifying the bad news. To keep the reader in a receptive mood, avoid expressions with punitive, demoralizing, or otherwise negative connotations. Stay away from such words as *cannot, claim, denied, error, failure, fault, impossible, mistaken, misunderstand, never, regret, rejected, unable, unwilling, unfortunately,* and *violate.*

SHOWING THAT THE MATTER WAS TREATED SERIOUSLY AND FAIRLY

In explaining reasons, demonstrate to the reader that you take the matter seriously, have investigated carefully, and are making an unbiased decision. Consumers are more accepting of disappointing news when they feel that their requests have been heard and that they have been treated fairly. Avoid passing the buck or blaming others within your organization. Such unprofessional behavior makes the reader lose faith in you and your company.

Cushioning the Bad News

Although you can't prevent the disappointment that bad news brings, you can reduce the pain somewhat by breaking the news sensitively. Be especially considerate when the reader will suffer personally from the bad news. A number of thoughtful techniques can cushion the blow.

POSITIONING THE BAD NEWS STRATEGICALLY

Techniques for cushioning bad news include positioning it strategically, using the passive voice, implying the refusal, and suggesting alternatives or compromises.

Instead of spotlighting it, sandwich the bad news between other sentences, perhaps among your reasons. Try not to let the refusal begin or end a paragraph—the reader's eye will linger on these high-visibility spots. Another technique that reduces shock is putting a painful idea in a subordinate clause: *Although another candidate was hired, we appreciate your interest in our organization and wish you every success in your job search.* Subordinate clauses often begin with words such as *although, as, because, if,* and *since.*

USING THE PASSIVE VOICE

Passive-voice verbs enable you to depersonalize an action. Whereas the active voice focuses attention on a person (*We don't give cash refunds*), the passive voice highlights the action (*Cash refunds are not given because . . .*). Use the passive voice for the bad news. In some instances you can combine passive-voice verbs and a subordinate clause: *Although franchise scoop shop owners cannot be required to lower their ice cream prices, we are happy to pass along your comments for their consideration.*

ACCENTUATING THE POSITIVE

As you learned earlier, messages are far more effective when you describe what you can do instead of what you can't do. Rather than *We will no longer allow credit card purchases*, try a more positive appeal: *We are now selling gasoline at discount cash prices.*

IMPLYING THE REFUSAL

It's sometimes possible to avoid a direct statement of refusal. Often, your reasons and explanations leave no doubt that a request has been denied. Explicit refusals may be unnecessary and at times cruel. In this refusal to contribute to a charity, for example, the writer never actually says *no*: *Because we will soon be moving into new offices in Glendale, all our funds are earmarked for relocation costs. We hope that next year we'll be able to support your worthwhile charity.* The danger of an implied refusal, of course, is that it is so subtle that the reader misses it. Be certain that you make the bad news clear, thus preventing the need for further correspondence.

SUGGESTING A COMPROMISE OR AN ALTERNATIVE

A refusal is not so depressing—for the sender or the receiver—if a suitable compromise, substitute, or alternative is available. In denying permission to a group of students to visit a historical private residence, for instance, this writer softens the bad news by proposing an alternative: *Although private tours of the grounds are not given, we do open the house and its gardens for one charitable event in the fall.* You can further reduce the impact of the bad news by refusing to dwell on it. Present it briefly (or imply it), and move on to your closing.

© Randy Glasbergen (www.glasbergen.com)

"Send him our toughest refusal letter, threaten him with legal action, and don't pull the punches. But put XOXOXO under my signature to show that we still love him as a customer."

Closing Pleasantly

After explaining the bad news sensitively, close the message with a pleasant statement that promotes goodwill. The closing should be personalized and may include a forward look, an alternative, good wishes, freebies, resale information, or an off-the-subject remark.

FORWARD LOOK

> Closings to bad-news messages might include a forward look, an alternative, good wishes, freebies, and resale or sales promotion information.

Anticipate future relations or business. A letter that refuses a contract proposal might read: *Thanks for your bid. We look forward to working with your talented staff when future projects demand your special expertise.*

ALTERNATIVE

If an alternative exists, end your letter with follow-through advice. For example, in a letter rejecting a customer's demand for replacement of landscaping plants, you might say: *I will be happy to give you a free inspection and consultation. Please call 746-8112 to arrange a date for my visit.*

GOOD WISHES

A letter rejecting a job candidate might read: *We appreciate your interest in our company, and we extend to you our best wishes in your search to find the perfect match between your skills and job requirements.*

FREEBIES

When customers complain—primarily about food products or small consumer items—companies often send coupons, samples, or gifts to restore confidence and to promote future business. In response to a customer's complaint about a frozen dinner, you could write: *Your loyalty and your concern about our frozen entrées is genuinely appreciated. Because we want you to continue enjoying our healthful and convenient dinners, we're enclosing a coupon that you can take to your local market to select your next Green Valley entrée.*

RESALE OR SALES PROMOTION

When the bad news is not devastating or personal, references to resale information or promotion may be appropriate: *The computer workstations you ordered are unusually popular because of their stain-, heat-, and scratch-resistant finishes. To help you locate hard-to-find accessories for these workstations, we invite you to visit our Web site where our online catalog provides a huge selection of surge suppressors, multiple outlet strips, security devices, and PC tool kits.*

Avoid endings that sound canned, insincere, inappropriate, or self-serving. Don't invite further correspondence (*If you have any questions, do not hesitate . . .*), and don't refer to the bad news. To review these suggestions for delivering bad news sensitively, take another look at Figure 8.2 on page 206.

◆ REFUSING ROUTINE REQUESTS AND CLAIMS

Every business communicator will occasionally have to say *no* to a request. Depending on how you think the receiver will react to your refusal, you can use the direct or the indirect pattern. If you have any doubt, use the indirect pattern and the following writing plan:

Writing Plan for Refusing Routine Requests and Claims

- *Buffer:* Start with a neutral statement on which both reader and writer can agree, such as a compliment, appreciation, a quick review of the facts, or an apology. Try to include a key idea or word that acts as a transition to the reasons.
- *Reasons:* Present valid reasons for the refusal, avoiding words that create a negative tone. Include resale or sales promotion material if appropriate.
- *Bad news:* Soften the blow by de-emphasizing the bad news, using the passive voice, accentuating the positive, or implying a refusal. Suggest a compromise, alternative, or substitute if possible. The alternative may be part of the bad news or part of the closing.
- *Closing:* Renew good feelings with a positive statement. Avoid referring to the bad news. Look forward to continued business.

Rejecting Requests for Favors, Money, Information, and Action

The reasons-before-refusal pattern works well when turning down requests for favors, money, information, or action.

Most of us prefer to be let down gently when we're being refused something we want. That's why the reasons-before-refusal pattern works well when you must turn down requests for favors, money, information, action, and so forth.

SAYING *NO* TO REQUESTS FROM OUTSIDERS

Requests for contributions to charity are common. Many big and small companies receive requests for contributions of money, time, equipment, and support. Although the causes may be worthy, resources are usually limited. In a letter from Forest Financial Services, shown in Figure 8.3, the company must refuse a request for a donation to a charity. Following the indirect strategy, the letter begins with a buffer acknowledging the request. It also praises the good works of the charity and uses those words as a transition to the second paragraph. In the second paragraph the writer explains why the company cannot donate. Notice that the writer reveals the refusal without actually stating it (*Because of sales declines and organizational downsizing, we're forced to take a much harder look at funding requests that we receive this year*). This gentle refusal makes it unnecessary to be more blunt in stating the denial.

In some donation refusal letters, the reasons may not be fully explained: *Although we can't provide financial support at this time, we all unanimously agree that the symphony orchestra contributes much to the community.* The emphasis is on the

FIGURE 8.3   **Refusing Donation Request**

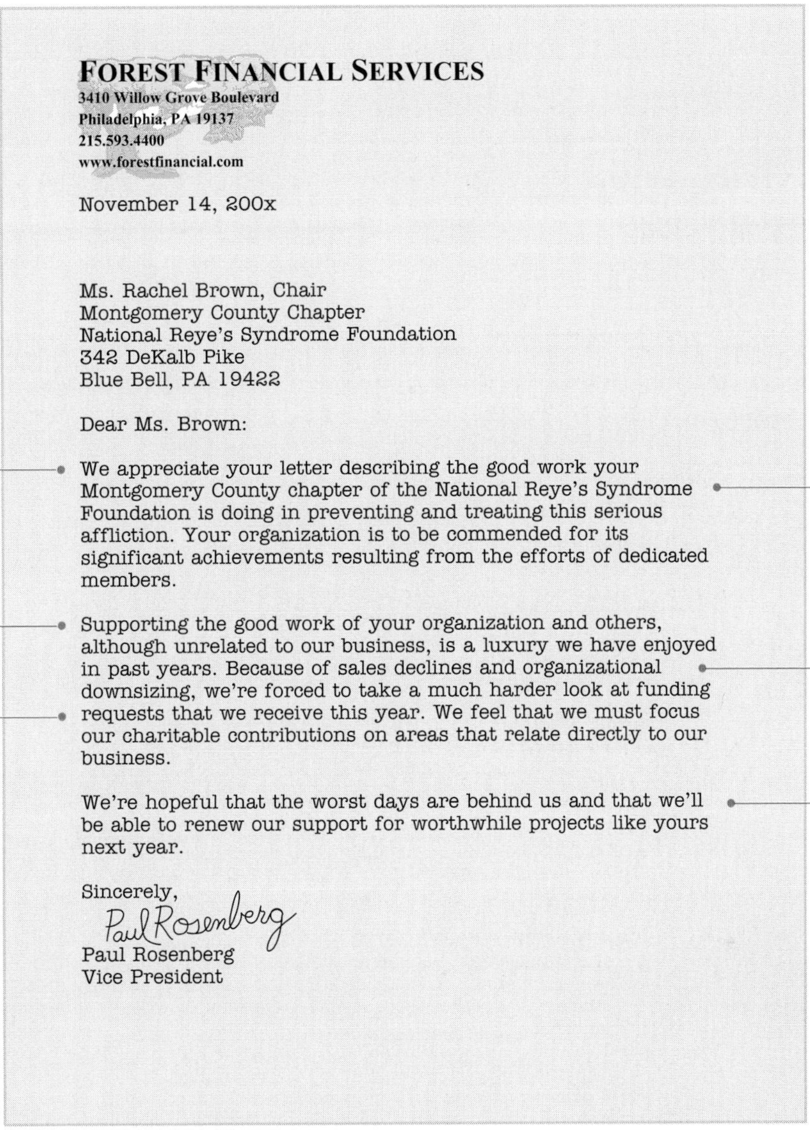

FOREST FINANCIAL SERVICES

3410 Willow Grove Boulevard
Philadelphia, PA 19137
215.593.4400
www.forestfinancial.com

November 14, 200x

Ms. Rachel Brown, Chair
Montgomery County Chapter
National Reye's Syndrome Foundation
342 DeKalb Pike
Blue Bell, PA 19422

Dear Ms. Brown:

Opens with praise and compliments — We appreciate your letter describing the good work your Montgomery County chapter of the National Reye's Syndrome Foundation is doing in preventing and treating this serious affliction. Your organization is to be commended for its significant achievements resulting from the efforts of dedicated members. — *Doesn't say* yes *or* no

Transitions with repetition of key idea (good work) — Supporting the good work of your organization and others, although unrelated to our business, is a luxury we have enjoyed in past years. Because of sales declines and organizational downsizing, we're forced to take a much harder look at funding requests that we receive this year. We feel that we must focus our charitable contributions on areas that relate directly to our business. — *Explains sales decline and cutback in gifts*

Reveals refusal without actually stating it —

We're hopeful that the worst days are behind us and that we'll be able to renew our support for worthwhile projects like yours next year. — *Closes graciously with forward look*

Sincerely,

Paul Rosenberg

Paul Rosenberg
Vice President

symphony's attributes rather than on an explanation for the refusal. In the letter shown in Figure 8.3, the writer felt a connection to the charity. Thus, he wanted to give a fuller explanation. If you were required to write frequent refusals, you might prepare a form letter, changing a few variables as needed. The refusal for a donation shown in Figure 8.3 could be adapted, using word processing equipment, to respond to other charity requests.

REFUSING INTERNAL REQUESTS

Internal request refusals focus on explanations and praise, maintaining a positive tone, and offering alternatives.

Just as managers must refuse requests from outsiders, they must also occasionally refuse requests from employees. In Figure 8.4 you see the first draft and revision of a message responding to a request from a key manager, Mark Stevenson. He wants permission to attend a conference. However, he can't attend the conference because the timing is bad; he must be present at budget planning meetings scheduled for the same two weeks. Normally, this matter would be discussed in person. But Mark has been traveling among branch offices, and he hasn't been in the office recently.

The vice president's first inclination was to send a quickie memo, as shown in Figure 8.4, and "tell it like it is." In revising, the vice president realized that this

FIGURE 8.4 • **Refusing an Internal Request**

before revision

DATE:	July 2, 200x
TO:	Mark Stevenson Manager, Telecommunications
FROM:	Ann Wells-Freed *AWF* VP, Management Information Systems
SUBJECT:	CONFERENCE REQUEST

We can't allow you to attend the conference in September, Mark. —• *Announces the bad news too quickly and painfully*
Perhaps you didn't know that budget-planning meetings are scheduled
for that month.

Your expertise is needed here to help keep our telecommunications • *Gives reasons, but includes a dangerous statement*
network on schedule. Without you, the entire system—which is shaky
at best—might fall apart. I'm sorry to have to refuse your request to
attend the conference. I know this is small thanks for the fine work
you have done for us. Please accept our humble apologies.

In the spring I'm sure your work schedule will be lighter, and we can —• *Makes a promise that might be difficult to keep*
release you to attend a conference at that time.

after revision

DATE:	July 2, 200x
TO:	Mark Stevenson Manager, Telecommunications
FROM:	Ann Wells-Freed *AWF* VP, Management Information Systems
SUBJECT:	REQUEST TO ATTEND SEPTEMBER CONFERENCE

The Management Council and I are extremely pleased with the • *Buffer: Includes sincere praise*
leadership you have provided in setting up live video transmission to
our regional offices. Because of your genuine professional commitment,
Mark, I can understand your desire to attend the conference of the
Telecommunication Specialists of America September 23 to 28 in Atlanta.

Transition:
Uses date to
move smoothly
from buffer
to reasons

The last two weeks in September have been set aside for budget planning. • *Reasons: Tells why refusal is necessary*
As you and I know, we've only scratched the surface of our
teleconferencing projects for the next five years. Since you are the
specialist and we rely heavily on your expertise, we need you here for
those planning sessions.

Bad news:
Implies refusal

If you're able to attend a similar conference in the spring and if our
workloads permit, we'll try to send you then. You're a valuable player,
Mark, and I'm grateful you're on our MIS team.

Closing:
Contains
realistic
alternative

message was going to hurt and that it had possible danger areas. Moreover, the memo misses a chance to give Mark positive feedback. An improved version of the memo starts with a buffer that delivers honest praise (*pleased with your leadership* and *your genuine professional commitment*). By the way, don't be stingy with compliments; they cost you nothing. As a philosopher once observed, *We don't live by bread alone. We need buttering up once in a while.* The buffer also includes the date of the meeting, used strategically to connect the reasons that follow. You will recall from Chapter 3 that repetition of a key idea is an effective transitional device to provide smooth flow between components of a message.

The middle paragraph provides reasons for the refusal. Notice that these reasons focus on positive elements: Mark is the specialist; the company relies on his expertise; and everyone will benefit if he passes up the conference. In this section it becomes obvious that the request will be refused. The writer is not forced to say, *No, you may not attend.* Although the refusal is implied, the reader gets the message.

The closing suggests a qualified alternative (*if our workloads permit, we'll try to send you then*). It also ends positively with gratitude for Mark's contributions to the organization and with another compliment (*you're a valuable player*). Notice that the improved version focuses on explanations and praise rather than on refusals and apologies.

The success of this message depends on attention to the entire writing process, not just on using a buffer or scattering a few compliments throughout.

BREAKING BAD NEWS TO CUSTOMERS

Businesses must occasionally respond to disappointed customers. In Chapter 6 you learned to use the direct strategy in granting claims and making adjustments because these were essentially good-news messages. But in some situations you have little good news to share. Sometimes your company is at fault, in which case an apology is generally in order. Other times the problem is with orders you can't fill, claims you must refuse, or credit you must deny. Messages with bad news for customers generally follow the same pattern as other negative messages. Customer letters, though, differ in one major way: they usually include resale or sales promotion information.

Controlling Damage With Disappointed Customers

All companies occasionally disappoint their customers. Merchandise is not delivered on time, a product fails to perform as expected, service is deficient, charges are erroneous, or customers are misunderstood. All businesses offering products or services must sometimes deal with troublesome situations that cause unhappiness to customers. Whenever possible, these problems should be dealt with immediately and personally. A majority of business professionals strive to control the damage and resolve such problems in the following manner:[11]

> When a customer problem arises and the company is at fault, many businesspeople call and apologize, explain what happened, and follow with a goodwill letter.

- Call the individual involved.
- Describe the problem and apologize.
- Explain why the problem occurred, what you are doing to resolve it, and how you will prevent it from happening again.
- Follow with a letter that documents the phone call and promotes goodwill.

Dealing with problems immediately is very important in resolving conflict and retaining goodwill. Written correspondence is generally too slow for problems that demand immediate attention. But written messages are important (1) when personal contact is impossible, (2) to establish a record of the incident, (3) to formally confirm follow-up procedures, and (4) to promote good relations.

A bad-news follow-up letter is shown in Figure 8.5. Consultant Maris Richfield found herself in the embarrassing position of explaining why she had given out the name of her client to a salesperson. The client, Data.com, Inc., had hired her firm, Richfield Consulting Services, to help find an appropriate service for outsourcing its payroll functions. Without realizing it, Maris had mentioned to a potential vendor (Payroll Services, Inc.) that her client was considering hiring an outside service to handle its payroll. An overeager salesperson from Payroll Services immediately called on Data.com, thus angering the client. The client had hired the consultant to avoid this very kind of intrusion. Data.com did not want to be hounded by vendors selling their payroll services.

When she learned of the problem, the first thing consultant Maris Richfield did was call her client to explain and apologize. She was careful to control her voice and rate of speaking. A low-pitched, deliberate pace gives the impression that you are thinking clearly, logically, and reasonably—not emotionally and certainly not irrationally. But she also followed up with the letter shown in Figure 8.5. The letter not only confirmed the telephone conversation but also added the right touch of formality. It sent the nonverbal message that the matter was being taken seriously and that it was important enough to warrant a written letter.

When something goes wrong in customer transactions and damage control is necessary, the first thing most businesspeople do is call the individual involved, discuss the problem, and apologize. Written messages follow up.

Denying Claims

Customers occasionally want something they're not entitled to or something you can't grant. They may misunderstand warranties or make unreasonable demands. Because these customers are often unhappy with a product or service, they are emotionally involved. Letters that say *no* to emotionally involved receivers will probably be your most challenging communication task. As publisher Malcolm Forbes observed, "To be agreeable while disagreeing—that's an art."[12]

In denying claims, writers use the reasons-before-refusal pattern to set an empathic tone and buffer the bad news.

Fortunately, the reasons-before-refusal plan helps you be empathic and artful in breaking bad news. Obviously, in denial letters you'll need to adopt the proper tone. Don't blame customers, even if they are at fault. Avoid *you* statements that sound preachy (*You would have known that cash refunds are impossible if you had read your contract*). Use neutral, objective language to explain why the claim must be refused. Consider offering resale information to rebuild the customer's confidence in your products or organization. In Figure 8.6 the writer denies a customer's claim for the difference between the price the customer paid for speakers and the price he saw advertised locally (which would have resulted in a cash refund of $151). Although the catalog service does match any advertised lower price, the price-matching policy applies only to *identical* models. This claim must be rejected because the advertisement the customer submitted showed a different, older speaker model.

The letter to Matthew Tyson opens with a buffer that agrees with a statement in the customer's letter. It repeats the key idea of product confidence as a transition to the second paragraph. Next comes an explanation of the price-matching policy. The writer does not assume that the customer is trying to pull a fast one. Nor does he suggest that the customer is a dummy who didn't read or understand the price-matching policy. The safest path is a neutral explanation of the policy along with precise distinctions between the customer's speakers and the older ones. The writer also gets a chance to resell the customer's speakers and demonstrate what a quality product they are. By the end of the third paragraph, it's evident to the reader that his claim is unjustified.

© TRBFOTO/PHOTODISC/GETTY IMAGES

FIGURE 8.5   **Bad-News Follow-Up Message**

RICHFIELD CONSULTING SERVICES

4023 Rodeo Drive Plaza, Suite 404   Voice: 213.499.8224
Beverly Hills, CA 90640   Web: www.richfieldconsulting.com

October 23, 200x

Ms. Angela Ranier
Vice President, Human Resources
Data.com, Inc.
21067 Pacific Coast Highway
Malibu, CA 90265

Dear Ms. Ranier:

You have every right to expect complete confidentiality in your transactions with an independent consultant. As I explained in yesterday's telephone call, I am distressed that you were called by a salesperson from Payroll Services, Inc. This should not have happened, and I apologize to you again for inadvertently mentioning your company's name in a conversation with a potential vendor, Payroll Services, Inc. *[Opens with agreement and apology]*

All clients of Richfield Consulting may be sure that we handle all their dealings in the strictest confidence. Because your company's payroll needs are so individual and because you have so many contract workers, I had to explain how your employees differed from those of other companies. The name of your company, however, should never have been mentioned. I can assure you that it will not happen again. I have informed Payroll Services that it had no authorization to call you directly, and its actions have forced me to reconsider using its services for my future clients. *[Explains what caused problem and how it was resolved]* *[Promises to prevent recurrence]*

A number of other payroll services offer excellent programs. I'm sure we can find the perfect partner to enable you to outsource your payroll responsibilities, thus allowing your company to focus its financial and human resources on its core business. I look forward to our next appointment when you may choose from a number of excellent payroll outsourcing firms. *[Closes with forward look]*

Sincerely yours,

Maris Richfield

Maris Richfield

Tips for Resolving Problems and Following Up
- Whenever possible, call or see the individual involved.
- Describe the problem and apologize.
- Explain why the problem occurred.
- Explain what you are doing to resolve it.
- Explain how it will not happen again.
- Follow up with a letter that documents the personal message.
- Look forward to positive future relations.

Refusing Credit

As much as companies want business, they can extend credit only when payment is likely to follow. Credit applications, from individuals or from businesses, are generally approved or disapproved on the basis of the applicant's credit history. This record is supplied by a credit-reporting agency, such as Experian, Equifax, or TransUnion.

FIGURE 8.6 ---- • **Denying a Claim**

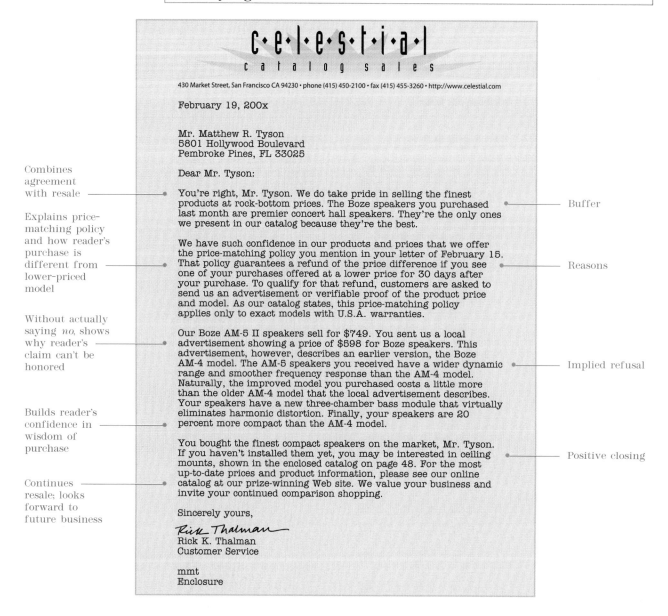

Combines agreement with resale — (connects to first paragraph)

Explains price-matching policy and how reader's purchase is different from lower-priced model — (connects to second paragraph)

Without actually saying *no*, shows why reader's claim can't be honored — (connects to third paragraph)

Builds reader's confidence in wisdom of purchase — (connects to third paragraph)

Continues resale; looks forward to future business — (connects to fourth paragraph)

Buffer — (connects to first paragraph)

Reasons — (connects to second paragraph)

Implied refusal — (connects to third paragraph)

Positive closing — (connects to fourth paragraph)

---

c·e·l·e·s·t·i·a·l
c a t a l o g   s a l e s

430 Market Street, San Francisco CA 94230 • phone (415) 450-2100 • fax (415) 455-3260 • http://www.celestial.com

February 19, 200x

Mr. Matthew R. Tyson
5801 Hollywood Boulevard
Pembroke Pines, FL 33025

Dear Mr. Tyson:

You're right, Mr. Tyson. We do take pride in selling the finest products at rock-bottom prices. The Boze speakers you purchased last month are premier concert hall speakers. They're the only ones we present in our catalog because they're the best.

We have such confidence in our products and prices that we offer the price-matching policy you mention in your letter of February 15. That policy guarantees a refund of the price difference if you see one of your purchases offered at a lower price for 30 days after your purchase. To qualify for that refund, customers are asked to send us an advertisement or verifiable proof of the product price and model. As our catalog states, this price-matching policy applies only to exact models with U.S.A. warranties.

Our Boze AM-5 II speakers sell for $749. You sent us a local advertisement showing a price of $598 for Boze speakers. This advertisement, however, describes an earlier version, the Boze AM-4 model. The AM-5 speakers you received have a wider dynamic range and smoother frequency response than the AM-4 model. Naturally, the improved model you purchased costs a little more than the older AM-4 model that the local advertisement describes. Your speakers have a new three-chamber bass module that virtually eliminates harmonic distortion. Finally, your speakers are 20 percent more compact than the AM-4 model.

You bought the finest compact speakers on the market, Mr. Tyson. If you haven't installed them yet, you may be interested in ceiling mounts, shown in the enclosed catalog on page 48. For the most up-to-date prices and product information, please see our online catalog at our prize-winning Web site. We value your business and invite your continued comparison shopping.

Sincerely yours,

Rick Thalman

Rick K. Thalman
Customer Service

mmt
Enclosure

After reviewing the applicant's record, a credit manager applies the organization's guidelines and approves or disapproves the application.

If you must deny credit to prospective customers, you have four goals in conveying the refusal:

- Avoiding language that causes hard feelings
- Retaining customers on a cash basis
- Preparing for possible future credit without raising false expectations
- Avoiding disclosures that could cause a lawsuit

Goals when refusing credit include maintaining customer goodwill and avoiding actionable language.

Because credit applicants are likely to continue to do business with an organization even if they are denied credit, you'll want to do everything possible to encourage that patronage. Thus, keep the refusal respectful, sensitive, and upbeat. A letter to a customer denying her credit application might begin as follows: *We genuinely appreciate your application of January 12 for a Fashion Express credit account.* To avoid possible litigation, many companies offer no explanation of the reasons for a credit refusal. Instead, they provide the name of the credit-reporting agency and suggest that inquiries be directed to it. In the following example notice the use of passive voice (*credit cannot be extended*) and a long sentence to de-emphasize the bad news:

> *After we received a report of your current credit record from Experian, it is apparent that credit cannot be extended at this time. To learn more about your record, you may call an Experian credit counselor at (212) 356-0922.*

A cordial closing looks forward to the possibility of a future reapplication:

> *Thanks, Ms. Love, for the confidence you've shown in Fashion Express. We invite you to continue shopping at our stores, and we look forward to your reapplication in the future.*

Some businesses do provide reasons explaining credit denials (*Credit cannot be granted because your firm's current and long-term credit obligations are nearly twice as great as your firm's total assets*). They may also provide alternatives, such as deferred billing or cash discounts. When the letter denies a credit application that accompanies an order, the message may contain resale information. The writer tries to convert the order from credit to cash. For example, if a big order cannot be filled on a credit basis, perhaps part of the order could be filled on a cash basis. Whatever form the bad-news letter takes, it's a good idea to have the message reviewed by legal counsel because of the litigation land mines awaiting unwary communicators in this area.

BREAKING BAD NEWS TO EMPLOYEES

A tactful tone and a reasons-first approach help preserve friendly relations with customers. These same techniques are useful when delivering bad news to employees. Bad news to employees might include increased health care costs, reduced benefits, downsizing, or a hiring freeze. It might involve telling employees about a relocation, declining profits, lost contracts, harmful lawsuits, public relations controversies, or a host of other problems and issues.

A primary goal in delivering bad news to employees is retaining their goodwill and trust.

If you must deliver bad news to employees, one of your primary goals is retaining their goodwill and trust. You are most likely to achieve this goal if you convey the bad news candidly, quickly, and sympathetically. Although you should use softening techniques, don't delay delivering bad news. Employee morale suffers when employees hear bad news through the grapevine rather than from management. You can also retain employee goodwill by explaining logically the reasons for the bad news and by using the techniques you have learned to soften the blow.

Printed memos are effective in delivering negative organizational news because they convey a formal tone and produce a permanent record.

When routine bad news must be delivered to employees, management may want to deliver the news personally. With large groups, however, a face-to-face presentation is generally impossible. Instead, organizations generally deliver bad news through printed memos. More effective than e-mail, printed memos achieve a formal, serious, and professional tone as well as provide a permanent record. The following writing plan helps writers soften negative organizational news while retaining employee goodwill.

Writing Plan for Announcing Bad News to Employees

- *Buffer:* Open with a neutral or positive statement that transitions to the reasons for the bad news. Consider mentioning the best news, a compliment, appreciation, agreement, or solid facts. Show understanding.
- *Reasons:* Explain the logic behind the bad news. Provide a rational explanation using positive words and displaying empathy. If possible, mention reader benefits.
- *Bad News:* Position the bad news so that it does not stand out. Be positive but don't sugarcoat the bad news. Use objective language.
- *Closing:* Provide information about an alternative, if one exists. If appropriate, describe what will happen next. Look forward positively.

The draft of the memo shown in Figure 8.7 announces a substantial increase in the cost of employee health care benefits. However, the memo suffers from many writing faults. It announces jolting news bluntly in the first sentence. Worse, it offers little or no explanation for the steep increase in costs. It also sounds insincere (*We did everything possible . . .*) and arbitrary. In a final miscue, the writer fails to give credit to the company for absorbing previous health cost increases.

The revision of this bad-news memo uses the indirect pattern and improves the tone considerably. Notice that it opens with a relevant, upbeat, neutral buffer regarding health care—but says nothing about increasing costs. For a smooth transition, the second paragraph begins with a key idea from the opening (*comprehensive package*). The reasons section explains rising costs with logical explanation. The bad news (*you will be paying $250 a month*) is clearly presented but presented in a dependent clause embedded within the paragraph. Throughout, the writer strives to show the fairness of the company's position. The ending, which does not refer to the bad news, emphasizes how much the company is paying and what a wise investment it is. Notice that the entire memo demonstrates a kinder, gentler approach than that shown in the first draft. Of prime importance in breaking bad news to employees is providing clear, convincing reasons that explain the decision.

ETHICS AND THE INDIRECT STRATEGY

You may worry that the indirect organizational strategy is unethical or manipulative because the writer deliberately delays the main idea. But consider the alternative. Breaking bad news bluntly can cause pain and hard feelings. By delaying bad news, you soften the blow somewhat, as well as ensure that your reasoning will be read while the receiver is still receptive. One expert communicator recognized the significance of the indirect strategy when she said, "People must believe the reasons why before they will listen to the details of what and when."[13] In using the indirect strategy, your motives are not to deceive the reader or to hide the news. Rather, your goal is to be a compassionate, yet effective communicator.

The indirect strategy is unethical only if the writer intends to deceive the reader.

The key to ethical communication lies in the motives of the sender. Unethical communicators *intend to deceive.* For example, Victoria's Secret, the clothing and lingerie chain, offered free $10 gift certificates. However, when customers tried to cash the certificates, they found that they were required to make a minimum purchase of $50 worth of merchandise.[14] For this misleading, deceptive, and unethical offer, the chain paid a $100,000 fine. Although the indirect strategy provides a setting in which to announce bad news, it should not be used to avoid or misrepresent the truth.

FIGURE 8.7 ─────── • ┃ **Announcing Bad News to Employees** ┃

before revision

Beginning January 1 your monthly payment for health care benefits will be increased to $250 a month.

Every year health care costs go up. Although we considered dropping other benefits, Midland decided that the best plan was to keep the present comprehensive package. Unfortunately, we can't do that unless we pass along some of the extra cost to you. Last year the company was forced to absorb the total increase in health care premiums. However, we can't continue down this destructive path.

We did everything possible to avoid the sharp increase in costs to you this year. A rate schedule describing the increases in payments for your family and dependents is enclosed.

Hits readers with bad news without any preparation

Offers no explanation

Sounds defensive and arbitrary

Fails to take credit for absorbing previous increases

after revision

interoffice
MEMORANDUM

DATE: October 2, 200x

TO: Fellow Employees

FROM: Isaak W. Brown, President   IWB

SUBJECT: Maintaining Quality Health Care

Begins with neutral but positive buffer that leads to reasons

Health care programs have always been an important part of our commitment to employees at Northern, Inc. We're proud that our total benefits package continues to rank among the best in the country.

Offers reasons explaining why costs are rising

Such a comprehensive package does not come cheaply. In the last decade health care premiums have risen nearly 10 percent every year. We're told that many factors fuel the cost spiral: higher hospital costs, increased use of prescription drugs, stricter state and government mandates, and costly defensive medicine techniques to avoid malpractice lawsuits.

Embeds bad news but doesn't sugarcoat it

Just two years ago our monthly health care cost for each employee was $415. It rose to $469 last year. We were able to absorb that jump without increasing your contribution. This year's hike to $539, however, forces us to ask you to share the increase. Although you will be paying $250 a month to maintain your current health care benefits, the major portion of your coverage is still paid by Northern.

Suggests some reader benefits to offset bad news

The enclosed rate schedule describes costs and benefits for families and dependents. You'll notice that we have been able to add a new convenient benefit. You may now order maintenance prescriptions by mail—up to a 90-day supply for a small co-pay. You can learn more about your benefits and find answers to your questions at the Northern intranet site.

Ends positively by stressing the company's major share of the costs

Northern continues to pay the major portion of your health care program because we think it's a wise investment. You can count on us to be constantly searching for ways to maintain current levels of benefits while controlling costs.

Enclosure

SUMMING UP AND LOOKING FORWARD

When faced with delivering bad news, you have a choice. You can announce it immediately, or you can delay it by presenting a buffer and reasons first. Many business communicators prefer the indirect strategy because it tends to preserve goodwill. In some instances, however, the direct strategy is effective in delivering bad news. In this chapter you learned the goals in communicating bad news and how to avoid creating legal problems. You studied many techniques for delivering bad news sensitively. Then, you learned to apply those techniques in refusing requests from outsiders (routine requests for favors, money, information,

and action) as well as refusing internal requests. You studied techniques for breaking bad news to customers, denying claims, refusing credit, and delivering bad news to employees. Finally, you were taught to distinguish unethical applications of the indirect strategy.

You have now completed the unit on corresponding at work, which included e-mail messages and memorandums, direct letters and goodwill messages, persuasive messages, and negative messages. In the next chapter, you will learn to report workplace data in informal reports.

CRITICAL THINKING

1. Nearly all respondents in a survey of business professionals said that every effort should be made to resolve business problems in person.[15] Why is this logical?

2. Consider times when you have been aware that others have used the indirect pattern in writing or speaking to you. How did you react?

3. Why is the "reasons" section of a bad-news message so important?

4. Some people feel that all employee news, good or bad, should be announced directly. Do you agree or disagree? Why?

5. You work for a large corporation with headquarters in a small town. Recently you received shoddy repair work and a huge bill from a local garage. Your car's transmission has the same problems that it did before you took it in for repair. You know that a complaint letter written on your corporation's stationery would be much more authoritative than one written on plain stationery. Should you use corporation stationery? Why or why not?

CHAPTER REVIEW

6. Explain a business communicator's four goals in communicating bad news.

7. List the four main parts of the indirect pattern for revealing bad news.

8. List six instances when a writer should announce bad news directly.

9. What is defamation? How is libel different from slander?

10. List seven possibilities for opening bad-news messages.

11. List at least five words that might affect readers negatively.

12. How can the passive voice be used effectively in bad-news messages? Provide an original example.

13. List five techniques for closing a bad-news message.

14. List four steps that many business professionals follow in resolving business problems.

15. What is one of the writer's primary goals in delivering bad news to employees?

WRITING IMPROVEMENT EXERCISES

Passive-Voice Verbs

Passive-voice verbs may be preferable in breaking bad news because they enable you to emphasize actions rather than personalities. Compare these two refusals:

Example   Active voice: I cannot authorize you to take three weeks of vacation in July.
Example   Passive voice: Three weeks of vacation in July cannot be authorized.

Revise the following refusals so that they use passive-voice instead of active-voice verbs.

16. We do not allow used merchandise to be returned or exchanged.

17. Managers may not advertise any job openings until those positions have first been posted internally.

18. Your car rental insurance does not cover large SUVs.

19. We cannot meet the sales income projected for the fourth quarter.

20. Titan Insurance Company will not process any claim not accompanied by documented proof showing that a physician treated the injuries.

Subordinate Clauses

You can further soften the effect of bad news by placing it in an introductory subordinate clause that begins with *although, since*, or *because*. The emphasis in a sentence is on the independent clause. Instead of saying *We cannot serve you on a credit basis*, try *Because we cannot serve you on a credit basis, we invite you to take advantage of our cash discounts and sale prices*. Revise the following so that the bad news is de-emphasized in a dependent clause that precedes an independent clause.

21. Unfortunately, we cannot accept personal checks or unauthorized credit. We encourage you to submit your credit application online before coming to the eBay auction.

22. We appreciate your interest in our organization, but we are unable to extend an employment offer to you at this time.

23. It is impossible for us to ship your complete order at this time. However, we are able to send the two armless task chairs immediately.

24. Air Pacific cannot possibly honor the $51 flight to Fiji that erroneously appeared on Travelocity. We are eager, however, to provide a compromise price to customers who booked the erroneous price.

Implied Refusals

Bad news can be de-emphasized by implying a refusal instead of stating it directly. Compare these refusals:

Example   Direct refusal: We cannot send you a price list, nor can we sell our lawn mowers directly to customers. We sell only through dealers, and your dealer is HomeCo.

Example   Implied refusal: Our lawn mowers are sold only through dealers, and your dealer is HomeCo.

Revise the following refusals so that the bad news is implied. If possible, use passive-voice verbs and subordinate clauses to further de-emphasize the bad news.

25. Because of the holiday period, all our billboard space was used this month. Therefore, we are sorry to say that we could not give your charitable group free display space. However, next month, after the holidays, we hope to display your message as we promised.

26. We have received your application to enroll your spouse as a dependent in the group insurance plan. But we must reject it because you just missed the deadline. Applications will not be accepted again until January 1, at which time you may enroll your wife.

27. We will not be able to make a pledge in the annual St. John's fund-raising campaign this year. At this time our cash is tied up in building a new production facility in Southport. We look forward to being able to support your campaign in coming years.

WRITING IMPROVEMENT CASES

8.1 Favor Refusal: Can't Share Software

Sue Wang must refuse the request of some staff engineers. They want to copy for home use the latest version of Adobe Photoshop, an expensive licensed software program that her department just received.

Your Task. Analyze Sue's message. It suffers from many writing faults that you have studied. List its weaknesses and then outline an appropriate writing plan. If your instructor directs, revise the message.

To: Staff Computer Users
From: Sue Wang, Manager, Document Production <swang@csb.com>
Subject: Software Sharing Violates the Law

Unfortunately, I cannot allow copies of our new Adobe Photoshop software to be made for home use. Or for any other use. Some staffers have asked for this privilege. Which is against the law.

This software program has many outstanding features, and I would be happy to demonstrate some of it to anyone who drops by the Document Production Department. Allowing this software to be copied violates company policy as well as the law. Like many licensed products today, it forbids and prohibits copying of all kinds. We have two copies, but we can't even make copies for other computers within our department. And especially not for home use! If you stop and think about it, it makes a lot of sense. Software companies would not be in business for long if it allowed wholesale copying. Eventually, they would not earn enough money to stay in business. Or to develop new software.

This memo is to inform you that we cannot allow copies of Adobe Photoshop to be made due to the fact that we agreed to limit its use to one single machine. Thank you for your cooperation.

1. List at least five weaknesses in this e-mail message.

2. Outline a plan for writing a refusal to a request.
   Buffer:

   Reasons:

   Bad news:

   Closing:

WRITING COACH
STEP-BY-STEP DEMONSTRATION

Refusing a Favor Request

Problem

As chief of regional marketing for LaserScope, a highly successful technology firm, you received a request from Emily Decker, feature writer for *Business Management Weekly*. Emily is researching an article about young sales stars. Your company has a number of high-flying sales reps pulling down six-figure salaries, based on their combined salary and commissions. But you can't single out sales reps, and you certainly can't reveal their salaries. You are surprised that anyone would make such a request. Many years ago sales reps and management reached an agreement to keep the terms of all their contracts strictly confidential. On the other hand, you would like very much to see your company featured in *Business Management Weekly*. You wonder how you can refuse the request but retain the possibility for public exposure. When you talk with Haley Adkinson, one of your product managers, she says, "Why not just send a fact sheet that tells a little something about the current top salespeople, and let it go at that?"

before revision

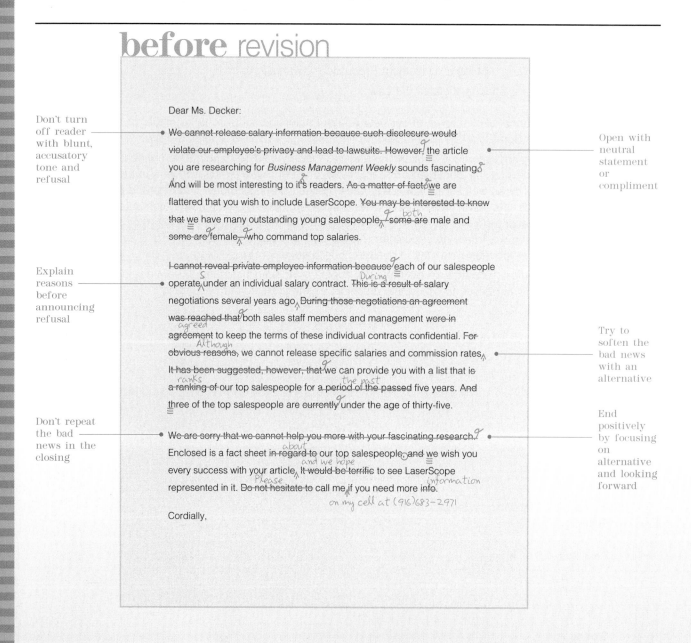

Don't turn off reader with blunt, accusatory tone and refusal

Open with neutral statement or compliment

Explain reasons before announcing refusal

Try to soften the bad news with an alternative

Don't repeat the bad news in the closing

End positively by focusing on alternative and looking forward

Dear Ms. Decker:

~~We cannot release salary information because such disclosure would violate our employee's privacy and lead to lawsuits. However,~~ the article you are researching for *Business Management Weekly* sounds fascinating. ~~And will be most interesting to it's readers. As a matter of fact,~~ we are flattered that you wish to include LaserScope. ~~You may be interested to know that~~ we have many outstanding young salespeople, ~~some are male and some are female,~~ both who command top salaries.

~~I cannot reveal private employee information because~~ each of our salespeople operate under an individual salary contract. ~~This is a result of~~ salary negotiations several years ago. ~~During those negotiations an agreement was reached that~~ both sales staff members and management ~~were in agreement~~ agreed to keep the terms of these individual contracts confidential. ~~For obvious reasons,~~ Although we cannot release specific salaries and commission rates. ~~It has been suggested, however, that~~ we can provide you with a list that ~~is~~ ~~a ranking of~~ ranks our top salespeople for a period of the ~~passed~~ past five years. ~~And~~ three of the top salespeople are ~~currently~~ under the age of thirty-five.

~~We are sorry that we cannot help you more with your fascinating research.~~ Enclosed is a fact sheet ~~in regard to~~ about our top salespeople, ~~and we wish you~~ and we hope every success with your article. ~~It would be terrific to see LaserScope represented in it.~~ ~~Do not hesitate to call me~~ Please if you need more ~~info.~~ information on my cell at (916)683-2971

Cordially,

Writing Plan

BUFFER
Start with a neutral statement.

Begin with a compliment, appreciation, or a quick review of the facts.

REASONS
Present valid reasons for refusal.

Explain logically why the request must be refused. Avoid words that create a negative tone.

BAD NEWS
De-emphasize the bad news.

Soften the bad news by using the passive voice, accentuating the positive, or implying the refusal.

Suggest a compromise, alternative, or substitute if possible.

CLOSING
Renew good feelings with a positive statement.

Avoid referring to the bad news. Look forward to continued relations.

---

after revision

LaserScope Enterprises
3457 Freeport Boulevard
Sacramento, CA 95823-3457

(916) (389-2000)
www.LASERSCOPE.COM

October 27, 200x

Ms. Emily Decker
2415 Jefferson Road
Rochester, NY 14623

Dear Ms. Decker:

The article you are now researching for *Business Management Weekly* sounds fascinating and will be most interesting to its readers. We are flattered that you wish to include some of LaserScope's top salespeople. We have many outstanding young salespeople, both male and female, who command top salaries.

Each of our salespeople operates under an individual salary contract. During salary negotiations several years ago, both sales staff members and management agreed to keep the terms of these individual contracts confidential. Although specific salaries and commission rates cannot be released, we can provide you with a ranked list of our top salespeople for the past five years. Three of the current top salespeople are under the age of thirty-five.

Enclosed is a fact sheet about our top salespeople. We wish you every success with your article, and we hope to see LaserScope represented in it. Please call me on my cell at (916) 683-2971 if you need more information.

Cordially,

Mitchell M. Haddad

Mitchell M. Haddad
Regional Marketing Chief

Enclosure

8.2 Request Refusal: Long-Time Customer Asks for Too Much

Analyze the following letter. List its weaknesses and outline a writing plan. Revise the letter if your instructor directs.

Current date

Ms. Ashley Puckett, Manager
Desert Design and Contracting
202 New Stine Road
N. Las Vegas, NV 89030

Dear Ms. Puckett:

Unfortunately, we cannot allow you to convert the payments you have been making on your Canon X1000 color copier toward its purchase, much as we would love to do so. We understand that you have been making regular payments for the past 14 months.

We operate under a firm company policy prohibiting such conversion of leasing monies. Perhaps you have noticed that we offer extremely low leasing and purchase prices. Obviously, these low prices would never be possible if we agreed to many proposals such as yours. Because we would like to stay in business, we cannot agree to your request asking us to convert all 14 months of rental payments toward the purchase of our popular new equipment.

We understand, Ms. Puckett, that you have had the Canon X1000 color copier for 14 months, and you claim that it has been reliable and versatile. We would like to tell you about another Canon model—one that is perhaps closer to your limited budget.

Sincerely,

1. List at least five weaknesses in this letter.

2. Outline a plan for writing a refusal to a request.
   Buffer:

   Reasons:

   Bad News:

   Closing:

8.3 Claim Denial: Bed Body Blots

Analyze the following letter. List its weaknesses and outline a writing plan. Then revise it so that it could be used to answer other, similar letters.

Current date

Mrs. Christina Esteves
340 South Cobb Drive
Marietta, GA 30060

Dear Mrs. Esteves:

I have before me your letter of September 22 demanding repair or replacement for your newly purchased BeautyTest mattress. You say that you enjoy sleeping on it, but in the morning when you and your husband get up, you claim that the mattress has body "blots" that remain all day.

Unfortunately, Mrs. Esteves, we can neither repair nor replace your mattress because those impressions are perfectly normal. If you will read your warranty carefully, you will find this statement: "Slight body impressions will appear with use and are not indicative of structural failure. The body-conforming coils and comfort-cushioning materials are beginning to work for you and impressions are caused by the natural settling of these materials."

When you purchased your mattress, I'm sure your salesperson told you that the BeautyTest mattress has a unique, scientifically designed system of individually pocketed coils that provide separate support for each person occupying the bed. This unusual construction, with those hundreds of independently operating coils, reacts to every body contour, providing luxurious comfort. At the same time, this system provides firm support. It is this unique design that's causing the body impressions that you see when you get up in the morning.

We never repair or replace a mattress when it merely shows slight impressions. We can, however, send our representative out to inspect your mattress, if it would make you feel better. Please call for an appointment at 1-800-433-9831. Remember, on a BeautyTest mattress you get the best night's rest possible.

Cordially,

1. List at least five weaknesses in this letter.

2. Outline a writing plain for refusing a claim and announcing bad news to customers.
   Buffer:
   Reasons:

   Bad news:

   Closing:

ACTIVITIES AND CASES

CRITICAL THINKING

8.4 Request Refusal: Thumbs Down on PDAs for Charleston Agents

George R. Hollings, president of Hollings Carolina Realty, is not keen on using technology to sell real estate. As you learned in Chapter 7, Activity 7.6, he was asked to purchase PDAs plus software and monthly updates for all 18 staff members of his firm. He did the math and figured that the cost would be something like $6,000 for the initial investment plus $4,000 per year for updates. That's a lot of money for technology that he's not convinced is needed. He appreciated the tactful, logical, and persuasive memo that he received from a talented agent requesting this PDA support. He wants to respond in writing because he can control exactly what he says and a written response is more forceful. His memo will also make a permanent record of this decision, in case agents make similar requests in the future. The more he ponders the request, the more Mr. Hollings thinks that this kind of investment in software and hardware should be made by agents themselves—not by the agency.

Your Task. Put yourself in the place of Mr. Hollings and write a refusal that retains the goodwill of the agent yet makes it clear that this request cannot be granted.

8.5 Request Refusal: Carnival Rejects Under-21 Crowd

The world's largest cruise line finds itself in a difficult position. Carnival climbed to the No. 1 spot by promoting fun at sea and pitching its appeal to younger customers who were drawn to on-board discos, swim-up bars, and hassle-free partying. But apparently the partying of high school and college students went too far. Roving bands of teens had virtually taken over some cruises in recent years. Travel agents complained of "drunken, loud behavior," as reported by Mike Driscall, editor of *Cruise Week*.

To crack down, Carnival raised the drinking age from 18 to 21 and required more chaperoning of school groups. Young individual travelers, however, were still unruly and disruptive. Thus, Carnival instituted a new policy, effective immediately. No one under 21 may travel unless accompanied by an adult over 25. Says Vicki Freed, Carnival's vice president for marketing, "We will turn them back at the docks, and they will not get refunds." As Eric Rivera, a Carnival marketing manager, you must respond to the inquiry of Sheryl Kiklas of All-World Travel, a New York travel agency that features special spring- and summer-break packages for college and high school students.

All-World Travel has been one of Carnival's best customers. However, Carnival no longer wants to encourage unaccompanied young people. You must refuse the request of Ms. Kiklas to help set up student tour packages. Carnival discourages even chaperoned tours. Its real market is now family packages. You must write to All-World Travel and break the bad news. Try to promote fun-filled, carefree cruises destined for sunny, exotic ports of call that remove guests from the stresses of everyday life. By the way, Carnival attracts more passengers than any other cruise line—over a million people a year from all over the world. Over 98 percent of Carnival's guests say that they were well satisfied.

Your Task. Write your letter to Sheryl Kiklas, All-World Travel Agency, 440 East Broadway, New York, NY 10014. Send her a schedule for spring and summer Caribbean cruises. Tell her you will call during the week of January 5 to help her plan special family tour packages.[16]

> **CRITICAL THINKING** — **INFOTRAC** — **WEB**

8.6 Request Refusal: Evict Loud Music Fan?

As the owner of Peachtree Business Plaza, you must respond to the request of Michael Vazquez, one of the tenants in your three-story office building. Mr. Vazquez, a CPA, demands that you immediately evict a neighboring tenant who plays loud music throughout the day, interfering with Mr. Vazquez's conversations with clients and with his concentration. The noisy tenant, Anthony Chomko, seems to operate an entertainment booking agency and spends long hours in his office. You know you can't evict Mr. Chomko because, as a legal commercial tenant, he is entitled to conduct his business. However, you might consider adding soundproofing, an expense that you would prefer to share with Mr. Chomko and Mr. Vazquez. You might also discuss limiting the time of day that Mr. Chomko could make noise.

Your Task. Before responding to Mr. Vazquez, you decide to find out more about commercial tenancy. Use InfoTrac and the Web to search the keywords "Commercial Eviction." Then develop a course of action. In writing to Mr. Vazquez, deny his request but retain his goodwill. Tell him how you plan to resolve the problem. Write to Michael Vazquez, CPA, Suite 230, Peachtree Business Plaza, 116 Krog Street, Atlanta, GA 30307. Your instructor may also ask you to write an appropriate message to Mr. Anthony Chomko, Suite 225.

8.7 Claim Denial: Refusing Wounded Buffalo and Pygmy Circus Refund

As manager of Promotions and Advertising, Five Flags Lake Point Park, you must respond to a recent letter. Nataleigh Haggard complained that she was "taken" by Five Flags when the park had to substitute performers for the Wounded Buffalo and Pygmy Circus "Summertime Slam" performance Sunday, July 4. Explain to her that the concert was planned by an independent promoter. Your only obligation was to provide the theater facility and advertising. Three days before the event, the promoter left town, taking with him all advance payments from financial backers. As it turned out, many of the artists he had promised to deliver were not even planning to attend.

Left with a messy situation, you decided on Thursday to go ahead with a modified version of the event since you had been advertising it and many would come expecting some kind of talent. At that time you changed your radio advertising to say that for reasons beyond your control, the Wounded Buffalo and Pygmy Circus bands would not be appearing. You described the new talent and posted signs at the entrance and in the parking lot announcing the change. Contrary to Ms. Haggard's claim, no newspaper advertising featuring Wounded Buffalo or the Pigs appeared on the day of the concert (at least you did not pay for any to appear that day). Somehow she must have missed your corrective radio advertising and signs at the entrance. You feel you made a genuine effort to communicate the changed program. In your opinion, most people who attended the concert thought that Five Flags had done everything possible to salvage a rather unfortunate situation.

Ms. Haggard wants a cash refund of $150 (two tickets at $75 each). Five Flags has a no-money-back policy on concerts after the event takes place. If Ms. Haggard had come to the box office before the event started, you could have returned her money. But she stayed to see the concert. She claims that she didn't know anything about the talent change until after the event was well underway. This sounds unlikely, but you don't quarrel with customers. Nevertheless, you can't give her cash back. You already took a loss on this event. But you can give two complimentary passes to Five Flags Lake Point Park.

Your Task. Write a refusal letter to Ms. Nataleigh Haggard, 9684 Middletown Road, Germantown, OH 45327. Invite her and a friend to return as guests under happier circumstances.

8.8 Customer Bad News: J. Crew Goofs on Cashmere Turtleneck

Who wouldn't want a cashmere zip turtleneck sweater for $18? At the J. Crew Web site, many delighted shoppers scrambled to order the bargain cashmere. Unfortunately, the price should have been $218! Before J. Crew officials could correct the mistake, several hundred e-shoppers had bagged the bargain sweater for their digital shopping carts.

When the mistake was discovered, J. Crew immediately sent an e-mail message to the soon-to-be disappointed shoppers. The subject line shouted "Big Mistake!" Emily Woods, chairwoman of J. Crew, began her message with this statement: "I wish we could sell such an amazing sweater for only $18. Our price mistake on your new cashmere zip turtleneck probably went right by you, but rather than charge you such a large difference, I'm writing to alert you that this item has been removed from your recent order."

As an assistant in the communication department at J. Crew, you saw the e-mail message that was sent to customers and you tactfully suggested that the bad news might have been broken differently. Your boss says, "OK, hot stuff. Give it your best shot."

Your Task. Although you have only a portion of the message, analyze the customer bad-news message sent by J. Crew. Using the principles suggested in this chapter, write an improved e-mail message. In the end, J. Crew decided to allow customers who ordered the sweater at $18 to reorder it for $118.80 to $130.80, depending on the size. Customers were given a special Web site to reorder (make up an address). Remember that J. Crew customers are youthful and hip. Keep your message upbeat.[17]

WEB

8.9 Bad-News Follow-Up: Worms in Her PowerBars!

In a recent trip to her local grocery store, Kelly Keeler decided for the first time to stock up on PowerBars. These are low-fat, high-carbohydrate energy bars that are touted as a highly nutritious snack food specially formulated to deliver long-lasting energy. Since 1986, PowerBar (*http://www.powerbar.com*) has been dedicated to helping athletes and active people achieve peak performance. It claims to be "the fuel of choice" for top athletes around the world. Kelly is a serious runner and participates in many track meets every year.

On her way to a recent meet, Kelly grabbed a PowerBar and unwrapped it while driving. As she started to take her first bite, she noticed something white and shiny in the corner of the wrapping. An unexpected protein source wriggled out of her energy bar—a worm! Kelly's first inclination was to toss it out the window and never buy another PowerBar. On second thought, though, she decided to tell the company. When she called the toll-free number on the wrapper, Sophie, who answered the phone, was incredibly nice, extremely apologetic, and very informative about what happened. "I'm very sorry you experienced an infested product," said Sophie.

She explained that the infamous Indian meal moth is a pantry pest that causes millions of dollars in damage worldwide. It feeds on grains or grain-based products, such as cereal, flour, dry pasta, crackers, dried fruits, nuts, spices, and pet food. The tiny moth eggs lie dormant for some time or hatch quickly into tiny larvae (worms) that penetrate food wrappers and enter products.

At its manufacturing facilities, PowerBar takes stringent measures to protect against infestation. It inspects incoming grains, supplies proper ventilation, and shields all grain-storage areas with screens to prevent insects from entering. It also uses light traps and electrocuters; these devices eradicate moths with the least environmental impact.

PowerBar President Brian Maxwell makes sure every complaint is followed up immediately with a personal letter. His letters generally tell customers that it is rare for infestations like this to occur. Entomologists say that the worms are not toxic and will not harm humans. Nevertheless, as President Maxwell says, "it is extremely disgusting to find these worms in food."

Your Task. For the signature of Brian Maxwell, PowerBar president, write a bad-news follow-up letter to Kelly Keeler, 932 Opperman Drive, Eagan, MN 55123. Keep the letter informal and personal. Explain how pests get into grain-based products and what you are doing to prevent infestation. You can learn more about the Indian meal moth by searching the Web. In your letter include a brochure titled "Notes About the Indian Meal Moth," along with a kit for Kelly to mail the culprit PowerBar to the company for analysis in Boise, Idaho. Also send a check reimbursing Kelly $26.85 for her purchase.[18]

8.10 Customer Bad News: Costly SUV Upgrade to a Ford Excursion

Steven Chan, a consultant from Oakland, California, was surprised when he picked up his rental car from Budget in Seattle over Easter weekend. He had reserved a full-size car, but the rental agent told him he could upgrade to a Ford Excursion for an additional $25 a day. "She told me it was easy to drive," Mr. Chan reported. "But when I saw it, I realized it was huge—like a tank. You could fit a full-size bed inside."

On his trip Mr. Chan managed to scratch the paint and damage the rear-door step. He didn't worry, though. He thought the damage would be covered because he had charged the rental on his American Express card. He knew that the company offered back-up car rental insurance coverage. To his dismay, he discovered that its car rental coverage excluded large SUVs. "I just assumed they'd cover it," he confessed. He wrote to Budget to complain about not being warned that certain credit cards may not cover damage to large SUVs or luxury cars.

Budget agents always encourage renters to sign up for Budget's own "risk product." But they don't feel that it is their responsibility to study the policies of customers' insurance carriers and explain what may or may not be covered. Moreover, they try to move customers into their rental cars as quickly as possible and avoid lengthy discussions of insurance coverage. Customers who do not purchase insurance are at risk. Mr. Chan does not make any claim against Budget, but he is upset about being "pitched" to upgrade to the larger SUV, which he didn't really want.[19]

Your Task. As a member of the communication staff at Budget, respond to Mr. Chan's complaint. Budget obviously is not going to pay for the SUV repairs, but it does want to salvage his goodwill and future business. Offer him a coupon worth two days' free rental of any full-size sedan. Write to Steven Chan, 5300 Park Ridge, Apt. 4A, Oakland, CA 93578

CRITICAL THINKING

8.11 Customer Bad News: McDonald's Squirms Over McAfrika Protests

The McAfrika burger sounded like a terrific new menu sandwich to fast-food giant McDonald's. Made from an authentic African recipe, the pita bread sandwich combined beef, cheese, tomatoes, and salad. But when launched in Norway, it triggered an avalanche of criticism and bad publicity. McDonald's was accused of "extreme insensitivity" in releasing the new sandwich when 12 million people are facing starvation in southern Africa.

Aid agencies trying to raise funds to avert famine in southern Africa were particularly vociferous in their complaints. They said the McAfrika marketing campaign was "insensitive, crass, and ill considered." Linn Aas-Hansen, of Norwegian Church Aid, complained that it was "inappropriate and distasteful to launch a hamburger called McAfrika when large portions of southern Africa are on the verge of starvation." To punctuate their protest, members of the aid group distributed "catastrophe crackers" outside McDonald's restaurants in Oslo. These crackers are protein-rich biscuits given to starving Africans.

Facing a public relations debacle, McDonald's Norway immediately began a damage-control strategy. Spokeswoman Margaret Brusletto apologized, saying that the name of the product and the timing of its launch were unfortunate. She said the company would consider sharing the proceeds from its sales with aid agencies. McDonald's also offered to allow aid agencies to leave collection boxes and fund-raising posters in its Norwegian restaurants that sold the McAfrika sandwich during its promotional sale.

McDonald's head office issued a statement saying, "All of the involved parties are happy with the solution. We hope this will put a wider focus on the important job that these organizations are doing, and McDonald's in Norway is pleased to be able to support this." Although the McAfrika was launched only in Norway, the protest made headlines in the United States and other countries.[20]

Your Task. As a member of the McDonald's corporate communication staff, you are given the task of drafting a letter to be sent to U.S. customers who have written to protest the McAfrika sandwich in Norway and in the

United States. Most of the letters ask McDonald's to withdraw the offending product, a request you must re-fuse. Address the letter to Mrs. Janice M. Clark, 35 South Washington, Carthage, IL 62325. Prepare your let-ter so that it can be sent to others.

CRITICAL THINKING

8.12 Bad News to Customers: The StairClimber or the LifeStep?

You are delighted to receive a large order from Greg Waller at New Bodies Gym. This order includes two Lifecycle Trainers (at $1,295 each), four Pro Abdominal Boards (at $295 each), three Tunturi Muscle Trainers (at $749 each), and three Dual-Action StairClimbers (at $1,545 each).

You could ship immediately except for one problem. The Dual-Action StairClimber is intended for home use, not for gym or club use. Customers like it because they say it's more like scaling a mountain than climb-ing a flight of stairs. With each step, users exercise their arms to pull or push themselves up. And its special cylinders absorb shock so that no harmful running impact results. However, this model is not what you would recommend for gym use. You feel Mr. Waller should order your premier stairclimber, the LifeStep (at $2,395 each). This unit has sturdier construction and is meant for heavy use. Its sophisticated electronics provide a selection of customer-pleasing programs that challenge muscles progressively with a choice of workouts. It also quickly multiplies workout gains with computer-controlled interval training. Electronic monitors inform users of step height, calories burned, elapsed time, upcoming levels, and adherence to fitness goals. For gym use the LifeStep is clearly better than the StairClimber. The bad news is that the LifeStep is considerably more expensive.

You get no response when you try to telephone Mr. Waller to discuss the problem. Should you ship what you can, or hold the entire order until you learn whether he wants the StairClimber or the LifeStep? Or perhaps you should substitute the LifeStep and send only two of them.

Your Task. Decide what to do and write a letter to Greg Waller, New Bodies Gym, 3402 Copeland Drive, Athens, OH 45701.

8.13 Credit Refusal: Cash Only at Gold's Gym and Fitness Center

As manager of Gold's Gym and Fitness Center, you must refuse the application of Becky Peniccia for an Ex-tended Membership. This is strictly a business decision. You liked Becky very much when she applied, and she seems genuinely interested in fitness and a healthful lifestyle. However, your Extended Membership plan qualifies the member for all your testing, exercise, recreation, yoga, and aerobics programs. This multiservice program is expensive for the club to maintain because of the huge staff required. Applicants must have a solid credit rating to join. To your disappointment, you learned that Becky's credit rating is decidedly nega-tive. Her credit report indicates that she is delinquent in payments to four businesses, including Desert Athletic Club, your principal competitor.

You do have other programs, including your Drop In and Work Out plan. It offers use of available facili-ties on a cash basis and enables a member to reserve space on the racquetball and handball courts. The member can also sign up for yoga and exercise classes, space permitting. Because Becky is far in debt, you would feel guilty allowing her to plunge in any more deeply.

Your Task. Refuse Becky Peniccia's credit application, but encourage her cash business. Suggest that she make an inquiry to the credit-reporting company Experian to learn about her credit report. She is eligible to receive a free credit report if she mentions this application. Write to Rebecca Peniccia, Box 103, Westgate Hills, 1402 Olive Avenue, Mesa, AZ 85301.

8.14 Credit Refusal: Risky Order for Cool Camera Phones

As a CellCity sales manager, you are delighted to land a sizable order for your new T-Mobile Nokia digital video camera phone. This great phone is too cool with its full-color LCD, multimedia player, speaker phone, and voice dialing.

The purchase order comes from Beech Grove Electronics, a retail distributor in Indianapolis. You send the order on to Pat Huckabee, your credit manager, for approval of the credit application attached. To your disappointment, Pat tells you that Beech Grove doesn't qualify for credit. Experian Credit Services reports that credit would be risky for Beech Grove.

Because you think you can be more effective in writing than on the telephone, you decide to write to Beech Grove with the bad news and offer an alternative. Suggest that Beech Grove order a smaller number of the camera phones. If it pays cash, it can receive a 2 percent discount. After Beech Grove has sold these fast-moving units, it can place another cash order through your toll-free order number. With your fast delivery system, its inventory will never be depleted. Beech Grove can get the camera phones it wants now and can replace its inventory almost overnight. Credit Manager Huckabee tells you that your company generally reveals to credit applicants the name of the credit-reporting service it used and encourages them to investigate their credit record.

Your Task. Write a credit refusal to Jacob Jackson, Beech Grove Electronics, 3590 Plainfield Road, Indianapolis, IN 46296

E-MAIL

8.15 Employee Bad News: Company Games Are Not Date Nights

As director of Human Resources at Weyerman Paper Company, you received an unusual request. Several employees asked that their spouses or friends be allowed to participate in Weyerman intramural sports teams. Although the teams play only once a week during the season, these employees claim that they can't afford more time away from friends and family. Over 100 employees currently participate in the eight coed volleyball, softball, and tennis teams, which are open to company employees only. The teams were designed to improve employee friendships and to give employees a regular occasion to have fun together.

If nonemployees were to participate, you're afraid that employee interaction would be limited. And while some team members might have fun if spouses or friends were included, you're not so sure all employees would enjoy it. You're not interested in turning intramural sports into "date night." Furthermore, the company would have to create additional teams if many nonemployees joined, and you don't want the administrative or equipment costs of more teams. Adding teams also would require changes to team rosters and game schedules. This could create a problem for some employees. You do understand the need for social time with friends and families, but guests are welcome as spectators at all intramural games. Besides, the company already sponsors a family holiday party and an annual company picnic.

Your Task. Write an e-mail or print memo to the staff denying the request of several employees to include nonemployees on Weyerman's intramural sports teams.

8.16 Employee Bad News: No Go for Tuition Reimbursement

Ashley Arnett, a hardworking bank teller, has sent a request asking that the company create a program to reimburse the tuition and book expenses for employees taking college courses. Although some companies have such a program, First Federal has not felt that it could indulge in such an expensive employee perk. Moreover, the CEO is not convinced that companies see any direct benefit from such programs. Employees improve their educational credentials and skills, but what is to keep them from moving that education and skill set to another employer? First Federal has over 200 employees. If even a fraction of them started classes, the company could see a huge bill for the cost of tuition and books. Because the bank is facing stiff competition and its profits are sinking, the expense of such a program is out of the question. In addition, it would involve administration—applications, monitoring, and record-keeping. It's just too much of a hassle. When employees were hard to hire and retain, companies had to offer employment perks. But with a soft economy, such inducements are unnecessary.

Your Task. As director of Human Resources, send an individual response to Ashley Arnett. The answer is a definite *no*, but you want to soften the blow and retain the loyalty of this conscientious employee.

E-MAIL

8.17 Employee Bad News: Suit Up or Ship Out

During the feverish dot-com boom days, "business casual" became the workplace norm. Like many other companies, Bear Stearns, the sixth largest securities firm in the United States, loosened its dress policies. It allowed employees to come to work in polo shirts, khaki pants, and loafers for two important reasons: It had to compete with Internet companies in a tight employment market, and it wanted to fit in with its casual dot-com customers. But when the dot-com bubble burst and the economy faltered, the casual workplace environment glorified by failed Internet companies fell out of favor.

Managers at Bear Stearns decided to reverse course and cancel the casual dress code that had been in effect for two years. Company spokesperson Elizabeth Ventura said, "Our employees should reflect the professionalism of our business." Some observers felt that relaxed dress codes carried over into relaxed work attitudes.

Particularly in difficult economic times, Bear Stearns believed that every aspect of the business, including dress, should reflect the serious attitude and commitment it had toward relations with clients. After the securities market plunged, Bear Stearns slashed 830 jobs, amounting to 7.5 percent of its workforce. This was the biggest cut in company history, and officials vowed to get serious about regaining market share.

To put into effect its more serious business tone, Bear Stearns decided to return to a formal dress code. For men, suits and ties would be required. For women, dresses, suits with skirts or slacks, or "equivalent attire" would be expected. Although Bear Stearns decided to continue to allow casual dress on Fridays, sports jackets would be required for men.

Despite the policy reversal, company officials downplayed the return to traditional, more formal attire. Spokesperson Ventura noted that the company's legal, administrative, and private client services departments had never adopted the casual dress code. In addition, she said, "We've always had a formal dress policy for meetings with clients."

To ease the transition, nearby Brooks Brothers Inc., a conservative clothing store, offered a special invitation. On September 20 it would stay open an extra hour to host an evening of wine, cheese, and shopping with discounts of 20 percent for Bear Stearns staffers.[21]

Your Task. As an assistant to John Jones, chairman of the Management and Compensation Committee, you have the challenging task of drafting a message to employees announcing the return to a formal dress code. He realizes that this is going to be a tough sell, but he's hoping that employees will recognize that difficult economic times require serious efforts and sacrifices. In the message to employees, he wants you to tell supervisors that they must speak to employees who fail to adhere to the new guidelines. You ask Mr. Jones whether he wants the message to open directly or indirectly. He says that Bear Stearns generally prefers directness in messages to employees, but he wants you to prepare two versions and he will choose one.

VIDEO RESOURCE

Video Library 2, *Building Workplace Skills*

Negative News: DawnSign Press. Named Small Business Owner of the Year in the state of California, Joe Dannis is a unique entrepreneur. In this video you'll learn how he started DawnSign Press, but you'll also see American Sign Language in action. Joe and many of his employees are deaf. As business communicators, you'll be exposed to a unique work environment and be inspired by Joe's success story. Notice that both deaf and hearing employees sign to each other. Pay attention to the nature of Joe's business and listen to his reasons for hiring both deaf and hearing employees.

As a staff employee at DawnSign Press, you were surprised but honored when owner Joe Dannis handed you a letter and asked you to answer it for him. The letter was from Melissa Thomas, a customer who had used one of DawnSign Press's books in a class and found it very helpful. However, she said that she was "profoundly disappointed" when she learned that Joe's business was not staffed by deaf people only. Melissa said that, as a deaf person herself, she had experienced great difficulty in finding employment. She felt that DawnSign Press

should set an example by hiring an all-deaf staff, thus providing jobs for many deserving people. She wants DawnSign Press to change its hiring policy.

Joe knows that you have studied business communication. That's why he asks you to prepare a letter that responds to this inquiry but that may also be used for any future ones. Because you have heard Joe talk about his employment philosophy, you realize that, in a perfect world, he would hire only deaf employees. But Joe is forced to hire hearing employees as well.

Your Task. For Joe's signature, prepare a bad-news message. Start indirectly, provide reasons, present the bad news (or imply it), and close pleasantly. You might wish to visit the DawnSign Press Web site (*http://www.dawnsign.com*) for more information. Address the draft to Ms. Melissa Thomas, 4752 Monroe Street, Toledo, OH 43623.

● GRAMMAR/MECHANICS CHECKUP—8

Commas 3

Review the Grammar/Mechanics Handbook Sections 2.10–2.15. Then study each of the following statements and insert necessary commas. In the space provided write the number of commas that you add; write *0* if no commas are needed. Also record the number of the G/M principle(s) illustrated. When you finish, compare your responses with those provided at the end of the book. If your answers differ, study carefully the principles shown in parentheses.

2 _____ (2.12)   **Example**   The CEO named Marianne Longhi, not Martin Jiang, to the board of directors.

_____

_____

_____

_____

1. "Perpetual optimism" said Colin Powell "is a force multiplier."
2. The featured speakers are Donna H. Cox Ph.D. and Pam Rankey M.B.A.
3. We interviewed Alexander Lee on June 2 didn't we?
4. Research shows that talking on a cell phone distracts drivers and quadruples their chances of getting into accidents such as rear-ending a car ahead of them.
5. The bigger the monitor the clearer the picture.

Review Commas 1, 2, 3

_____

6. As you may know information chips are already encoded in the visas of people who need them for work travel or study in this country.

_____

7. We think however that the new passports will be issued only to diplomats and other government employees beginning in August.

_____

8. To fill the vacant position we hope to hire Kimberly Creek-Lea who is currently working in Palm Beach Gardens.

_____

9. All things considered our conference will attract more participants if it is held in a resort setting such as Las Vegas Scottsdale or Orlando.

_____

10. If you examine the log closely you will see that 15 orders were shipped on Thursday; on Friday only 4.

_____

11. In the past ten years we have promoted over 30 well-qualified individuals many of whom started in accounting.

_____

12. Donald DuBay who spoke to our class last week is the author of a book titled *The Digital Workplace.*

_____

13. A recent study of productivity that was conducted by authoritative researchers revealed that workers in the United States are more productive than workers in Europe or Japan.

_____

14. America's secret productivity weapons according to the report were not bigger companies more robots or even brainier managers.

_____

15. As a matter of fact the report said that America's productivity resulted from a capitalistic system of unprotected hands-off competition.

● GRAMMAR/MECHANICS CHALLENGE—8

The following memo has faults in grammar, punctuation, spelling, capitalization, number form, repetition, wordiness, and other problems. Correct the errors with standard proofreading marks (see Appendix B) or revise the message online at **Guffey Xtra!**

DATE: August 5, 200x

TO: Arthur W. Rose, Vice President

FROM: Jessica Thomas, Market Research

SUBJECT: ANALYSIS OF GATORADE XL

Here is a summery of the research of James Willis' and myself. Regarding the reduced sugar sports drink being introduced by our No. 1 compittior, Gatorade.

In just under a years time Gatorade developed this new drink, it combines together a mixture of 50 percent sugar and 50 percent artificial sweetener. Apparently Gatorade plans to spend over $8 million to introduce the drink, and to assess consumers reactions to it. It will be tested on the shelfs of convience stores grocerys and other mass merchants in five citys in Florida.

The companys spokesperson said, "The 'X' stands for excelent taste, and the 'L' stands for less sugar." Aimed at young adult's who don't like the taste of artificial sweeteners but who want to control calories. The new sports drink is a hybrid sugar and diet drink. Our studys show that simular drinks tryed in this country in the 1980's were unsucessful. On the other hand a 50 calorie low sugar sports drink introduced in Canada two year ago was well received, similarly in Japan a 40 calorie soda is now marketed sucessfully by Coca-Cola.

However our research in regard to trends and our analysis of Gatorade XL fails to indicate that this countrys consumers will be interested in a midcalorie sports drink. Yet Wall Streets response to Gatorades announcement of it's new drink was not unfavorable.

In view of the foregoing the writer and her colleague are of the opinion that we should take a wait and see attitude. Toward the introduction of our own low sugar sports drink.

COMMUNICATION WORKSHOP
MULTICULTURAL ISSUES

PRESENTING BAD NEWS
IN OTHER CULTURES

To minimize disappointment, Americans generally prefer to present negative messages indirectly. Other cultures may treat bad news differently, as illustrated in the following:

- In Germany business communicators occasionally use buffers but tend to present bad news directly.

- British writers also tend to be straightforward with bad news, seeing no reason to soften its announcement.

- In Latin countries the question is not how to organize negative messages but whether to present them at all. It's considered disrespectful and impolite to report bad news to superiors. Thus, reluctant employees may fail to report accurately any negative messages to their bosses. `

- In Thailand the negativism represented by a refusal is completely alien; the word *no* does not exist. In many cultures negative news is offered with such subtleness or in such a positive light that it may be overlooked or misunderstood by literal-minded Americans.

- In many Asian and some Latin cultures, one must look beyond an individual's actual words to understand what's really being communicated. One must consider the communication style, the culture, and especially the context.

  I agree might mean *I agree with 15 percent of what you say*.

  We might be able to could mean *Not a chance*.

  We will consider could mean *WE will, but the real decision maker will not*.

  That is a little too much might equate to *That is outrageous*.[22]

  Yes, might mean *Yes, I'm listening*, or *Yes, you have a good point* or *Yes, I see, but I don't necessarily agree*.[23]

Career Application. Interview fellow students or work colleagues who are from other cultures. Collect information regarding the following:

- How is negative news handled in their cultures?

- How would typical business communicators refuse a request for a business favor (such as a contribution to a charity)?

- How would typical business communicators refuse a customer's claim?

- How would an individual be turned down for a job?

Your Task

Report the findings of your interviews in class discussion or in a memo report. In addition, collect samples of foreign business letters. You might ask foreign students, your campus admissions office, or local export/import companies whether they would be willing to share business letters from other countries. Compare letter styles, formats, tone, and writing strategies. How do these elements differ from those in typical North American business letters?

REPORTING WORKPLACE DATA

9 CHAPTER

INFORMAL REPORTS

OBJECTIVES

- Describe business report basics, including functions, organizational patterns, formats, and delivery methods.

- Follow guidelines for developing informal reports, including determining the problem and purpose, gathering data, using an appropriate writing style, composing effective headings, and being objective.

- Describe six kinds of informal reports.

- Write information and progress reports.

- Write justification/recommendation reports.

- Write feasibility reports.

- Write minutes of meetings and summaries.

"You can have brilliant ideas, but if you can't get them across, your ideas won't get you anywhere.[1]*"*

Lee Iacocca, American industrialist and former chairman of Chrysler Corporation

Savvy business report writers are eager to follow the advice of Lee Iacocca by doing what is necessary to get their ideas across. They are able to simplify facts so that anyone can understand these facts in reports. Why do you need to learn how to write reports? As a business and professional communicator, you'll probably have your share of reports to write. Reports are a fact of life in business today. With increasing emphasis on performance and profits, businesspeople analyze the pros and cons of problems, studying alternatives and assessing facts, figures, and details. This analysis results in reports.

Management decisions in many organizations are based on information submitted in the form of reports. Reports may be submitted in writing, orally, or digitally. Increasingly, workplace information is presented in a PowerPoint talk accompanied by a written report. You'll learn about making oral presentations in Chapter 12.

In this chapter we'll concentrate on informal written reports. These reports tend to be short (usually eight or fewer pages), use memo or letter format, and are personal in tone. You'll learn about the functions, patterns, formats, and writing styles of typical business reports. You'll also learn to write good reports by examining basic techniques and by analyzing appropriate models.

Informal reports are relatively short (eight or fewer pages) and are usually written in memo or letter format.

PHOTOS: © PHOTODISC COLLECTION/GETTY IMAGES; © ROYALTY-FREE/ CORBIS; © JULES FRAZIER/PHOTODISC/GETTY IMAGES

UNDERSTANDING REPORT BASICS

Because of their abundance and diversity, business reports are difficult to define. They may range from informal half-page trip reports to formal 200-page financial forecasts. Reports may be presented orally in front of a group or electronically via e-mail or a Web site. Some reports appear as words on paper in the form of memos and letters. Others are primarily numerical data, such as tax reports or profit-and-loss statements. Some reports provide information only; others analyze and make recommendations. Although reports vary greatly in length, content, form, and formality level, they all have one common purpose: *to answer questions and solve problems.*

Business reports are systematic attempts to answer questions and solve problems.

Functions of Reports

In terms of what they do, most reports fit into two broad categories: informative reports and analytical reports.

INFORMATIVE REPORTS

Informative reports present data without analysis or recommendations.

Reports that present data without analysis or recommendations are primarily informative. Although writers collect and organize facts, they are not expected to analyze the facts for readers. A trip report describing an employee's visit to a conference, for example, simply presents information. Other reports that present information without analysis involve routine operations, compliance with regulations, and company policies and procedures.

ANALYTICAL REPORTS

Analytical reports provide data, analyses, conclusions, and, if requested, recommendations.

Reports that provide data, analyses, and conclusions are analytical. If requested, writers also supply recommendations. Analytical reports may intend to persuade readers to act or to change their beliefs. Assume you're writing a feasibility report that compares several potential locations for a tapas restaurant. After analyzing and discussing alternatives, you might recommend one site, thus attempting to persuade readers to accept this choice.

Organizational Patterns

Like letters and memos, reports may be organized directly or indirectly. The reader's expectations and the content of a report determine its pattern of development, as illustrated in Figure 9.1.

DIRECT PATTERN

When the purpose for writing is presented close to the beginning, the organizational pattern is direct. Informative reports, such as the letter report shown in Figure 9.2, are usually arranged directly. They open with an introduction, followed by the facts and a summary. In Figure 9.2 the writer explains a legal services plan. The letter report begins with an introduction. Then it presents the facts, which are divided into three subtopics identified by descriptive headings. The letter ends with a summary and a complimentary close.

Analytical reports may also be organized directly, especially when readers are supportive or are familiar with the topic. Many busy executives prefer this pattern because it gives them the results of the report immediately. You should be aware, though, that unless readers are familiar with the topic, they may find the direct pattern confusing. Some readers prefer the indirect pattern because it seems logical and mirrors the way we solve problems.

Randy Glasbergen.
www.glasbergen.com

**"Your report was a bit unfocused, so
I trimmed it down from 300 pages
to one strong paragraph."**

FIGURE 9.1 ———— • **Audience Analysis and Report Organization**

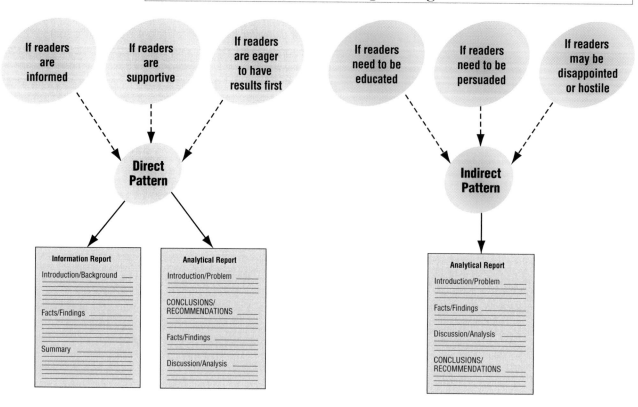

INDIRECT PATTERN

The indirect pattern is appropriate for analytical reports that seek to persuade or that convey bad news.

When the conclusions and recommendations, if requested, appear at the end of the report, the organizational pattern is indirect. Such reports usually begin with an introduction or description of the problem, followed by facts and interpretation from the writer. They end with conclusions and recommendations. This pattern is helpful when readers are unfamiliar with the problem. It's also useful when readers must be persuaded or when they may be disappointed in or hostile toward the report's findings. The writer is more likely to retain the reader's interest by first explaining, justifying, and analyzing the facts and then making recommendations. This pattern also seems most rational to readers because it follows the normal thought process: problem, alternatives (facts), solution.

Formats

How you format a report depends on its length, topic, audience, and purpose.

The format of a report is governed by its length, topic, audience, and purpose. After considering these elements, you'll probably choose from among the following four formats.

LETTER FORMAT

Use letter format for short (usually eight or fewer pages) informal reports addressed outside an organization. Prepared on a company's letterhead stationery, a letter report contains a date, inside address, salutation, and complimentary close, as shown in Figure 9.2. Although they may carry information similar to that found in correspondence, letter reports usually are longer and show more careful organization than most letters. They also include headings.

MEMO FORMAT

For short informal reports that stay within organizations, memo format is appropriate. Memo reports begin with essential background information, using standard

FIGURE 9.2

Information Report—Letter Format

 Center for Consumers of Legal Services
480 Congress St.
Portland, ME 04101

January 17, 200x

Ms. Christine Agostinho, Secretary
Bancroft Village Homeowners' Association
3902 Oak Hill Drive
Westbrook, ME 04092

Dear Ms. Agostinho:

As executive director of the Center for Consumers of Legal Services, I'm pleased to send you this information describing how your homeowners' association can sponsor a legal services plan for its members. After an introduction with background data, this report will discuss three steps necessary for your group to start its plan.

Introduction

A legal services plan promotes preventive law by letting members talk to attorneys whenever problems arise. Prompt legal advice often avoids or prevents expensive litigation. Because groups can supply a flow of business to the plan's attorneys, groups can negotiate free consultation, follow-up, and discounts.

Two kinds of plans are commonly available. The first, a free plan, offers free legal consultation along with discounts for services when the participating groups are sufficiently large to generate business for the plan's attorneys. These plans actually act as a substitute for advertising for the attorneys. The second common type is the prepaid plan. Prepaid plans provide more benefits, but members must pay annual fees, usually of $200 or more a year. More than 30 million people are covered by legal services plans today, and a majority belong to free plans.

Since you inquired about a free plan for your homeowners' association, the following information describes how to set up such a program.

Determine the Benefits Your Group Needs

The first step in establishing a free legal services plan is to meet with the members of your group to decide what benefits they want. Typical benefits include the following:

Free consultation. Members may consult a participating attorney—by phone or in the attorney's office—to discuss any matter. The number of consultations is unlimited, provided each is about a separate matter. Consultations are generally limited to 30 minutes, but they include substantive analysis and advice.

Free document review. Important papers—such as leases, insurance policies, and installment sales contracts—may be reviewed with legal counsel. Members may ask questions and receive an explanation of terms.

Uses letterhead stationery for an informal report addressed to an outsider

Presents introduction and facts without analysis or recommendations

Arranges facts of report into sections with descriptive headings

Emphasizes benefits in paragraph headings with boldface type

Tips for Letter Reports
- Use letter format for short informal reports sent to outsiders.
- Organize the facts into divisions with consistent headings.
- Single-space the body.
- Double-space between paragraphs.
- Leave two blank lines above each side heading.
- Create side margins of 1 to 1¼ inches.
- Add a second-page heading, if necessary, consisting of the addressee's name, the page number, and the date.

headings: *Date, To, From,* and *Subject.* Like letter reports, memo reports differ from regular memos in length, use of headings, and deliberate organization.

MANUSCRIPT FORMAT

For longer, more formal reports, use manuscript format. These reports are usually printed on plain paper instead of letterhead stationery or memo forms. They begin with

FIGURE 9.2 • **Continued**

Identifies second and succeeding pages with headings

Ms. Christine Agostinho   Page 2   January 17, 200x

Discount on additional services. For more complex matters, participating attorneys will charge members 75 percent of the attorney's normal fee. However, some organizations choose to charge a flat fee for commonly needed services.

Select the Attorneys for Your Plan

Groups with geographically concentrated memberships have an advantage in forming legal plans. These groups can limit the number of participating attorneys and yet provide adequate service. Generally, smaller panels of attorneys are advantageous.

Assemble a list of candidates, inviting them to apply. The best way to compare prices is to have candidates submit their fees. Your group can then compare fee schedules and select the lowest bidder, if price is important. Arrange to interview attorneys in their offices.

Uses parallel side headings for consistency and readability

After selecting an attorney or a panel, sign a contract. The contract should include the reason for the plan, what the attorney agrees to do, what the group agrees to do, how each side can end the contract, and the signature of both parties. You may also wish to include references to malpractice insurance, assurance that the group will not interfere with the attorney–client relationship, an evaluation form, a grievance procedure, and responsibility for government filings.

Publicize the Plan to Your Members

Members won't use a plan if they don't know about it, and a plan will not be successful if it is unused. Publicity must be vocal and ongoing. Announce it in newsletters, meetings, bulletin boards, and flyers.

Persistence is the key. All too frequently, leaders of an organization assume that a single announcement is all that's needed. They expect members to see the value of the plan and remember that it's available. Most organization members, though, are not as involved as the leadership. Therefore, it takes more publicity than the leadership usually expects in order to reach and maintain the desired level of awareness.

Summary

A successful free legal services plan involves designing a program, choosing the attorneys, and publicizing the plan. To learn more about these steps or to order a $25 how-to manual, call me at (207) 772-9901.

Includes complimentary close and signature

Sincerely,

Christopher D. Kelley

Christopher D. Kelley, Esq.
Executive Director

pas

a title followed by systematically displayed headings and subheadings. You will see examples of proposals and formal reports using manuscript formats in Chapter 10.

PRINTED FORMS

Prepared forms are often used for repetitive data, such as monthly sales reports, performance appraisals, merchandise inventories, expense claims, and personnel and financial reports. Standardized headings on these forms save time for the writer. Preprinted forms also make similar information easy to locate and ensure that all necessary information is provided.

Report Delivery

Once reports are written, you must decide what channel to use to deliver them to your readers. Written business reports can be delivered in the following ways:

In Person. If you are located close to the reader, deliver your report in person. This delivery method works especially well when you'd like to comment on the report or clarify its purpose. Delivering a report in person also makes the report seem more important or urgent.

Written reports can be delivered in person, by mail, or electronically.

By Mail. Many reports are delivered via mail. You can send your reports by inter-office mail, U.S. Postal Service delivery, or commercial delivery service such as UPS or FedEx.

By Fax. You can fax your report to your reader. Be sure to include a cover page that identifies the sender and introduces the report.

By E-Mail. Reports in any format can be attached to an e-mail message. When using this channel, you will introduce the report and refer clearly to the attachment in the body of your e-mail message.

Online. You might choose to make your report available online. Many report writers today are making their reports available to their readers on the Web. One common method for doing this involves saving the report in Portable Document Format (PDF) and then uploading it to the company's Web site. This is an inexpensive method of delivery and allows an unlimited number of readers access to the report. If the report contains sensitive or confidential information, access to the document can be password protected.

GUIDELINES FOR DEVELOPING INFORMAL REPORTS

Your natural tendency in preparing a report is to sit down and begin writing immediately. If you follow this urge, however, you will very likely have to backtrack and start again. Reports take planning, beginning with defining the project and gathering data. The following guidelines will help you plan your project.

Determining the Problem and Purpose

Begin the report-writing process by determining your purpose for writing the report.

The first step in writing a report is understanding the problem or assignment clearly. This includes coming up with a statement of purpose. Ask yourself: Am I writing this report to inform, to analyze, to solve a problem, or to persuade? The answer to this question should be a clear, accurate statement identifying your purpose. In informal reports the statement of purpose may be only one sentence; that sentence usually

To solve a world-class traffic problem, the city of Boston undertook one of the largest, most technologically difficult and environmentally challenging highway projects in U.S. history. Known as The Big Dig, the project involved expanding the interstate system through downtown Boston. Before gaining approval and implementing plans for any big project, teams define the project, gather data, develop specifications, and write many reports. Business reports, which are systematic attempts to answer questions and solve problems, always begin with the collection of solid facts.

© LISA POOLE/AP WIDE WORLD PHOTOS

becomes part of the introduction. Notice how the following introductory statement describes the purpose of the report:

> *This report presents data regarding the feasibility of and costs involved with opening an on-site day care facility for use by employees with children.*

After writing a statement of purpose, analyze who will read your report. If your report is intended for your immediate supervisors and they are supportive of your project, you need not include extensive details, historical development, definition of terms, or persuasion. Other readers, however, may require background data and persuasive strategies.

The expected audience for your report influences your writing style, research methods, vocabulary, areas of emphasis, and communication strategy. Remember, too, that your audience may consist of more than one set of readers. Reports are often distributed to secondary readers who may need more details than the primary reader does.

Gathering Data

The facts for reports are often obtained from company records, observation, surveys, interviews, printed material, and electronic resources.

One of the most important steps in the process of writing a report is that of researching and gathering data. A good report is based on solid, accurate, verifiable facts. Typical sources of factual information for informal reports include (1) company records; (2) observation; (3) surveys, questionnaires, and inventories; (4) interviews; (5) printed material; and (6) electronic resources.

COMPANY RECORDS

Many business-related reports begin with an analysis of company records and files. From these records you can observe past performance and methods used to solve previous problems. You can collect pertinent facts that will help determine a course of action.

OBSERVATION

Another logical source of data for many problems lies in personal observation and experience. For example, if you were writing a report on the need for a company e-mail and Internet-use policy, you might observe how much employees are using e-mail and the Web for personal use.

SURVEYS, QUESTIONNAIRES, AND INVENTORIES

Data from groups of people can be collected most efficiently and economically by using surveys, questionnaires, and inventories. For example, if you were part of a committee investigating the success of an employee carpooling program, you might begin by using a questionnaire to survey use of the program by employees.

INTERVIEWS

Interviews provide rich, accurate first-hand information because questions can be explained.

Talking with individuals directly concerned with the problem produces excellent first-hand information. For example, if you are researching whether your company should install wireless technology, you could interview an expert in wireless technology about the pros and cons. Interviews also allow for one-on-one communication, thus giving you an opportunity to explain your questions and ideas in eliciting the most accurate information.

PRINTED MATERIAL

Although we're seeing a steady movement away from print to electronic data, print sources are still the most visible part of most libraries. Much information is available only in print. Print sources include books, newspapers, and periodicals, such as magazines and journals.

ELECTRONIC RESOURCES

Special sources of electronic data may include mailing lists, discussion boards, and weblogs (blogs).

An extensive source of current and historical information is available electronically by using a computer to connect to the Web, electronic databases, and other online resources. From a personal or office computer you can access storehouses of information provided by the government, newspapers, magazines, and companies. Business researchers are also using such electronic tools as mailing lists, discussion boards, and weblogs (or "blogs") to conduct research. For short, informal reports the most usable data will probably be found in online resources. Chapter 10 gives you more detailed suggestions about online research and electronic research tools.

Developing an Appropriate Writing Style

Like other business messages, reports can range from informal to formal, depending on their purpose, audience, and setting. Research reports from consultants to their clients tend to be rather formal. Such reports must project an impression of objectivity, authority, and impartiality. But a report to your boss describing a trip to a conference would probably be informal. You can see the differences between formal and informal styles in Figure 9.3.

An informal writing style includes first-person pronouns, contractions, active-voice verbs, short sentences, and familiar words.

In this chapter we are most concerned with an informal writing style. Your short reports will probably be written for familiar audiences and involve noncontroversial topics. You may use first-person pronouns (*I, we, me, my, us, our*) and contractions (*I'm, we'll, they're, didn't*). You'll emphasize active-voice verbs and strive for shorter sentences using familiar words.

Whether you choose a formal or informal writing style, remember to apply the writing techniques you've learned in earlier chapters. The same techniques you've been using to compose effective memos, letters, and e-mail messages can be applied to developing outstanding reports. Like all business documents, business reports must be clear and concise. They should be written using inclusive language, precise verbs, concrete nouns, and vivid adjectives. Avoid using outdated expressions, needless adverbs, slang, and clichés in your reports. Finally, proofread all business reports

FIGURE 9.3   • **Report Writing Styles**

	Informal Writing Style	Formal Writing Style
Use	Short, routine reports Reports for familiar audiences Noncontroversial reports Most reports for company insiders	Theses Research studies Controversial or complex reports (especially to outsiders)

Effect	Feeling or warmth, personal involvement,
	   closeness
		Impression of objectivity, accuracy,
		   professionalism, fairness
		Distance created between writer and reader

Characteristics	Use of first-person pronouns (*I, we, me,
	   my, us, our*)
	Use of contractions (*can't, don't*)
	Emphasis on active-voice verbs
	   (*I conducted the study*)
	Shorter sentences; familiar words
	Occasional use of humor, metaphors
	Occasional use of colorful speech
	Acceptance of author's opinions and ideas
		Absence of first-person pronouns; use of
		   third-person (*the researcher, the writer*)
		Absence of contractions (*cannot, do not*)
		Use of passive-voice verbs (*the study
		   was conducted*)
		Complex sentences; long words
		Absence of humor and figures of speech
		Reduced use of colorful adjectives and adverbs
		Elimination of "editorializing" (author's
		   opinions, perceptions)

carefully to make sure that they contain no errors in spelling, grammar, punctuation, names and numbers, or format.

Using Effective Headings

Good headings are helpful to both the report reader and the writer. For the reader they serve as an outline of the text, highlighting major ideas and categories. They also act as guides for locating facts and pointing the way through the text. Moreover, headings provide resting points for the mind and for the eye, breaking up large chunks of text into manageable and inviting segments. For the writer, headings force organization of the data into meaningful blocks. To learn more about designing readable headings, as well as to pick up other tips on designing documents, see Figure 9.4.

Functional heads show the outline of a report; talking heads describe the content.

You may choose functional or talking heads. Functional heads (such as *Background*, *Findings*, *Staffing*, and *Projected Costs*) describe functions or general topics. They show the outline of a report but provide little insight for readers. Functional

FIGURE 9.4 ———————

┌───┐
│ • **Ten Tips for Designing Better Documents** │
└───┘

Desktop publishing packages, high-level word processing programs, and advanced printers now make it possible for you to turn out professional-looking documents. The temptation, though, is to overdo it by incorporating too many features in one document. Here are ten tips for applying good sense and good design principles in "publishing" your documents:

- **Analyze your audience.** Avoid overly flashy type, colors, and borders for conservative business documents. Also consider whether your readers will be reading painstakingly or merely browsing. Lists and headings help readers who are in a hurry.

- **Choose an appropriate type size.** For most business memos, letters, and reports, the body text should be 10 to 12 points tall (a point is 1/72 of an inch). Larger type looks amateurish, and smaller type is hard to read.

- **Use a consistent type font.** Although your software may provide a variety of fonts, stay with a single family of type within one document. The most popular fonts are Times Roman and Arial. For emphasis and contrast, you may vary the font size and weight with **bold**, *italic*, ***bold italic***, and other selections.

- **Generally, don't justify right margins.** Textbooks, novels, newspapers, magazines, and other long works are usually set with justified (even) right margins. However, for shorter works ragged-right margins are recommended because such margins add white space and help readers locate the beginnings of new lines. Slower readers find ragged-right copy more legible.

- **Separate paragraphs and sentences appropriately.** The first line of a paragraph should be indented or preceded by a blank line. To separate sentences, typists have traditionally left two spaces. This spacing is still acceptable, but most writers now follow printers' standards and leave only one space.

- **Design readable headlines.** Presenting headlines and headings in all caps is generally discouraged because solid blocks of capital letters interfere with recognition of word patterns. To further improve readability, select a sans serif typeface (one without cross strokes or embellishment), such as Arial.

- **Strive for an attractive page layout.** In designing title pages or graphics, provide for a balance between print and white space. Also consider placing the focal point (something that draws the reader's eye) at the optical center of a page—about three lines above the actual center. Moreover, remember that the average reader scans a page from left to right and top to bottom in a Z pattern. Plan your visuals accordingly.

- **Use graphics and clip art with restraint.** Charts, original drawings, and photographs can be scanned into documents. Ready-made clip art and graphics can also be inserted into documents. Use such images, however, only when they are well drawn, relevant, purposeful, and appropriately sized.

- **Avoid amateurish results.** Many beginning writers, eager to display every graphic device a program offers, produce busy, cluttered documents. Too many typefaces, ruled lines, images, and oversized headlines will overwhelm readers. Strive for simple, clean, and forceful effects.

- **Develop expertise.** Learn to use the desktop publishing features of your current word processing software, or investigate one of the special programs, such as QuarkXPress, Adobe's InDesign, and Corel's Ventura. Although the learning curve for many of these programs is steep, such effort is well spent if you will be producing newsletters, brochures, announcements, visual aids, and promotional literature.

heads are useful for routine reports. They're also appropriate for sensitive or controversial topics that might provoke emotional reactions. Functional heads are used in the progress report shown in Figure 9.5.

Talking heads (such as *Employees Challenged by Shortage of Parking* or *Long-Term Parking Solutions*) describe content and provide more information to the reader. Many of the examples in this chapter use talking heads, including the information report in Figure 9.2. To provide even greater clarity, you can make headings both functional and descriptive, such as *Recommendations: Shuttle and New Structures*. Whether your headings are talking or functional, keep them brief and clear. To create the most effective headings, follow a few basic guidelines:

- **Use appropriate heading levels.** The position and format of a heading indicate its level of importance and relationship to other points.
- **Strive for parallel construction within levels.** All headings at a given level should be grammatically similar. Use balanced expressions such as *Current Costs* and *Future Costs* rather than *Current Costs* and *Costs Expected in the Future*.
- **For short reports use first- and second-level headings.** Many business reports contain only one or two levels of headings. For such reports use first-level headings (centered, bolded) and/or second-level headings (flush left, bolded).
- **Capitalize and underline carefully.** Most writers use all capital letters (without underlines) for main titles, such as the report, chapter, and unit titles. For first- and second-level headings, they capitalize only the first letter of main words. For additional emphasis, they use a bold font. Don't enclose headings in quotation marks.
- **Keep headings short but clear.** Try to make your headings brief (no more than eight words) but understandable. Experiment with headings that concisely tell who, what, when, where, and why.
- **Don't use headings as antecedents for pronouns** such as *this, that, these*, and *those*. For example, when the heading reads *Digital Images*, don't begin the next sentence with *These are often used to add interest to company Web sites.*
- **Include at least one heading per report page.** Headings increase the readability and attractiveness of report pages. Use at least one per page to break up blocks of text.

Being Objective

Reports are convincing only when the facts are believable and the writer is credible. You can build credibility in a number of ways:

- **Present both sides of an issue.** Even if you favor one possibility, discuss both sides and show through logical reasoning why your position is superior. Remain impartial, letting the facts prove your point.
- **Separate fact from opinion.** Suppose a supervisor wrote, *Our department works harder and gets less credit than any other department in the company.* This opinion is difficult to prove, and it damages the credibility of the writer. A more convincing statement might be, *Our productivity has increased 6 percent over the past year, and I'm proud of the extra effort my employees are making.* After you've made a claim or presented an important statement in a report, ask yourself, *Is this a verifiable fact?* If the answer is *no*, rephrase your statement to make it sound more reasonable.
- **Be sensitive and moderate in your choice of language.** Don't exaggerate. Instead of saying *most people think . . .* , it might be more accurate to say *Some people think . . . .* Better yet, use

Reports are more believable if the author is impartial, separates fact from opinion, uses moderate language, and cites sources.

Randy Glasbergen.
www.glasbergen.com

"It says our reports stink. We all have to go to writing class to learn to be more objective and sensitive."

specific figures such as *Sixty percent of employees agree* . . . . Also avoid using labels and slanted expressions. Calling someone a *loser*, a *control freak*, or an *elitist* demonstrates bias. If readers suspect that a writer is prejudiced, they may discount the entire argument.

- **Cite sources.** Tell your readers where the information came from. For example, *In a telephone interview with Blake Spence, director of transportation, October 15, he said* . . . OR: *The Wall Street Journal (August 10, p. 40) reports that* . . . . By referring to respected sources, you lend authority and credibility to your statements. Your words become more believable and your argument, more convincing. You will learn how to properly document your sources in Chapter 10.

SIX KINDS OF INFORMAL REPORTS

Informal business reports generally fall into one of six categories. In many instances the boundaries of the categories overlap; distinctions are not always clear-cut. Individual situations, goals, and needs may make one report take on some characteristics of a report in another category. Still, these general categories, presented here in a brief overview, are helpful to beginning writers. Later you'll learn how to fully develop each of these reports.

Information and progress reports generally present data without analysis.

- **Information reports.** Reports that collect and organize information are informative or investigative. They may record routine activities such as daily, weekly, and monthly reports of sales or profits. They may investigate options, performance, or equipment. Although they provide information, they do not analyze that information.

- **Progress reports.** Progress reports monitor the headway of unusual or nonroutine activities. For example, progress reports would keep management informed about a committee's preparations for a trade show 14 months from now. Such reports usually answer three questions: (1) Is the project on schedule? (2) Are corrective measures needed? (3) What activities are next?

- **Justification/recommendation reports.** Justification and recommendation reports are similar to information reports in that they present information. However, they

This greenhouse at the famous Keukenhof Gardens in Holland became a key point in the justification report of a tour organizer. In supporting his inclusion of the Keukenhof in a proposed itinerary for an American travel company, the writer argued that tourists can never be rained out. In addition to the 70 acres of outdoor gardens, thousands of flowers bloom under glass. Justification and recommendation reports are most persuasive when their recommendations are supported by solid facts.

DR. MARY ELLEN GUFFEY

Justification/recommendation and feasibility reports attempt to solve problems by presenting data, drawing conclusions, and making recommendations.

offer analysis in addition to data. They attempt to solve problems by evaluating options and offering recommendations. These reports are often solicited; that is, the writer has been asked to investigate and report.

- **Feasibility reports.** When a company must decide whether to proceed with a plan of action, it may require a feasibility report. For example, should a company invest thousands of dollars to expand its Web site? A feasibility report would examine the practicality of implementing the proposal.

Minutes of meetings and summaries organize and condense information for quick reading and reference.

- **Minutes of meetings.** A record of the proceedings of a meeting is called "the minutes." This record is generally kept by a secretary or recorder. Minutes may be kept for groups that convene regularly, such as clubs, committees, and boards of directors.
- **Summaries.** A summary condenses the primary ideas, conclusions, and recommendations of a longer report or publication. Employees may be asked to write summaries of technical reports. Students may be asked to write summaries of periodical articles or books to sharpen their writing skills. Executive summaries condense long reports such as business plans and proposals.

We'll now look more closely at each of these report categories, beginning with information reports.

INFORMATION REPORTS

Writers of information reports provide information without drawing conclusions or making recommendations. Some information reports are highly standardized, such as police reports, hospital admittance reports, monthly sales reports, or government regulatory reports. Other information reports are more personalized, as illustrated in the letter report shown in Figure 9.2. Information reports generally contain three parts: introduction, body (findings), and conclusion. The body may have many subsections. Consider these suggestions for writing information reports:

- In the introduction explain why you are writing. For some reports, describe what methods and sources were used to gather information and why they are credible. Provide any special background information that may be necessary. Preview what is to follow.

Organize information chronologically, alphabetically, topically, geographically, journalistically, from simple to complex, or from most to least important.

- In the findings section organize the facts in a logical sequence. You might group information in one of these patterns: (1) chronological, (2) alphabetical, (3) topical, (4) geographical, (5) journalism style (*who, what, when, where, why,* and *how*), (6) simple-to-complex, or (7) most to least important. Organizational strategies will be explained in detail in Chapter 10.

In the two-page information report shown in Figure 9.2, Christopher Kelley responds to an inquiry about prepaid legal services. In the introduction he explains the purpose of the report and previews the organization of the report. In the findings/facts section, he arranges the information topically. He uses the summary to emphasize the three main topics previously discussed.

PROGRESS REPORTS

Progress reports tell management whether projects are on schedule.

Continuing projects often require progress reports to describe their status. These reports may be external (advising customers regarding the headway of their projects) or internal (informing management of the status of activities). Progress reports typically follow this pattern of development:

- Specify in the opening the purpose and nature of the project.
- Provide background information if the audience requires filling in.
- Describe the work completed.

- Explain the work currently in progress, including personnel, activities, methods, and locations.
- Anticipate problems and possible remedies.
- Discuss future activities and provide the expected completion date.

As a location manager in the film industry, Katherine Granado frequently writes progress reports, such as the one shown in Figure 9.5. Producers want to be

FIGURE 9.5

Progress Report—Memo Format

QuaStar Productions
Interoffice Memo

DATE: February 7, 200x

TO: Mark Bidema, Executive Producer

FROM: Katherine Granado, Location Manager *KG*

SUBJECT: Sites for *Bodega Bay* Telefilm

Identifies project and previews report

This memo describes the progress of my search for an appropriate rustic home, villa, or ranch to be used for the wine country sequences in the telefilm *Bodega Bay*. Three sites will be available for you to inspect on February 21, as you requested.

Background: In preparation for this assignment, I consulted Director Damien Fitzgerald, who gave me his preferences for the site. He suggested a picturesque ranch home situated near vineyards, preferably with redwoods in the background. I also consulted Producer Meghan Friederichs, who told me that the site must accommodate 55 to 70 production crew members for approximately three weeks of filming. Valerie Hannah, telefilm accountant, requested that the cost of the site not exceed $24,000 for a three-week lease.

Saves space by integrating headings into paragraphs

Work Completed: For the past eight days I have searched the Russian River area in the Northern California wine country. Possible sites include turn-of-the-century estates, Victorian mansions, and rustic farmhouses in the towns of Duncans Mills, Sebastopol, and Guerneville. One exceptional site is the Country Meadow Inn, a 97-year-old farmhouse nestled among vineyards with a breathtaking view of valleys, redwoods, and distant mountains.

Work to Be Completed. In the next five days, I'll search the Sonoma County countryside, including several wineries such as Geyser Peak, Canyon Road, and Rodney Strong. Many old wineries contain charming structures that may present exactly the degree of atmosphere and mystery we need. These wineries have the added advantage of easy access. I will also inspect possible structures at the Armstrong Redwoods State Reserve and the Kruse Rhododendron Reserve, both within 100 miles of Guerneville. I've made an appointment with the director of state parks to discuss our project, use of state lands, restrictions, and costs.

Tells the bad news as well as the good

Anticipated Problems: You should be aware of two complications for filming in this area.

1. Property owners seem unfamiliar with the making of films and are suspicious of short-term leases.

2. Many trees won't have leaves again until May. You may wish to change the filming schedule somewhat.

By February 14 you'll have my final report describing the three most promising locations. Arrangements will be made for you to visit these sites February 21.

Concludes by giving completion date and describing what follows

Tips for Writing Progress Reports
- Identify the purpose and the nature of the project immediately.
- Supply background information only if the reader must be educated.
- Describe the work completed.
- Discuss the work in progress, including personnel, activities, methods, and locations.
- Identify problems and possible remedies.
- Consider future activities.
- Close by telling the expected date of completion.

informed of what she's doing, and a phone call doesn't provide a permanent record. Notice that her progress report identifies the project and provides brief background information. She then explains what has been completed, what is yet to be completed, and what problems she expects.

JUSTIFICATION/RECOMMENDATION REPORTS

Justification/recommendation reports analyze a problem, discuss options, and present a recommendation, solution, or action to be taken.

Both managers and employees must occasionally write reports that justify or recommend something, such as buying equipment, changing a procedure, hiring an employee, consolidating departments, or investing funds. Large organizations sometimes prescribe how these reports should be organized; they use forms with conventional headings. When you are free to select an organizational plan yourself, however, let your audience and topic determine your choice of direct or indirect structure.

Direct Pattern

For nonsensitive topics and recommendations that will be agreeable to readers, you can organize directly according to the following sequence:
* In the introduction identify the problem or need briefly.
* Announce the recommendation, solution, or action concisely and with action verbs.
* Explain more fully the benefits of the recommendation or steps to be taken to solve the problem.
* Discuss pros, cons, and costs.
* Conclude with a summary specifying the recommendation and necessary action.

Jonathan Crider applied the preceding process in writing the recommendation report shown in Figure 9.6. Jonathan is operations manager in charge of a fleet of trucks for a large parcel delivery company in Charleston, South Carolina. When he heard about a new Goodyear smart tire with an electronic chip, Jonathan thought his company should give the new tire a try. His recommendation report begins with a short introduction to the problem followed by his two recommendations. Then he explains the product and how it would benefit his company. He concludes by highlighting his recommendation and specifying the action to be taken.

Indirect Pattern

When a reader may oppose a recommendation or when circumstances suggest caution, don't be in a hurry to reveal your recommendation. Consider using the following sequence for an indirect approach to your recommendations:
* Make a general reference to the problem, not to your recommendation, in the subject line.
* Describe the problem or need your recommendation addresses. Use specific examples, supporting statistics, and authoritative quotes to lend credibility to the seriousness of the problem.
* Discuss alternative solutions, beginning with the least likely to succeed.
* Present the most promising alternative (your recommendation) last.
* Show how the advantages of your recommendation outweigh its disadvantages.
* Summarize your recommendation. If appropriate, specify the action it requires.
* Ask for authorization to proceed if necessary.

FIGURE 9.6

• Justification/Recommendation Report—Memo Format

Interoffice Memo   ***Pacific Trucking, Inc.***

DATE: July 19, 200x

TO: Symone Fisher, Vice President

FROM: Jonathan Crider, Operations Manager   *JC*

SUBJECT: Pilot Testing Smart Tires

Next to fuel, truck tires are our biggest operating cost. Last year we spent $211,000 replacing and retreading tires for 495 trucks. This year the costs will be greater because prices have jumped at least 12 percent and because we've increased our fleet to 550 trucks. Truck tires are an additional burden since they require labor-intensive paperwork to track their warranties, wear, and retread histories. To reduce our long-term costs and to improve our tire tracking system, I recommend that we do the following:

• Purchase 24 Goodyear smart tires
• Begin a one-year pilot test on four trucks

How Smart Tires Work

Smart tires have an embedded computer chip that monitors wear, performance, and durability. The chip also creates an electronic fingerprint for positive identification of a tire. By passing a handheld sensor next to the tire, we can learn where and when a tire was made (for warranty and other information), how much tread it had originally, and its serial number.

How Smart Tires Could Benefit Us

Although smart tires are initially more expensive than other tires, they could help us improve our operations and save us money in four ways:

1. **Retreads.** Goodyear believes that the wear data is so accurate that we should be able to retread every tire three times, instead of our current two times. If that's true, in one year we could save at least $27,000 in new tire costs.
2. **Safety.** Accurate and accessible wear data should reduce the danger of blowouts and flat tires. Last year, drivers reported six blowouts.
3. **Record keeping and maintenance.** Smart tires could reduce our maintenance costs considerably. Currently, we use an electric branding iron to mark serial numbers on new tires. Our biggest headache is manually reading those serial numbers, decoding them, and maintaining records to meet safety regulations. Reading such data electronically could save us thousands of dollars in labor.
4. **Theft protection.** The chip can be used to monitor each tire as it leaves or enters the warehouse or yard, thus discouraging theft.

Summary and Action

Specifically, I recommend that you do the following:
• Authorize the special purchase of 24 Goodyear smart tires at $450 each, plus one electronic sensor at $1,200
• Approve a one-year pilot test in our Atlanta territory that equips four trucks with smart tires and tracks their performance

Left annotations:
Applies memo format for short informal internal report

Presents recommendations immediately

Justifies recommendations by explaining product and benefits

Explains recommendations in more detail

Right annotations:
Introduces problem briefly

Enumerates items for maximum impact and readability

Specifies action to be taken

Tips for Memo Reports
• Use memo format for most short (eight or fewer pages) informal reports within an organization.
• Leave side margins of 1 to 1¼ inches.
• Sign your initials on the *FROM* line.
• Use an informal, conversational style.
• Include talking (descriptive) or functional side headings to organize a report into logical divisions.
• For a receptive audience, put recommendations first.
• For an unreceptive audience, put recommendations last.

FEASIBILITY REPORTS

Feasibility reports analyze
whether a proposal or plan will
work.

Feasibility reports examine the practicality and advisability of following a course of action. They answer this question: Will this plan or proposal work? Feasibility reports typically are internal reports written to advise on matters such as consolidating departments, offering a wellness program to employees, or hiring an outside firm to handle a company's accounting or computing operations. These reports may also be written by consultants called in to investigate a problem. The focus in these reports is on the decision: stopping or proceeding with the proposal. Since your role is not to persuade the reader to accept the decision, you'll want to present the decision immediately. In writing feasibility reports, as shown in Figure 9.7, consider these suggestions:

* Announce your decision immediately.
* Describe the background and problem necessitating the proposal.
* Discuss the benefits of the proposal.
* Describe any problems that may result.
* Calculate the costs associated with the proposal, if appropriate.
* Show the time frame necessary for implementing the proposal.

FIGURE 9.7   **Feasibility Report—Memo Format**

DATE: March 12, 200x

TO: Shannon O'Donnell, Vice President

FROM: Allison Myers-Whitman, Human Resources Manager *amw*

SUBJECT: FEASIBILITY OF AN E-MAIL AND INTERNET MONITORING PROGRAM

The plan calling for implementing an employee e-mail and Internet monitoring program is workable, and I think it could be fully implemented by May 1. This report discusses the background, benefits, problems, costs, and time frame involved in executing the plan.

Reveals decision immediately

Outlines organization of the report

Background: Current Misuse of E-Mail and the Internet. We currently provide all employees with a company e-mail account to use for interoffice correspondence and for communicating with outside clients. E-mail is a fast, efficient, and cost-effective means of communication when used correctly. We also allow employees full Internet access to help them perform their job duties more effectively. However, we have received numerous reports that many employees are using e-mail and the Internet for personal reasons, resulting in lowered productivity, higher costs, and a strain on our network. These problems were submitted to an outside consultant, who suggested an e-mail and Internet monitoring program.

Describes problem and background

Benefits of Plan: Appropriate Use of E-Mail and the Internet. The proposed plan calls for installing e-mail and Internet monitoring software such as EmployeeMonitoring (http://www.employeemonitoring.net/), UntraView Plus (http://www.awarenesstech.com/), or Spector CNE (http://www.spectorcne.com/). We would fully disclose to employees that this software will be monitoring their e-mail and Internet activity. We will also conduct training to teach employees what e-mail and Internet use is considered appropriate and inappropriate. The software will limit any liability that may result from charges of sexual harassment, workplace harassment, or cyberstalking. It will help us avoid copyright infringement from employees illegally downloading software. In addition, the software can help ensure our credibility and professional reputation.

Evaluates positive and negative aspects of proposal objectively

Problems of Plan: Difficulty in Convincing Employees to Accept the Plan. One of the biggest problems will be convincing employees to accept this new policy without feeling as if their privacy is being violated. However, I believe that, with the help of our consultant, we can communicate the reasons for this policy in a way that employees will understand. In addition, if we provide adequate training, we can help employees understand appropriate and inappropriate use of e-mail and the Internet on the job.

Costs. Implementing the employee e-mail and monitoring plan involves two direct costs. The first is the initial cost of the software, which will be $200 to $500, depending on the package we choose. The second cost involves employee training, including the cost of the trainer. I estimate initial training will cost approximately $800. I believe, however, that the costs involved are within the estimates planned for this project.

Time Frame. Selecting the software package to purchase will take about two weeks. Preparing a training program will require another three weeks. Once the program is started, I expect a breaking-in period of at least three months. By May 1 the e-mail and Internet monitoring program will be fully implemented and showing positive results in increased productivity, decreased costs, lowered liability, and improved network performance.

Presents costs and schedule; omits unnecessary summary

MINUTES OF MEETINGS

Minutes provide a summary of the proceedings of meetings. Formal, traditional minutes, illustrated in Figure 9.8, are written for large groups and legislative bodies. If you are the secretary or recorder of a meeting, you'll want to write minutes that do the following:

- Provide the name of the group, as well as the date, time, and place of the meeting.
- Identify the names of attendees and absentees, if appropriate.
- Describe the disposition of previous minutes.
- Record old business, new business, announcements, and reports.
- Include the precise wording of motions; record the vote and action taken.
- Conclude with the name and signature of the person recording the minutes.

FIGURE 9.8

Minutes of Meeting—Report Format

International Association of Administrative Professionals
Planning Committee Meeting
March 14, 2008, 10 a.m.
Conference Room B, Marriott Century Hotel

Shows attendees and absentees

Present: Leah Bustillo, Eric Evangelista, Harrison Farr, Ritu Garewal, Sean Langevin, Nicole Parsay, Michelle Tse

Absent: Benjamin Mobley

Call to Order/Approval of Agenda/Approval of Minutes

Notes approval of agenda and describes disposition of previous minutes

The meeting was called to order by Chair Nicole Parsay at 10:05 a.m. The agenda was unanimously approved as distributed. Minutes from the February 1 meeting were read and approved.

Reports of Officers and Committees

Michelle Tse reported on convention exhibits and her desire to involve more companies and products during this year's international convention. Discussion followed regarding how this might be accomplished.
MOTION: That IAAP office staff develop a list of possible convention exhibitors. The list should be submitted at the next meeting. (Bustillo/Garewal). PASSED 7–0.

Unfinished Business

Describes discussion; does not record every word

Leah Bustillo and Harrison Farr reviewed the information distributed at the last meeting about hotels being considered for the Denver conference. Leah said that the Brown Palace Hotel has ample conference rooms and remodeled interiors. Harrison reported that the Adams Mark Hotel also has excellent banquet facilities, adequate meeting facilities, and rooms at $169 per night.
MOTION: To recommend that IAAP hold its International Convention at the Adams Mark Hotel in Denver, July 17–20, 2008. (Evangelista/Parsay). PASSED 6–1.

Highlights motions, showing name of person making motion and person seconding it

New Business

Describes new business and announcements

The chair announced three possible themes for the convention, all of which focused on technology and the changing role of administrative assistants. Sean Langevin suggested the following possible title: "Vision Without Boundaries." Leah Bustillo suggested a communication theme. Several other possibilities were discussed. The chair appointed a subcommittee of Sean and Leah to bring to the next committee meeting two or three concrete theme ideas.

Harrison Farr thinks that IAAP should be doing more to help members stay ahead in the changing workplace. He suggested workshops to polish skills in word processing, project management, Web research, presentations, and scheduling software.
MOTION: To recommend to IAAP that it investigate offering fee-based technology workshops at the national and regional conventions. (Garewal/Tse). PASSED 5–2.

Adjournment

Records meeting adjournment and next meeting date and time

There being no further business, it was moved, seconded, and carried that the meeting be adjourned. The meeting was adjourned at 11:50 a.m. by Nicole Parsay. The next meeting will be held on April 15 at 10 a.m. at the Marriott Century Hotel.

Respectfully submitted,

Harrison Farr

Harrison Farr, Secretary

Includes name and signature of person recording minutes

Randy Glasbergen.
www.glasbergen.com

**"Here are the minutes of our last meeting.
Some events have been fictionalized
for dramatic purposes."**

Notice in Figure 9.8 that secretary Farr tries to summarize discussions rather than capture every comment. However, when a motion is made, he records it verbatim. He also shows in parentheses the name of the individual making the motion and the person who seconded it. By using all capital letters for *MOTION* and *PASSED*, he makes these important items stand out for easy reference.

Informal minutes are usually shorter and easier to read than formal minutes. They may be formatted with three categories: summaries of topics discussed, decisions reached, and action items (showing the action item, the person responsible, and the due date).

SUMMARIES

> A summary condenses the primary ideas, conclusions, and recommendations of a longer publication.

A summary compresses the main points from a book, report, article, Web site, meeting, or convention. A summary saves time because it can reduce a report or article 85 to 95 percent. Employees are sometimes asked to write summaries that condense technical reports, periodical articles, or books so that their staffs or superiors may grasp the main ideas quickly. Students may be asked to write summaries of articles, chapters, or books to sharpen their writing skills and to confirm their knowledge of reading assignments. In writing a summary, you'll follow these general guidelines:

- Identify completely the article, book, or item being summarized (author's name, document title, publication title, and date of publication).
- Present the goal or purpose of the document being summarized. Why was it written?
- Highlight the research methods (if appropriate), findings, conclusions, and recommendations.
- Omit illustrations, examples, and references.
- Improve readability by including descriptive (talking) or functional headings.
- Include bulleted or enumerated items to provide high "skim" value.
- Include your reactions or an overall evaluation of the document if asked to do so.

> An executive summary presents an overview of a longer report or proposal and focuses on key points.

An *executive summary* summarizes a long report, proposal, or business plan. It concentrates on what management needs to know from a longer report. The executive summary shown in Figure 9.9 summarizes main points from a business plan prepared by Bluewater Koi fish farm. This company wants to expand, and it needs $72,000 to acquire additional land for three fish ponds. To secure financial backing, Bluewater wrote a business plan explaining its operation, service, product, marketing, and finances. Part of that business plan is an executive summary, which you see in Figure 9.9.

FIGURE 9.9

Executive Summary (excerpt from business plan)

EXECUTIVE SUMMARY

Bluewater Koi Expansion Plan

Summarizes purpose of longer report

The purpose of this business plan is to acquaint venture capitalists with Bluewater Koi fish farm and to solicit support for an expansion plan to be undertaken over the next two years. This report will do the following:
- Profile the current Bluewater Koi operation
- Explain the need for expansion to meet market demands
- Summarize expansion costs and expected payback

Uses headings to improve readability

Business Profile

Bluewater Creek is a 45-acre ornamental fish farm located in South Alabama. Bluewater specializes in breeding and selling koi, which are exotic and beautifully colored carp developed in Japan. Koi are collected by hobbyists and usually live in lushly landscaped fish ponds indoors or outside. Although a grand champion koi in Asia has sold for over a million dollars, the koi sold at Bluewater Creek range in price from $2.20 to $90 each. Bluewater had total sales of $347,000 last year in its retail and wholesale operations. The fish at Bluewater are grown in five surface ponds, and the operation ranges from breeding to shipping.

Provides overview of main points

Expansion to Meet Market Demands

Follows sequence of longer report

Bluewater has enjoyed increasing sales and profits since its inception as a fish hatchery in 1981. It has developed a large clientele, selling to retailers and wholesalers through its print catalog and its Web site. Fish quality and health are of utmost importance at Bluewater. Because koi are susceptible to viruses, Bluewater has adopted a policy of not buying or reselling fish from other U.S. growers. As a result, all Bluewater koi are bred and grown on site. This policy, coupled with constantly increasing sales, makes it necessary to acquire a 9-acre farm to accommodate three additional growing ponds.

Financial Needs and Payback

Acquiring the 9-acre farm is expected to cost $38,000. An additional $12,000 is needed to move 60,000 cubic yards of earth to enable the ponds to reach the natural water table necessary for maintaining water levels in the ponds. Other expenses include $22,000 to expand the breeding operation, which involves matching high-quality male and female brood fish imported from Japan. Artificial spawning yields high hatching rates. But this practice is labor intensive. Equally laborious is the following culling process in which only the best colored, patterned, and conformed fish are kept. A total investment of $72,000 will enable Bluewater to complete its needed expansion. Projected annual sales and costs indicate that Bluewater should be able to repay the loan in five years.

Focuses on most important parts of business plan, including marketing, finances, and payback

© PHOTODISC COLLECTION

Breeding beautifully colored koi for collectors is a profitable but hazardous and costly business. Commercial growers need acreage to build breeding and growing ponds, expensive equipment to monitor water quality and prevent diseases, and caring personnel to oversee the intricate breeding program. To secure financial backing, business such as Bluewater Koi submit proposals that often include executive summaries, such as that shown in Figure 9.9.

SUMMING UP AND LOOKING FORWARD

This chapter presented six types of informal business reports: information reports, progress reports, justification/recommendation reports, feasibility reports, minutes of meetings, and summaries. Information reports generally provide data only. Justification/recommendation and feasibility reports are more analytical in that they evaluate the information, draw conclusions, and make recommendations. This chapter discussed four formats for reports. Letter format is used for reports sent outside an organization; Format is used for internal reports. Formal reports are formatted on plain paper with a manuscript design, while routine reports may be formatted on prepared forms. The chapter presented numerous model documents illustrating the many kinds of reports and their formats.

All of the examples in this chapter are considered relatively informal. Longer, more formal reports are necessary for major investigations and research. These reports and proposals, along with suggestions for research methods, are presented in Chapter 10.

CRITICAL THINKING

1. Why are reports necessary to businesses, and why do today's businesspeople write so many?

2. How do business reports differ from business letters?

3. How are informative reports different from analytical reports? Give an original example of each.

4. Of the reports presented in this chapter, discuss those that require indirect development versus those that require direct development.

5. How are the reports that you write for your courses similar to those presented here? How are they different?

CHAPTER REVIEW

6. What is the first step when beginning the process of report writing? What question should you ask yourself in the beginning?

7. List six kinds of informal reports. Be prepared to describe each.

8. List four formats suitable for reports. Be prepared to discuss each.

9. From the lists you made in Questions 7 and 8, select a report category and appropriate format for each of the following situations.

   a. Your supervisor asks you to review the Web site of one of your competitors and to write a report that condenses the important content.

   b. You want to tell management about an idea you have for consolidating two departments in order to eliminate redundancy and lower expenses.

c. You are in charge of developing a new procedure for processing payroll. Your boss wants to know what you have done thus far.

d. You are asked to record the proceedings of a meeting of your college's student association.

e. As Accounting Department manager, you have been asked to describe for all employees your procedure for processing expense claims.

f. As a security officer, you are writing a report of an office break-in.

g. At a Web-based retail company, your supervisor asks you to investigate ways to reduce the number of steps that customers must go through to place an online order. She wants your report to examine the problem and offer solutions.

10. If you were about to write the following reports, where would you gather information? Be prepared to discuss the specifics of each choice.

a. You are a student representative on a curriculum committee. You are asked to study the course requirements in your major and make recommendations.

b. As department manager, you must write job descriptions for several new positions you wish to establish in your department.

c. You are proposing a new company Internet-use policy to management.

d. You must document the progress of a 12-month campaign to alter the image of Levi-Strauss jeans.

11. List and explain four ways you can build credibility in a business report.

12. What one factor distinguishes reports developed directly from those developed indirectly?

13. What is the difference between a functional head and a talking head? Give an example of each for a report about employee reactions to a proposed reduction in health benefits.

14. What should the minutes of a meeting include?

15. What should a summary of a long article or report contain?

WRITING IMPROVEMENT EXERCISES

Evaluating Headings and Titles

Identify the following report headings and titles as **talking** or **functional/descriptive**. Discuss the usefulness and effectiveness of each.

16. Background

17. Need for Changing Passwords Regularly

18. Annual Budget

19. How Instant Messaging Can Improve Corporate Communication

20. Solution: Promoting an Employee Carpool Program

21. Solving Our Networking Problems With an Extranet

22. Comparing Copier Volume, Ease of Use, and Speed

23. Alternatives

ACTIVITIES AND CASES

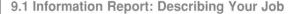

9.1 Information Report: Describing Your Job

Your instructor wants to learn about your employment. Select a position you now hold or one that you have held in the past. If you have not been employed, choose a campus, professional, or community organization to which you belong.

Your Task. Write an information report describing your employment. As an introduction describe the company and its products or services, its ownership, and its location. As the main part of the report, describe your position, including its tasks and the skills required to perform these tasks. Summarize by describing the experience you gained. Your memo report should be single-spaced and 1½ to 2 pages long and should be addressed to your instructor.

WEB

9.2 Information Report: Searching for Career Information

Gather information about a career or position in which you might be interested. Learn about the nature of the job. Discover whether certification, a license, or experience is required. One of the best places to search is the latest *Occupational Outlook Handbook*. Use a search engine such as Google (*http://www.google.com*) to locate the handbook, sponsored by the U.S. Bureau of Labor Statistics. Click the *OOH Search/A-Z Index* link; then search for a specific job title or search the alphabetic list for an occupation.

Your Task. Write an information report to your instructor that describes your target career area. Discuss the nature of the work, working conditions, necessary qualifications, and the future job outlook for the occupation. Include information about typical salary ranges and career paths. If your instructor wants an extended report, collect information about two companies where you might apply. Investigate each company's history, products and/or services, size, earnings, reputation, and number of employees. Describe the functions of an employee working in the position you have investigated. To do this, interview one or more individuals who are working in that position. Devote several sections of your report to the specific tasks, functions, duties, and opinions of these individuals. You can make this into a recommendation report by drawing conclusions and making recommendations. One conclusion that you could draw relates to success in this career area. Who might be successful in this field?

WEB

9.3 Information Report: Exploring a Possible Place to Work

You are thinking about taking a job with a Fortune 500 company, and you want to learn as much as possible about the company.

Your Task. Select a Fortune 500 company (or any other company that interests you), and collect information about it on the Web. Visit *www.hoovers.com* for basic facts. Then take a look at the company's Web site; check its background, news releases, and annual report. Learn about its major product, service, or emphasis. Find its Fortune 500 ranking (if applicable), its current stock price (if listed), and its high and low range for the year. Look up its profit-to-earnings ratio. Track its latest marketing plan, promotion, or product. Identify its home office, major officers, and number of employees. Find out about the company's future plans. In a memo report to your instructor, summarize your research findings. Explain why this company would be a good or bad employment choice.

9.4 Progress Report: Making Headway Toward Your Degree

You agreed with your parents (or spouse, partner, relative, or friend) that you would submit a progress report at this time describing the progress you have made toward your educational goal (employment, certificate, or degree).

Your Task. In memo format write a progress report that fulfills your promise to describe your progress toward your educational goal. Address your progress report to your parents, spouse, partner, relative, or friend. In your memo (1) describe your goal; (2) summarize the work you have completed thus far; (3) discuss thoroughly the work currently in progress, including your successes and anticipated obstacles; and (4) forecast your future activities in relation to your scheduled completion date.

9.5 Progress Report: Keeping Your Supervisor Updated

As office manager for the Animal Rescue Foundation (*www.arf.net*), a nonprofit organization that rescues and finds homes for abandoned and abused animals, you have been asked to come up with ways to increase community awareness of your organization. For the past month you have been meeting with business and community leaders, conducting Web research, and visiting with representatives from other nonprofit organizations. Your supervisor has just asked you to prepare a written report to outline what you have accomplished so far.

Your Task. In memo format write a progress report to your supervisor. In your memo (1) state whether the project is on schedule; (2) summarize the activities you have completed thus far; (3) discuss thoroughly the work currently in progress; and (4) describe your future activities. Also let your supervisor know any obstacles you've encountered and whether the project is on schedule.

E-MAIL

9.6 Progress Report:Connecting With E-Mail

If you are working on a long report for either this chapter or Chapter 10, keep your instructor informed of your progress.

Your Task. Send your instructor a report via e-mail detailing the progress you are making on your long report assignment. Discuss (1) the purpose of the report, (2) the work already completed, (3) the work currently in progress, and (4) your schedule for completing the report.

CRITICAL THINKING

9.7 Justification/Recommendation Report: Expanding the Company Library

Despite the interest in online publications, managers and employees at your company still like to browse through magazines in the company library. Andy Kivel, the company librarian, wants to add business periodicals to the library subscription list and has requested help from various company divisions.

Your Task. You've been asked to recommend four periodicals in your particular specialty (accounting, marketing, etc.). Visit your library and use appropriate indexes and guides to select four periodicals to recommend. Write a memo report to Mr. Kivel describing the particular readership, usual contents, and scope of each periodical. To judge each adequately, you should examine several issues. Explain why you think each periodical should be ordered and who would read it. Convince the librarian that your choices would be beneficial to your department.

TEAM

9.8 Justification/Recommendation Report: Solving a Campus Problem

In any organization, room for improvement always exists. Your college campus is no different. You are the member of a student task force that has been asked to identify problems and suggest solutions.

Your Task. In groups of two to five, investigate a problem on your campus, such as inadequate parking, slow registration, poor class schedules, inefficient bookstore, weak job-placement program, unrealistic degree requirements, or lack of internship programs. Within your group develop a solution to the problem. If possible, consult the officials involved to ask for their input in arriving at a feasible solution. Do not attack existing programs; instead, strive for constructive discussion and harmonious improvements. After reviewing persuasive techniques discussed in Chapter 7, write a justification/recommendation report in memo or letter format. Address your report to the college president.

CRITICAL THINKING   **TEAM**   **WEB**   **INFOTRAC**

9.9 Justification/Recommendation Report: Developing a Company E-Mail and Web-Use Policy

As a manager in a midsized financial services firm, you are aware that members of your department frequently use e-mail and the Internet for private messages, shopping, games, and other personal activities. In addition to the strain on your company's computer network, you worry about declining productivity, security problems, and liability issues. When you walked by one worker's computer and saw what looked like pornography on the screen, you knew you had to do something. Although workplace privacy is a controversial issue for unions and employee-rights groups, employers have legitimate reasons for wanting to know what is happening on their computers. A high percentage of lawsuits involve the use and abuse of e-mail. You think that the executive council should establish some kind of e-mail and Web-use policy. The council is generally receptive to sound suggestions, especially if they are inexpensive. You decide to talk with other managers about the problem and write a justification/recommendation report.

Your Task. In teams of two to five, discuss the need for an e-mail and Web-use policy. Using InfoTrac and the Web, find sample policies used by other firms. Look for examples of companies struggling with lawsuits over e-mail abuse. Find information about employers' rights to monitor employees' e-mail and Web use. Use this research to determine what your company's e-mail and Web-use policy should cover. Each member of the team should present and support his or her ideas regarding what should be included in the policy and how to best present your ideas to the executive council. Write a convincing justification/recommendation report in memo or letter format to the executive council based on the conclusions you draw from your research and discussion. Decide whether you should be direct or indirect.

CRITICAL THINKING

9.10 Feasibility Report: Professional Business Organization

To fulfill a student project in your department, you have been asked to submit a letter report to the dean evaluating the feasibility of starting a Phi Beta Lambda (*http://www.fbla-pbl.org/*) chapter on campus.

Your Task. Find out how many business students are on your campus, the benefits Phi Beta Lambda would provide for students, how one goes about starting a chapter, and whether a faculty sponsor is needed. Assume that you conducted an informal survey of business students. Of the 39 who filled out the survey, 31 said they would be interested in joining. Write a report in memo or letter format to the dean outlining the practicality and advisability of starting a Phi Beta Lambda chapter on your college campus.

CRITICAL THINKING

9.11 Feasibility Report: Improving Employee Fitness

Your company is considering ways to promote employee fitness and morale.

Your Task. Select a possible fitness program that seems reasonable for your company. Consider a softball league, bowling teams, a basketball league, lunchtime walks, lunchtime fitness speakers and demos, company-sponsored health club memberships, a workout room, a fitness center, nutrition programs, and so on. Assume that your supervisor has tentatively agreed to one of the programs and has asked you to write a memo report investigating its feasibility.

9.12 Minutes: Recording the Proceedings of a Meeting

Attend an open meeting of an organization at your school, in your community, or elsewhere. Assume that you are asked to record the proceedings.

Your Task. Record the meeting proceedings in formal or informal minutes. Review the chapter to be sure you include all the data necessary for minutes. Focus on motions, votes, decisions reached, and action taken.

INFOTRAC   **WEB**

9.13 Summary: Using Weblogs for Research

Your supervisor has just learned about the popularity of using weblogs (or "blogs") as research tools. This is the first he's heard of this new communication tool, and he wants to learn more. He asks you to conduct Internet research to see what has been written on the subject.

Your Task. Using InfoTrac or the Web, find an article that discusses the use of weblogs in the workplace for research purposes. In a memo report addressed to your boss, Charlie Shi, summarize the primary ideas, conclusions, and recommendations presented in the article. Be sure to identify the author, article name, journal, and date of publication in your summary.

INFOTRAC   **WEB**

9.14 Executive Summary: Keeping the Boss Informed

Like many executives, your boss is too rushed to read long journal articles. But she is eager to keep up with developments in her field. Assume she has asked you to help her stay abreast of research in her field. She asks you to submit to her one executive summary every month on an article of interest.

Your Task. In your field of study, select a professional journal, such as the *Journal of Management*. Using an InfoTrac Advanced search or a Web search, look for articles in your target journal. Select an article that is at least five pages long and is interesting to you. Write an executive summary in memo format. Include an introduction that might begin with *As you requested, I am submitting this executive summary of . . . .* Identify the author, article name, journal, and date of publication. Explain what the author intended to do in the study or article. Summarize three or four of the most important findings of the study or article. Use descriptive rather than functional headings. Summarize any recommendations made. Your boss would also like a concluding statement indicating your reaction to the article. Address your memo to Martha Laham.

9.15 Report Topics

A list of over 90 report topics is available at your book companion site (*http://guffey.swlearning.com*). The topics are divided into the following categories: accounting, finance, human resources, marketing, information systems, management, and general business/education/campus issues. You can collect information for many of these reports by using InfoTrac and the Web. Your instructor may assign them as individual or team projects. All involve critical thinking in collecting and organizing information into logical reports.

GRAMMAR/MECHANICS CHECKUP—9

Semicolons and Colons

Review Sections 2.16–2.19 in the Grammar/Mechanics Handbook. Then study each of the following statements. Insert any necessary punctuation. Use the delete sign to omit unnecessary punctuation. In the space provided indicate the number of changes you made and record the number of the G/M principle(s) illustrated. (When you replace one punctuation mark with another, count it as one change.) If you make no changes, write *0*. This exercise concentrates on semicolon and colon use, but you will also be responsible for correct comma use. When you finish, compare your responses with those shown at the end of the book. If your responses differ, study carefully the specific principles shown in parentheses.

2	(2.16a)	**Example**	Gonzalo Cino's job is to make sure that his company has enough cash to meet its obligations; moreover, he is responsible for finding ways to reduce operating expenses.

1. Short-term financing refers to a period of one year or less long-term financing on the other hand refers to a period of more than one year.

2. Cash resulting from holiday product sales does not arrive until January therefore our cash flow becomes critical in November and December.

3. We must negotiate short-term financing during the following months October November and December.

4. Large American corporations that offer a variety of financial services are, Bank of America and Citibank.

5. Although some firms rarely need to borrow short-term money many businesses find that they require significant credit to pay for current production and sales costs.

6. A supermarket probably requires no short-term credit a seasonal company such as a ski resort however typically would need considerable short-term credit.

7. We offer three basic types of short-term lines of credit commercial paper and single-payer credit.

8. Speakers at the conference on credit include the following businesspeople Lynne Krause financial manager American International Investments Patrick Coughlin comptroller NationsBank and Shannon Daly legal counsel Fidelity National Financial.

9. The prime interest rate is set by one or more of the nation's largest banks and this rate is offered to a bank's best customers.

10. Many methods are used to calculate finance charges for example average daily balance adjusted balance two-cycle average daily balance and previous balance.

11. Hot Topic, which is a small clothing retailer with a solid credit rating recently applied for a loan but Union Bank refused the loan application because the bank was short on cash.

12. When Hot Topic was refused by Union Bank its financial managers submitted applications to: Chemical Bank, Washington Mutual, and Wells Fargo.

13. The cost of financing capital investments at the present time is very high therefore Hot Topic's managers elected to postpone certain expansion projects.

14. If interest rates reach as high as 18 percent the cost of borrowing becomes prohibitive and many businesses are forced to reconsider or abandon projects that require financing.

15. Several investors decided to pool their resources then they could find attractive investments for large-scale projects.

GRAMMAR/MECHANICS CHALLENGE—9

The following progress report has faults in grammar, punctuation, spelling, number form, wordiness, and word use. Use standard proofreading marks (see Appendix B) to correct the errors. When you finish, your instructor can show you the revised version of this report.

DATE: November 9, 200x

TO: Mark Edelstein, President

FROM: Darmisha Pierson, Development Officer

SUBJECT: Progress Report on Construction of Seattle Branch Office

Construction of Vintage Realtys Seattle Branch Office has entered Phase three. Although we are 1 week behind the contractors original schedule the building should be already for occupancie on March 10.

Past Progress

Phaze one involved development of the architects plans, this process was completed onJune 5. Phaze two involved submission of the plan's for county building department approval. Each of the plans were then given to the following 2 contractors for the purpose of eliciting estimates, David Gray Construction, and Millennium Builders. The lowest bidder was David Gray Construction, consequently this firm began construction on July 15.

Present Status

Phase three includes initial construction processes. We have completed the following steps as of November 9:

* Demolition of existing building at 11485 NW 27 Avenue
* Excavation of foundation footings for the building and for the surrounding wall
* Steel reinforcing rods installed in building pad and wall
* Pouring of concrete foundation

David Gray Construction indicated that he was 1 week behind schedule for these reasons. The building inspectors required more steel reinforcement then was showed on the architects blueprints. In addition excavation of the footings required more time then the contractor anticipated because the 18 inch footings were all below grade.

Future Schedule

In spite of the fact that we lost time in Phase 3 we are substantially on target for the completion of this office building by March 1. Phase 4 include the following activities, framing drywalling and installation of plumbing.

COMMUNICATION ∿∿∿WORKSHOP
COLLABORATION

LAYING THE GROUNDWORK
FOR TEAM WRITING PROJECTS

The chances are that you can look forward to some kind of team writing in your future career. You may collaborate voluntarily (seeking advice and differing perspectives) or involuntarily (through necessity or by assignment). Working with other people can be frustrating, particularly when some team members don't carry their weight or when conflict breaks out. Team projects, though, can be harmonious, productive, and rewarding when members establish ground rules at the outset and adhere to guidelines such as those presented here.

Preparing to Work Together
Before you discuss the project, talk about how your group will function.

- Limit the size of your team, if possible, to two to five members. Larger groups have more difficulties. An odd number is usually preferable to avoid ties in voting.

- Name a team leader (to plan and conduct meetings), a recorder (to keep a record of group decisions), and an evaluator (to determine whether the group is on target and meeting its goals).

- Decide whether your team will be governed by consensus (everyone must agree) or by majority rule.

- Compare schedules of team members, and set up the best meeting times. Plan to meet often. Avoid other responsibilities during meetings. Team meetings can take place face-to-face or virtually.

- Discuss the value of conflict. By bringing conflict into the open and encouraging confrontation, your team can prevent personal resentment and group dysfunction. Conflict can actually create better final documents by promoting new ideas and avoiding "groupthink."

- Discuss how you will deal with members who are not pulling their share of the load.

Planning the Document
Once you've established ground rules, you're ready to discuss the project and resulting document. Be sure to keep a record of the decisions your team makes.

- Establish the document's specific purpose and identify the main issues involved.

- Decide on the final form of the document. What parts will it have?

- Discuss the audience(s) for the document and what appeal would help it achieve its purpose.

- Develop a work plan. Assign jobs. Set deadlines.

- Decide how the final document will be written: individuals working separately on assigned portions, one person writing the first draft, the entire group writing the complete document together, or some other method.

Collecting Information
The following suggestions help teams gather accurate information:

- Brainstorm for ideas as a group.

- Decide who will be responsible for gathering what information.

- Establish deadlines for collecting information.
- Discuss ways to ensure the accuracy and currency of the information collected.

Organizing, Writing, and Revising

As the project progresses, your team may wish to modify some of its earlier decisions.

- Review the proposed organization of your final document, and adjust it if necessary.
- Write the first draft. If separate team members are writing segments, they should use the same word processing program to facilitate combining files.
- Meet to discuss and revise the draft(s).
- If individuals are working on separate parts, appoint one person (probably the best writer) to coordinate all the parts, striving for consistent style and format.

Editing and Evaluating

Before the document is submitted, complete these steps:

- Give one person responsibility for finding and correcting grammatical and mechanical errors.
- Meet as a group to evaluate the final document. Does it fulfill its purpose and meet the needs of the audience?

Career Application. Select a report topic from this chapter or Chapter 10. Assume that you must prepare the report as a team project. If you are working on a long report, your instructor may ask you to prepare individual progress reports as you develop your topic.

Your Task

- Form teams of two to five members.
- Prepare to work together by using the suggestions provided here.
- Plan your report by establishing its purpose, analyzing the audience, identifying the main issues, developing a work plan, and assigning tasks.
- Collect information, organize the data, and write the first draft.
- Decide how the document will be revised, edited, and evaluated.

Your instructor may assign grades not only on the final report but also on your team effectiveness and your individual contribution, as determined by fellow team members.

© PHOTODISC COLLECTION/GETTY IMAGES

CHAPTER 10

PROPOSALS AND FORMAL REPORTS

Basically, our goal is to organize the world's information and to make it universally accessible and useful.[1]

Larry Page, cofounder and CEO of Google

OBJECTIVES

Identify and explain the parts of informal and formal proposals.

Describe the preparatory steps for writing a formal report.

Learn to collect data from secondary sources including print and electronic sources.

Understand how to use Web browsers, search tools, and blogs to locate reliable data.

Discuss how to generate primary data from surveys, interviews, observation, and experimentation.

Understand the need for accurate documentation of data.

Describe how to organize report data, create an outline, and make effective headings.

Illustrate data using tables, charts, and graphs.

Describe and sequence the parts of a formal report.

UNDERSTANDING BUSINESS PROPOSALS

You may not be writing for the world, but you have the same goal as Larry Page when writing business proposals and formal reports: to make them accessible and useful to your readers. In this chapter you'll learn how to achieve this goal. Our discussion will start with proposals.

Proposals are written offers to solve problems, provide services, or sell equipment. Some proposals are internal, often taking the form of justification and recommendation reports. You learned about these reports in Chapter 9. Most proposals, however, are external and are a critical means of selling equipment and services that generate income for many companies.

External proposals may be divided into two categories: solicited and unsolicited. Enterprising companies looking for work might submit unsolicited proposals, but most proposals are solicited. When firms know exactly what they want, they prepare a request for proposal (RFP), specifying their requirements. Government agencies as well as private businesses use RFPs to solicit competitive bids from vendors.

> Proposals are persuasive offers to solve problems, provide services, or sell equipment.

> Both large and small companies today often use requests for proposals (RFPs) to solicit competitive bids on projects.

For example, let's say that sports shoe manufacturer New Balance wants to upgrade the computers and software in its human resources department. If it knows exactly what it wants, it would prepare a request for proposals (RFP) specifying its requirements. It then publicizes this RFP, and companies interested in bidding on the job submit proposals. Both large and small companies are increasingly likely to use RFPs to solicit competitive bids on their projects. This enables them to compare "apples to apples." That is, they can compare prices from different companies on their projects. They also want the legal protection offered by proposals, which are legal contracts.

Many companies earn a sizable portion of their income from sales resulting from proposals. That's why creating effective proposals is especially important today. In writing proposals, the most important thing to remember is that proposals are sales presentations. They must be persuasive, not merely mechanical descriptions of what you can do. You may recall from Chapter 7 that effective persuasive sales messages (1) emphasize benefits for the reader, (2) "toot your horn" by detailing your expertise and accomplishments, and (3) make it easy for the reader to understand and respond.

INFORMAL PROPOSALS

Informal proposals may contain an introduction, background information, the proposal, staffing requirements, a budget, and an authorization request.

Proposals may be informal or formal; they differ primarily in length and format. Informal proposals are often presented in short (two- to four-page) letters. Sometimes called *letter proposals*, they contain six principal parts: introduction, background, proposal, staffing, budget, and authorization request. The informal letter proposal shown in Figure 10.1 illustrates all six parts of a letter proposal. This proposal is addressed to a Honolulu dentist who wants to improve patient satisfaction.

Introduction

Most proposals begin by explaining briefly the reasons for the proposal and by highlighting the writer's qualifications. To make your introduction more persuasive, you need to provide a "hook" to capture the reader's interest. One proposal expert suggests these possibilities:[2]

Effective proposal openers "hook" readers by promising extraordinary results or resources or by identifying key benefits, issues, or outcomes.

- Hint at extraordinary results, with details to be revealed shortly.
- Promise low costs or speedy results.
- Mention a remarkable resource (well-known authority, new computer program, well-trained staff) available exclusively to you.
- Identify a serious problem (worry item) and promise a solution, to be explained later.
- Specify a key issue or benefit that you feel is the heart of the proposal.

For example, in the introduction of the proposal shown in Figure 10.1, Travis Garcia focused on what the customer was looking for. He analyzed the request of the Honolulu dentist, Dr. Arbon, and decided that she was most interested in specific recommendations for improving service to her patients. But Garcia didn't hit on this hook until he had written a first draft and had come back to it later. Indeed, it's often a good idea to put off writing the introduction to a proposal until after you have completed other parts. For longer proposals the introduction also outlines the organization of the material to come.

Although writers may know what goes into the proposal introduction, many face writer's block before they get started. When she worked as a proposals manager at Hewlett-Packard, Mary Piecewicz recognized that writer's block was a big problem for sales representatives on a proposal team. They simply didn't know how to get started. Piecewicz offered the following advice: "To conquer writer's block, begin with a bulleted list of what the customer is looking for. This list is like a road map; it gets you started and keeps you headed in the right direction."[3]

FIGURE 10.1   • **Informal Proposal**

ALA MOANA RESEARCH

Pacific Rim Market Research Consultants

600 Ala Moana Boulevard
Honolulu, HI 96813
(818) 523-8933
www.alamoanaresearch.com

June 2, 200x

Leilani Arbon, D.D.S.
1450 Kapiolani Boulevard
Honolulu, HI 96814

Dear Dr. Arbon:

Helping you improve your practice is of the highest priority to us at Ala • Moana Research. That's why we are pleased to submit the following proposal outlining our plan to help you more effectively meet your patients' needs by analyzing their views about your practice.

Background and Goals

We understand that you have been incorporating a total quality management system in your practice. Although you have every reason to believe your patients are pleased with the service you provide, you would like to give them an opportunity to discuss what they like and possibly don't like about your service. Specifically, your purposes are to survey your patients to (1) • determine the level of their satisfaction with you and your staff, (2) elicit their suggestions for improvement, (3) learn more about how they discovered you, and (4) compare your "preferred" and "standard" patients.

Proposed Plan

On the basis of our experience in conducting many local and national customer satisfaction surveys, Ala Moana Research proposes the following plan:

Survey. We will develop a short but thorough questionnaire probing the data you desire. Although the survey instrument will include both open-ended and closed questions, it will concentrate on the latter. Closed questions enable respondents to answer easily; they also facilitate systematic data analysis. The questionnaire will measure patient reactions to such elements as courtesy, professionalism, accuracy of billing, friendliness, and waiting time. After you approve it, the questionnaire will be sent to a carefully selected sample of 300 patients whom you have separated into groupings of "preferred" and "standard."

Analysis. Data from the survey will be analyzed by demographic segments, such as patient type, age, and gender. Our experienced team of experts, using state-of-the-art computer systems and advanced statistical measures, will study the (1) degree of patient satisfaction, (2) reasons for satisfaction or dissatisfaction, and (3) relationship between the responses of your "preferred" and "standard" patients. Moreover, our team will give you specific suggestions for making patient visits more pleasant.

Report. You will receive a final report with the key findings clearly spelled out, Dr. Arbon. Our expert staff will also draw conclusions based on these findings. The report will include tables summarizing all responses, broken down into groups of "preferred" and "standard" clients.

Marginal annotations (left):
- Uses opening paragraph in place of introduction
- Announces heart of proposal
- Divides total plan into logical segments for easy reading

Marginal annotations (right):
- Grabs attention with "hook" that focuses on key benefit
- Identifies four purposes of survey
- Describes procedure for solving problem or achieving goals

Background, Problem, Purpose

In the background section of a proposal, the writer discusses the problem and goals of the project.

The background section identifies the problem and discusses the goals or purposes of the project. In an unsolicited proposal your goal is to convince the reader that a problem exists. Thus, you must present the problem in detail, discussing such factors as monetary losses, failure to comply with government regulations, and loss of customers. In a solicited proposal your aim is to persuade the reader that you understand the problem completely. Thus, if you are responding to an RFP, this means repeating its language. For example, if the RFP asks for the *design and installation of a wireless communications network*, you would use the same language in explaining the purpose of your proposal. This section might include segments titled *Basic Requirements*, *Most Critical Tasks*, and *Most Important Secondary Problems*.

Proposal, Plan, Schedule

The proposal section must give enough information to secure the contract but not so much detail that the services are not needed.

In the proposal section itself, you should discuss your plan for solving the problem. In some proposals this is tricky because you want to disclose enough of your plan

FIGURE 10.1 _____ | **· Continued** |

Includes ——— second-page heading

Promotes ——— credentials and expertise of key people

Closes by ——— repeating key qualifications and main benefits

Dr. Leilani Arbon   Page 2   June 2, 200x

Schedule. With your approval, the following schedule has been arranged for your patient satisfaction survey:

Questionnaire development and mailing	August 1–6
Deadline for returning questionnaire	August 24
Data tabulation and processing	August 24–26
Completion of final report	September 1

Staffing

Ala Moana Research is a nationally recognized, experienced research consulting firm specializing in survey investigation. I have assigned your customer satisfaction survey to Dr. Kenneth Tong, our director of research. Dr. Tong was trained at Brigham Young University Hawaii and has successfully supervised our research program for the past nine years. Before joining Ala Moana Research, he was a marketing analyst with Johnson & Johnson.

Assisting Dr. Tong will be a team headed by Nancy Baughman, our vice president for operations. Ms. Baughman earned a bachelor's degree in computer science and a master's degree in marketing from the University of Hawaii, where she was elected to Mu Kappa Tau, a national marketing honor society. Within our organization she supervises our computer-aided telephone interviewing (CAT) system and manages our 30-person professional interviewing staff.

Budget

	Estimated Hours	Rate	Total
Professional and administrative time			
Questionnaire development	3	$150/hr.	$ 450
Questionnaire mailing	4	40/hr.	160
Data processing and tabulation	12	40/hr.	480
Analysis of findings	15	150/hr.	2,250
Preparation of final report	5	150/hr.	750
Mailing costs			
300 copies of questionnaire			120
Postage and envelopes			270
Total costs			$4,480

Authorization

We are convinced, Dr. Arbon, that our professionally designed and administered patient satisfaction survey will enhance your practice. Ala Moana Research can have specific results for you by September 1 if you sign the enclosed duplicate copy of this letter and return it to us with a retainer of $2,300 so that we may begin developing your survey immediately. The rates in this offer are in effect only until October 1.

Sincerely,

Travis Garcia

Travis Garcia, President

TEG:mem
Enclosure

Uses past-tense verbs to show that work has already started on the project

Builds credibility by describing outstanding staff and facilities

Itemizes costs carefully because a proposal is a contract offer

Makes response easy

Provides deadline

to secure the contract without giving away so much information that your services aren't needed. Without specifics, though, your proposal has little chance, so you must decide how much to reveal. Tell what you propose to do and how it will benefit the reader. Remember, too, that a proposal is a sales presentation. Sell your methods, product, and "deliverables"—items that will be left with the client. In this section some writers specify how the project will be managed and how its progress will be audited. Most writers also include a schedule of activities or timetable showing when events will take place.

Staffing

The staffing section promotes the credentials and expertise of the project leaders and support staff.

The staffing section of a proposal describes the credentials and expertise of the project leaders. It may also identify the size and qualifications of the support staff, along with other resources such as computer facilities and special programs for analyzing

© BEN MARGOT/STAFF/AP WIDE WORLD PHOTO

Trade show business consumes more than $1.5 billion today. Every day hundreds of shows go on in every major city around the globe. One of the world's largest shows is the annual Macworld Conference and Expo, where companies can sell, market, or promote products, services, peripherals, or solutions for the Mac OS platform. Designing exhibit booths for events such as Macworld has become a huge business. To compete for business, companies that design and sell trade booths submit proposals that describe the problem (how to attract visitors to their booth), plan (strategy for designing and constructing the exhibit booth), staffing, and budget.

statistics. The staffing section is a good place to endorse and promote your staff. In longer proposals some firms follow industry standards and include staff qualifications and generic résumés of key people in an appendix. Using generic rather than actual résumés ensures privacy for individuals and also protects the company in case the staff changes after a proposal has been submitted to a client.

Budget

> Because a proposal is a legal contract, the budget must be carefully researched.

A central item in most proposals is the budget, a list of project costs. You need to prepare this section carefully because it represents a contract; you can't raise the price later—even if your costs increase. You can—and should—protect yourself with a deadline for acceptance. In the budget section some writers itemize hours and costs; others present a total sum only. A proposal to install a complex wireless network might, for example, contain a detailed line-by-line budget. In the proposal shown in Figure 10.1, Travis Garcia felt that he needed to justify the budget for his firm's patient satisfaction survey, so he itemized the costs. But the budget included for a proposal to conduct a one-day diversity awareness seminar for employees might be presented as a lump sum only. Your analysis of the project will help you decide what kind of budget to prepare.

© Randy Glasbergen.
www.glasbergen.com

"I haven't read your proposal yet, Bob, but I already have some great ideas on how to improve it."

Authorization Request

Informal proposals often close with a request for approval or authorization. In addition, the closing should remind the reader of key benefits and motivate action. It might also include a deadline date beyond which the offer is invalid. At some companies, such as Hewlett-Packard, authorization to proceed is not part of the proposal. Instead, it is usually discussed after the customer has received the proposal. In this way the customer and the sales account manager are able to negotiate terms before a formal agreement is drawn.

FORMAL PROPOSALS

Formal proposals respond to big projects and may contain 200 or more pages.

Formal proposals differ from informal proposals not in style but in tone, structure, format, and length. Formal proposals respond to big projects and may range from 5 to 200 or more pages. To facilitate comprehension and reference, they are organized into many parts. In addition to the six basic parts just described, formal proposals contain some or all of the following additional parts: copy of the RFP, letter or memo of transmittal, abstract and/or executive summary, title page, table of contents, list of figures, and appendix. In addition, the tone used in formal proposals is often more formal than the tone used in informal proposals.

The primary differences between formal and informal proposals are tone, structure, format, and length.

Well-written proposals win contracts and business for companies and individuals. In fact, many companies depend entirely on proposals to generate their income. Companies such as Microsoft, Hewlett-Packard, and IBM employ staffs of people who do nothing but prepare proposals to compete for new business. For more information about industry standards and resources, visit the Web site of the Association of Proposal Management Professionals at *http://www.apmp.org*.

PREPARING TO WRITE FORMAL REPORTS

Formal reports discuss the results of a process of thorough investigation and analysis.

Formal reports are similar to formal proposals in length, organization, and serious tone. Instead of making an offer, however, formal reports represent the end product of thorough investigation and analysis. They present organized information to decision makers in business, industry, government, and education. Although formal reports in business are seen infrequently, they serve an important function. They provide management with vital data for decision making. In this section we will consider the entire process of writing a formal report: preparing to write, researching secondary data, generating primary data, documenting data, organizing and outlining data, illustrating data, and presenting the final report.

Like proposals and informal reports, formal reports begin with a definition of the project. Probably the most difficult part of this definition is limiting the scope of the report. Every project has limitations. If you are writing a formal report, decide at the outset what constraints influence the range of your project and how you will achieve your purpose. How much time do you have for completing your report? How accessible are the data you need? How thorough should your research be?

If you are writing about low morale among swing-shift employees, for example, how many of your 475 employees should you interview? Should you limit your research to company-related morale factors, or should you consider external factors over which the company has no control? In investigating adjustable-rate mortgages, should you focus on a particular group, such as first-time homeowners in a specific area, or should you consider all mortgage holders? The first step in writing a report, then, is determining the precise boundaries of the topic.

The planning of every report begins with a statement of purpose explaining the goal, significance, and limitations of the report.

Once you have defined the project and limited its scope, write a statement of purpose. Preparing a written statement of purpose is a good idea because it defines the focus of the report and provides a standard that keeps the project on target. The statement of purpose should describe the goal, significance, and limitations of the report. In writing useful statements of purpose, choose action verbs telling what you intend to do: *analyze, choose, investigate, compare, justify, evaluate, explain, establish, determine*, and so on. Notice how the following statement pinpoints the research and report and uses action verbs:

> The purpose of this report is to explore employment possibilities for entry-level paralegal workers in the city of Phoenix. It will consider typical salaries, skills required, opportunities, and working conditions. This research is significant because of the increasing number of job openings in the paralegal field. This report will not consider legal secretarial employment, which represents a different employment focus.

RESEARCHING SECONDARY DATA

One of the most important steps in the process of writing a report is that of gathering information (research). Because a report is only as good as its data, you'll want to spend considerable time collecting data before you begin writing.

Primary data come from firsthand experience and observation; secondary data, from reading.

Data fall into two broad categories, primary and secondary. Primary data result from firsthand experience and observation. Secondary data come from reading what others have experienced and observed. Coca-Cola and Pepsi-Cola, for example, produce primary data when they stage taste tests and record the reactions of consumers. These same sets of data become secondary after they have been published and, let's say, a newspaper reporter uses them in an article about soft drinks. Secondary data are easier and cheaper to develop than primary data, which might involve interviewing large groups or sending out questionnaires.

You're going to learn first about secondary data because that's where nearly every research project should begin. Often, something has already been written about your topic. Reviewing secondary sources can save time and effort and prevent you from "reinventing the wheel." Most secondary material is available either as print resources or electronically in databases and on the Web.

Print Resources

Although researchers are increasingly turning to electronic data, some data are available only in print.

Although we're seeing a steady movement away from print to electronic data, print sources are still the most visible parts of most libraries. Because some information is available only in print, you may want to use some of the following print resources.

If you are an infrequent library user, begin your research by talking with a reference librarian about your project. These librarians won't do your research for you, but they will steer you in the right direction. And they are very accommodating. Several years ago a *Wall Street Journal* poll revealed that librarians are thought to be among the friendliest, most approachable people in the working world. Many libraries help you understand their computer, cataloging, and retrieval systems by providing brochures, handouts, and workshops.

BOOKS

Books provide historical, in-depth data; periodicals provide limited but current coverage.

Although quickly outdated, books provide excellent historical, in-depth data on a large variety of subjects. Books can be located through print catalogs or online catalogs. Most automated systems today enable you to learn not only whether a book is in the library but also whether it is currently available.

PERIODICALS

Magazines, pamphlets, and journals are called *periodicals* because of their recurrent or periodic publication. Journals are compilations of scholarly articles. Articles in journals and other periodicals will be extremely useful to you because they are concise, limited in scope, current, and can supplement information in books.

PRINT, CD-ROM, AND WEB-BASED BIBLIOGRAPHIC INDEXES

The Readers' Guide to Periodical Literature is a valuable index of general-interest magazine article titles. It includes such magazines as *Time, Newsweek, The New Yorker*, and *U.S. News & World Report*. More useful to business writers, though, will be the titles of articles appearing in business and industrial magazines and newspapers (such as *Forbes, Fortune, The Economist, BusinessWeek, Barron's*, and *The Wall Street Journal*). For an index of these publications, consult the *Business Periodicals Index*. Most indexes today are available in print, CD-ROM, and Web versions for easy searching.

Electronic Databases

Most researchers today begin by looking in electronic databases.

As a writer of business reports today, you will probably begin your secondary research with electronic resources. Although some databases are still presented on CD-ROM, information is increasingly available in online databases. These online databases have become a staple of secondary research. Most writers turn to them first because they are fast, cheap, and easy to use. This means that you can conduct detailed searches without ever leaving your office, home, or dorm room.

Commercial databases offer articles, reports, and other information online.

A database is a collection of information stored electronically so that it is accessible by computer and digitally searchable. Databases provide both bibliographic (titles of documents and brief abstracts) and full-text documents. Most researchers prefer full-text documents. Various databases contain a rich array of magazine, newspaper, and journal articles, as well as newsletters, business reports, company profiles, government data, reviews, and directories. Provided with this textbook is access to Infotrac, a Web-centered database that is growing rapidly. At this writing, it offers nearly 18 million magazine and journal articles from such publications as *Time, The New York Times*, and *The Wall Street Journal*. Web-based documents are enriched with charts, graphs, bold and italic fonts, color, and pictures. Other well-known databases are EBSCO Business Source Premier, ABI/Inform, and LexisNexis.

The World Wide Web

The World Wide Web is a collection of hypertext pages that offer information and links on trillions of pages.

The best-known area of the Internet is the World Wide Web. Growing at a dizzying pace, the Web includes an enormous collection of specially formatted documents called *Web pages* located at Web sites around the world. With trillions of pages of information available on the Web, chances are that if you have a question, an answer exists online. Web offerings include online databases, magazines, newspapers, library resources, sound and video files, and many other information resources. You can expect to find such items as product and service facts, public relations material, mission statements, staff directories, press releases, current company news, government information, selected article reprints, collaborative scientific project reports, stock research, financial information, and employment information. Creators of Web pages use a special system of codes (HTML, i.e., Hypertext Markup Language) to format their offerings. The crucial feature of these hypertext pages is their use of links to other Web pages. These hyperlinks (or links) are identified by underlined words and phrases or, occasionally, images. When clicked, the links open up related Web pages. These pages immediately download to your computer screen, thus creating a vast web of resources at your fingertips.

© FLYING COLOURS LTD./DIGITAL VISION/GETTY IMAGES

Financial analysts, stock investors, and other business researchers require a steady stream of information, much of which is available online. For example, Bloomberg.com offers real-time financial and market data, information about interest rates and currency rates, relevant news stories, stock charts and analyses, and other information to corporations, individuals, news organizations, and financial and legal professionals around the world. Because this information is on the Web, it can be accessed 24 hours a day, seven days a week.

The Web is unquestionably one of the greatest sources of information now available to anyone needing facts quickly and inexpensively. But finding that information can be frustrating and time-consuming. The constantly changing contents of the Web and its lack of organization frustrate researchers. Moreover, content is not always reliable. Check out the Communication Workshop at the end of this chapter to learn more about what questions to ask in assessing the quality of a Web document. The problem of gathering information is complicated by the fact that the total amount of information on the Web grows daily at the rate of over 7 million pages.[4] Thus, to succeed in your search for information and answers, you need to understand how to browse the Web and use search tools. You also need to understand how to evaluate the information you find.

WEB BROWSERS AND URLS

Web browsers are software programs that access Web pages and their links.

Searching the Web requires a Web browser, such as Microsoft Internet Explorer, Netscape, or Firefox. Browsers are software programs that enable you to view the graphics and text of, as well as access links to, Web pages. To locate the Web page of a specific organization, you need its Web site address or URL (Uniform Resource Locator). URLs are case and space sensitive, so be sure to type the address exactly as it is printed. For most companies, the URL is *http://www.xyzcompany.com*. Your goal is to locate the top-level Web page of an organization's site. On this page you'll generally find an overview of the site contents or a link to a site map. If you can't guess a company's URL, you can usually find it quickly using Google (*www.google.com*).

SEARCH TOOLS

A search tool is a service that indexes, organizes, and often rates and reviews Web pages.

The Web is packed with amazing information. Instead of visiting libraries or searching reference books when you need to find something, you can now turn to the Web for all kinds of facts. However, you'll need a good search tool, such as Google, Yahoo!, or AskJeeves. A search tool is a service that indexes, organizes, and often rates and reviews Web pages. Some search tools rely on people to maintain a catalog of Web sites or pages. Others use software to identify key information. They all begin a search based on the keywords that you enter. The most-used search tool at this writing is Google. It has developed a cult-like following with its "uncanny ability to sort through millions of Web pages and put the sites you really want at the top of its results pages."[5]

WEB SEARCH TIPS AND TECHNIQUES

You must know how to use search tools to make them most effective.

To conduct a thorough Web search for the information you need, use these tips and techniques:

- **Use two or three search tools.** Different Internet search engines turn up different results. However, at this writing, Google consistently turns up more reliable "hits" than other search tools.
- **Know your search tool.** When connecting to a search service for the first time, always read the description of its service, including its FAQs (Frequently Asked Questions), Help, and How to Search sections.
- **Understand case sensitivity.** Generally use lowercase for your searches, unless you are searching for a term that is typically written in upper- and lowercase, such as a person's name.
- **Use nouns as search words and as many as eight words in a query.** The right keywords—and more of them—can narrow your search considerable.
- **Use quotation marks.** When searching for a phrase, such as *cost benefit analysis*, most search tools will retrieve documents having all or some of the terms. This AND/OR strategy is the default of most search tools. To locate occurrences of a specific phrase, enclose it in quotation marks.
- **Omit articles and prepositions.** Known as "stop words," articles and prepositions do not add value to a search. Instead of *request for proposal*, use *proposal request*.

- **Proofread your search words.** Make sure you're searching for the right thing by proofreading your search words carefully. For example, searching for *sock market* will come up with substantially different results than searching for *stock market*.
- **Save the best.** To keep better track of your favorite Web sites, save them as bookmarks or favorites.
- **Keep trying.** If a search produces no results, check your spelling. Try synonyms and variations on words. Try to be less specific in your search term. If your search produces too many hits, try to be more specific. Think of words that uniquely identify what you're looking for, and use as many relevant keywords as possible. Use a variety of search tools, and repeat your search a few days later.

Weblogs (Blogs)

Weblogs, or "blogs," can be used to generate primary or secondary data.

One of the newest ways to locate secondary information on the Web is through the use of weblogs, which are more commonly referred to a "blogs." According to Wikipedia, a blog is a "web-based publication consisting primarily of periodic articles (normally in reverse chronological order)."[6] Blogs are used by business researchers, students, politicians, the media, and many others to share and gather information. Marketing firms and their clients are looking closely at blogs because blogs can produce unbiased consumer feedback faster and more cheaply than such staples of consumer research as focus groups and surveys.[7] Employees and executives at companies such as Google, Sun Microsystems, IBM, and Hewlett-Packard maintain blogs. They use blogs to communicate internally with employees and externally with clients.[8]

A blog is basically an online diary or journal that allows visitors to leave public comments. In April 2005 writers had posted 8.7 million blogs, up from 2 million at the same time in 2004,[9] and 40,000 new blogs appear every day.[10] With so many people using blogs, these online journals allow you to get up-to-the-minute information straight from the source, whether it's market data, financial information, product analysis, employment information, or technology trends. According to Jeff Weiner, Yahoo senior vice president, "Never in the history of market research has there been a tool like this."[11] Although blogs represent an amazing new information stream, be sure to evaluate all blog content using the checklist provided in the Communication Workshop at the end of this chapter.

GENERATING PRIMARY DATA

Business reports often rely on primary data from firsthand experience.

Although you'll begin a business report by probing for secondary data, you'll probably need primary data to give a complete picture. Business reports that solve specific current problems typically rely on primary, firsthand data. If, for example, management wants to discover the cause of increased employee turnover in its Las Vegas office, it must investigate conditions in Las Vegas by collecting recent information. Providing answers to business problems often means generating primary data through surveys, interviews, observation, or experimentation. In addition to generating secondary data, blogs can also be used to generate primary data.

Surveys

Surveys yield efficient and economical primary data for reports.

Surveys collect data from groups of people. When companies develop new products, for example, they often survey consumers to learn their needs. The advantages of surveys are that they gather data economically and efficiently. Surveys can be mailed to participants, or they can be administered online. Both mailed and online surveys reach big groups nearby or at great distances. Moreover, people responding to mailed and online surveys have time to consider their answers, thus improving the accuracy of the data.

Mailed surveys, of course, have disadvantages. Most of us rank them with junk mail, so response rates may be no higher than 2 percent. Online surveys also have disadvantages, although response rates tend to be higher. Furthermore, those who do respond to either mailed or online surveys may not represent an accurate sample of the overall population, thus invalidating generalizations from the group. Let's say, for example, that an insurance company sends out a survey questionnaire asking about provisions in a new policy. If only older people respond, the survey data cannot be used to generalize what people in other age groups might think. A final problem with surveys has to do with truthfulness. Some respondents exaggerate their incomes or distort other facts, thus causing the results to be unreliable. Nevertheless, surveys may be the best way to generate data for business and student reports.

Interviews

Interviews with experts produce useful report data, especially when little has been written about a topic.

Some of the best report information, particularly on topics about which little has been written, comes from individuals. These individuals are usually experts or veterans in their fields. Consider both in-house and outside experts for business reports. Tapping these sources will call for in-person, telephone, or online interviews. To elicit the most useful data, try these techniques:

- **Locate an expert.** Ask managers and individuals working in an area whom they consider to be most knowledgeable. Check membership lists of professional organizations, and consult articles about the topic or related topics. Search business-related blogs to find out who the experts are in your area of interest. You could also post an inquiry to an Internet *newsgroup*. An easy way to search newsgroups in a topic area is through the browse groups now indexed by the popular search tool Google (*http://groups.google.com*). Most people enjoy being experts or at least recommending them.

- **Prepare for the interview.** Learn about the individual you're interviewing, and make sure you can pronounce the interviewee's name correctly. Research the background and terminology of the topic. Let's say you're interviewing a corporate communication expert about producing an in-house newsletter. You ought to be familiar with terms such as *font* and software such as QuarkXpress and Adobe InDesign. In addition, be prepared by making a list of questions that pinpoint your focus on the topic. Ask the interviewee if you may record the talk.

- **Maintain a professional attitude.** Call before the interview to confirm the arrangements, and then arrive on time. Bring what you need to take notes, and dress professionally. Use your body language to convey respect.

- **Make your questions objective and friendly.** Adopt a courteous and respectful attitude. Don't get into a debating match with the interviewee. Remember that you're there to listen, not to talk! Use open-ended questions (*What are your predictions for the future of the telecommunications industry?*), rather than yes-or-no questions (*Do you think we'll see more video e-mail in the future?*) to draw experts out.

- **Watch the time.** Tell interviewees in advance how much time you expect to need for the interview. Don't overstay your appointment.

- **End graciously.** Conclude the interview with a general question, such as *Is there anything you'd like to add?* Express your appreciation, and ask permission to telephone later if you need to verify points. Send a thank-you note within a day or two after the interview.

Observation and Experimentation

Some of the best report data come from firsthand observation and experimentation.

Some kinds of primary data can be obtained only through firsthand observation and experimentation. If you determine that the questions you have require observational data, then you need to plan the observations carefully. One of the most important questions to ask is what or whom you're observing and how often those observations are necessary to provide reliable data. For example, if you want to learn more about

Experimentation inspired today's innovative running shoe, Nike Free. Researchers at Nike started with the observation that many top athletes train barefoot to increase performance. The research team then spent years experimenting in the Nike Sports Research lab and discovered that a bare foot lands more evenly, resulting in less stress and better alignment. The information the researchers collected, considered primary data, led to the development of the highly successful Nike Free athletic shoe.[12]

© PRNewsFOTO/NIKE, INC.

an organization's customer service phone service, you probably need to use observation techniques, along with interviews and perhaps even surveys. You'll want to answer questions such as, *How long does a typical caller wait before a customer service rep answers the call?* and *Is the service consistent?*

Observation produces rich data, but that information is especially prone to charges of subjectivity. One can interpret an observation in many ways. Thus, to make observations more objective, try to quantify them. For example, record customer telephone wait-time for 60-minute periods at different times throughout a week. This will give you a better picture than just observing for an hour on a Friday before a holiday.

Experimentation produces data suggesting causes and effects. Informal experimentation might be as simple as a pretest and posttest in a college course. Did students expand their knowledge as a result of the course? More formal experimentation is undertaken by scientists and professional researchers who control variables to test their effects. Assume, for example, that the Hershey Company wants to test the hypothesis (which is a tentative assumption) that chocolate lifts people out of the doldrums. An experiment testing the hypothesis would separate depressed individuals into two groups: those who ate chocolate (the experimental group) and those who did not (the control group). What effect did chocolate have? Such experiments are not done haphazardly, however. Valid experiments require sophisticated research designs and careful attention to matching the experimental and control groups.

DOCUMENTING DATA

Whether you collect data from primary or secondary sources, the data must be documented; that is, you must indicate where the data originated. Using the ideas of someone else without giving credit is called *plagiarism* and is unethical. Even if you *paraphrase* (put the information in your own words), the ideas must be documented. You'll learn more about paraphrasing in this section.

Purposes of Documentation

As a careful writer, you should properly document your data for the following reasons:

- **To strengthen your argument.** Including good data from reputable sources will convince readers of your credibility and the logic of your reasoning.

Report writers document their
sources to strengthen an argument, protect themselves from
charges of plagiarism, and help
readers locate data.

- **To instruct the reader.** Citing references enables readers to pursue a topic further and make use of the information themselves.
- **To protect yourself against charges of plagiarism.** Acknowledging your sources keeps you honest. Plagiarism, which is illegal and unethical, is the act of using others' ideas without proper documentation.

Plagiarism of words or ideas is a serious charge and can lead to loss of a job. Recent stories about the fates of journalists such as Jayson Blair of *The New York Times* illustrate that plagiarism is serious business.[13] You can avoid charges of plagiarism as well as add clarity to your work by knowing what to document and by developing good research habits.

Learning What to Document

Give credit when you use
another's ideas, when you borrow
facts that are not common knowledge, and when you quote or
paraphrase another's words.

When you write business or academic reports, you are continually dealing with other people's ideas. You are expected to conduct research, synthesize ideas, and build on the work of others. But you are also expected to give proper credit for borrowed material. To avoid plagiarism, you must give credit whenever you use the following:[14]

- Another person's ideas, opinions, examples, or theory
- Any facts, statistics, graphs, and drawings that are not common knowledge
- Quotations of another person's actual spoken or written words
- Paraphrases of another person's spoken or written words

Information that is common knowledge requires no documentation. For example, the following statement requires no documentation. *The Wall Street Journal is a popular business newspaper.* Statements that are not common knowledge, however, must be documented. For example, *Eight of the nation's top ten fastest-growing large cities (100,000 or more population) since Census 2000 lie in the Western states of Arizona, Nevada, and California* would require a citation because most people do not know this fact. Cite sources for proprietary information such as statistics organized and reported by a newspaper or magazine. Also use citations to document direct quotations and ideas that you summarize in your own words.

Developing Good Research Habits

Report writers who are gathering information should record documentation data immediately after locating the information. This information can then be used in footnotes, endnotes, or in-text citations; and it can be listed in a bibliography or works-cited list at the end of the report. Here are some tips for gathering the documentation data you need from some of the most popular types of resources:

- For a book, record the title, author(s), publisher, place of publication, year of publication, and pages cited.
- For newspaper, magazine, and journal articles, record the publication title, article title, author(s), issue/volume number, date, and pages cited.
- For online newspaper and magazine articles, record the author(s), article title, publication title, date the article was written, the exact URL, and the date you retrieved the article.
- For an entire Web site, record the name of the company or organization sponsoring the site, the URL, and the date you retrieved the page.

You can learn more about what types of documentation information to record during your research by studying the formal report in Figure 10.17 and by consulting Appendix C.

Developing the Fine Art of Paraphrasing

Paraphrasing involves putting an
original passage into your own
words.

In writing business or academic reports and using the ideas of others, you will probably rely heavily on paraphrasing, which means restating an original passage in your own words and in your own style. To do a good job of paraphrasing, follow these steps:

- Read the original material carefully to comprehend its full meaning.
- Write your own version without looking at the original.
- Do not repeat the grammatical structure of the original, and do not merely replace words with synonyms.
- Reread the original to be sure you covered the main points but did not borrow specific language.

Knowing When and How to Quote

On occasion you will want to use the exact words of a source. Anytime you use the exact words from a source, you must enclose the words in quotation marks. Be careful when doing this that you don't change the wording of the quoted material in any way.

Also beware of overusing quotations. Documents that contain pages of spliced-together quotations suggest that writers have few ideas of their own. Wise writers and speakers use direct quotations for three purposes only:

- To provide objective background data and establish the severity of a problem as seen by experts
- To repeat identical phrasing because of its precision, clarity, or aptness
- To duplicate exact wording before criticizing

Use quotations only to provide background data, to cite experts, to repeat precise phrasing, or to duplicate exact wording before criticizing.

When you must use an exact quotation, try to summarize and introduce it in your own words. Readers want to know the gist of a quotation before they tackle it. For example, to introduce a quotation discussing the shrinking staffs of large companies, you could precede it with your words: *In predicting employment trends, Charles Waller believes the corporation of the future will depend on a small core of full-time employees.* To introduce quotations or paraphrases, use wording such as the following:

> According to Waller, ...
> Waller argues that . . . .
> In his recent study, Waller reported . . . .

Use quotation marks to enclose exact quotations, as shown in the following: "The current image," says Charles Waller, "of a big glass-and-steel corporate headquarters on landscaped grounds directing a worldwide army of tens of thousands of employees may soon be a thing of the past."

Using Citation Formats

Guidelines for MLA and APA citation formats may be found in Appendix C; guidelines for electronic citations are at the Guffey student Web site.

You can direct readers to your sources with parenthetical notes inserted into the text and with bibliographies or works-cited lists. The most common citation formats are those presented by the Modern Language Association (MLA) and the American Psychological Association (APA). Learn more about how to use these formats in Appendix C. For the most up-do-date citation formats for electronic references, check the Guffey student Web site. You will find model citation formats for online magazine, newspaper, and journal articles, as well as for Web references.

ORGANIZING AND OUTLINING DATA

Once you've collected the data for a report and recorded that information on notes or printouts, you're ready to organize it into a coherent plan of presentation. First, you should decide on an organizational strategy, and then, following your plan, you'll want to outline the report. Poorly organized reports lead to frustration; therefore, it's important to organize your report carefully so that readers will understand, remember, or be persuaded.

Organizational Strategies

The readability and effectiveness of a report are greatly enhanced by skillful organization of the information presented. As you begin the process of organization, ask yourself two important questions: (1) Where should I place the conclusions/recommendations? and (2) How should I organize the findings?

WHERE TO PLACE THE CONCLUSIONS AND RECOMMENDATIONS

In the direct strategy, conclusions and recommendations come first; in the indirect strategy, they are last.

As you recall from earlier instruction, the direct strategy presents main ideas first. In formal reports that would mean beginning with your conclusions and recommendations. For example, if you were studying five possible locations for a proposed shopping center, you would begin with the recommendation of the best site. Use this strategy when the reader is supportive and knowledgeable. However, if the reader is not supportive or needs to be informed, the indirect strategy may be better. This strategy involves presenting facts and discussion first, followed by conclusions and recommendations. Since formal reports often seek to educate the reader, this order of presentation is often most effective. Following this sequence, a study of possible locations for a shopping center would begin with data regarding all proposed sites followed by analysis of the information and conclusions drawn from that analysis.

HOW TO ORGANIZE THE FINDINGS

After collecting your facts, you need a coherent plan for presenting them. We describe here three principal organizational patterns: chronological, geographical, and topical. You will find these and other patterns summarized in Figure 10.2. The pattern you choose depends on the material collected and the purpose of your report.

Organize report findings chronologically, geographically, topically, or by one of the methods shown in Figure 10.2.

- **Chronological sequence.** Information sequenced along a time frame is arranged chronologically. This plan is effective for presenting historical data or for describing a procedure. Agendas, minutes of meetings, progress reports, and procedures are usually organized by time. A description of the development of a multinational company, for example, would be chronological. A report explaining how to obtain federal funding for a project might be organized chronologically. Often topics are arranged in a past-to-present or present-to-past sequence.
- **Geographical or spatial arrangement.** Information arranged geographically or spatially is organized by physical location. For instance, a report analyzing a company's national sales might be divided into sections representing different geographical areas such as the East, South, Midwest, West, and Northwest.
- **Topical or functional arrangement.** Some subjects lend themselves to arrangement by topic or function. A report analyzing changes in the management hierarchy of an organization might be arranged in this manner. First, the report would consider the duties of the CEO followed by the functions of the general manager, business manager, marketing manager, and so forth.

Outlines and Headings

Most writers agree that the clearest way to show the organization of a report topic is by recording its divisions in an outline. Although the outline is not part of the final report, it is a valuable tool of the writer. It reveals at a glance the overall organization of the report. As you learned in Chapter 3, outlining involves dividing a topic into major sections and supporting those with details. Figure 10.3 shows an abbreviated outline of a report about forms of business ownership. Rarely is a real outline so perfectly balanced; some sections are usually longer than others. Remember, though, not to put a single topic under a major component. If you have only one subpoint, integrate it with the main item above it or reorganize. Use details, illustrations, and evidence to support subpoints.

FIGURE 10.2   **Organizational Patterns for Report Findings**

Pattern	Development	Use
Chronology	Arrange information in a time sequence to show history or development of topic.	Useful in showing time relationships, such as 5-year profit figures or a series or events leading to a problem
Geography/ Space	Organize information by regions or areas.	Appropriate for topics that are easily divided into locations, such as East Coast, West Coast, etc.
Topic/ Function	Arrange by topics or functions.	Works well for topics with established categories, such as a report about categories of company expenses
Compare/ Contrast	Present problem and show alternative solutions. Use consistent criteria. Show how the solutions are similar and different.	Best used for "before and after" scenarios or for problems with clear alternatives
Journalism Pattern	Arrange information in paragraphs devoted to *who, what, when, where, why*, and *how*. May conclude with recommendations.	Useful with audiences that need to be educated or persuaded
Value/Size	Start with the most valuable, biggest, or most important item. Discuss other items in descending order.	Useful for classifying information in, for example, a realtor's report on home values
Importance	Arrange from most important to least importance or build from least to most important.	Appropriate when persuading the audience to take a specific action or change a belief
Simple/ Complex	Begin with simple concept; proceed to more complex idea.	Useful for technical or abstract topics
Best Case/ Worst Case	Describe the best and possibly the worst possible outcomes.	Useful when dramatic effect is needed to achieve results; helpful when audience is uninterested or uninformed
Convention	Organize the report using a prescribed plan that all readers understand.	Useful for many operational and recurring reports such as weekly sales reports

FIGURE 10.3   **Outline Format**

Forms of Business Ownership

I. Sole proprietorship (*first main topic*)
   A. Advantages of sole proprietorship (*first subdivision of Topic I*)
      1. Minimal capital requirements (*first subdivision of Topic A*)
      2. Control by owner (*second subdivision of Topic A*)
   B. Disadvantages of sole proprietorship (*second subdivision of Topic I*)
      1. Unlimited liability (*first subdivision of Topic B*)
      2. Limited management talent (*second subdivision of Topic B*)

II. Partnership (*second main topic*)
   A. Advantages of partnership (*first subdivision of Topic II*)
      1. Access to capital (*first subdivision of Topic A*)
      2. Management talent (*second subdivision of Topic A*)
      3. Ease of formation (*third subdivision of Topic A*)
   B. Disadvantages of partnership (*second subdivision of Topic II*)
      1. Unlimited liability (*first subdivision of Topic B*)
      2. Personality conflicts (*second subdivision of Topic B*)

The main points used to outline a report often become the main headings of the written report. In Chapter 9 you studied tips for writing talking and functional headings. Formatting those headings depends on what level they represent. Major headings, as you can see in Figure 10.4, are centered and typed in bold font. Second-level headings start at the left margin, and third-level headings are indented and become part of a paragraph.

ILLUSTRATING DATA

After collecting information and interpreting it, you need to consider how best to present it to your audience. If your report contains complex data and numbers, you may want to consider using graphics such as tables and charts. Appropriate graphics clarify data, create visual interest, and make numerical data meaningful. By simplifying complex ideas and emphasizing key data, well-constructed graphics make key information more understandable and easier to remember. In contrast, readers tend to be bored and confused by text paragraphs packed with complex data and numbers. The same information summarized in a table or chart becomes clear.

Effective graphics clarify numerical data and simplify complex ideas.

FIGURE 10.4

Levels of Headings in Reports

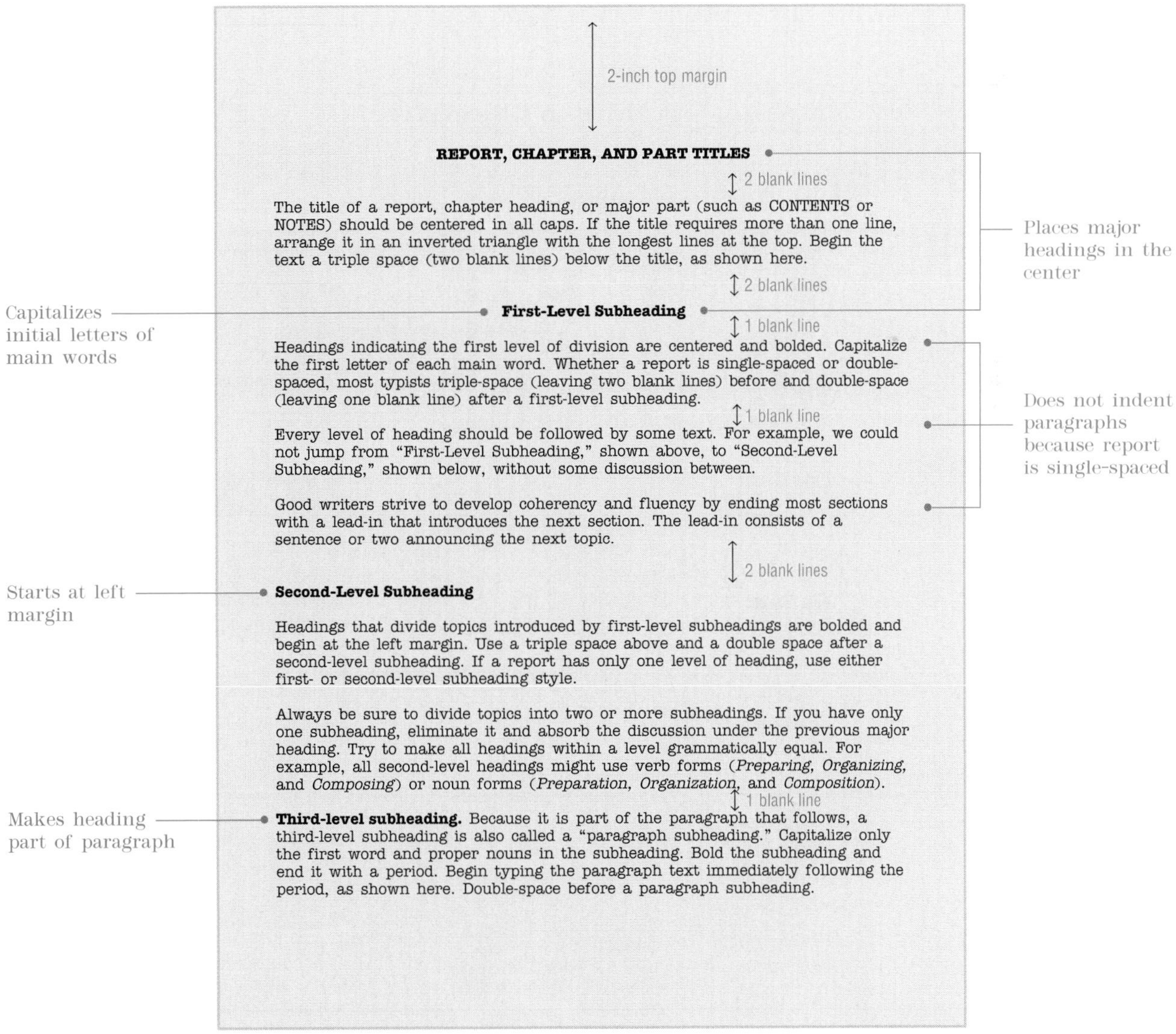

2-inch top margin

REPORT, CHAPTER, AND PART TITLES

↕ 2 blank lines

The title of a report, chapter heading, or major part (such as CONTENTS or NOTES) should be centered in all caps. If the title requires more than one line, arrange it in an inverted triangle with the longest lines at the top. Begin the text a triple space (two blank lines) below the title, as shown here.

Places major headings in the center

↕ 2 blank lines

First-Level Subheading

↕ 1 blank line

Capitalizes initial letters of main words

Headings indicating the first level of division are centered and bolded. Capitalize the first letter of each main word. Whether a report is single-spaced or double-spaced, most typists triple-space (leaving two blank lines) before and double-space (leaving one blank line) after a first-level subheading.

↕ 1 blank line

Every level of heading should be followed by some text. For example, we could not jump from "First-Level Subheading," shown above, to "Second-Level Subheading," shown below, without some discussion between.

Does not indent paragraphs because report is single-spaced

Good writers strive to develop coherency and fluency by ending most sections with a lead-in that introduces the next section. The lead-in consists of a sentence or two announcing the next topic.

↕ 2 blank lines

Second-Level Subheading

Starts at left margin

Headings that divide topics introduced by first-level subheadings are bolded and begin at the left margin. Use a triple space above and a double space after a second-level subheading. If a report has only one level of heading, use either first- or second-level subheading style.

Always be sure to divide topics into two or more subheadings. If you have only one subheading, eliminate it and absorb the discussion under the previous major heading. Try to make all headings within a level grammatically equal. For example, all second-level headings might use verb forms (*Preparing, Organizing,* and *Composing*) or noun forms (*Preparation, Organization,* and *Composition*).

↕ 1 blank line

Makes heading part of paragraph

Third-level subheading. Because it is part of the paragraph that follows, a third-level subheading is also called a "paragraph subheading." Capitalize only the first word and proper nouns in the subheading. Bold the subheading and end it with a period. Begin typing the paragraph text immediately following the period, as shown here. Double-space before a paragraph subheading.

Because data can be shown in many different forms (for example, in a chart, table, or graph), you need to recognize how to match the appropriate graphic with your objective. In addition, you need to know how to incorporate graphics into your reports.

Matching Graphics and Objectives

In developing the best graphics, you should first decide what data you want to highlight. Chances are you will have many points you would like to show in a table or chart. But which graphics are most appropriate to your objectives? Tables? Bar charts? Pie charts? Line charts? Surface charts? Flowcharts? Organization charts? Pictures?

Figure 10.5 summarizes appropriate uses for each type of graphic. Notice that tables are appropriate when you must report exact figures and values. However, if you want to compare one item with others or demonstrate changes in quantitative data over time, bar and line charts are better. To show the parts of a whole and the proportions of all the parts, you might draw a pie chart. If you must show a process such as how a product is made, a flow chart works well. An organization chart defines elements in a hierarchy such as the line of command in business management. Photographs, maps, and illustrations are most useful to create authenticity, to spotlight a location, and to show an item in use.

FIGURE 10.5

Matching Graphics to Objectives

Selecting an appropriate graphic form depends on the purpose that it serves.

Graphic		Objective
Table	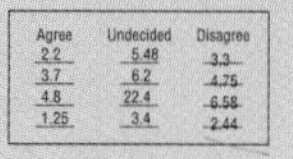	To show exact figures and values
Bar Chart	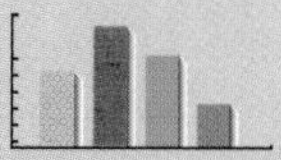	To compare one item with others
Line Chart	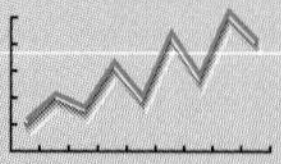	To demonstrate changes in quantitative data over time
Pie Chart		To visualize a whole unit and the proportions of its components
Flowchart	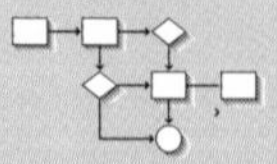	To display a process or procedure
Organization Chart	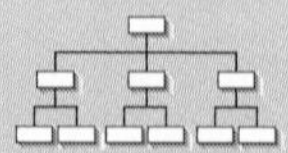	To define a hierarchy of elements
Photograph, Map, Illustration		To create authenticity, to spotlight a location, and to show an item in use

FIGURE 10.6 —————● **Table Summarizing Precise Data**

Figure 1
MPM ENTERTAINMENT COMPANY
Income by Division (in millions of dollars)

	Theme Parks	Motion Pictures	DVDs and Videos	Total
2003	$15.8	$39.3	$11.2	$66.3
2004	18.1	17.5	15.3	50.9
2005	23.8	21.1	22.7	67.6
2006	32.2	22.0	24.3	78.5
2007 (projected)	35.1	21.0	26.1	82.2

Source: *Industry Profiles* (New York: DataPro, 2006), 225.

Tables

Tables permit the systematic presentation of large amounts of data, whereas charts enhance visual comparisons.

Probably the most frequently used visual aid in reports is the table. Because a table presents quantitative or verbal information in systematic columns and rows, it can clarify large quantities of data in small spaces. The disadvantage is that tables do not readily display trends. In making tables, you will be constructing rows and columns. A row is a list of items presented straight across a table. Each row must have a row heading. In Figure 10.6, the row headings are years. Columns are lists of items presented vertically.

Here are specific tips for making good tables:
- Provide a descriptive title at the top of the table.
- Arrange items in a logical order (alphabetical, chronological, geographical, highest to lowest), depending on what you want to emphasize.
- Provide clear headings for the rows and columns.
- Identify the units in which figures are given (percentages, dollars, units per worker hour, and so forth) in the table title, in the column or row head, with the first item in a column, or in a note at the bottom.
- Use *N/A* (not available) for missing data.
- Make long tables easier to read by shading alternate lines or by leaving a blank line after groups of five.
- Place tables as close as possible to the place where they are mentioned in the text.

Bar Charts

Bar charts enable readers to compare related items, see changes over time, and understand how parts relate to a whole.

Although they lack the precision of tables, bar charts enable you to make emphatic visual comparisons by using horizontal or vertical bars of varying lengths. Bar charts can be used to compare related items, illustrate changes in data over time, and show segments as part of a whole. Figures 10.7 through 10.10 show vertical, horizontal, grouped, and segmented bar charts that highlight some of the data shown in the MPM Entertainment Company table (Figure 10.6). Note how the varied bar charts present information in different ways.

Many suggestions for tables also hold true for bar charts. Here are a few additional tips:
- Keep the length and width of each bar and segment proportional.
- Include a total figure in the middle of a bar or at its end if the figure helps the reader and does not clutter the chart.
- Start dollar or percentage amounts at zero.
- Avoid showing too much information, which produces clutter and confusion.
- Place each bar chart as close as possible to the place where it is mentioned in the text.

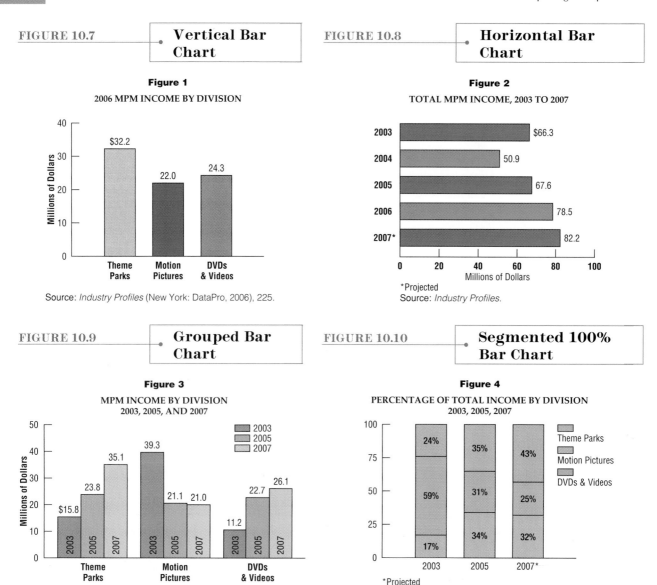

FIGURE 10.7
Vertical Bar Chart

Figure 1
2006 MPM INCOME BY DIVISION

Source: *Industry Profiles* (New York: DataPro, 2006), 225.

Horizontal Bar Chart
FIGURE 10.8

Figure 2
TOTAL MPM INCOME, 2003 TO 2007

*Projected
Source: *Industry Profiles.*

Grouped Bar Chart
FIGURE 10.9

Figure 3
MPM INCOME BY DIVISION
2003, 2005, AND 2007

Source: *Industry Profiles.*

Segmented 100% Bar Chart
FIGURE 10.10

Figure 4
PERCENTAGE OF TOTAL INCOME BY DIVISION
2003, 2005, 2007

*Projected
Source: *Industry Profiles.*

Line Charts

Line charts illustrate trends and changes in data over time.

The major advantage of line charts is that they show changes over time, thus indicating trends. The vertical axis is typically the dependent variable (such as dollars), and the horizontal axis is the independent one (such as years). Figures 10.11 through 10.13 show line charts that reflect income trends for the three divisions of MPM. Notice that line charts do not provide precise data, such as the 2006 MPM DVD and video income. Instead, they give an overview or impression of the data. Experienced report writers use tables to list exact data; they use line charts or bar charts to spotlight important points or trends.

Simple line charts (Figure 10.11) show just one variable. Multiple line charts compare items, such as two or more data sets, using the same variable (Figure 10.12). Segmented line charts (Figure 10.13), also called *surface charts*, illustrate how the components of a whole change over time.

Here are tips for preparing line charts:
- Begin with a grid divided into squares.
- Arrange the time component (usually years) horizontally across the bottom; arrange values for the other variable vertically.
- Draw small dots at the intersections to indicate each value at a given year.
- Connect the dots and add color if desired.

FIGURE 10.11
Simple Line Chart

FIGURE 10.12
Multiple Line Chart

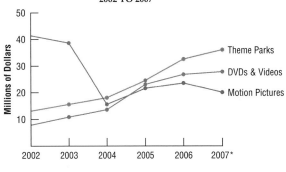

Figure 5
MOTION PICTURE REVENUES
2002 TO 2007

*Projected
Source: *Industry Profiles.*

Figure 6
COMPARISON OF DIVISION REVENUES
2002 TO 2007

*Projected
Source: *Industry Profiles.*

FIGURE 10.13
Segmented Line (Surface) Chart

FIGURE 10.14
Pie Chart

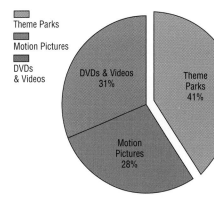

Figure 7
COMPARISION OF DIVISION REVENUES
2002 TO 2007

*Projected
Source: *Industry Profiles.*

Figure 8
2006 MPM INCOME BY DIVISION

Source: *Industry Profiles.*

- To prepare a segmented (surface) chart, plot the first value (say, DVD and video income) across the bottom; add the next item (say, motion picture income) to the first figures for every increment; for the third item (say, theme park income) add its value to the total of the first two items. The top line indicates the total of the three values.
- Place each line chart as close as possible to the place where it is mentioned in the text.

Pie Charts

Pie charts are most useful in showing the proportion of parts to a whole.

Pie, or circle, charts enable readers to see a whole and the proportion of its components, or wedges. Although less flexible than bar or line charts, pie charts are useful in showing percentages, as Figure 10.14 illustrates. Notice that a wedge can be "exploded" or popped out for special emphasis, as seen in Figure 10.14. For the most effective pie charts, follow these suggestions:

- Begin at the 12 o'clock position, drawing the largest wedge first. (Computer software programs don't always observe this advice, but if you're drawing your own charts, you can.)

- Include, if possible, the actual percentage or absolute value for each wedge.
- Use four to eight segments for best results; if necessary, group small portions into one wedge called "Other."
- Distinguish wedges with color, shading, or cross-hatching.
- Keep all labels horizontal.
- Place each pie chart as close as possible to the place where it is mentioned in the text.

Flowcharts

Flowcharts use standard symbols to illustrate a process or procedure.

Procedures are simplified and clarified by diagramming them in a flowchart, as shown in Figure 10.15. Whether you need to describe the procedure for handling a customer's purchase order or outline steps in solving a problem, flowcharts help the reader visualize the process. Traditional flowcharts use the following symbols:

- **Ovals:** to designate the beginning and end of a process
- **Diamonds:** to denote decision points
- **Rectangles:** to represent major activities or steps

Software programs such as SmartDraw!, EasyDraw, and ConceptDraw can be used to create professional-quality flowcharts.

Organization Charts

Many large organizations are so complex that they need charts to show the chain of command, from the boss down to the line managers and employees. Organization charts like the one in Figure 10.16 provide such information as who reports to whom, how many subordinates work for each manager (the span of control), and what channels of official communication exist. These charts may illustrate a company's structure, for example, by function, customer, or product. They may also be organized by the work being performed in each job or by the hierarchy of decision making.

Photographs, Maps, and Illustrations

Some business reports include photographs, maps, illustrations, and other graphics to serve specific purposes. Photos, for example, add authenticity and provide a

FIGURE 10.15   • **Flowchart**

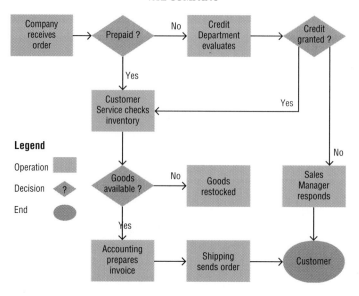

FIGURE 10.16   • **Organization Chart**

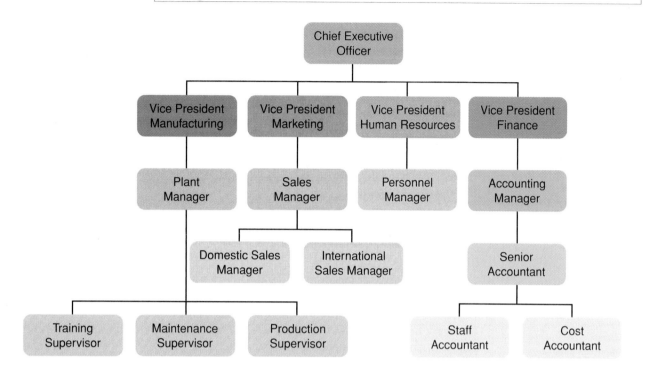

visual record. An environmental engineer may use photos to document hazardous waste sites. Maps enable report writers to depict activities or concentrations geographically, such as dots indicating sales reps in states across the country. Illustrations and diagrams are useful in indicating how an object looks or operates. A drawing showing the parts of a printer with labels describing their functions, for example, is more instructive than a photograph or verbal description. With today's computer technology, photographs, maps, illustrations, and other graphics can be scanned and inserted directly into business reports.

Incorporating Graphics in Reports

Used appropriately, graphics make reports more interesting and easier to understand. In putting graphics into your reports, follow these suggestions for best effects:

* **Evaluate the audience.** Consider the reader, the content, your schedule, and your budget.
* **Use restraint.** Don't overuse color or decorations. Too much color can be distracting and confusing.
* **Be accurate and ethical.** Double-check all graphics for accuracy of figures and calculations. Be certain that your visuals aren't misleading—either accidentally or intentionally. Also be sure to cite sources when you use someone else's facts.
* **Introduce a graph meaningfully.** Refer to every graphic in the text, and place the graphic close to the point where it is mentioned. Most important, though, help the reader understand the significance of the graphic.
* **Choose an appropriate caption or heading style.** Like reports, graphics may use functional or talking heads. These were discussed in Chapter 9.

Using Your Computer to Produce Charts

Computer software programs enable you to produce top-quality graphics quickly and cheaply.

Designing effective, accurate bar charts, pie charts, figures, and other graphics is easy with today's software. Spreadsheet programs such as Excel, as well as presentation graphics programs such as PowerPoint, allow even nontechnical people to design high-quality graphics. These graphics can be printed directly on paper for written reports or used for transparency masters and slides for oral presentations. The benefits of preparing visual aids on a computer are near-professional quality, shorter preparation time, and substantial cost savings.

PRESENTING THE FINAL REPORT

Long reports are generally organized into three major divisions: (1) prefatory parts, (2) body, and (3) supplementary parts. Following is a description of the order and content of each part. Refer to the model formal report in Figure 10.17 for illustrations of most of these parts.

Prefatory Parts (Preceding the Body of Report)

TITLE PAGE

A report title page, as illustrated in Figure 10.17, begins with the name of the report typed in uppercase letters (no underscore and no quotation marks). Next comes *Prepared for* (or *Submitted to*) and the name, title, and organization of the individual receiving the report. Lower on the page is *Prepared by* (or *Submitted by*) and the author's name plus any necessary identification. The last item on the title page is the date of submission. All items after the title appear in a combination of upper- and lowercase letters. The information on the title page should be evenly spaced and balanced on the page for a professional look.

LETTER OR MEMO OF TRANSMITTAL

> A letter or memo of transmittal presents an overview of the report, suggests how to read it, describes limitations, acknowledges assistance, and expresses appreciation.

Generally written on organization letterhead stationery, a letter or memo of transmittal introduces a formal report. You will recall that letters are sent to outsiders and memos to insiders. A transmittal letter or memo follows the direct pattern and is usually less formal than the report itself. For example, the letter or memo may use contractions and first-person pronouns such as *I* and *we*. The transmittal letter or memo typically (1) announces the topic of the report and tells how it was authorized; (2) briefly describes the project; (3) highlights the report's findings, conclusions, and recommendations, if the reader is expected to be supportive; and (4) closes with appreciation for the assignment, instructions for the reader's follow-up actions, acknowledgment of help from others, or offers of assistance in answering questions. If a report is going to different readers, a special transmittal letter or memo should be prepared for each, anticipating what each reader needs to know in using the report.

TABLE OF CONTENTS

The table of contents shows the headings in a report and their page numbers. It gives an overview of the report topics and helps readers locate them. You should wait to prepare the table of contents until after you've completed the report. For short reports include all headings. For longer reports you might want to list only first- and second-level headings. Leaders (spaced or unspaced dots) help guide the eye from the heading to the page number. Items may be indented in outline form or typed flush with the left margin.

LIST OF FIGURES

For reports with several figures or illustrations, you may wish to include a list of figures to help readers locate them. This list may appear on the same page as the table of contents, space permitting. For each figure or illustration, include a title and page number.

FIGURE 10.17   **Model Format Report**

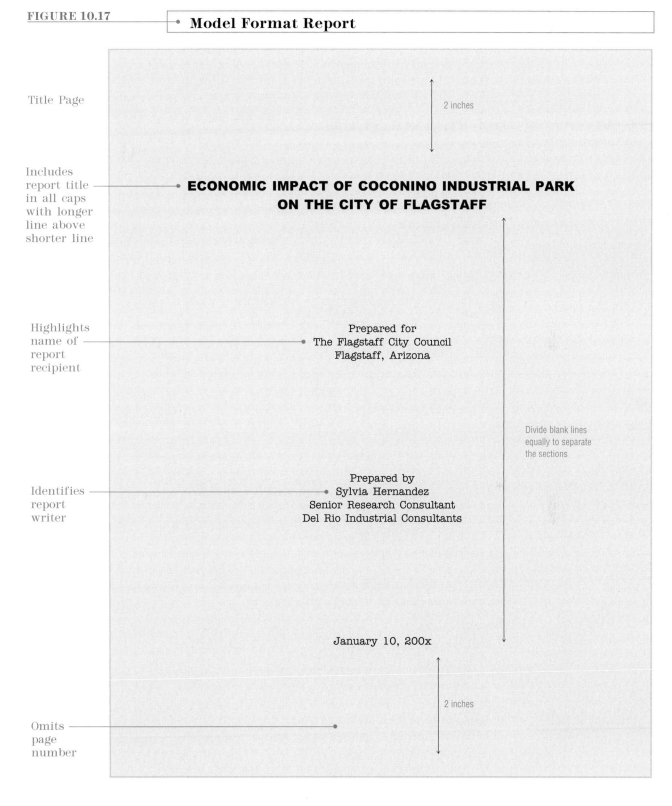

Title Page

2 inches

Includes
report title
in all caps
with longer
line above
shorter line

**ECONOMIC IMPACT OF COCONINO INDUSTRIAL PARK
ON THE CITY OF FLAGSTAFF**

Highlights
name of
report
recipient

Prepared for
The Flagstaff City Council
Flagstaff, Arizona

Divide blank lines
equally to separate
the sections

Identifies
report
writer

Prepared by
Sylvia Hernandez
Senior Research Consultant
Del Rio Industrial Consultants

January 10, 200x

2 inches

Omits
page
number

The title page is usually arranged in four evenly balanced areas. If the report is to be bound on the left, move the left margin and center point ¼ inch to the right. Notice that no page number appears on the title page, although it is counted as page i. In designing the title page, be careful to avoid anything unprofessional—such as too many type fonts, italics, oversized print, and inappropriate graphics. Keep the title page simple and professional. This model report uses MLA documentation style. However, it is not double-spaced, the recommended format for research papers using MLA style. Instead, this model is single-spaced, which saves space and is more appropriate for business reports.

FIGURE 10.17   • **Letter of Transmittal**

DEL RIO INDUSTRIAL CONSULTANTS

110 West Route 66   www.delrio.com
Flagstaff, Arizona 86001   (928) 774-1101

January 12, 200x

City Council
City of Flagstaff
211 West Aspen Avenue
Flagstaff, AZ 86001

Dear Council Members:

Announces report and identifies authorization

The attached report, requested by the Flagstaff City Council in a letter to Goldman-Lyon & Associates dated October 20, describes the economic impact of Coconino Industrial Park on the city of Flagstaff. We are confident you will find the results of this study useful in evaluating future development of industrial parks within the city limits.

Gives broad overview of report purposes

This study was designed to examine economic impact in three areas:

- Current and projected tax and other revenues accruing to the city from Coconino Industrial Park

- Current and projected employment generated by the park

- Indirect effects on local employment, income, and economic growth

Describes primary and secondary research

Primary research consisted of interviews with 15 Coconino Industrial Park tenants and managers, in addition to a 2006 survey of over 5,000 CIP employees. Secondary research sources included the Annual Budget of the City of Flagstaff, county and state tax records, government publications, periodicals, books, and online resources. Results of this research, discussed more fully in this report, indicate that Coconino Industrial Park exerts a significant beneficial influence on the Flagstaff metropolitan economy.

Offers to discuss report; expresses appreciation

We would be pleased to discuss this report and its conclusions with you at your request. My firm and I thank you for your confidence in selecting our company to prepare this comprehensive report.

Sincerely,

Sylvia Hernandez

Sylvia Hernandez
Senior Research Consultant

SMH:mef
Attachment

Uses Roman numerals for prefatory pages

ii

A letter or memo of transmittal announces the report topic and explains who authorized it. It briefly describes the project and previews the conclusions, if the reader is supportive. Such messages generally close by expressing appreciation for the assignment, suggesting follow-up actions, acknowledging the help of others, or offering to answer questions. The margins for the transmittal should be the same as for the report, about 1 to 1¼ inches on all sides. The letter should be left-justified. A page number is optional.

FIGURE 10.17

Table of Contents and List of Figures

TABLE OF CONTENTS

Uses leaders to guide eye from heading to page number

Indents secondary headings to show levels of outline

LIST OF FIGURES

Includes tables and figures in one list for simplified numbering

Because the table of contents and the list of figures for this report are small, they are combined on one page. Notice that the titles of major report parts are in all caps, while other headings are a combination of upper- and lowercase letters. This duplicates the style within the report. Advanced word processing capabilities enable you to generate a contents page automatically, including leaders and accurate page numbering—no matter how many times you revise. Notice that the page numbers are right-justified.

FIGURE 10.17   • **Executive Summary**

EXECUTIVE SUMMARY

Opens directly with major research findings

The city of Flagstaff can benefit from the development of industrial parks like the Coconino Industrial Park. Both direct and indirect economic benefits result, as shown by this in-depth study conducted by Del Rio Industrial Consultants. The study was authorized by the Flagstaff City Council when Goldman-Lyon & Associates sought the City Council's approval for the proposed construction of a G-L industrial park. The City Council requested evidence demonstrating that an existing development could actually benefit the city.

Identifies data sources

Our conclusion that the city of Flagstaff benefits from industrial parks is based on data supplied by a survey of 5,000 Coconino Industrial Park employees, personal interviews with managers and tenants of CIP, city and state documents, and professional literature.

Summarizes organization of report

Analysis of the data revealed benefits in three areas:

- **Revenues.** The city of Flagstaff earned nearly $2 million in tax and other revenues from the Coconino Industrial Park in 2006. By 2012 this income is expected to reach $3.4 million (in constant 2006 dollars).

- **Employment.** In 2006, CIP businesses employed a total of 7,035 workers, who earned an average wage of $56,579. By 2012, CIP businesses are expected to employ directly nearly 15,000 employees who will earn salaries totaling over $998 million.

- **Indirect benefits.** Because of the multiplier effect, by 2012 Coconino Industrial Park will directly and indirectly generate a total of 38,362 jobs in the Flagstaff metropolitan area.

Condenses recommendations

On the basis of these findings, it is recommended that development of additional industrial parks be encouraged to stimulate local economic growth.

iv

For readers who want a quick overview of the report, the executive summary presents its most important elements. Executive summaries focus on the information the reader requires for making a decision related to the issues discussed in the report. The summary may include some or all of the following elements: purpose, scope, research methods, findings, conclusions, and recommendations. Its length depends on the report it summarizes. A 100-page report might require a 10-page summary. Shorter reports may contain 1-page summaries, as shown here. Unlike letters of transmittal (which may contain personal pronouns and references to the writer), the executive summary of a long report is formal and impersonal. It uses the same margins as the body of the report. See Chapter 9 for additional discussion of executive summaries.

FIGURE 10.17   • Page 1

PROBLEM

This study was designed to analyze the direct and indirect economic impact of Coconino Industrial Park on the city of Flagstaff. Specifically, the study seeks answers to these questions:

Uses a bulleted list for clarity and ease of reading

Lists three problem questions

- What current tax and other revenues result directly from this park? What tax and other revenues may be expected in the future?

- How many and what kinds of jobs are directly attributable to the park? What is the employment picture for the future?

- What indirect effects has Coconino Industrial Park had on local employment, incomes, and economic growth?

BACKGROUND

Describes authorization for report and background of study

The development firm of Goldman-Lyon & Associates commissioned this study of Coconino Industrial Park at the request of the Flagstaff City Council. Before authorizing the development of a proposed Goldman-Lyon industrial park, the City Council requested a study examining the economic effects of an existing park. Members of the City Council wanted to determine to what extent industrial parks benefit the local community, and they chose Coconino Industrial Park as an example.

For those who are unfamiliar with it, Coconino Industrial Park is a 400-acre industrial park located in the city of Flagstaff about 4 miles from the center of the city. Most of the area lies within a specially designated area known as Redevelopment Project No. 2, which is under the jurisdiction of the Flagstaff Redevelopment Agency. Planning for the park began in 1994; construction started in 1996.

The original goal for Coconino Industrial Park was development for light industrial users. Land in this area was zoned for uses such as warehousing, research and development, and distribution. Like other communities, Flagstaff was eager to attract light industrial users because such businesses tend to employ a highly educated workforce, are quieter, and do not pollute the environment. The city of Flagstaff recognized the need for light industrial users and widened an adjacent highway to accommodate trucks and facilitate travel by workers and customers coming from Flagstaff.

1

The first page of a formal report generally contains the title printed 2 inches from the top edge. Titles for major parts of a report are centered in all caps. In this model document we show functional heads, such as *PROBLEM, BACKGROUND, FINDINGS,* and *CONCLUSIONS.* However, most business reports would use talking heads or a combination such as *FINDINGS REVEAL REVENUE AND EMPLOYMENT BENEFITS.* First-level subheadings (such as *Revenues* on page 2) are printed with bold upper- and lowercase letters. Second-level subheadings (such as *Distribution* on page 3) begin at the side, are bolded, and are written in upper- and lowercase letters. See Figure 10.4 for an illustration of heading formats.

FIGURE 10.17

• Page 2

The park now contains 14 building complexes with over 1.25 million square feet of completed building space. The majority of the buildings are used for office, research and development, marketing and distribution, or manufacturing uses. Approximately 50 acres of the original area are yet to be developed.

Uses functional heads — Data for this report came from a 2006 survey of over 5,000 Coconino Industrial Park employees; interviews with 15 CIP tenants and managers; the Annual Budget of the City of Flagstaff; county and state tax records; current books, articles, journals; and online resources. Projections for future revenues resulted from analysis of past trends and "Estimates of Revenues for Debt Service Coverage, Redevelopment Project Area 2" (Miller 79).

Provides specifics for data sources —
DISCUSSION OF FINDINGS

Previews organization of report — The results of this research indicate that major direct and indirect benefits have accrued to the city of Flagstaff and surrounding metropolitan areas as a result of the development of Coconino Industrial Park. The research findings presented here fall into three categories: (a) revenues, (b) employment, and (c) indirect effects.

Revenues

Coconino Industrial Park contributes a variety of tax and other revenues to the city of Flagstaff, as summarized in Figure 1. Current revenues are shown, along with projections to the year 2012. At a time when the economy is unstable, revenues from an industrial park such as Coconino can become a reliable income stream for the city of Flagstaff.

Places figure close to textual reference —
Figure 1

REVENUES RECEIVED BY THE CITY OF FLAGSTAFF
FROM COCONINO INDUSTRIAL PARK

Current Revenues and Projections to 2012

	2006	2012
Sales and use taxes	$904,140	$1,335,390
Revenues from licenses	426,265	516,396
Franchise taxes	175,518	229,424
State gas tax receipts	83,768	112,134
Licenses and permits	78,331	112,831
Other revenues	94,039	141,987
Total	$1,762,061	$2,448,162

Source: Arizona State Board of Equalization Bulletin.
Phoenix: State Printing Office, 2006, 103.

2

Notice that this formal report is single-spaced. Many businesses prefer this space-saving format. However, some organizations prefer double-spacing, especially for preliminary drafts. If you single-space, do not indent paragraphs. If you double-space, do indent the paragraphs. Page numbers may be centered 1 inch from the bottom of the page or placed 1 inch from the upper right corner at the margin. Your word processor can insert page numbers automatically. Strive to leave a minimum of 1 inch for top, bottom, and side margins. References follow the parenthetical citation style (or in-text citation style) of the Modern Language Association (MLA). Notice that the author's name and a page reference appear in parentheses. The complete bibliographic entry for any in-text citation appears at the end of report in the works-cited section.

FIGURE 10.17 | **Page 3**

Continues
interpreting
figures
in table

Includes
ample
description
of electronic
reference

Sets stage
for next
topics to be
discussed

Sales and Use Revenues

As shown in Figure 1, the city's largest source of revenues from CIP is the sales and use tax. Revenues from this source totaled $904,140 in 2006, according to figures provided by the Arizona State Board of Equalization (28). Sales and use taxes accounted for more than half of the park's total contribution to the city of $1,762,061.

Other Revenues

Other major sources of city revenues from CIP in 2006 include alcohol licenses, motor vehicle in lieu fees, trailer coach licenses ($426,265), franchise taxes ($175,518), and state gas tax receipts ($83,768). Although not shown in Figure 1, other revenues may be expected from the development of recently acquired property. The U.S. Economic Development Administration has approved a grant worth $975,000 to assist in expanding the current park eastward on an undeveloped parcel purchased last year. Revenues from leasing this property may be sizeable.

Projections

Total city revenues from CIP will nearly double by 2012, producing an income of $2.45 million. This estimate is based on an annual growth rate of 0.65 percent, as projected by the Bureau of Labor Statistics and reported at the Web site of Infoplease.com ("Economic Outlook Through 2012").

Employment

One of the most important factors to consider in the overall effect of an industrial park is employment. In Coconino Industrial Park the distribution, number, and wages of people employed will change considerably in the next six years.

Distribution

A total of 7,035 employees currently work in various industry groups at Coconino Industrial Park. The distribution of employees is shown in Figure 2. The largest number of workers (58 percent) is employed in manufacturing and assembly operations. In the next largest category, the computer and electronics industry employs 24 percent of the workers. Some overlap probably exists because electronics assembly could be included in either group. Employees also work in publishing (9 percent), warehousing and storage (5 percent), and other industries (4 percent).

Although the distribution of employees at Coconino Industrial Park shows a wide range of employment categories, it must be noted that other industrial parks would likely generate an entirely different range of job categories.

3

Only the most important research findings are interpreted and discussed for readers. The depth of discussion depends on the intended length of the report, the goal of the writer, and the expectations of the reader. Because the writer wants this report to be formal in tone, she avoids *I* and *we* in all discussions.

As you type a report, avoid widows and orphans (ending a page with the first line of a paragraph or carrying a single line of a paragraph to a new page). Strive to start and end pages with at least two lines of a paragraph, even if a slightly larger bottom margin results.

FIGURE 10.17

• Page 4

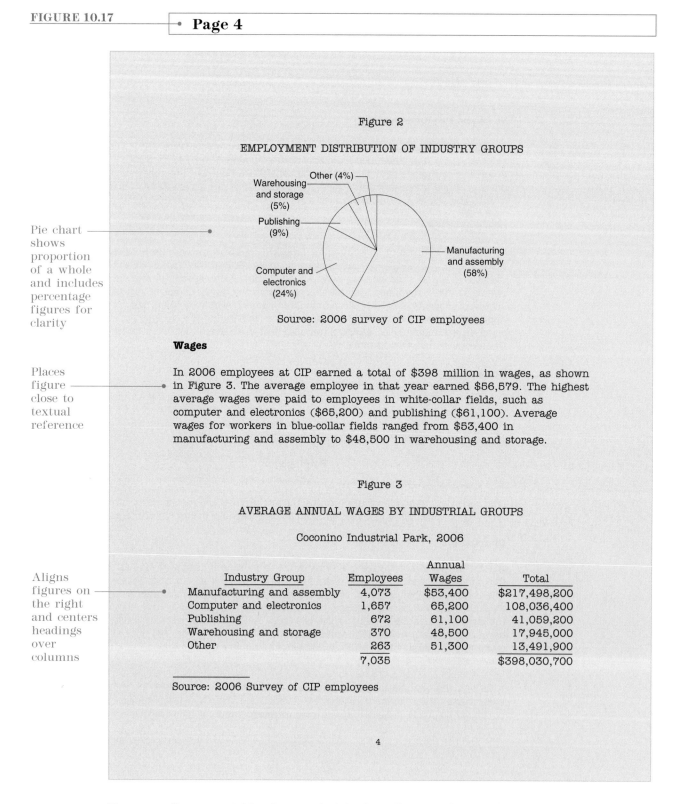

Figure 2

EMPLOYMENT DISTRIBUTION OF INDUSTRY GROUPS

Other (4%)
Warehousing and storage (5%)
Publishing (9%)
Manufacturing and assembly (58%)
Computer and electronics (24%)

Source: 2006 survey of CIP employees

Pie chart shows proportion of a whole and includes percentage figures for clarity

Wages

In 2006 employees at CIP earned a total of $398 million in wages, as shown in Figure 3. The average employee in that year earned $56,579. The highest average wages were paid to employees in white-collar fields, such as computer and electronics ($65,200) and publishing ($61,100). Average wages for workers in blue-collar fields ranged from $53,400 in manufacturing and assembly to $48,500 in warehousing and storage.

Places figure close to textual reference

Figure 3

AVERAGE ANNUAL WAGES BY INDUSTRIAL GROUPS

Coconino Industrial Park, 2006

Industry Group	Employees	Annual Wages	Total
Manufacturing and assembly	4,073	$53,400	$217,498,200
Computer and electronics	1,657	65,200	108,036,400
Publishing	672	61,100	41,059,200
Warehousing and storage	370	48,500	17,945,000
Other	263	51,300	13,491,900
	7,035		$398,030,700

Source: 2006 Survey of CIP employees

Aligns figures on the right and centers headings over columns

4

If you use figures or tables, be sure to introduce them in the text (for example, *as shown in Figure 3*). Although it's not always possible, try to place figures and tables close to the spot where they are first mentioned. To save space, you can print the title of a figure at its side. Because this report contains few tables and figures, the writer named them all "Figures" and numbered them consecutively.

FIGURE 10.17

> **Page 5**

Clarifies information and tells what it means in relation to original research questions

Projections

By 2012 Coconino Industrial Park is expected to more than double its number of employees, bringing the total to over 15,000 workers. The total payroll in 2012 will also more than double, producing over $998 million (using constant 2006 dollars) in salaries to CIP employees. These projections are based on an 8 percent growth rate (Miller 78), along with anticipated increased employment as the park reaches its capacity.

Future development in the park will influence employment and payrolls. One CIP project manager stated in an interview that much of the remaining 50 acres is planned for medium-rise office buildings, garden offices, and other structures for commercial, professional, and personal services (Novak). Average wages for employees are expected to increase because of an anticipated shift to higher-paying white-collar jobs. Industrial parks often follow a similar pattern of evolution (Badri 41). Like many industrial parks, CIP evolved from a warehousing center into a manufacturing complex.

Summarizes conclusions and recommendations

CONCLUSIONS AND RECOMMENDATIONS

Analysis of tax revenues, employment data, personal interviews, and professional literature leads to the following conclusions and recommendations about the economic impact of Coconino Industrial Park on the city of Flagstaff:

Uses a numbered list for clarity and ease of reading

1. Sales tax and other revenues produced nearly $1.8 million in income to the city of Flagstaff in 2006. By 2012 sales tax and other revenues are expected to produce $2.5 million in city income.

2. CIP currently employs 7,035 employees, the majority of whom are working in manufacturing and assembly. The average employee in 2006 earned $56,579.

3. By 2012 CIP is expected to employ more than 15,000 workers producing a total payroll of over $998 million.

4. Employment trends indicate that by 2012 more CIP employees will be engaged in higher-paying white-collar positions.

On the basis of these findings, we recommend that the City Council of Flagstaff authorize the development of additional industrial parks to stimulate local economic growth.

5

After discussing and interpreting the research findings, the writer articulates what she considers the most important conclusions and recommendations. Longer, more complex reports may have separate sections for conclusions and resulting recommendations. In this report they are combined. Notice that it is unnecessary to start a new page for the conclusions.

FIGURE 10.17   **Works Cited**

Arranges
references
in alpha-
betical order

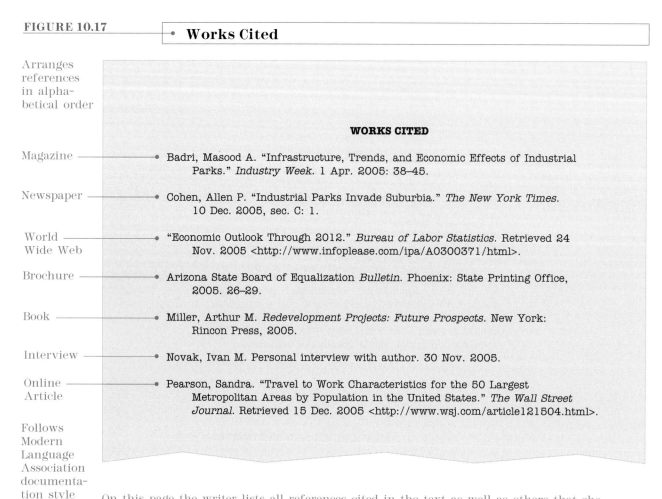

WORKS CITED

Magazine ——————• Badri, Masood A. "Infrastructure, Trends, and Economic Effects of Industrial
                        Parks." *Industry Week.* 1 Apr. 2005: 38–45.

Newspaper ——————• Cohen, Allen P. "Industrial Parks Invade Suburbia." *The New York Times.*
                        10 Dec. 2005, sec. C: 1.

World ——————————• "Economic Outlook Through 2012." *Bureau of Labor Statistics.* Retrieved 24
Wide Web   Nov. 2005 <http://www.infoplease.com/ipa/A0300371/html>.

Brochure ——————• Arizona State Board of Equalization *Bulletin.* Phoenix: State Printing Office,
                        2005. 26–29.

Book ————————————• Miller, Arthur M. *Redevelopment Projects: Future Prospects.* New York:
                        Rincon Press, 2005.

Interview ——————• Novak, Ivan M. Personal interview with author. 30 Nov. 2005.

Online ————————• Pearson, Sandra. "Travel to Work Characteristics for the 50 Largest
Article   Metropolitan Areas by Population in the United States." *The Wall Street
                        Journal.* Retrieved 15 Dec. 2005 <http://www.wsj.com/article121504.html>.

Follows
Modern
Language
Association
documenta-
tion style

On this page the writer lists all references cited in the text as well as others that she examined during her research. The writer lists these citations following the MLA referencing style. Notice that all entries are arranged alphabetically. Book and periodical titles are italicized, but they could be underlined. When referring to online items, she shows the full name of the citation and then identifies the URL as well as the date on which she accessed the electronic reference. This works-cited page is shown with single-spacing, which is preferable for business reports. However, MLA style recommends double-spacing for research reports, including the works-cited page. MLA style also shows "Works Cited" in upper- and lowercase letters. However, the writer preferred to use all caps to be consistent with other headngs in this business report.

EXECUTIVE SUMMARY

As you learned in Chapter 9, the purpose of an executive summary is to present an overview of a longer report to people who may not have time to read the entire document. This time-saving device summarizes the purpose, key points, findings, and conclusions. An executive summary is usually no longer than 10 percent of the original document. Thus, a 20-page report might require a 2-page executive summary. Chapter 9 discussed how to write an executive summary and included an example in Figure 9.9. You can see another executive summary in Figure 10.17.

Body of Report

The body of a report includes an introduction; discussion of findings; and summary, conclusions, or recommendations.

The main section of a report is the body. It generally begins with an introduction, includes a discussion of findings, and concludes with a summary and possibly recommendations.

INTRODUCTION

The body of a formal report starts with an introduction that sets the scene and announces the subject. Because they contain many parts serving different purposes, formal reports have a degree of repetition. The same information may be included in the letter or memo of transmittal, executive summary, and introduction. To avoid sounding repetitious, try to present the information slightly differently in each section.

A good report introduction typically covers the following elements, although not necessarily in this order:

- **Background.** Describe the events leading up to the problem or need.
- **Problem or purpose.** Explain the report topic and specify the problem or need that motivated the report.
- **Significance.** Tell why the topic is important. You may wish to quote experts or cite secondary sources to establish the importance of the topic.
- **Scope.** Clarify the boundaries of the report, defining what will be included or excluded.
- **Sources and methods.** Describe your secondary sources. Also explain how you collected primary data.
- **Summary.** Include a summary of findings, if the report is written directly.
- **Organization.** Preview the major sections of the report to follow, thus providing coherence and transition for the reader.

DISCUSSION OF FINDINGS

This is the main section of the report and contains numerous headings and sub-headings. This section discusses, analyzes, interprets, and evaluates the research findings or solution to the initial problem. This is where you show the evidence that justifies your conclusions. It is unnecessary to use the title *Discussion of Findings*; many business report writers prefer to begin immediately with the major headings into which the body of the report is divided. As summarized in Figure 10.2, you may organize the findings chronologically, geographically, topically, or by some other method. Regardless of the organizational pattern, present your findings logically and objectively. Avoid the use of first-person pronouns (*I, we*). Include tables, charts, and graphs if necessary to illustrate findings. Analytic and scientific reports may include another section titled *Implications of Findings*, in which the findings are analyzed and related to the problem. Less formal reports contain the author's analysis of the research findings within the *Discussion* section.

SUMMARY, CONCLUSIONS, RECOMMENDATIONS

The conclusion to a report tells what the findings mean, particularly in terms of solving the original problem. If the report has been largely informational, it ends with a summary of the data presented. If the report analyzes research findings, then it ends with conclusions drawn from the analyses. An analytic report frequently poses research questions. The conclusion to such a report reviews the major findings and answers the research questions. If a report seeks to determine a course of action, it may end with conclusions and recommendations. Recommendations regarding a course of action may be placed in a separate section or incorporated with the conclusions.

Supplementary Parts of Report

WORKS CITED, REFERENCES, OR BIBLIOGRAPHY

Endnotes, a bibliography, and appendixes may appear after the body of the report.

Readers look in the bibliography section to locate the sources of ideas mentioned in a report. Your method of report documentation determines how this section is developed. If you use the Modern Language Association (MLA) referencing format, all citations would be listed alphabetically in the "Works Cited." If you use the American Psychological Association (APA) format, your list would be called "References."

Regardless of the format, you must include the author, title, publication, date of publication, page number, and other significant data for all sources used in your report. For electronic references include the URL and the date you accessed the information online. To see electronic and other citations, examine the list of references at the end of Figure 10.17, which follows the MLA documentation style. See Appendix C for more information on documentation formats.

APPENDIX

The appendix contains any supplementary or supporting information needed to clarify the report. This information is relevant to some readers but not to all. Extra information that might be included in an appendix are such items as survey forms, a survey cover letter, correspondence relating to the report, maps, other reports, and optional tables. Items in the appendix are labeled Appendix A, Appendix B, and so forth; and these items should be referenced in the body of the report.

SUMMING UP AND LOOKING FORWARD

Proposals are written offers to solve problems, provide services, or sell equipment. Both small and large businesses today write proposals to generate income. Informal proposals may be as short as 2 pages; formal proposals may be 200 pages or more. Regardless of the size, proposals contain standard parts that must be developed persuasively.

Formal reports present well-organized information systematically. The information may be collected from primary or secondary sources. All ideas borrowed from others must be documented. Good reports contain appropriate headings to help guide readers through the report. In addition, formal reports often contain tables, charts, and graphs to illustrate data.

Written reports are vital to decision makers. But oral reports can be equally important. In Chapter 12 you will learn how to organize and make professional oral presentations. Before discussing oral reports, however, you'll learn how to communicate effectively in person, by telephone, and in meetings in Chapter 11.

CRITICAL THINKING

1. Why is proposal writing an important function in many businesses?

2. Discuss this statement, made by three well-known professional business writers: "Nothing you write will be completely new."[15]

3. Is information obtained on the Web as reliable as information obtained from journals, newspapers, and magazines? Explain.

4. Should all reports be written so that they follow the sequence of investigation—that is, description of the initial problem, analysis of issues, data collection, data analysis, and conclusions? Why or why not?

5. Distinguish between primary and secondary data. Which data are more likely to be useful in a business report?

CHAPTER REVIEW

6. What is the difference between a solicited and an unsolicited proposal. Give an example of when each would be written.

7. What are the six principal parts of an informal proposal? Be prepared to explain each.

8. How are formal proposals different from informal proposals?

9. What is the first step in writing a formal report?

10. List four sources of secondary information, and be prepared to discuss how valuable each might be in writing a formal report about outsourcing your company's payroll function.

11. Define these terms: *browser, URL, search tool.*

12. What are weblogs (blogs) and how can they be used for research?

13. Pie charts are most helpful in showing what? Line charts are most effective in showing what?

14. List three reasons for documenting data in a business report.

15. List the parts of a formal report. Be prepared to discuss each.

ACTIVITIES AND CASES

TEAM

10.1 Researching Secondary and Primary Data

In teams, discuss how you would collect information for each of the following report topics. Would your research be primary, secondary, or a combination of methods? What resources would be most useful—-books, articles, the Web, interviewing, surveys?

a. The history of unions in the United States

b. Which public relations firm will best improve the image of a company so that its stock price increases

c. The cause of the high absenteeism in one department of a company

d. The latest Occupational Safety and Health Administration (OSHA) rulings that might affect your small business

e. The traffic count at a possible location for a new coffee shop

f. What do school board members feel about the criticism of snack foods being sold to students?

g. The costs and features of a new network system for your company

h. How users are reacting to a new digital imaging software that was recently released

i. How to meet international quality standards (ISO certification) so that you can sell your products in Europe

INFOTRAC   **WEB**

10.2 Gathering and Documenting Data: Biotechnology Alters Foods

California is home to the nation's most diverse and valuable agricultural industry. Many of its crops are sold in Japanese and European markets where customers are extremely wary of genetically modified foods. Despite that fact, sources in the state capital are reporting that the biotech industry is actively seeking sponsors for a bill in the state legislature that would preempt the right of counties to ban genetically engineered crops. As an intern working for the Organic Consumers Association, the nation's largest public interest group dedicated to a healthy and sustainable food system, you have been asked to gather data about the dangers of genetically engineered crops. The organization plans to write a report to the state government about this issue.

Your Task. Conduct a keyword search using three different search tools on the Web. Select three articles you think would be most pertinent to the organization's argument. Save them using the strategies for managing data, and create a bibliography. Conduct the same keyword search with InfoTrac. Save the three most pertinent articles, and add these items to your bibliography. In a short memo to your instructor, summarize what you've found and describe its value. Attach the bibliography.

(INFOTRAC) (WEB)

10.3 Writing a Survey: Studying Employee Use of Instant Messaging

Instant messaging (IM) is a popular way to exchange messages in real time. It offers the convenience of telephone conversations and e-mail. Best of all, it allows employees to contact anyone in the world while retaining a written copy of the conversation—without a whopping telephone bill! But instant messaging is risky for companies. They may lose trade secrets or confidential information over insecure lines. They also may be liable if inappropriate material is exchanged. Moreover, IM opens the door to viruses that can infect a company's entire computer system.

Your boss just read an article stating that 40 percent of companies now use IM for business and up to 90 percent of employees use IM WITHOUT their manager's knowledge or authorization. He asks you to prepare a survey of your 48-member staff to learn how many are using IM. He wants to know what type of IM software they have downloaded, how many hours a day they spend on IM, what are the advantages of IM, and so forth. The goal is not to identify those using or abusing IM. Instead, the goal is to learn when, how, and why it is being used so that appropriate policies can be designed.

Your Task. Use InfoTrac or the Web to learn more about instant messaging. Then prepare a short employee survey. Include an appropriate introduction that explains the survey and encourages a response. Should you ask for names on the survey? How can you encourage return of the forms? Your instructor may wish to expand this survey into a report by having you produce fictitious survey results, analyze the findings, draw conclusions, and make recommendations.

10.4 Outlining: Explaining Weblogs

Your boss has been hearing a lot about weblogs (blogs) lately and wonders if this is something your company should start using for research and communication. He has asked you to write a short report on how blogs can be used in a business environment. He also wonders if a blogging policy would be needed. Here are some ideas you gathered from your Internet research:

Although some companies worry that blogs could be used to expose company secrets or violate securities laws, many companies are encouraging their employees to take part in blogging. The corporate world has found that blogging is an effective way to communicate with customers and clients, to encourage internal interaction, and make them look more approachable and "human" to the outside world. Blogs can also be used by employees for research, for data collection, and for keeping up with what competitors are doing. Some companies have both external and internal blogs, and some even allow employees to set up personal blogs.

Companies that use blogs should probably have policies or guidelines governing their use. Companies might adopt guidelines that require employees to use first-person pronouns and to be honest. Microsoft tells employees to avoid writing blog entries when they're upset or emotional. Other companies provide lists of topics that should be avoided in blogs, such as anything that should remain confidential, private, or secret or anything that is embarrassing, libelous, or illegal. Above all, any policy should state that employees are responsible for their own posts.

Various tools can be used to set up blogs. Some of the most popular include Google's Blogger.com, Microsoft's MSN Spaces, and Yahoo's 360 service. These tools make setting up blogs easy to do. They help users publish text entries, add photos, publish links to other blogs and Web pages, and establish privacy if desired. They also provide themes and various editing tools that can help corporate blogs look professional.

Your Task. Select the most important information and organize it into an outline such as that shown in Figure 10.3. You should have three main topics with three subdivisions under each. Assume that you will gather more information later. Add a title.

TEAM

10.5 Selecting Graphics

In teams identify the best graphic (table, bar chart, line chart, pie chart, flowchart, organization chart, illustration, map) to illustrate the following data:

a. Figure showing the process of converting grapes into wine

b. Figures showing what proportion of every state tax dollar is spent on education, social services, transportation, debt, and other expenses

c. Data showing the academic, administrative, and operation divisions of a college, from the president to department chairs and division managers

d. Figures showing the operating revenue of a company for the past five years

e. Figures comparing the sales of PDAs (personal digital assistants), cell phones, and laptop computers over the past five years

f. Percentages showing the causes of forest fires (lightning, 73 percent; arson, 5 percent; campfires, 9 percent; and so on) in the Rocky Mountains

g. Figure comparing the costs of cable, DSL, and satellite Internet service in ten major metropolitan areas of the United States for the past ten years (the boss wants to see exact figures)

h. Figure showing the distribution of West Nile virus in humans by state

10.6 Evaluating Graphics in Publications

From *U.S. News & World Report, USA Today, BusinessWeek*, a textbook, or some other publication, locate one example each of a table, a pie chart, a line chart, a bar chart, and an organization chart. Bring copies of these visual aids to class. How effectively could the data have been expressed in words, without the graphics? Is the appropriate graphic form used? How is the graphic introduced in the text? Do you think the graphic is misleading or unethical in any way? Your instructor may ask you to submit a memo discussing visual aids.

10.7 Studying Graphics in Annual Reports

In a memo to your instructor, evaluate the effectiveness of graphics in three to five corporation annual reports. Critique their readability, clarity, and success in visualizing data. How were they introduced in the text? What suggestions would you make to improve them? Do you feel the graphics presented the data accurately and ethically?

10.8 Developing Bibliography Skills

Select a business topic that interests you. Prepare a bibliography of at least five current magazine or newspaper articles, three books, and five online references that contain relevant information regarding the topic. Your instructor may ask you to divide your bibliography into sections: *Books, Periodicals, Online Resources.*

You may also be asked to annotate your bibliography, that is, to compose a brief description of each reference, such as this:

Armstrong, David. "Airlines Could Allow Chatter: FCC Reconsidering Ban on In-Flight Calls, Starting to Ask Passengers What They Think." *San Francisco Chronicle*, 28 April 2005, C1.

> This article discusses the efforts the Federal Communications Commission (FCC), which regulates telecommunications, and the Federal Aviation Administration (FAA), which oversees civil airline safety. What efforts are these agencies making to allow airline passengers to use personal cell phones during flights? For this to happen, each organization would have to lift bans on using personal electronic devices on commercial aircraft. They are asking for public comment to determine whether passengers are interested in this service.

WEB

10.9 Proposals: Comparing Real Proposals

Many new companies with services or products to offer would like to land corporate or government contracts. But they are intimidated by the proposal (RFP process). You have been asked for help by your friend Chloe, who has started her own designer uniform company. Her goal is to offer her colorful yet functional uniforms to hospitals and clinics. Before writing a proposal, however, she wants to see examples and learn more about the process.

Your Task. Use the Web to find at least two examples of business proposals. Don't waste time on sites that want to sell templates or books. Find actual examples. Then prepare a memo to Chloe in which you do the following:
a. Identify two sites with sample business proposals.
b. Outline the parts of each proposal.
c. Compare the strengths and weaknesses of each proposal.
d. Draw conclusions. What can Chloe learn from these examples?

TEAM   **CRITICAL THINKING**

10.10 Proposal: Looking for Clients for Your Business

In university towns, sports medicine is increasingly popular. A new medical clinic, SportsMed Institute, is opening its doors in your hometown; and a mutual friend has recommended your small business to the administrator of the clinic. You have received a letter asking you to provide information about your service. The new medical clinic specializes in sports medicine, physical therapy, and cardiac rehabilitation services. It is interested in retaining your company, rather than hiring its own employees to perform the service your company offers.

Your Task. Working in teams, first decide what service you will offer. It could be landscaping, uniform supply, laundry of uniforms, general cleaning, computerized no-paper filing system, online medical supplies, patient transportation, supplemental hospice care, temporary office support, or food service. As a team, develop a letter proposal outlining your plan, staffing, and budget. Use persuasion to show why contracting your services is better than hiring in-house employees. In the proposal letter, request a meeting with the administrative board. In addition to a written proposal, you may be expected to make an oral presentation that includes visual aids and/or handouts. Send your proposal to Dr. Douglas Zlock, Director, SportsMed Institute. Supply a local address.

10.11 Unsolicited Proposal: Working From Home

You have been working as a computer programmer for your company since its inception in 1998. Every day you commute from your home, almost two hours round trip. Most of your work is done at a computer terminal with little or no human contact. You would prefer to eliminate the commute time, and you believe that this time could be better spent working on your programming. You believe your job would be perfect for telecommuting. With a small investment in the proper equipment, you could do all of your work at home, perhaps reporting to the office once a week for meetings and other activities.

Your Task. Research the costs and logistics of telecommuting, and present your proposal to your supervisor, Cynthia Barry. Because this is an unsolicited proposal, you'll need to be even more persuasive. Convince your supervisor that the company will benefit from this telecommuting arrangement.

TEAM   **CRITICAL THINKING**

10.12 Proposal: Starting Your Own Business

You and your buddies have a terrific idea for a new business in your town. For example, you might want to propose to Starbucks the concept of converting some of its coffee shops into Internet cafes. Or you might propose to the city or another organization a better Web site, which you and your team would design and maintain. You might want to start a word processing business that offers production, editing, and printing services. Often businesses, medical centers, attorneys, and other professionals have overload transcribing or word processing to farm out to a service.

Your Task. Working in teams, explore entrepreneurial ventures based on your experience and expertise. Write a proposal to secure approval and funding. Your report should include a transmittal letter, as well as a description of your proposed company, its product or service, a market analysis, an operations and management plan, and a financial plan.

TEAM

10.13 Formal Report: Intercultural Communication

U.S. businesses are expanding into foreign markets with manufacturing plants, sales offices, and branch offices abroad. Unfortunately, most Americans have little knowledge of or experience with people from other cultures. To prepare for participation in the global marketplace, you are to collect information for a report focused on an Asian, Latin American, African, or European country where English is not regularly spoken. Before selecting the country, though, consider consulting your campus international student program for volunteers who are willing to be interviewed. Your instructor may make advance arrangements seeking international student volunteers.

Your Task. In teams of two to four, collect information about your target country from the library, the Web, and other sources. If possible, invite an international student representing your target country to be interviewed by your group. As you conduct primary and secondary research, investigate the topics listed in Figure 10.18.[16] Confirm what you learn in your secondary research by talking with your interviewee. When you complete your research, write a report for the CEO of your company (make up a name and company). Assume that your company plans to expand its operations abroad. Your report should advise the company's executives of social customs, family life, attitudes, appropriate business attire, religions, economic institutions, and values in the target country. Remember that your company's interests are business oriented; don't dwell on tourist information. Write your report individually or in teams.

CRITICAL THINKING

10.14 Formal Report: Readability of Insurance Policies

The Urban Life Insurance Company is concerned about the readability of its policies. State legislators are beginning to investigate complaints of policyholders who say they can't understand their insurance policies. One judge lambasted insurers, saying, "The language in these policies is bureaucratic gobbledygook, jargon, double-talk, a form of officialese, federalese, and insurancese that does not qualify as English. The burden upon organizations is to write policies in a manner designed to communicate rather than to obfuscate." Taking the initiative in improving its policies, Urban Life hires you as a consultant to study its standard policy and make recommendations.

Examine a life, fire, auto, or health insurance policy that you or a friend or relative holds. Select one that is fairly complex. Study the policy for jargon, confusing language, long sentences, and unclear antecedents. Evaluate its format, print size, paper and print quality, amount of white space, and use of headings. Does it have an index or glossary? Are difficult terms defined? How easy is it to find specifics, should a policyholder want to check something?

In addition to the data you collect from your own examination of the policy, Urban Life gives you the following data from a recent policyholder survey:

Response to statement: "I am able to read and understand the language and provisions of my policy."

Age Group	Strongly Agree	Agree	Undecided	Disagree	Strongly Disagree
18–34	2%	9%	34%	41%	14%
35–49	2	17	38	33	10
50–64	1	11	22	35	31
65+	1	2	17	47	33

Your Task. Prepare a report for Neal Skapura, vice president, Urban Life Insurance Company, discussing your analysis, conclusions, and recommendations for improving its basic policy.

FIGURE 10.18   • **Intercultural Interview Topics and Questions**

Social Customs

1. How do people react to strangers? Friendly? Hostile? Reserved?

2. How do people greet each other?

3. What are the appropriate manners when you enter a room? Bow? Nod? Shake hands with everyone?

4. How are names used for introductions? Is it appropriate to inquire about one's occupation or family?

5. What are the attitudes toward touching?

6. How does one express appreciation for an invitation to another's home? Bring a gift? Send flowers? Write a thank-you note? Are any gifts taboo?

7. Are there any customs related to how or where one sits?

8. Are any facial expressions or gestures considered rude?

9. How close do people stand when talking?

10. What is the attitude toward punctuality in social situations? In business situations?

11. What are acceptable eye contact patterns?

12. What gestures indicate agreement? Disagreement?

Family Life

1. What is the basic unit of social organization? Basic family? Extended family?

2. Do women work outside of the home? In what occupations?

Housing, Clothing, and Food

1. Are there differences in the kind of housing used by different social groups? Differences in location? Differences in furnishings?

2. What occasions require special clothing?

3. Are some types of clothing considered taboo?

4. What is appropriate business attire for men? For women?

5. How many times a day do people eat?

6. What types of places, food, and drink are appropriate for business entertainment? Where is the seat of honor at a table?

Class Structure

1. Into what classes is society organized?

2. Do racial, religious, or economic factors determine social status?

3. Are there any minority groups? What is their social standing?

Political Patterns

1. Are there any immediate threats to the political survival of the country?

2. How is political power manifested?

3. What channels are used for expression of popular opinion?

4. What information media are important?

5. Is it appropriate to talk politics in social situations?

Religion and Folk Beliefs

1. To which religious groups do people belong? Is one predominant?

2. Do religious beliefs influence daily activities?

3. Which places have sacred value? Which objects? Which events?

4. How do religious holidays affect business activities?

Economic Institutions

1. What are the country's principal products?

2. Are workers organized in unions?

3. How are businesses owned? By family units? By large public corporations? By the government?

4. What is the standard work schedule?

5. Is it appropriate to do business by telephone?

6. How has technology affected business procedures?

7. Is participatory management used?

8. Are there any customs related to exchanging business cards?

9. How is status shown in an organization? Private office? Secretary? Furniture?

10. Are businesspeople expected to socialize before conducting business?

Value Systems

1. Is competitiveness or cooperation more prized?

2. Is thrift or enjoyment of the moment more valued?

3. Is politeness more important than factual honesty?

4. What are the attitudes toward education?

5. Do women own or manage businesses? If so, how are they treated?

6. What are your people's perceptions of Americans? Do Americans offend you? What has been hardest for you to adjust to in America? How could Americans make this adjustment easier for you?

10.15 Formal Report: Fast-Food Checkup

The national franchising headquarters for a fast-food chain has received complaints about the service, quality, and cleanliness of one of its restaurants in your area. You have been sent to inspect and to report on what you see.

Your Task. Select a nearby fast-food restaurant. Visit on two or more occasions. Make notes about how many customers were served, how quickly they received their food, and how courteously they were treated. Observe the number of employees and supervisors working. Note the cleanliness of observable parts of the restaurant. Inspect the restroom as well as the exterior and surrounding grounds. Sample the food. Your boss is a stickler for details; she has no use for general statements such as *The restroom was not clean.* Be specific. Draw conclusions. Are the complaints justified? If improvements are necessary, make recommendations. Address your report to Samantha M. Murray, President.

INFOTRAC   **WEB**

10.16 Formal Report: Consumer Product Investigation

Study a consumer product that you might consider buying. Are you, or is your family or your business, interested in purchasing a DVD player, computer, digital camera, espresso machine, car, SUV, hot tub, or some other product?

Your Task. Use at least five primary and five secondary sources in researching your topic. Your primary research will be in the form of interviews with individuals (owners, users, salespeople, technicians) in a position to comment on attributes of your product. Secondary research will be in the form of print or electronic sources, such as magazine articles, owner manuals, and Web sites. Be sure to use InfoTrac and the Web to find appropriate articles. Your report should analyze and discuss at least three comparable models or versions of the target product. Decide what criteria you will use to compare the models, such as price, features, warranty, service, and so forth. The report should include these components: letter of transmittal, table of contents, executive summary, introduction (including background, purpose, scope of the study, and research methods), findings (organized by comparison criteria), summary of findings, conclusions, recommendations, and bibliography. Address the report to your instructor. You may work individually, in pairs, or in teams.

INFOTRAC   **WEB**

10.17 Formal Report: Communication Skills on the Job

Collect information regarding communication skills used by individuals in a particular career field (accounting, management, marketing, office administration, paralegal, and so forth). Interview three or more individuals in a specific occupation in that field. Determine how much and what kind of writing they do. Do they make oral presentations? How much time do they spend in telephone communication? Do they use e-mail? If so, how much and for what? What other technology do they use for communication? What recommendations do they have for training for this position?

Your Task. Write a report that discusses the findings from your interviews. What conclusions can you draw regarding communication skills in this field? What recommendations would you make for individuals entering this field? Your instructor may ask you to research the perception of businesspeople over the past ten years regarding the communication skills of employees. To gather such data, conduct library or online research.

10.18 More Proposal and Report Topics

A list with over 90 report topics is available at the companion site for this book (*http://guffey.swlearning.com*). The topics are divided into the following categories: accounting, finance, human resources, marketing, information systems, management, and general business/education/campus issues. You can collect information for many of these reports by using InfoTrac and the Web. Your instructor may assign them as individual or team projects. All involve critical thinking in organizing information, drawing conclusions, and making recommendations. The topics include assignments appropriate for proposals, business plans, and formal reports.

GRAMMAR/MECHANICS CHECKUP—10

Apostrophes

Review Sections 2.20–2.22 in the Grammar/Mechanics Handbook. Then study each of the following statements. Underscore any inappropriate form. Write a correction in the space provided and record the number of the G/M principle(s) illustrated. If a sentence is correct, write *C*. When you finish, compare your responses with those at the back of the book. If your answers differ, study carefully the principles shown in parentheses.

years'　　　　(2.20b)　　　　**Example**　　In just two <u>years</u> time, Marti earned her M.B.A. degree.

1. Amanda Sullivans proposal was accepted.

2. The company plans to double its earnings in three years time.

3. All employees in the Human Resources Department must take their two weeks vacation before January 1.

4. The attorneys agreed that Judge Millers comments were justified.

5. Several employees records were accidentally removed from the files.

6. The last witness testimony was the most convincing to the jury members.

7. Lisas smoking led to health problems.

8. I always get my moneys worth at my favorite restaurant.

9. Three local companies went out of business last month.

10. In one months time we hope to have our new Web site up and running.

11. I need my boss signature on this expense claim.

12. Only one legal secretaries document was error-free.

13. Five applicants will be interviewed on Friday.

14. My companys stock price rose dramatically last month.

15. In three months several businesses opening hours will change.

GRAMMAR/MECHANICS CHALLENGE—10

The following executive summary has faults in grammar, punctuation, spelling, number form, wordiness, and word use. Correct the errors with standard proofreading marks (see Appendix B) or revise the message online at **Guffey Xtra!** When you finish, your instructor may show you the revised version of this summary.

EXECUTIVE SUMMARY

Problem

The U.S. tuna industry must expand it's markets abroad particularly in regard to Japan. One of the largest consumer's of tuna in the world. Although consumption of tuna is decreasing in the United States they are increasing in Japan. The problem that is for the american tuna industry is developing apropriate marketing strategies to boost its current sale's in Japanese markets. Even tho Japan produces much of it's tuna domesticly, they must still relie on imported tuna to meet costumer demand.

Summary of Findings

This report analyzes the Japanese market which currently consumes six hundred thousand tons of tuna per year, and is growing rapidly. In Japan, tuna is primarilly used for sashimi (raw fish) and caned tuna. Tuna is consumed in the food service industry and in home's. Much of this tuna is supplied by imports which at this point in time total about 35% of sales. Our findings indicate that not only will this expand, but the share of imports will continue to grow. The trend is alarming to Japanese tuna industry leaders, because this important market, close to a $billion a year, is increasingly subject to the influence of foriegn imports. Declining catches by Japans own Tuna fleet as well as a sharp upward turn in food preference by affluent Japanese consumers, has contributed to this trend. The demand for sashimi alone in Japan has increased in the amount of 15% in the past two year's.

The U.S. tuna industry are in the perfect position to meet this demand. Fishing technique's has been developed that maximize catch rate's, while minimizing danger to the enviroment. Modern packaging procedures assure that the tuna reaches Japan in the freshest possible condition. Let it be said that Japanese consumers have rated the qaulity of American tuna high. Which has increased demand.

Recommendations

Based on our analisys we reccommend the following 6 marketing strategys for the U.S. Tuna industry.

1. Farm greater supplys of tuna to export.
2. Establish new fisheries around the World.
3. We should market our own value added products.
4. Sell fresh tuna direct to the Tokyo Central Wholesale market.
5. Sell to other Japanese markets also.
6. Direct sales should be made to Japanese Supermarket chains.

COMMUNICATION ⫴⫴⫴ WORKSHOP
TECHNOLOGY

TRASH OR TREASURE
ASSESSING THE QUALITY OF WEB DOCUMENTS

Many users think that documents found by a World Wide Web search tool have somehow been previously validated by a trustworthy authority. Others think that, because the Web is the most current and most accessible source of information, its documents must be the most reliable available. Wrong on both counts! Almost anyone with a computer and an Internet connection can publish almost anything on the Web. In every Web domain, reliable sites and unreliable ones compete for your attention.

Unlike the contents of the journals, magazines, and newspapers found in research-oriented libraries, the contents of many Web sites have not been carefully scrutinized by experienced editors and peer writers. To put it another way, print journals, magazines, and newspapers have traditionally featured reasonably unbiased, trustworthy articles; all too many Web sites, however, have another goal in mind. They are above all else interested in promoting a cause or in selling a product.

To use the Web meaningfully, you must learn to scrutinize carefully what you find in the documents it offers. The following checklist will help you distinguish Web trash from Web treasure.

Checklist for Assessing the Quality of a Web Page

Authority

- ☑ Who publishes or sponsors this Web page?
- ☑ Is the author or sponsor clearly identified?
- ☑ What makes the author or sponsor of the page an authority?
- ☑ Is information about the author or creator available?
- ☑ If the author is an individual, is he or she affiliated with a reputable organization?
- ☑ Is contact information, such as an e-mail address, available?
- ☑ To what domain (.com, .org, .edu, .gov, .net, .biz, .tv) does the site containing it belong?
- ☑ Is the site based in the United States or abroad (usually indicated by .uk, .ca, .ru, or other designation in the URL)?
- ☑ Is the site "personal" (often indicated by "~" or "%" in the site's URL)?

Currency

- ☑ What is the date of the Web page?
- ☑ When was the last time the Web page was updated?
- ☑ Is some of the information obviously out of date?

Content

- ☑ Is the purpose of the page to entertain, inform, convince, or sell?
- ☑ How would you classify this page (e.g., news, personal, advocacy, reference)?
- ☑ Is the objective or purpose of the Web page clear?
- ☑ Who is the intended audience of the page, based on its content, tone, and style?
- ☑ Can you judge the overall value of the content as compared with other resources on this topic?
- ☑ Does the content seem to be comprehensive (does it cover everything about the topic)?
- ☑ Is the site easy to navigate?

☑ What other sites does the Web page link to? These may give you a clue to the credibility of the target page.

☑ Does the page contain distracting graphics or fill your screen with unwanted pop-ups?

Accuracy

☑ Do the facts that are presented seem reliable to you?

☑ Do you find spelling, grammar, or usage errors?

☑ Does the page have broken links or graphics that don't load?

☑ Do you see any evidence of bias?

☑ Are footnotes or other documentation necessary? If so, have they been provided?

☑ If the site contains statistics or other data, are the source, date, and other pertinent information disclosed?

☑ Are advertisements clearly distinguished from content?

Career Application. As interns at a news-gathering service, you have been asked to assess the quality of the following Web sites. Which of these could you recommend as sources of valid information?

- Beef Nutrition (*http://www.beefnutrition.org*)

- Edmunds—Where Smart Car Buyers Start (*http://www.edmunds.com*)

- I Hate Windows (*http://www.ihatewindowsxp.com*)

- EarthSave International (*http://www.earthsave.org*)

- The Vegetarian Resource Group (*http://www.vrg.org*)

- The White House (*http://www.whitehouse.org*)

- The White House (*http://www.whitehouse.gov*)

- National Anti-Vivisection Society (*http://www.navs.org*)

- Dow: A Chemical Company on the Global Playground (*http://www.dowethics.com*)

- Smithsonian Institution (*http://www.si.edu*)

- Drudge Report (*http://www.drudgereport.com*)

- American Cancer Society (*http://www.cancer.org*)

- CraigsList (*http://www.craigslist.com*)

Your Task

If you are working with a team, divide the preceding list among team members. If you are working individually, select four of the sites. Answer the questions in the preceding checklist as you evaluate each site. Summarize your evaluation of each site in a memo report to your instructor or in team or class discussion.

DEVELOPING SPEAKING AND TECHNOLOGY SKILLS

CHAPTER 11

COMMUNICATING IN PERSON, IN MEETINGS, BY TELEPHONE, AND DIGITALLY

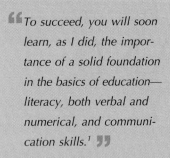

" To succeed, you will soon learn, as I did, the importance of a solid foundation in the basics of education— literacy, both verbal and numerical, and communication skills.[1] *"*

Alan Greenspan,
chairman, Federal Reserve

OBJECTIVES

- Discuss improving face-to-face workplace communication including using your voice as a communication tool.

- Specify procedures for promoting positive workplace relations through conversation.

- Review techniques for responding professionally to workplace criticism and for offering constructive criticism on the job.

- Outline procedures for planning, leading, and participating in productive business meetings, including professional etiquette techniques, resolving conflict, and handling dysfunctional group members.

- Explain ways to polish your professional telephone skills, including traditional phones and cell phones.

- List techniques for making the best use of voice mail, including proper voice mail etiquette.

- Describe a variety of digital workplace communication tools, including voice conferencing, videoconferencing, Web conferencing, instant messaging, wireless technology, and blogging.

Strong oral communication skills can help you be hired and succeed on the job.

Alan Greenspan, chairman of the Federal Reserve, would agree that oral communication skills consistently rank at or near the top of competencies valued by employers. Companies are looking for employees who can interact successfully with customers, work smoothly with coworkers, and provide meaningful feedback to managers. Expressing yourself well and communicating effectively with others are skills that are critical to job placement, workplace performance, career advancement, and organizational success.

Earlier in this book you studied the communication process, effective listening techniques, and nonverbal communication skills. Many intervening chapters helped you develop good writing skills. The next two chapters will round out your communication expertise by focusing on oral communication skills. In your business or professional

PHOTOS: © ROYALTY-FREE/CORBIS

career, you will be judged not only by what you say but also by the way you say it. In this chapter we'll help you become more successful when you communicate in person, in meetings, by telephone, and digitally.

IMPROVING FACE-TO-FACE WORKPLACE COMMUNICATION

One-dimensional communication technologies cannot replace the richness or effectiveness of face-to-face communication.

Because today's technologies provide many alternate communication channels, you may think that face-to-face communication is no longer essential or even important in business and professional transactions. You've already learned that e-mail is now the preferred communication channel because it is faster, cheaper, and easier than telephone, mail, or fax. Yet, despite their popularity and acceptance, alternate communication technologies can't replace the richness or effectiveness of face-to-face communication.[2] Imagine that you want to tell your boss how you solved a problem. Would you settle for a one-dimensional phone call, a fax, or an e-mail when you could step into her office and explain in person?

Face-to-face conversation has many advantages. It allows you to be persuasive and expressive because you can use your voice and body language to make a point. You are less likely to be misunderstood because you can read feedback and make needed adjustments. In conflict resolution, you can reach a solution more efficiently and cooperate to create greater levels of mutual benefit when communicating face-to-face.[3] Moreover, people want to see each other to satisfy a deep human need for social interaction. For numerous reasons communicating in person remains the most effective of all communication channels. In this chapter you'll explore helpful business and professional interpersonal speaking techniques, starting with viewing your voice as a communication tool. You'll also explore ways to use technology to communicate effectively in the workplace.

Using Your Voice as a Communication Tool

Like an actor, you can change your voice to make it a more powerful communication tool.

It's been said that language provides the words, but your voice is the music that makes words meaningful.[4] You may believe that a beautiful or powerful voice is unattainable. After all, this is the voice you were born with and it can't be changed. Actually, the voice is a flexible instrument. Actors hire coaches to help them eliminate or acquire accents or proper inflection for challenging roles. For example, Nicole Kidman, who

© MARK LENNIHAN/AP WIDE WORLD PHOTOS

One of the most important figures in popular culture, Oprah Winfrey has cultivated a distinct speaking style. To use your voice as a communication tool, pay attention to how you sound. Practice techniques that improve your pronunciation, voice quality, pitch, volume, and emphasis.

speaks with an Australian accent, often takes on other accents, including American Southern and South African, for film roles. Celebrities, business executives, and everyday people consult voice and speech therapists to help them shake bad habits or just help them speak so that they can be understood and not sound less intelligent than they are. Rather than consult a high-paid specialist, you can pick up useful tips for using your voice most effectively by learning how to control such elements as pronunciation, voice quality, pitch, volume, rate, and emphasis.

PRONUNCIATION

Proper pronunciation means saying words correctly and clearly with the accepted sounds and accented syllables.

Pronunciation involves saying words correctly and clearly with the accepted sounds and accented syllables. You'll be at a distinct advantage in your job if, through training and practice, you learn to pronounce words correctly. How can you improve your pronunciation skills? The best ways are to listen carefully to educated people, to look words up in the dictionary, and to practice.

VOICE QUALITY

The quality of your voice sends a nonverbal message to listeners. It identifies your personality and your mood. Some voices sound enthusiastic and friendly, conveying the impression of an upbeat person who is happy to be with the listener. But voices can also sound controlling, patronizing, slow-witted, angry, bored, or childish. This doesn't mean that the speaker necessarily has that attribute. It may mean that the speaker is merely carrying on a family tradition or pattern learned in childhood. To check your voice quality, record your voice and listen to it critically. Is it projecting a positive quality about you?

PITCH

Effective speakers use a relaxed, controlled, well-pitched voice to attract listeners to their message. *Pitch* refers to sound vibration frequency; that is, it indicates the highness or lowness of a sound. Voices are most engaging when they rise and fall in conversational tones. Flat, monotone voices are considered boring and ineffectual.

VOLUME AND RATE

Speaking in a moderately low-pitched voice at about 125 words a minute makes you sound pleasing and professional.

Volume indicates the degree of loudness or the intensity of sound. Just as you adjust the volume on your radio or television set, you should adjust the volume of your speaking to the occasion and your listeners. *Rate* refers to the pace of your speech. If you speak too slowly, listeners are bored and their attention wanders. If you speak too quickly, listeners may not be able to understand you. Most people normally talk at about 125 words a minute. Monitor the nonverbal signs of your listeners and adjust your volume and rate as needed.

EMPHASIS

By emphasizing or stressing certain words, you can change the meaning you are expressing. To make your message interesting and natural, use emphasis appropriately.

"Uptalk," in which sentences sound like questions, makes speakers seem weak and tentative.

Some speakers today are prone to *uptalk*. This is a habit of using a rising inflection at the end of a sentence resulting in a singsong pattern that makes statements sound like questions. Once used exclusively by teenagers, uptalk is increasingly found in the workplace with negative results. When statements sound like questions, speakers seem weak and tentative. Their messages lack conviction and authority. On the job, managers afflicted by uptalk may have difficulty convincing staff members to follow directions because their voice inflection implies that other valid options are available. If you want to sound confident and competent, avoid uptalk.

Promoting Positive Workplace Relations Through Conversation

In the workplace, conversations may involve giving and taking instructions, providing feedback, exchanging ideas on products and services, participating in performance appraisals, or engaging in small talk about such things as families and sports. Face-to-face conversation helps people work together harmoniously and feel that they are part of the larger organization. Our goal here is to provide you with several guidelines that promote positive workplace conversations, both in the office and at work-related social functions.

USE CORRECT NAMES AND TITLES

Although the world seems increasingly informal, it's still wise to use titles and last names when addressing professional adults (*Ms. O'Malley, Mr. Santiago*). In some organizations senior staff members will speak to junior employees on a first-name basis, but the reverse may not be encouraged. Probably the safest plan is to ask your superiors how they want to be addressed. Customers and others outside the organization should always be addressed initially by title and last name. Wait for an invitation to use first names.

When you meet strangers, do you have trouble remembering their names? You can improve your memory considerably if you associate the person with an object, place, color, animal, job, adjective, or some other memory hook. For example, *technology pro Gina, L.A. Matt, silver-haired Mr. Elliott, baseball fan John, programmer Tanya, traveler Ms. Choi.* The person's name will also be more deeply imbedded in your memory if you use it immediately after being introduced, in subsequent conversation, and when you part.

CHOOSE APPROPRIATE TOPICS

You will be most effective in workplace conversations if you use correct names and titles, choose appropriate topics, avoid negative and judgmental remarks, and give sincere and specific praise.

In some workplace activities, such as social gatherings or interviews, you will be expected to engage in small talk. Be sure to stay away from controversial topics with someone you don't know very well. Avoid politics, religion, or controversial current event items that can start heated arguments. To initiate appropriate conversations, read newspapers and listen to radio and TV shows discussing current events. Subscribe to e-newsletters that deliver relevant news to you via e-mail. Make a mental note of items that you can use in conversation, taking care to remember where you saw or heard the news items so that you can report accurately and authoritatively. Try not to be defensive or annoyed if others present information that upsets you.

AVOID NEGATIVE REMARKS

Workplace conversations are not the place to complain about your colleagues, your friends, the organization, or your job. No one enjoys listening to whiners. What's more, your criticism of others may come back to haunt you. A snipe at your boss or a complaint about a fellow worker may reach him or her, sometimes embellished or distorted with meanings you did not intend. Be circumspect in all negative judgments. Remember, some people love to repeat statements that will stir up trouble or set off internal workplace wars. Don't give them the ammunition!

LISTEN TO LEARN

In conversations with managers, colleagues, subordinates, and customers, train yourself to expect to learn something from what you are hearing. Being attentive is not only instructive but also courteous. Beyond displaying good manners, you'll probably find that your conversation partner has information that you don't have. Being receptive and listening with an open mind means not interrupting or prejudging. Let's say you want very much to be able to work at home for part of your workweek. You try to explain your ideas to your boss, but he cuts you off shortly after you start. He

Office parties and other social functions provide excellent opportunities to relax and to get to know your coworkers better. When attending these functions, keep your conversations positive and professional.

says, *It's out of the question; we need you here every day.* Suppose instead he says, *I have strong reservations about your telecommuting, but maybe you'll change my mind*; and he settles in to listen to your presentation. Even if your boss decides against your request, you will feel that your ideas were heard and respected.

GIVE SINCERE AND SPECIFIC PRAISE

The Greek philosopher Xenophon once said, *The sweetest of all sounds is praise.* Probably nothing promotes positive workplace relationships better than sincere and specific praise. Whether the compliments and appreciation are traveling upward to management, downward to workers, or horizontally to colleagues, everyone responds well to recognition. Organizations run more smoothly and morale is higher when people feel appreciated. In your workplace conversations, look for ways to recognize good work and good people. Try to be specific. Instead of *You did a good job in leading that meeting*, say something more specific, such as *Your excellent leadership skills certainly kept that meeting short, focused, and productive.*

ACT PROFESSIONALLY IN SOCIAL SITUATIONS

You will likely attend many work-related social functions during your career, including dinners, picnics, holiday parties, and other events. It's important to remember that your actions at these events can help or harm your career. Dress appropriately, and avoid or limit alcohol consumption. Choose appropriate conversation topics, and make sure that your voice and mannerisms communicate that you're glad to be there.

Accepting and Responding Professionally to Workplace Criticism

As much as most of us hate giving criticism, we dislike receiving it even more. Yet, it's normal to both give and receive criticism on the job. The criticism may be given informally, for example, during a casual conversation with a supervisor or coworker. Or the criticism may be given formally, for example, during a performance evaluation. The important thing is that you are able to accept and respond professionally when receiving criticism.

When being criticized, you may feel that you are being attacked. You can't just sit back and relax. Your heart beats faster, your temperature shoots up, your face reddens, and you respond with the classic "fight or flight" syndrome. You want to instantly retaliate or escape from the attacker. But focusing on your feelings distracts you from hearing the content of what is being said, and it prevents you from responding professionally. Some or all of the following suggestions will guide you in reacting positively to criticism so that you can benefit from it:

When being criticized, you should listen, paraphrase, and clarify what is said; if you agree, apologize or explain what you will do differently.

- **Listen without interrupting.** Even though you might want to protest, make yourself hear the speaker out.
- **Determine the speaker's intent.** Unskilled communicators may throw "verbal bricks" with unintended negative-sounding expressions. If you think the intent is positive, focus on what is being said rather than reacting to poorly chosen words.
- **Acknowledge what you are hearing.** Respond with a pause, a nod, or a neutral statement such as *I understand you have a concern.* This buys you time. Do not disagree, counterattack, or blame, which may escalate the situation and harden the speaker's position.
- **Paraphrase what was said.** In your own words restate objectively what you are hearing.
- **Ask for more information if necessary.** Clarify what is being said. Stay focused on the main idea rather than interjecting side issues.
- **Agree—if the comments are accurate.** If an apology is in order, give it. Explain what you plan to do differently. If the criticism is on target, the sooner you agree, the more likely you will be able to engender respect from the other person.

If you feel you are being criticized unfairly, disagree respectfully and constructively; look for a middle position.

- **Disagree respectfully and constructively—if you feel the comments are unfair.** After hearing the criticism, you might say, *May I tell you my perspective?* Or you could try to solve the problem by saying, *How can we improve this situation in a way you believe we can both accept?* If the other person continues to criticize, say, *I want to find a way to resolve your concern. When do you want to talk about it next?*
- **Look for a middle position.** Search for a middle position or a compromise. Be genial even if you don't like the person or the situation.

Learn what you can from workplace criticism to improve your performance on the job.

- **Learn from criticism.** Most work-related criticism is given with the best of intentions. You should welcome the opportunity to correct your mistakes and to learn from them. Responding positively and professionally to workplace criticism can help improve your job performance. As Winston Churchill said, "All men make mistakes, but only wise men learn from their mistakes."[5]

Offering Constructive Criticism on the Job

No one likes to receive criticism, and most of us don't like to give it either. But in the workplace, cooperative endeavors demand feedback and evaluation. How are we doing on a project? What went well? What failed? How can we improve our efforts? Today's workplace often involves team projects. As a team member, you will be called on to judge the work of others. In addition to working on teams, you can also expect to become a supervisor or manager one day. As such, you will need to evaluate subordinates. Good employees seek good feedback from their supervisors. They want and need timely, detailed observations about their work to reinforce what they do well and help them overcome weak spots. But making that feedback palatable and constructive is not always easy. Depending on your situation, you may find some or all of the following suggestions helpful when you must deliver constructive criticism:

Offering constructive criticism is easier if you plan what you will say, focus on improvement, offer to help, be specific, discuss the behavior and not the person, speak privately face-to-face, and avoid anger.

- **Mentally outline your conversation.** Think carefully about what you want to accomplish and what you will say. Find the right words and deliver them at the right time and in the right setting.
- **Generally, use face-to-face communication.** Most constructive criticism is better delivered in person rather than in e-mail messages or memos. Personal feedback offers an opportunity for the listener to ask questions and give explanations. Occasionally, however, complex situations may require a different strategy. You might prefer to write out your opinions and deliver them by telephone or in writing. A written document enables you to organize your thoughts, include all the details, and be sure of keeping your cool. Remember, though, that written documents create permanent records—for better or worse.

- **Focus on improvement.** Instead of attacking, use language that offers alternative behavior. Use phrases such as *Next time, you could . . . .*
- **Offer to help.** Criticism is accepted more readily if you volunteer to help in eliminating or solving the problem.
- **Be specific.** Instead of a vague assertion such as *Your work is often late*, be more specific: *The specs on the Riverside job were due Thursday at 5 p.m., and you didn't hand them in until Friday.* Explain how the person's performance jeopardized the entire project.
- **Avoid broad generalizations.** Don't use words such as *should, never, always*, and other encompassing expressions as they may cause the listener to shut down and become defensive.
- **Discuss the behavior, not the person.** Instead of *You seem to think you can come to work any time you want*, focus on the behavior: *Coming to work late means that we have to fill in with someone else until you arrive.*
- **Use the word *we* rather than *you.*** *We need to meet project deadlines* is better than saying. *You need to meet project deadlines.* Emphasize organizational expectations rather than personal ones. Avoid sounding accusatory.
- **Encourage two-way communication.** Even if well-planned, criticism is still hard to deliver. It may surprise or hurt the feelings of the employee. Consider ending your message with, *It can be hard to hear this type of feedback. If you would like to share your thoughts, I'm listening.*
- **Avoid anger, sarcasm, and a raised voice.** Criticism is rarely constructive when tempers flare. Plan in advance what you will say and deliver it in low, controlled, and sincere tones.
- **Keep it private.** Offer praise in public; offer criticism in private. "Setting an example" through public criticism is never a wise management policy.

PLANNING AND PARTICIPATING IN PRODUCTIVE BUSINESS AND PROFESSIONAL MEETINGS

Because you can expect to attend many workplace meetings, learn to make them efficient, satisfying, and productive.

As businesses become more team oriented and management becomes more participatory, people are attending more meetings than ever. Despite heavy reliance on e-mail and the growing use of wireless devices to stay connected, meetings are still the most comfortable way to exchange information. Yet, many meetings are a waste of time. One survey showed that a quarter of U.S. workers would rather go to the dentist than attend a boring meeting.[6] Regardless, meetings are here to stay. Our task, then, is to make them efficient, satisfying, and productive.

Meetings consist of three or more individuals who gather to pool information, solicit feedback, clarify policy, seek consensus, and solve problems. For you, however, meetings have another important purpose. They represent opportunities. Because they are a prime tool for developing staff, they are career-critical. The inability to run an effective meeting can sink a career, warns *The Wall Street Journal*.[7] The head of a leadership training firm echoed this warning when he said, "If you can't orchestrate a meeting, you're of little use to the corporation."[8] At meetings, judgments are formed and careers are made. Therefore, instead of treating meetings as thieves of your valuable time, try to see them as golden opportunities to demonstrate your leadership, communication, and problem-solving skills. So that you can make the most of these opportunities, here are techniques for planning and conducting successful meetings. You will also learn how to be a valuable meeting participant.

Before the Meeting

Benjamin Franklin once said, "By failing to prepare, you are preparing to fail."[9] If you are in charge of a meeting, give yourself plenty of preparation time to guarantee the meeting's success. Before the meeting, determine your purpose, decide how and where to meet, organize an agenda, decide who to invite, and prepare the meeting location and materials.

DETERMINING YOUR PURPOSE

Call meetings only when necessary, and invite only key people.

Before you do anything else, you must decide the purpose of your meeting and whether a meeting is even necessary. No meeting should be called unless the topic is important, can't wait, and requires an exchange of ideas. If the flow of information is strictly one way and no immediate feedback will result, then don't schedule a meeting. For example, if people are merely being advised or informed, send an e-mail, memo, or letter. Leave a telephone or voice mail message, but don't call a costly meeting. Remember, the real expense of a meeting is the lost productivity of all the people attending. To decide whether the purpose of the meeting is valid, it's a good idea to consult the key people who will be attending. Ask them what outcomes are desired and how to achieve those goals. This consultation also sets a collaborative tone and encourages full participation.

DECIDING HOW AND WHERE TO MEET

Once you've determined that a meeting is necessary, you must decide whether to meet face-to-face or virtually. If you decide to meet face-to-face, reserve a meeting room. If you decide to meet virtually, make any necessary advance arrangements for your voice conference, videoconference, or Web conference. These electronic tools will be discussed later in the chapter.

ORGANIZING AN AGENDA

Before a meeting, pass out a meeting agenda showing topics to be discussed and other information.

Prepare an agenda of topics to be discussed during the meeting. Also include any reports or materials that participants should read in advance. For continuing groups, you might also include a copy of the minutes of the previous meeting. To keep meetings productive, limit the number of agenda items. Remember, the narrower the focus, the greater the chances for success. Consider putting items that will be completed quickly near the beginning of the agenda to give the group a sense of accomplishment. Save emotional topics for the end. You should distribute the agenda at least two days in advance of the meeting. A good agenda, as illustrated in Figure 11.1, covers the following information:
- Date and place of meeting
- Start time and end time
- Brief description of each topic, in order of priority, including names of individuals who are responsible for performing some action
- Proposed allotment of time for each topic
- Any premeeting preparation expected of participants

INVITING PARTICIPANTS

Problem-solving meetings should involve five or fewer people.

The number of meeting participants is determined by the purpose of the meeting, as shown in Figure 11.2. If the meeting purpose is motivational, such as an awards ceremony for sales reps of Mary Kay Cosmetics, then the number of participants is unlimited. But to make decisions, according to studies at 3M Corporation, the best number is five or fewer participants.[10] Ideally, those attending should be people who will make the decision and people with information necessary to make the decision. Also attending should be people who will be responsible for implementing the decision and representatives of groups who will benefit from the decision. Let's say, for example, that the CEO of sportswear manufacturer Timberland is strongly committed to community service. He wants his company to participate more fully in community service. So he might meet with managers, employee representatives, and community leaders to decide how his employees could volunteer to refurbish a school, build affordable housing, or volunteer at a clinic.[11]

PREPARING THE MEETING LOCATION AND MATERIALS

If you're meeting face-to-face, decide the layout of the room. To maximize collaboration and participation, try to arrange tables and chairs in a circle or a square so that all participants can see one another.[12] Set up any presentation equipment that

FIGURE 11.1   **Typical Meeting Agenda**

AGENDA
Quantum Travel International
Staff Meeting
October 13, 200x
1 to 2 p.m.
Conference Room, Fifth Floor

		Person	**Proposed Time**
I. Call to order; roll call			
II. Approval of agenda			
III. Approval of minutes from previous meeting			
IV. Committee reports			
	A. Web site update	Ben	5 minutes
	B. Tour packages	Robin	10 minutes
V. Old business			
	A. Equipment maintenance	Debra	5 minutes
	B. Client escrow accounts	Roya	5 minutes
	C. Internal newsletter	Jami	5 minutes
VI. New business			
	A. New accounts	Suang	5 minutes
	B. Pricing policy for trips	Marcus	15 minutes
VII. Announcements			
VIII. Chair's summary, adjournment			

will be needed. Make copies of documents that will be handed out during the meeting. Arrange for refreshments.

During the Meeting

Meetings can be less boring, more efficient, and more productive if leaders and participants recognize how to get the meeting started, move it along, handle conflict, and deal with dysfunctional participants. Whether you're the meeting leader or a participant, it's important to act professionally during the meeting. Figure 11.3 outlines etiquette tips for both meeting leaders and participants. Following are additional guidelines to adhere to during the meeting to guarantee its success.

GETTING THE MEETING STARTED

Start meetings on time and open with a brief introduction.

To avoid wasting time and irritating attendees, always start meetings on time—even if some participants are missing. Waiting for latecomers causes resentment and sets a bad precedent. For the same reasons, don't give a quick recap to anyone who

FIGURE 11.2   **Meeting Purpose and Number of Participants**

Purpose	Ideal Size
Intensive problem solving	5 or fewer
Problem identification	10 or fewer
Information reviews and presentations	30 or fewer
Motivational	Unlimited

These graphic designers hold weekly meetings in their loft office to brainstorm ideas to share with their current and future clients. Business meetings give groups a chance to collaborate to solve problems, make decisions, and come up with creative ideas. Whether you're meeting face-to-face or virtually, it's important to prepare ahead of time, to show up on time, and to contribute positively during the meeting.

© PHOTODISC COLLECTION/GETTY IMAGES

Meeting leaders and participants should follow professional meeting etiquette at all times.

arrives late. At the appointed time, open the meeting by having all participants introduce themselves if necessary. Then continue with a three- to five-minute introduction that includes the following:

- Goal and length of the meeting
- Background of topics or problems
- Possible solutions and constraints
- Tentative agenda
- Ground rules to be followed

FIGURE 11.3   • **Etiquette Checklist for Meeting Leaders and Participants**

Meeting Leader

© C SQUARED STUDIOS/PHOTODISC/GETTY IMAGES

✓ Start and end the meeting on time.
✓ Introduce yourself and urge participants to introduce themselves.
✓ Make everyone feel welcome and valued.
✓ Maintain control of the group members and discussion.
✓ Make sure that everyone participates.
✓ Stick to the agenda.
✓ Encourage everyone to follow the ground rules.
✓ Schedule breaks for longer meetings.

Meeting Participants

✓ Arrive on time and stay until the meeting ends, unless you've made prior arrangements to arrive late or leave early.
✓ Leave the meeting only for breaks and emergencies.
✓ Come to the meeting prepared.
✓ Turn off cell phones and pagers.
✓ Follow the ground rules.
✓ If you're on the agenda as a presenter, do not go over your allotted time.
✓ Do not exhibit nonverbal behavior that suggests you're bored, frustrated, angry, or negative in any way.
✓ Do not interrupt others or cut anyone off.
✓ Make sure your comments, especially negative comments, are about ideas, not people.
✓ Listen carefully to what other meeting participants are saying.
✓ Participate fully.
✓ Do not go off on tangents; be sure that you stick to the topic being discussed.
✓ Do not engage in side conversations.
✓ Clean up after yourself when leaving the meeting.
✓ Complete any follow-up work that you're assigned in a timely manner.

Ted Goff (www.tedgoff.com)

"Wow! This meeting lasted longer than I thought. It appears the year is now 2053."

A typical set of ground rules might include arriving on time, communicating openly, being supportive, listening carefully, participating fully, confronting conflict frankly, turning off cell phones and pagers, and following the agenda. Participants should also determine how decisions will be made. More formal groups follow parliamentary procedures based on Robert's Rules of Order. After establishing basic ground rules, the leader should ask whether participants agree thus far. The next step is to assign one attendee to take minutes and one to act as a recorder. The recorder stands at a flipchart or whiteboard and lists the main ideas being discussed and agreements reached.

MOVING THE MEETING ALONG

After the preliminaries, the leader should say as little as possible. Like a talk show host, an effective leader makes "sure that each panel member gets some air time while no one member steals the show."[13] Remember that the purpose of a meeting is to exchange views, not to hear one person, even the leader, do all the talking. If the group has one member who monopolizes, the leader might say, *Thanks, Gary, for that perspective, but please hold your next point while we hear how Rachel would respond to that.* This technique also encourages quieter participants to speak up.

Keep the meeting moving by avoiding issues that sidetrack the group.

To avoid allowing digressions to sidetrack the group, try generating a "Parking Lot" list. This is a list of important but divergent issues that should be discussed at a later time. Another way to handle digressions is to say, *Look, folks, we're veering off track here. Let's get back to the central issue of . . . .* It's important to adhere to the agenda and the time schedule. Equally important, when the group seems to have reached a consensus, is to summarize the group's position and check to see whether everyone agrees.

DEALING WITH CONFLICT

When a conflict develops between two members, allow each to make a complete case before the group.

Conflict is a normal part of every workplace. Although conflict may cause you to feel awkward and uneasy, conflict is not always negative. In fact, conflict in the workplace can even be desirable. When managed properly, conflict can improve decision making, clarify values, increase group cohesiveness, stimulate creativity, decrease tensions, and reduce dissatisfaction. Unresolved conflict, however, can destroy productivity and seriously reduce morale.

In meetings, conflict typically develops when people feel unheard or misunderstood. If two people are in conflict, the best approach is to encourage each to make a complete case while group members give their full attention. Let each one question the other. Then, the leader should summarize what was said, and the group should offer comments. The group may modify a recommendation or suggest alternatives before reaching consensus on a direction to follow. You'll find more suggestions for dealing with conflict in the Communication Workshop, "Eight Steps to Resolving Workplace Conflicts," at the end of this chapter.

HANDLING DYSFUNCTIONAL GROUP MEMBERS

When individuals are performing in a dysfunctional role (such as blocking discussion, monopolizing the conversation, attacking other speakers, joking excessively, not paying attention, or withdrawing), they should be handled with care and tact. The following specific techniques can help a meeting leader control some group members and draw others out.[14]

- **Lay down the rules in an opening statement.** Give a specific overall summary of topics, time allotment, and expected behavior. Warn that speakers who digress will be interrupted.

To control dysfunctional behavior, team leaders should establish rules and seat problem people strategically.

- **Seat potentially dysfunctional members strategically.** Experts suggest seating a difficult group member immediately next to the leader. It's easier to bypass a person in this position. Make sure the person with dysfunctional behavior is not seated in a power point, such as at the end of table or across from the leader.
- **Avoid direct eye contact.** In American society direct eye contact is a nonverbal signal that encourages talking. Thus, when asking a question of the group, look only at those whom you wish to answer.
- **Assign dysfunctional members specific tasks.** Ask a potentially disruptive person, for example, to be the group recorder.
- **Ask members to speak in a specific order.** Ordering comments creates an artificial, rigid climate and should be done only when absolutely necessary. But such a regimen ensures that everyone gets a chance to participate.
- **Interrupt monopolizers.** If a difficult member dominates a discussion, wait for a pause and then break in. Summarize briefly the previous comments or ask someone else for an opinion.
- **Encourage nontalkers.** Give only positive feedback to the comments of reticent members. Ask them direct questions about which you know they have information or opinions.
- **Give praise and encouragement** to those who seem to need it, including the distracters, the monopolizers, the blockers, and the withdrawn.

Ending the Meeting and Following Up

How do you know when to stop a meeting? Many factors determine when a meeting should be adjourned, including (1) when the original objectives have been accomplished, (2) when the group has reached an impasse, or (3) when the agreed-upon ending time occurs. To show respect for participants, the leader should be sure the meeting stops at the promised time. It may be necessary to table (postpone for another meeting) some unfinished agenda items. Concluding a meeting effectively helps participants recognize what was accomplished so that they feel that the meeting was worthwhile. Effective leaders perform a number of activities in ending a meeting and following up.

CONCLUDING THE MEETING

End the meeting with a summary of accomplishments and a review of action items; follow up by distributing meeting minutes and reminding participants of their assigned tasks.

When the agreed-upon stopping time arrives or when the objectives have been met, discussion should stop. The leader should summarize what has been decided and who is going to do what. Deadlines for action items should also be established. It may be necessary to ask people to volunteer to take responsibility for completing action items agreed to in the meeting. No one should leave the meeting without a full understanding of what was accomplished. One effective technique that encourages full participation is "once around the table." Everyone is asked to summarize briefly his or her interpretation of what was decided and what happens next. Of course, this closure technique works best with smaller groups.

An effective leader concludes by asking the group to set a time for the next meeting. The leader should also assure the group that a report will follow and thank participants for attending. Participants should vacate the meeting room once the meeting is over, especially if another group is waiting to enter. The room should be returned to a neat and orderly appearance.

DISTRIBUTING MINUTES

If minutes were taken during the meeting, they should be keyed in an appropriate format. You'll find guidelines for preparing meeting minutes in Chapter 9. Minutes should be distributed within a couple of days after the meeting. Send the minutes to all meeting participants and to anyone else who needs to know what was accomplished and discussed during the meeting.

COMPLETING ASSIGNED TASKS

It is the leader's responsibility to see that what was decided at the meeting is accomplished. The leader may need to call people to remind them of their assignments and also to volunteer to help them if necessary. Meeting participants should complete any assigned tasks by the agreed-upon deadline.

IMPROVING TELEPHONE, CELL PHONE, AND VOICE MAIL SKILLS

For most businesses, telephones—both traditional and wireless—are a primary contact with the outside world.

Despite the heavy reliance on e-mail, the telephone is still an extremely important piece of equipment in offices. With the addition of today's wireless technology, it doesn't matter whether you are in or out of the office. You can always be reached by phone. As a business communicator, you can be more productive, efficient, and professional by following some simple suggestions. In this chapter we'll focus on traditional telephone techniques as well as cell phone use and voice mail efficiency.

Making Telephone Calls Efficiently and Professionally

You can make productive telephone calls by planning an agenda, identifying the purpose, being cheerful and accurate, being professional and courteous, and avoiding rambling.

Before making a telephone call, decide whether the intended call is really necessary. Could you find the information yourself? If you wait a while, would the problem resolve itself? Perhaps your message could be delivered more efficiently by some other means. Some companies have found that telephone calls are often less important than the work they interrupted. Alternatives to telephone calls include instant messaging, e-mail, memos, or calls to voice mail systems. If you must make a telephone call, consider using the following suggestions to make it fully productive:

- **Plan a mini-agenda.** Have you ever been embarrassed when you had to make a second telephone call because you forgot an important item the first time? Before placing a call, jot down notes regarding all the topics you need to discuss. Following an agenda guarantees not only a complete call but also a quick one. You'll be less likely to wander from the business at hand while rummaging through your mind trying to remember everything.

- **Use a three-point introduction.** When placing a call, immediately (1) name the person you are calling, (2) identify yourself and your affiliation, and (3) give a brief explanation of your reason for calling. For example: *May I speak to Jeremy Johnson? This is Paula Soltani of Coughlin and Associates, and I'm seeking information about a software program called ZoneAlarm Internet Security.* This kind of introduction enables the receiving individual to respond immediately without asking further questions.

- **Be brisk if you are rushed.** For business calls when your time is limited, avoid questions such as *How are you?* Instead, say, *Lauren, I knew you'd be the only one who could answer these two questions for me.* Another efficient strategy is to set a "contract" with the caller: *Look, Lauren, I have only ten minutes, but I really wanted to get back to you.*

- **Be cheerful and accurate.** Let your voice show the same kind of animation that you radiate when you greet people in person. In your mind try to envision the individual answering the telephone. A smile can certainly affect the tone of your voice; therefore, even though the individual can't see you, smile at that person. Speak with a tone that is enthusiastic, respectful, and attentive. Moreover, be accurate about what you say. *Hang on a second; I'll be right back* rarely is true. It's better to say, *It may take me two or three minutes to get that information. Would you prefer to hold or have me call you back?*

- **Be professional and courteous.** Remember that you're representing yourself and your company when you make phone calls. Use professional vocabulary and courteous language. Say *thank you* and *please* during your conversations. Don't eat, drink, or chew gum while talking on the phone, which can often be heard

on the other end. Articulate your words clearly so that the receiver can understand you. Avoid doing other work during the phone call so that you can focus entirely on the conversation.
- **Bring it to a close.** The responsibility for ending a call lies with the caller. This is sometimes difficult to do if the other person rambles on. You may need to use suggestive closing language, such as the following: (1) *I've certainly enjoyed talking with you,* (2) *I've learned what I needed to know, and now I can proceed with my work,* (3) *Thanks for your help,* (4) *I must go now, but may I call you again in the future if I need . . .?* or (5) *Should we talk again in a few weeks?*
- **Avoid telephone tag.** If you call someone who's not in, ask when it would be best for you to call again. State that you will call at a specific time—and do it. If you ask a person to call you, give a time when you can be reached—and then be sure you are in at that time.
- **Leave complete voice mail messages.** Remember that there's no rush when you leave a voice mail message. Always enunciate clearly. And be sure to provide a complete message, including your name, telephone number, and the time and date of your call. Explain your purpose so that the receiver can be ready with the required information when returning your call.

Receiving Telephone Calls Professionally

With a little forethought you can project a professional image and make your telephone a productive, efficient work tool. Developing good telephone manners also reflects well on you and on your organization.
- **Answer promptly and courteously.** Try to answer the phone on the first or second ring if possible. Smile as you pick up the phone.
- **Identify yourself immediately.** In answering your telephone or someone else's, provide your name, title or affiliation, and a greeting. For example, *Juan Salinas, Digital Imaging Corporation. How may I help you?* Force yourself to speak clearly and slowly. Remember that the caller may be unfamiliar with what you are saying and fail to recognize slurred syllables.
- **Be responsive and helpful.** If you are in a support role, be sympathetic to callers' needs and show that you understand their situations. Instead of *I don't know,* try *That's a good question; let me investigate.* Instead of *We can't do that,* try *That's a tough one; let's see what we can do.* Avoid *No* at the beginning of a sentence. It sounds especially abrasive and displeasing because it suggests total rejection.
- **Be cautious when answering calls for others.** Be courteous and helpful, but don't give out confidential information. It's better to say, *She's away from her desk* or *He's out of the office* than to report a colleague's exact whereabouts. Also be tight lipped about sharing company information with strangers. Security experts insist that employees answering telephones must become guardians of company information.[15]
- **Take messages carefully.** Few things are as frustrating as receiving a potentially important phone message that is illegible. Repeat the spelling of names and verify telephone numbers. Write messages legibly and record their time and date. Promise to give the messages to intended recipients, but don't guarantee return calls.
- **Leave the line respectfully.** If you must put a call on hold, let the caller know and give an estimate of how long you expect the call to be on hold. Give the caller the option of holding. Say *Would you prefer to hold, or would you like me to call you back?* If the caller is on hold for a long period of time, check back periodically so that the caller doesn't think that he or she has been forgotten or that the call has been disconnected.
- **Explain what you're doing when transferring calls.** Give a reason for transferring, and identify the extension to which you are directing the call in case the caller is disconnected.

You can improve your telephone reception skills by identifying yourself, being responsive and helpful, and taking accurate messages.

Cell phones are now used globally to help business communicators keep in touch with colleagues and clients, whether they're in the office or on the road. U.S. businesspeople traveling abroad can purchase or lease global cell phones that allow worldwide roaming.[16]

© DIGITAL VISION/GETTY IMAGES

Using Cell Phones for Business

Cell phones are essential workplace communication tools, but they must be used without offending others.

Cell phones enable you to conduct business from virtually anywhere at any time. More than a plaything or a mere convenience, the cell phone has become an essential part of communication in today's workplace. The U.S. government reported that in late 2004, for the first time, the number of U.S. cell phone users surpassed the number of landline telephone users, and the number of cell phone users has continued to grow.[17] Today's smart cell phones are used for much more than making and receiving calls. High-end cell phones can be used to store contact information, make to-do lists, keep track of appointments and important dates, send and receive e-mail, send and receive text and multimedia messages, get news and stock quotes from the Internet, take pictures and videos, synchronize with Outlook and other software applications, and many other functions.

With so many people using cell phones, it's important to understand proper use and etiquette. How are they best used? When is it acceptable to take calls? Where should calls be made? Most of us have experienced thoughtless and rude cell phone behavior. To avoid offending, smart business communicators practice cell phone etiquette, as outlined in Figure 11.4. In projecting a professional image, they are careful about location, time, and volume in relation to their cell phone calls.

LOCATION

Use good judgment in placing or accepting cell phone calls. Some places are dangerous or inappropriate for cell phone use. Turn off your cell phone when entering a conference room, interview, theater, place of worship, or any other place where it could be distracting or disruptive to others. Taking a call in a crowded room or bar makes it difficult to hear and reflects poorly on you as a professional. Taking a call while driving can be dangerous, leading some states to ban cell phone use while driving. A bad connection also makes a bad impression. Static or dropped signals create frustration and miscommunication. Don't sacrifice professionalism for the sake of a garbled phone call. It's smarter to turn off your phone in an area where the signal is weak and when you are likely to have interference. Use voice mail and return the call when conditions are better. Also be careful about using your cell phone to discuss private or confidential company information.

FIGURE 11.4 ┤• **Practicing Courteous and Responsible Cell Phone Use**

Business communicators find cell phones to be enormously convenient and real time-savers. But rude users have generated a backlash against inconsiderate callers. Here are specific suggestions for using cell phones safely and responsibly:

- **Be courteous to those around you.** Don't force those near you to hear your business. Don't step up to a service counter, such as at a restaurant, bank, or post office, while talking on your cell phone. Don't carry on a cell phone conversation while someone is waiting on you. Think first of those in close proximity instead of those on the other end of the phone. Apologize and make amends gracefully for occasional cell phone blunders.
- **Observe wireless-free quiet areas.** Don't allow your cell phone to ring in theaters, restaurants, museums, classrooms, important meetings, and similar places. Use the cell phone's silent/vibrating ring option. A majority of travelers prefer that cell phone conversations *not* be held on most forms of public transportation.
- **Speak in low, conversational tones.** Microphones on cell phones are quite sensitive, thus making it unnecessary to talk loudly. Avoid "cell yell."
- **Take only urgent calls.** Make full use of your cell phone's caller ID feature to screen incoming calls. Let voice mail take those calls that are not pressing.
- **Drive now, talk later.** Pull over if you must make a call. Talking while driving increases the chance of accidents four-fold, about the same as driving while intoxicated. Some companies are implementing cell phone policies that prohibit employees from using cell phones while driving for company business.
- **Choose a professional ringtone.** These days you can download a variety of ringtones, from classical to rap to the *Star Wars* theme. Choose a ringtone that will sound professional.

TIME

Often what you are doing is more important than whatever may come over the air waves to you on your phone. For example, when you are having an important discussion with a business partner, customer, or superior, it is rude to allow yourself to be interrupted by an incoming call. It's also poor manners to practice multitasking while on the phone. What's more, it's dangerous. Although you might be able to read and print out e-mail messages, deal with a customer at the counter, and talk on your cell phone simultaneously, it's impolite and risky. Lack of attention results in errors. If a phone call is important enough to accept, then it's important enough to stop what you are doing and attend to the conversation.

VOLUME

Many people raise their voices when using their cell phones. "Cell yell" results, much to the annoyance of anyone nearby. Raising your voice is unnecessary since most phones have excellent microphones that can pick up even a whisper. If the connection is bad, louder volume will not improve the sound quality. As in face-to-face conversations, a low, modulated voice sounds professional and projects the proper image.

Making the Best Use of Voice Mail

Because telephone calls can be disruptive, most businesspeople are making extensive use of voice mail to intercept and screen incoming calls. Voice mail links a telephone system to a computer that digitizes and stores incoming messages. Some systems also

© Randy Glasbergen.
www.glasbergen.com

"Thank you for calling. Please leave a message. In case I forget to check my messages, please send your message as an audio file to my e-mail, then send me a fax to remind me to check my e-mail, then call back to remind me to check my fax."

provide functions such as automated attendant menus, allowing callers to reach any associated extension by pushing specific buttons on a touch-tone telephone.

Voice mail is quite efficient for message storage. Because as many as half of all business calls require no discussion or feedback, the messaging capabilities of voice mail can mean huge savings for businesses. Incoming information is delivered without interrupting potential receivers and without all the niceties that most two-way conversations require. Stripped of superfluous chitchat, voice mail messages allow communicators to focus on essentials. Voice mail also eliminates telephone tag, inaccurate message-taking, and time-zone barriers.

However, voice mail should not be overused. Individuals who screen all incoming calls cause irritation, resentment, and needless telephone tag. Both receivers and callers can use etiquette guidelines to make voice mail work most effectively for them.

> Voice mail eliminates telephone tag, inaccurate message-taking, and time-zone barriers; it also allows communicators to focus on essentials.

ON THE RECEIVER'S END

Your voice mail should project professionalism and should provide an efficient mechanism for your callers to leave messages for you. Here are some voice mail etiquette tips to follow:

- **Don't overuse voice mail.** Don't use voice mail as a means to avoid taking phone calls. It's better to answer calls yourself than to let voice mail messages build up.
- **Set the number of rings appropriately.** Set your voice mail to ring as few times as possible before picking up. This shows respect for your callers' time.
- **Prepare a professional, concise, friendly greeting.** Make your mechanical greeting sound warm and inviting, both in tone and content. Your greeting should be in your own voice, not a computer-generated voice. Identify yourself and your organization so that callers know they have reached the right number. Thank the caller and briefly explain that you are unavailable. Invite the caller to leave a message or, if appropriate, call back. Here's a typical voice mail greeting: *Hi! This is Larry Lopez of Proteus Software, and I appreciate your call. You've reached my voice mailbox because I'm either working with customers or talking on another line at the moment. Please leave your name, number, and reason for calling so that I can be prepared when I return your call.* Give callers an idea of when you will be available, such as *I'll be back at 2:30* or *I'll be out of my office until Wednesday, May 20.* If you screen your calls as a time-management technique, try this message: *I'm not near my phone right now, but I should be able to return calls after 3:30.*
- **Test your message.** Call your number and assess your message. Does it sound inviting? Sincere? Professional? Understandable? Are you pleased with your tone? If not, record your message again until it conveys the professional image you want.
- **Change your message.** Update your message regularly, especially if you travel for your job.
- **Respond to messages promptly.** Check your messages regularly, and try to return all voice mail messages within one business day.
- **Plan for vacations and other extended absences.** If you will not be picking up voice mail messages for an extended period, let callers know how they can reach someone else if needed.

ON THE CALLER'S END

When leaving a voice mail message, you should follow these tips:

- **Be prepared to leave a message.** Before calling someone, be prepared for voice mail. Decide what you're going to say and what information you're going to include in your message. If necessary, write your message down before calling.
- **Leave a concise, thorough message.** When leaving a message, always identify yourself using your complete name and affiliation. Mention the date and time you called and a brief explanation of your reason for calling. Always leave a

complete phone number, including the area code, even if you think the receiver already has it. Tell the receiver the best time to return your call. Don't ramble.

- **Use a professional and courteous tone.** When leaving a message, make sure that your tone is professional, enthusiastic, and respectful. Smile when leaving a message to add warmth to your voice.
- **Speak slowly and articulate.** You want to make sure that your receiver will be able to understand your message. Speak slowly and pronounce your words carefully, especially when providing your phone number. The receiver should be able to write information down without having to replay your message.
- **Be careful with confidential information.** Don't leave confidential or private information in a voice mail message. Remember that anyone could gain access to this information.
- **Don't make assumptions.** If you don't receive a call back within a day or two after leaving a message, don't get angry or frustrated. Assume that the message wasn't delivered or that it couldn't be understood. Call back and leave another message, or send the person an e-mail message.

OTHER DIGITAL COMMUNICATION TOOLS IN THE WORKPLACE

As you learned in Chapter 1, technology has dramatically changed the way we communicate in the workplace. In addition to e-mail, telephones, and cell phones, many tools allow businesspeople to react rapidly, share information, and work together at any time of the day and from anywhere in the world. Whether in the office, on the road, or halfway around the world, business communicators can be connected to virtual team members, office colleagues, company databases, and application programs. Some of the most significant technologies revolve around conferencing tools.

VOICE CONFERENCING

Digital communication tools, such as voice conferencing, videoconferencing, Web conferencing, instant messaging, wireless technology, and blogging, have become the norm in today's global business environment.

One of the simplest communication tools is *voice conferencing* (also called *audioconferencing*, *teleconferencing*, or simply *conference calling*). One or more people in a work area use an enhanced speakerphone to confer with others by telephone. Voice conferencing enables people at both ends to speak and be heard simultaneously. Thanks to cell phones, you can even participate in a conference call from an airplane or your home. Although voice conferencing is not as glitzy as other collaboration tools, it is the mainstay of the entire teleconferencing industry. Because it is simple and effective, more people use it than any other of the collaboration meeting tools.

Videoconferencing allows business communicators to take part in meetings with globally dispersed colleagues in real time. Today videoconferencing is used by companies, educational institutions, and governments around the world.

© TRIANGLE IMAGES/DIGITAL VISION/GETTY IMAGES

VIDEOCONFERENCING

If meeting participants need to see each other, they use *videoconferencing*. This tool combines video, audio, and communications networking technologies for real-time interaction. Participants generally meet in special conference rooms equipped with cameras and screens for transmitting images and documents. Because participants do not have to journey to distant meetings, organizations reduce travel expenses, travel time, and employee fatigue. Increasingly, however, many business communicators prefer desktop videoconferencing because they can do it from their own PCs. Videoconferencing is widely used for business, training, and educational purposes. It allows groups of people to see and communicate with each other from anywhere in the world.

WEB CONFERENCING

Participants can take part in "real life" meetings from the comfort of their offices. Web conferencing is similar to videoconferencing but usually without the transmission of pictures of the participants. They use their computers to access an online virtual meeting room where they can present PowerPoint slides or share spreadsheets or Word documents, just as they might do in a face-to-face meeting. They can even demonstrate products and make changes in real time during a meeting. Software such as WebEx and Microsoft Live Meeting makes Web conferencing easy and effective. Notice how SideKick used Web conferencing to meet virtually and design a new athletic shoe, as shown in Figure 11.5.

INSTANT MESSAGING (IM)

Once used almost exclusively by teenagers, instant messaging is now increasingly accepted as a communication tool in the workplace. A recent Nemertes Research survey found that 73 percent of businesses said their employees already use instant messaging or will within the next year.[18] In our fast-paced world, many business communicators find that even e-mail is not swift enough. Instead, they rely on instant messaging to deliver messages immediately and directly to the receiver's desktop. Instant messaging is especially useful for back-and-forth online conversations, such as a customer communicating with a tech support person to solve a problem. Businesses

---

FIGURE 11.5   • **Web Conferencing in Practice**

Here's how SideKick Enterprises sets up a virtual meeting to design a new athletic shoe.

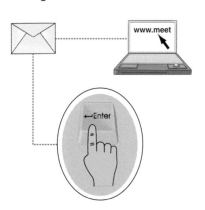

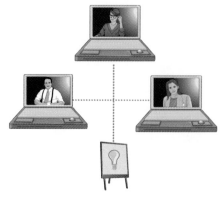

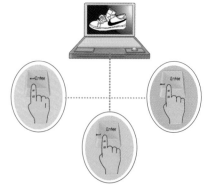

2. Virtual Meeting. When the Web conference begins, participants see live videos of each others' faces on their computer screens. They look at photos of athletic shoes, share ideas, sketch designs on a shared "virtual whiteboard," and review contract terms.

1. E-Mail Contact. Matt M., president of SideKick, a shoe company located in Los Angeles, sends an e-mail to Lisa G., chief designer at NYConcepts, located in New York, to discuss a new athletic shoe. The e-mail includes a date for the meeting and a link to launch the session.

3. Design Collaboration. NYConcepts designers and SideKick managers use peer-to-peer software that allows them to share spaces on each others' computers. The software enables them to take turns modifying the designs, and it also tracks all the changes.

use instant messaging to communicate with customers, colleagues, and clients across the world or down the hall. Sending an instant message is faster than e-mail and cheaper than a phone call, two factors that have led to its popularity.

WIRELESS TECHNOLOGY

Through the use of wireless technology, business communicators can stay in touch with anyone anywhere in the world. Instead of being tied to a desktop PC or land-line phone, many business communicators now carry wireless laptops, cell phones, personal digital assistants (PDAs), and handheld computers. They use these tools to read and send e-mail, conduct Web research, create and share files, and use application programs. Wireless Fidelity, better known as Wi-Fi, makes wireless communication possible through the use of local area networks that use high-frequency radio signals or infrared waves to send and receive data. Wi-Fi "hot spots" can now be found across the United States and internationally.

WEBLOGS (BLOGS)

You learned about weblogs, or blogs, in Chapter 10. A type of interactive online journal, blogs allow companies of all sizes to share information, promote products, respond to customer concerns, and monitor competitors' actions. Corporations, small businesses, educational institutions, and government agencies worldwide are now using blogs to exchange information with employees, customers, students, and the general public. For example, IBM, American Airlines, and DaimlerChrysler employees around the world use intranet blogs to discuss business strategies, solve problems, and communicate with management.[19] The Web site Bluefly.com uses its blog, Flypaper.bluefly.com, to post fashion-related information and news items aimed at fashion-conscious women, which has proven to be beneficial to sales. Melissa Payner, CEO of Bluefly, reports that visitors to the blog, who then click over to Bluefly, are more likely to purchase something than those who browse to Bluefly.com directly.[20]

◆ SUMMING UP AND LOOKING FORWARD

In this chapter you studied how to improve communication in the workplace. You learned how to use your voice as a communication tool, how to promote positive workplace relations through conversation, and how to give and take constructive criticism on the job. The chapter also presented techniques for planning and participating in productive business and professional meetings, both face-to-face and virtual. You learned how to polish your professional telephone, cell phone, and voice mail skills, including making and receiving productive telephone calls. Finally, you learned about a variety of tools available to communicate digitally in the workplace, including voice conferencing, videoconferencing, Web conferencing, instant messaging, wireless technology, and blogging.

The next chapter covers an additional facet of oral communication, that of making presentations. Learning to speak before groups is important to your career success because you will probably be expected to do so occasionally. You'll learn helpful techniques and get practice applying them so that you can control stage fright in making polished presentations.

◆ CRITICAL THINKING

1. Is face-to-face communication always preferable to one-dimensional channels of communication such as e-mail and fax? Why or why not?

2. In what ways can conflict be a positive force in the workplace?

3. How can business meetings help you advance your career?

4. Why do so many people hate voice mail when it is an efficient system for recording messages?

5. Commentators are constantly predicting that new communications media will destroy old ones. Do you think e-mail and instant messaging will kill off phone calls? Why or why not?

CHAPTER REVIEW

6. Why do employers want to hire employees with excellent communication skills?

7. Name five elements that you control in using your voice as a communication tool.

8. What topics should be avoided in workplace conversations?

9. If you are criticized at work, what are nine ways you can respond and benefit professionally?

10. List six techniques that you consider most important when delivering constructive criticism.

11. What is a meeting agenda and what should it include?

12. List ten etiquette guidelines for meeting participants that you feel are most important.

13. List eight tactics that a meeting leader can use in dealing with dysfunctional participants.

14. Name six ways callers can practice courteous and responsible cell phone use.

15. List and describe six tools that can be used to communicate digitally in the workplace.

ACTIVITIES AND CASES

TEAM

11.1 Voice Quality

Recording your voice gives you a chance to learn how your voice sounds to others and provides an opportunity for you to improve its effectiveness. Don't be surprised if you fail to recognize your own voice.

Your Task. Record yourself reading a newspaper or magazine article.
a. If you think your voice sounds a bit high, practice speaking slightly lower.
b. If your voice is low or expressionless, practice speaking slightly louder and with more inflection.
c. Ask a colleague, teacher, or friend to provide feedback on your pronunciation, pitch, volume, rate, and professional tone.

E-MAIL   **TEAM**

11.2 Surviving a Social Business Function

The idea of attending a social business function provokes anxiety in many businesspeople. What should you talk about? What should you wear? How can you make sure you maintain your professionalism?

Your Task. In groups of two to four, discuss appropriate behavior in four social situations. Decide appropriate attire, suitable topics of conversation, and other etiquette guidelines that you should follow. Present your decisions regarding the following social functions to your instructor in a memo or e-mail message:

a. Company picnic
b. Holiday party
c. Formal dinner
d. Business luncheon

11.3 Delivering and Responding to Criticism

Develop your skills in handling criticism by joining with a partner to role-play critical messages you might deliver and receive on the job.

Your Task. Designate one person "A" and the other "B." A describes the kinds of critical messages she or he is likely to receive on the job and identifies who might deliver them. In Scenario 1, B takes the role of the critic and delivers the criticism in an unskilled manner. A responds using techniques described in this chapter. In Scenario 2, B again is the critic but delivers the criticism using techniques described in this chapter. A responds again. Then A and B reverse roles and repeat Scenarios 1 and 2.

TEAM

11.4 Discussing Workplace Criticism

In the workplace, criticism is often delivered thoughtlessly.

Your Task. In teams of two or three, describe a time when you were criticized by an untrained superior or colleague. What made the criticism painful? What goal do you think the critic had in mind? How did you feel? How did you respond? Considering techniques discussed in this chapter, how could the critic have improved his or her delivery? How does the delivery technique affect the way a receiver responds to criticism? Your instructor may ask you to submit a memo or e-mail analyzing an experience in which you were criticized.

11.5 Analyzing a Meeting

You've learned a number of techniques in this chapter for planning and participating in meetings. Here's your chance to put your knowledge to work.

Your Task. Attend a structured meeting of a college, social, business, community, or other organization. Compare the manner in which the meeting is conducted with the suggestions presented in this chapter. Why did the meeting succeed or fail? Prepare a memo for your instructor or be ready to discuss your findings in class.

11.6 Planning a Meeting

Assume that the next meeting of your Associated Students Organization (ASO) will discuss preparations for a careers day in the spring. The group will hear reports from committees working on speakers, business recruiters, publicity, reservations of campus space, setup of booths, and any other matters you can think of.

Your Task. As president of your ASO, prepare an agenda for the meeting. Compose your introductory remarks to open the meeting. Your instructor may ask you to submit these two documents or use them in staging an actual meeting in class.

INFOTRAC

11.7 Leading a Meeting

Your boss is unhappy at the way some employees lead meetings. Because he knows that you have studied this topic, he asks you to send him a memo or e-mail listing specific points that he can use in an in-house training session in which he plans to present ideas on how to conduct business meetings.

Your Task. Using InfoTrac, locate articles providing tips on leading meetings. Two particularly good articles are Dennis Kremer's "Rules for Improved Meetings" (Article No. A126850123) and Jim Olsztynski's "Productive Meetings vs. Bull Sessions" (Article No. A125714406). Prepare a memo to your boss, Michael Hicks, outlining eight or more points on how to lead a meeting. Include at least five tips that are not found in this chapter.

11.8 Improving Telephone Skills by Role-Playing

Acting out the roles of telephone caller and receiver is an effective technique for improving skills. To give you such practice, your instructor will divide the class into pairs.

Your Task. For each scenario take a moment to read and rehearse your role silently. Then play the role with your partner. If time permits, repeat the scenarios, changing roles.

Partner 1

A. You are the personnel manager of Wireless World, Inc. Call Susan Campbell, office manager at Digitron Corporation. Inquire about a job applicant, Lisa Chung, who listed Ms. Campbell as a reference.

B. Call Ms. Campbell again the following day to inquire about the same job applicant, Lisa Chung. Ms. Campbell answers today, but she talks on and on, describing the applicant in great detail. Tactfully close the conversation.

C. You are now the receptionist for Cyrus Artemis, of Artemis Imports. Answer a call for Mr. Artemis, who is working in another office, at Ext. 2219, where he will accept calls.

D. You are now Cyrus Artemis, owner of Artemis Imports. Call your attorney, Maria Solomon-Williams, about a legal problem. Leave a brief, incomplete message.

E. Call Ms. Solomon-Williams again. Leave a message that will prevent telephone tag.

Partner 2

A. You are the receptionist for Digitron Corporation. The caller asks for Susan Campbell, who is home sick today. You don't know when she will be able to return. Answer the call appropriately.

B. You are now Ms. Campbell, office manager. Describe Lisa Chung, an imaginary employee. Think of someone with whom you've worked. Include many details, such as her ability to work with others, her appearance, her skills at computing, her schooling, her ambition, and so forth.

C. You are now an administrative assistant for attorney Maria Solomon-Williams. Call Cyrus Artemis to verify a meeting date Ms. Solomon-Williams has with Mr. Artemis. Use your own name in identifying yourself.

D. You are now the receptionist for attorney Maria Solomon-Williams. Ms. Solomon-Williams is skiing in Aspen and will return in two days, but she doesn't want her clients to know where she is. Take a message.

E. Take a message again.

WEB   **CRITICAL THINKING**

11.9 Web Conferencing: Holding Your Meetings Online

You've just discovered that one of the hottest trends today is using Web conferencing to hold virtual meetings. You really like the idea and would like to propose it to your supervisor, but you have no idea what tools can be used. You want to conduct research to find out more before making your proposal.

Your Task. Use a search tool such as Google (*http://www.google.com*) to locate two tools that can be used for Web conferencing. For this purpose you should definitely consider commercial sites that provide virtual meeting software. Watch any demonstrations, take free trials, and evaluate what you see. In an e-mail or memo to your supervisor, Karen Hanson, submit a proposal that includes information about the two best sites that you find. Provide a short description of each tool, and explain why you think your company could benefit from Web conferencing.

INFOTRAC   **WEB**

11.10 Blogging: Who's Doing It?

Your company will be launching a new product shortly, and it is wondering whether a weblog (blog) is a possibility for announcing it.

Your Task. Your boss asks you to use the Web or InfoTrac to find examples of three organizations that have used weblogs recently to announce new products or services. In a class discussion or in an e-mail to your instructor, list three blogs and explain briefly who announced what. Do you think these announcements were successful? Why or why not?

GRAMMAR/MECHANICS CHECKUP–11

Other Punctuation

Although this checkup concentrates on Sections 2.23–2.29 in the Grammar/ Mechanics Handbook, you may also refer to other punctuation principles. Insert any necessary punctuation. In the space provided, indicate the number of changes you make and record the number of the G/M principle(s) illustrated. Count each mark separately; for example, a set of parentheses counts as 2. If you make no changes, write *O*. When you finish, compare your responses with those provided at the end of the book. If your responses differ, study carefully the specific principles shown in parentheses.

2   (2.27)   **Example**   (De-emphasize.) Several cities chosen by *CNN/Money* as the best places to live in the United States Alexandria, Chesapeake, Chantilly, and Reston are in Virginia.

1. (Emphasize.) The scholarship committee has invited three recipients Matt Conover, Debbie Lee, and Traci Peerson to speak at the awards ceremony.

2. Could you please Dr. Kerlin be sure that my insurance papers have been filed

3. (De-emphasize.) Our June financial figures see Appendix A show a sharp increase in operating expenses.

4. To determine whether to spell Web site as one word or two, consult our company style book.

5. Northwestern, Stanford, and Harvard these universities have three of the best M B A programs in the country.

6. Warren Buffet said, "Why not invest your assets in companies you really like

7. Have you read The Wall Street Journal article entitled Oracle's Ellison Gives $115 Million to Harvard Study

8. (Emphasize.) The biggest wine-producing states California, Washington, and Oregon are all located on the Pacific Coast.

9. Have you received replies from Mr Francisco M Arce, Ms Brenda Marini, and Dr Patricia Franzoia

10. I enjoyed the chapter entitled The Almost Perfect Meeting that appeared in Emily Post's book called The Etiquette Advantage in Business.

11. Donald Trump said, "Generally I like other people to fire, because it's always a lousy task" however he has fired many people himself.

12. In business the word speculator, may be defined as one who attempts to make profits by anticipating price changes.

13. Devon described the filthy factory floor as gross.

14. Is today's meeting at 2 p m

15. Wow You've been working out haven't you

GRAMMAR/MECHANICS CHALLENGE—11

The following report of meeting minutes has faults in grammar, punctuation, spelling, number form, wordiness, and word use. Use standard proofreading marks (see Appendix B) to correct the errors. When you finish, your instructor can show you the revised version of this summary.

Honolulu-Pacific Federal Interagency Board
Policy Board Committee
Room 25, 310 Ala Moana Boulevard, Honolulu
February 4, 200x

Present:　　Debra Chinnapongse, Tweet Jackson, Irene Kishita, Barry Knaggs, Kevin
　　　　　　　Poepoe, and Ralph Mason

Absent:　　Alex Watanabe

The meeting was call to order by Chair Kevin Poepo at 9:02 a.m. in the morning.
Minutes fromthe January 6thmeeting was read and approve.

Old Business

Debra Chinnapongse discussed the cost of the annual awards luncheon. That honors
outstanding employees. The ticket price ticket does not cover all the expenses incured.
Major expenses include: awards, leis, and complementary lunches for the judges, VIP
guests and volunteers. Honolulu-Pacific Federal Interagency Board can not continue to
make up the difference between income from tickets and costs for the luncheon.
Ms. Chinnapongse reported that it had come to her attention that other interagency
boards relied on members contributions for their awards' programs.

MOTION: To send a Letter to board members asking for there contributions to support
the annual awards luncheon. (Chinapongse/Kishita). PASSED 6-0.

Reports

Barry Knaggs reported that the homeland defense committee sponsored a get acquainted
meeting in November. More than eighty people from various agencys attended.

The Outreach Committee reports that they have been asked to assist the Partnership
for Public Service, a non profit main land organization in establishing a speakers
bureau of Hawaiian Federal employees. It would be available to speak at schools and
colleges about Federal jobs and employment.

New Business

The chair announced a Planning Meeting to be held in March regarding revising the
emergency dismissal plan. In other New Business Ralph Mason reported that the staff
had purchased fifty tickets for members, and our committees to attend the Zig Ziglar
seminar in the month of March.

Next Meeting

The next meeting of the Policy Boare Committee will be held in early Aprl at the Fleet
and Industrial Supply Center, Pearl harbor. At that time the meeting will include a tour
of the Red Hill under ground fuel storage facility.

The meeting adjourned at 10:25 am by Keven Poepoe.

Respectfully submitted,

COMMUNICATION WORKSHOP
CAREER SKILLS

EIGHT STEPS TO RESOLVING
WORKPLACE CONFLICTS

"People who never experience conflict on the job are either living in a dream world, blind to their surroundings, or in solitary confinement," says communication expert Dianna Booher.[21] Although all workplaces experience conflict from time to time, some people think that workplace conflict is escalating.

Several factors may be tied to increasing problems at work. One factor is our increasingly diverse workforce. Sharing ideas that stem from a variety of backgrounds, experiences, and personalities may lead to better problem solving, but it can also lead to conflict. Another factor related to increased conflict is the trend toward participatory management. In the past only bosses had to resolve problems, but now more employees are making decisions and facing conflict. This is particularly true of teams. Working together harmoniously involves a great deal of give and take, and conflict may result if some people feel that they are being taken advantage of.

Not all conflict is negative or dysfunctional. In fact, conflict can serve a number of healthy functions. In groups, conflict can increase involvement and cohesiveness. When people clash over differing views, they can become more committed to their purpose and to each other. Handled properly, conflict can provide an outlet for hostility and can increase group productivity.[22]

When problems arise in the workplace, it's important for everyone to recognize that conflict is a normal occurrence[23] and that it should be confronted and resolved. Effective conflict resolution requires good listening skills, flexibility, and a willingness to change. Individuals must be willing to truly listen and seek to understand rather than immediately challenge the adversary. In many workplace conflicts, involving a third party to act as a mediator is necessary. Although problems vary greatly, the following eight steps offer a good basic process for resolving conflicts.[24]

- **Arrange a meeting.** Find a time when both parties are willing to have a conversation in a nonthreatening environment.

- **Listen to each side.** Each individual should describe the situation from his or her perspective. To be sure you understand the other person's side, listen carefully. If the other person doesn't seem to be listening to you, you need to set the example and be the first to listen.

- **Understand the other person's point of view and paraphrase before responding.** Once you listen, it's much easier to understand the other's position. Show your understanding by asking questions and paraphrasing. This will also verify what you think the other person means. To promote empathic communication, follow this rule: No one may respond without first accurately summarizing the other person's previous remarks.

- **Show a concern for the relationship and look for common ground.** By focusing on the problem, not the person, you can build, maintain, and even improve the relationship. Show an understanding of the other person's situation and needs. Show an overall willingness to come to an agreement. Learn what you have in common, and look for a solution to which both sides can agree.

- **Begin problem solving.** Brainstorm together to develop multiple options for resolving the conflict. Try to see each other as allies, rather than opponents, in solving the problem. Spend time identifying the interests of both sides.

- **Reach an agreement based on what's fair.** Seek to determine a standard of fairness that is acceptable to both sides. Ensure that both parties are agreeable to the chosen solution.

- **Record the solution.** It is important to formalize the agreement in some way.
- **Implement the solution and follow up.** Meet again on an agreed-upon date to ensure a satisfactory resolution of the conflict. The deadline makes it more likely that both parties will follow through on their part of the deal.

Career Application. As leader of your work team, you were recently confronted by an angry fellow team member. Laura, a story editor on your film production team, is upset because, for the third time in as many weeks, she was forced to give up part of her weekend for work. This time it was for a black-tie affair that everyone in the office tried to duck. Laura is particularly angry with Bob, who should have represented the team at this awards dinner. But he uttered the magic word: *family.* "Bob says he has plans with his family, and it's like a get-out-of-jail-free card," Laura complains to you. "I don't resent him or his devotion to his family. But I do resent it when my team constantly expects me to give up my personal time because I don't have kids. That's my choice, and I don't think I should be punished for it."[25]

Your Task

Using the principles outlined here, work out a conflict resolution plan for Laura and Bob. Your instructor may wish to divide your class into three-person teams to role-play Laura, Bob, and the team leader. Add any details to make a realistic scenario.

- What are the first steps in resolving this conflict?
- What arguments might each side present?
- What alternatives might be offered?
- What do you think is the best solution?
- How could the solution be implemented with the least friction?

CHAPTER 12

MAKING EFFECTIVE AND PROFESSIONAL ORAL PRESENTATIONS

Public speaking skills have risen to the top of nearly every company's wish list of executive attributes.[1]

Hal Lancaster, *Wall Street Journal* columnist

OBJECTIVES

- Discuss two important first steps in preparing effective oral presentations.

- Explain the major elements in organizing the content of a presentation, including the introduction, body, and conclusion.

- Identify techniques for gaining audience rapport, including using effective imagery, providing verbal signposts, and sending appropriate nonverbal messages.

- Discuss types of visual aids, including multimedia slides, handouts, and overhead transparencies.

- Explain how to design an impressive multimedia presentation, including selecting a template, building bullet points, adding multimedia effects, producing speaker's notes, moving your presentation to the Web, and avoiding being upstaged by your slides.

- Specify delivery techniques for use before, during, and after a presentation.

- Explain effective techniques for adapting oral presentations to international and cross-cultural audiences.

Organizations today are increasingly interested in hiring people with good presentation skills. Why? The business world is changing. Technical skills aren't enough to guarantee success. You also need to be able to communicate ideas effectively in presentations to customers, vendors, members of your team, and management. Your presentations will probably be made to inform, influence, or motivate action.

One study revealed that a primary predictor of business success and upward mobility is how much you enjoy public speaking and how effective you are at it.[2] Speaking skills are useful at every career stage. You might, for example, have to make a sales pitch before customers or speak to a professional gathering. You might need to describe your company's expansion plans to your banker, or you might need to persuade management to support your proposed marketing strategy. In today's workplace the opportunities to make these presentations are increasing, even for nonmanagement employees.[3]

This chapter prepares you to use speaking skills in making effective and professional oral presentations. You'll learn what to do before, during, and after your presentation; how to design effective visual aids and multimedia presentations; and how to adapt a presentation for an international audience.

PHOTOS: © PHOTODISC COLLECTION/GETTY IMAGES; © TRIANGLE IMAGES/ DIGITAL VISION/GETTY IMAGES; © TRIANGLE IMAGES/DIGITAL VISION/ GETTY IMAGES

Today's work environments require employees to fully develop their presentation skills so that they are prepared to share information in informal settings as well as in more formal presentations. Preparing for a team presentation involves deciding what you want to accomplish, understanding your audience, gathering information, and working together to develop a polished performance.

© STOCKBYTE/GETTY IMAGES

GETTING READY FOR AN ORAL PRESENTATION

In getting ready for an oral presentation, you probably feel a great deal of anxiety. For many people fear of speaking before a group is almost as great as the fear of dying. Jerry Seinfeld spoke about this fear during a monologue in Episode 61 of *Seinfeld*: "According to most studies, people's number one fear is public speaking. The number two fear is death. Death is number two!!! Now, this means, to the average person, if you have to go to a funeral, you're better off in the casket than doing the eulogy!!"[4]

The good news is that for any presentation, you can reduce your fears and lay the foundation for a professional performance by focusing on five areas: preparation, organization, audience rapport, visual aids, and delivery.

Knowing Your Purpose

Preparing for an oral presentation means identifying your purpose and understanding the audience.

The most important part of your preparation is deciding your purpose. What do you want to accomplish? Do you want to sell a health care program to a prospective client? Do you want to persuade management to increase the marketing budget? Do you want to inform customer service reps of three important ways to prevent miscommunication? Do you want to give advice to graduating high school seniors? Whether your goal is to persuade, to inform, or to entertain, you must have a clear idea of where you are going. At the end of your presentation, what do you want your listeners to believe, remember, or do?

Shannon Daly, a loan officer at First Fidelity Trust, faced such questions as she planned a talk for a class in small-business management. (You can see the outline for her talk in Figure 12.3 on page 349.) Shannon's former business professor had asked her to return to campus and give the class advice about borrowing money from banks in order to start new businesses. Because Shannon knew so much about this topic, she found it difficult to extract a specific purpose statement for her presentation. After much thought she narrowed her purpose to this: *To inform potential entrepreneurs about three important factors that loan officers consider before granting start-up loans to launch small businesses.* Her entire presentation focused on ensuring that the class members understood and remembered three principal ideas.

Understanding Your Audience

A second key element in preparation is analyzing your audience, anticipating its reactions, and making appropriate adaptations. Audiences may fall into four categories, as summarized in Figure 12.1. By anticipating your audience, you have a better idea of how to organize your presentation. A friendly audience, for example, will respond to humor and personal experiences. A neutral audience requires an even, controlled delivery style. The talk would probably be filled with facts, statistics, and expert opinions. An uninterested audience that is forced to attend requires a brief presentation. Such an audience might respond best to humor, cartoons, colorful visuals, and startling statistics. A hostile audience demands a calm, controlled delivery style with objective data and expert opinion. Whatever type of audience you'll have, remember that the most important thing to do is to plan your presentation so that it focuses on audience benefits. The members of your audience will want to know what's in it for them.

Audience analysis issues include size, age, gender, experience, attitude, and expectations.

Other elements, such as age, gender, education, experience, professional background, and audience size will affect your style and message content. Analyze the following questions to help you determine your organizational pattern, delivery style, and supporting material.

- *Who is my audience and how will this topic appeal to them?*
- *How can I relate this information to their needs?*
- *How can I gain credibility and earn respect so that they accept my message?*

FIGURE 12.1   • **Succeeding With Four Audience Types**

Audience Members	Organizational Pattern	Delivery Style	Supporting Material
Friendly They like you and your topic.	Use any pattern. Try something new. Involve the audience.	Be warm, pleasant, and open. Use lots of eye contact and smiles.	Include humor, personal examples, and experiences.
Neutral They are calm, rational; their minds are made up but they think they are objective.	Present both sides of the issue. Use pro/con or problem/solution patterns. Save time for audience questions.	Be controlled. Do nothing showy. Use confident, small gestures.	Use facts, statistics, expert opinion, and comparison and contrast. Avoid humor, personal stories, and flashy visuals.
Uninterested They have short attention spans; they may be there against their will.	Be brief—no more than three points. Avoid topical and pro/con patterns that seem lengthy to the audience.	Be dynamic and entertaining. Move around. Use large gestures.	Use humor, cartoons, colorful visuals, powerful quotations, and startling statistics.
	Avoid darkening the room, standing motionless, passing out handouts, using boring visuals, or expecting the audience to participate.		
Hostile They want to take charge or to ridicule the speaker; they may be defensive, emotional.	Organize using a noncontroversial pattern, such as a topical, chronological, or geographical strategy.	Be calm and controlled. Speak evenly and slowly.	Include objective data and expert opinion. Avoid anecdotes and humor.
	Avoid a question-and-answer period, if possible; otherwise, use a moderator or accept only written questions.		

- *What would be most effective in making my point? Facts? Statistics? Personal experiences? Expert opinion? Humor? Cartoons? Graphic illustrations? Demonstrations? Case histories? Analogies?*
- *What measures must I take to ensure that this audience remembers my main points?*

ORGANIZING CONTENT FOR A POWERFUL IMPACT

Good organization and intentional repetition help your audience understand and retain what you say.

Once you have determined your purpose and analyzed the audience, you're ready to collect information and organize it logically. Good organization and conscious repetition are the two most powerful keys to audience comprehension and retention. In fact, many speech experts recommend the following admittedly repetitious, but effective, plan:

Step 1: Tell them what you're going to say.
Step 2: Say it.
Step 3: Tell them what you've just said.

Randy Glasbergen.
www.glasbergen.com

"Always start your presentation with a joke, but be careful not to offend anyone! Don't mention religion, politics, race, age, money, technology, men, women, children, plants, animals, food..."

In other words, repeat your main points in the introduction, body, and conclusion of your presentation. Although it sounds deadly, this strategy works surprisingly well. Let's examine how to construct the three parts of an effective presentation.

Capturing Attention in the Introduction

How many times have you heard a speaker begin with, *It's a pleasure to be here, I'm honored to be asked to speak,* or *I'm going to do my presentation on . . . .* Boring openings such as these get speakers off to a dull start. Avoid such banalities by striving to accomplish three goals in the introduction to your presentation:

- Capture listeners' attention and get them involved.
- Identify yourself and establish your credibility.
- Preview your main points.

Attention-grabbing openers include questions, startling facts, jokes, anecdotes, and quotations.

Many professional speakers consider the introduction to be one of the most important parts of a presentation. If you're able to appeal to listeners and involve them in your presentation right from the start, you're more likely to hold their attention until the finish. However, if you're unable to grab the audience members' attention in the beginning, they may never hear what you have to say. To secure your audience's attention, consider some of the same techniques that you used to open sales letters: a question, a startling fact, a joke, a story, or a quotation. Some speakers achieve involvement by opening with a question or command that requires audience members to raise their hands or stand up. Ten techniques for effectively capturing and maintaining your audience's attention are described in Figure 12.2.

To establish your credibility, you need to describe your position, knowledge, education, or experience—whatever qualifies you to speak. Try also to connect with your audience. Listeners are particularly drawn to speakers who reveal something of themselves and identify with them. A consultant addressing office workers might describe how he started as a temporary worker; a CEO might tell a funny story in which the joke is on herself. Use humor if you can pull it off (not everyone can), and self-effacing humor is probably best.

FIGURE 12.2

Ten Winning Techniques for Gaining and Keeping Audience Attention

Experienced speakers know how to capture the attention of an audience and how to maintain that attention during a presentation. You can give your presentations a boost by trying these ten proven techniques.

- **A promise.** Begin with a promise that keeps the audience expectant. For example, *By the end of this presentation, you will know how you can increase your sales by 50 percent!*
- **Drama.** Open by telling an emotionally moving story or by describing a serious problem that involves the audience. Throughout your talk include other dramatic elements, such as a long pause after a key statement. Change your vocal tone or pitch. Professionals use high-intensity emotions such as anger, joy, sadness, and excitement.
- **Eye contact.** As you begin, command attention by surveying the entire audience to take in all listeners. Take two to five seconds to make eye contact with as many people as possible.
- **Movement.** Leave the lectern area whenever possible. Walk around the conference table or between the aisles of your audience. Try to move toward your audience, especially at the beginning and end of your talk.
- **Questions.** Keep listeners active and involved with rhetorical questions. Ask for a show of hands to get each listener thinking. The response will also give you a quick gauge of audience attention.
- **Demonstrations.** Include a member of the audience in a demonstration. For example, *I'm going to show you exactly how to implement our four-step customer courtesy process, but I need a volunteer from the audience to help me.*
- **Samples/gimmicks.** If you're promoting a product, consider using items to toss out to the audience or to award as prizes to volunteer participants. You can also pass around product samples or promotional literature. Be careful, though, to maintain control.
- **Visuals.** Give your audience something to look at besides yourself. Use a variety of visual aids in a single session. Also consider writing the concerns expressed by your audience on a flipchart or on the board as you go along.
- **Dress.** Enhance your credibility with your audience by dressing professionally for your presentation. Professional dress will help you look more competent and qualified, which will make your audience more likely to listen to you and take you seriously.
- **Self-interest.** Review your entire presentation to ensure that it meets the critical *What's-in-it-for-me* audience test. Remember that people are most interested in things that benefit them.

During the time when the Macarena was a popular dance, Vice President Al Gore addressed the Democratic National Convention. He used the introduction of his speech to make fun of himself and his reputation of being boring. He said, ". . . this is some crowd. I've been watching you doing the Macarena on television. And if I could have your silence, I would like to demonstrate for you the Al Gore version of the Macarena." He then stood perfectly still for several seconds, after which he said, "Would you like to see it again?"[5]

After capturing attention, introducing yourself, and establishing your credibility, you'll want to preview the main points of your topic, perhaps with a visual aid. You may wish to put off actually writing your introduction, however, until after you have organized the rest of the presentation and crystallized your principal ideas.

Take a look at Shannon Daly's introduction, shown in Figure 12.3, to see how she integrated all the elements necessary for a good opening.

FIGURE 12.3

Oral Presentation Outline

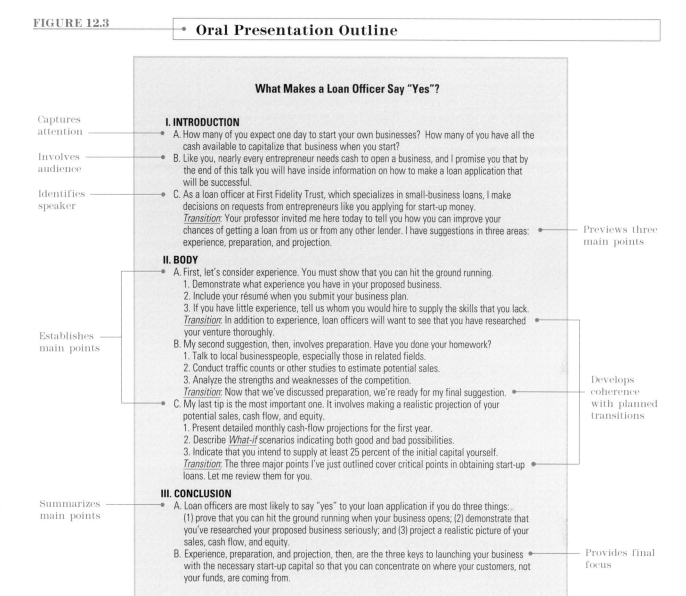

What Makes a Loan Officer Say "Yes"?

Captures attention

Involves audience

Identifies speaker

I. INTRODUCTION

A. How many of you expect one day to start your own businesses? How many of you have all the cash available to capitalize that business when you start?

B. Like you, nearly every entrepreneur needs cash to open a business, and I promise you that by the end of this talk you will have inside information on how to make a loan application that will be successful.

C. As a loan officer at First Fidelity Trust, which specializes in small-business loans, I make decisions on requests from entrepreneurs like you applying for start-up money.
Transition: Your professor invited me here today to tell you how you can improve your chances of getting a loan from us or from any other lender. I have suggestions in three areas: experience, preparation, and projection.

Previews three main points

Establishes main points

II. BODY

A. First, let's consider experience. You must show that you can hit the ground running.
1. Demonstrate what experience you have in your proposed business.
2. Include your résumé when you submit your business plan.
3. If you have little experience, tell us whom you would hire to supply the skills that you lack.
Transition: In addition to experience, loan officers will want to see that you have researched your venture thoroughly.

B. My second suggestion, then, involves preparation. Have you done your homework?
1. Talk to local businesspeople, especially those in related fields.
2. Conduct traffic counts or other studies to estimate potential sales.
3. Analyze the strengths and weaknesses of the competition.
Transition: Now that we've discussed preparation, we're ready for my final suggestion.

C. My last tip is the most important one. It involves making a realistic projection of your potential sales, cash flow, and equity.
1. Present detailed monthly cash-flow projections for the first year.
2. Describe *What-if* scenarios indicating both good and bad possibilities.
3. Indicate that you intend to supply at least 25 percent of the initial capital yourself.
Transition: The three major points I've just outlined cover critical points in obtaining start-up loans. Let me review them for you.

Develops coherence with planned transitions

Summarizes main points

III. CONCLUSION

A. Loan officers are most likely to say "yes" to your loan application if you do three things: (1) prove that you can hit the ground running when your business opens; (2) demonstrate that you've researched your proposed business seriously; and (3) project a realistic picture of your sales, cash flow, and equity.

B. Experience, preparation, and projection, then, are the three keys to launching your business with the necessary start-up capital so that you can concentrate on where your customers, not your funds, are coming from.

Provides final focus

Organizing the Body

The best oral presentations focus on a few key ideas.

The biggest problem with most oral presentations is a failure to focus on a few principal ideas. Thus, the body of your short presentation (20 or fewer minutes) should include a limited number of main points, say, two to four. Develop each main point with adequate, but not excessive, explanation and details. Too many details can obscure the main message, so keep your presentation simple and logical. Remember, listeners have nothing written to look back over should they become confused.

When Shannon Daly began planning her presentation, she realized immediately that she could talk for hours on her topic. She also knew that listeners are not good at separating major and minor points. Thus, instead of submerging her listeners in a sea of information, she sorted out a few principal ideas. In the mortgage business, loan officers generally ask the following three questions of each applicant for a small business loan: (1) Are you ready to "hit the ground running" in starting your business? (2) Have you done your homework? and (3) Have you made realistic projections of potential sales, cash flow, and equity investment? These questions would become her main points, but Shannon wanted to streamline them further so that her audience would be sure to remember them. She capsulized the questions in three words: *experience, preparation*, and *projection*. As you can see in Figure 12.3,

Shannon prepared a sentence outline showing these three main ideas. Each is supported by examples and explanations.

How to organize and sequence main ideas may not be immediately obvious when you begin working on a presentation. In Chapter 10 (Figure 10.2), you studied a number of patterns for organizing written reports. Those patterns—reviewed, amplified, and illustrated here—are equally appropriate for oral presentations.

Organize your report by time, geography, function, importance, or some other method that is logical to the receiver.

- **Chronology.** Example: A presentation describing the history of a problem, organized from the first sign of trouble to the present.
- **Geography/space.** Example: A presentation about the changing diversity of the workforce, organized by regions in the country (East Coast, West Coast, and so forth).
- **Topic/function/conventional grouping.** Example: A presentation discussing amenities offered to coach passengers, organized by names of airlines.
- **Comparison/contrast (pro/con).** Example: A presentation comparing organic farming methods with those of modern industrial farming.
- **Journalism pattern.** Example: A presentation describing how identity thieves can ruin your good name. Organized by *who, what, when, where, why*, and *how*.
- **Value/size.** Example: A presentation describing fluctuations in housing costs, organized by prices of homes.
- **Importance.** Example: A presentation describing five reasons that a consumer should pay bills online, organized from the most important reason to the least important.
- **Problem/solution.** Example: A company faces a problem such as high turnover. A solution such as adding more flexible time-off benefits is offered.
- **Simple/complex.** Example: A presentation explaining genetic modification of plants, organized from simple seed production to complex gene introduction.
- **Best case/worst case.** Example: A presentation analyzing whether two companies should merge, organized by the best-case results (improved market share, profitability, employee morale) opposed to the worst-case results (devalued stock, lost market share, employee malaise).

In the presentation shown in Figure 12.3, Shannon arranged the main points by importance, placing the most important point last where it had maximum effect. When organizing any presentation, prepare a little more material than you think you will actually need. Savvy speakers always have something useful in reserve (such as an extra handout, transparency, or idea)—just in case they finish early and must fill the remaining time.

Summarizing in the Conclusion

Nervous speakers often rush to wrap up their presentations because they can't wait to flee the stage. But listeners will remember the conclusion more than any part of a speech. That's why you should spend some time to make it most effective. Strive to achieve three goals:

Effective conclusions summarize main points and allow the speaker to exit gracefully.

- Summarize the main themes of the presentation.
- Provide a final, action-oriented focus that tells your listeners how they can use the information you presented or what you want them to do.
- Include a statement that allows you to depart the podium gracefully and leaves a lasting impression.

When it's time to end your presentation, be careful not to introduce any new material. Anything important should have been included in the body of your presentation. The conclusion is the time to summarize that information, not to bring up new details.

Some speakers end blandly with comments such as *I guess that's about all I have to say* or *That's it*. This makes the speaker look unprofessional and unprepared. Skilled speakers alert the audience that they are finishing. They use phrases such as, *As I end this presentation* or *It's time for me to stop*. Then they proceed immediately to the conclusion. Skilled speakers try to avoid using the cliché phrase *In conclusion* to end their presentations; for some audience members that's a signal to stop listening. Audiences become justly irritated with a speaker who announces the conclusion but then talks on for ten more minutes.

A straightforward summary should review major points and focus on what you want the listeners to do, think, or remember. You might say, *In bringing my presentation to a close, I will restate my major purpose . . . .* Or, *In summary, my major purpose has been to . . . .; in support of my purpose, I have presented three major points. They are (a) . . . , (b) . . . , and (c) . . . .* Notice how Shannon Daly, in the conclusion shown in Figure 12.3, summarized her three main points and provided a final focus to listeners.

If you are promoting a recommendation, you might end as follows: *In order to increase our sales by at least 25 percent, I recommend that we retain Matrixx Marketing to conduct a telemarketing campaign beginning September 1 at a cost of X dollars. To complete this recommendation, I suggest that we (a) finance this campaign from our operations budget, (b) develop a persuasive message describing our new product, and (c) name Tonya Padilla to oversee the project.* Avoid using phrases such as *I think, I believe,* or *I feel,* which will weaken your presentation.

In your conclusion you might want to use an anecdote, an inspiring quotation, or a statement that ties in the opener and offers a new insight. Whatever you choose, be sure to include a closing thought that indicates you are finished. For example, *This concludes my presentation. After investigating many marketing firms, we are convinced that Matrixx is the best for our purposes. Your authorization of my recommendations will mark the beginning of a very successful campaign for our new product.*

HOW THE BEST SPEAKERS BUILD AUDIENCE RAPPORT

Good speakers are adept at building audience rapport. They form a bond with the audience; they entertain as well as inform. They keep their audience involved throughout the presentation. How do they do it? Based on observations of successful and unsuccessful speakers, we learn that the good ones use a number of verbal and nonverbal techniques to connect with the audience. Some of their helpful techniques include providing effective imagery, supplying verbal signposts, and using body language strategically.

Effective Imagery

You'll lose your audience quickly if your talk is filled with abstractions, generalities, and dry facts. To enliven your presentation and enhance comprehension, try using some of these techniques:

Use analogies, metaphors, similes, personal anecdotes, personalized statistics, and worst- and best-case scenarios instead of dry facts.

- **Analogies.** A comparison of similar traits between dissimilar things can be effective in explaining and drawing connections. For example, *Product development is similar to the process of conceiving, carrying, and delivering a baby.* Or, *Putting together an effective business presentation is similar to directing and producing an award-winning theatrical play.*
- **Metaphors.** A comparison between otherwise dissimilar things without using the words *like* or *as* results in a metaphor. For example, *Our competitor's CEO is a snake when it comes to negotiating.* Or, *The discussion board is the heart of an online class.*
- **Similes.** A comparison that includes the words *like* or *as* is a simile. For example, *Graduating at the top of his class was like hitting a grand slam in the bottom of the ninth inning to win the World Series.* Or, *She's as relaxed as someone who just spent a day at the spa.*
- **Personal anecdotes.** Nothing connects you faster or better with your audience than a good personal story. In a talk about identity theft, you could reveal your own experiences with having your identity stolen.
- **Personalized statistics.** Although often misused, statistics stay with people—particularly when they relate directly to the audience. A speaker addressing a

group of first-year medical school students might say, *Look at the people seated on each side of you. Only one of you will still be here at the end of the academic year.* If possible, simplify and personalize facts. For example, *The sales of Coca-Cola totaled 2 billion cases last year. That means that six full cases of Coke were consumed by every man, woman, and child in the United States.*

- **Worst- and best-case scenarios.** Hearing the worst that could happen can be effective in driving home a point. For example, *If we do nothing to make our network more secure now, it's just a matter of time before a hacker gets in and steals confidential company information. Can you imagine what would happen if customers learned that their account information had gotten into the wrong hands? However, if we take the necessary steps now, we can ensure that our network is safe and protected against fraud and other security threats.*

Verbal Signposts

Speakers must remember that listeners, unlike readers of a report, cannot control the rate of presentation or flip back through pages to review main points. As a result, listeners get lost easily. Knowledgeable speakers help the audience recognize the organization and main points in an oral message with verbal signposts. They keep listeners on track by including helpful previews, summaries, and transitions, such as these:

Knowledgeable speakers provide verbal signposts to indicate when they are previewing, summarizing, or switching directions.

- Previewing
  The next segment of my talk presents three reasons for . . . .
  Let's now consider two causes of . . . .

- Summarizing
  Let me review with you the major problems I've just discussed.
  You see, then, that the most significant factors are . . . .

- Switching directions
  Thus far we've talked solely about . . . ; now let's move to . . . .
  I've argued that . . . and . . . , but an alternate view holds that . . . .

You can further improve any oral presentation by including appropriate transitional expressions such as *first, second, next, then, therefore, moreover, on the other hand, on the contrary,* and *in summary.* These expressions lend emphasis and tell listeners where you are headed. Notice in Shannon Daly's outline, in Figure 12.3 on page 349, the specific transitional elements that were designed to help listeners recognize each new principal point.

Nonverbal Messages

The way you look, how you move, and how you speak affect the success of your presentation.

Although what you say is most important, the nonverbal messages you send can also have a powerful effect on how well your message is received. How you look, how you move, and how you speak can make or break your presentation. The following suggestions focus on nonverbal tips to ensure that your verbal message is well received.

- **Look professional.** Like it or not, you will be judged by your appearance. For everything but small in-house presentations, be sure you dress professionally. A general rule of thumb is that you should dress at least as well as the best-dressed person in the audience. However, even if you know that your audience will be dressed casually, showing up in professional attire will help you build credibility. You'll feel better about yourself too!

- **Animate your body.** Be enthusiastic and let your body show it. Stand with good posture to show confidence. Emphasize ideas to enhance points about size, number, and direction. Use a variety of gestures, but don't consciously plan them in advance.

© ANDERSEN ROSS/BRAND X PICTURES/GETTY IMAGES

During any presentation you'll communicate to your audience both verbally and nonverbally. Use your dress, facial expressions, posture, and gestures to add professionalism, poise, and impact to your presentation.

- **Punctuate your words.** You can keep your audience interested by varying your tone, volume, pitch, and pace. Use pauses before and after important points. Allow the audience to take in your ideas.
- **Use appropriate eye contact.** Maintaining eye contact with your audience shows that you're confident and prepared. In addition, looking at audience members, rather than looking at your notes or your computer screen, helps them feel more involved.
- **Get out from behind the podium.** Avoid being planted behind the podium. Movement makes you look natural and comfortable and helps you connect more with your audience. You might pick a few places in the room to walk to. Even if you must stay close to your visual aids, make a point of leaving them occasionally so that the audience can see your whole body.
- **Vary your facial expression.** Begin with a smile, but change your expressions to correspond with the thoughts you are voicing. You can shake your head to show disagreement, roll your eyes to show disdain, look heavenward for guidance, or wrinkle your brow to show concern or dismay. To see how speakers convey meaning without words, mute the sound on your TV and watch the facial expressions of a talk show personality, newscaster, or politician.

PLANNING VISUAL AIDS

Before you make a business presentation, consider this wise Chinese proverb: "Tell me, I forget. Show me, I remember. Involve me, I understand." Your goals as a speaker are to make listeners understand, remember, and act on your ideas. To get them interested and involved, include effective visual aids. Some experts say that we acquire 85 percent of all our knowledge visually. Therefore, an oral presentation that incorporates visual aids is far more likely to be understood and retained than one lacking visual enhancement.

Visual aids clarify points, improve comprehension, and aid retention.

Good visual aids have many purposes. They emphasize and clarify main points, thus improving comprehension and retention. They increase audience interest, and they make the presenter appear more professional, better prepared, and more persuasive. Furthermore, research shows that the use of visual aids actually shortens presentations.[6] Visual aids are particularly helpful for inexperienced speakers because the audience concentrates on the aid rather than on the speaker. Good visuals also serve to jog the memory of a speaker, thus improving self-confidence, poise, and delivery.

Types of Visual Aids

Fortunately for today's speakers, many forms of visual media are available to enhance a presentation. When deciding what types of visual aids to include in your presentation, you should consider the cost, the ease of preparation, the degree of formality desired, and the potential effectiveness. Figure 12.4 describes the pros and cons for a number of visual aids and can guide you in selecting the best visual aid for any speaking occasion. Three of the most popular visuals are multimedia slides, handouts, and overhead transparencies.

MULTIMEDIA SLIDES

With today's excellent software programs—such as Microsoft PowerPoint, Apple Keynote, Lotus Freelance Graphics, Corel Presentations, and Astound Presentation—you can create dynamic, colorful presentations with your PC. The output from these programs is generally shown on a PC monitor, a TV monitor, an LCD (liquid crystal display)

FIGURE 12.4 — • **Consider the Pros and Cons for Visual Aid Options**

Medium	Pros	Cons
Multimedia slides	Creates professional appearance with many color, art, graphic, and font options. Easy to use and transport via removable disk, Web download, or e-mail attachment. Inexpensive to update.	Presents potential incompatibility issues. Requires costly projection equipment and practice for smooth delivery. Tempts user to include razzle-dazzle features that may fail to add value.
Transparencies	Gives professional appearance with little practice. Easy to (1) prepare, (2) update and maintain, (3) locate reliable equipment, and (4) limit information shown at one time.	Appears to some as an outdated presentation method. Holds speaker captive to the machine. Provides poor reproduction of photos and some graphics.
Handouts	Encourages audience participation. Easy to maintain and update. Enhances recall because audience keeps reference material.	Increases risk of unauthorized duplication of speaker's material. Can be difficult to transport. May cause speaker to lose audience's attention.
Flipcharts or whiteboards	Provides inexpensive option available at most sites. Easy to (1) create, (2) modify on the spot, (3) record comments from the audience, and (4) combine with more high-tech visuals in the same presentation.	Requires graphics talent. Difficult for larger audiences to see. Prepared flipcharts are cumbersome to transport and easily worn with use.
Video	Gives an accurate representation of the content; strong indication of forethought and preparation.	Creates potential for compatibility issues related to computer video formats. Expensive to create and update.
Objects for demonstration	Offers a realistic reinforcement of message content. Increases audience participation with close observation.	Leads to extra work and expense in transporting and replacing worn objects. Limited use with larger audiences.

panel, or a screen. With a little expertise and advanced equipment, you can create a multimedia presentation that includes audio, video clips, and hyperlinks, as described in the following discussion of electronic presentations. Multimedia slides can also be uploaded to a Web site or broadcast live over the Internet.

HANDOUTS

To maintain control, distribute handouts after you finish speaking.

You can enhance and complement your presentations by distributing pictures, outlines, brochures, articles, charts, summaries, or other supplements. Speakers who use multimedia presentation programs often prepare a handout that has images of their slides along with notes to distribute to viewers. Timing the distribution of any handout, though, is tricky. If given out during a presentation, your handouts tend to distract the audience, causing you to lose control. Thus, it's probably best to discuss most handouts during the presentation but delay distributing them until after you finish. If you plan to give your audience handouts at the end, tell them near the beginning of the presentation.

OVERHEAD TRANSPARENCIES

Student and professional speakers alike rely on the overhead projector for many reasons. Most meeting areas are equipped with projectors and screens. Moreover, acetate transparencies for the overhead are cheap, effortlessly prepared on a computer or copier, easy to transport, and simple to use. What's more, because rooms need not be darkened, a speaker using transparencies can maintain eye contact with the audience. A word of caution, though: stand to the side of the projector so that you don't obstruct the audience's view. Also make sure that the information on your transparencies can be seen by all audience members.

DESIGNING AN IMPRESSIVE MULTIMEDIA PRESENTATION

Microsoft PowerPoint has become the business standard for presenting, defending, and selling ideas.

Whether making a presentation to a dozen people sitting around a conference table or speaking to an audience of 500 in a large auditorium, smart speakers choose to put their key points on screen to underscore and reinforce them. As a result, software programs such as PowerPoint have become the business standard for presenting, defending, and selling ideas most effectively. Business speakers use multimedia presentations because they are economical, flexible, and easy to prepare. Changes can be made right up to the last minute. The medium provides a wide variety of visual and auditory enhancements to keep audience attention and to emphasize important information. Most significant, though, such presentations, when done well, can make even amateurs look like real pros.

Randy Glasbergen.
www.glasbergen.com

GLASBERGEN

"My presentation lacks power and it has no point. I assumed the software would take care of that!"

Critics say that PowerPoint is too regimented and produces "bullet-pointed morons."

Yet, PowerPoint has its critics. They charge that the program dictates the way information is structured and presented. PowerPoint stifles "the storyteller, the poet, the person whose thoughts cannot be arranged in the shape of an AutoContent slide."[7] PowerPoint, say its detractors, is turning the nation's businesspeople into a "mindless gaggle of bullet-pointed morons."[8] Although storytellers and poets may find that PowerPoint smothers their creativity, business speakers know that it increases audience enjoyment, enhances comprehension, and promotes retention. PowerPoint speakers, however, are effective only when they are skillful. To stay clear of the "bullet-pointed moron" category, you must learn about creating your presentation, building bullet points, and adding multimedia effects.

Creating Your Presentation

All presentation programs require you to (1) select or create a template that will serve as the background for your presentation and (2) make each individual slide by selecting a layout that best conveys your message. You can use one of the templates provided with your presentation software program, download one from many Web sites, or create one from scratch.

Novice and even advanced users choose existing templates because they are designed by professionals who know how to combine harmonious colors, borders, bullet styles, and fonts for pleasing visual effects. If you prefer, you can alter existing templates so they better suit your needs. Adding a corporate logo, adjusting the color scheme to better match the colors used on your organization's Web site, or selecting a different font are just some of the ways you can customize existing templates.

Overused templates and clip art produce "visual clichés" that bore audiences.

Be careful, though, of what one expert labels "visual clichés."[9] Overused templates and even clip art that comes with PowerPoint can weary viewers who have seen them repeatedly in presentations. Instead of using a standard template, key in "Power-Point Template" in your favorite search engine. You will see hundreds of template options available as free downloads. Unless your employer requires that presentations all have the same look, your audience will most likely appreciate fresh templates that complement the purpose of your presentation and provide visual variety.

Whether you create your own template or choose one designed by professionals, consider these principles when evaluating color options. Warm colors—reds, oranges, and yellows—are best to highlight important elements. Blue is associated with calmness; yellow signals caution; red can mean stop, financial loss, or danger; and green relates to nature, go, and money.

Background and text colors depend on the lightness of the room.

The color for backgrounds and text depends on where the presentation will be given. Use light text on a dark background for presentations in darkened rooms. Use dark text on a light background for computer presentations in lighted rooms. Avoid using a dark font on a dark background, such as red text on a dark blue background. Likewise, avoid using a light font on a light background, such as white text on a pale blue background or yellow text on a white background. Dark on dark and light on light results in low contrast, making the slides difficult to read. Figure 12.5 shows two of the many different template designs you have to choose from.

In selecting the best layout for each slide, you again can choose from the layout options that are part of your presentation program, or you can create a layout from scratch by adding your own elements to each slide. Figure 12.6 illustrates some of the many layout options for creating your slides. You can alter layouts by repositioning, resizing, or changing the fonts for the placeholders in which your title, bulleted list, organization chart, video clip, photograph, or other elements appear.

When working as a team to prepare a slide presentation, be sure that each member is using the same template. That way when team members merge their individual

FIGURE 12.5   **Selecting a Slide Template**

You may choose from a variety of predesigned templates or design your own. Lighter backgrounds are better in darkened rooms, whereas darker backgrounds are better in lighted rooms.

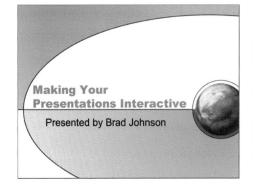

FIGURE 12.6

Selecting a Slide Layout

You may choose from a
variety of slide layout
plans, or you may design
your own slide layout to
fit your material.

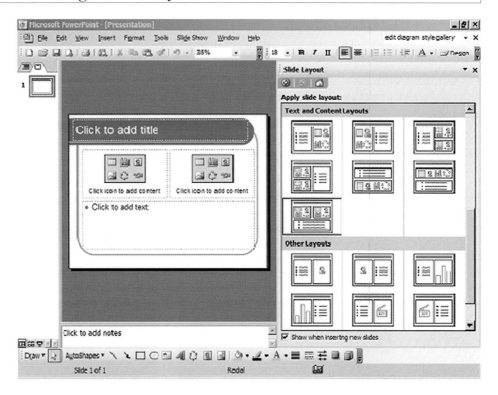

sections into one presentation file, no one will be surprised about how the slides look. To maintain a consistent look throughout the presentation, only one team member should be in charge of making color, font, or other global formatting changes to the slide and title masters. Team members should be encouraged to follow the global formatting established by the master slides. In addition, team members should understand that making global changes one time using the master slides is a definite plus. It prevents the hassles associated with changing many individual slides.

Building Bullet Points

Bullet points should be short
phrases that are parallel.

When you prepare your slides, translate the major headings in your presentation outline into titles for slides. Then build bullet points using short phrases. In Chapter 5 you learned to improve readability by using graphic highlighting techniques, including bullets, numbers, and headings. In preparing a PowerPoint presentation, you will use those same techniques.

Let's say, for example, that Brad wants to persuade the seven trainers in his department to use more audience participation when giving training seminars. He has to convince them that trainee feedback describing some sessions as "one-way information dumps" is proof that improvement is needed. Brad wants to emphasize how trainers and trainees can benefit by including audience-involvement techniques. Here is a portion of the text he wrote.

Text of Presentation

Today's audience members interact with wireless phones, instant messaging, blogs, and other communication media. So when they come to one of your training sessions, they often expect you to include two-way dialog and interactivity through audience-involvement techniques. Such techniques include asking the trainees to guess a statistic before revealing it, dividing the trainees into small groups to discuss an issue, and encouraging participation with giveaways. In addition to meeting audience expectations, incorporating interactivity into a presentation also benefits the speaker. Audience-involvement techniques can be used to reinforce key points and to add variety to the presentation by changing the pace and giving audiences a "break" from listening to just one person. Interactivity also helps the speaker build rapport with the audience and encourages audience members to get to know each other.

Text can be converted to bullet points by experimenting with key phrases that are concise and balanced grammatically.

To convert the preceding text into bullet points, Brad started with a title and then listed the main ideas that related to that title as illustrated in the left slide of Figure 12.6. He worked with the list until all the items were parallel (in the same grammatical structure). That meant considerable experimenting with different wording. Brad went through many revisions before creating the revised slide pictured on the right of Figure 12.7. Notice that Brad revised the title to promote reader benefits. Notice also that the bullet points are concise and parallel. They should be key phrases, not complete sentences. Finally, adding graphics illustrates the point and adds interest.

| FIGURE 12.7 | **Revising Slide to Improve Bullet Points and Add Illustration** |

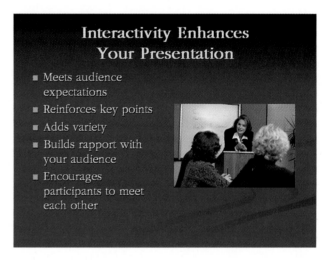

Before Revision   **After Revision**

The "before" slide does not use parallel wording; the "after" slide improves wording and includes an illustration for added punch.

PowerPoint's *Animation* feature will allow Brad to focus viewer's attention on each point of this bulleted slide. By choosing from a variety of effects such as "fly" in from the top or "wipe" right, he can time the display of each bullet point to coordinate with his comments on each point. In addition, when Brad moves from slide to slide, he can use *Slide Transition* effects. Such effects for a new slide appearing on screen include checkerboard effects, dissolving, or fading slowly. Most experts agree that using too many different animation and transition effects can be distracting. Therefore, Brad needs to choose effects that will help his audience focus on his message, not the technology.

For the most readable slides, apply the *Rule of Seven*. Each slide should include no more than seven words in a line, no more than seven total lines, and no more than 7 x 7 or 49 total words. If possible, use fewer words. Remember that presentation slides depict an idea graphically or provide an overview; they don't tell the whole story. That's the job of the presenter.

Adding Multimedia and Other Effects

Multimedia elements include sound, animation, video, and other visual elements.

Few approaches are more mind numbing to your audience than displaying endless slides of bulleted lists. Thanks to the multimedia features available on presentation programs, you can include sound, animation, video, and other visual elements to enhance your content and make your presentation more effective. For example, video clips can add excitement and depth to a presentation. You might use video to capture attention

FIGURE 12.8

Using a Diagram Gallery Option to Convert the Bulleted List From Figure 12.7 to an Animated Diagram

The slide at the right was created using the *Radial Diagram* option from the PowerPoint *Diagram Gallery.*

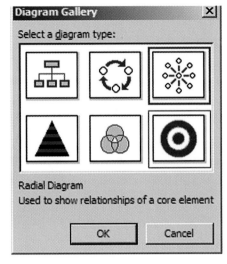

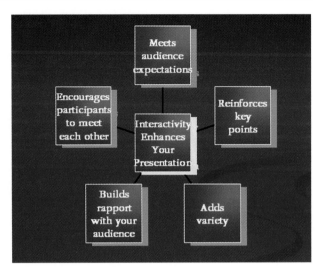

in a stimulating introduction, to show the benefits of a product in use, or to bring the personality of a distant expert or satisfied customer right into the meeting room. Audio can also be used to enliven a presentation. Sound or music can be used to gain your audience's attention, to illustrate a key point, or to hear what a product sounds like.

Another way to enliven a presentation is with photographic images. These images are easy to obtain thanks to stock photos that can be purchased online and to the prevalence of low-cost scanners and digital cameras. Furthermore, animated flowcharts present processes, operations, and sequences more accurately than do bulleted lists.

PowerPoint, for example, has a *Diagram Gallery* feature that offers users many interesting options for presenting information. Figure 12.8 illustrates six common diagram types. The accompanying slide shows how Brad chose the radial diagram option to present the bulleted list shown in Figure 12.7. When Brad displays this slide, he will animate the boxes so that the center box appears first. Subsequent boxes will appear timed with his explanation of each.

Numeric information is more easily grasped in charts or graphs than in a listing of numbers. Moreover, in most programs, you can animate your graphs and charts. Say, for instance, you have four columns in your bar chart. You can control the entry of each column by determining in what order and how each column appears on the screen. The goal is to use animation strategically to introduce elements of the presentation as they unfold in your spoken remarks. Figure 12.9 shows how a chart can be used to illustrate a concept discussed in Brad's presentation.

Most programs are also capable of generating hyperlinks ("hot spots" on the screen) that allow you to jump instantly to sources outside your presentation. With a click of your mouse, you could take your audience "live" to a Web site that contains up-to-the-minute data related to your presentation. Hyperlinks can also be used to link to a Word document, Excel spreadsheet, or any other type of document that you want participants to see. Hyperlinks can enhance interest in your presentation by adding interactive features and a wide variety of multimedia elements.

Be warned, though, that using multimedia effects or visual enhancements just because you can is never a good enough reason to include them. Every multimedia and visual effect you use should enhance your message and engage your audience. Using too many "bells and whistles" is annoying and may cause your audience to remember the entertaining slides rather than the key points.

Use animation to introduce elements of a presentation as they unfold in your spoken remarks.

FIGURE 12.9

Using a Bar Chart to Illustrate a Concept

This slide was created using PowerPoint's *Insert, Chart* function. The information presented here is more exciting and easier to comprehend than if it had been presented in a bulleted list.

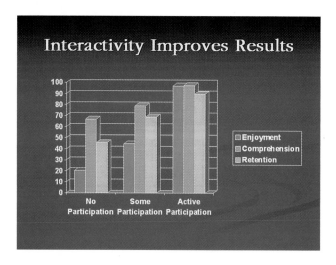

Producing Speaker's Notes and Handouts

You also have a variety of options for printing hard-copy versions of your presentation. One excellent option is to make speaker's notes, which can be an effective aid for practicing and delivering your talk. To create speaker's notes while designing your slides in PowerPoint, type any comments or outline material in the "Click to add notes" section that appears at the bottom of each slide. Once this is done, you can print "Notes Pages" using the *Print* option. Each printed page will show the slide image on the top half of the printout, with your supporting comments for the abbreviated material in your slides below. You might find that using these speaker notes during your presentation can help you better synchronize your presentation with the slide content. Speaker's notes can also be printed as handouts for your audience or displayed on the Web if you want to give viewers more detailed information. Printed handouts may include up to nine miniature versions of your slides per page. These miniatures are handy if you want to preview your talk to a sponsoring organization or if you want to supply the audience with a summary handout of your presentation.

Moving Your Presentation to the Web

Internet options for slide presentations range from posting slides online to conducting a live Web conference with slides, narration, and speaker control.

You have a range of alternatives, from simple to complex, for moving your multimedia presentation to the Internet. The simplest option is posting your slides online for others to access. Even if you are giving a face-to-face presentation, attendees appreciate these *electronic handouts* because they don't have to lug them home. You can also e-mail your PowerPoint presentation as an attachment to attendees.

The most complex option for moving your multimedia presentation to the Internet involves a Web conference or live broadcast. Web presentations with slides, narration, and speaker control have emerged as a way for anyone who has access to the Internet to attend your presentation without leaving the office. For example, you could initiate a meeting via a conference call, narrate using a telephone, and have participants see your slides from the browsers on their computers. If you prefer, you could skip the narration and provide a prerecorded presentation. Web-based presentations have many applications, including providing access to updated training or sales data whenever needed. Business communicators often find that Web conferences can be more persuasive and more detailed than phone calls or e-mail messages. In addition, Web conferencing can save a company money since it eliminates travel expenses.[10]

Avoiding Being Upstaged by Your Slides

One expert urges speakers to "use their PowerPresence in preference to their Power-Point."[11] Although multimedia presentations can add excitement to the presentation, they cannot replace solid, well-researched content. In developing a presentation, don't expect your slides to carry the show. Your goal is to avoid letting PowerPoint "steal your thunder." Here are suggestions for keeping control in your slide presentation:

To avoid making PowerPoint the main event, a speaker should look at the audience, not the screen; leave the lights on; and use other visualization techniques.

- Use your slides primarily to summarize important points. For each slide have one or more paragraphs of narration to present to your audience.
- Remember that your responsibility is to *add value* to the information you present. Explain the analyses leading up to the major points and what each point means.
- Look at the audience, not the screen.
- As you show new elements on a slide, allow the audience time to absorb the information; then paraphrase and elaborate on what they have seen. Do NOT read verbatim from a slide.
- Leave the lights as bright as you can. Make sure the audience can see your face and eyes.
- Use a radio remote control (not infrared) so that you can stand near the screen or near your audience rather than remain tethered to your computer. Radio remotes allow you to be up to 50 feet away from your laptop.
- Maintain a connection with the audience by using a laser pointer to highlight slide items to discuss.
- Don't rely totally on PowerPoint. Help the audience visualize your points by using other techniques. Drawing a diagram on a whiteboard or flipchart can be more engaging than showing slide after slide of static drawings. Showing real objects is a welcome relief from slides.
- In case of equipment failure, bring backups of your presentation. You can print your presentation on acetate transparencies or bring handouts of your slides as discussed earlier. Transferring your presentation to a CD, DVD, or USB flash drive that could run from any available computer device (laptop, PDA, or handheld) might prove useful as well. Finally, e-mail a copy of your presentation to yourself so that you're able to access the file if needed.

Above all, remember that your slides merely supply a framework for your presentation. Your audience came to see and hear you!

POLISHING YOUR DELIVERY AND FOLLOWING UP

Once you've organized your presentation and prepared visuals, you're ready to practice delivering it. Here are suggestions for selecting a delivery method, along with specific techniques to use before, during, and after your presentation.

Delivery Method

Inexperienced speakers often feel that they must memorize an entire presentation to be effective. Unless you are an experienced performer, however, you will sound wooden and unnatural. What's more, forgetting your place can be disastrous! That's why we don't recommend memorizing an entire oral presentation. However, memorizing significant parts—the introduction, the conclusion, and perhaps a meaningful quotation—can be dramatic and impressive.

If memorizing won't work, is reading your presentation the best plan? Definitely not! Reading to an audience is boring and ineffective. Because reading suggests that you don't know your topic well, the audience loses confidence in your expertise. Reading also prevents you from maintaining eye contact. You can't see audience reactions; consequently, you can't benefit from feedback. Finally, reading makes for a dull presentation!

Presentations delivered using the "notes" method are more convincing than those that are memorized or read.

Neither the memorizing nor the reading method creates convincing presentations. The best plan, by far, is a *notes* method. Plan your presentation carefully and talk from note cards or an outline containing key sentences and major ideas. If you're using PowerPoint, you might choose to create speaker's notes pages, as discussed earlier, to help you stay synchronized with your bullet points. Your notes should be neither entire paragraphs nor single words. Instead, they should contain a complete sentence or two to introduce each major idea. Below the topic sentence(s), outline subpoints and illustrations.

Whether you choose to use note cards, a printed outline, or speaker's notes, you should practice with them. By preparing and then practicing with your notes, you can talk to your audience in a conversational manner. Practice will also help you become skilled at handling your notes while using a remote control to advance your PowerPoint slides, which can be tricky. Notes will keep you on track and prompt your memory, but only if you have rehearsed the presentation thoroughly. Even when using notes, you should look at your audience more than you look at your notes.

Randy Glasbergen. www.glasbergen.com

"Fear of public speaking is quite common. If dressing up as Speaker Man makes you feel more confident, then so be it."

Delivery Techniques

Stage fright is both natural and controllable.

Nearly everyone experiences some degree of stage fright when speaking before a group. "The typical person is uncomfortable in a presentation forum. Neither rank nor personality is a differentiator," says corporate speech consultant Dianna Booher.[12] Being afraid is quite natural and results from actual physiological changes occurring in

---

FIGURE 12.10

Conquer Stage Fright With These Techniques

Ever get nervous before giving a speech? Everyone does! And it's not all in your head, either. When you face something threatening or challenging, your body reacts in what psychologists call the *fight-or-flight response*. This response provides your body with increased energy to deal with threatening situations. You can't eliminate the physiological symptoms altogether, but you can reduce their effects with the following techniques:

- **Breathe deeply.** Use deep breathing to ease your fight-or-flight symptoms. Inhale to a count of ten, hold this breath to a count of ten, and exhale to a count of ten. Concentrate on your counting and your breathing; both activities reduce your stress.

- **Convert your fear.** Don't view your sweaty palms and dry mouth as evidence of fear. Interpret them as symptoms of exuberance, excitement, and enthusiasm to share your ideas.

- **Know your topic.** Feel confident about your topic. Select a topic that you know well and that is relevant to your audience.

- **Use positive self-talk.** Remind yourself that you know your topic and are prepared. Tell yourself that the audience is on your side—because it is!

- **Shift the spotlight to your visuals.** At least some of the time the audience will be focusing on your slides, transparencies, handouts, or whatever you have prepared—and not on you.

- **Ignore any stumbles.** Realize that it's OK to make an occasional mistake. If you make a mistake, don't apologize to your audience. Keep going. The audience will forget any mistakes quickly.

- **Don't admit you're nervous.** Never tell your audience that you're nervous. They will probably never notice!

- **Feel proud when you finish.** You'll be surprised at how good you feel when you finish. Take pride in what you've accomplished, and your audience will reward you with applause and congratulations. And, of course, your body will call off the fight-or-flight response and return to normal!

- **Reward yourself.** After the presentation is over, take time to reward yourself for a job well done. Go out to dinner, take the rest of the day off, go shopping, or do anything else that makes you happy. You've earned it!

your body. Faced with a frightening situation, your body responds with the fight-or-flight response, discussed more fully in Figure 12.10. Typical physical responses include a dry mouth, a pounding heart, sweaty palms, butterflies in the stomach, trembling hands, or a shortage of breath. If you've ever felt any of these symptoms before speaking in front of a group, you're not alone! The good news is that you can learn to control and reduce stage fright, as well as to incorporate techniques for effective speaking, by using the following strategies and techniques before, during, and after your presentation.

Before Your Presentation

Although you may not look forward to a presentation, you can reduce your apprehension and increase your confidence before your talk by following these tips:

Thorough preparation, extensive rehearsal, and stress-reduction techniques can lessen stage fright.

- **Prepare thoroughly.** One of the most effective strategies for reducing stage fright is knowing your subject thoroughly. Research your topic diligently and prepare a careful sentence outline. Those who try to "wing it" usually suffer the worst butterflies—and make the worst presentations.
- **Rehearse repeatedly.** When you rehearse, practice your entire presentation—not just the first half. Place your outline sentences on note cards or PowerPoint speaker's notes pages. You may also wish to include transitional sentences to help you move to the next topic. Use these cards or notes pages as you practice, and include your visual aids in your rehearsal. Rehearse alone or before friends and family. Ask them to provide you constructive, honest feedback. Also try rehearsing on audio- or videotape so that you can evaluate your effectiveness.
- **Time yourself.** Most audiences tend to get restless during longer talks. Thus, try to complete your presentation in no more than 20 minutes. If you have a time limit, don't go over it. Set a timer during your rehearsal to measure your speaking time.
- **Request a lectern.** Every beginning speaker needs the security of a high desk or lectern from which to deliver a presentation. It serves as a note holder and a convenient place to rest wandering hands and arms. Don't, however, lean on it.
- **Check the room.** Before you talk, make sure that a lectern has been provided. If you are using sound equipment or a projector, be certain they are operational. Check electrical outlets and the position of the viewing screen. Ensure that the seating arrangement is appropriate to your needs.
- **Greet members of the audience.** Try to make contact with a few members of the audience when you enter the room, while you are waiting to be introduced, or when you walk to the podium. Your body language should convey friendliness, confidence, and enjoyment.
- **Practice stress reduction.** If you feel tension and fear while you are waiting your turn to speak, use stress-reduction techniques, such as deep breathing. Additional techniques to help you conquer stage fright are presented in Figure 12.10.

During Your Presentation

By following these suggestions during your presentation, you can apply techniques used by professionals to win over the audience, feel comfortable, and look polished:

- **Dress professionally.** Dressing professionally for a presentation will make you look more credible to your audience. You'll also feel more confident.
- **Begin with a pause.** When you first approach the audience, take a moment to adjust your notes and make yourself comfortable. Establish your control of the situation.
- **Present your first sentence from memory.** By memorizing your opening, you can immediately establish rapport with the audience through eye contact. You'll also sound confident and knowledgeable.

Eye contact, a moderate tone of voice, and natural movements enhance a presentation.

- **Maintain eye contact.** If the size of the audience overwhelms you, pick out two individuals on the right and two on the left. Talk directly to these people. If you're presenting to a smaller audience, try to make eye contact with everyone in the room at least once during your presentation.

You want to be your best during your presentation. Begin by researching your topic, preparing your visuals, and practicing thoroughly before your talk. Dress professionally on the day of your presentation. During your presentation maintain eye contact with your audience and use appropriate hand gestures.

- **Control your voice and vocabulary.** This means speaking in moderated tones but loudly enough to be heard. Eliminate verbal static, such as *uh, like, you know,* and *um.* Silence is preferable to meaningless fillers when you are thinking of your next idea.
- **Show enthusiasm.** If you're not excited about your topic, how can you expect your audience to be? Show passion for your topic through your tone, facial expressions, and gestures. Adding variety to your voice also helps to keep your audience alert and interested.
- **Put the brakes on.** Many novice speakers talk too rapidly, displaying their nervousness and making it difficult for audience members to understand their ideas. Slow down and listen to what you are saying.
- **Move naturally.** You can use the lectern to hold your notes so that you are free to move about casually and naturally. Avoid fidgeting with your notes, your clothing, or items in your pockets. Learn to use your body to express a point.
- **Use visual aids effectively.** Discuss and interpret each visual aid for the audience. Move aside as you describe it so that it can be seen fully. Use a pointer if necessary.
- **Avoid digressions.** Stick to your outline and notes. Don't suddenly include clever little anecdotes or digressions that occur to you on the spot. If it's not part of your rehearsed material, leave it out so that you can finish on time.
- **Summarize your main points.** Conclude your presentation by reiterating your main points or by emphasizing what you want the audience to think, do, or remember. Once you have announced your conclusion, proceed to it directly.

After Your Presentation

The time to answer questions, distribute handouts, and reiterate main points is after a presentation.

Concluding gracefully and answering questions skillfully can reinforce your message as well as make you look credible and professional. The following tips help you know what to do after your presentation:

- **Distribute handouts.** If you prepared handouts with data the audience will not need during the presentation, pass them out when you finish.
- **Encourage questions.** If the situation permits a question-and-answer period, announce it at the beginning of your presentation. Then, when you finish, ask for questions. Set a time limit for questions and answers. If you don't know the answer to a question, don't make one up. Instead, offer to find the answer within a day or two. If you make such a promise to your audience, be sure to follow through.

Once your presentation is over, you might ask your audience for questions. If you've planned a question-and-answer session, it's best to tell your audience at the beginning of your presentation so that they can start formulating questions. This also helps prevent interruptions during your presentation.

- **Repeat questions.** Although the speaker may hear the question, audience members often do not. Begin each answer with a repetition of the question. This also gives you thinking time. Then, direct your answer to the entire audience, not just to the person who originally asked the question.
- **Reinforce your main points.** You can use your answers to restate your primary ideas (*I'm glad you brought that up because it gives me a chance to elaborate on . . .*). In answering questions, avoid becoming defensive or debating the questioner.
- **Keep control.** Don't allow one individual to take over. Keep the entire audience involved.
- **Avoid *Yes, but* answers.** The word *but* immediately cancels any preceding message. Try replacing it with *and*. For example, *Yes, X has been tried. And Y works even better because . . . .*
- **End with a summary and appreciation.** To signal the end of the session before you take the last question, say something like *We have time for just one more question.* As you answer the last question, try to work it into a summary of your main points. Then, express appreciation to the audience for the opportunity to talk with them.

ADAPTING TO INTERNATIONAL AND CROSS-CULTURAL AUDIENCES

Every good speaker adapts to the audience, and cross-cultural presentations call for special adjustments and sensitivity. When working with an interpreter or speaking before individuals whose English is limited, you'll need to be very careful about your language. You might have to speak more slowly, use simple English, avoid jargon and clichés, and use short sentences.

Beyond these basic language adaptations, however, more fundamental sensitivity is often necessary. In organizing a presentation for a cross-cultural audience, think twice about delivering your main idea up front. Many people (notably those in Japanese, Latin American, and Arabic cultures) consider such directness to be brash and inappropriate. Remember that others may not share our cultural emphasis on straightforwardness.[13]

Addressing cross-cultural audiences requires a speaker to consider audience expectations and cultural conventions.

Also consider breaking your presentation into short, discrete segments. Such organization enables participants to ask questions and digest what has been presented. This technique is especially effective in cultures where people communicate in

© STEWART COHEN/DIGITAL VISION/GETTY IMAGES

"loops." In the Middle East, for example, Arab speakers "mix circuitous, irrelevant (by American standards) conversations with short dashes of information that go directly to the point." Presenters who are patient, tolerant, and "mature" (in the eyes of the audience) will make the sale or win the contract.[14]

Match your presentation to the expectations of your audience. In Germany, for instance, successful presentations tend to be dense with facts and precise statistics. Americans might say *around 30 percent* while a German presenter might say *30.4271958 percent*. Make sure, too, that you dress appropriately for your audience.

You should also be aware that some cultures prefer greater formality than Americans exercise. Writing on a flipchart or transparency seems natural and spontaneous in this country. Abroad, though, such informal techniques may suggest that the speaker does not value the audience enough to prepare proper visual aids in advance.[15]

This caution aside, you'll still want to use visual aids to communicate your message. These visuals should be written in both languages, so that you and your audience understand them. Never use numbers without writing them out for all to see. If possible, say numbers in both languages. Distribute translated handouts, summarizing your important information, when you finish. Finally, be careful of your body language. Looking people in the eye suggests intimacy and self-confidence in this country, but in other cultures such eye contact may be considered disrespectful.

SUMMING UP AND LOOKING FORWARD

This chapter presented techniques for making effective oral presentations. Good presentations begin with analyses of your purpose and your audience. Organizing the content involves preparing an effective introduction, body, and closing. The introduction should capture the listener's attention, identify the speaker, establish credibility, and preview the main points. The body should discuss two to four main points, with appropriate explanations, details, and verbal signposts to guide listeners. The conclusion should review the main points, provide a final focus, and allow the speaker to leave the podium gracefully.

You can improve audience rapport by using effective imagery including analogies, metaphors, similes, personal anecdotes, statistics, and worst/best-case scenarios. In illustrating a presentation, use simple, easily understood visual aids to emphasize and clarify main points. If you employ PowerPoint, you can enhance the presentation by using templates, layout designs, bullet points, and multimedia elements. Don't allow your PowerPoint slides, however, to "steal your thunder."

In delivering your presentation, outline the main points on note cards and rehearse repeatedly. During the presentation consider beginning with a pause and presenting your first sentence from memory. Dress professionally, make eye contact, control your voice, show enthusiasm for your topic, speak and move naturally, and avoid digressions. After your talk distribute handouts and answer questions. End gracefully and express appreciation.

The final two chapters of this book focus on your ultimate goal—getting a job or advancing in your career. In Chapter 13 you'll learn how to write a persuasive résumé and other employment documents. In Chapter 14 you'll discover how to ace an employment interview.

CRITICAL THINKING

1. Why is it necessary to repeat key points in an oral presentation?
2. How can a speaker make the most effective use of visual aids?
3. If PowerPoint is so effective, why are people speaking out against using it in presentations?
4. How can speakers prevent electronic presentation software from upstaging them?
5. What techniques are most effective for reducing stage fright?

CHAPTER REVIEW

6. What is the most important thing to do as you prepare your presentation? What should you ask yourself before you do anything else?

7. Why is it important to analyze your audience when preparing your presentation?

8. Name three goals to be achieved in the introduction of an oral presentation.

9. What should the conclusion to an oral presentation include?

10. Name three ways for a speaker to use verbal signposts in a presentation. Illustrate each.

11. List ten ways that an oral presentation may be organized.

12. What should you consider when deciding what types of visual aids to use during your presentation?

13. How is the Rule of Seven applied in preparing bulleted points?

14. What delivery method is most effective for speakers?

15. How might presentations before international or cross-cultural audiences be altered to be most effective?

ACTIVITIES AND CASES

12.1 Critiquing a Speech

Your Task. Visit your library and select a speech from *Vital Speeches of Our Day*. You can also listen to a variety of famous speeches online at *http://www.historychannel.com/speeches/archive1.html*. (**Note:** If this link doesn't work, use a search tool such as *http://www.google.com* to search for "Speech Transcripts.") Write a memo report to your instructor critiquing the speech in terms of the following:

a. Effectiveness of the introduction, body, and conclusion

b. Evidence of effective overall organization

c. Use of verbal signposts to create coherence

d. Emphasis of two to four main points

e. Effectiveness of supporting facts (use of examples, statistics, quotations, and so forth)

f. Focus on audience benefits

g. Enthusiasm for the topic

12.2 Knowing Your Audience

Your Task. Select a recent issue of *Fortune*, *The Wall Street Journal*, *Fast Company*, *BusinessWeek*, *The Economist*, or another business periodical approved by your instructor. Based on your analysis of your classmates, select an article that will appeal to them and that you can relate to their needs. Submit to your instructor a one-page summary that includes the following: (a) the author, article title, source, issue date, and page reference; (b) a one-paragraph article summary; (c) a description of why you believe the article will appeal to your classmates; and (d) a summary of how you can relate the article to their needs.

12.3 Preparing an Oral Presentation From an Article

Your Task. Select a business-related newspaper or magazine article and prepare an oral report based on it. Submit your outline, introduction, and conclusion to your instructor, or present the report to your class. You might use the same article you used for Activity 12.2. If you are required to present the report to your class, your instructor will set criteria such as length of time.

12.4 Overcoming Stage Fright

What makes you most nervous when making a presentation before class? Being tongue-tied? Fearing all eyes on you? Messing up? Forgetting your ideas and looking silly?

Your Task. Discuss the previous questions as a class. Then, in groups of three or four, talk about ways to overcome these fears. Your instructor may ask you to write a memo (individual or collective) summarizing your suggestions, or you may break out of your small groups and report your best ideas to the entire class.

12.5 Investigating Oral Communication in Your Field

One of the best sources of career information is someone in your field.

Your Task. Interview one or two individuals in your professional field. How is oral communication important in this profession? Does the need for oral skills change as one advances? What suggestions can these people make to newcomers to the field for developing proficient oral communication skills? Present your findings to your class.

INFOTRAC   **WEB**

12.6 Discovering New Presentation Tips

Your Task. Using InfoTrac or the Web, perform a search for "business presentations." Read at least three articles that provide suggestions for giving business presentations. If possible, print the most relevant findings. Select at least eight good tips or techniques that you did NOT learn from this chapter. Your instructor may ask you to bring them to class for discussion or submit a short memo report outlining your tips.

12.7 Outlining an Oral Presentation

One of the hardest parts of preparing an oral presentation is developing the outline.

Your Task. Select an oral presentation topic from the list in Activity 12.10 or suggest an original topic. Prepare an outline for your presentation using the following format.

Title _____

Purpose _____

	I.	INTRODUCTION
Gain attention of audience		A.
Involve audience		B.
Establish credibility		C.
Preview main points		D.
Transition	II.	BODY
Main point		A.
Illustrate, clarify, contrast		1.
		2.
		3.
Transition		
Main point		B.
Illustrate, clarify, contrast		1.
		2.
		3.
Transition		
Main point		C.
Illustrate, clarify, contrast		1.
		2.
		3.
Transition	III.	CONCLUSION
Summarize main points		A.
Provide final focus		B.
Encourage questions		C.

INFOTRAC — **WEB**

12.8 Exploring the New World of Web Conferencing

Your boss at the Home Realty Company is interested in learning more about Web conferencing but doesn't have time to do the research herself. She asks you to find out the following:

a. In terms of revenue, how big is the Web conferencing industry?

b. Who are the leading providers of Web conferencing tools?

c. What are the typical costs associated with holding a Web conference?

d. How are other realtors using Web conferencing?

Your Task. Using InfoTrac and the Internet, locate articles and Web sites that will provide the information your boss has outlined. Be prepared to role-play an informal presentation to your boss in which you begin with an introduction, answer the four questions in the body, and present a conclusion.

INFOTRAC — **WEB**

12.9 Researching Job-Application Information

Your Task. Using InfoTrac or the Web, perform a search for one of the following topics. Find as many articles as you can. Then organize and present a five- to ten-minute informative talk to your class.

a. Do recruiters prefer one- or two-page résumés?

b. How do applicant-tracking systems work?

c. How are inflated résumés detected and what are the consequences?

d. What's new in writing cover letters in job applications?

e. How can the Web be used most effectively during the job search?

f. What are some new rules for résumés?

12.10 Choosing a Topic for an Oral Presentation

Your Task. Select a topic from the following list or from the report topics at the end of Chapter 10. For an expanded list of report topics, go to **Guffey Xtra!** (*http://guffeyxtra.swlearning.com*). Prepare a five- to ten-minute oral presentation. Consider yourself an expert who has been called in to explain some aspect of the topic before a group of interested people. Since your time is limited, prepare a concise yet forceful presentation with effective visual aids.

a. What is the career outlook in a field of your choice? Consider job growth, compensation, and benefits. What kind of academic or other experience is typically required in your field?

b. What information and tools are available online to someone searching for full-time employment? In what ways can the Web help someone during a job search?

c. How can attendance be improved at sporting events at your school?

d. What simple network security tips can your company use to avoid problems?

e. What is telecommuting, and for what kinds of workers is it an appropriate work alternative?

f. What criteria should parents use in deciding whether their young child should attend public, private, parochial, or home school?

g. What travel location would you recommend for college students during the holidays or in the summer?

h. What is the economic outlook for a given product, such as domestic cars, laptop computers, digital cameras, fitness equipment, or a product of your choice?

i. How can your company or educational institution improve its image?

j. What are the Webby Awards, and what criteria do the judges use to evaluate Web sites?

k. What brand and model of computer and printer represent the best buy for college students today?

l. What franchise would offer the best investment opportunity for an entrepreneur in your area?

m. How should a job candidate dress for an interview?

n. What should a guide to proper cell phone use include?

o. Are internships worth the effort?

p. Why should a company have a written e-mail and Internet-use policy?

q. Where should your organization hold its next convention?

r. What is your opinion of the statement "Advertising steals our time, defaces the landscape, and degrades the dignity of public institutions"?[16]

s. How can businesspeople reduce the amount of e-mail spam they receive?

t. What is the outlook for real estate (commercial or residential) investment in your area?

u. What are the pros and cons of videoconferencing for [name an organization]?

v. What do the personal assistants for celebrities do, and how does one become a personal assistant? (Investigate the Association of Celebrity Personal Assistants.)

w. What kinds of gifts are appropriate for businesses to give clients and customers during the holiday season?

x. What scams are on the Federal Trade Commission's List of Top 10 Consumer Scams, and how can consumers avoid falling for them?

y. How are businesses and conservationists working together to protect the world's dwindling tropical forests?

z. Should employees be able to use computers in a work environment for anything other than work-related business?

VIDEO RESOURCE

Video Library 1, *Building Workplace Skills*
Effective On-the-Job Oral Presentations. Watch this video to see how businesspeople apply Guffey's writing process in developing a persuasive oral presentation.

GRAMMAR/MECHANICS CHECKUP—12

Capitalization

Review Sections 3.01–3.16 in the Grammar/Mechanics Handbook. Then study each of the following statements. Draw three underlines below any lowercase letter that should be capitalized. Draw a slash (/) through any capital letter that you wish to change to lowercase. Indicate in the space provided the number of changes you made in each sentence and record the number of the G/M principle(s) illustrated. If you made no changes, write *0*. When you finish, compare your responses with those provided at the back of the book. If your responses differ, study carefully the principles in parentheses.

5   (3.01, 3.06a)   **Example**   Once the Management Team and the Union members finally agreed, mayor Johnson signed the Agreement.

1. All united passengers will exit the Plane at gate 3b when they reach the key west international airport.

2. Personal tax rates for japanese citizens are low by International standards; rates for japanese corporations are high, according to Iwao Nakatani, an Economics Professor at Osaka university.

3. Stephanie, an aspiring Entrepreneur, hopes to open her own Consulting Firm one day.

4. Randy plans to take courses in Psychology, Math, History, and english next semester.

5. Did you see the *BusinessWeek* article entitled "harry potter and the endless cash"?

6. Although I recommend the dell inspiron 2200, you may purchase any Notebook Computer you choose.

7. According to a Federal Government report, any regulation of State and County banking must receive local approval.

8. The vice president of the united states said, "we continue to look for Foreign invesment opportunities."

9. The Comptroller of Zarconi Industries reported to the President and the Board of Directors that the securities and exchange commission was beginning an investigation of their Company.

10. My Father, who lives near death valley, says that the Moon and Stars are especially brilliant on a cold, clear night.

11. Our Marketing Director met with Karin Bloedorn, Manager of the Advertising Sales Department, to plan an Ad Campaign for our newly redesigned Wireless Phone.

12. In the Spring our Admissions Director plans to travel to venezuela, colombia, and ecuador to recruit new Students.

13. To reach Belle Isle park, which is located on an Island in the Detroit river, tourists pass over the Douglas MacArthur bridge.

14. On page 8 of the report, you'll find a list of all employees with Master's degrees in our accounting department.

15. Please consult figure 3.2 in chapter 5 for U.S. census bureau figures regarding non-english-speaking residents.

GRAMMAR/MECHANICS CHALLENGE—12

The following executive summary of a report has faults in grammar, punctuation, spelling, number form, wordiness, and word use. Correct the errors with standard proofreading marks (see Appendix B) or revise the message online at **Guffey Xtra!**.

EXECUTIVE SUMMARY
Purpose of Report

The purposes of this report is (1) To determine the Sun coast university campus communitys awareness of the campus recycling program and (2) To recommend ways to increase participation. Sun Coasts recycling program was intended to respond to the increasing problem of waste disposal, to fulfil it's social responsibility as an educational institution, and to meet the demands of legislation that made it a requirement for individuals and organizations to recycle.

A Survey was conducted in an effort to learn about the campus communities recycling habits and to make an assessment of the participation in the recycling program that is current. 220 individuals responded to the Survey but twenty-seven Surveys could not be used. Since Sun coast universitys recycling program include only aluminum, glass, paper and plastic at this point in time these were the only materials considered in this Study.

Recycling at Sun coast

Most Survey respondants recognized the importance of recycling, they stated that they do recycle aluminum, glass, paper and plastic on a regular basis either at home or at work. However most respondants displayed a low-level of awareness, and use of the on campus program. Many of the respondants was unfamilar with the location of the bins around campus; and therefore had not participated in the Recycling Program. Other responses indicated that the bins were not located in convenent locations.

Reccommendations for increasing recycling participation

Recommendations for increasing participation in the Program include the following;

1. relocating the recycling bins for greater visability

2. development of incentive programs to gain the participation of on campus groups

3. training student volunteers to give on campus presentations that give an explanation of the need for recycling, and the benefits of using the Recycling Program

4. we should increase Advertising in regard to the Program

COMMUNICATION WORKSHOP
COLLABORATION

TECHNIQUES FOR TAKING PART IN
EFFECTIVE AND PROFESSIONAL TEAM PRESENTATIONS

You may find that you are assigned to a team that must prepare and deliver an oral presentation. This can happen in the classroom and on the job. If you've been part of any team efforts before, you also know that such projects can be very frustrating—particularly when some team members don't carry their weight or when members cannot resolve conflict. On the other hand, team projects can be harmonious and productive when members establish ground rules and follow guidelines related to preparing, planning, collecting information for, organizing, rehearsing, and evaluating team projects. Here are steps to take to ensure that your team presentation is a success.

- **Prepare to work together.** Before you begin working on the presentation, you should (1) compare schedules of team members in order to set up the best meetings times, (2) plan to meet often, and (3) discuss how you will deal with team members who are not contributing to the project.

- **Plan the presentation.** You need to make a number of decisions in the beginning about the presentation. These include agreeing on (1) the specific purpose of the presentation, (2) who your audience is, (3) how long the presentation will be, (4) what types of visuals will be included, and (5) the basic structure and content of the presentation.

- **Make assignments.** Once you have a clear understanding of what your presentation will cover, give each team member a written assignment that details his or her responsibilities for researching content, producing visuals, developing handout materials, building transitions between segments, and showing up for team meetings and rehearsals.

- **Collect information.** To gather or generate information, teams can brainstorm together, conduct interviews, or search the Web for information. The team should decide on deadlines for collecting information and should discuss how to ensure the accuracy and currency of the information collected. Team members should exchange periodic progress reports on how their research is coming along.

- **Organize and develop the presentation.** Once all research has been gathered, it's time for the team to start working on the presentation. Decide on the organization of the presentation, compose a draft of the presentation in writing, and prepare PowerPoint slides and other visual aids. The team should meet often to discuss and revise the presentation and to determine which team member will be responsible for delivering what parts of the presentation. Be sure each member builds a transition to the next presenter's topic and launches it smoothly. Strive for logical connections between segments.

- **Edit, rehearse, and evaluate.** Before the presentation is made, it's important to rehearse several times as a team. Make sure that transitions from speaker to speaker are smooth. For example, you might say, *Now that I've discussed how to prepare for the meeting, Renee is going to discuss how to get the meeting started.* Decide who will be responsible for advancing slides during the presentation. Practice fielding questions if you plan to have a question-and-answer session. Decide how you're going to dress so that you look professional and complementary. Look over your PowerPoint slides to make sure that the design, format, and vocabulary are consistent.

- **Deliver the presentation.** On the day of the presentation, show up on time and in appropriate attire. Deliver your part of the presentation with professionalism and enthusiasm. Remember that your audience is judging the team on its performance, not the individuals. Do what you can to make your team shine!

Career Application. You have just been named to a team that is to produce an organizational five-year plan for your company. You know this assignment will end with an oral presentation to management and stockholders. Your first reaction is dismay. You've been on teams before in the classroom, and you know how frustrating they can be. But you decide that if you must take on this task, you want to make sure you know what you are doing and that you'll contribute positively to this team effort.

Your Task

In small groups or with the entire class, discuss what traits and actions make effective and ineffective team members. How can one contribute positively to a team? How should teams deal with members who aren't contributing or who have negative attitudes? What should team members do to ensure that the final presentation is professional, well coordinated, and effective?

COMMUNICATING FOR EMPLOYMENT

PHOTOS: © IMAGE 100/ROYALTY-FREE/CORBIS; © DIGITAL VISION/GETTY IMAGES; © DIGITAL VISION/GETTY IMAGES

CHAPTER 13

THE JOB SEARCH, RÉSUMÉS, AND COVER LETTERS

" *Think not of yourself as the architect of your career but as the sculptor. Expect to have to do a lot of hard hammering and chiseling and scraping and polishing.*[1] "

Bertie Charles Forbes, founder of *Forbes* magazine

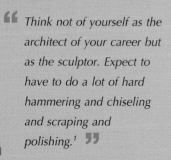

OBJECTIVES

- Prepare for employment by identifying your interests, evaluating your assets, recognizing the changing nature of jobs, choosing a career path, and studying traditional and electronic job-search techniques.

- Compare and contrast chronological and functional résumés.

- Organize and format the parts of a résumé to produce a persuasive product.

- Identify techniques that prepare a résumé for today's technologies, including preparing a scannable résumé, an embedded résumé, and an e-portfolio.

- Write a persuasive cover letter to accompany your résumé.

Whether you are looking for an internship, applying for a full-time position, searching for a part-time job, competing for a promotion, or changing careers, you'll be more successful if you understand employment strategies and how to promote yourself with a winning résumé. The reality is that the job market is highly competitive, and you must do everything you can to outshine your competition. The better prepared you are, the more confident you'll feel during your search. This chapter provides expert current advice in preparing for employment, searching the job market, writing a persuasive résumé, and developing an effective cover letter. What you learn here can lead to a successful job search and maybe even your dream job.

PREPARING FOR EMPLOYMENT

Finding a satisfying career requires learning about yourself, the job market, and the employment process.

You may think that the first step in finding a job is writing a résumé. Wrong! The job-search process actually begins long before you are ready to prepare your résumé. Regardless of the kind of employment you seek, you must invest time and effort getting ready. You can't hope to find the position of your dreams without (1) knowing yourself, (2) knowing the job market, and (3) knowing the employment process.

One of the first things you should do is obtain career information and choose a specific job objective. At the same time, you should be studying the job market and becoming aware of substantial changes in the nature of work. You'll want to understand how to use the latest Web resources in your job search. Finally, you'll need to design a persuasive résumé and cover letter appropriate for small businesses as well as for larger organizations that may be using résumé-scanning programs. Following these steps, summarized in Figure 13.1 and described in this chapter, gives you a master plan for landing a job you really want.

Identifying Your Interests

Analyzing your likes and dislikes helps you make wise employment decisions.

The employment process begins with introspection. This means looking inside yourself to analyze what you like and dislike so that you can make good employment choices. Career counselors charge large sums for helping individuals learn about themselves. You can do the same kind of self-examination—without spending a cent. For guidance in choosing a field that eventually proves to be satisfying, answer the following questions. If you have already chosen a field, think carefully about how your answers relate to that choice.

Answering specific questions can help you choose a career.

- *Do you enjoy working with people, data, or things?*
- *Would you like to work for someone else or be your own boss?*
- *How important are salary, benefits, technology support, and job stability?*
- *How important are working environment, colleagues, and job stimulation?*
- *Would you rather work for a large or a small company?*
- *Must you work in a specific city, geographical area, or climate?*
- *Are you looking for security, travel opportunities, money, power, or prestige?*
- *How would you describe the perfect job, boss, and coworkers?*

FIGURE 13.1   **The Employment Search**

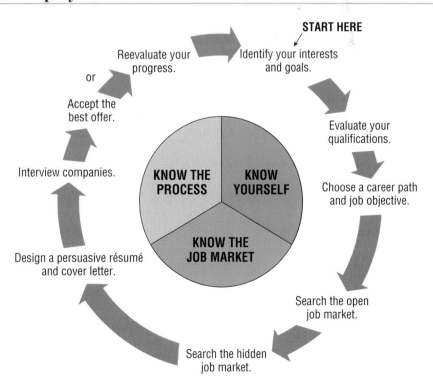

Evaluating Your Qualifications

Decide what qualifications you possess and how you can prove them.

In addition to your interests, assess your qualifications. Employers today want to know what assets you have to offer them. Your responses to the following questions will target your thinking as well as prepare a foundation for your résumé. Remember, though, that employers seek more than empty assurances; they will want proof of your qualifications.

Randy Glasbergen.
www.glasbergen.com

"We found someone overseas who can drink coffee and talk about sports all day for a fraction of what we're paying you."

- *What technology skills can you offer?* Employers are often interested in specific computer software programs.
- *What other skills have you acquired in school, on the job, or through activities?* How can you demonstrate these skills?
- *Do you work well with people? Do you enjoy team-work?* What proof can you offer? Consider extracurricular activities, clubs, class projects, and jobs.
- *Are you a leader, self-starter, or manager?* What evidence can you offer?
- *Do you speak, write, or understand another language?*
- *Do you learn quickly? Are you creative? Do you take initiative? Are you flexible?* How can you demonstrate these characteristics?
- *Do you communicate well in speech and in writing?* How can you verify these talents?

Recognizing the Changing Nature of Jobs

People feel less job security after downsizing, outsourcing, and offshoring of jobs.

As you learned in Chapter 1, the nature of the workplace is changing. One of the most significant changes involves the concept of the "job." Following the downsizing of corporations and the outsourcing and offshoring of jobs in recent years, companies are employing fewer people in permanent positions.

Other forms of employment are replacing traditional jobs. In many companies teams complete special projects and then disband. Work may also be outsourced to a group that's not even part of an organization. Because new technologies can

Employees who are most valuable to their employers are willing to broaden their skills through training, show flexibility in adapting to a changing work environment, and work successfully with fellow employees or on a team. These employees have the best chance of job security and career advancement.

© STOCKBYTE PLATINUM/GETTY IMAGES

spring up overnight making today's skills obsolete, employers are less willing to hire people into jobs with narrow descriptions. Instead, they are hiring contingency employees who work temporarily and then leave. What's more, big companies are no longer the main employers. People work for smaller companies, or they are starting their own businesses. By 2020 small, privately owned companies are expected to comprise 25 percent of U.S. businesses.[2]

The workplace has also become more flexible. Working from home or other remote locations, called *telecommuting*, is growing in popularity. Changing technology and environmental concerns have led to this trend. Today more than 60 percent of workers have positions that do not require them to be in a specific physical location.[3] Furthermore, these positions are most likely technical in nature. Skilled jobs are quickly replacing semiskilled and unskilled jobs as technology skills become more important at all levels.

Jobs are becoming more flexible and less permanent.

What do these changes mean for you? For one thing, you should probably no longer think in terms of a lifelong career with a single company. Don't count on regular pay raises, promotions, and a comfortable retirement income. You should also become keenly aware that a career that relies on yesterday's skills is headed for trouble. You're going to need updated, marketable skills that serve you well as you move from job to job. Upgrading your skills through constant retraining is the best career strategy for the twenty-first century. People who learn quickly and adapt to change will always be in demand even in a climate of surging change.[4]

Choosing a Career Path

The employment picture today is much different from that of a decade or two ago. By the time you are 30, you can expect to have had five to seven jobs. The average employee will have worked at 12 to 15 jobs over the course of a career, staying an average of 3.6 years at each job.[5] Some of you probably have not yet settled on your first career choice; others are returning to college to retrain for a new career. Although you may be changing jobs in the future, you still need to train for a specific career area now. In choosing an area, you'll make the best decisions when you can match your interests and qualifications with the requirements and rewards in specific careers. Where can you find the best career data? Here are some suggestions:

Career information can be obtained at campus career centers and libraries, from the Web, in classified ads, and from professional organizations.

- **Visit your campus career center.** Most have literature, inventories, software programs, and Internet connections that allow you to investigate such fields as accounting, finance, office technology, information systems, hotel management, and so forth.
- **Search the Web.** Many job-search sites on the Web offer career-planning information and resources. You'll learn about some of the best sites in the next section.
- **Use your library.** Many print and online resources are especially helpful. Consult *O*NET Occupational Information Network*, *Dictionary of Occupational Titles*, *Occupational Outlook Handbook*, and *The Jobs Rated Almanac* for information about job duties, qualifications, salaries, and employment trends.

Summer and part-time jobs and internships are good opportunities to learn about different careers.

- **Take a summer job, internship, or part-time position in your field.** Nothing is better than trying out a career by actually working in it or in a related area. Many companies offer internships and temporary or part-time jobs to begin training college students and to develop relationships with them. These relationships sometimes blossom into permanent positions.
- **Interview someone in your chosen field.** People are usually flattered when asked to describe their careers. Inquire about needed skills, required courses, financial and other rewards, benefits, working conditions, future trends, and entry requirements.
- **Monitor the classified ads.** Early in your college career, begin monitoring want ads and Web sites of companies in your career area. Check job availability, qualifications sought, duties, and salary range. Don't wait until you're about to graduate to see how the job market looks.

- **Join professional organizations in your field.** Frequently, they offer student membership status and reduced rates. You'll get inside information on issues, career news, and possibly jobs.
- **Join student clubs.** Many colleges and universities sponsor student organizations that provide opportunities for students to network, hear guest speakers, and explore career options.

Searching for a Job Electronically

Employment Web sites list many jobs, but finding a job electronically requires more work than simply clicking a mouse.

Another significant change in the workplace involves the way we find jobs. Searching for a job electronically has become a common, but not always fruitful, approach. With all the publicity given to employment Web sites, you might think that electronic job searching has totally replaced traditional methods. Not so! Although Web sites such as *http://www.collegerecruiter.com* and *http://hotjobs.yahoo.com*, shown in Figure 13.2, list millions of jobs, actually landing a job is much harder than just clicking a mouse.

Both recruiters and job seekers complain about online job boards. Corporate recruiters say that the big job boards bring a flood of candidates, many of whom are not suited for the listed jobs. Job candidates grumble that listings are frequently out-of-date and fail to produce leads. Applicants worry about the privacy of information posted online. Despite these issues, job seekers go to both the big boards and beyond searching for jobs and advice.

USING THE BIG JOB BOARDS

Although they may not actually find a position at one of the big employment Web sites, many job seekers use them to gather job-search information, such as résumé, interviewing, and salary tips. These Webs sites serve as a jumping-off point in most searches. And, who knows—you might get lucky and be hired for the job of your dreams from an online site. With over 40,000 job boards and employment Web sites

FIGURE 13.2 — • **Job Boards Jump Start a Job Search**

Commercial job boards such as *College Recruiter* and *Yahoo! HotJobs* not only list millions of job openings but also provide excellent tips for conducting job searches, writing résumés, organizing cover letters, and preparing for job interviews.

Yahoo! image reproduced with permission of Yahoo! Inc. © 2005 by Yahoo! Inc. YAHOO! and the YAHOO! logo are trademarks of Yahoo! Inc.
College Recruiter image courtesy of Collegerecruiter.com.

deluging the Internet, it's hard to know where to start. We've listed a few of the best-known online job sites here:[6]

- **Monster** (*http://www.monster.com*) offers access to information on more than 1 million jobs worldwide. You may search for jobs by keyword, company name, geographic location, and job category. Many consider it to be the Web's premier job site.
- **CareerBuilder** (*http://www.careerbuilder.com*) claims to be the nation's largest employment network. At this writing it lists 225,000 jobs and has over 100,000 client companies posting jobs. Users can search for these jobs by keyword, geographic location, and job type. They can also search for positions within specific salary ranges.
- **CareerJournal** (*http://www.CareerJournal.com*), sponsored by *The Wall Street Journal*, lists over 75,000 executive positions from over 10,000 companies.
- **College Recruiter** (*http://www.CollegeRecruiter.com*) claims to be the "highest traffic entry-level job site" for students and graduates. It lists over 60,000 jobs from more than 5,000 client companies.
- **Yahoo! Hot Jobs** (*http://hotjobs.yahoo.com*) claims to be the leader in the online recruiting industry and says that job seekers voted it the "Best General Purpose Job Board for Job Seekers."

BEYOND THE BIG JOB BOARDS

Disillusioned job seekers increasingly turn their backs on the big online job boards but not on electronic job-searching tactics. Savvy candidates know how to use their computers to search for jobs at Web sites such as the following:

- **Corporate Web sites.** Probably the best way to find a job online is at a company's own Web site. One poll found that 70 percent of job seekers felt they were more likely to obtain an interview if they posted their résumés on corporate sites. In addition to finding a more direct route to decision makers, job seekers thought that they could keep their job searches more private at corporate Web sites than at big job board sites.[7]
- **Association Web sites.** Online job listings have proved to be the single-most popular feature of many professional organizations such as the International Association of Administrative Professionals, the American Institute of Certified Public Accountants, the National Association of Sales Professionals, the National Association of Legal Assistants, and the Association of Information Technology Professionals. Although you pay a fee, the benefits of joining a professional association in your career field are enormous.
- **Local employment Web sites.** Pam Dixon, author of *Job Searching Online for Dummies*, recommends using local, community-based employment sites such as *http://www.craigslist.com* because "they're not out to make a buck."[8] Many employers use these sites because listing job openings is free and often results in high-quality applicants. Many job seekers prefer these sites because they can look for positions in very specific geographic locations, and they often find job postings that aren't listed anywhere else.
- **Niche Web sites.** If you want a job in a specialized field, look for a niche Web site. You'll find employment sites that have been created for individuals seeking positions in such fields as accounting, office administration, and computer technology. Employment Web sites for specific target populations, such as disabled job applicants or recent college graduates, also exist.
- **Search engine Google.** If you're in a hurry, just name a city and a job title as search terms in Google (*www.google.com*), and its powerful search engine will find jobs collected from the three big job boards.[9]

Thousands of job boards listing millions of jobs now flood the Internet. The harsh reality, however, is that landing a job still depends largely on personal contacts. One employment expert said, "Online recruiting is a little like computer dating. People

Job prospects may be more promising at the Web sites of corporations, professional organizations, employers' organizations, and niche fields.

Many jobs are listed on the Web, but most hiring is still done through personal contact.

Traditional job-search techniques include checking classified ads, examining announcements in professional publications, and developing your own personal network of people who may help you find the right position. Maintaining communication with the people in your network is made easier by the rich array of communication options available today, including cell phones, e-mail, instant messaging, voice mail, and fax.

© HOBY FINN/PHOTODISC/GETTY IMAGES

may find dates that way, but they don't get married that way."[10] Another professional placement expert said, "If you think just [posting] your résumé will get you a job, you're crazy. [Electronic services are] just a supplement to a core strategy of networking your buns off."[11]

Searching for a Job Using Traditional Techniques

Finding the perfect job requires an early start and a determined effort. Whether you use traditional or online job search techniques, you should be prepared to launch an aggressive campaign. What's more, you can't start too early. Some universities now require first- and second-year students to take an employment seminar called "Reality 101." Students are told early on that a college degree alone doesn't guarantee a job. They are cautioned that grade point averages make a difference to employers. They are also advised of the importance of experience, such as internships and participation in campus activities and clubs. Traditional job-search techniques, such as those described here, continue to be critical in landing jobs.

- **Check classified ads in local and national newspapers.** Be aware, though, that classified ads are only one small source of jobs.
- **Check announcements in publications of professional organizations.** If you do not have a student membership, ask your professors to share current copies of professional journals, newsletters, and so on. Your college library is another good source.
- **Contact companies in which you're interested, even if you know of no current opening.** Write an unsolicited letter and include your résumé. Follow up with a telephone call. Check the company's Web site for employment possibilities and procedures. Put on professional business attire and deliver copies of your résumé in person.
- **Sign up for campus interviews with visiting company representatives.** Campus recruiters may open your eyes to exciting jobs and locations.
- **Ask for advice from your professors.** They often have contacts and ideas for expanding your job search.
- **Develop your own network of contacts.** Networking still accounts for most of the jobs found by candidates. Therefore, plan to spend a considerable portion

of your job-search time developing a personal network. The Communication Workshop at the end of this chapter gives you step-by-step instructions for traditional networking as well as some ideas for online networking.

THE PERSUASIVE RÉSUMÉ

After using both traditional and online resources to learn about the employment market and to develop job leads, you'll focus on writing a persuasive résumé. Such a résumé does more than merely list your qualifications. It packages your assets into a convincing advertisement that sells you for a specific job. The goal of a persuasive résumé is winning an interview. Even if you are not in the job market at this moment, preparing a résumé now has advantages. Having a current résumé makes you look well organized and professional should an unexpected employment opportunity arise. Moreover, preparing a résumé early can help you recognize weak areas and give you time to bolster them. Even after you've accepted a position, it's a good idea to keep your résumé up-to-date. You never know when an opportunity might come along!

Choosing a Résumé Style

See our comprehensive collection of résumé styles beginning on page 390.

Résumés usually fall into two categories: chronological and functional. In this section we present basic information as well as inside tips on how to choose an appropriate résumé style, how to determine its length, and how to arrange its parts. You'll also learn about adding a summary of qualifications, which busy recruiters increasingly want to see. Models of the résumés in the following discussion are shown in our comprehensive résumé section beginning on page 390.

CHRONOLOGICAL

Chronological résumés focus on job history with the most recent positions listed first.

The most popular résumé format is the chronological résumé, shown in Figures 13.6 through 13.9 in our résumé collection. It lists work history job by job, starting with the most recent position. Recruiters favor the chronological format because such résumés quickly reveal a candidate's education and experience record. Recruiters are familiar with the chronological résumé, and as many as 85 percent of employers prefer to see a candidate's résumé in this format.[12] The chronological style works well for candidates who have experience in their field of employment and for those who show steady career growth, but it is less appropriate for people who have changed jobs frequently or who have gaps in their employment records. For college students and others who lack extensive experience, the functional résumé format may be preferable.

FUNCTIONAL

Because functional résumés focus on skills, they may be more advisable for graduates with little experience.

The functional résumé, shown in Figure 13.10, focuses attention on a candidate's skills rather than on past employment. Like a chronological résumé, the functional résumé begins with the candidate's name, address, telephone number, job objective, and education. Instead of listing jobs, though, the functional résumé groups skills and accomplishments in special categories, such as *Supervisory and Management Skills* or *Retailing and Marketing Experience*. This résumé style highlights accomplishments and can de-emphasize a negative employment history. People who have changed jobs frequently, who have gaps in their employment records, or who are entering an entirely different field may prefer the functional résumé. Recent graduates with little or no related employment experience often find the functional résumé useful. Older job seekers who want to de-emphasize a long job history and job hunters who are afraid of appearing overqualified may also prefer the functional format. Be aware, though, that online job boards may insist on chronological format. In addition, some recruiters are suspicious of functional résumés, thinking the candidate is hiding something.

Deciding on Length

Recruiters may say they prefer one-page résumés, but many choose to interview those with longer résumés.

Experts simply do not agree on how long a résumé should be. Conventional wisdom has always held that recruiters prefer one-page résumés. That's because busy recruiters are said to give no more than 30 seconds to each résumé they peruse. A carefully controlled study of 570 recruiters, however, revealed that they *claimed* they preferred one-page résumés. But the recruiters actually *chose* to interview the applicants with two-page résumés.[13] Recruiters who are serious about candidates often prefer a full picture with the kind of details that can be provided in a two-page résumé.

Randy Glasbergen.
www.glasbergen.com

"What do you mean, it's not a good résumé? It's the most expensive one they had on eBay!"

The entire question may become moot as more and more recruiters encourage online résumés, which are not restricted by page lengths. Perhaps the best advice is to make your résumé as long as needed to sell your skills to recruiters and hiring managers. Individuals with more experience will naturally have longer résumés. Those with fewer than ten years of experience, those making a major career change, and those who have had only one or two employers will likely have a one-page résumé. Those with ten years or more of related experience may have a two-page résumé. Finally, some senior-level managers and executives with a lengthy history of major accomplishments might have a résumé that is three pages or longer.[14]

Arranging the Parts

The parts of résumés should be arranged with the most important qualifications first.

Although résumés have standard parts, their arrangement and content should be strategically planned. The most persuasive résumés emphasize skills and achievements aimed at a particular job or company. They show a candidate's most important qualifications first, and they de-emphasize any weaknesses. In arranging the parts, try to create as few headings as possible; more than six generally looks cluttered. No two résumés are ever exactly alike, but most writers consider including all or some of these items: main heading, career objective, summary of qualifications, education, experience, capabilities and skills, awards and activities, personal information, and references.

MAIN HEADING

Your résumé, whether it's chronological or functional, should always begin with your name; add your middle initial for an even more professional look. Following your name, list your contact information, including your complete address, area code and phone number, and e-mail address. If possible, include a telephone number where messages may be left for you. The outgoing message at this number should be in your voice, it should mention your full name, and it should be concise and professional. Don't give a number that is always busy because you're using a modem on that line. Prospective employers tend to call the next applicant when no one answers. For your e-mail address, be sure it sounds professional instead of something like *toosexy4you@hotmail.com* or *sixpackguy@yahoo.com*. Also be sure that you're using a personal e-mail address. Putting your work e-mail address on your résumé announces to prospective employers that you're using your current employer's resources to look for another job. Keep the main heading as uncluttered and simple as possible. Format your name so that it stands out on the page. Finally, don't include the word *résumé*; it's like putting the word *letter* above correspondence.

CAREER OBJECTIVE

Career objectives are most appropriate for specific, targeted positions, but they may limit a broader job search.

Opinion is divided about the effect of including a career objective on a résumé. Recruiters think such statements indicate that a candidate has made a commitment to a career and is sure about what he or she wants to do. Career objectives, of course, make the recruiter's life easier by quickly classifying the résumé. But such declarations can also disqualify a candidate if the stated objective doesn't match a company's job description.[15] In addition, many hiring managers find that career objectives are poorly written, vague, or self-serving.[16] Such objectives end up harming more than helping a job applicant. However, a well-written objective that explains specifically what the applicant can do to meet the organization's needs can add value to a chronological or functional résumé.

If you decide to include a career objective on your résumé, you must keep several things in mind in order to make it powerful. First of all, your objective should be specific. Make sure the objective is not so general that it's meaningless. A typical example of a vague objective is *A challenging position in the accounting field with opportunity for growth.* This objective can be improved by adding detail, such as the job title, the area of specialization, and the type of company. A person applying for an auditor position might include the following objective: *An auditor position in an internal corporate accounting department where my accounting skills, computer experience, knowledge of GAAP, and attention to detail will help the company run efficiently and ensure that its records are kept accurately.* Aggressive job applicants today prepare individual résumés that are targeted for each company or position sought. Thanks to word processing, the task is easy.

Your objective should also focus on the employer's needs. Therefore, it should be written from the employer's perspective, not your own. Focus on how you can contribute to the organization, not on what the organization can do for you. A typical self-serving objective is *To obtain a meaningful and rewarding position that enables me to learn more about the graphic design field and allows for advancement.* Instead, show how you'll add value to the organization with an objective such as *Position with advertising firm designing Web sites, publications, logos, and promotional displays for clients, where creativity, software knowledge, and proven communication skills can be used to build client base and expand operations.*

Also be careful that your career objective doesn't downplay your talents. For example, some consultants warn against using the words *entry-level* in your objective, as these words emphasize lack of experience or show poor self-confidence. Finally, your objective should be concise. Try to limit your objective to no more than two or three lines. Avoid using complete sentences and the pronoun *I.*

If you choose to omit the career objective, be sure to discuss your objectives and goals in your cover letter. Savvy job seekers are also incorporating their objectives into a summary of qualifications, which is discussed next.

SUMMARY OF QUALIFICATIONS

A summary of qualifications section lists your most impressive accomplishments and qualifications in one concise bulleted list.

In Chapter 10 you learned about writing executive summaries that condense the information in long reports for busy executives. Recruiters are also busy, and smart job seekers add a summary of qualifications to their résumés to save the time of recruiters and hiring managers. Once a job is advertised, a hiring manager may get hundreds or even thousands of résumés in response. A summary at the top of your résumé makes it easier to read and may help ensure that your most impressive qualifications are not overlooked by a recruiter, who may be skimming résumés quickly. A well-written summary motivates the recruiter to read further.

A summary of qualifications will include three to eight bulleted statements that prove you're the ideal candidate for the position. When formulating these statements, consider your experience in the field, your education, your unique skills, awards you've won, certifications, and any other accomplishments that you want to highlight. Include numbers wherever possible. Target the most important qualifications an employer will be looking for in the person hired for this position. You'll find examples of summaries of qualifications in Figures 13.6, 13.7, 13.8, 13.9, and 13.11 in the résumé models found in our collection starting on page 390.

A summary of qualifications is more likely to be included in the chronological résumé of an experienced job candidate. It is less likely to be found in a functional résumé.

EDUCATION

The education section shows degrees and GPA but does not list all courses a job applicant has taken.

The next component in a chronological résumé is your education—if it is more note-worthy than your work experience. In this section you should include the name and location of schools, dates of attendance, major fields of study, and degrees received. By the way, once you've attended college, you don't need to list high school infor-mation on your résumé. Your grade point average and/or class ranking may be im-portant to prospective employers. One way to enhance your GPA is to calculate it in your major courses only (for example, *3.6/4.0 in major*). It is not unethical to show-case your GPA in your major—as long as you clearly indicate what you are doing. If your GPA is low, you might choose to omit it. Remember, however, that many em-ployers will assume your GPA is lower than a 3.0 if you omit it.[17]

Under *Education* you might be tempted to list all the courses you took, but such a list makes for very dull reading. Refer to courses only if you can relate them to the position sought. When relevant, include certificates earned, seminars attended, work-shops completed, and honors earned. If your education is incomplete, include such statements as *B.S. degree expected 6/08* or *80 units completed in 120-unit program*. Title this section *Education, Academic Preparation*, or *Professional Training*. If you're preparing a functional résumé, you'll probably put the education section below your skills summaries, as Kevin Touhy has done in Figure 13.10 on page 394.

WORK EXPERIENCE OR EMPLOYMENT HISTORY

The work experience section of a résumé should list specifics and quantify achievements.

If your work experience is significant and relevant to the position sought, this infor-mation should appear before education. List your most recent employment first and work backward, including only those jobs that you think will help you win the targeted position. A job application form may demand a full employment history, but your ré-sumé may be selective. Be aware, though, that time gaps in your employment his-tory will probably be questioned in the interview. For each position show the following:

- Employer's name, city, and state
- Dates of employment
- Most important job title
- Significant duties, activities, accomplishments, and promotions

When listing your dates of employment, be sure to include both months and years. Some employers are suspicious when they see only years listed. In addition, if you're currently employed, make that clear. For example, you could write your dates of employment as *March 2004 to present*.

Describe your employment achievements concisely but concretely. Avoid gen-eralities such as *Worked with customers*. Be more specific, with statements such as *Served 40 or more retail customers a day; Successfully resolved problems about custom stationery orders;* or *Acted as intermediary among customers, printers, and suppliers*. If possible, quantify your accomplishments, such as *Conducted study of equipment needs of 100 small businesses in Houston; Personally generated orders for sales of $90,000 annually;* or *Keyed all the production models for a 250-page em-ployee procedures manual*. One professional recruiter said, "I spend a half hour every day screening 50 résumés or more, and if I don't spot some [quantifiable] results in the first 10 seconds, the résumé is history."[18]

Your employment achievements and job duties will be easier to read if you place them in a bulleted list. When writing these bullet points, don't try to list every single thing you've done on the job; instead, keep the prospective employer's needs in mind. Make sure your list of job duties shows what you have to contribute and how you're qualified for the position you're applying for. Do not make your bullet points complete sentences, and avoid using personal pronouns (*I, me, my*) in them. If you've per-formed a lot of the same duties for multiple employers, you don't have to repeat them.

In addition to technical skills, employers seek individuals with communication, management, and interpersonal capabilities. This means you'll want to select work ex-periences and achievements that illustrate your initiative, dependability, responsibility,

FIGURE 13.3

Strengthen Your Résumé With Action Verbs

accelerated	enabled	introduced	reviewed
achieved	encouraged	managed	revitalized
analyzed	engineered	organized	screened
collaborated	established	originated	served
conceptualized	expanded	overhauled	spearheaded
constructed	expedited	pioneered	spurred
converted	facilitated	reduced	strengthened
designed	improved	resolved	targeted
directed	increased	restructured	transformed

resourcefulness, flexibility, and leadership. Employers also want people who can work together in teams. Thus, include statements such as *Collaborated with interdepartmental task force in developing 10-page handbook for temporary workers* and *Headed student government team that conducted most successful voter registration in campus history.*

Statements describing your work experience can be made forceful and persuasive by using action verbs, such as those listed in Figure 13.3 and illustrated in Figure 13.4. Starting each of your bullet points with an action verb will help ensure that your bulleted lists are parallel.

CAPABILITIES AND SKILLS

Emphasize the skills and aptitudes that prove you're qualified for a specific position.

Recruiters want to know specifically what you can do for their companies. Therefore, list your special skills, such as *Proficient in preparing federal, state, and local payroll tax returns as well as franchise and personal property tax returns.* Include your ability to use the Internet, software programs, office equipment, and communication technology tools. If you speak a foreign language or use sign language, include it on your résumé. Describe proficiencies you have acquired through training and experience, such as *Certified in computer graphics and Web design through an intensive 350-hour classroom program.* Use expressions such as *competent in, skilled in, proficient with, experienced in,* and *ability to*; for example, *Competent in writing, editing, and proofreading reports, tables, letters, memos, manuscripts, and business forms.*

You'll also want to highlight exceptional aptitudes, such as working well under stress, learning computer programs quickly, and interacting with customers. If possible, provide details and evidence that back up your assertions; for example, *Mastered PhotoShop in 25 hours with little instruction.* Search for examples of your writing, speaking, management, organizational, and interpersonal skills—particularly those talents

FIGURE 13.4

Using Action Verbs to Strengthen Your Résumé

Identified weaknesses in internships and **researched** five alternate programs
Reduced delivery delays by an average of three days per order
Streamlined filing system, thus reducing 400-item backlog to 0
Organized holiday awards program for 1,200 attendees and 140 awardees
Created a 12-point checklist for use when requesting temporary workers
Designed five posters announcing new employee suggestion program
Calculated shipping charges for overseas deliveries and **recommended** most economical rates
Managed 24-station computer network linking data in three departments
Distributed and **explained** voter registration forms to over 500 prospective student voters
Praised by top management for enthusiastic teamwork and achievement
Secured national recognition from American Cancer Society for fund-raising project

that are relevant to your targeted job. For recent graduates, this section can be used to give recruiters evidence of your potential. Instead of *Capabilities*, the section might be called *Skills and Abilities*.

Those job hunters preparing a functional résumé will place more focus on skills than on any other section. A well-written functional résumé groups skills into categories such as *Accounting/Finance, Skills, Management/Leadership Skills, Communication/ Teamwork Skills*, and *Computer/Technology Skills*. Each skills category includes a bulleted list of achievements and experience that demonstrate the skill, including specific numbers whenever possible. These skills categories should be placed in the beginning of the résumé, where they'll be highlighted, followed by education and work experience. The action verbs shown in Figures 13.3 and 13.4 can also be used when constructing a functional résumé.

AWARDS, HONORS, AND ACTIVITIES

Awards, honors, and activities are appropriate for the résumé.

If you have three or more awards or honors, highlight them by listing them under a separate heading. If not, put them with activities or in the education or work experience section if appropriate. Include awards, scholarships (financial and other), fellowships, dean's list, honors, recognition, commendations, and certificates. Be sure to identify items clearly. Your reader may be unfamiliar, for example, with Greek organizations, honoraries, and awards; tell what they mean. Instead of saying *Recipient of Star award*, give more details: *Recipient of Star award given by Pepperdine University to outstanding graduates who combine academic excellence and extracurricular activities.*

It's also appropriate to include school, community, volunteer, and professional activities. Employers are interested in evidence that you are a well-rounded person. This section provides an opportunity to demonstrate leadership and interpersonal skills. Strive to use action statements. For example, instead of saying *Treasurer of business club*, explain more fully: *Collected dues, kept financial records, and paid bills while serving as treasurer of 35-member business management club.*

PERSONAL DATA

Omit personal data not related to job qualifications.

Today's résumés omit personal data, such as birth date, marital status, height, weight, national origin, health, and religious affiliation. Such information doesn't relate to genuine occupational qualifications, and recruiters are legally barred from asking for such information. Some job seekers do, however, include hobbies or interests (such as skiing or photography) that might grab the recruiter's attention or serve as conversation starters. Naturally, you shouldn't mention dangerous pastimes (such as bungee jumping or motorcycle racing) or time-consuming interests. You could also indicate your willingness to travel or to relocate since many companies will be interested.

Randy Glasbergen.
www.glasbergen.com

"Allen is an incredible, wonderful, fun, generous, exciting, kind, loving, brilliant, very special human being. This personal reference from your dog is quite impressive."

REFERENCES

Listing references directly on a résumé takes up valuable space. Moreover, references are not normally instrumental in securing an interview—few companies check them before the interview. Instead, recruiters prefer that you bring to the interview a list of individuals willing to discuss your qualifications. Therefore, you should prepare a separate list, such as that in Figure 13.5, when you begin your job search. Ask three to five instructors, your current employer or previous employers, colleagues or subordinates, and other professional contacts whether they would be willing to

References are unnecessary for the résumé, but they should be available for the interview.

FIGURE 13.5 ─────── • **Sample Reference List**

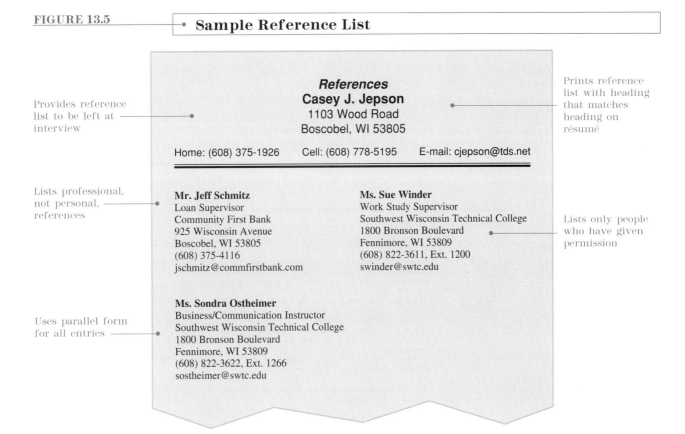

Provides reference list to be left at interview

Lists professional, not personal, references

Uses parallel form for all entries

Prints reference list with heading that matches heading on résumé

Lists only people who have given permission

References
Casey J. Jepson
1103 Wood Road
Boscobel, WI 53805

Home: (608) 375-1926　　　Cell: (608) 778-5195　　　E-mail: cjepson@tds.net

Mr. Jeff Schmitz
Loan Supervisor
Community First Bank
925 Wisconsin Avenue
Boscobel, WI 53805
(608) 375-4116
jschmitz@commfirstbank.com

Ms. Sue Winder
Work Study Supervisor
Southwest Wisconsin Technical College
1800 Bronson Boulevard
Fennimore, WI 53809
(608) 822-3611, Ext. 1200
swinder@swtc.edu

Ms. Sondra Ostheimer
Business/Communication Instructor
Southwest Wisconsin Technical College
1800 Bronson Boulevard
Fennimore, WI 53809
(608) 822-3622, Ext. 1266
sostheimer@swtc.edu

answer inquiries regarding your qualifications for employment. Be sure, however, to provide them with an opportunity to refuse. No reference is better than a negative one.

Do not include personal or character references, such as friends, family, or neighbors, because recruiters rarely consult them. Companies are more interested in the opinions of objective individuals who know how you perform professionally and academically. One final note: most recruiters see little reason for including the statement *References furnished upon request*. It's unnecessary and takes up precious space.

In Figures 13.6 through 13.10, you'll find a collection of models for chronological and functional résumés. Use these models to help you organize the content and format of your own persuasive résumé.

© STOCKBYTE PLATINUM/GETTY IMAGES

With careful research and planning, you can put together a persuasive and professional résumé that will win you interviews. Traditionally hard copies of résumés were mailed to employers. Although you may still submit your résumé by mail today, it's more likely that you'll fax it, e-mail it, or post it online. Always remember, though, to bring several copies of your traditional print-based résumé with you to job interviews.

FIGURE 13.6

Chronological Résumé: Recent College Graduate With Related Experience

Courtney Castro uses a chronological résumé to highlight her work experience, most of which is related directly to the position she seeks. Although she is a recent graduate, she has accumulated experience in two part-time jobs and one full-time job. She includes a summary of qualifications to highlight her skills, experience, and interpersonal traits aimed at a specific position.

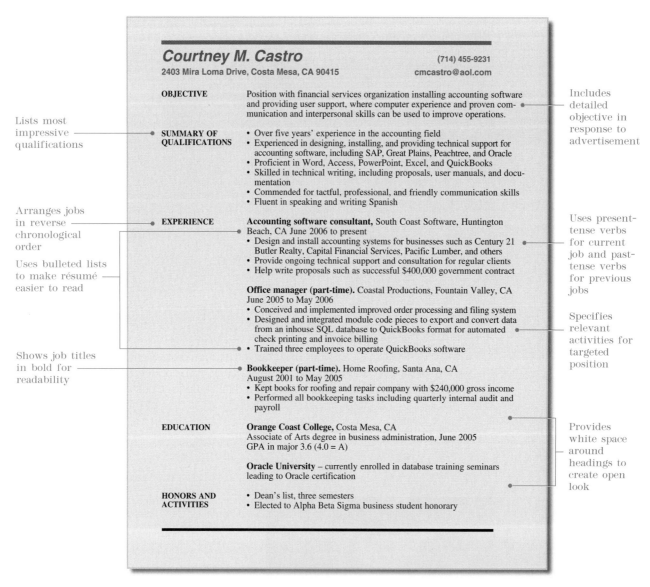

Lists most impressive qualifications

Arranges jobs in reverse chronological order

Uses bulleted lists to make résumé easier to read

Shows job titles in bold for readability

Includes detailed objective in response to advertisement

Uses present-tense verbs for current job and past-tense verbs for previous jobs

Specifies relevant activities for targeted position

Provides white space around headings to create open look

Courtney M. Castro
2403 Mira Loma Drive, Costa Mesa, CA 90415
(714) 455-9231
cmcastro@aol.com

OBJECTIVE Position with financial services organization installing accounting software and providing user support, where computer experience and proven communication and interpersonal skills can be used to improve operations.

SUMMARY OF QUALIFICATIONS
- Over five years' experience in the accounting field
- Experienced in designing, installing, and providing technical support for accounting software, including SAP, Great Plains, Peachtree, and Oracle
- Proficient in Word, Access, PowerPoint, Excel, and QuickBooks
- Skilled in technical writing, including proposals, user manuals, and documentation
- Commended for tactful, professional, and friendly communication skills
- Fluent in speaking and writing Spanish

EXPERIENCE
Accounting software consultant, South Coast Software, Huntington Beach, CA June 2006 to present
- Design and install accounting systems for businesses such as Century 21 Butler Realty, Capital Financial Services, Pacific Lumber, and others
- Provide ongoing technical support and consultation for regular clients
- Help write proposals such as successful $400,000 government contract

Office manager (part-time). Coastal Productions, Fountain Valley, CA June 2005 to May 2006
- Conceived and implemented improved order processing and filing system
- Designed and integrated module code pieces to export and convert data from an inhouse SQL database to QuickBooks format for automated check printing and invoice billing
- Trained three employees to operate QuickBooks software

Bookkeeper (part-time). Home Roofing, Santa Ana, CA August 2001 to May 2005
- Kept books for roofing and repair company with $240,000 gross income
- Performed all bookkeeping tasks including quarterly internal audit and payroll

EDUCATION
Orange Coast College, Costa Mesa, CA
Associate of Arts degree in business administration, June 2005
GPA in major 3.6 (4.0 = A)

Oracle University – currently enrolled in database training seminars leading to Oracle certification

HONORS AND ACTIVITIES
- Dean's list, three semesters
- Elected to Alpha Beta Sigma business student honorary

FIGURE 13.7

Chronological Résumé: Current College Student With Limited Experience

To highlight her skills and capabilities, Casey placed them in the summary of qualifications at the top of her résumé. She used the tables feature of her word processing program to help her format. Because she wanted to describe her skills and experience fully, she used two pages.

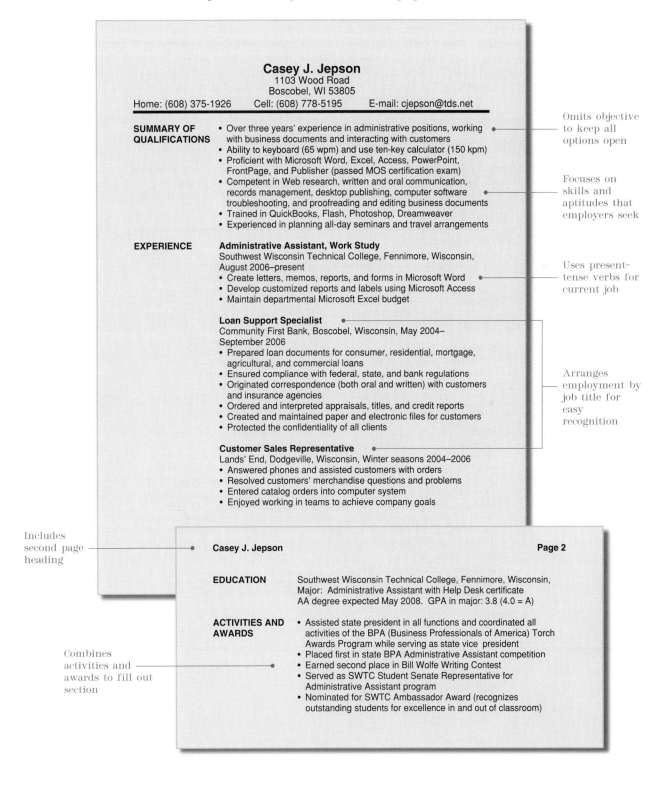

Casey J. Jepson
1103 Wood Road
Boscobel, WI 53805
Home: (608) 375-1926   Cell: (608) 778-5195   E-mail: cjepson@tds.net

SUMMARY OF QUALIFICATIONS	• Over three years' experience in administrative positions, working with business documents and interacting with customers • Ability to keyboard (65 wpm) and use ten-key calculator (150 kpm) • Proficient with Microsoft Word, Excel, Access, PowerPoint, FrontPage, and Publisher (passed MOS certification exam) • Competent in Web research, written and oral communication, records management, desktop publishing, computer software troubleshooting, and proofreading and editing business documents • Trained in QuickBooks, Flash, Photoshop, Dreamweaver • Experienced in planning all-day seminars and travel arrangements

Omits objective to keep all options open

Focuses on skills and aptitudes that employers seek

EXPERIENCE

Administrative Assistant, Work Study
Southwest Wisconsin Technical College, Fennimore, Wisconsin, August 2006–present
• Create letters, memos, reports, and forms in Microsoft Word
• Develop customized reports and labels using Microsoft Access
• Maintain departmental Microsoft Excel budget

Uses present-tense verbs for current job

Loan Support Specialist
Community First Bank, Boscobel, Wisconsin, May 2004–September 2006
• Prepared loan documents for consumer, residential, mortgage, agricultural, and commercial loans
• Ensured compliance with federal, state, and bank regulations
• Originated correspondence (both oral and written) with customers and insurance agencies
• Ordered and interpreted appraisals, titles, and credit reports
• Created and maintained paper and electronic files for customers
• Protected the confidentiality of all clients

Arranges employment by job title for easy recognition

Customer Sales Representative
Lands' End, Dodgeville, Wisconsin, Winter seasons 2004–2006
• Answered phones and assisted customers with orders
• Resolved customers' merchandise questions and problems
• Entered catalog orders into computer system
• Enjoyed working in teams to achieve company goals

Includes second page heading

Casey J. Jepson   **Page 2**

EDUCATION   Southwest Wisconsin Technical College, Fennimore, Wisconsin, Major: Administrative Assistant with Help Desk certificate
AA degree expected May 2008. GPA in major: 3.8 (4.0 = A)

ACTIVITIES AND AWARDS
• Assisted state president in all functions and coordinated all activities of the BPA (Business Professionals of America) Torch Awards Program while serving as state vice president
• Placed first in state BPA Administrative Assistant competition
• Earned second place in Bill Wolfe Writing Contest
• Served as SWTC Student Senate Representative for Administrative Assistant program
• Nominated for SWTC Ambassador Award (recognizes outstanding students for excellence in and out of classroom)

Combines activities and awards to fill out section

FIGURE 13.8

Chronological Résumé: Current University Student With Limited Related Experience

Rick's résumé answers an advertisement specifying skills for a staff accountant. In responding to the ad, he targeted his objective and shaped his statements to the precise job requirements mentioned by the employer.

To produce this attractive print-based résumé, he employed italics, bold, and scalable font features from his word processing program. He realized that this résumé might not be scannable and could not be embedded in an e-mail message. That's why he was ready with a scannable version that shortened the line length and stripped the fancy formatting in case he had to submit it electronically.

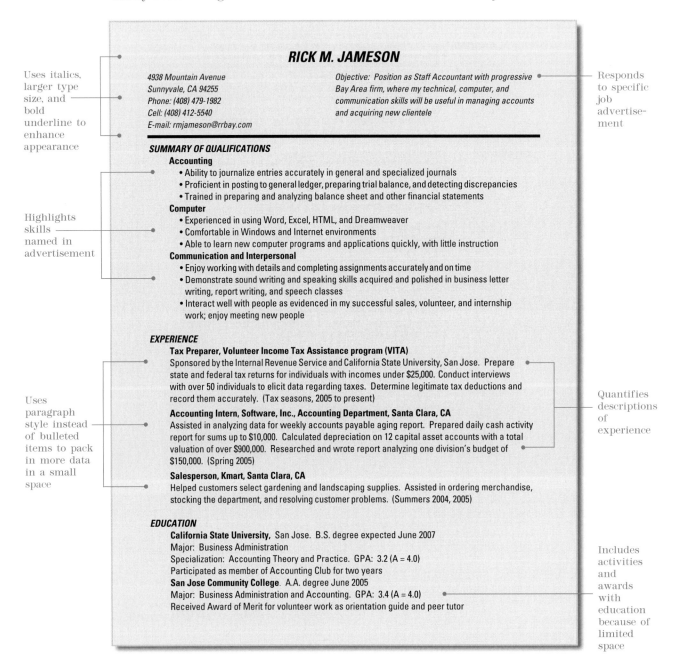

Uses italics, larger type size, and bold underline to enhance appearance

Highlights skills named in advertisement

Uses paragraph style instead of bulleted items to pack in more data in a small space

Responds to specific job advertisement

Quantifies descriptions of experience

Includes activities and awards with education because of limited space

RICK M. JAMESON

4938 Mountain Avenue
Sunnyvale, CA 94255
Phone: (408) 479-1982
Cell: (408) 412-5540
E-mail: rmjameson@rrbay.com

Objective: Position as Staff Accountant with progressive Bay Area firm, where my technical, computer, and communication skills will be useful in managing accounts and acquiring new clientele

SUMMARY OF QUALIFICATIONS

Accounting
- Ability to journalize entries accurately in general and specialized journals
- Proficient in posting to general ledger, preparing trial balance, and detecting discrepancies
- Trained in preparing and analyzing balance sheet and other financial statements

Computer
- Experienced in using Word, Excel, HTML, and Dreamweaver
- Comfortable in Windows and Internet environments
- Able to learn new computer programs and applications quickly, with little instruction

Communication and Interpersonal
- Enjoy working with details and completing assignments accurately and on time
- Demonstrate sound writing and speaking skills acquired and polished in business letter writing, report writing, and speech classes
- Interact well with people as evidenced in my successful sales, volunteer, and internship work; enjoy meeting new people

EXPERIENCE

Tax Preparer, Volunteer Income Tax Assistance program (VITA)
Sponsored by the Internal Revenue Service and California State University, San Jose. Prepare state and federal tax returns for individuals with incomes under $25,000. Conduct interviews with over 50 individuals to elicit data regarding taxes. Determine legitimate tax deductions and record them accurately. (Tax seasons, 2005 to present)

Accounting Intern, Software, Inc., Accounting Department, Santa Clara, CA
Assisted in analyzing data for weekly accounts payable aging report. Prepared daily cash activity report for sums up to $10,000. Calculated depreciation on 12 capital asset accounts with a total valuation of over $900,000. Researched and wrote report analyzing one division's budget of $150,000. (Spring 2005)

Salesperson, Kmart, Santa Clara, CA
Helped customers select gardening and landscaping supplies. Assisted in ordering merchandise, stocking the department, and resolving customer problems. (Summers 2004, 2005)

EDUCATION

California State University, San Jose. B.S. degree expected June 2007
Major: Business Administration
Specialization: Accounting Theory and Practice. GPA: 3.2 (A = 4.0)
Participated as member of Accounting Club for two years
San Jose Community College. A.A. degree June 2005
Major: Business Administration and Accounting. GPA: 3.4 (A = 4.0)
Received Award of Merit for volunteer work as orientation guide and peer tutor

FIGURE 13.9

Chronological Résumé: University Graduate With Substantial Experience

Because Rachel has many years of experience and seeks executive-level employment, she highlights her experience by placing it before her education. Her summary of qualifications highlight her most impressive experience and skills. This chronological two-page résumé shows the steady progression of her career to executive positions, a movement that impresses and reassures recruiters.

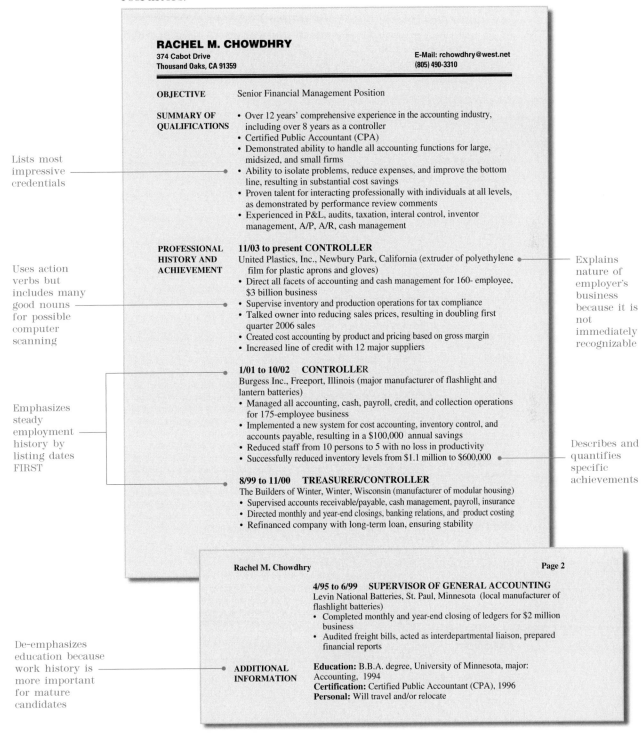

Lists most impressive credentials

Uses action verbs but includes many good nouns for possible computer scanning

Emphasizes steady employment history by listing dates FIRST

De-emphasizes education because work history is more important for mature candidates

Explains nature of employer's business because it is not immediately recognizable

Describes and quantifies specific achievements

RACHEL M. CHOWDHRY
374 Cabot Drive
Thousand Oaks, CA 91359

E-Mail: rchowdhry @west.net
(805) 490-3310

OBJECTIVE — Senior Financial Management Position

SUMMARY OF QUALIFICATIONS
- Over 12 years' comprehensive experience in the accounting industry, including over 8 years as a controller
- Certified Public Accountant (CPA)
- Demonstrated ability to handle all accounting functions for large, midsized, and small firms
- Ability to isolate problems, reduce expenses, and improve the bottom line, resulting in substantial cost savings
- Proven talent for interacting professionally with individuals at all levels, as demonstrated by performance review comments
- Experienced in P&L, audits, taxation, interal control, inventor management, A/P, A/R, cash management

PROFESSIONAL HISTORY AND ACHIEVEMENT

11/03 to present CONTROLLER
United Plastics, Inc., Newbury Park, California (extruder of polyethylene film for plastic aprons and gloves)
- Direct all facets of accounting and cash management for 160- employee, $3 billion business
- Supervise inventory and production operations for tax compliance
- Talked owner into reducing sales prices, resulting in doubling first quarter 2006 sales
- Created cost accounting by product and pricing based on gross margin
- Increased line of credit with 12 major suppliers

1/01 to 10/02 CONTROLLER
Burgess Inc., Freeport, Illinois (major manufacturer of flashlight and lantern batteries)
- Managed all accounting, cash, payroll, credit, and collection operations for 175-employee business
- Implemented a new system for cost accounting, inventory control, and accounts payable, resulting in a $100,000 annual savings
- Reduced staff from 10 persons to 5 with no loss in productivity
- Successfully reduced inventory levels from $1.1 million to $600,000

8/99 to 11/00 TREASURER/CONTROLLER
The Builders of Winter, Winter, Wisconsin (manufacturer of modular housing)
- Supervised accounts receivable/payable, cash management, payroll, insurance
- Directed monthly and year-end closings, banking relations, and product costing
- Refinanced company with long-term loan, ensuring stability

Rachel M. Chowdhry   Page 2

4/95 to 6/99 SUPERVISOR OF GENERAL ACCOUNTING
Levin National Batteries, St. Paul, Minnesota (local manufacturer of flashlight batteries)
- Completed monthly and year-end closing of ledgers for $2 million business
- Audited freight bills, acted as interdepartmental liaison, prepared financial reports

ADDITIONAL INFORMATION
Education: B.B.A. degree, University of Minnesota, major: Accounting, 1994
Certification: Certified Public Accountant (CPA), 1996
Personal: Will travel and/or relocate

FIGURE 13.10

Functional Résumé: Recent University Graduate With Unrelated Part-Time Experience

Recent graduate Kevin Touny chose this functional format to de-emphasize his meager work experience and emphasize his potential in sales and marketing. This version of his résumé is more generic than one targeted for a specific position. Yet, it emphasizes his strong points with specific achievements and includes an employment section to satisfy recruiters.

The functional format presents ability-focused topics. It illustrates what the job seeker can do for the employer instead of narrating a history of previous jobs. Although recruiters prefer chronological résumés, the functional format is a good choice for new graduates, career changers, and those with employment gaps.

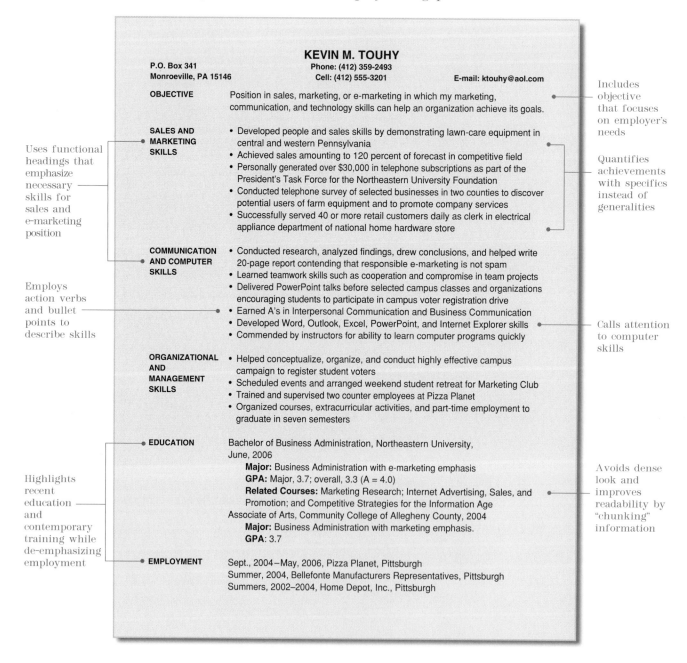

Uses functional headings that emphasize necessary skills for sales and e-marketing position

Employs action verbs and bullet points to describe skills

Highlights recent education and contemporary training while de-emphasizing employment

Includes objective that focuses on employer's needs

Quantifies achievements with specifics instead of generalities

Calls attention to computer skills

Avoids dense look and improves readability by "chunking" information

KEVIN M. TOUHY

P.O. Box 341
Monroeville, PA 15146
Phone: (412) 359-2493
Cell: (412) 555-3201
E-mail: ktouhy@aol.com

OBJECTIVE
Position in sales, marketing, or e-marketing in which my marketing, communication, and technology skills can help an organization achieve its goals.

SALES AND MARKETING SKILLS
• Developed people and sales skills by demonstrating lawn-care equipment in central and western Pennsylvania
• Achieved sales amounting to 120 percent of forecast in competitive field
• Personally generated over $30,000 in telephone subscriptions as part of the President's Task Force for the Northeastern University Foundation
• Conducted telephone survey of selected businesses in two counties to discover potential users of farm equipment and to promote company services
• Successfully served 40 or more retail customers daily as clerk in electrical appliance department of national home hardware store

COMMUNICATION AND COMPUTER SKILLS
• Conducted research, analyzed findings, drew conclusions, and helped write 20-page report contending that responsible e-marketing is not spam
• Learned teamwork skills such as cooperation and compromise in team projects
• Delivered PowerPoint talks before selected campus classes and organizations encouraging students to participate in campus voter registration drive
• Earned A's in Interpersonal Communication and Business Communication
• Developed Word, Outlook, Excel, PowerPoint, and Internet Explorer skills
• Commended by instructors for ability to learn computer programs quickly

ORGANIZATIONAL AND MANAGEMENT SKILLS
• Helped conceptualize, organize, and conduct highly effective campus campaign to register student voters
• Scheduled events and arranged weekend student retreat for Marketing Club
• Trained and supervised two counter employees at Pizza Planet
• Organized courses, extracurricular activities, and part-time employment to graduate in seven semesters

EDUCATION
Bachelor of Business Administration, Northeastern University, June, 2006
  Major: Business Administration with e-marketing emphasis
  GPA: Major, 3.7; overall, 3.3 (A = 4.0)
  Related Courses: Marketing Research; Internet Advertising, Sales, and Promotion; and Competitive Strategies for the Information Age
Associate of Arts, Community College of Allegheny County, 2004
  Major: Business Administration with marketing emphasis.
  GPA: 3.7

EMPLOYMENT
Sept., 2004–May, 2006, Pizza Planet, Pittsburgh
Summer, 2004, Bellefonte Manufacturers Representatives, Pittsburgh
Summers, 2002–2004, Home Depot, Inc., Pittsburgh

FIGURE 13.11   **Scannable Résumé**

Leticia P. Lopez prepared this "plain Jane" résumé free of graphics and fancy formatting so that it would scan well if read by a computer. Within the résumé, she includes many job titles, skills, traits, and other descriptive keywords that scanners are programmed to recognize. To improve accurate scanning, she avoided bullets, italics, underlining, and columns. If she had more information to include, she could go on to a second page since a résumé to be scanned need not be restricted to one page.

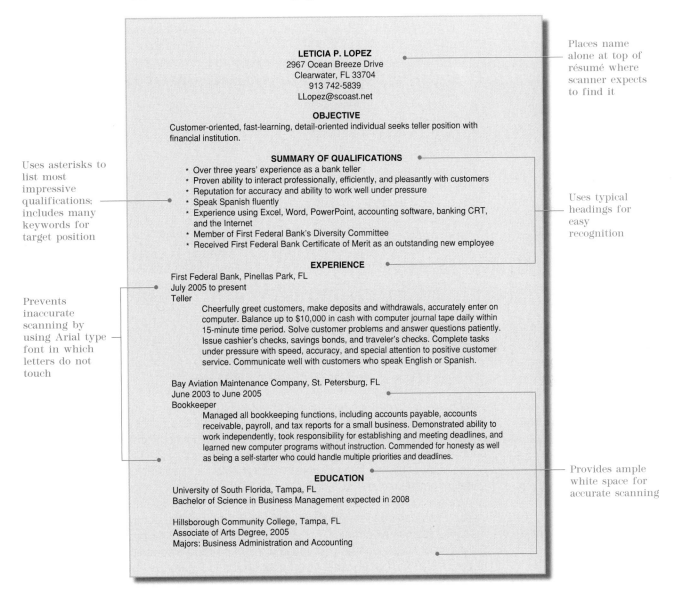

LETICIA P. LOPEZ
2967 Ocean Breeze Drive
Clearwater, FL 33704
913 742-5839
LLopez@scoast.net

Places name alone at top of résumé where scanner expects to find it

OBJECTIVE
Customer-oriented, fast-learning, detail-oriented individual seeks teller position with financial institution.

SUMMARY OF QUALIFICATIONS
* Over three years' experience as a bank teller
* Proven ability to interact professionally, efficiently, and pleasantly with customers
* Reputation for accuracy and ability to work well under pressure
* Speak Spanish fluently
* Experience using Excel, Word, PowerPoint, accounting software, banking CRT, and the Internet
* Member of First Federal Bank's Diversity Committee
* Received First Federal Bank Certificate of Merit as an outstanding new employee

Uses asterisks to list most impressive qualifications; includes many keywords for target position

Uses typical headings for easy recognition

EXPERIENCE
First Federal Bank, Pinellas Park, FL
July 2005 to present
Teller

Cheerfully greet customers, make deposits and withdrawals, accurately enter on computer. Balance up to $10,000 in cash with computer journal tape daily within 15-minute time period. Solve customer problems and answer questions patiently. Issue cashier's checks, savings bonds, and traveler's checks. Complete tasks under pressure with speed, accuracy, and special attention to positive customer service. Communicate well with customers who speak English or Spanish.

Prevents inaccurate scanning by using Arial type font in which letters do not touch

Bay Aviation Maintenance Company, St. Petersburg, FL
June 2003 to June 2005
Bookkeeper

Managed all bookkeeping functions, including accounts payable, accounts receivable, payroll, and tax reports for a small business. Demonstrated ability to work independently, took responsibility for establishing and meeting deadlines, and learned new computer programs without instruction. Commended for honesty as well as being a self-starter who could handle multiple priorities and deadlines.

EDUCATION
University of South Florida, Tampa, FL
Bachelor of Science in Business Management expected in 2008

Provides ample white space for accurate scanning

Hillsborough Community College, Tampa, FL
Associate of Arts Degree, 2005
Majors: Business Administration and Accounting

OPTIMIZING YOUR RÉSUMÉ FOR TODAY'S TECHNOLOGIES

Thus far we've aimed our résumé advice at human readers. However, the first reader of your résumé may well be a computer. Hiring organizations today use a variety of methods to process incoming résumés. Some organizations still welcome traditional print-based résumés that may include attractive formatting. Larger organizations, however, must deal with thousands of incoming résumés. Increasingly, they are placing those résumés directly into searchable databases. So that you can optimize your chances, you may need three versions of your résumé: (1) a traditional print-based résumé, (2) a scannable résumé, and (3) an embedded résumé for e-mailing. You should also be aware of the significant role of résumé keywords. Finally, you may decide to create an e-portfolio to showcase your qualifications.

Because résumés are increasingly becoming part of searchable databases, you may need three versions.

Designing a Traditional Print-Based Résumé

Traditional print-based résumés are attractively formatted to maximize readability. You can create a professional-looking résumé by using your word processing program to highlight your qualifications. The examples in this chapter provide ideas for simple layouts that are easily duplicated. You can also examine résumé templates for design and format ideas. Their inflexibility, however, leads to frustration as you try to force your skills and experience into a predetermined template sequence. What's more, recruiters who read hundreds of résumés can usually spot a template-based résumé. Instead, create your own original résumé that fits your unique qualifications.

Your print-based résumé should use an outline format with headings and bullet points to present information in an orderly, uncluttered, easy-to-read format. An attractive print-based résumé is necessary (1) when you are competing for a job that does not require electronic submission, (2) to present in addition to an electronic submission, and (3) to bring with you to job interviews. Even if a résumé is submitted electronically, nearly every job candidate will want to have an attractive traditional résumé handy for human readers.

Preparing a Scannable Résumé

Increasing use of scanners requires job candidates to prepare computer-friendly résumés.

To screen incoming résumés, many mid- and large-sized companies use automated applicant-tracking software. These systems scan an incoming résumé with optical character recognition (OCR) looking for keywords. The most sophisticated programs enable recruiters and hiring managers to search for keywords, rank résumés based on the number of "hits," and generate reports. Information from your résumé is stored, usually from six months to a year.

Before sending your résumé, find out whether the recipient uses scanning software. If you can't tell from the job announcement, call the company to ask whether it scans résumés electronically. If you don't get a clear answer and you have even the slightest suspicion that your résumé might be read electronically, you'll be smart to prepare a plain, scannable version as shown in Figure 13.11 on page 395.

TIPS FOR MAXIMIZING SCANNABILITY

Scannable résumés use plain formatting, large fonts, quality printing, and white space.

A scannable résumé must sacrifice many of the graphic enhancements you might have used to make your traditional print résumé attractive. To maximize scannability:

- **Use 10- to 14-point type.** Because touching letters or unusual fonts are likely to be misread, it's safest to use a large, well-known font, such as 12-point Times New Roman or Arial. This may mean that your résumé will require two pages. After printing, inspect your résumé to see whether any letters touch—especially in your name.

- **Avoid unusual typefaces, underlining, and italics.** Moreover, don't use borders, shading, or other graphics to highlight text. These features don't scan well. Most applicant-tracking programs, however, can accurately read bold print, solid bullets, and asterisks.
- **Be sure that your name is the first line on the page.** Don't use fancy layouts that may confuse a scanner. Reports generated by applicant-tracking software usually assume that the first line of a résumé contains the applicant's name.
- **List each phone number on its own line.** Your land and cell phone numbers should appear on separate lines to improve recognition.
- **Provide white space.** To ensure separation of words and categories, leave plenty of white space. For example, instead of using parentheses to enclose a telephone area code, insert blank spaces, such as 212 799-2415. Leave blank lines around headings.
- **Avoid double columns.** When listing job duties, skills, computer programs, and so forth, don't tabulate items into two- or three-column lists. Scanners read across and may convert tables into nonsensical output.
- **Use smooth white paper, black ink, and quality printing.** Avoid colored or textured paper, and use a high-quality laser or ink-jet printer.
- **Don't fold or staple your résumé.** Send it in a large envelope so that you can avoid folds. Words that appear on folds may not be scanned correctly.

TIPS FOR MAXIMIZING "HITS"

Scanners produce "hits" when they recognize targeted keywords such as nouns describing skills, traits, tasks, and job titles.

In addition to paying attention to the physical appearance of your résumé, you must also be concerned with keywords that produce "hits" or recognition by the scanner. To maximize hits:

- **Focus on specific keywords.** Study carefully any advertisements and job descriptions for the position you want. Select keywords that describe skills, traits, tasks, and job titles. Because interpersonal traits are often requested by employers, consult Figure 13.12. It shows the most frequently requested interpersonal traits, as reported by Resumix, a pioneer in résumé-scanning software.
- **Incorporate words from the advertisement or job description.** Describe your experience, education, and qualifications in terms associated with the job advertisement or job description for this position.

FIGURE 13.12

Interpersonal Keywords Most Requested by Employers Using Résumé-Scanning Software*

Ability to delegate	Ethical	Persuasive
Ability to implement	Flexible	Problem solving
Ability to plan	Follow instructions	Public speaking
Ability to train	Follow through	Results oriented
Accurate	Follow up	Safety conscious
Adaptable	High energy	Self-accountable
Aggressive work	Industrious	Self-managing
Analytical ability	Innovative	Setting priorities
Assertive	Leadership	Supportive
Communication skills	Multitasking	Takes initiative
Competitive	Open communication	Team building
Creative	Open minded	Team player
Customer oriented	Oral communication	Tenacious
Detail minded	Organizational skills	Willing to travel

*Reported by Resumix, a leading producer of résumé-scanning software.
Source: Joyce Lain Kennedy and Thomas J. Morrow, *Electronic Résumé Revolution* (New York: John Wiley & Sons), 70. Reprinted by permission of John Wiley & Sons, Inc.

- **Use typical headings.** Include expected categories such as Objective, Summary of Qualifications, Education, Work Experience, Skills, and Accomplishments. Scanning software looks for such headings.
- **Use accurate names.** Spell out complete names of schools, degrees, and dates.
- **Be careful of abbreviations.** Minimize unfamiliar abbreviations, but maximize easily recognized abbreviations—especially those within your field, such as CAD, JPG, or JIT. When in doubt, though, spell out! Computers are less confused by whole words.
- **Describe interpersonal traits and attitudes.** Hiring managers look for keywords and phrases such as *time management skills, dependability, high energy, leadership, sense of responsibility*, and *team player*.
- **Use more than one page if necessary.** Computers can easily handle more than one page so include as much as necessary to describe your qualifications and maximize hits.

Preparing an Embedded Résumé for E-Mailing

An embedded résumé, as seen in Figure 13.13, is one that is stripped of formatting and placed within the body of an e-mail message. An embedded résumé may also be called a plain-text résumé or an electronic résumé. Regardless of its name, this format is increasingly requested because employers worry about viruses and word processing incompatibilities in attachments. Employers don't want to open attachments. They prefer embedded résumés that are immediately searchable and avoid the scanning step.[19] Many online job boards also require embedded résumés. Thus, you should be prepared with a plain-text résumé that can be pasted directly into an e-mail message. To create an embedded plain-text résumé:

Employers prefer embedded résumés because these plain-text documents are immediately searchable and they do not require employers to open attachments, which might carry viruses or create software incompatibilities.

- **Follow all the tips for a scannable résumé.** A résumé that will be embedded into an e-mail message requires the same attention to content, formatting, and keywords as that recommended for a scannable résumé.
- **Consider reformatting with shorter lines.** Many e-mail programs wrap lines longer than 60 characters. To avoid having your résumé look as if a chain saw attacked it, use a short line length (such as 4 inches).
- **Think about using keyboard characters to enhance format.** In addition to using capital letters and asterisks, you might use spaced equals signs (= = =) and tildes (~ ~ ~) to create separating lines that highlight résumé categories.
- **Move all text to the left.** Do not center items; start all text at the left margin. Remove tabs.
- **Save your résumé in plain text (.txt) or rich text format (.rtf).** Saving your résumé in one of these formats will ensure that it can be read when pasted in an e-mail message.
- **Test your résumé before sending it to an employer.** After preparing and saving your résumé, copy and paste a copy of it into an e-mail message and send it to yourself and check to see whether any non-ASCII characters appear. They may show up as question marks, square blocks, or other odd characters. Make any necessary changes.

When sending an embedded résumé to an employer, be sure that your subject line clearly describes the purpose of your message. In addition, use the professional e-mail techniques you learned in Chapter 5.

Creating an E-Portfolio

An e-portfolio offers links to examples of a job candidate's performance, talents, and accomplishments in digitized form.

As the workplace becomes increasingly digitized, you have yet another way to display your qualifications to prospective employers—the digitized e-portfolio. Resourceful job candidates in other fields—particularly writers, models, artists, and graphic artists—created print portfolios to illustrate their qualifications and achievements. Now business and professional job candidates are using electronic portfolios to show off their talents.

An e-portfolio is a collection of digitized materials that provides viewers with a snapshot of a candidate's performance, talents, and accomplishments. It may include

FIGURE 13.13   **• Embedded Résumé**

To be sure her résumé would transmit well when embedded within an e-mail message, Leticia prepared a special version with all lines starting at the left margin. She used a 4-inch line length to avoid awkward line breaks. To set off her major headings, she used the tilde character on her keyboard. She saved the document as a text file (.txt or .rtf) so that it could be read by different computers. At the end she included a statement saying that an attractive, fully formatted hard copy of her résumé was available on request.

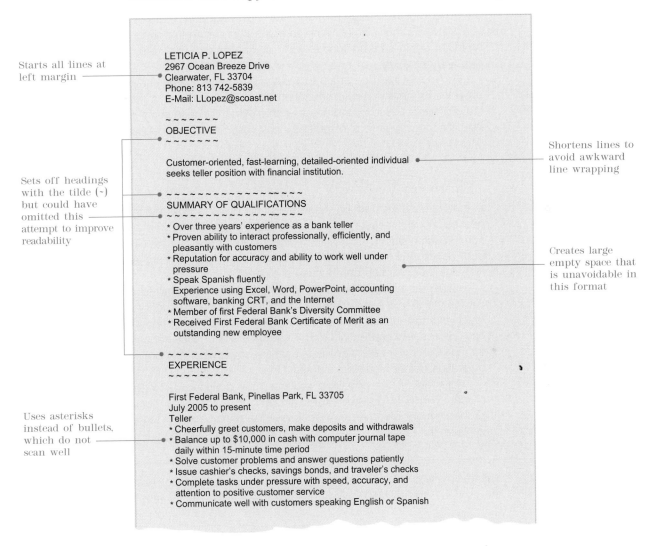

Starts all lines at left margin

Sets off headings with the tilde (~) but could have omitted this attempt to improve readability

Uses asterisks instead of bullets, which do not scan well

Shortens lines to avoid awkward line wrapping

Creates large empty space that is unavoidable in this format

LETICIA P. LOPEZ
2967 Ocean Breeze Drive
Clearwater, FL 33704
Phone: 813 742-5839
E-Mail: LLopez@scoast.net

~ ~ ~ ~ ~ ~ ~
OBJECTIVE
~ ~ ~ ~ ~ ~ ~

Customer-oriented, fast-learning, detailed-oriented individual seeks teller position with financial institution.

~ ~ ~ ~ ~ ~ ~ ~ ~ ~ ~ ~ ~ ~ ~ ~
SUMMARY OF QUALIFICATIONS
~ ~ ~ ~ ~ ~ ~ ~ ~ ~ ~ ~ ~ ~ ~ ~

* Over three years' experience as a bank teller
* Proven ability to interact professionally, efficiently, and
  pleasantly with customers
* Reputation for accuracy and ability to work well under
  pressure
* Speak Spanish fluently
  Experience using Excel, Word, PowerPoint, accounting
  software, banking CRT, and the Internet
* Member of first Federal Bank's Diversity Committee
* Received First Federal Bank Certificate of Merit as an
  outstanding new employee

~ ~ ~ ~ ~ ~ ~
EXPERIENCE
~ ~ ~ ~ ~ ~ ~

First Federal Bank, Pinellas Park, FL 33705
July 2005 to present
Teller
* Cheerfully greet customers, make deposits and withdrawals
* Balance up to $10,000 in cash with computer journal tape
  daily within 15-minute time period
* Solve customer problems and answer questions patiently
* Issue cashier's checks, savings bonds, and traveler's checks
* Complete tasks under pressure with speed, accuracy, and
  attention to positive customer service
* Communicate well with customers speaking English or Spanish

a copy of your résumé, reference letters, special achievements, awards, certificates, work samples, a complete list of your courses, thank-you letters, and anything else that touts your accomplishments. An advanced portfolio might include links to electronic copies of your artwork, film projects, blueprints, and photographs of classwork that might otherwise be difficult to share with potential employers. Moreover, you can include attention-getting effects such as color, animation, sound, and graphics.

E-portfolios are generally presented at Web sites, where they are available around the clock to employers. Some colleges and universities not only make Web site space available for student e-portfolios, but also provide instruction and resources for scanning photos, digitizing images, and preparing graphics. E-portfolios may also be burned onto CDs and DVDs that you mail to prospective employers.

Job candidates generally offer e-portfolios at Web sites, but they may also burn them onto a CD or a DVD.

E-portfolios have many advantages. At Web sites they can be viewed whenever convenient for an employer. Let's say you are talking on the phone with an employer in another city who wants to see a copy of your résumé. You can simply refer the employer to the Web address where your résumé resides. E-portfolios can also be seen by many individuals in an organization without circulating a paper copy. But the real reason for preparing an e-portfolio is that it shows off your talents and qualifications more thoroughly than a print résumé does.

APPLYING THE FINAL TOUCHES TO YOUR RÉSUMÉ

Because your résumé is probably the most important message you will ever write, you'll revise it many times. With so much information in concentrated form and with so much riding on its outcome, your résumé demands careful polishing, proofreading, and critiquing.

As you revise, be certain to verify all the facts, particularly those involving your previous employment and education. Don't be caught in a mistake, or worse, distortion of previous jobs and dates of employment. These items likely will be checked. And the consequences of puffing up a résumé with deception or flat-out lies are simply not worth the risk.

Being Honest and Ethical

A résumé is expected to showcase a candidate's strengths and minimize weaknesses. For this reason, recruiters expect a certain degree of self-promotion. But some résumé writers step over the line that separates honest self-marketing from deceptive half-truths and flat-out lies. Distorting facts on a résumé is unethical; lying is illegal. Either practice can destroy a career.

Given the competitive job market, it might be tempting to puff up your résumé. What's more, you wouldn't be alone in telling fibs or outright whoppers. One study found that 44 percent of applicants lied about their work histories, 23 percent fabricated licenses or credentials, and 41 percent falsified their educational backgrounds.[20] Although recruiters can't check everything, most will verify previous employment and education before hiring candidates. Over half will require official transcripts.

After hiring, the checking process may continue. If hiring officials find a discrepancy in GPA or prior experience and the error is an honest mistake, they will probably meet with the new-hire to hear an explanation. If the discrepancy wasn't a mistake, they will likely fire the person immediately. No job seeker wants to be in the

© JOE RAYMOND/AP WIDE WORLD PHOTOS

Newly appointed Notre Dame football coach George O'Leary resigned in disgrace after admitting that he had lied about his academic and athletic credentials on his résumé. His revelation touched off a wave of investigations into résumés and biographical sketches. Several coaches, athletic directors, and even the president of the U.S. Olympic Committee lost their jobs over long-forgotten lies or half-truths in their résumés. Once a lie becomes part of your résumé, it's difficult to correct later.

unhappy position of explaining résumé errors or defending misrepresentation. Avoiding the following common problems can keep you off the hot seat:

- **Inflated education, grades, or honors.** Some job candidates claim degrees from colleges or universities when in fact they merely attended classes. Others increase their grade point averages or claim fictitious honors. Any such dishonest reporting is grounds for dismissal when discovered.
- **Enhanced job titles.** Wanting to elevate their status, some applicants misrepresent their titles. For example, one technician called himself a "programmer" when he had actually programmed only one project for his boss. A mail clerk who assumed added responsibilities conferred upon herself the title of "supervisor." Even when the description seems accurate, it's unethical to list any title not officially granted.
- **Puffed-up accomplishments.** Some job seekers inflate their employment experience or achievements. One clerk, eager to make her photocopying duties sound more important, said that she assisted the *vice president in communicating and distributing employee directives*. An Ivy League graduate who spent the better part of six months watching rented videos on his VCR described the activity as *Independent Film Study*. That statement may have helped win an interview, but it lost him the job. In addition to avoiding puffery, guard against taking sole credit for achievements that required the efforts of many people. When recruiters suspect dubious claims on résumés, they nail applicants with specific—and often embarrassing—questions during their interviews.

Randy Glasbergen.
www.glasbergen.com

"I typed up my résumé on the computer. The spell-checker accidentally changed 'Mid-State Junior College' to 'Harvard'."

- **Altered employment dates.** Some candidates extend the dates of employment to hide unimpressive jobs or to cover up periods of unemployment and illness. Let's say that several years ago Emily was unemployed for fourteen months between working for Company A and being hired by Company B. To make her employment history look better, she adds seven months to her tenure with Company A and seven months to Company B. Now her employment history has no gaps, but her résumé is dishonest and represents a potential booby trap for her.

Polishing Your Résumé

As you continue revising, look for other ways to improve your résumé. For example, consider consolidating headings. By condensing your information into as few headings as possible, you'll produce a clean, professional-looking document. Study other résumés for valuable formatting ideas. Ask yourself what graphics highlighting techniques you can use to improve readability: capitalization, underlining, indenting, and bulleting. Experiment with headings and styles to achieve a pleasing, easy-to-read message. Moreover, look for ways to eliminate wordiness. For example, instead of *Supervised two employees who worked at the counter*, try *Supervised two counter employees*. Review Chapter 4 for more tips on writing concisely.

In addition to making your résumé concise, make sure that you haven't included any of the following information, which doesn't belong on a résumé:

- Any basis for discrimination (age, marital status, gender, national origin, religion, race, marital status, number of children, disability)
- A photograph
- Reasons for leaving previous jobs
- The word *Résumé*

- Your Social Security number
- Salary history or requirements
- High school information
- References
- Full addresses of schools or employers (include city and state only)

Above all, make sure your print-based résumé look professional. Avoid anything humorous or "cute," such as a help-wanted poster with your name or picture inside. Eliminate the personal pronoun *I*. The abbreviated, objective style of a résumé should not include personal pronouns. Use good-quality paper in a professional color, such as white, off-white, or light gray. Print your résumé using a first-rate laser or ink-jet printer. Be prepared with a résumé for people to read as well as one for a computer to read.

Proofreading Your Résumé

In addition to being well written, a résumé must be carefully formatted and meticulously proofread.

After revising, you must proofread, proofread, and proofread again for spelling, mechanics, content, and format. Then, have a knowledgeable friend or relative proofread it yet again. This is one document that must be perfect. Because the job market is so competitive, one typo, misspelled word, or grammatical error could eliminate you from consideration.

By now you may be thinking that you'd like to hire someone to write your résumé. Don't! First, you know yourself better than anyone else could know you. Second, you'll end up with either a generic or a one-time résumé. A generic résumé in today's highly competitive job market will lose out to a targeted résumé nine times out of ten. Equally useless is a one-time résumé aimed at a single job. What if you don't get that job? Because you will need to revise your résumé many times as you seek a variety of jobs, be prepared to write (and rewrite) it yourself.

Sending Your Résumé

Send your résumé in the format the employer requests.

Read the job listing carefully to make sure you know how the employer wants you to submit your résumé. Not following the prospective employer's instructions can eliminate you from consideration before your résumé is even reviewed.

If you're mailing your résumé the traditional way, don't send it on its own. A résumé should always be accompanied by a cover letter, which will be discussed in the next section. The résumé and cover letter should be printed on the same high-quality paper. It's best to mail them in a large envelope to prevent folding.

In this fast-paced world, employers increasingly want information immediately. We've already discussed how to send your résumé embedded in an e-mail message. An employer, however, might prefer that you attach your résumé to an e-mail message. To do this, save your résumé as a text (.txt) or a rich text format (.rtf) file first. Remember that a cover letter, discussed later in the chapter, must accompany any e-mail résumé. To include your cover letter, (1) you may type your cover letter along with your résumé in the body of your e-mail message, or (2) you may attach them. If you choose the second option, be sure that your subject line and e-mail message clearly and professionally explain the purpose of your message; also include a reference to your attachment in the body of your e-mail message. Type your full name at the bottom of your message.

Finally, an employer may request that you fax your résumé. The key to success in a faxed document is white space. Without it, characters blur. Underlines blend with the words above, and bold print may look like an ink blot. If you are faxing your printed résumé, select a font with adequate space between characters. Thinner fonts—such as Times, Palatino, New Century Schoolbook, Arial, and Bookman—are clearer than thicker ones. Use a 12-point or larger font, and avoid underlines, which may look broken or choppy when faxed. Include a fax cover sheet and a cover letter. Again, a résumé should never be faxed on its own. To be safe, get a transmission report to ensure that all pages were transmitted satisfactorily, or call or e-mail the employer to verify that your fax went through. Finally, follow up with your polished, printed résumé.

● THE PERSUASIVE COVER LETTER

Cover letters introduce résumés, relate writer strengths to reader benefits, and seek an interview.

Job candidates often labor over their résumés but treat the cover letter as an afterthought. This critical mistake could destroy a job search. Even if an advertisement doesn't request one, be sure to distinguish your application with a persuasive cover letter (also called a *letter of application*). It has three purposes: (1) introducing the résumé, (2) highlighting your strengths in terms of benefits to the reader, and (3) gaining an interview. In many ways your cover letter is a sales letter; it sells your talent and tries to beat the competition. It will, accordingly, include many of the techniques you learned for sales letters in Chapter 7, especially if your letter is unsolicited.

Recruiting professionals disagree about how long to make a cover letter. Many prefer short letters with no more than three paragraphs. Others desire longer letters that supply more information, thus giving them a better opportunity to evaluate a candidate's qualifications. These recruiters argue that hiring and training new employees is expensive and time-consuming; therefore, they welcome extra data to guide them in making the best choice the first time. Follow your judgment in writing a brief or a longer cover letter. If you feel, for example, that you need space to explain in more detail what you can do for a prospective employer, do so.

Regardless of its length, a cover letter should have three primary parts: (1) an opening that introduces the message and identifies the position, (2) a body that sells the candidate and focuses on the employer's needs, and (3) a closing that requests an interview and motivates action. When putting your cover letter together, remember that the biggest mistake job seekers make when writing cover letters is making them sound too generic. You should, therefore, write a personalized, targeted cover letter for every position you apply for.

Gaining Attention in the Opening

The opening in a cover letter gains attention by addressing the receiver by name.

Your cover letter will be more appealing, and will more likely be read, if it begins by addressing the reader by name. Rather than sending your letter to the *Human Resources Department*, try to identify the name of the appropriate individual. Call the organization for the name of the person in charge of hiring for the position, and always verify spelling. If you cannot find the name of a person to address, you might use the simplified letter style and replace the salutation with a subject line such as "Application for Position of . . . ."

A cover letter addressed to someone by name is more likely to be read, especially if it's unsolicited. If you don't know the name of the person in charge of hiring, make the effort to find out by calling the employer.

© JAVIER PIERINI/DIGITAL VISION/GETTY IMAGES

How you open your cover letter depends largely on whether the application is solicited or unsolicited. If an employment position has been announced and applicants are being solicited, you can use a direct approach. If you do not know whether a position is open and you are prospecting for a job, use an indirect approach. Whether direct or indirect, the opening should attract the attention of the reader. Strive for openings that are more imaginative than *Please consider this letter an application for the position of . . .* or *I would like to apply for . . . .*

OPENINGS FOR SOLICITED JOBS

Here are some of the best techniques to open a cover letter for a job that has been announced:

Openers for solicited jobs refer to the source of the information, the job title, and qualifications for the position.

- **Refer to the name of an employee in the company.** Remember that employers always hope to hire known quantities rather than complete strangers:

  Mitchell Sims, a member of your Customer Service Department, told me that IntriPlex is seeking an experienced customer service representative. The enclosed summary of my qualifications demonstrates my preparation for this position.

  At the suggestion of Ms. Jennifer Larson of your Human Resources Department, I submit my qualifications for the position of staffing coordinator.

- **Refer to the source of your information precisely.** If you are answering an advertisement, include the exact position advertised and the name and date of the publication. For large organizations it's also wise to mention the section of the newspaper where the ad appeared:

  Your advertisement in Section C-3 of the June 1 *Daily News* for an accounting administrator greatly appeals to me. With my accounting training and computer experience, I believe I could serve Quad Graphics well.

  From your company's Web site, I learned about your need for a sales representative for the Ohio, Indiana, and Illinois regions. I am very interested in this position and believe that my education and experience are appropriate for the opening.

  Susan Butler, placement director at Sierra University, told me that DataTech has an opening for a technical writer with knowledge of Web design and graphics.

- **Refer to the job title and describe how your qualifications fit the requirements.** Human resources directors are looking for a match between an applicant's credentials and the job needs:

  Will an honors graduate with a degree in recreation and two years of part-time experience organizing social activities for a convalescent hospital qualify for your position of activity director?

  Because of my specialized training in computerized accounting at Boise State University, I am confident that I have the qualifications you described in your advertisement for a cost accountant trainee.

OPENINGS FOR UNSOLICITED JOBS

If you are unsure whether a position actually exists, you may wish to use a more persuasive opening. Since your goal is to convince this person to read on, try one of the following techniques:

Openers for unsolicited jobs show interest in and knowledge of the company, as well as spotlight reader benefits.

- **Demonstrate interest in and knowledge of the reader's business.** Show the hiring officer that you have done your research and that this organization is more than a mere name to you:

  Because Signa HealthNet, Inc., is organizing a new information management team for its recently established group insurance division, could you use the services of a well-trained information systems graduate who seeks to become a professional systems analyst?

- Show how your special talents and background will benefit the company. Human resource managers need to be convinced that you can do something for them:

  Could your rapidly expanding publications division use the services of an editorial assistant who offers exceptional language skills, an honors degree from the University of Maine, and two years' experience in producing a campus literary publication?

In applying for an advertised job, Kendra Hawkins wrote the solicited cover letter shown in Figure 13.14. Notice that her opening identifies the position and the newspaper completely so that the reader knows exactly what advertisement Kendra means. Using features on her word processing program, Kendra designed her own letterhead that uses her name and looks like professionally printed letterhead paper.

FIGURE 13.14 ┈┈┈┈┈┈┈ • **Solicited Cover Letter**

Kendra A. Hawkins

1770 Hawthorne Place, Boulder, CO 80304
(303) 492–1244 khawkins@yahoo.com • ─── Uses personally designed letterhead

May 23, 200x

Ms. Courtney L. Donahue
Director, Human Resources   • ─── Addresses proper person by name and title
Del Rio Enterprises
4839 Mountain View Avenue
Denver, CO 82511

Dear Ms. Donahue:

Your advertisement for an assistant product manager, appearing May 22 in Section C of the *Denver Post*, immediately caught my attention • ─── Identifies job and exact page where ad appeared
because my education and training closely parallel your needs.

According to your advertisement, the job includes "assisting in the coordination of a wide range of marketing programs as well as analyzing sales results and tracking marketing budgets." A recent internship at • ─── Relates writer's experiences to job requirements
Ventana Corporation introduced me to similar tasks. Assisting the marketing manager enabled me to analyze the promotion, budget, and overall sales success of two products Ventana was evaluating. My ten-page report examined the nature of the current market, the products' life cycles, and their sales/profit return. In addition to this research, I helped formulate a product merchandising plan and answered consumers' questions at a local trade show.

Intensive course work in marketing and management, as well as proficiency in computer spreadsheets and databases, has given me the kind • ─── Discusses schooling
of marketing and computer training that Del Rio probably demands in a product manager. Moreover, my recent retail sales experience and participation in campus organizations have helped me develop the kind of • ─── Discusses experience
customer service and interpersonal skills necessary for an effective product manager.

After you have examined the enclosed résumé for details of my qualifi- • ─── Refers reader to résumé
cations, I would be happy to answer questions. Please call me at (303) 492-1244 to arrange an interview at your convenience so that we may discuss how my marketing experience, computer training, and interpersonal skills could contribute to Del Rio Enterprises. • ─── Asks for interview and repeats main qualifications

Sincerely,

Kendra A. Hawkins

Kendra A. Hawkins

Enclosure

FIGURE 13.15

> **Unsolicited Cover Letter**

Uses personal
business style
with return
address above date

2250 Turtle Creek Drive
Monroeville, PA 15146
May 29, 200x

Mr. Richard M. Jannis
Vice President, Operations
Sports World, Inc.
4907 Allegheny Boulevard
Pittsburgh, PA 16103

Dear Mr. Jannis:

Shows
resourcefulness
and knowledge of
company

Today's *Pittsburgh Examiner* reports that your organization plans to
expand its operations to include national distribution of sporting goods,
and it occurs to me that you will be needing highly motivated, self-
starting sales representatives and marketing managers. Here are three
significant qualifications I have to offer:

Keeps letter brief
to retain reader's
attention

Uses bulleted list
to make letter
easier to read

- Four years of formal training in business administration, including specialized courses in sales management, retailing, marketing
  promotion, and consumer behavior

- Practical experience in demonstrating and selling consumer products, as well as successful experience in telemarketing

- Excellent communication skills and a strong interest in most areas of sports (which helped me become a sportscaster at Penn
  State radio station WGNF)

Refers to enclosed
résumé

May we talk about how I can put these qualifications, and others summarized in the enclosed résumé, to work for Sports World as it develops
its national sales force? I'll call during the week of June 5 to discuss
your company's expansion plans and the opportunity for an interview.

Takes initiative
for follow-up

Sincerely yours,

Donald W. Vinton

Donald W. Vinton

Enclosure

More challenging are unsolicited cover letters, such as Donald Vinton's shown
in Figure 13.15. Because he hopes to discover or create a job, his opening must
grab the reader's attention immediately. To do that, he capitalizes on company information appearing in an online article. Donald purposely kept his cover letter short
and to the point because he anticipated that a busy executive would be unwilling to
read a long, detailed letter. Donald's unsolicited letter "prospects" for a job. Some
job candidates feel that such letters may be even more productive than efforts to secure advertised jobs, since "prospecting" candidates face less competition and show
initiative. Notice that Donald's letter uses a personal business letter format with his
return address above the date.

Selling Your Strengths in the Body

The body of the cover letter
promotes the candidate's
qualifications for the targeted job.

Once you have captured the attention of the reader and identified your purpose in
the letter opening, you should use the body of the letter to promote your qualifications
for this position. If you are responding to an advertisement, you'll want to explain how

your preparation and experience fill the stated requirements. If you are prospecting for a job, you may not know the exact requirements. Your employment research and knowledge of your field, however, should give you a reasonably good idea of what is expected for this position.

It's also important to stress reader benefits. In other words, you should describe your strong points in relation to the needs of the employer. Hiring officers want you to tell them what you can do for their organizations. This is more important than telling what courses you took in college or what duties you performed in your previous jobs. Instead of *I have completed courses in business communication, report writing, and technical writing*, try this:

> Courses in business communication, report writing, and technical writing have helped me develop the research and writing skills required of your technical writers.

Choose your strongest qualifications and show how they fit the targeted job. Remember that students with little experience are better off spotlighting their education and its practical applications, as these candidates did:

> Because you seek an architect's apprentice with proven ability, I submit a drawing of mine that won second place in the Sinclair College drafting contest last year.

> Composing e-mail messages, business letters, memos, and reports in my business communication and office technology courses helped me develop the writing, language, proofreading, and computer skills mentioned in your ad for an administrative assistant.

Employers seek employees who are team players, take responsibility, show initiative, and learn easily.

In the body of your letter, you may choose to discuss relevant personal traits. Employers are looking for candidates who, among other things, are team players, take responsibility, show initiative, and learn easily. Don't just list several personal traits though; instead, include documentation that proves you possess these traits. Notice how the following paragraph uses action verbs to paint a picture of a promising candidate:

> In addition to developing technical and academic skills at Mid-State University, I have gained interpersonal, leadership, and organizational skills. As vice president of the business students' organization, Gamma Alpha, I helped organize and supervise two successful fund-raising events. These activities involved conceptualizing the tasks, motivating others to help, scheduling work sessions, and coordinating the efforts of 35 diverse students in reaching our goal. I enjoyed my success with these activities and look forward to applying such experience in your management trainee program.

Finally, in this section or the next, you should refer the reader to your résumé. Do so directly or as part of another statement, as shown here:

> As you will notice from my enclosed résumé, I will graduate in June with a bachelor's degree in business administration.

> Please refer to the attached résumé for additional information regarding my education, experience, and references.

Motivating Action in the Closing

The closing of a cover letter confidently requests an interview and makes it easy to respond.

After presenting your case, you should conclude by asking confidently for an interview. Don't ask for the job. To do so would be presumptuous and naive. In requesting an interview, you might suggest reader benefits or review your strongest points. Sound sincere and appreciative. Remember to make it easy for the reader to agree by supplying your telephone number and the best times to call you. In addition, keep in mind that some hiring officers prefer that you take the initiative to call them.

Avoid expressions like *I hope*, which will weaken your closing. Here are possible endings:

> This brief description of my qualifications and the additional information on my résumé demonstrate my genuine desire to put my skills in accounting to work for you. Please call me at (405) 488-2291 before 10 a.m. or after 3 p.m. to arrange an interview.

> To add to your staff an industrious, well-trained administrative assistant with proven word processing and communication skills, call me at (350) 492-1433 to arrange an interview. I can meet with you at any time convenient to your schedule.

> I look forward to the opportunity to discuss my qualifications more fully in an interview. I can be reached on my cell phone at (213) 458-4030.

> Next week, after you have examined the enclosed résumé, I will call you to discuss the possibility of arranging an interview.

Sending Your Cover Letter by E-Mail or by Fax

> Serious job candidates will send a professional cover letter even if the résumé is submitted online, by e-mail, or by fax.

Many applicants using technology make the mistake of not including cover letters with their résumés submitted via e-mail or by fax. A résumé that arrives without a cover letter makes the receiver wonder what it is and why it was sent. Recruiters want you to introduce yourself, and they also are eager to see some evidence that you can write. Some candidates either skip the cover letter or think they can get by with one-line cover letters such as this: *Please see attached résumé, and thanks for your consideration.*

If you are serious about landing the job, take the time to prepare a professional cover letter. If you're sending your résumé via e-mail, you may use the same cover letter you would send by land mail but shorten it a bit. As illustrated in Figure 13.16,

---

FIGURE 13.16   **E-Mail Cover Letter**

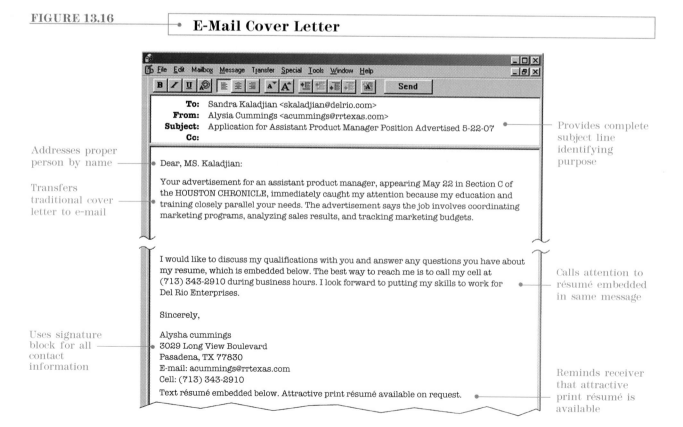

Provides complete subject line identifying purpose

Addresses proper person by name

Transfers traditional cover letter to e-mail

Calls attention to résumé embedded in same message

Uses signature block for all contact information

Reminds receiver that attractive print résumé is available

an inside address is unnecessary for an e-mail recipient. Also move your return address from the top of the letter to just below your name. Include your e-mail address and phone number. Remove tabs, bullets, underlining, and italics that might be problematic in e-mail messages. If you're submitting your résumé by fax, you can use the same cover letter you would send by land mail.

Final Tips for Successful Cover Letters

Look for ways to reduce the overuse of "I."

As you revise your cover letter, notice how many sentences begin with *I*. Although it's impossible to talk about yourself without using *I*, you can reduce "I" domination with this writing technique. Make activities and outcomes, and not yourself, the subjects of sentences. For example, rather than *I took classes in business communication and computer applications*, say *Classes in business communication and computer applications prepared me to . . .* Instead of *I enjoyed helping customers*, say *Helping customers was a real pleasure*.

A cover letter should look professional and suggest quality.

Like the résumé, your cover letter must look professional and suggest quality. This means using a traditional letter style, such as block or modified block. Also, be sure to print it on the same quality paper as your résumé. As with your résumé, proofread it several times yourself; then have a friend read it for content and mechanics. Don't rely on spell check to find all the errors. Just like your résumé, your cover letter must be perfect.

SUMMING UP AND LOOKING FORWARD

In today's competitive job market, an employment search begins with identifying your interests, evaluating your qualifications, and choosing a career path. Finding the perfect job will mean a concentrated effort devoted to searching online job listings, checking classified advertisements, and networking. In applying for jobs, you'll want to submit a persuasive résumé that sells your skills and experience. Whether you choose a chronological or a functional résumé style, you should tailor your assets to fit the position sought. If you think your résumé might be scanned, emphasize keywords and keep the format simple. A persuasive cover letter should introduce your résumé and describe how your skills and experiences match those required.

Now, if your résumé and cover letter have been successful, you'll proceed to the employment interview, one of life's most nerve-wracking experiences. The last chapter in this book provides helpful suggestions for successful interviewing and follow-up communication.

CRITICAL THINKING

1. How has the concept of the job changed, and how will it affect your employment search?

2. Why is it better to have professional rather than personal references?

3. Some job candidates think that applying for unsolicited jobs can be more fruitful than applying for advertised openings. Discuss the advantages and disadvantages of letters that "prospect" for jobs.

4. What are the advantages and disadvantages of searching for a job using one of the major online job boards such as Monster.com?

5. Ethical Issue: At work, fellow employee Chris lets it slip that he did not complete the degree he claims on his résumé. You have never liked Chris, but he does satisfactory work. You are both competing for the same promotion. You are considering writing an anonymous note to the boss telling him to verify Chris's degree. Use the tools on page 78 to decide whether this is an ethical action.

CHAPTER REVIEW

6. List five questions that you should ask yourself to identify your employment interests.

7. In addition to using the big job boards on the Web, list five other types of Web sites on which to find jobs.

8. How are most jobs likely to be found? Through the classified ads? Employment agencies? Networking? Explain.

9. What is the ultimate goal of your résumé?

10. Describe a chronological résumé and discuss its advantages.

11. Describe a functional résumé and discuss its advantages and disadvantages.

12. List five tips for writing an effective career objective on your résumé.

13. Describe a summary of qualifications, and explain why it is increasingly popular on résumés.

14. On a chronological résumé what information should you include for the jobs you list?

15. In addition to technical skills, what traits and characteristics do employers seek?

16. List suggestions for creating a résumé that will be scanned by a computer.

17. Explain how to embed a résumé in an e-mail message.

18. What is an e-portfolio and what are its advantages?

19. What are the three purposes of a cover letter?

20. How can you make it easy for a recruiter to reach you?

WRITING IMPROVEMENT CASES

13.1 Revising Brenda's Résumé
One effective way to improve your writing skills is to critique and edit the résumé of someone else.

Your Task. Analyze the following poorly organized résumé. List its weaknesses. Your instructor may ask you to revise sections of this résumé before showing you an improved version.

Résumé of Brenda Ann Trudell
5349 West Plaza Place
Tulsa, OK 74115-3394
Home: 834-4583 Cell: 594-2985
E-mail: supahsnugglykitty@aol.com

OBJECTIVE: I would like to find an entry-level position with a large corporation that offers opportunity for advancement

SKILLS: Word processing, Internet browsers (Explorer and Yahoo), Excel, Powerpoint, typing 25 w.a.m, Excel, database, spreadsheet.

EDUCATION

Langston University, Tulsa, Oklahoma. Now working on B.B.A. Major: Management; GPA in major is 3.5. Expected degree date: June, 2008. Interested in human recourses management. Took Labor Relations as well as Hiring Practices.

EXPERIENCE

Administrative Assistant, 2006 to present. Marsh and McLennan, Inc., Tulsa. I greet clients as they come in the door and answer the phone when they call. I type up letters, memos, and reports. I make coffee and keep the break room clean. Have to be accurate and friendly. The owner of Marsh and McLennan said I was reliable and flexible.

Peterson Controls Inc., Tulsa. I held a Management trainee Internship from July to October, 2005. I helped design various documents and also processed weekly and monthly information for payroll. I helped prepare graphs to illustrate payroll deduction data. I answered calls on the telephone, directed them, and photocopied and collated data and distributed it as needed.

Langston University, Tulsa. I marketed the Business Club to Langston students and organized volunteers and supplies. Official title: Business Club Recruiter. I did this for three years. I'm proud to be able to help increase club membership, and I developed people skills.

Community Service: March of Dimes Drive, Central Park High School; All Souls Unitarian Church, assistant director of Children's Choir.

1. List at least six weaknesses in this résumé.

13.2 Revising Brenda's Cover Letter

The following cover letter accompanies Brenda Trudell's résumé (Activity 13.1).

Your Task. Analyze each section of the following cover letter written by Brenda and list its weaknesses. Your instructor may ask you to revise this letter before showing you an improved version.

Dear Human Resources Director:

Please consider this letter as an application for the position of assistant manager that I saw at your Web site. Although I am working part time and trying to finish my degree program, I think a position at your industry-leading firm would be beneficial and would certainly look good on my résumé.

I have been studying management at Langston University for four years. I have taken courses in business law, management, finance, accounting, and marketing, but I am most interested in my management courses. I am especially interested in human resources management.

I have been an active student member of the Business Club, in addition to my course work. I liked the Business Club because it gave me a chance to be the recruiter, and I learned a lot from this experience. I also worked at Marsh and McLennan as an administrative assistant. I should mention that I have had another internship, which was at Peterson Controls. I worked in general management, but I am more interested in human resources management.

I am a competent, reliable, well-organized person who gets along pretty well with others. I feel that I have a strong foundation in management as a result of my course work and my experience. I hope you will agree that, along with my personal qualities and my desire to succeed, I qualify for the position, which begins March 1, with your company.

Yours very truly,

1. List at least six weaknesses in the cover letter.

ACTIVITIES AND CASES

E-MAIL

13.3 Identifying Your Employment Interests

Your Task. In a memo or e-mail addressed to your instructor, answer the questions in the section "Identifying Your Interests" at the beginning of the chapter. Draw a conclusion from your answers. What kinds of career, company, position, and location seem to fit your self-analysis?

13.4 Evaluating Your Qualifications

Your Task. Prepare four worksheets that inventory your qualifications in the areas of employment, education, capabilities and skills, and honors and activities. Use active verbs when appropriate.

a. **Employment.** Begin with your most recent job or internship. For each position list the following information: employer; job title; dates of employment (months and years); and three to five duties, activities, or accomplishments. Emphasize activities related to your job goal. Strive to quantify your achievements.

b. **Education.** List degrees, certificates, and training accomplishments. Include courses, seminars, or skills that are relevant to your job goal. Calculate your grade point average in your major.

c. **Capabilities and skills.** List all capabilities and skills that recommend you for the job you seek. Use words such as *skilled, competent, trained, experienced*, and *ability to*. Also list five or more qualities or interpersonal skills necessary for a successful individual in your chosen field. Write action statements demonstrating that you possess some of these qualities. Empty assurances aren't good enough; try to show evidence (*Developed teamwork skills by working with a committee of eight to produce a . . .*).

d. **Awards, honors, and activities.** Explain any awards so that the reader will understand them. List campus, community, and professional activities that suggest you are a well-rounded individual or possess traits relevant to your target job.

WEB

13.5 Choosing a Career Path

Many people know surprisingly little about the work done in various occupations and the training requirements.

Your Task. Use the online *Occupational Outlook Handbook* at *http://www.bls.gov/oco*, prepared by the Bureau of Labor Statistics, to learn more about an occupation of your choice. Find the description of a position for which you could apply now or after you graduate. Learn about what workers do, the nature of the job, working conditions, training and education needed, earnings, and expected job outlook. Print the pages from the *Occupational Outlook Handbook* that describe employment in the area in which you are interested. If your instructor directs, attach these copies to the cover letter you will write in Activity 13.10.

WEB

13.6 Locating Salary Information

What salary can you expect in your chosen career?

Your Task. Visit Salary.com at *www.salary.com* and create a detailed salary report using the Salary Wizard. Base your selections on the kind of employment you are seeking now or will be seeking after you graduate. Use your current geographic area or the location you'd like to work after graduation. Bring a printout of your personalized salary report to class. Be prepared to discuss your report during a class discussion and to submit your printout to your instructor.

WEB

13.7 Searching the Job Market

Where are the jobs? Even though you may not be in the market at the moment, become familiar with the kinds of available positions because job awareness should become an important part of your education.

Your Task. Clip or print a job advertisement or announcement from (a) the classified section of a newspaper, (b) a job board on the Web, (c) a company Web site, or (d) a professional association listing. Select an advertisement or announcement describing the kind of employment you are seeking now or plan to seek when you graduate. Save this advertisement or announcement to attach to the résumé you will write in Activity 13.9.

WEB

13.8 Posting a Résumé on the Web

Learn about the procedure for posting résumés at job boards on the Web.

Your Task. Prepare a list of at least three online employment sites where you could post your résumé. Describe the procedure involved and the advantages for each site.

13.9 Writing Your Résumé

Your Task. Using the data you developed in Activity 13.4, write your résumé. Aim it at a full-time job, part-time position, or internship. Attach a job listing for a specific position (from Activity 13.7). Also prepare a separate list of at least three references. Revise your résumé until it is perfect.

13.10 Preparing Your Cover Letter

Your Task. Write a cover letter introducing your résumé. Again, revise it until it is perfect.

E-MAIL   **INFOTRAC**

13.11. Special Tips for Today's Résumé Writers

Your Task. Using InfoTrac, research the topic of employment résumés. Read at least three recent articles. In an e-mail or memo to your instructor list eight or more good tips that are not covered in this chapter. Pay special attention to advice concerning the preparation of online résumés. The subject line of your memo should be *Special Tips for Today's Résumé Writers.*

• GRAMMAR/MECHANICS CHECKUP—13

Number Style

Review Sections 4.01–4.13 in the Grammar/Mechanics Handbook. Then study each of the following pairs. Assume that these expressions appear in the context of letters, reports, or memos. Write *a* or *b* in the space provided to indicate the preferred number style and record the number of the G/M principle illustrated. When you finish, compare your response with those at the end of the book. If your responses differ, study carefully the principles in parentheses.

a _____ (4.01a) | **Example** (a) three cell phones | (b) 3 cell phones

1. (a) fifteen employees | (b) 15 employees
2. (a) Third Avenue | (b) 3rd Avenue
3. (a) 24 newspapers | (b) twenty-four newspapers
4. (a) September 1st | (b) September 1
5. (a) thirty dollars | (b) $30
6. (a) on the 15th of July | (b) on the fifteenth of July
7. (a) at 4:00 p.m. | (b) at 4 p.m.
8. (a) 3 200-page reports | (b) three 200-page reports
9. (a) over fifty years ago | (b) over 50 years ago
10. (a) 2,000,000 people | (b) 2 million people
11. (a) fifteen cents | (b) 15 cents
12. (a) a thirty-day warranty | (b) a 30-day warranty
13. (a) 2/3 of the e-mails | (b) two thirds of the e-mails
14. (a) two printers for 15 employees | (b) 2 printers for 15 employees
15. (a) 6 of the 130 messages | (b) six of the 130 messages

GRAMMAR/MECHANICS CHALLENGE—13

The following résumé (shortened for this exercise) has faults in grammar, punctuation, spelling, number form, verb form, wordiness, and word use. Correct the errors with standard proofreading marks (see Appendix B) or revise the message online at **Guffey Xtra!**

MEGAN A. RYAN

2450 1st Street

Miami, Flor., 33133

EDUCATION

Coastal Community College, Miami, Florida

Degree expected approximately in June of 2008

Major Office Technology

EXPERIENCE:

- **Office Assistant.** Host Systems, Miami. 2006 too pressent. Responsible for entering data on Macintosh computer. I had to insure accuracy and completness of data that was to be entered. Another duty was maintaining a clean and well-organized office. I also served as Office Courier.

- **Lechter's Housewares.** Miami Shores. 2nd Asst. Mgr I managed store in absence of mgr. and asst. mgr. I open and close registers. Ballanced daily reciepts. Ordered some mds. I also had to supervise 2 employes, earning rabid promotion.

- **Clerk typist.** Caribean Cruises Miami. 2001–02. (part time) Entered guest data on IBM PC. Did personalized followup letters to customer inquirys. Was responsible for phones. I also handled all errands as courier.

STRENGTHS

Computer, transcription, poofreading.

Can type 50 words/per/minute.

I am a fast learner, and very accurate.

Word, Excell, InterNet

COMMUNICATION WORKSHOP
CAREER SKILLS

NETWORK YOUR WAY
TO A JOB IN THE HIDDEN MARKET

Although many jobs appear on online job boards and in classified ads, even more are not advertised at all. The "hidden" job market accounts for as many as 75 percent of all positions available.[21] Companies don't always announce openings publicly because it's time-consuming to interview all the applicants, many of whom aren't qualified. What's more, even when a job is advertised, companies dislike hiring "strangers." They are more comfortable hiring a person they know.

Smart job seekers won't count on the Internet or a newspaper's classified section to land a job. *Workforce Management*, along with countless other human resources experts, admitted that "most new hires come by word of mouth and employee referrals."[22] The key to finding a good job, then, is converting yourself from a "stranger" into a known quantity. Probably the best way to become a known quantity is by networking. You can use either traditional methods or online resources.

Traditional Networking

- **Step 1: Develop a list.** Make a list of anyone who would be willing to talk with you about finding a job. List your friends, relatives, former employers, former coworkers, members of your church, people in social and athletic clubs, present and former teachers, neighbors, and friends of your parents. Also consider asking your campus career center for alumni contacts who will talk with students.

- **Step 2: Make contacts.** Call the people on your list or, even better, try to meet with them in person. To set up a meeting, say *Hi, Uncle Chuck! I'm looking for a job and I wonder if you could help me out. When could I come over to talk about it?* During your visit be friendly, well organized, polite, and interested in what your contact has to say. Provide a copy of your résumé, and try to keep the conversation centered on your job-search area. Your goal is to get two or more referrals. In pinpointing your request, ask two questions: *Do you know of anyone who might have an opening for a person with my skills?* or, *Do you know of anyone else who might know of someone who would?*

- **Step 3: Follow up on your referrals.** Call the people whose names are on your referral list. You might say something like, *Hello. I'm Justin Hall, a friend of Erica Palomino. She suggested that I call and ask you for help. I'm looking for a position as a management trainee, and she thought you might be willing to spare a few minutes and steer me in the right direction.* Don't ask for a job. During your referral interview ask how the individual got started in this line of work, what he or she likes best (or least) about the work, what career paths exist in the field, and what problems must be overcome by a newcomer. Most important, ask how a person with your background and skills might get started in the field. Send an informal thank-you note to anyone who helps you in your job search, and stay in touch with the most promising contacts. Ask whether you may call every three weeks or so during your job search.

Online Networking

As with traditional networking, the goal of online networking is to make connections with people who are advanced in their fields. Ask for their advice about finding a job. Most people like talking about themselves, and asking them about their experiences is an excellent way to begin an online correspondence that might lead to "electronic mentoring," a letter of recommendation from an expert in the field, or information on an internship opportunity. Making online connections with industry professionals is a great way to keep tabs on the latest business trends and potential job leads. Here are possible online networking sources:

- **Career networking groups.** Familiarize yourself with the options available for building your own professional network. Current favorites include *http://www.linkedin.com/*, *http://ryze.com/*, *http://zerodegrees.com/*, and *http://itsnotwhatyouknow.com/*. Some of these sites are fee based while others are free. Typically, joining a network requires creating a password, filling in your profile, and adding your business contacts. At some sites, you can specify search criteria to locate and then contact individuals directly. At other sites both parties' e-mail addresses are hidden. The site then acts as an intermediary connecting people only after they agree to share their contact information. Once you've connected with an individual, the content of your discussions and the follow-up will be similar to that of traditional networking. The medium, however, will center on electronic communication through e-mail and chatroom discussions.

- **Discussion groups and mailing lists.** Two especially good discussion group resources for beginners are Yahoo! Groups (*http://groups.yahoo.com*) and Google Groups (*http://groups.google.com/*). You may choose from groups in a variety of fields including business and computer technology. For example, if you click the Business/Finance listing, you will see listings for more specialized groups. Click Employment and Work, and you will find career groups including construction, customer service, office administration, court reporting, and interior design.

- **Weblogs ("blogs").** Blogs are the latest trend for networking and sharing information. A quick Web search will result in hundreds of career-related blogs and blogs in your field of study. Many companies, such as Microsoft, also maintain employment-related blogs. A good list of career-related blogs can be found at *http://www.quintcareers.com/career-related_blogs.html*. You can also search a worldwide blog directory at *http://www.blogcatalog.com/*. Once you locate a relevant blog, you can read recent postings, search archives, and make replies.

Career Application. Everyone who enters the job market must develop a personal network. Assume you are ready to change jobs or look for a permanent position.

Your Task
To begin developing your personal network, do one of the following:

- Conduct at least one referral interview and report your experience to your class.

- Join one professional discussion group or mailing list. Ask your instructor to recommend an appropriate group for your field. Take notes on group discussions, and describe your reactions and findings to your class.

- Find a weblog related to your career or your major. After monitoring the blog for several days, describe your experience to your class.

CHAPTER 14

EMPLOYMENT INTERVIEWING AND FOLLOW-UP MESSAGES

"Interviewing, like acting, requires solid preparation with the goal of delivering a flawless performance that just rolls off your tongue and gets the employer applauding as you outshine all the other auditioners.[1]"

Joyce Lain Kennedy, nationally syndicated careers columnist

OBJECTIVES

- Differentiate among screening, one-on-one, panel, group, sequential, and stress interviews.

- Describe what to do before the interview to make an impressive initial contact.

- Explain how to prepare for employment interviews, including researching the target company.

- Recognize how to control nonverbal messages and how to fight interview fears.

- Be prepared to answer common interview questions and know how to close an interview.

- Outline the activities that take place after an interview, including thanking the interviewer and contacting references.

- Write follow-up letters and other employment messages.

Job interviews, for most of us, are intimidating; no one enjoys being judged and, possibly, rejected. Should you expect to be nervous about an upcoming job interview? Of course! Everyone is uneasy about being scrutinized and questioned. But think of how much *more* nervous you would be if you had no idea what to expect in the interview and if you were unprepared.

This chapter presents different kinds of interviews and shows you how to prepare for them. You'll learn how to gather information about an employer, as well as how to reduce nervousness, control body language, and fight fear during an interview. You'll pick up tips for responding to recruiters' favorite questions and learn how to cope with illegal questions and salary matters. Moreover, you'll receive pointers on significant questions you can ask during an interview. Finally, you'll learn what you should do as a successful follow-up to an interview.

Yes, you can expect to be nervous during the interview process. But you can also expect to ace an interview when you know what's coming and when you prepare thoroughly. Remember, it's often the degree of preparation that determines who gets the job. You can become a more skillful player in the interview game if you know what to do before, during, and after the interview. First, though, you need to know what types of interviews you might encounter in your job search.

© TRIANGLE IMAGES/PHOTODISC/GETTY IMAGES

The primary goal of an interviewer is to learn whether you have the skills, training, experience, and interest necessary to fulfill the requirements of the position. Although you may meet with just one interviewer, many interviews today are conducted by small teams or panels.

© STOCKBYTE PLATINUM/GETTY IMAGES

TYPES OF EMPLOYMENT INTERVIEWS

Job applicants generally face two kinds of interviews: screening interviews and hiring/placement interviews. You must succeed in the first to proceed to the second. Once you make it to the hiring/placement interview, you'll find a variety of interview styles, including one-on-one, panel, group, sequential, and stress interviews. You will be better prepared if you know what to expect in these different types of interviews.

Screening Interviews

Screening interviews are intended to eliminate those who fail to meet minimum requirements.

Screening interviews do just that—they screen candidates to eliminate those who fail to meet minimum requirements. Many companies use screening interviews as a way to save time and money by screening out lesser-qualified candidates before scheduling face-to-face interviews. Most screening interviews take place on the telephone.[2] In addition, some screening interviews take place during job fairs, and recruiters often conduct screening interviews when they visit college campuses. Finally, some companies conduct screening interviews online. For example, Lowe's Home Improvement has applicants access a Web site where they answer a series of ethics-related questions, and Wal-Mart uses an online multiple-choice questionnaire to screen cashiers, stockers, and customer service representatives.[3]

During a screening interview you will likely be asked to provide details about the education and experience listed on your résumé, so you must be prepared to sell your qualifications. Remember that the person conducting the screening interview is trying to determine whether you should move on to the next step in the interview process.

A screening interview may be as short as five minutes. Even though it may be short, don't treat it casually. If you don't perform well during the screening interview, it may be your last interview with that organization. You can use the tips that follow in this chapter to succeed during the screening process.

Hiring/Placement Interviews

In hiring/placement interviews, recruiters try to learn how the candidate would fit into their organization.

The most promising candidates selected from screening interviews will be invited to hiring/placement interviews. Although these interviews are the real thing, in some ways they are like a game. Trained interviewers try to uncover any negative information that will eliminate a candidate. The candidate, of course, tries to minimize faults and emphasize strengths to avoid being eliminated. More common, however, are interviewers who genuinely want to learn how the candidate would fit into their organization. Conducted in depth, hiring/placement interviews may take many forms.

Randy Glasbergen.
www.glasbergen.com

"I wouldn't say my computer skills are outdated. I prefer to think of them as 'classic.'"

ONE-ON-ONE INTERVIEWS

In one-on-one interviews, which are the most common type, you can expect to sit down with a company representative and talk about the job and your qualifications. If the representative is the hiring manager, questions will be specific and job related. If the representative is from human resources, the questions will probably be more general.

PANEL INTERVIEWS

Also called team interviews, panel interviews are common with companies that rule by consensus. Many panel interviews are conducted by teams of two or more people. With panel interviews, begin to think in terms of "we" instead of "I." Explain how you contributed to a team effort instead of emphasizing individual achievements. Strive to stay focused, summarize important points, and ask good questions. Remember to direct your answers to all panel members, not just to the person who asked the question. Maintaining eye contact with everyone during the interview is important.[4]

GROUP INTERVIEWS

Some companies interview several candidates for the same position at the same time. These employers use this technique to measure leadership skills and communication styles. During a group interview stay focused on the interviewer, and treat the other candidates with respect.[5]

SEQUENTIAL INTERVIEWS

Sequential interviews allow a candidate to meet with two or more interviewers on a one-on-one basis over the course of several hours or days. You must listen carefully and respond positively to all interviewers. Sell your qualifications to each one; don't assume that any interviewer knows what was said in a previous interview.[6]

STRESS INTERVIEWS

Stress interviews are meant to test your reactions during nerve-racking situations. You may be forced to wait a long time before being greeted by the interviewer, you may be given a test with an impossible time limit, or you may be treated rudely by one or more of the interviewers. Another stress interview technique is to have interviewers ask questions at a rapid rate. If asked rapid-fire questions from many directions, take the time to slow things down. For example, *I would be happy to answer your question, Ms. X, but first I must finish responding to Mr. Z.* If greeted with silence, another stress technique, you might say, *Would you like me to begin the interview? Let me tell you about myself.* Or ask a question such as *Can you give me more information about the position?* The best way to handle stress questions is to remain calm and give carefully considered answers. However, you might want to give second thoughts to whether you want to work for an organization in which stress is so important that it becomes part of the interview process.

No matter what interview structure you encounter, you must know what to do before, during, and after the interview to succeed.

Once you've sent out your résumé, your first contact with an employer will likely be by telephone. When taking or returning employer calls, make sure you're in a quiet place where you can focus exclusively on the caller. Making a good impression during this initial contact is imperative.

© RYAN McVAY/PHOTODISC/GETTY IMAGES

BEFORE THE INTERVIEW

Once you've sent out at least one résumé or filled out at least one job application, you must consider yourself an active job seeker. Being active in the job market means that you must be prepared to be contacted by potential employers. Here are tips for sounding and acting professionally once an interview is scheduled.

Ensuring Professional Phone Contact

Even with the popularity of e-mail, most employers will contact job applicants by phone to set up interviews. Therefore, once you're actively looking for a job, anytime the phone rings, it could be a potential employer. Don't make the mistake of letting an unprofessional voice mail message or a lazy roommate ruin your chances. Here's how you can avoid such problems:

- Invest in a good answering machine or voice mail service. Make sure that your outgoing message is concise and professional, with no distracting background sounds. It should be in your own voice and include your full name for clarity. You'll find more tips for creating professional outgoing messages in Chapter 11.
- Tell those who might answer your phone at home about your job search. Explain to them the importance of acting professionally and taking complete messages. Family members or roommates can affect the first impression an employer has of you.
- If you have children, prevent them from answering the phone during your job search. Children of all ages are not known for taking good messages!
- If you've put your cell phone number on your résumé, don't answer your cell phone unless you're in a good location to carry on a conversation with an employer.
- Use voice mail to screen calls. By screening incoming calls, you can be totally in control when you return a prospective employer's call.

Make the First Conversation Impressive

Job seekers who sound flustered, unprepared, or unprofessional when an employer calls may ruin their chances with that company.

Whether you answer the phone directly or return an employer's call, make sure you're prepared for the conversation. Remember that this is the first time the employer has heard your voice. Here are tips to make that first impression a positive one:

- Keep a list near the telephone of positions for which you have applied.
- Treat any call from an employer just like an interview. Use a professional tone and businesslike language. Be polite and enthusiastic, and sell your qualifications.

- If caught off guard by the call, ask whether you can call back in a few minutes. Organize your materials and yourself.
- Have a copy of your résumé available so that you can answer any questions that come up. Also have your list of references, a calendar, and a notepad handy.
- Be prepared for a screening interview. As discussed earlier, this might occur during the first phone call.
- Take good notes during the phone conversation. Obtain accurate directions, and verify the spelling of your interviewer's name. If you'll be interviewed by more than one person, get all of their names.
- Ask the employer to send you a copy of the job description and other company information, which you can use to prepare for the interview.
- Before you hang up, reconfirm the date and time of your interview. You could say something like *I look forward to meeting with you next Wednesday at 2 p.m.*

Researching the Target Company

Before your interview, take time to research the target company, prepare success stories, and plan what you will wear.

Once you've scheduled an interview, it's time to start preparing for it. One of the most important steps in effective interviewing is gathering detailed information about a prospective employer. Never enter an interview cold. Recruiters are impressed by candidates who have done their homework. When asked about the biggest mistake a candidate can make during an interview, Kate Aiken, senior director of college recruiting for the Gap Inc., said, "Not knowing enough about our company."[7]

Visit the library or search the Web for information and articles about the target company or its field, service, or product. Visit the company's Web site and read everything. Call the company to request annual reports, catalogs, or brochures. Ask about the organization and possibly the interviewer. Learn something about the company's mission and goals, size, number of employees, customers, competitors, culture, management structure and names of leaders, reputation in the community, financial condition, future plans, strengths, and weaknesses.

Analyze the company's advertising, including sales and marketing brochures. One candidate, a marketing major, spent a great deal of time pouring over brochures from an aerospace contractor. During his initial interview, he shocked and impressed the recruiter with his knowledge of the company's guidance systems. The candidate had, in fact, relieved the interviewer of his least-favorite task—explaining the company's complicated technology.

Blogs can provide authentic information about a company's culture, current happenings, and future plans.

Weblogs, or blogs, are also good sources for company research. Many employees maintain both formal and informal blogs, where they share anecdotes and information about their employers. You can use these blogs to learn about a company's culture, its current happenings, and its future plans. Many job seekers find that they can get a more realistic picture of a company's day-to-day culture by reading blogs than they would by reading news articles or company Web site information.[8]

In learning about a company, you may uncover information that convinces you that this is not the company for you. It's always better to learn about negatives early in the process. More likely, though, the information you collect will help you tailor your application and interview responses to the organization's needs. You know how flattered you feel when an employer knows about you and your background. That feeling works both ways. Employers are pleased when job candidates take an interest in them. Be ready to put in plenty of effort in investigating a target employer because this effort really pays off at interview time.

Preparing and Practicing

After you have learned about the target organization, study the job description or job listing. It not only helps you write a focused résumé but also enables you to match your education, experience, and interests with the employer's position. Finding out the duties and responsibilities of the position will help you practice your best response strategies. Obtain as much specific information as possible. What are the functions of an individual in this position? What is the typical salary range? What career paths are generally open to this individual?

One of the best ways to prepare for an interview involves itemizing your (1) most strategic skills, (2) greatest areas of knowledge, (3) strongest personality traits, and (4) key accomplishments. Write this information down and practice relating these strengths to the kinds of questions frequently asked in interviews. Here are some specific tips for preparation:

> Practice success stories that emphasize your most strategic skills, areas of knowledge, strongest personality traits, and key accomplishments.

- **Prepare success stories.** One of the most important things you can do before an interview is to prepare and practice success stories. Success stories are specific examples of your educational and work-related experience that demonstrate your accomplishments and achievements. Look over the job description and your résumé to determine what skills, training, personal characteristics, and experience you want to emphasize during the interview. Then prepare a success story for each one. Incorporate numbers, such as dollars saved or percentage of sales increase, whenever possible. Success stories should be detailed but brief. One career expert recommends preparing these success stories as if they were 30-second radio spots.[9] Practice telling your success stories; then in the interview be certain to find a place to insert them.

- **Practice answers to possible questions.** Imagine the kinds of questions you may be asked and work out sample answers. Although you can't anticipate precise questions, you can expect to be asked about your education, skills, experience, and availability. Recite answers to typical interview questions in a mirror, with a friend, while driving in your car, or in spare moments. Keep practicing until you have the best responses down pat.

- **Record yourself.** Consider videotaping or tape recording a practice session to see and hear how you really come across. Do you look and sound enthusiastic?

- **Expect to explain problem areas on your résumé.** For example, if you have little or no experience, you might emphasize your recent training and up-to-date skills. If you have gaps in your résumé, be prepared to answer questions about them positively and truthfully.

- **Take a trial trip.** If you're not sure where the employer is located, take a trial trip to the company before the day of your interview. You'll learn how long it will take you to get there, what the parking situation is, and other important information. Best of all, a trial trip will save you from getting lost on the way to the interview!

- **Decide how you will dress professionally.** What you wear to a job interview still matters. Even if some employees in the organization dress casually, you should

What you wear to an interview matters! To help you make that all-important positive first impression, take time to put together an attractive and conservative outfit. Professional attire shows that you're serious and helps you look competent. Think about it. Which of these three candidates would impress you the least?

© DIGITAL VISION/GETTY IMAGES

look qualified, competent, and successful. One young applicant complained to his girlfriend about having to wear a suit for an interview when everyone at the company dressed casually. She replied, "You don't get to wear the uniform, though, until you make the team!" Avoid loud colors; strive for a coordinated, natural appearance. Favorite "power" colors for interviews are gray and dark blue. Cover tattoos and conceal body piercings; these can be a turn-off for many interviewers. Don't overdo jewelry, and make sure that what you do wear is understated and conservative. Above all, make sure that what you wear projects professionalism and shows that you have respect for the interview situation.

- **Gather what you will bring with you.** Decide what you should bring with you to the interview, and get everything ready the night before. You should plan to bring copies of your résumé, your reference lists, a notebook and pen, money for parking and tolls, and samples of your work if appropriate. Place everything in a businesslike briefcase to add that final professional touch to your look.

ON THE DAY OF YOUR INTERVIEW

The big day has arrived! Ideally you are fully prepared for your interview. Now you need to make sure that everything goes smoothly. That means arriving on time, sending positive nonverbal messages, and handling that fear you're likely to feel.

Traveling to and Arriving at Your Interview

Allow ample time to arrive unflustered, and be congenial to everyone who greets you.

On the morning of your interview, give yourself plenty of time to groom and dress. Then give yourself ample time to get to the employer's office. If something unexpected happens that will cause you to be late, such as an accident or bridge closure, call the interviewer right away to explain what is happening. Most interviewers will be understanding, and your call will show that you're responsible. On the way to the interview, don't smoke, don't eat anything messy or smelly, and don't load up on perfume or cologne. Arrive at the interview five or ten minutes early. If possible, check your appearance before going in.

When you enter the office, be courteous and congenial to everyone. Remember that you are being judged not only by the interviewer but by the receptionist and anyone else who sees you before and after the interview. They will notice how you sit, what you read, and how you look. Introduce yourself to the receptionist, and wait to be invited to sit. You may be asked to fill out a job application while you're waiting. You'll find tips for doing this effectively later in this chapter.

Greet the interviewer confidently, and don't be afraid to initiate a handshake. Doing so exhibits professionalism and confidence. Extend your hand, look the interviewer directly in the eye, smile pleasantly, and say, *I'm pleased to meet you, Mr. Agnos. I am Constance Reid.* In this culture a firm, not crushing, handshake sends a nonverbal message of poise and assurance. Once introductions have taken place, wait for the interviewer to offer you a chair. Make small talk with upbeat comments, such as *This is a beautiful headquarters* or *I'm very impressed with the facilities you have here.* Don't immediately begin rummaging in your briefcase for your résumé. Being at ease and unrushed suggest that you are self-confident.

© Ted Goff
www.tedgoff.com

"I'm in the middle of a job interview. What are you doing?"

Sending Positive Nonverbal Messages

Send positive nonverbal messages by arriving on time, being courteous, dressing professionally, greeting the interviewer confidently, controlling your body movements, making eye contact, listening attentively, and smiling.

You've already sent nonverbal messages to your interviewer by arriving on time, being courteous, dressing professionally, and greeting the interviewer confidently. You'll continue to send nonverbal messages throughout the interview. Remember that what comes out of your mouth and what's written on your résumé are not the only messages an interviewer receives from you. Nonverbal messages also create powerful impressions on people. Here are suggestions that will help you send the right nonverbal messages during interviews:

- **Control your body movements.** Keep your hands, arms, and elbows to yourself. Don't lean on a desk. Keep your feet on the floor. Don't cross your arms in front of you. Keep your hands out of your pockets.
- **Exhibit good posture.** Sit erect, leaning forward slightly. Don't slouch in your chair; at the same time, don't look too stiff and uncomfortable. Good posture demonstrates confidence and interest.
- **Use appropriate eye contact.** A direct eye gaze, at least in North America, suggests interest and trustworthiness. If you're being interviewed by a panel, remember to maintain eye contact with all interviewers.
- **Use gestures effectively.** Nod to show agreement and interest. Gestures should be used as needed, but don't overdo it.
- **Smile enough to convey a positive attitude.** Have a friend give you honest feedback on whether you generally smile too much or not enough.
- **Listen attentively.** Show the interviewer you're interested and attentive by listening carefully to the questions being asked. This will also help you answer questions appropriately.
- **Turn off your cell phone.** There's nothing more embarrassing than having your cell phone ring during an interview. Turn it off or leave it at home.
- **Don't chew gum.** Chewing gum during an interview is distracting and unprofessional.
- **Sound enthusiastic and interested—but sincere.** The tone of your voice has an enormous effect on the words you say. Avoid sounding bored, frustrated, or sarcastic during an interview. Employers want employees who are enthusiastic and interested.
- **Avoid "empty" words.** Filling your answers with verbal pauses such as *um*, *uh*, *like*, and *basically* communicates that you're not prepared. Also avoid annoying distractions such as clearing your throat repeatedly or sighing deeply.

Above all, remember that employers want to hire people who have confidence in their own abilities. Let your body language, posture, dress, and vocal tone prove that you're self-assured.

Fighting Fear

Expect to be nervous before and during the interview. It's natural! Other than public speaking, employment interviews are the most dreaded events in people's lives. One of the best ways to overcome fear is to know what happens in a typical interview. You can further reduce your fears by following these suggestions.

Fight fear by practicing, preparing thoroughly, breathing deeply, and knowing that you are in charge for part of the interview.

- **Practice interviewing.** Try to get as much interviewing practice as you can—especially with real companies. The more times you experience the interview situation, the less nervous you will be.
- **Prepare thoroughly.** Research the company. Know how you will answer the most frequently asked questions. Be ready with success stories. Rehearse your closing statement. One of the best ways to reduce butterflies is to know that you have done all you can to be ready for the interview.
- **Breathe deeply.** Take deep breaths, particularly if you feel anxious while waiting for the interviewer. Deep breathing makes you concentrate on something other than the interview and also provides much-needed oxygen.

- **Know that you're not alone.** Everyone feels some level of anxiety during a job interview. Interviewers expect some nervousness, and a skilled interviewer will try to put you at ease.
- **Remember that it's a two-way street.** The interviewer isn't the only one who is gleaning information. You have come to learn about the job and the company. In fact, during some parts of the interview, you will be in charge. This should give you courage.

DURING THE INTERVIEW

During the interview you'll be answering questions and asking your own questions. The interviewer will be trying to learn more about you, and you should learn more about the job and the organization. Although you may be asked some unique questions, many interviewers ask standard, time-proven questions, which means that you can prepare your answers ahead of time.

How you answer questions can be as important as the answers themselves.

The way you answer questions can be almost as important as what you say. Use the interviewer's name and title from time to time when you answer. *Ms. Lyon, I would be pleased to tell you about....* People like to hear their own names. Be sure you are pronouncing the name correctly, and don't overuse this technique. Avoid answering questions with a simple *yes* or *no*; elaborate on your answers to better sell yourself.

Occasionally it may be necessary to refocus and clarify vague questions. Some interviewers are inexperienced and ill at ease in the role. You may even have to ask your own question to understand what was asked (*By _____ do you mean _____?*). Consider closing out some of your responses with *Does that answer your question?* or *Would you like me to elaborate on any particular experience?*

Stay focused on the skills and traits that employers seek; don't reveal weaknesses.

Always aim your answers at the key characteristics interviewers seek: expertise and competence, motivation, interpersonal skills, decision-making skills, enthusiasm for the job, and a pleasing personality. Remember to stay focused on your strengths. Don't reveal weaknesses, even if you think they make you look human. You won't be hired for your weaknesses, only for your strengths.

Use good English, and enunciate clearly. Remember, you will definitely be judged by how well you communicate. Avoid slurred words such as *gonna* and *din't*, as well as slangy expressions such as *yeah, like*, and *ya know*. As you practice answering expected interview questions, it's always a good idea to make a tape recording. Is your speech filled with verbal static?

Randy Glasbergen.
www.glasbergen.com

"Yes, I think I have good people skills. What kind of idiot question is that?"

You can't expect to be perfect in an employment interview. No one is. But you can avert sure disaster by avoiding certain topics and behaviors such as those described in Figure 14.1.

Answering Questions

You can anticipate a large percentage of the questions you will be asked in an interview.

Employment interviews are all about questions, and many of the questions interviewers ask are not new. You can actually anticipate a large percentage of all questions that will be asked before you ever walk into an interview room. Although you can't anticipate every question, you can prepare for different types.

This section presents questions that may be asked during employment interviews. You'll find get-acquainted questions; questions to measure your interest, experience, and accomplishments; questions about the future; challenging questions; and money

FIGURE 14.1 • **Twelve Interview Actions to Avoid**

1. **Don't be late or too early.** Arrive five to ten minutes before your scheduled interview.
2. **Don't be rude.** Treat everyone you come into contact with warmly and respectfully.
3. **Don't ask for the job.** Asking for the job is naïve, undignified, and unprofessional. Wait to see how the interview develops.
4. **Don't criticize anyone or anything.** Don't criticize your previous employer, supervisors, colleagues, or job. The tendency is for interviewers to wonder if you would speak about their companies similarly.
5. **Don't be a threat to the interviewer.** Avoid suggesting directly or indirectly that your goal is to become head honcho, a path that might include the interviewer's job.
6. **Don't act unprofessionally.** Don't discuss controversial subjects, and don't use profanity. Don't talk too much.
7. **Don't emphasize salary or benefits.** Don't bring up salary, vacation, or benefits during the first interview. Leave this up to the interviewer.
8. **Don't focus on your imperfections.** Never dwell on your liabilities or talk negatively about yourself.
9. **Don't interrupt.** Interrupting is not only impolite but also prevents you from hearing a complete question or remark.
10. **Don't bring someone along.** Don't bring a friend or relative with you to the interview. If someone must drive you, ask that person to drop you off and come back later.
11. **Don't appear impatient.** Your entire focus should be on the interview. Don't glance at your watch, which can imply that you're late for another appointment.
12. **Don't act desperate.** A sure way to turn off an interviewer is to act too desperate. Don't focus on why you *need* the job; focus on how you'll add value to the organization.

questions. You'll also find examples of situational, behavioral, and brain teaser questions, as well as illegal interview questions. To get you thinking about how to respond, we've provided an answer or discussion for one or more of the questions in each group. As you read the remaining questions in each group, think about how you could respond most effectively.

QUESTIONS TO GET ACQUAINTED

After opening introductions, recruiters generally try to start the interview with personal questions that put you at ease. They are also striving to gain an overview to see whether you will fit into the organization's culture. When answering these questions, keep the employer's needs in mind and try to incorporate success stories.

1. Tell me about yourself.

Prepare for get-acquainted questions by practicing a short formula response.

Experts agree that you must keep this answer short (one to two minutes tops) but on target. Use this chance to promote yourself. Stick to educational, professional, or business-related strengths; avoid personal or humorous references. Be ready with at least three success stories illustrating characteristics important to this job. Demonstrate responsibility you have been given; describe how you contributed as a team player. Try practicing this formula: *I have completed _____ degree with a major in _____. Recently I worked for _____ as a _____. Before that I worked for _____ as a _____. My strengths are _____ (interpersonal) and _____ (technical).* Try rehearsing your response in 30-second segments devoted to your education, your work experience, and your qualities/skills.

2. What are your greatest strengths?

Stress your strengths that are related to the position, such as *I am well organized, thorough, and attentive to detail.* Tell success stories and give examples that illustrate these qualities: *My supervisor says that my research is exceptionally thorough. For example, I recently worked on a research project in which I . . . .*

3. Do you prefer to work by yourself or with others? Why?

> This question can be tricky. Provide a middle-of-the-road answer that not only suggests your interpersonal qualities but also reflects an ability to make independent decisions and work without supervision.

4. What was your major in college, and why did you choose it?

5. What are some things you do in your spare time? Hobbies? Sports?

QUESTIONS TO GAUGE YOUR INTEREST

Recruiters want to know how interested you are in this organization and in this specific position.

Interviewers want to understand your motivation for applying for a position. Although they'll realize that you are probably interviewing for other positions, they still want to know why you're interested in this particular position with this organization. These types of questions help them determine your level of interest.

1. Why do you want to work for (name of company)?

> Questions like this illustrate why you must research an organization thoroughly before the interview. The answer to this question must prove that you understand the company and its culture. This is the perfect place to bring up the company research you did before the interview. Show what you know about the company, and discuss why you desire to become a part of this organization. Describe your desire to work for this organization not only from your perspective but also from its point of view. What do you have to offer?

2. Why are you interested in this position?

3. What do you know about our company?

4. Why do you want to work in the _____ industry?

5. What interests you about our products (services)?

QUESTIONS ABOUT YOUR EXPERIENCE AND ACCOMPLISHMENTS

After questions about your background and education and questions that measure your interest, the interview generally becomes more specific with questions about your experience and accomplishments. Remember to show confidence when you answer these questions. If you're not confident in your abilities, why should an employer be?

1. Why should we hire you when we have applicants with more experience or better credentials?

Employers will hire a candidate with less experience and fewer accomplishments if he or she can demonstrate the skills required.

> In answering this question, remember that employers often hire people who present themselves well instead of others with better credentials. Emphasize your personal strengths that could be an advantage with this employer. Are you a hard worker? How can you demonstrate it? Have you had recent training? Some people have had more years of experience but actually have less knowledge because they have done the same thing over and over. Stress your experience using the latest methods and equipment. Be sure to mention your computer training and use of the Internet and Web. Tell success stories. Emphasize that you are open to new ideas and learn quickly. Above all, show that you're confident in your abilities.

2. Describe the most rewarding experience of your career so far.

3. How do your education and professional experiences prepare you for this position?

4. What were your major accomplishments in each of your past jobs?

5. What was a typical workday like?

6. What job functions did you enjoy most? Least? Why?

7. Tell me about your computer skills.

8. Who was the toughest boss you ever worked for and why?

9. What were your major achievements in college?

10. Why did you leave your last position? Or, why are you leaving your current position?

QUESTIONS ABOUT THE FUTURE

Questions that look into the future tend to stump some candidates, especially those who have not prepared adequately. Employers ask these questions to see whether you are goal oriented and to determine whether your goals are realistic.

1. Where do you expect to be five (or ten) years from now?

   When asked about the future, show ambition and interest in succeeding with this company.

   Formulate a realistic plan with respect to your present age and situation. The important thing is to be prepared for this question. It's a sure kiss of death to respond that you'd like to have the interviewer's job! Instead, show an interest in the current job and in making a contribution to the organization. Talk about the levels of responsibility you'd like to achieve. One employment counselor suggests showing ambition but not committing to a specific job title. Suggest that you hope to have learned enough to have progressed to a position where you will continue to grow. Keep your answer focused on educational and professional goals, not personal goals.

2. If you got this position, what would you do to be sure you fit in?

3. This is a large (or small) organization. Do you think you'd like that environment?

4. Do you plan to continue your education?

5. What do you predict for the future of the _____ industry?

6. How do you think you can contribute to this company?

7. What would you most like to accomplish if you get this position?

8. How do you keep current with what is happening in your profession?

CHALLENGING QUESTIONS

The following questions may make you uncomfortable, but the important thing to remember is to answer truthfully without dwelling on your weaknesses. As quickly as possible, convert any negative response into a discussion of your strengths.

1. What is your greatest weakness?

   Strive to convert a discussion of your weaknesses to topics that show your strengths.

   It's amazing how many candidates knock themselves out of the competition by answering this question poorly. Actually, you have many choices. You can present a strength as a weakness (*Some people complain that I'm a workaholic or too attentive to details*). You can mention a corrected weakness (*I found that I really needed to learn about conducting Web research, so I took a course*). You could cite an unrelated skill (*I really need to brush up on my Spanish*). You can cite a learning objective (*One of my long-term goals is to learn more about international management. Does your company have any plans to expand overseas?*). Another possibility is to reaffirm your qualifications (*I have no weaknesses that affect my ability to do this job*).

2. What type of people do you have no patience for?

   Avoid letting yourself fall into the trap of sounding overly critical. One possible response is, *I've always gotten along well with others. But I confess that I can be irritated by complainers who don't accept responsibility.*

3. If you could live your life over, what would you change and why?

4. How would your former (or current) supervisor describe you as an employee?

5. What do you want the most from your job? Money? Security? Power?

6. What is your grade point average, and does it accurately reflect your abilities?

7. Have you ever used drugs?

8. Who in your life has influenced you the most and why?

9. What are you reading right now?

10. Describe your ideal work environment.

QUESTIONS ABOUT MONEY

Remember that nearly all salaries are negotiable, depending on your qualifications. Knowing the typical salary range for the target position helps. The recruiter can tell you the salary ranges—but you will have to ask. If you've had little experience, you will probably be offered a salary somewhere between the low point and the midpoint in the range. With more experience, you can negotiate for a higher figure. A word of caution, though. One personnel manager warns that candidates who emphasize money are suspect because they may leave if offered a few thousand dollars more elsewhere. Here are some typical money questions:

1. How much money are you looking for?

   > One way to handle salary questions is to ask politely to defer the discussion until it's clear that a job will be offered to you (*I'm sure when the time comes, we'll be able to work out a fair compensation package. Right now, I'd rather focus on whether we have a match*). Another possible response is to reply candidly that you can't know what to ask until you know more about the position and the company. If you continue to be pressed for a dollar figure, give a salary range with an annual dollar amount. Be sure to do research before the interview so that you know what similar jobs are paying in your geographic region. For example, check a Web site such as *http://www.salary.com*.

   Defer a discussion of salary until later in the interview when you know more about the job and whether it will be offered.

2. How much are you presently earning?
3. How much do you think you're worth?
4. How much money do you expect to earn within the next ten years?
5. Are you willing to take a pay cut from your current (or previous) job?
6. Would you take a lesser amount during a probationary period?

Salary is an important interview topic. To give you more experience in handling it skillfully, we provide a Communication Workshop titled, "Let's Talk Money: Negotiating a Salary." It includes eight rules to guide you in bargaining your way to the best possible starting salary.

In addition to traditional interview questions about your background, interest, and future plans, you must be prepared to answer more difficult questions. Many interviews today use situational and behavioral questions to better evaluate a candidate's strengths and abilities.

© COMSTOCK/JUPITER IMAGES

SITUATIONAL QUESTIONS

Many employers find that situational and behavioral interview questions give them useful information about job candidates.

Situational questions help employers test your thought processes and logical thinking. When using situational questions, interviewers will describe a hypothetical situation and ask how you would handle it. Situational questions will differ based on the type of position you are interviewing for.[10] Knowledge of the position and the company culture will help you respond favorably to these questions. Even if the situation sounds negative, keep your response positive. Here are just a few examples:

1. You receive a call from an irate customer who complains about the service she received last night at your restaurant. She is demanding her money back. How would you handle the situation?

2. If you were aware that a coworker was falsifying data, what would you do?

3. Your supervisor has just told you that she is dissatisfied with your work, but you think it's acceptable. How would you resolve the conflict?

4. Your supervisor has told you to do something a certain way, and you know that way is wrong and that there's a far better way to complete the task. What would you do?

5. A work colleague has told you in confidence that she suspects another colleague of stealing. What would your actions be?

6. You have noticed that communication between upper management and first-level employees is eroding. How would you solve this problem?

BEHAVIORAL QUESTIONS

Interviewers use behavioral questions, which require you to tell success stories, because past performance tends to be an accurate predictor of future success.[11] Behavioral questions usually start with something like *Describe a time when . . . or Tell me about a time when . . . .* To respond effectively, learn to use the storytelling or STAR technique. Ask yourself, what the Situation or Task was, what Action you took, and what the Results were.[12] Practice using this method to recall specific examples of your skills and accomplishments. To be fully prepared, develop a coherent and articulate STAR narrative for every bullet point on your résumé. When answering behavioral questions, describe only education- and work-related situations or tasks, and try to keep them as current as possible. Here are just a few examples of behavioral questions:

1. Tell me about a time you solved a difficult problem.

   Tell a concise story explaining the situation or task, what you did, and the result. For example, *When I was at Ace Products, we continually had a problem of excessive back orders. After analyzing the situation, I discovered that orders went through many unnecessary steps. I suggested that we eliminate much paperwork. As a result, we reduced back orders by 30 percent.* Go on to emphasize what you learned and how you can apply that learning to this job. Practice your success stories in advance so that you will be ready.

2. Describe a situation in which you were able to use persuasion to successfully convince someone to see things your way.

   The recruiter is interested in your leadership and teamwork skills. You might respond, *I've learned to appreciate the fact that the way you present an idea is just as important as the idea itself. When trying to influence people, I put myself in their shoes and find some way to frame my idea from their perspective. I remember when I . . . .*

3. Describe a time when you had to analyze information and make a recommendation.

4. Describe a time that you worked successfully as part of a team.

5. Tell me about a time you dealt with confidential information.

6. Give me an example of a time when you were under stress to meet a deadline.

7. Tell me about a time when you had to go above and beyond the call of duty in order to get a job done.

8. Tell me about a time you were able to successfully deal with another person even when that individual may not have personally liked you (or vice versa).

9. Give me an example of when you showed initiative and took the lead.

10. Tell me about a recent situation in which you had to deal with an upset customer or coworker.

BRAIN TEASER QUESTIONS

Brain teaser questions are popular in the high-tech, consulting, finance, insurance, and manufacturing fields.[13] Job duties in these and other fields tend to change so rapidly that employers need employees who are flexible, creative, and able to learn quickly. Brain teaser questions help interviewers measure how smart you are, how well you reason, how well you solve problems, and how well you can think under pressure. Some brain teaser questions have correct answers, but most do not. The most important thing to do when asked a brain teaser question is to think before you speak. If it helps, repeat what you've heard, or ask the interviewer to repeat the question. Ask questions if necessary to clarify the problem. If all else fails, give a unique answer.[14] Because some employers are using these questions in interviews, you should be prepared for them. You'll find many Web sites that give examples of brain teaser questions and possible answers. Blogs are another good source to learn more about this type of interview question; many job seekers share their interview experiences in blogs, including specific questions they are asked. Here are some examples of brain teaser questions:

1. If you had to remove 1 of the 50 U.S. states, what would it be and why?

   This question has no right answer; it measures your ability to defend an answer.

2. A businessman devises a business plan for buying and selling coconuts. He calculates that by buying coconuts for $5 a dozen and selling them for $3 a dozen, in less than a year he will be a millionaire. His business plan and calculations are accurate. How is this possible?

   This question tests the ability to put aside assumptions. We assume he starts with no money, but this can only be possible if he started with more money. The answer is that the businessman started off with more than a million dollars.

3. If you had an infinite supply of water and a 5-quart and 3-quart pail, how would you measure exactly 4 quarts?

4. A rope ladder hangs over the side of a ship. The rungs are 1 foot apart, and the ladder is 12 feet long. The tide is rising at 4 inches an hour. How long will it take before the first four rungs of the ladder are under water?[15]

Brain teaser questions help interviewers know how well you reason under pressure.

Some brain teaser questions have no answer; they test your ability to defend a position.

© TRIANGLE IMAGES/DIGITAL VISION/GETTY IMAGES

Although brain teaser questions may have no specific answer, they give recruiters an opportunity to see how well a candidate can answer under pressure. They also test the candidate's ability to defend a position. Such questions are accepted in fields that require critical thinking and well-developed communication skills, such as high-tech, consulting, finance, and insurance.

These and other brain teaser questions can be found in John Kador's fascinating *How to Ace the Brain Teaser Interview* (McGraw-Hill, 2005).

ILLEGAL AND INAPPROPRIATE QUESTIONS

Federal laws prohibit employment discrimination based on gender, age, religion, color, race, national origin, and disability. In addition, many state and city laws exist that prohibit employment discrimination based on such factors as sexual preference.[16] Therefore, it's inappropriate for interviewers to ask any question related to these areas. These questions become illegal, though, only when a court of law determines that the employer is asking them with the intent to discriminate.[17] Nevertheless, you may face an inexperienced or unscrupulous interviewer who does ask some of these inappropriate or illegal questions. How should you react? First, remember that many of these questions are asked innocently by interviewers who may be ignorant of the law and may just be trying to get to know you better.[18]

If you find the question harmless and if you want the job, go ahead and answer it. If you think that answering it would damage your chance to be hired, try to deflect the question tactfully with a response such as *Could you tell me how my marital status relates to the responsibilities of this position?* or *I prefer to keep my personal and professional lives separate.* If you're uncomfortable answering a question, try to determine the reason behind it; you might answer *I don't let my personal life interfere with my ability to do my job* or *Are you concerned with my availability to work overtime?* Another option, of course, is to respond to any inappropriate or illegal question by confronting the interviewer and threatening a lawsuit or refusing to answer. However, you could not expect to be hired under these circumstances.

Here are some inappropriate and illegal questions that you may or may not want to answer:

1. What is your marital status? Are you married? Do you live with anyone? Do you have a boyfriend (or girlfriend)? (However, employers can ask your marital status after hiring for tax and insurance forms.)

2. Do you have any disabilities? Have you had any recent illnesses? (But it is legal to ask if the person can perform specific job duties, such as *Can you carry a 50-pound sack up a 10-foot ladder five times daily?*)

3. I notice you have an accent. Where are you from? What is the origin of your last name? What is your native language? (However, it's legal to ask what languages you speak fluently if language ability is related to the job.)

4. Have you ever filed a worker's compensation claim or been injured on the job?

5. Have you ever had a drinking problem or been addicted to drugs? (But it is legal to ask if a person uses illegal drugs.)

6. Have you ever been arrested? (But it is legal to ask *Have you ever been convicted of _____?* when the crime is related to the job.)

7. How old are you? What is your date of birth? When did you graduate from high school? (But it is legal to ask *Are you 16 years (or 18 years or 21 years) old or older?* depending on the age requirements for the position.)

8. Of what country are you a citizen? Where were you born? (But it is legal to ask *Are you a citizen of the United States?* or *Can you legally work in the United States?*)

9. What is your maiden name? (But it is legal to ask *What is your full name?* or *Have you worked under another name?*)

10. Do you have children? Do you plan to have children? Do you have adequate child-care arrangements? (However, employers can ask for dependent information for tax and insurance purposes after you're hired.)

11. How much do you weigh? How tall are you? (However, employers can ask you about your height and weight if minimum standards are necessary to safely perform a job.)[19]

You may respond to an inappropriate or illegal question by asking tactfully how it relates to the responsibilities of the position.

You may answer inappropriate questions if they seem harmless, or you may confront the interviewer.

End the interview by thanking the interviewer, reviewing your strengths for this position, and inquiring about what action will follow. Ask whether you may leave another copy of your résumé and a list of your references. You might also ask when you can expect to hear from the company, Finally, say, "If I don't hear from you by then, may I call you?"

© TRIANGLE IMAGES/DIGITAL VISION/GETTY IMAGES

CLOSING THE INTERVIEW

Once the interview nears conclusion, start thinking how to end on a positive note. It's easy to become flustered after a challenging interview, so be sure to practice questions that you plan to ask. Also focus on how to leave a lasting positive impression.

Asking Your Own Questions

Your questions should impress the interviewer but also provide valuable information about the job.

At some point in the interview, usually near the end, you will be asked whether you have any questions. The worst thing you can do is say *No*, which suggests that you're not interested in the position. Instead, ask questions that will help you gain information and will impress the interviewer with your thoughtfulness and interest in the position. Remember, though, that this interview is a two-way street. You must be happy with the prospect of working for this organization. You want a position for which your skills and personality are matched. Use this opportunity to find out whether this job is right for you. Also remember that you don't have to wait for the interviewer to ask you for questions. You can ask your own questions throughout the interview to learn more about the company and position.

1. What will my duties be (if not already discussed)?
2. Tell me what it's like working here in terms of the people, management practices, workloads, expected performance, and rewards.
3. What training programs are available from this organization? What specific training will be given for this position?
4. Who would be my immediate supervisor?
5. What is the organizational structure, and where does this position fit in?
6. Is travel required in this position?
7. How is job performance evaluated?
8. Assuming my work is excellent, where do you see me in five years?
9. How long do employees generally stay with this organization?
10. What are the major challenges for a person in this position?
11. What do you see in the future of this organization?

12. What do you like best about working for this organization?

13. Can I have a tour of the facilities?

14. When do you expect to make a decision?

Ending Positively

After you have asked your questions, the interviewer will signal the end of the interview, usually by standing up or by expressing appreciation that you came. If not addressed earlier, you should at this time find out what action will follow. Demonstrate your interest in the position by asking when it will be filled or what the next step will be. Too many candidates leave the interview without knowing their status or when they will hear from the recruiter. Don't be afraid to say that you want the job!

> End the interview by thanking the interviewer, reviewing your strengths for this position, and asking what action will follow.

Before you leave, summarize your strongest qualifications, show your enthusiasm for obtaining this position, and thank the interviewer for a constructive interview and for considering you for the position. Ask the interviewer for a business card, which will provide the information you need to write a thank-you letter, which is discussed later. Shake the interviewer's hand with confidence, and acknowledge anyone else you see on the way out. Be sure to thank the receptionist. Leaving the interview gracefully and enthusiastically will leave a lasting impression on those responsible for making the final hiring decision.

AFTER THE INTERVIEW

After leaving the interview, immediately make notes of what was said in case you are called back for a second interview. Write down key points that were discussed, the names of people you spoke with, and other details of the interview. Ask yourself what went really well and what could have been improved. Note your strengths and weaknesses during the interview so that you can work to improve in future interviews. Next, write down your follow-up plans. To whom should you send thank-you letters? Will you contact the employer by phone? If so, when? Then be sure to follow up on those plans, beginning with writing a thank-you letter and contacting your references.

Thanking Your Interviewer

> A follow-up thank-you letter shows your good manners and your enthusiasm for the job.

After a job interview you should always send a thank-you letter, also called a follow-up letter. This courtesy sets you apart from other applicants, most of whom will not bother. Your letter also reminds the interviewer of your visit as well as suggesting your good manners and genuine enthusiasm for the job. Follow-up letters are most effective if sent immediately after the interview. In your letter refer to the date of the interview, the exact job title for which you were interviewed, and specific topics discussed. Avoid worn-out phrases, such as *Thank you for taking the time to interview me*. Be careful, too, about overusing *I*, especially to begin sentences. Most important, show that you really want the job and that you are qualified for it. Notice how the letter in Figure 14.2 conveys enthusiasm and confidence.

If you've been interviewed by more than one person, send a separate letter to each interviewer. It's also a good idea to send a thank-you letter to the receptionist and to the person who set up the interview. Your thank-you letter will probably make more of an impact if prepared in proper business format and sent by regular mail. However, if you know the decision will be made quickly, send your letter via e-mail. Whatever channel you choose to send your letter, make sure it's formatted and written professionally, using the techniques you learned earlier in this textbook.

FIGURE 14.2   • **Interview Follow-Up Letter**

Christopher D. Wiley

3592 Channel Islands Boulevard, Ventura, CA 90630
(805) 483-6734, cwiley@mail.com

May 28, 200x

Mr. Eric C. Nielson
Comstock Images & Technology
3201 State Street
Santa Barbara, CA 93104

Dear Mr. Nielson:

Talking with you Thursday, May 27, about the graphic designer
position was both informative and interesting.

Thanks for describing the position in such detail and for introducing me
to Ms. Ouchi, the senior designer. Her current project designing an
annual report in four colors sounds fascinating as well as quite
challenging.

Now that I've learned in greater detail the specific tasks of your
graphic designers, I'm more than ever convinced that my computer and
creative skills can make a genuine contribution to your graphic
productions. My training in design and layout using Photoshop and
InDesign ensures that I could be immediately productive on your staff.

You will find me an enthusiastic and hardworking member of any team
effort. As you requested, I'm enclosing additional samples of my work.
I'm eager to join the graphics staff at your Santa Barbara
headquarters, and I look forward to hearing from
you soon.

Sincerely,

Christopher D. Wiley

Christopher D. Wiley

Enclosures

Annotations (left margin):
- Mentions the interview date and specific job title
- Highlights specific skills for the job
- Shows appreciation, good manners, and perseverance—traits that recruiters value

Annotations (right margin):
- Personalizes the message by referring to topics discussed in the interview
- Reminds reader of interpersonal skills as well as enthusiasm and eagerness for this job

© Ted Goff
www.tedgoff.com

"Why do all your references scream
and slam down the phone when
I mention your name?"

Contacting Your References

Once you've thanked your interviewer, it's time to alert
your references that they may be contacted by the employer. You might also have to request a letter of recommendation to be sent to the employer by a certain
date. As discussed in Chapter 13, you should have already asked permission to use these individuals as references, and you should have supplied them with a
copy of your résumé, highlighted with sales points.

In order to provide the best possible recommendation, your references need information. What position have you applied for with what company? What
should they stress to the prospective employer? Let's
say you're applying for a specific job that requires a letter of recommendation. Professor Orenstein has already
agreed to be a reference for you. To get the best letter

of recommendation from Professor Orenstein, help her out. Write a letter telling her about the position, its requirements, and the recommendation deadline. Include a copy of your résumé. You might remind her of a positive experience with you that she could use in the recommendation. Remember that recommenders need evidence to support generalizations. Give them appropriate ammunition, as the student has done in the following request:

Dear Professor Orenstein:

In a reference request, identify the target position and company.

Recently I interviewed for the position of administrative assistant in the Human Resources Department of Host International. Because you kindly agreed to help me, I am now asking you to write a letter of recommendation to Host.

Specify the job requirements so that the recommender knows what to stress.

The position calls for good organizational, interpersonal, and writing skills, as well as computer experience. To help you review my skills and training, I enclose my résumé. As you may recall, I earned an A in your business communication class; and you commended my long report for its clarity and organization.

Provide a stamped, addressed envelope.

Please send your letter to Mr. James Jenkins at Host International before July 1 in the enclosed stamped, addressed envelope. I'm grateful for your support, and I promise to let you know the results of my job search.

Sincerely,

Kari M. Ryan

After you've received a job offer, be sure to let your references know. Write a brief, personal note to all of your references, thanking them for the role they played in your job search. They'll appreciate the courtesy, which will make them much more likely to serve as references for you in future job searches.

Following Up

If you don't hear from the interviewer within five days, or at the specified time, call him or her. Practice saying something like, *I'm wondering what else I can do to convince you that I'm the right person for this job* or *I'm calling to find out the status of your search for the _____ position.* You could also e-mail the interviewer to find out how the decision process is going. When following up, it's important to sound professional and courteous. Sounding desperate, angry, or frustrated that you haven't been contacted yet can ruin your chances. The following follow-up e-mail message would impress the interviewer:

Dear Ms. Jamison:

A follow-up letter should sound courteous, not angry or desperate.

I enjoyed my interview with you last Thursday for the receptionist position. You should know that I'm very interested in this opportunity with Coastal Enterprises. Because you mentioned that you might have an answer this week, I'm eager to know how your decision process is coming along. I look forward to hearing from you.

Sincerely,

Carlos Mendez

Depending on the response you get to your first follow-up request, you may have to follow up additional times. Keep in mind, though, that some employers won't tell you about their hiring decision unless you're the one hired.[20]

Don't harass the interviewer, and don't force a decision. If you don't hear back from an employer within several weeks after following up, it's best to assume that you didn't get the job and to continue with your job search.

In addition to studying résumés, many employers review application forms to determine which candidates should be brought in for interviews. It pays to make your application form as neat and professional as possible. Many employers will view the way you fill out this form as an indication of the quality of your work and your ability to follow directions.

© DIGITAL VISION/GETTY IMAGES

OTHER EMPLOYMENT LETTERS AND DOCUMENTS

Although the résumé and cover letter are your major tasks, other important letters and documents are often required during the employment process. You may need to write follow-up letters or fill out employment applications. You might also have to write a letter of resignation when leaving a job. Because each of these tasks reveals something about you and your communication skills, you'll want to put your best foot forward.

Application Form

When applying for jobs, keep with you a card summarizing your important data.

Some organizations require job candidates to fill out job application forms instead of, or in addition to, submitting résumés. This practice permits them to gather and store standardized data about each applicant.

- Carry a card summarizing vital statistics not included on your résumé. If you are asked to fill out an application form in an employer's office, you will need a handy reference to the following data: graduation dates, beginning and ending dates of all employment; salary history; full names, titles, and present work addresses of former supervisors; full addresses and phone numbers of current and previous employers; and full names, occupational titles, occupational addresses, and telephone numbers of persons who have agreed to serve as references.
- Look over all the questions before starting.
- Fill out the form neatly, using blue or black ink. Many career counselors recommend printing your responses; cursive handwriting can be difficult to read.
- Answer all questions honestly. Write *Not applicable* or *N/A* if appropriate.
- Use accurate spelling, grammar, and punctuation.
- If asked for the position desired, give a specific job title or type of position. Writing *Anything* or *Open* will make you look unfocused and will make it difficult for employers to know what you're qualified for or interested in.
- Be prepared for a salary question. Unless you know what comparable employees are earning in the company, the best strategy is to suggest a salary range or to write *Negotiable* or *Open*.
- Be prepared to explain the reasons for leaving previous positions. Use positive or neutral phrases such as *Relocation, Seasonal, To accept a position with more responsibility, Temporary position*, or *Career change*. Avoid words or phrases such as *Fired, Quit, Didn't get along with supervisor*, or *Pregnant*.

Remember that your completed job application will be judged by the employer. Make sure that it looks neat and professional. An application that contains errors, is incomplete, is wrinkled or dirty, or is difficult to read may eliminate you from consideration.

Application or Résumé Follow-Up Letter

If your résumé or application generates no response within a reasonable time, you may decide to send a short follow-up letter such as the following. Doing so (1) jogs the memory of the personnel officer, (2) demonstrates your serious interest, and (3) allows you to emphasize your qualifications or to add new information.

Dear Ms. Lopez:

Open by reminding the reader of your interest.

Please know I am still interested in becoming an administrative support specialist with Quad, Inc.

Use this opportunity to review your strengths or to add new qualifications.

Since I submitted an application [*or* résumé] in May, I have completed my degree and have been employed as a summer replacement for office workers in several downtown offices. This experience has honed my word processing and communication skills. It has also introduced me to a wide range of office procedures.

Close by looking forward positively; avoid accusations that make the reader defensive.

Please keep my application in your active file and let me know when I may put my formal training, technical skills, and practical experience to work for you.

Sincerely,

Jessica F. Olney

Rejection Follow-Up Letter

If you didn't get the job and you think it was perfect for you, don't give up. Employment specialists encourage applicants to respond to a rejection. The candidate who was offered the position may decline, or other positions may open up. In a rejection follow-up letter, it's OK to admit you're disappointed. Be sure to add, however, that you're still interested and will contact the company again in a month in case a job opens up. Then follow through for a couple of months—but don't overdo it. You should be professional and persistent, but not a pest. Here's an example of an effective rejection follow-up letter:

Dear Mr. O'Neal:

Subordinate your disappointment to your appreciation at being notified promptly and courteously.

Although I'm disappointed that someone else was selected for your accounting position, I appreciate your promptness and courtesy in notifying me.

Emphasize your continuing interest. Express confidence in meeting the job requirements.

Because I firmly believe that I have the technical and interpersonal skills needed to work in your fast-paced environment, I hope you will keep my résumé in your active file. My desire to become a productive member of your Transamerica staff remains strong.

Refer to specifics of your interview. If possible, tell how you are improving your skills.

I enjoyed our interview, and I especially appreciate the time you and Ms. Goldstein spent describing your company's expansion into international markets. To enhance my qualifications, I've enrolled in a course in International Accounting at CSU.

Take the initiative; tell when you will call for an update.

Should you have an opening for which I am qualified, you may reach me at (818) 719-3901. In the meantime, I will call you in a month to discuss employment possibilities.

Sincerely,

Douglas P. Sawacki

Job Acceptance and Rejection Letters

When all your hard work pays off, you will be offered the position you want. Although you will likely accept the position over the phone, it's a good idea to follow up with an acceptance letter to confirm the details and to formalize the acceptance. Your acceptance letter might look like this:

Dear Ms. Scarborough:

Confirm your acceptance of the position with enthusiasm.

It was a pleasure talking with you earlier today. As I mentioned, I am delighted to accept the position of web designer with Innovative Creations, Inc., in your Seattle office. I look forward to becoming part of the IC team and to starting work on a variety of exciting and innovative projects.

Review salary and benefits details.

As we agreed, my starting salary will be $46,000, with a full benefits package including health and life insurance, retirement plan, stock options, and three weeks of vacation per year.

Include the specific starting date.

I look forward to starting my position with Innovative Creations on September 15, 2008. Before that date I will send you the completed tax and insurance forms you need. Thanks again for everything, Ms. Scarborough.

Likewise, you might want to write a letter when you decide to turn down a job offer. This letter should thank the employer and explain briefly that you are turning it down. Taking the time to extend this courtesy could help you in the future if this employer has a position you really want. Here's an example of a job rejection letter:

Thank the employer for the job offer and decline the offer without giving specifics.

Thank you very much for offering me the position of sales representative with Bendall Pharmaceuticals. It was a difficult decision to make, but I have accepted a position with another company.

Express gratitude and best wishes for the future.

I appreciate your taking the time to interview me, and I wish Bendall much success in the future.

Resignation Letter

After you've been in a position for a period of time, you may find it necessary to leave. Perhaps you've been offered a better position, or maybe you've decided to return to school full-time. Whatever the reason, you should leave your position gracefully and tactfully. Although you'll likely discuss your resignation in person with your supervisor, it's a good idea to document your resignation by writing a formal letter. Many resignation letters are placed in personnel files; therefore, it should be formatted and written using the professional business letter writing techniques you learned earlier. Here is an example of a basic letter of resignation:

Dear Ms. Patrick:

Confirm the exact date of your resignation. Remind the employer of your contributions.

This letter serves as formal notice of my resignation from Allied Corporation, effective Friday, August 15. I've enjoyed serving as your office assistant for the past two years, and I am grateful for everything I've learned during my employment with Allied.

Offer assistance to prepare for your resignation.

Please let me know what I can do over the next two weeks to help you prepare for my departure. I would be happy to help with finding and training my replacement.

Offer thanks and end with a forward-looking statement.

Thanks again for providing such a positive employment experience. I will long remember my time here.

Although this employee gave a standard two-week notice, you may find that a longer notice is necessary. The higher and more responsible your position, the longer the notice you should give your employer.

SUMMING UP AND LOOKING FORWARD

Whether you face a screening interview or a hiring/placement interview, you must be well prepared. You can increase your chances of success and reduce your anxiety considerably by knowing how interviews are typically conducted and by researching the target company thoroughly. Practice answering typical questions, including situational, behavioral, and brain teaser ones. Consider tape recording or videotaping a mock interview so that you can check your body language and improve your answering techniques.

Close the interview by thanking the interviewer, reviewing your main strengths for this position, and asking what the next step is. Follow up with a thank-you letter and a follow-up call or message, if appropriate. Prepare other employment-related documents as needed,

including application forms, application and résumé follow-up letters, rejection follow-up letters, job acceptance and rejection letters, and resignation letters.

For more information about all kinds of interviewing, visit **Guffey Xtra!** (*http://guffeyxtra.swlearning.com*). You'll find a complete online chapter with additional advice for successful employment and other interviewing.

You have now completed 14 chapters of rigorous instruction aimed at developing your skills so that you can be a successful business communicator in today's rapidly changing world of information. Remember that this is but a starting point. Your skills as a business communicator will continue to grow on the job as you apply the principles you have learned and expand your expertise.

CRITICAL THINKING

1. Is it normal to be nervous about an employment interview, and what can be done to overcome this fear?

2. What can you do to improve the first impression you make at an interview?

3. In employment interviews, do you think that behavioral questions (such as *Tell me about a business problem you have had and how you solved it*) are more effective than traditional questions (such as *Tell me what you are good at*)? Why?

4. Why is it important to avoid discussing salary early in an interview?

5. Why should a job candidate write a thank-you letter after an interview?

CHAPTER REVIEW

6. Briefly describe the different types of hiring/placement interviews you may encounter.

7. If you have sent out your résumé to many companies, what information should you keep near your telephone and why?

8. You've scheduled an interview with a large local company. What kind of information should you seek about this company, and where could you expect to find it?

9. What are success stories? Why should you prepare several of these before going to an interview?

10. Name at least six interviewing behaviors you can exhibit that send positive nonverbal messages.

11. What is your greatest fear of what you might do or what might happen to you during an employment interview? How can you overcome your fears?

12. Should you be candid with an interviewer when asked about your weaknesses?

13. How should you respond if you are asked why a company should hire you when it has applicants with more experience or better credentials?

14. How should you respond to questions you feel are inappropriate or illegal?

15. List various kinds of follow-up letters.

ACTIVITIES AND CASES

WEB

14.1 Researching an Organization

An important part of your preparation for an interview is finding out about the target company.

Your Task. Select an organization where you would like to be employed. Assume you've been selected for an interview. Using resources described in this chapter, locate information about the organization's leaders and their business philosophy. Find out about the organization's accomplishments, setbacks, finances, products, customers, competition, and advertising. Prepare a summary report documenting your findings.

WEB

14.2 Learning What Jobs Are Really About Through Weblogs

Weblogs, or blogs, are becoming an important tool in the employment search process. By accessing blogs, job seekers can learn more about a company's culture and day-to-day activities.

Your Task. Using the Web, locate a blog that's maintained by an employee of a company you'd like to work for. Monitor the blog for at least a week. Prepare a short report that summarizes what you learned about the company through reading the blog postings. Include a statement of whether this information would be valuable during your job search.

14.3 Building Interview Skills

Successful interviews require diligent preparation and repeated practice. To be best prepared, you need to know what skills are required for your targeted position. In addition to computer and communication skills, employers generally want to know whether a candidate works well with a team, accepts responsibility, solves problems, is efficient, meets deadlines, shows leadership, saves time and money, and is a hard worker.

Your Task. Consider a position for which you are eligible now or one for which you will be eligible when you complete your education. Identify the skills and traits necessary for this position. If you prepared a résumé in Chapter 13, be sure that it addresses these targeted areas. Now prepare interview worksheets listing at least ten technical and other skills or traits you think a recruiter will want to discuss in an interview for your targeted position.

14.4 Preparing Success Stories

You can best showcase your talents if you are ready with your own success stories that show how you have developed the skills or traits required for your targeted position.

Your Task. Using the worksheets you prepared in Activity 14.3, prepare success stories that highlight the required skills or traits. Select three to five stories to develop into answers to potential interview questions. For example, here's a typical question: *How does your background relate to the position we have open?* A possible response: *As you know, I have just completed an intensive training program in _____. In addition, I have over three years of part-time work experience in a variety of business settings. In one position I was selected to manage a small business in the absence of the owner. I developed responsibility and customer-service skills in filling orders efficiently, resolving shipping problems, and monitoring key accounts. I also inventoried and organized products worth over $200,000. When the owner returned from a vacation to Florida, I was commended for increasing sales and was given a bonus in recognition of my efforts.* People relate to and remember stories. Try to shape your answers into memorable stories.

14.5 Polishing Answers to Interview Questions

Practice makes perfect in interviewing. The more often you rehearse responses to typical interview questions, the closer you are to getting the job.

Your Task. Select three questions from each of these question categories discussed in this chapter: Questions to Get Acquainted, Questions to Gauge Your Interest, Questions About Your Experience and Accomplishments, Questions About the Future, and Challenging Questions. Write your answers to each set of questions. Try to incorporate skills and traits required for the targeted position, and include success stories where appropriate. Polish these answers and your delivery technique by practicing in front of a mirror or into a tape recorder.

WEB — **TEAM**

14.6 Learning to Answer Situational Interview Questions

Situational interview questions can vary widely from position to position. You should know enough about a position to understand some of the typical situations you would encounter on a regular basis.

Your Task. Use your favorite search tool to locate typical job descriptions of a position you're interested in. Based on these descriptions, develop a list of six to eight typical situations someone in this position would face; then write situational interview questions for each of these scenarios. In pairs of two students, role-play interviewer and interviewee alternating with your listed questions.

WEB — **TEAM**

14.7 Developing Skill With Behavioral Interview Questions

Behavioral interview questions are increasingly popular, and you will need a little practice before you can answer them easily.

Your Task. Use your favorite search tool to locate lists of behavioral questions on the Web. Select five skills areas such as communication, teamwork, and decision making. For each skill area find three behavioral questions that you think would be effective in an interview. In pairs of two students, role-play interviewer and interviewee, alternating with your listed questions. You goal is to answer effectively in one or two minutes. Remember to use the STAR method when answering.

WEB — **TEAM**

14.8 Preparing to Ace Brain Teaser Interview Questions

You may be confronted with a brain teaser question or two during an interview. So as not to be caught off guard, you can familiarize yourself with typical brain teaser questions so that you're ready for them.

Your Task. Use your favorite search tool to locate lists of brain teaser questions and suggested answers on the Web. Select five or six brain teaser questions that you find interesting. In groups of three or four students, role-play interviewer and interviewee, alternating with your selected questions. You goal is to answer these questions creatively and confidently.

WEB

14.9 Answering Puffball and Killer Questions in a Virtual Interview

Two Web sites offer excellent interview advice. At *http://interview.monster.com* you can improve your interviewing skills in virtual interviews You'll find questions, answers, and explanations for interviews in job fields ranging from administrative support to human resources to technology. At *http://www.wetfeet.com/advice/interviewing.asp* you can learn how to answer résumé-based questions and how to handle preinterview jitters, and see dozens of articles filled with helpful tips.

Your Task. Visit one or both of the targeted Web sites. If these URLs have been changed, use your favorite search tool to locate "Monster Interviews" and "WetFeet Interviews."

14.10 Creating an Interview Cheat Sheet

Even the best-rehearsed applicants sometimes forget to ask the questions they prepared, or they fail to stress their major accomplishments in job interviews. Sometimes applicants are so rattled they even forget the interviewer's name. To help you keep your wits during an interview, make a "cheat sheet" that summarizes key facts, answers, and questions. Use it before the interview and also review it as the interview is ending to be sure you have covered everything that is critical.

Your Task. Prepare a cheat sheet with the following information:

Day and time of interview:
Meeting with: (Name of interviewer(s), title, company, city, state, zip, telephone, cell, fax, pager, e-mail)
Major accomplishments: (four to six)
Management or work style: (four to six)
Things you need to know about me: (three to four items)
Reason I left my last job:
Answers to difficult questions: (four to five answers)
Questions to ask interviewer:
Things I can do for you:

14.11 Handling Inappropriate and Illegal Interview Questions

Although some questions are considered illegal by the government, many interviewers will ask them anyway—whether intentionally or unknowingly. Being prepared is important.

Your Task. How would you respond in the following scenario? Let's assume you are being interviewed at one of the top companies on your list of potential employers. The interviewing committee consists of a human resources manager and the supervising manager of the department where you would work. At various times during the interview, the supervising manager has asked questions that made you feel uncomfortable. For example, he asked whether you were married. You know this question is illegal, but you saw no harm in answering it. But then he asked how old you were. Since you started college early and graduated in three and a half years, you are worried that you may not be considered mature enough for this position. But you have most of the other qualifications required, and you are convinced you could succeed on the job. How should you answer this question?

14.12 Knowing What to Ask

When it is your turn to ask questions during the interview process, be ready.

Your Task. Decide on three to five questions that you would like to ask during an interview. Write these questions out and practice asking them so that you sound confident and sincere.

TEAM

14.13 Practicing Answering Interview Questions

One of the best ways to understand interview dynamics and to develop confidence is to role-play the parts of interviewer and candidate.

Your Task. Choose a partner for this activity. Make a list of two interview questions for each of the nine interview question categories presented in this chapter. In team sessions you and your partner will role-play an actual interview. One acts as interviewer; the other is the candidate. Prior to the interview, the candidate tells the interviewer what job and company he or she is applying to. For the interview, the interviewer and candidate should dress appropriately and sit in chairs facing each other. The interviewer greets the candidate and makes the candidate comfortable. The candidate gives the interviewer a copy of his or her résumé. The interviewer asks three (or more depending on your instructor's time schedule) questions from the candidate's list. The interviewer may also ask follow-up questions if appropriate. When finished, the interviewer ends the meeting graciously. After one interview, reverse roles and repeat.

14.14 Videotaping an Interview

Seeing how you look during an interview can help you improve your body language and presentation style. Your instructor may act as the interviewer, or an outside businessperson may be asked to conduct mock interviews in your classroom.

Your Task. Engage a student or campus specialist to videotape each interview. Review your performance, and critique it looking for ways to improve. Your instructor may ask class members to offer comments and suggestions on individual interviews.

14.15 Saying Thanks for the Interview

You've just completed an exciting employment interview, and you want the interviewer to remember you.

Your Task. Write a follow-up thank-you letter to Ronald T. Ranson, Human Resources Development, Electronic Data Sources, 1328 Peachtree Plaza, Atlanta, GA 30314 (or a company of your choice). Make up any details needed.

14.16 Refusing to Take No for an Answer

After an excellent interview with Electronic Data Sources (or a company of your choice), you're disappointed to learn that someone else was hired. But you really want to work for EDS.

Your Task. Write a follow-up letter to Ronald T. Ranson, Human Resources Development, Electronic Data Sources, 1328 Peachtree Plaza, Atlanta, GA 30314 (or a company of your choice). Indicate that you are disappointed but still interested.

14.17 Following Up After Submitting Your Résumé

A month has passed since you sent your résumé and cover letter in response to a job advertisement. You're still interested in the position and would like to find out whether you still have a chance.

Your Task. Write a follow-up letter that doesn't offend the reader or damage your chances of employment.

14.18 Requesting a Reference

Your favorite professor has agreed to be one of your references. You've just arrived home from a job interview that went well, and you must ask your professor to write a letter of recommendation.

Your Task. Write to the professor requesting that a letter of recommendation be sent to the company where you interviewed. Explain that the interviewer asked that the letter be sent directly to him. Provide data about the job description and about yourself so that the professor can target its content.

14.19 Saying *Yes* to a Job Offer

Your dream has come true: you've just been offered an excellent position. Although you accepted the position on the phone, you want to send a formal acceptance letter.

Your Task. Write a job acceptance letter to an employer of your choice. Include the specific job title, your starting date, and details about your compensation package. Make up any necessary details.

(INFOTRAC)　(WEB)　(E-MAIL)

14.20 Searching for Advice

You can find wonderful, free, and sometimes entertaining information about job-search strategies, career tips, and interview advice on the Web.

Your Task. Use InfoTrac or a Web search tool to locate articles or links to job-search and résumé sites. Make a list of at least five good job-search pointers—ones that were not covered in this chapter. Send an e-mail message to your instructor describing your findings, or post your findings to a class discussion board to share with your classmates.

VIDEO RESOURCE

Video Library 1, *Building Workplace Skills*

Sharpening Your Interview Skills. In the video titled "Sharpening Your Interview Skills," you see the job interview of Betsy Chin. Based on what you learned in this chapter and your own experience, critique her performance. What did she do well and what could she improve?

GRAMMAR/MECHANICS CHECKUP—PUNCTUATION REVIEW

Review Sections 1.17 and 2.01–2.29 in the Grammar/Mechanics Handbook. Study the following groups of sentences. In the space provided write the letter of the one that is correctly punctuated. When you finish, compare your responses with those at the end of the book. If your responses differ, study carefully the principles in parentheses.

1. a. We specialize in network design, however we also offer troubleshooting and consulting.

    b. We realize that downtime is not an option; therefore, you can count on us for reliable, competent service.

    c. Our factory-trained and certified technicians perform repair at your location, or in our own repair depot for products under warranty and out of warranty.

2. a. Our accounting team makes a point of analyzing your business operations, and getting to know what's working for you and what's not.

    b. We are dedicated to understanding your business needs over the long term, and taking an active role when it comes to creating solutions.

    c. We understand that you may be downsizing or moving into new markets, and we want to help you make a seamless transition.

3. a. If you are growing, or connecting to new markets, our team will help you accomplish your goals with minimal interruptions.

    b. When you look at our organization chart, you will find the customer at the top.

    c. Although we offer each customer a dedicated customer account team we also provide professional general services.

4. a. The competition is changing; therefore, we have to deliver our products and services more efficiently.

    b. Although delivery systems are changing; the essence of banking remains the same.

    c. Banks will continue to be available around the corner, and also with the click of a mouse.

5. a. One of the reasons we are decreasing the number of our ATMs, is that two thirds of the bank's customers depend on tellers for transactions.

    b. We are looking for an article entitled, "Online Banking."

    c. Banks are at this time competing with nontraditional rivals who can provide extensive financial services.

6. a. We care deeply about the environment; but we also care about safety and good customer service.

    b. The president worked with environmental concerns; the vice president focused on customer support.

    c. Our Web site increases our productivity, it also improves customer service.

7. a. Employees who will be receiving salary increases are: Terri, Mark, Rob, and Ellen.

    b. The following employees are eligible for bonuses: Robin, Jeff, Bill, and Jose.

    c. Our consulting firm is proud to offer Web services for: site design, market analysis, e-commerce, and hosting.

8. a. All secretaries' computers were equipped with Excel.

    b. Both attorneys statements confused the judge.

    c. Some members names and addresses must be rekeyed.

9. a. Our committee considered convention sites in Scottsdale, Arizona, Palm Springs, California; and Dallas, Texas.

    b. Serena was from Columbus, Ohio; Josh was from Denver, Colorado, and Rachel was from Seattle, Washington.

    c. The following engineers were approved: J. W. Ellis, civil; Dr. Thomas Lee, structural; and W. R. Verey, mechanical.

10. a. The package from Albany, New York was never delivered.

    b. We have scheduled an inspection tour on Tuesday, March 5, at 4 p.m.

    c. Send the check to M. E. Williams, 320 Summit Ridge, Ogden, Utah 84404 before the last mail pickup.

• GRAMMAR/MECHANICS CHALLENGE—14

The following letter has faults in grammar, punctuation, spelling, capitalization, wordiness, and other problems. Correct the errors with standard proofreading marks (see Appendix B) or revise the message online at **Guffey Xtra!**

4201 North Harrison
Shawnee, OK 74801
June 4, 200x

Mr. Anthony R. Masters
Human Resources Department
Biolage Enterprises
7246 South May Avenue
Oklahoma City, OK 73159

Dear Mr. Master:

I appriciate the opportunity for the interview yesterday for the newly-listed Position of Sales Trainee. It was really a pleasure meeting yourself and learning more about Biolage Enterprises, you have a fine staff and a sophisticated approach to marketing.

You're organization appears to be growing in a directional manner that parralels my interests' and career goals. The interview with yourself and your staff yesterday confirmed my initale positive impressions of Biolage Enterprises and I want to reiterate my strong interest in working with and for you. My prior Retail sales experience as a sales associate with Sears; plus my recent training in Microsoft Word and Excel would enable me to make progress steadily through your programs of training and become a productive member of your sales team in no time at all.

Again, thank-you for your kind and gracius consideration. In the event that you need any additional information from me, all you have to do is give me a call me at (405) 391-7792.

Sincerly yours,

CAREER SKILLS

LET'S TALK MONEY
NEGOTIATING A SALARY

When to talk about salary causes many job applicants concern. The important thing to remember is that almost all salaries are negotiable. Research conducted by the Society for Human Resource Management and CareerJournal.com shows that approximately 90 percent of human resource professionals say salaries are negotiable, and 78 percent of employees report negotiating salary.[21] If you've proved your worth throughout the interview process, employers will want to negotiate with you. To negotiate effectively, though, you must be prepared for salary questions, and you should know what you're worth. You also need to know basic negotiation strategies. As negotiation expert Chester L. Karrass said, "In business, you don't get what you deserve, you get what you negotiate."[22] The following negotiating rules, recommended by various career experts, can guide you to a better beginning salary.[23]

Rule No. 1: Avoid discussing salary for as long as possible in the interview process.

The longer you delay salary discussion, the more time you will have to convince the employer that you're worth what you're asking for. Ideally you should try to avoid discussing salary until you know for sure that the interviewing company is making a job offer. The best time for you to negotiate your salary is between the time you're offered the position and the time you accept it. Wait for the employer to bring salary up first. If salary comes up and you are not sure whether the job is being offered to you, it's time for you to be blunt. Here are some things you could say:

> *Are you making me a job offer?*
> *What salary range do you pay for positions with similar requirements?*
> *I'm very interested in the position, and my salary would be negotiable.*
> *Tell me what you have in mind for the salary range.*

Rule No. 2: Know in advance the probable salary range for similar jobs in similar organizations.

Many job-search Web sites provide salary information. But it's probably better for you to call around in your area to learn what similar jobs are paying. The important thing here is to think in terms of a wide range. Let's say you are hoping to start at between $45,000 and $50,000. To an interviewer, you might say, *I was looking for a salary in the high forties to the low fifties*. This technique is called bracketing. In addition, stating your salary range in an annual dollar amount sounds more professional than asking for an hourly wage. Be sure to consider such things as geographic location, employer size, industry standards, the strength of the economy, and other factors to make sure that the range you come up with is realistic.

Rule No. 3: When negotiating, focus on what you're worth, not on what you need.

Throughout the interview and negotiation process, focus continually on your strengths. Make sure that the employer knows everything of value that you'll bring to the organization. You have to prove that you're worth what you're asking for. Employers pay salaries based on what you'll accomplish on the job and contribute to the organization. When negotiating your salary, focus on how the company will benefit from these contributions.

Don't bring personal issues into the negotiation process. No employer will be willing to pay you more because you have bills to pay, mouths to feed, or debt to get out of.

Rule No. 4: Never say *no* to a job before it is offered.

Why would anyone refuse a job offer before it's made? It happens all the time. Let's say you were hoping for a salary of, say, $45,000. The interviewer tells you that the salary scheduled for this job is $40,000. You respond, *Oh, that's out of the question!* Before you were offered the job, you have, in effect, refused it. Instead, wait for the job offer; then start negotiating your salary.

Rule No. 5: Ask for a higher salary first, and consider benefits.

Within reason, always try to ask for a higher salary first. This will leave room for this amount to decrease during negotiations until it's closer to your original expectations. Remember to consider the entire compensation package when negotiating. You may be willing to accept a lower salary if benefits such as insurance, flexible hours, time off, and retirement are attractive.

Rule No. 6: Be ready to bargain if offered a low starting salary.

Many salaries are negotiable. Companies are often willing to pay more for someone who interviews well and fits their culture. If the company seems right to you and you are pleased with the sound of the open position but you have been offered a low salary, say, *That is somewhat lower than I had hoped but this position does sound exciting. If I were to consider this, what sorts of things could I do to quickly become more valuable to this organization?* Also discuss such things as bonuses based on performance or a shorter review period. You could say something like, *Thanks for the offer. The position is very much what I wanted in many ways, and I am delighted at your interest. If I start at this salary, may I be reviewed within six months with the goal of raising the salary to ____?*

Another possibility is to ask for more time to think about the low offer. Tell the interviewer that this is an important decision and you need some time to consider the offer. The next day you can call and say, *I am flattered by your offer, but I cannot accept because the salary is lower than I would like. Perhaps you could reconsider your offer or keep me in mind for future openings.*

Rule No. 7: Be honest.

Be honest throughout the entire negotiation process. Don't inflate the salaries of your previous positions to try to get more money. Don't tell an employer that you've received other job offers unless it's true. These lies can be grounds for being fired later on.

Rule No. 8: Get the final offer in writing.

Once you've agreed on a salary and compensation package, get the offer in writing. You should also follow up with a position acceptance letter, as discussed earlier in the chapter.

Career Application. You've just passed the screening interview and have been asked to come in for a personal interview with the human resources representative and the hiring manager of a company where you are very eager to work. Although you are delighted with the company, you have promised yourself that you will not accept any position that pays less than $45,000 to start.

Your Task
In teams of two, role-play the position of interviewer and interviewee. The interviewer sets the scene by discussing preliminaries and offers a salary of $42,500. The interviewee responds to preliminary questions and to the salary offer of $42,500. Then, reverse roles so that the interviewee becomes the interviewer, and repeat the scenario.

Appendix A

REFERENCE GUIDE TO DOCUMENT FORMATS

Business documents carry two kinds of messages. Verbal messages are conveyed by the words chosen to express the writer's ideas. Nonverbal messages are conveyed largely by the appearance of a document. If you compare an assortment of letters and memos from various organizations, you will notice immediately that some look more attractive and more professional than others. The nonverbal message of the professional-looking documents suggests that they were sent by people who are careful, informed, intelligent, and successful. Understandably, you're more likely to take seriously documents that use professional formatting techniques.

Over the years certain practices and conventions have arisen regarding the appearance and formatting of business documents. Although these conventions offer some choices (such as letter and punctuation styles), most business documents follow standardized formats. To ensure that your documents carry favorable nonverbal messages about you and your organization, you'll want to give special attention to the appearance and formatting of your letters, envelopes, and e-mail messages.

Spacing and Punctuation

For some time typists left two spaces after end punctuation (periods, question marks, and so forth). This practice was necessary, it was thought, because typewriters did not have proportional spacing and sentences were easier to read if two spaces separated them. Professional typesetters, however, never followed this practice because they used proportional spacing, and readability was not a problem. Fortunately, today's word processors now make available the same fonts used by typesetters.

The question of how many spaces to leave after concluding punctuation is one of the most frequently asked questions at the Modern Language Association Web site (*http://www.mla.org*). MLA experts point out that most publications in this country today have the same spacing after a punctuation mark as between words on the same line. Influenced by the look of typeset publications, many writers now leave only one space after end punctuation. As a practical matter, however, it is not wrong to use two spaces.

Letter Placement

The easiest way to place letters on the page is to use the defaults of your word processing program. These are usually set for side margins of 1¼ inch. Many companies today find these margins acceptable.

If you want to adjust your margins to better balance shorter letters, use the following chart:

Words in Body of Letter	Side Margins	Blank Lines After Date
Under 200	1½ inches	4 to 10
Over 200	1 inch	2 to 3

Experts say that a "ragged" right margin is easier to read than a justified (even) margin. You might want to turn off the justification feature of your word processing program if it automatically justifies the right margin.

Letter Parts

Professional-looking business letters are arranged in a conventional sequence with standard parts. Following is a discussion of how to use these letter parts properly. Figure A.1 illustrates the parts of a block style letter. (See Chapter 6 for additional discussion of letters and their parts.)

LETTERHEAD

Most business organizations use 8½ × 11-inch paper printed with a letterhead displaying their official name, street address, Web address, e-mail address, and telephone and fax numbers. The letterhead may also include a logo and an advertising message.

DATELINE

On letterhead paper you should place the date one blank line below the last line of the letterhead or 2 inches from the top edge of the paper (line 13). On plain paper place the date immediately below your return address. Since the date goes on line 13, start the return address an appropriate number of lines above it. The most common dateline format is as follows: *June 9, 2007*. Don't use *th* (or *rd, nd* or *st*) when the date is written this way. For European or military correspondence, use the following dateline format: *9 June 2007*. Notice that no commas are used.

ADDRESSEE AND DELIVERY NOTATIONS

Delivery notations such as *FAX TRANSMISSION, FEDERAL EXPRESS, MESSENGER DELIVERY, CONFIDENTIAL*, or *CERTIFIED MAIL* are typed in all capital letters two blank lines above the inside address.

INSIDE ADDRESS

Type the inside address—that is, the address of the organization or person receiving the letter—single-spaced, starting at the left margin. The number of lines between the dateline and the inside address depends on the size of the letter body, the type size (point or pitch size), and the length of the typing lines. Generally, one to nine blank lines are appropriate.

Be careful to duplicate the exact wording and spelling of the recipient's name and address on your documents. Usually, you can copy this information from the letterhead of the correspondence you are answering. If, for example, you are responding to *Jackson & Perkins Company*, don't address your letter to *Jackson and Perkins Corp.*

Always be sure to include a courtesy title such as *Mr., Ms., Mrs., Dr.*, or *Professor* before a person's name in the inside address—for both the letter and the envelope. Although many women in business today favor *Ms.*, you'll want to use whatever title the addressee prefers.

Remember that the inside address is not included for readers (who already know who and where they are). It's there to help writers accurately file a copy of the message.

In general, avoid abbreviations such as *Ave.* or *Co.* unless they appear in the printed letterhead of the document being answered.

ATTENTION LINE

An attention line allows you to send your message officially to an organization but to direct it to a specific individual, officer, or department. However, if you know an individual's complete name, it's always better to use it as the first line of the

FIGURE A.1 | **Block and Modified Block Letter Styles**

Block Style
Mixed Punctuation

Letterhead

Island Graphics
893 Dillingham Boulevard
Honolulu, HI 96817-8817

(808)493-2310
http://www.islandgraphics.com

↓ Dateline is 2 inches from the top or 1 blank line below letterhead

Dateline — September 13, 200x

↓ 1 to 9 blank lines

Inside address — Mr. T. M. Wilson, President
Visual Concept Enterprises
1901 Kaumualii Highway
Lihue, HI 96766

↓ 1 blank line

Salutation — Dear Mr. Wilson:

↓ 1 blank line

Subject line — SUBJECT: BLOCK LETTER STYLE

↓ 1 blank line

This letter illustrates block letter style, about which you asked. All typed lines begin at the left margin. The date is usually placed 2 inches from the top edge of the paper or one blank line below the last line of the letterhead, whichever position is lower.

Body — This letter also shows mixed punctuation. A colon follows the salutation, and a comma follows the complimentary close. Open punctuation requires no colon after the salutation and no comma following the close; however, open punctuation is seldom seen today.

If a subject line is included, it appears one blank line below the salutation. The word *SUBJECT* is optional. Most readers will recognize a statement in this position as the subject without an identifying label. The complimentary close appears one blank line below the end of the last paragraph.

↓ 1 blank line

Complimentary close — Sincerely,

Mark H. Wong

↓ 3 blank lines

Signature block — Mark H. Wong
Graphics Designer

↓ 1 blank line

Reference initials — MHW:pil

↓ 1 blank line

cc: Stacy Shirley

**Modified block style
Mixed punctuation**

In the modified block style letter shown at the left, the date is centered or aligned with the complimentary close and signature block, which start at the center. Mixed punctuation includes a colon after the salutation and a comma after the complimentary close, as shown above and at the left.

inside address and avoid an attention line. Here are two common formats for attention lines:

MultiMedia Enterprises   MultiMedia Enterprises
931 Calkins Road   Attention: Marketing Director
Rochester, NY 14301   931 Calkins Road
                                          Rochester, NY 14301
ATTENTION MARKETING DIRECTOR

Attention lines may be typed in all caps or with upper- and lowercase letters. The colon following *Attention* is optional. Notice that an attention line may be placed two lines below the address block or printed as the second line of the inside address. You'll want to use the latter format if you're composing on a word processor because the address block may be copied to the envelope and the attention line will not interfere with the last-line placement of the zip code. Mail can be sorted more easily if the zip code appears in the last line of a typed address.

Whenever possible, use a person's name as the first line of an address instead of putting that name in an attention line. Some writers use an attention line because they fear that letters addressed to individuals at companies may be considered private. They worry that if the addressee is no longer with the company, the letter may be forwarded or not opened. Actually, unless a letter is marked *Personal* or *Confidential*, it will very likely be opened as business mail.

SALUTATION

For most letter styles place the letter greeting, or salutation, one blank line below the last line of the inside address or the attention line (if used). If the letter is addressed to an individual, use that person's courtesy title and last name (*Dear Mr. Lanham*). Even if you are on a first-name basis (*Dear Leslie*), be sure to add a colon (not a comma or a semicolon) after the salutation. Do not use an individual's full name in the salutation (not *Dear Mr. Leslie Lanham*) unless you are unsure of gender (*Dear Leslie Lanham*).

For letters with attention lines or those addressed to organizations, the selection of an appropriate salutation has become more difficult. Formerly, writers used *Gentlemen* generically for all organizations. With increasing numbers of women in business management today, however, *Gentlemen* is problematic. Because no universally acceptable salutation has emerged as yet, you could use *Ladies and Gentlemen* or *Gentlemen and Ladies*.

One way to avoid the salutation dilemma is to address a document to a specific person. Another alternative is to use the simplified letter style (shown in Figure A.2), which conveniently omits the salutation (and the complimentary close).

SUBJECT AND REFERENCE LINES

Although experts suggest placing the subject line one blank line below the salutation, some organizations actually place it above the salutation. Use whatever style your organization prefers. Reference lines often show policy or file numbers; they generally appear one blank line above the salutation. Use initial capital letters for the main words or all capital letters.

BODY

Most business letters and memorandums are single-spaced, with double spacing between paragraphs. Very short messages may be double-spaced with indented paragraphs.

FIGURE A.2 —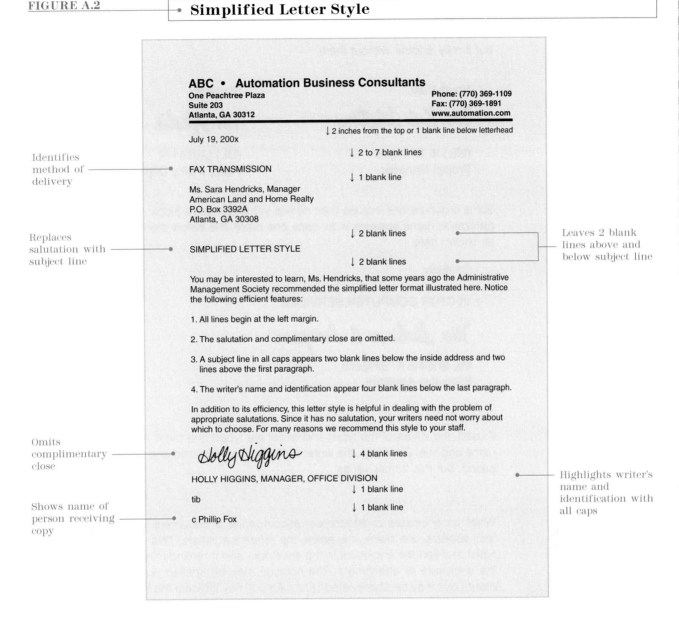

Simplified Letter Style

Identifies method of delivery

Replaces salutation with subject line

Omits complimentary close

Shows name of person receiving copy

Leaves 2 blank lines above and below subject line

Highlights writer's name and identification with all caps

COMPLIMENTARY CLOSE

Typed one blank line below the last line of the letter, the complimentary close may be formal (*Very truly yours*) or informal (*Sincerely* or *Cordially*). The simplified letter style omits a complimentary close.

SIGNATURE BLOCK

In most letter styles the writer's typed name and optional identification appear three or four blank lines below the complimentary close. The combination of name, title, and organization information should be arranged to achieve a balanced look. The name and title may appear on the same line or on separate lines, depending on the length of each. Use commas to separate categories within the same line, but not to conclude a line.

Sincerely yours,

Jeremy M. Wood

Jeremy M. Wood, Manager
Technical Sales and Services

Cordially yours,

Casandra Baker-Murillo

Casandra Baker-Murillo
Executive Vice President

Courtesy titles (*Ms.*, *Mrs.*, or *Miss*) should be used before names that are not readily distinguishable as male or female. They should also be used before names containing only initials and international names. The title is usually placed in parentheses, but it may appear without them.

Yours truly,

Ms. K.C. Tripton

(Ms.) K. C. Tripton
Project Manager

Sincerely,

Mr. Leslie Hill

(Mr.) Leslie Hill
Public Policy Department

Some organizations include their names in the signature block. In such cases the organization name appears in all caps one blank line below the complimentary close, as shown here:

Cordially,

VECTOR COMPUTER SERVICES

Ms. Shelina A. Simpson

Ms. Shelina A. Simpson
Executive Assistant

REFERENCE INITIALS

If used, the initials of the typist and writer are typed one blank line below the writer's name and title. Generally, the writer's initials are capitalized and the typist's are lowercased, but this format varies.

ENCLOSURE NOTATION

When an enclosure or attachment accompanies a document, a notation to that effect appears one blank line below the reference initials. This notation reminds the typist to insert the enclosure in the envelope, and it reminds the recipient to look for the enclosure or attachment. The notation may be spelled out (*Enclosure, Attachment*), or it may be abbreviated (*Enc., Att.*). It may indicate the number of enclosures or attachments, and it may also identify a specific enclosure (*Enclosure: Form 1099*).

COPY NOTATION

If you make copies of correspondence for other individuals, you may use *cc* to indicate carbon copy, *pc* to indicate photocopy, or merely *c* for any kind of copy. A colon following the initial(s) is optional.

SECOND-PAGE HEADING

When a letter extends beyond one page, use plain paper of the same quality and color as the first page. Identify the second and succeeding pages with a heading consisting of the name of the addressee, the page number, and the date. Use the following format or the one shown in Figure A.3:

Ms. Sara Hendricks   2   May 3, 200x

Both headings appear six blank lines (1 inch) from the top edge of the paper followed by two blank lines to separate them from the continuing text. Avoid using a second page if you have only one line or the complimentary close and signature block to fill that page.

FIGURE A.3 • **Second-Page Heading**

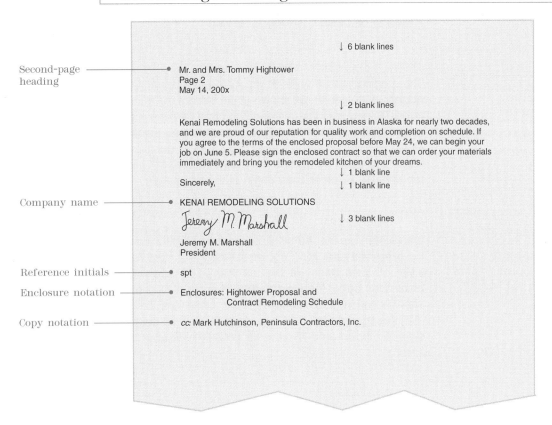

Second-page heading

Company name

Reference initials

Enclosure notation

Copy notation

PLAIN-PAPER RETURN ADDRESS

If you prepare a personal or business letter on plain paper, place your address immediately above the date. Do not include your name; you will type (and sign) your name at the end of your letter. If your return address contains two lines, arrange the date so that it appears 2 inches from the top. Avoid abbreviations except for a two-letter state abbreviation.

580 East Leffels Street
Springfield, OH 45501
December 14, 2007

Ms. Ellen Siemens
Escrow Department
TransOhio First Federal
1220 Wooster Boulevard
Columbus, OH 43218-2900

Dear Ms. Siemens:

For letters in the block style, type the return address at the left margin. For modified block style letters, start the return address at the center to align with the complimentary close.

Letter Styles

Business letters are generally prepared in one of three formats. The most popular is the block style, but the simplified style has much to recommend it.

BLOCK STYLE

In the block style, shown in Figure A.1, all lines begin at the left margin. This style is a favorite because it is easy to format.

MODIFIED BLOCK STYLE

The modified block style differs from block style in that the date and closing lines appear in the center, as shown at the bottom of Figure A.1. The date may be (1) centered, (2) begun at the center of the page (to align with the closing lines), or (3) backspaced from the right margin. The signature block—including the complimentary close, writer's name and title, or organization identification—begins at the center. The first line of each paragraph may begin at the left margin or may be indented five or ten spaces. All other lines begin at the left margin.

SIMPLIFIED STYLE

Introduced by the Administrative Management Society a number of years ago, the simplified letter style, shown in Figure A.2, requires little formatting. Like the block style, all lines begin at the left margin. A subject line appears in all caps two blank lines below the inside address and two blank lines above the first paragraph. The salutation and complimentary close are omitted. The signer's name and identification appear in all caps four blank lines below the last paragraph. This letter style is efficient and avoids the problems of appropriate salutations and courtesy titles.

PUNCTUATION STYLES

Two punctuation styles are available for letters. *Mixed* punctuation, shown in Figure A.1, requires a colon after the salutation and a comma after the complimentary close. *Open* punctuation contains no punctuation after the salutation or complimentary close. It is seldom used in business today. With mixed punctuation, be sure to use a colon—not a comma or semicolon—after the salutation. Even when the salutation is a first name, the colon is appropriate.

Envelopes

An envelope should be of the same quality and color of stationery as the letter it carries. Because the envelope introduces your message and makes the first impression, you need to be especially careful in addressing it. Moreover, how you fold the letter is important.

RETURN ADDRESS

The return address is usually printed in the upper left corner of an envelope, as shown in Figure A.4. In large companies some form of identification (the writer's initials, name, or location) may be placed above the company name and address. This identification helps return the letter to the sender in case of nondelivery.

On an envelope without a printed return address, single-space the return address in the upper left corner. Beginning on line 3 on the fourth space (½ inch) from the left edge, print the writer's name, title, company, and mailing address.

MAILING ADDRESS

On legal-sized No. 10 envelopes (4⅛ × 9½ inches), begin the address on line 13 about 4¼ inches from the left edge, as shown in Figure A.4. For small envelopes (3⅝ × 6½ inches), begin typing on line 12 about 2½ inches from the left edge.

FIGURE A.4 • **Envelope Formats**

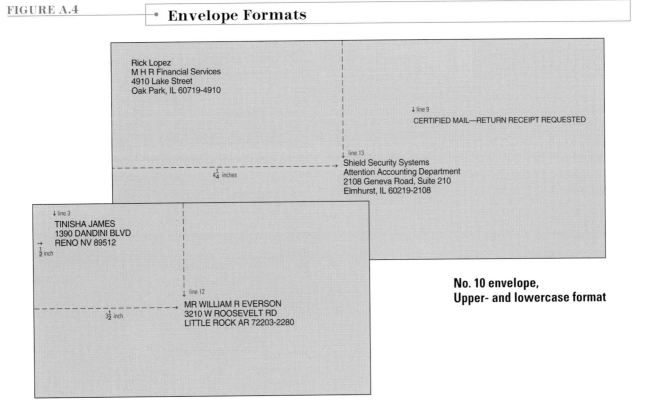

Rick Lopez
M H R Financial Services
4910 Lake Street
Oak Park, IL 60719-4910

↓ line 9
CERTIFIED MAIL—RETURN RECEIPT REQUESTED

↓ line 13
Shield Security Systems
Attention Accounting Department
2108 Geneva Road, Suite 210
Elmhurst, IL 60219-2108

$4\frac{1}{4}$ inches

↓ line 3
TINISHA JAMES
1390 DANDINI BLVD
RENO NV 89512
$\frac{1}{2}$ inch

↓ line 12
MR WILLIAM R EVERSON
3210 W ROOSEVELT RD
LITTLE ROCK AR 72203-2280

$3\frac{1}{2}$ inch

**No. 10 envelope,
Upper- and lowercase format**

No. $6\frac{3}{4}$ envelope, Postal Service uppercase format

The U.S. Postal Service recommends that addresses be typed in all caps without any punctuation. This Postal Service style, shown in the small envelope in Figure A.4, was originally developed to facilitate scanning by optical character readers. Today's OCRs, however, are so sophisticated that they scan upper- and lowercase letters easily. Many companies today do not follow the Postal Service format because they prefer to use the same format for the envelope as for the inside address. If the same format is used, writers can take advantage of word processing programs to "copy" the inside address to the envelope, thus saving keystrokes and reducing errors. Having the same format on both the inside address and the envelope also looks more professional and consistent. For those reasons you may choose to use the familiar upper- and lowercase combination format. But you will want to check with your organization to learn its preference.

In addressing your envelopes for delivery in this country or in Canada, use the two-letter state and province abbreviations shown in Figure A.5. Notice that these abbreviations are in capital letters without periods.

FOLDING

The way a letter is folded and inserted into an envelope sends additional nonverbal messages about a writer's professionalism and carefulness. Most businesspeople follow the procedures shown here, which produce the least number of creases to distract readers.

For large No. 10 envelopes, begin with the letter face up. Fold slightly less than one third of the sheet toward the top, as shown in the following diagram. Then fold down the top third to within 6¾ inch of the bottom fold. Insert the letter into the envelope with the last fold toward the bottom of the envelope.

FIGURE A.5

Abbreviations of States, Territories, and Provinces

State or Territory	Two-Letter Abbreviation	State or Territory	Two-Letter Abbreviation
Alabama	AL	North Carolina	NC
Alaska	AK	North Dakota	ND
Arizona	AZ	Ohio	OH
Arkansas	AR	Oklahoma	OK
California	CA	Oregon	OR
Canal Zone	CZ	Pennsylvania	PA
Colorado	CO	Puerto Rico	PR
Connecticut	CT	Rhode Island	RI
Delaware	DE	South Carolina	SC
District of Columbia	DC	South Dakota	SD
Florida	FL	Tennessee	TN
Georgia	GA	Texas	TX
Guam	GU	Utah	UT
Hawaii	HI	Vermont	VT
Idaho	ID	Virgin Islands	VI
Illinois	IL	Virginia	VA
Indiana	IN	Washington	WA
Iowa	IA	West Virginia	WV
Kansas	KS	Wisconsin	WI
Kentucky	KY	Wyoming	WY
Louisiana	LA		
Maine	ME	**Canadian Province**	
Maryland	MD	Alberta	AB
Massachusetts	MA	British Columbia	BC
Michigan	MI	Labrador	LB
Minnesota	MN	Manitoba	MB
Mississippi	MS	New Brunswick	NB
Missouri	MO	Newfoundland	NF
Montana	MT	Northwest Territories	NT
Nebraska	NE	Nova Scotia	NS
Nevada	NV	Ontario	ON
New Hampshire	NH	Prince Edward Island	PE
New Jersey	NJ	Quebec	PQ
New Mexico	NM	Saskatchewan	SK
New York	NY	Yukon Territory	YT

For small No. 6¾ envelopes, begin by folding the bottom up to within ⅓ inch of the top edge. Then fold the right third over to the left. Fold the left third to within ⅓ inch of the last fold. Insert the last fold into the envelope first.

E-Mail Messages

Although e-mail is a developing communication medium, formatting and usage are becoming more standardized. The following suggestions, illustrated in Figure A.6 and also in Figure 5.2 in Chapter 5 on page 106, may guide you in setting up the parts of any e-mail message. Always check, however, with your organization so that you can follow its practices.

TO LINE

Include the receiver's e-mail address after *To*. If the receiver's address is recorded in your address book, you just have to click on it. Be sure to enter all addresses very carefully since one mistyped letter prevents delivery.

FROM LINE

Most mail programs automatically include your name and e-mail address after *From*.

CC AND *BCC*

Insert the e-mail address of anyone who is to receive a copy of the message. *Cc* stands for carbon copy or courtesy copy. Don't be tempted, though, to send needless copies just because it's so easy. *Bcc* stands for blind carbon copy. Some writers use *bcc* to send a copy of the message without the addressee's knowledge. Writers are also using the *bcc* line for mailing lists. When a message is being sent to a number of people and their e-mail addresses should not be revealed, the *bcc* line works well to conceal the names and addresses of all receivers.

FIGURE A.6 **E-Mail Message**

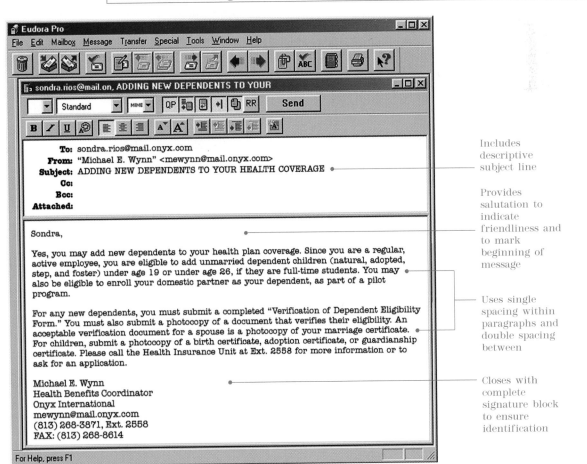

Includes descriptive subject line

Provides salutation to indicate friendliness and to mark beginning of message

Uses single spacing within paragraphs and double spacing between

Closes with complete signature block to ensure identification

SUBJECT

Identify the subject of the e-mail message with a brief but descriptive summary of the topic. Be sure to include enough information to be clear and compelling. Capitalize the initial letters of principal words, or capitalize the entire line.

SALUTATION

Include a brief greeting, if you like. Some writers use a salutation such as *Dear Sondra* followed by a comma or a colon. Others are more informal with *Hi, Sondra!*, or *Good morning* or *Greetings*. Some writers treat an e-mail message like a memo and skip the salutation entirely. See Chapter 5 on page 105 for a more complete discussion of e-mail salutations.

MESSAGE

Cover just one topic in your message, and try to keep your total message under two or three screens in length. Single-space and be sure to use both upper- and lower-case letters. Double-space between paragraphs.

COMPLIMENTARY CLOSE

Because e-mail messages are not memos, they may include a friendly complimentary close, such as *Cheers*, *Best wishes*, or *Warm regards*. Such a closing is optional, but it does introduce warmth to a rather cold communication channel. It also signals the end of a message, which is helpful when long sets of messages are included in a transmission thread.

SIGNATURE BLOCK

An e-mail signature block has become the equivalent of your business card. Include as much information as people will need to contact you electronically or otherwise. Smart e-mail writers insert a complete signature block that includes some or all of the following information: name, title, department, organization, address of organization, e-mail address, telephone, cell phone, and fax. Why insert your e-mail address in your signature? Many programs do not include your address automatically, and forwarded messages may drop it.

Consider preparing different signature combinations for colleagues, customers, or others. An e-mail to a fellow employee may require just your name. Most messages, however, require a more complete signature block. Receivers are grateful to have all of your contact information in one handy block.

ATTACHMENT

Use the attachment window or button to select the path and file name of any file you wish to send with your e-mail message. You can also attach a Web page to your message.

Appendix B

INSITE CORRECTION SYMBOLS AND PROOFREADING MARKS

In marking your papers, your instructor may use the following symbols or abbreviations to indicate writing weaknesses. Studying these symbols and suggestions will help you understand your instructor's remarks. Knowing this information can also help you evaluate and improve your own memos, e-mail, letters, reports, and other writing. These symbols are part of a customized version of InSite, an online grading, research, and writing tool your instructor may use. Many of the symbols are reinforced with InSite remediation quizzes, written by your author, to help build your skills. These symbols are keyed to your Grammar/Mechanics Handbook and to the text.

Adj	Hyphenate two or more adjectives that are joined to create a compound modifier before a noun. See G/M 1.17e.
Adv	Use adverbs, not adjectives, to describe or limit the action. See G/M 1.17d.
Apos	Use apostrophes to show possession. See G/M 2.20.
Assgn	Follow the assignment instructions.
Awk	Recast to avoid awkward expression.
Bias	Use inclusive, bias-free language. See Ch. 2, page 42.
Cap	Use capitalization appropriately. See G/M 3.01–3.16.
CmConj	Use a comma before the coordinating conjunction in a compound sentence. See G/M 2.05.
CmDate	Use commas appropriately in dates, addresses, geographical names, degrees, and long numbers. See G/M 2.04.
CmIn	Use commas to set off internal sentence interrupters. See G/M 2.06c.
CmIntr	Use commas to separate introductory clauses and certain phrases from independent clauses. See G/M 2.06.
CmSer	Use commas to separate three or more items (words, phrases, or short clauses) in a series. See G/M 2.01.
Coh	Improve coherence between ideas. Repeat key ideas, use pronouns, or use transitional expressions. See Ch. 3, pages 68–69.
Cl	Improve the clarity of ideas or expression so that the point is better understood.
CS	Avoid comma-splice sentences, Do not use a comma to splice (join) two independent clauses. See Ch. 3, page 62.
CmUn	Avoid unnecessary commas. See G/M 2.15.
:	Use a colon after a complete thought that introduces a list of items. Use a colon in business letter salutations and to introduce long quotations. See G/M 2.17–2.19.
Direct	Use the direct strategy by emphasizing the main idea. See Ch. 3, page 59.
Dash	Use a dash to set off parenthetical elements, to emphasize sentence interruptions, or to separate an introductory list from a summarizing statement. See G/M 2.26.

DM	Avoid dangling modifiers by placing modifiers close to the words they describe or limit. See Ch. 3, pages 67–68.
Frag	Avoid fragments by expressing ideas in complete sentences. A fragment is a broken-off part of a sentence. See Ch. 3, page 62.
Filler	Avoid fillers such as *there are* or long lead-ins such as *this is to inform you that.* See Ch. 4, page 83.
Format	Choose an appropriate format for this document.
GH	Use graphic highlighting (bullets, lists, indentions, or headings) to enhance readability. See Ch. 5, pages 102–103.
MM	Avoid misplaced modifiers by placing modifiers close to the words they describe or limit. See Ch. 3, pages 67–68.
Num	Use number or word form appropriately. See G/M 4.01–4.13.
Ob	Avoid stating the obvious.
Org	Improve organization by grouping similar ideas.
Par	Express ideas in parallel form. See Ch. 3, page 66.
Paren	Use parentheses to set off nonessential sentence elements such as explanations, directions, questions, or references. See G/M 2.27.
Period	Use one period to end a statement, command, indirect question, or polite request. See G/M 2.23.
Pos	Express an idea positively rather than negatively. See Ch. 2, pages 41–42.
PosPro	Use possessive-case pronouns to show ownership. See G/M 1.07 and 1.08d.
Pro	Use nominative-case pronouns as subjects of verbs and as subject complements. Use objective-case pronouns as objects of prepositions and verbs. See G/M 1.07–1.08.
ProAgr	Make pronouns agree in number and gender with the words to which they refer (their antecedents). See G/M 1.09.
ProVag	Be sure that pronouns such as *it, which, this*, and *that* refer to clear antecedents. See G/M 1.09.
?	Use a question mark after a direct question and after statements with questions appended. See G/M 2.24.
Quo	Use quotation marks to enclose the exact words of a speaker or writer, to distinguish words used in a special sense, or to enclose titles of articles, chapters, or other short works. See G/M 2.28.
Redun	Avoid expressions that repeat meaning or include unnecessary words. See Ch. 4, page 83.
RunOn	Avoid run-on (fused) sentences. A sentence with two independent clauses must be joined by a coordinating conjunctions (*and, or, nor, but*) or by a semicolon (;). See Ch. 3, page 62.
Sp	Check misspelled words.
Self	Use *self*-ending pronouns only when they refer to previously mentioned nouns or pronouns. See G/M 1.08h.
;	Use a semicolon to join closely related independent clauses. A semicolon is also an option to join separate items in a series when one or more of the items contain internal commas. See G/M 2.16.
Shift	Avoid a confusing shift in verb tense, mood, or voice. See G/M 1.15c.
Trans	Use an appropriate transition. See Ch. 3, page 69, and Ch. 12, page 352.
Tone	Use a conversational, positive, and courteous tone that promotes goodwill. See Ch. 2, pages 40–41.
You	Focus on developing the "you" view. See Ch. 2, pages 39–40.
VbTnse	Use present-tense, past-tense, and part-participle forms correctly. See G/M 1.13
VbMood	Use the subjunctive mood to express hypothetical (untrue) ideas. See G/M 1.12.
VbVce	Use active- and passive-voice verbs appropriately. See G/M 1.11.

VbAgr	Make verbs agree with subjects. See G/M 1.10.
WC	Focus on precise word choice. See Ch. 4, page 85.
Wordy	Avoid wordiness including fillers, long lead-ins, redundancies, compound prepositions, wordy noun phrases, and empty words. See Ch. 4, page 82.

Proofreading Marks

Proofreading Mark	Draft Copy	Final Copy
⸗ Align horizontally	TO: Rick Munoz	TO: Rick Munoz
‖ Align vertically	166.32 132.45	166.32 132.45
≣ Capitalize	Coca-cola runs on ms-dos	Coca-Cola runs on MS-DOS
⊂ Close up space	meeting at 3 p. m.	meeting at 3 p.m.
⟧⟦ Center	⟧Recommendations⟦	Recommendations
⟨ Delete	in my final judgement	in my judgment
ⱽ Insert apostrophe	our companys product	our company's product
⋀ Insert comma	you will of course	you will, of course,
⫶ Insert hyphen	tax free income	tax-free income
⨀ Insert period	Ms Holly Hines	Ms. Holly Hines
⸾ Insert quotation mark	shareholders receive a bonus.	shareholders receive a "bonus."
# Insert space	wordprocessing program	word processing program
/ Lowercase (remove capitals)	the Vice President HUMAN RESOURCES	the vice president Human Resources
⊏ Move to left	⊏I. Labor costs	I. Labor costs
⊐ Move to right	A. Findings of study⊐	A. Findings of study
⊘ Spell out	aimed at 2 depts	aimed at two departments
¶ Start new paragraph	¶Keep the screen height of your computer at eye level.	Keep the screen height of your computer at eye level.
⋯ Stet (don't delete)	officials talked openly	officials talked openly
∿ Transpose	accounts recievable	accounts receivable
bf Use boldface	Conclusions bf	**Conclusions**
ital Use italics	The Perfect Résumé ital	*The Perfect Résumé*

Appendix C

DOCUMENTATION FORMATS

For many reasons business writers are careful to properly document report data. Citing sources strengthens a writer's argument, as you learned in Chapter 10. Acknowledging sources also shields writers from charges of plagiarism. Moreover, good references help readers pursue further research.

Before we discuss specific documentation formats, you must understand the difference between *source* notes and *content* notes. Source notes identify quotations, paraphrased passages, and author references. They lead readers to the sources of cited information, and they must follow a consistent format. Content notes, on the other hand, enable writers to add comments, explain information not directly related to the text, or refer readers to other sections of a report. Because content notes are generally infrequent, most writers identify them in the text with a raised asterisk (*). At the bottom of the page, the asterisk is repeated with the content note following. If two content notes appear on one page, a double asterisk identifies the second reference.

Your real concern will be with source notes. These identify quotations or paraphrased ideas in the text, and they direct readers to a complete list of references (a bibliography) at the end of your report. Researchers have struggled for years to develop the perfect documentation system, one that is efficient for the writer and crystal clear to the reader. As a result, many systems exist, each with its advantages. The important thing for you is to adopt one system and use it consistently.

Students frequently ask, *But what documentation system is most used in business?* Actually, no one method dominates. Many businesses have developed their own hybrid systems. These companies generally supply guidelines illustrating their in-house style to employees. Before starting any research project on the job, you'll want to inquire about your organization's preferred documentation style. You can also look in the files for examples of previous reports.

References are usually cited in two places: (1) a brief citation appears in the text, and (2) a complete citation appears in a bibliography at the end of the report. The two most common formats for citations and bibliographies are those of the Modern Language Association (MLA) and the American Psychological Association (APA). Each has its own style for textual references and bibliography lists. For more discussion and examples of citations for electronic formats, go to your student Web site (*http://guffey.swlearning.com*).

Modern Language Association Format

Writers in the humanities frequently use the MLA format, as illustrated in Figure C.1. In parentheses close to the textual reference appears the author's name and page cited. If no author is known, a shortened version of the source title is used. At the end of the report, the writer lists alphabetically all references in a bibliography called *Works Cited*. To see a long report illustrating MLA documentation, turn to Figure 10.17 in Chapter 10. For more information consult Joseph Gibaldi, *MLA Handbook for Writers of Research Papers*, 6e (New York: The Modern Language Association of America, 2003).

FIGURE C.1 **• Portions of MLA Text Page and Bibliography**

Peanut butter was first delivered to the world by a St. Louis physician in 1890. As discussed at the Peanut Advisory Board's Web site, peanut butter was originally promoted as a protein substitute for elderly patients ("History"). However, it was the 1905 Universal Exposition in St. Louis that truly launched peanut butter. Since then, annual peanut butter consumption has zoomed to 3.3 pounds a person in the United States (Barrons 46). America's farmers produce 1.6 million tons of peanuts annually, about half of which is used for oil, nuts, and candy. Lisa Gibbons, executive secretary of the Peanut Advisory Board, says that "peanuts in some form are in the top four candies: Snickers, Reese's Peanut Butter Cups, Peanut M & Ms, and Butterfingers" (Meadows 32).

Works Cited

Barrons, Elizabeth Ruth. "A Comparison of Domestic and International Consumption of Legumes." *Journal of Economic Agriculture* 23 (2004): 45–49.

"History of Peanut Butter." *Peanut Advisory Board.* Retrieved 19 Jan. 2006 <http://www.peanutbutterlovers.com/History/index.html>.

Meadows, Mark Allen. "Peanut Crop Is Anything but Peanuts at Home and Overseas." *Business Monthly*, 30 Sept. 2005, 31–34.

MLA IN-TEXT FORMAT

In-text citations generally appear close to the point where they are mentioned. If the citation appears at the end of the sentence, it is placed inside the closing period. Follow these guidelines:

- Include the last name of the author(s) and the page number. Omit a comma, as (Smith 310).
- If the author's name is mentioned in the text, cite only the page number in parentheses. Do not include either the word *page* or the abbreviations *p.* or *pp.*
- If no author is known, refer to the document title or a shortened version of it, as ("Facts at Fingertips" 102).

MLA BIBLIOGRAPHIC FORMAT

In the list of works cited, include all references cited in a report. Some writers include all works consulted. A portion of an MLA bibliography is shown in Figure C.1. A more complete list of model references appears in Figure C.2. These business models use single spacing. However, MLA format suggests double spacing for the entire paper, including the list of works cited. Following are selected guidelines summarizing important points regarding MLA bibliographic format:

- Use italics or underscores for the titles of books, magazines, newspapers, and journals. Check with your organization or instructor for guidance. Capitalize all important words.
- Enclose the titles of magazine, newspaper, and journal articles in quotation marks. Include volume and issue numbers for journals only.
- For Internet citations, include a retrieval date. Although MLA format does not include the words *Retrieved* or *Accessed*, such wording helps distinguish the retrieval date from the document date.

FIGURE C.2

MLA Bibliography Sample References

Works Cited

American Airlines. *2005 Annual Report*. Fort Worth, TX: AMR Corporation. •————— Annual report

Berss, Marcia. "Protein Man." *Forbes* 24 Oct. 2004: 65–66. •————— Magazine article

Connors, H. Lee. "Saturn's Orbit Still High With Consumers."
　　Marketing News Online. 31 Aug. 2005. 1 Sept. 2005 •————— Magazine article, online
　　<http://www.marketingnews.com/08-31-05.htm>.

"Globalization Often Means That the Fast Track Leads Overseas." *The Washington* •————— Newspaper article, no author
　　Post 17 June 2005: A10.

Lancaster, Hal. "When Taking a Tip From a Job Network, Proceed With Caution." •————— Newspaper article, one author
　　The Wall Street Journal 7 Feb. 2005: B1.

Markoff, John. "Voluntary Rules Proposed to Help Insure Privacy for Internet
　　Users." *New York Times on the Web* 5 June 2005. 9 June 2005
　　<http://www.nytimes.com/library/tech/06/05/biztech/articles/05privacy.html>. •————— Newspaper article, online

PG.com. 2005. Procter & Gamble home page. 28 Nov. 2005 <http://www.pg.com>. •————— Entire Internet site

Pinkerton Investigation Services. *The Employer's Guide to Investigation Services*, •————— Brochure
　　3rd ed. Atlanta: Pinkerton Information Center, 2005.

Rivera, Francisco. Personal interview. 16 May 2006. •————— Interview

Rose, Richard C., and Echo Montgomery Garrett. *How to Make a Buck and Still Be*
　　a Decent Human Being. New York: HarperCollins, 2004. •————— Book, two authors

"Spam: How to Eliminate It From Your Workplace." *SmartPros*. 8 Aug. 2003. •————— Internet document, no author
　　12 Sept. 2005 <http://accounting.smartpros.com/x10434.xml>.

U.S. Dept. of Labor. *Child Care as a Workforce Issue*. Washington, DC. GPO, 2005. •————— Government publication

"Wendy's International, Inc.," *Hoover's Online*. 2005. Hoover's Inc. 9 Nov. 2005
　　<http://www.hoovers.com/wendy's-ID_11621-free-co-factsheet.xhtml>. •————— Article from online database

Wetherbee, James C., Nicholas P. Vitalari, and Andrew Milner. "Key Trends in
　　Systems Development in Europe and North America." *Journal of Global*
　　Information Management 3.2 (2004): 5–20. ["3.2" signifies volume 3, issue 2] •————— Journal article with volume and issue numbers

Yellen, Mike.<myellen022@yahoo.com> "Managing Managers and Cell Phones."
　　Online posting. 26 June 2005. Technical Writers Listserv. 9 Sept. 2005   Online posting (listservs and
　　<http://www.techwr-l.com/techwhirl/archives/>. •————— newsgroups)

Note 1: If a printed document is viewed electronically and you have no reason to believe the electronic version is different from the print version, use the same format as for the print citation. More extensive information about electronic documentation formats can be found at *http://guffey.swlearning.com.*

Note 2: To prevent confusion, you might add the word *Accessed* or *Retrieved* preceding the date you accessed an online source.

Note 3: Although MLA style prescribes double-spacing for the works cited, we show single spacing to conserve space and to represent preferred business usage.

American Psychological Association Format

Popular in the social and physical sciences, the American Psychological Association (APA) documentation style uses parenthetic citations. That is, each author reference is shown in parentheses when cited in the text, as shown in Figure C.3. At the end of the report, all references are listed alphabetically in a bibliography called *References*. For more information about APA formats, see the *Concise Rules of APA Style* (Washington, DC: American Psychological Association, 2005).

APA IN-TEXT FORMAT

Within the text, document each specific textual source with a short description in parentheses. Following are selected guidelines summarizing important elements of APA style:

- Include the last name of the author(s), date of publication, and page number, as (Jones, 2002, p. 36). Use "n.d." if no date is available.
- If no author is known, refer to the first few words of the reference list entry and the year, as (Computer Privacy, 2003, p. 59).
- Omit page numbers for general references, but always include page numbers for direct quotations.

APA BIBLIOGRAPHIC FORMAT

List all citations alphabetically in a section called *References*. A portion of an APA bibliography is shown in Figure C.3. A more complete list of model references appears in Figure C.4. APA style requires specific capitalization and electronic guidelines, some of which are summarized here:

- Include an author's name with the last name first followed by initials, such as *Smith, M. A.* First and middle names are not used.

FIGURE C.3 → **Portions of APA Text Page and Bibliography**

Peanut butter was first delivered to the world by a St. Louis physician in 1890. As discussed at the Peanut Advisory Board's Web site, peanut butter was originally promoted as a protein substitute for elderly patients (History, n.d.). However, it was the 1905 Universal Exposition in St. Louis that truly launched peanut butter. Since then, annual peanut butter consumption has zoomed to 3.3 pounds a person in the United States (Barrons, 2004, p. 46). America's farmers produce 1.6 million tons of peanuts annually, about half of which is used for oil, nuts, and candy. Lisa Gibbons, executive secretary of the Peanut Advisory Board, says that "peanuts in some form are in the top four candies: Snickers, Reese's Peanut Butter Cups, Peanut M & Ms, and Butterfingers" (Meadows, 2005, p. 32).

References

Barrons, E. (2004, November). A comparison of domestic and international consumption of legumes. *Journal of Economic Agriculture, 23*(3), 45–49.

History of peanut butter. (n.d.). Peanut Advisory Board. Retrieved January 19, 2006, from http://www.peanutbutterlovers.com/History/index.html

Meadows, M. (2005, September 30). Peanut crop is anything but peanuts at home and overseas. *Business Monthly, 14,* 31–34.

FIGURE C.4

Model APA Bibliography Sample References

References

American Airlines. (2005). *2005 Annual Report*. Fort Worth, TX: AMR Corporation. •————— Annual report

Atamian, R. M., & Ferranto, M. (2003). *Driving market forces*. New York: •————— Book, two authors
    HarperCollins.

Berss, M. (2004, October 24). Protein man. *Forbes, 154*, 65–66. •————— Magazine article

Cantrell, M. R., & Watson, H. (2004, January 10). Violence in today's workplace ————— Magazine article, viewed
    [Electronic version]. *Office Review, 26* (1), 24–29. •————— electronically

Globalization often means that the fast track leads overseas. (2004, June 16). *The* •————— Newspaper article, no author
    Washington Post, p. A10.

Lancaster, H. (2005, February 7). When taking a tip from a job network, proceed •————— Newspaper article, one author
    with caution. *The Wall Street Journal*, p. B1.

Lang, R. T. (2004, March 2). Most people fail to identify nonverbal signs. *The New*
    York Times. Retrieved November 15, 2001, from http://www.nytimes.com •————— Newspaper article, online

Moon, J. (2002). Solid waste disposal. *Microsoft Encarta 2000* [CD-ROM]. •————— CD-ROM encyclopedia article
    Redmond, WA: Microsoft.

Pinkerton Investigation Services. (2005). *The employer's guide to investigation*
    services (3rd ed.) [Brochure]. Atlanta: Pinkerton Information Center. •————— Brochure

Wetherbee, J. C., Vitalari, N. P., & Milner, A. (2004, May). Key trends in systems
    development in Europe and North America. *Journal of Global Information* ————— Journal article with volume
    Management, 3 (2), 5–20. ["*3* (2)" signifies volume 3, series or issue 2] •————— and issue numbers

Wilson, G., & Simmons, P. (2004). *Plagiarism: What it is, and how to avoid it.* •————— World Wide Web document
    Retrieved July 4, 2005, from Biology Program Guide 2001/2002 at the ————— with author and date
    University of British Columbia Web site: http://www.zoology.ubc/ca/bpg/
    plagiarism.htm

WWW user survey reveals consumer trends. (n.d.). Retrieved August 2, 2005, from •————— World Wide Web document,
    http://www.cc.gatech.edu/gvu/user_surveys/survey2004-10/ ————— no author, no date

Yudkin, M. (2005, August 24). The marketing minute: Truth is always in season •————— Message to online forum or
    [Msg. ID:ruf6kt0aiu5eui6523qsrofhu70h21evoj@4ax.com]. Message posted to ————— discussion group
    news://biz.ecommerce

- Show the date of publication in parentheses immediately after the author's name, as *Smith, M. A. (2002).*
- Italicize the titles of books. Use "sentence-style" capitalization. This means that only the first word of a title, proper nouns, and the first word after an internal colon is capitalized.
- Do not italicize, underscore, or use quotation marks for the titles of magazine and journal articles. Use sentence-style capitalization for article titles.
- Italicize the names of magazines and journals. Capitalize the initial letters of all important words.
- To reference a published article that you viewed only in its electronic form, add in brackets after the article title [Electronic version]. Use this form only if the electronic version is identical to the published version.
- To reference an online article that you have reason to believe has been changed (e.g., the format is different from that of the print version or page numbers are not indicated), add the date you retrieved the document and the URL. Do not include a period after a URL that appears at the end of a line.

Citing Electronic Sources

Standards for researchers using electronic sources are still emerging. When citing electronic media, you should hold the same goals as for print sources. That is, you try to give credit to the authors and to allow others to locate easily the same or updated information. However, traditional formats for identifying authors, publication dates, and page numbers become confusing when applied to sources on the Internet. Strive to give correct credit for electronic sources by including the author's name (when available), document title, Web page title, Web address, and retrieval date. Formats for some electronic sources are shown here. More extensive information about electronic documentation formats may be found at *http://guffey.swlearning.com*.

GRAMMAR/MECHANICS HANDBOOK

Because many students need a quick review of basic grammar and mechanics, we provide a number of resources in condensed form. The Grammar/Mechanics Handbook, which offers you a rapid systematic review, consists of four parts:

- **Grammar/Mechanics Diagnostic Test.** This 65-point pretest helps you assess your strengths and weaknesses in eight areas of grammar and mechanics. Your instructor may later give you a posttest to assess your improvement.
- **Grammar/Mechanics Profile.** The G/M Profile enables you to pinpoint specific areas in which you need remedial instruction or review.
- **Grammar Review With Reinforcement and Editing Exercises.** A concise set of guidelines reviews basic principles of grammar, punctuation, capitalization, and number style. The review also provides reinforcement and quiz exercises that help you interact with the principles of grammar and test your comprehension. The guidelines not only provide a study guide for review but will also serve as a reference manual throughout the writing course. The grammar review can be used for classroom-centered instruction or for self-guided learning.
- **Confusing Words and Frequently Misspelled Words.** A list of selected confusing words, along with a list of 160 frequently misspelled words, completes the Grammar/Mechanics Handbook.

Some of you want all the help you can get in improving your language skills. For additional assistance with grammar and language fundamentals, *Essentials of Business Communication*, 7e, offers you unparalleled interactive and print resources at **Guffey Xtra!**:

- **Your Personal Language Trainer.** In this self-paced learning tool, Dr. Guffey acts as your personal trainer in helping you pump up your language muscles. *Your Personal Language Trainer* provides the rules plus hundreds of sentence applications so that you can try out your knowledge and build your skills with immediate feedback and explanations.
- **Sentence Competency Skill Builders** offer interactive exercises similar to the grammar/mechanics checkups in this book. These drills focus on common writing weaknesses so that you can learn to avoid them.
- **Speak Right!** reviews frequently mispronounced words. You'll hear correct pronunciations from Dr. Guffey so that you will never be embarrassed by mispronouncing these terms.
- **Spell Right!** presents frequently misspelled words along with exercises to help you improve your skills.
- **Advanced Grammar/Mechanics Checkups** take you to the next level in developing language confidence. These self-teaching exercises provide challenging sentences that test your combined grammar, punctuation, spelling, and usage skills.

More comprehensive treatment of grammar, punctuation, and usage can be found in Clark and Clark's *A Handbook for Office Workers* or Guffey's *Business English*.

The first step in your systematic review of grammar and mechanics involves completing a diagnostic pretest found on the next page.

GRAMMAR/MECHANICS DIAGNOSTIC PRETEST

This diagnostic pretest is intended to reveal your strengths and weaknesses in using the following:

plural nouns	adjectives	punctuation
possessive nouns	adverbs	capitalization style
pronouns	prepositions	number style
verbs	conjunctions	

The pretest is organized into sections corresponding to the preceding categories. In Sections A through H, each sentence is either correct or has one error related to the category under which it is listed. If a sentence is correct, write *C*. If it has an error, underline the error and write the correct form in the space provided. When you finish, check your answers with your instructor and fill out the Grammar/Mechanics Profile at the end of the test.

A. PLURAL NOUNS

copies

Example   All CPAs must keep backup <u>copys</u> of their files.

1. Since the early 2000s, most attornies have invested in software packages that detect computer viruses.
2. Four freshmans discussed the pros and cons of using laptops and cell phones in their classes.
3. Both of Mark's sister-in-laws worked as secretaries at different companies.
4. Neither the Cortezes nor the Morris's knew about the changes in beneficiaries.
5. All job candidates are asked whether they can work on Sunday's.

B. POSSESSIVE NOUNS

6. We sincerely hope that the jurys judgment reflects the stories of all the witnesses.
7. In a little over two months time, the analysts finished their reports.
8. Ms. Hartmans staff is responsible for all accounts receivable for customers purchasing electronics parts.
9. At the next stockholders meeting, we will discuss benefits for employees and dividends for shareholders.
10. For the past 90 days, employees in the sales department have complained about Mr. Logan smoking.

C. PRONOUNS

me

Example   Whom did you ask to replace Francisco and <u>I</u>?

11. The chief and myself were quite willing to send copies to whoever requested them.
12. Much of the project assigned to Samantha and I had to be reassigned to Matt and them.
13. Although it's CPU was noisy, the computer worked for Jeremy and me.
14. Just between you and me, only you and I know that she will be transferred.
15. My friend and I applied at GM because of their excellent benefits.

D. VERB AGREEMENT

has

Example   The list of payments <u>have</u> to be approved by the boss.

16. This cell phone and its calling plan costs much less than I expected.
17. A description of the property, together with several other legal documents, were submitted by my attorney.
18. There are a wide range of proposals for taming spam.
19. Neither the manager nor the employees in the office think the solution is fair.
20. Because of the holiday, our committee were unable to meet.

E. VERB MOOD, VOICE, AND TENSE

21. If I was in charge, I would certainly change things.
22. To make a copy, first open the disk drive door and then you insert the disk.
23. If I could chose any city, I would select Hong Kong.
24. Those contracts have laid on his desk for more than two weeks.
25. The auditors have went over these accounts carefully, and they have found no discrepancies.

F. ADJECTIVES AND ADVERBS

26. Until we have a more clearer picture of what is legal, we will proceed cautiously.
27. Britney thought she had done good in her job interview.
28. A recently appointed official was in charge of monitoring peer to peer file-sharing systems.
29. Robert only has two days before he must submit his end-of-the-year report.
30. The architects submitted there drawings in a last-minute attempt to beat the deadline.

G. PREPOSITIONS AND CONJUNCTIONS

31. Can you tell me where the meeting is scheduled at?
32. It seems like we have been taking this pretest forever.
33. Our investigation shows that cell phones may be cheaper then landlines.
34. My courses this semester are totally different than last semester's.
35. Do you know where this shipment is going to?

H. COMMAS

For each of the following sentences, insert any necessary commas. Count the number of commas that you added. Write that number in the space provided. All punctuation must be correct to receive credit for the sentence. If a sentence requires no punctuation, write C.

1

Example   Because of developments in theory and computer applications, management is becoming more of a science.

36. For example management determines how orders assignments and responsibilities are delegated to employees.
37. Your order Ms. Lee will be sent from Memphis Tennessee on July 1.
38. When you need service on any of your equipment we will be happy to help you Mr. Lopez.
39. Michelle Wong who is the project manager at TeleCom suggested that I call you.
40. You have purchased from us often and your payments in the past have always been prompt.

I. COMMAS AND SEMICOLONS 1

Add commas and semicolons to the following sentences. In the space provided, write the number of punctuation marks that you added.

41. The salesperson turned in his report however he did not indicate the time period it covered.

42. Interest payments on bonds are tax deductible dividend payments are not.

43. We are opening a branch office in Scottsdale and hope to be able to serve all your needs from that office by the middle of January.

44. As suggested by the committee we must first secure adequate funding then we may consider expansion.

45. When you begin to research a report consider many sources of information namely the Internet, books, periodicals, government publications, and databases.

J. COMMAS AND SEMICOLONS 2

46. After our chief had the printer repaired it jammed again within the first week although we treated it carefully.

47. Our experienced courteous staff has been trained to anticipate your every need.

48. In view of the new law that went into effect on April 1 our current liability insurance must be increased therefore we need to adjust our budget.

49. As stipulated in our contract your agency will supervise our graphic arts and purchase our media time.

50. As you know Ms. Mears we aim for long-term business relationships not quick profits.

K. OTHER PUNCTUATION

Each of the following sentences may require colons, question marks, quotation marks, periods, parentheses, and underscores, as well as commas and semicolons. Add the appropriate punctuation to each sentence. Then in the space provided, write the total number of marks that you added or changed.

Example Fully recharging your digital camera's battery (see page 6 of the instruction manual) takes only 90 minutes.

2

51. The following members of the department volunteered to help on Saturday Kim Carlos Dan and Sylvia.

52. Mr Phillips, Miss Reed, and Mrs Garcia usually arrived at the office by 830 a m.

53. We recommend that you use hearing protectors see the warning on page 8 when using this electric drill.

54. Did the president really say "All employees may take Friday off

55. We are trying to locate an edition of Newsweek that carried an article titled Who Is Reading Your E-Mail

L. CAPITALIZATION

For each of the following sentences, underline any letter that should be capitalized. In the space provided, write the number of words you marked.

4.

Example vice president daniels devised a procedure for expediting purchase orders from area 4 warehouses.

56. although english was his native language, he also spoke spanish and could read french.

57. on a trip to the east coast, uncle henry visited the empire state building.

58. karen enrolled in classes in history, german, and sociology.

59. the business manager and the vice president each received a new dell computer.

60. james lee, the president of kendrick, inc., will speak to our conference in the spring.

M. NUMBER STYLE

Decide whether the numbers in the following sentences should be written as words or as figures. Each sentence either is correct or has one error. If it is correct, write *C*. If it has an error, underline it and write the correct form in the space provided.

five _____   **Example**   The bank had <u>5</u> branches in three suburbs.

_____

_____

_____

_____

_____

61. More than 2,000,000 people have visited the White House in the past five years.

62. Of the 28 viewer comments we received regarding our TV commercial, only three were negative.

63. We set aside forty dollars for petty cash, but by December 1 our fund was depleted.

64. The meeting is scheduled for May 5th at 3 p.m.

65. In the past five years, nearly fifteen percent of the population changed residences at least once.

GRAMMAR/MECHANICS PROFILE

In the spaces at the right, place a check mark to indicate the number of correct answers you had in each category of the Grammar/Mechanics Diagnostic Pretest.

		NUMBER CORRECT				
		5	4	3	2	1
1–5	Plural Nouns	___	___	___	___	___
6–10	Possessive Nouns	___	___	___	___	___
11–15	Pronouns	___	___	___	___	___
16–20	Verb Agreement	___	___	___	___	___
21–25	Verb Mood, Voice, and Tense	___	___	___	___	___
26–30	Adjectives and Adverbs	___	___	___	___	___
31–35	Prepositions and Conjunctions	___	___	___	___	___
36–40	Commas	___	___	___	___	___
41–45	Commas and Semicolons 1	___	___	___	___	___
46–50	Commas and Semicolons 2	___	___	___	___	___
51–55	Other Punctuation	___	___	___	___	___
56–60	Capitalization	___	___	___	___	___
61–65	Number Style	___	___	___	___	___

Note: 5 = have excellent skills; 4 = need light review; 3 = need careful review; 2 = need to study rules; 1 = need serious study and follow-up reinforcement.

GRAMMAR REVIEW

PARTS OF SPEECH (1.01)

1.01 Functions. English has eight parts of speech. Knowing the functions of the parts of speech helps writers better understand how words are used and how sentences are formed.

a. **Nouns:** name persons, places, things, qualities, concepts, and activities (for example, *Kevin, Phoenix, computer, joy, work, banking*).

b. **Pronouns:** substitute for nouns (for example, *he, she, it, they*).

c. **Verbs:** show the action of a subject or join the subject to words that describe it (for example, *walk, heard, is, was jumping*).

d. **Adjectives:** describe or limit nouns and pronouns and often answer the questions *what kind? how many?* and *which one?* (for example, *red* car, *ten* items, *good* manager).

e. **Adverbs:** describe or limit verbs, adjectives, or other adverbs and frequently answer the questions *when? how? where?* or *to what extent?* (for example, *tomorrow, rapidly, here, very*).

f. **Prepositions:** join nouns or pronouns to other words in sentences (for example, desk *in* the office, ticket *for* me, letter *to* you).

g. **Conjunctions:** connect words or groups of words (for example, you *and* I, Mark *or* Jill).

h. **Interjections:** express strong feelings (for example, *Wow! Oh!*).

NOUNS (1.02–1.06)

Nouns name persons, places, things, qualities, concepts, and activities. Nouns may be classified into a number of categories.

1.02 Concrete and Abstract. Concrete nouns name specific objects that can be seen, heard, felt, tasted, or smelled. Examples of concrete nouns are *telephone, dollar, IBM,* and *tangerine*. Abstract nouns name generalized ideas such as qualities or concepts that are not easily pictured. *Emotion, power,* and *tension* are typical examples of abstract nouns.

   Business writing is most effective when concrete words predominate. It's clearer to write *We need 16-pound copy paper* than to write *We need office supplies*. Chapter 4 provides practice in developing skill in the use of concrete words.

1.03 Proper and Common. Proper nouns name specific persons, places, or things and are always capitalized (*General Electric, Baltimore, Jennifer*). All other nouns are common nouns and begin with lowercase letters (*company, city, student*). Rules for capitalization are presented in Sections 3.01–3.16.

1.04 Singular and Plural. Singular nouns name one item; plural nouns name more than one. From a practical view, writers seldom have difficulty with singular nouns. They may need help, however, with the formation and spelling of plural nouns.

1.05 Guidelines for Forming Noun Plurals

a. Add *s* to most nouns (*chair, chairs; mortgage, mortgages; Monday, Mondays*).

b. Add *es* to nouns ending in *s, x, z, ch,* or *sh* (*bench, benches; boss, bosses; box, boxes; Lopez, Lopezes*).

c. Change the spelling in irregular noun plurals (*man, men; foot, feet; mouse, mice; child, children*).

d. Add *s* to nouns that end in *y* when *y* is preceded by a vowel (*attorney, attorneys; valley, valleys; journey, journeys*).

e. Drop the *y* and add *ies* to nouns ending in *y* when *y* is preceded by a consonant (*company, companies; city, cities; secretary, secretaries*).

f. Add *s* to the principal word in most compound expressions (*editors in chief, fathers-in-law, bills of lading, runners-up*).

g. Add *s* to most numerals, letters of the alphabet, words referred to as words, degrees, and abbreviations (*5s, 2000s, Bs, ands, CPAs, qts.*).

h. Add *'s* only to clarify letters of the alphabet that might be misread, such as *A's, I's, M's,* and *U's* and *i's, p's,* and *q's*. An expression like *c.o.d.s* requires no apostrophe because it would not easily be misread.

1.06 Collective Nouns. Nouns such as *staff, faculty, committee, group,* and *herd* refer to a collection of people, animals, or objects. Collective nouns may be considered singular or plural depending on their action. See Section 1.10i for a discussion of collective nouns and their agreement with verbs.

REVIEW EXERCISE A—NOUNS

In the space provided for each item, write *a* or *b* to complete the following statements accurately. When you finish, compare your responses with those provided. Answers are provided for odd-numbered items. Your instructor has the remaining answers. For each item on which you need review, consult the numbered principle shown in parentheses.

1. Two of the contest (a) *runner-ups*, (b) *runners-up* protested the judges' choice.
2. Several (a) *attorneys*, (b) *attornies* worked on the case together.
3. Please write to the (a) *Davis's*, (b) *Davises* about the missing contract.
4. The industrial complex has space for nine additional (a) *companys*, (b) *companies*.
5. That accounting firm employs two (a) *secretaries*, (b) *secretarys* for five CPAs.
6. Four of the wooden (a) *benches*, (b) *benchs* must be repaired.
7. The home was constructed with numerous (a) *chimneys*, (b) *chimnies*.
8. Tours of the production facility are made only on (a) *Tuesdays*, (b) *Tuesday's*.
9. We asked the (a) *Lopez's*, (b) *Lopezes* to contribute to the fund-raising drive.
10. Both my (a) *sister-in-laws*, (b) *sisters-in-law* agreed to the settlement.
11. The stock market is experiencing abnormal (a) *ups and downs*, (b) *up's and down's*.
12. Three (a) *mouses*, (b) *mice* were seen near the trash cans.
13. This office is unusually quiet on (a) *Sundays*, (b) *Sunday's*.
14. Several news (a) *dispatchs*, (b) *dispatches* were released during the strike.
15. Two major (a) *countries*, (b) *countrys* will participate in arms negotiations.
16. Some young children have difficulty writing their (a) *bs and ds*, (b) *b's and d's*.
17. The (a) *board of directors*, (b) *boards of directors* of all the major companies participated in the surveys.
18. In their letter the (a) *Metzes*, (b) *Metzs* said they intended to purchase the property.
19. In shipping we are careful to include all (a) *bill of sales*, (b) *bills of sale*.
20. Over the holidays many (a) *turkies*, (b) *turkeys* were consumed.

---

1. b (1.05f) 3. b (1.05b) 5. a (1.05e) 7. a (1.05d) 9. b (1.05b) 11. a (1.05g) 13. a (1.05a) 15. a (1.05e) 17. b (1.05f) 19. b (1.05f) (Only odd-numbered answers are provided. Consult your instructor for the others.)

PRONOUNS (1.07–1.09)

Pronouns substitute for nouns. They are classified by case.

1.07 Case. Pronouns function in three cases, as shown in the following chart.

Nominative Case *(Used for subjects of verbs and subject complements)*	**Objective Case** *(Used for objects of prepositions and objects of verbs)*	**Possessive Case** *(Used to show possession)*
I	me	my, mine
we	us	our, ours
you	you	your, yours
he	him	his
she	her	her, hers
it	it	its
they	them	their, theirs
who, whoever	whom, whomever	whose

1.08 Guidelines for Selecting Pronoun Case

a. Pronouns that serve as subjects of verbs must be in the nominative case:

He and *I* (not *Him* and *me*) decided to apply for the jobs.

b. Pronouns that follow linking verbs (such as *am, is, are, was, were, be, being, been*) and rename the words to which they refer must be in the nominative case.

It must have been *she* (not *her*) who placed the order. (The nominative-case pronoun *she* follows the linking verb *been* and renames *it*.)

If it was *he* (not *him*) who called, I have his number. (The nominative-case pronoun *he* follows the linking verb *was* and renames *it*.)

c. Pronouns that serve as objects of verbs or objects of prepositions must be in the objective case:

Mr. Andrews asked *them* to complete the proposal. (The pronoun *them* is the object of the verb *asked*.)

All computer printouts are sent to *him*. (The pronoun *him* is the object of the preposition *to*.)

Just between you and *me*, profits are falling. (The pronoun *me* is one of the objects of the preposition *between*.)

d. Pronouns that show ownership must be in the possessive case. Possessive pronouns (such as *hers, yours, ours, theirs*, and *its*) require no apostrophes:

I bought a cheap cell phone, but *yours* (not *your's*) is expensive.

All parts of the machine, including *its* (not *it's*) motor, were examined.

The house and *its* (not *it's*) contents will be auctioned.

Don't confuse possessive pronouns and contractions. Contractions are shortened forms of subject–verb phrases (such as *it's* for *it is*, *there's* for *there is*, and *they're* for *they are*).

e. When a pronoun appears in combination with a noun or another pronoun, ignore the extra noun or pronoun and its conjunction. In this way pronoun case becomes more obvious:

The manager promoted Jeff and *me* (not *I*). (Ignore *Jeff and*.)

f. In statements of comparison, mentally finish the comparative by adding the implied missing words:

Next year I hope to earn as much as *she*. (The verb *earns* is implied here: . . . *as much as she earns*.)

g. Pronouns must be in the same case as the words they replace or rename. When pronouns are used with appositives, ignore the appositive:

A new contract was signed by *us* (not *we*) employees. (Temporarily ignore the appositive *employees* in selecting the pronoun.)

We (not *us*) citizens have formed our own organization. (Temporarily ignore the appositive *citizens* in selecting the pronoun.)

h. Pronouns ending in *self* should be used only when they refer to previously mentioned nouns or pronouns:

The CEO *himself* answered the telephone.

Robert and *I* (not *myself*) are in charge of the campaign.

i. Use objective-case pronouns as objects of the prepositions *between, but, like*, and *except*:

Everyone but John and *him* (not *he*) qualified for the bonus.

Employees like Miss Gillis and *her* (not *she*) are hard to replace.

j. Use *who* or *whoever* for nominative-case constructions and *whom* or *whomever* for objective-case constructions. In making the correct choice, it's sometimes helpful to substitute *he* for *who* or *whoever* and *him* for *whom* or *whomever*:

For *whom* was this book ordered? (*This book was ordered for him/whom?*)

Who did you say would drop by? (*Who/he . . . would drop by?*)

Deliver the package to *whoever* opens the door. (In this sentence the clause *whoever opens the door* functions as the object of the preposition *to*. Within the clause itself *whoever* is the subject of the verb *opens*. Again, substitution of *he* might be helpful: *He/Whoever opens the door.*)

1.09 Guidelines for Making Pronouns Agree With Their Antecedents. Pronouns must agree with the words to which they refer (their antecedents) in gender and in number.

a. Use masculine pronouns to refer to masculine antecedents, feminine pronouns to refer to feminine antecedents, and neuter pronouns to refer to antecedents without gender:

The man opened *his* office door. (Masculine gender applies.)

A woman sat at *her* desk. (Feminine gender applies.)

This computer and *its* programs fit our needs. (Neuter gender applies.)

b. Use singular pronouns to refer to singular antecedents:

Common-gender pronouns (such as *him* or *his*) traditionally have been used when the gender of the antecedent is unknown. Sensitive writers today, however, prefer to recast such constructions to avoid the need for common-gender pronouns. Study these examples for alternatives to the use of common-gender pronouns:*

Each student must submit *a* report on Monday.

All students must submit *their* reports on Monday.

Each student must submit *his or her* report on Monday. (This alternative is least acceptable since it is wordy and calls attention to itself.)

c. Use singular pronouns to refer to singular indefinite subjects and plural pronouns for plural indefinite subjects. Words such as *anyone, something*, and *anybody* are considered indefinite because they refer to no specific person or object. Some indefinite pronouns are always singular; others are always plural.

Always Singular			**Always Plural**
anybody	everyone	somebody	both
anyone	everything	someone	few
anything	neither		many
each	nobody		several
either	no one		

Somebody in the group of touring women left *her* (not *their*) purse in the museum.

Either of the companies has the right to exercise *its* (not *their*) option to sell stock.

d. Use singular pronouns to refer to collective nouns and organization names:

The engineering staff is moving *its* (not *their*) facilities on Friday. (The singular pronoun *its* agrees with the collective noun *staff* because the members of *staff* function as a single unit.)

---

*See Chapter 2, page 42, for additional discussion of common-gender pronouns and inclusive language.

Jones, Cohen, & James, Inc., *has* (not *have*) canceled *its* (not *their*) contract with us. (The singular pronoun *its* agrees with *Jones, Cohen, & James, Inc.*, because the members of the organization are operating as a single unit.)

e. Use a plural pronoun to refer to two antecedents joined by *and*, whether the antecedents are singular or plural:

Our company president and our vice president will be submitting *their* expenses shortly.

f. Ignore intervening phrases—introduced by expressions such as *together with, as well as*, and *in addition to*—that separate a pronoun from its antecedent:

One of our managers, along with several salespeople, is planning *his* retirement. (If you wish to emphasize both subjects equally, join them with *and*: One of our managers *and* several salespeople are planning *their* retirements.)

g. When antecedents are joined by *or* or *nor*, make the pronoun agree with the antecedent closest to it.

Neither Jackie nor Kim wanted *her* (not *their*) desk moved.

REVIEW EXERCISE B—PRONOUNS

In the space provided for each item, write *a, b,* or *c* to complete the statement accurately. When you finish, compare your responses with those provided. For each item on which you need review, consult the numbered principle shown in parentheses.

1. Send e-mail copies of the policy to the manager or (a) *me*, (b) *myself.*
2. James promised that he would call; was it (a) *him*, (b) *he* who left the message?
3. Much preparation for the seminar was made by Mrs. Washington and (a) *I*, (b) *me* before the brochures were sent out.
4. The Employee Benefits Committee can be justly proud of (a) *its*, (b) *their* achievements.
5. A number of inquiries were addressed to Jeff and (a) *I*, (b) *me*, (c) *myself.*
6. (a) *Who*, (b) *Whom* did you say the letter was addressed to?
7. When you visit Sears Savings Bank, inquire about (a) *its*, (b) *their* certificates.
8. Copies of all reports are to be reviewed by Mr. Sanders and (a) *I*, (b) *me*, (c) *myself.*
9. Apparently one of the female applicants forgot to sign (a) *her*, (b) *their* application.
10. Both the printer and (a) *it's*, (b) *its* cover are missing.
11. I've never known any man who could work as fast as (a) *him*, (b) *he.*
12. Just between you and (a) *I*, (b) *me*, the stock price will fall by afternoon.
13. Give the supplies to (a) *whoever*, (b) *whomever* ordered them.
14. (a) *Us*, (b) *We* employees have been given an unusual voice in choosing benefits.
15. On her return from Mexico, Mrs. Sanchez, along with many other passengers, had to open (a) *her*, (b) *their* luggage for inspection.
16. Either James or Robert will have (a) *his*, (b) *their* work reviewed next week.
17. Any woman who becomes a charter member of this organization will be able to have (a) *her*, (b) *their* name inscribed on a commemorative plaque.
18. We are certain that (a) *our's*, (b) *ours* is the smallest smart phone available.
19. Everyone has completed the reports except Debbie and (a) *he*, (b) *him.*
20. Lack of work disturbs Mr. Thomas as much as (a) *I*, (b) *me.*

1. a (1.08h)   3. b (1.08c)   5. b (1.08c, 1.08e)   7. a (1.09d)   9. a (1.09b)   11. b (1.08f)
13. a (1.08j)   15. a (1.09f)   17. a (1.09b)   19. b (1.08i)

CUMULATIVE EDITING QUIZ 1

Use proofreading marks (see Appendix B) to correct errors in the following sentences. All errors must be corrected to receive credit for the sentence. Check with your instructor for the answers.

Example   Nicholas and ~~him~~ *he* made all ~~there~~ *their* money in the 1990's.

1. Just between you and I, whom do you think would make the best manager?
2. Either Stacy or me is responsible for correcting all errors in news dispatchs.
3. Several attornies asked that there cases be postponed.
4. One of the secretarys warned Bill and I to get the name of whomever answered the phone.
5. The committee sent there decision to the president and I last week.
6. Who should Susan or me call to verify the three bill of sales received today?
7. Several of we employees complained that it's keyboard made the new computer difficult to use.
8. All the CEO's agreed that the low interest rates of the early 2000s could not continue.
9. Every customer has a right to expect there inquirys to be treated courteously.
10. You may send you're contribution to Eric or myself or to whomever is listed as your representative.

VERBS (1.10–1.15)

Verbs show the action of a subject or join the subject to words that describe it.

1.10 Guidelines for Agreement With Subjects. One of the most troublesome areas in English is subject–verb agreement. Consider the following guidelines for making verbs agree with subjects.

a. A singular subject requires a singular verb:

The stock market *opens* at 10 a.m. (The singular verb *opens* agrees with the singular subject *market*.)

He *doesn't* (not *don't*) work on Saturday.

b. A plural subject requires a plural verb:

On the packing slip several items *seem* (not *seems*) to be missing.

c. A verb agrees with its subject regardless of prepositional phrases that may intervene:

This list of management objectives *is* extensive. (The singular verb *is* agrees with the singular subject *list*.)

Every one of the letters *shows* (not *show*) proper form.

d. A verb agrees with its subject regardless of intervening phrases introduced by *as well as, in addition to, such as, including, together with*, and similar expressions:

An important memo, together with several contracts, *was* misplaced. (The singular verb *was* agrees with the singular subject *memo*.)

The president as well as several other top-level executives *approves* of our proposal. (The singular verb *approves* agrees with the subject *president*.)

e. A verb agrees with its subject regardless of the location of the subject:

Here *is* one of the contracts about which you asked. (The verb *is* agrees with its subject *one*, even though it precedes *one*. The adverb *here* cannot function as a subject.)

There *are* many problems yet to be resolved. (The verb *are* agrees with the subject *problems*. The word *there* does not function as a subject.)

In the next office *are* several printers. (In this inverted sentence the verb *are* must agree with the subject *printers*.)

f. Subjects joined by *and* require a plural verb:

Analyzing the reader and organizing a strategy *are* the first steps in letter writing. (The plural verb *are* agrees with the two subjects, *analyzing* and *organizing*.)

The tone and the wording of the letter *were* persuasive. (The plural verb *were* agrees with the two subjects, *tone* and *wording*.)

g. Subjects joined by *or* or *nor* may require singular or plural verbs. Make the verb agree with the closer subject:

Neither the memo nor the report *is* ready. (The singular verb *is* agrees with *report*, the closer of the two subjects.)

h. The following indefinite pronouns are singular and require singular verbs: *anyone, anybody, anything, each, either, every, everyone, everybody, everything, many a, neither, nobody, nothing, someone, somebody*, and *something*:

Either of the alternatives that you present *is* acceptable. (The verb *is* agrees with the singular subject *either*.)

i. Collective nouns may take singular or plural verbs, depending on whether the members of the group are operating as a unit or individually:

Our management team *is* united in its goal.

The faculty *are* sharply *divided* on the tuition issue. (Although acceptable, this sentence sounds better recast: The faculty *members* are sharply divided on the tuition issue.)

j. Organization names and titles of publications, although they may appear to be plural, are singular and require singular verbs.

Clark, Anderson, and Horne, Inc., *has* (not *have*) hired a marketing consultant.

Thousands of Investment Tips is (not *are*) again on the best-seller list.

1.11 Voice. Voice is that property of verbs that shows whether the subject of the verb acts or is acted upon. Active-voice verbs direct action from the subject toward the object of the verb. Passive-voice verbs direct action toward the subject.

Active voice: Our employees *send* many e-mail messages.
Passive voice: Many e-mail messages *are sent* by our employees.

Business writing that emphasizes active-voice verbs is generally preferred because it is specific and forceful. However, passive-voice constructions can help a writer be tactful. Strategies for effective use of active- and passive-voice verbs are presented in Chapter 3.

1.12 Mood. Three verb moods express the attitude or thought of the speaker or writer toward a subject: (1) the indicative mood expresses a fact; (2) the imperative mood expresses a command; and (3) the subjunctive mood expresses a doubt, a conjecture, or a suggestion.

Indicative: I *am looking* for a job.
Imperative: *Begin* your job search with the want ads.
Subjunctive: I wish I *were* working.

Only the subjunctive mood creates problems for most speakers and writers. The most common use of subjunctive mood occurs in clauses including *if* or *wish*. In such clauses substitute the subjunctive verb *were* for the indicative verb *was*:

If he *were* (not *was*) in my position, he would understand.

Mr. Simon acts as if he *were* (not *was*) the boss.

We wish we *were* (not *was*) able to ship your order.

The subjunctive mood may be used to maintain goodwill while conveying negative information. The sentence *We wish we were able to ship your order* sounds more pleasing to a customer than *We cannot ship your order*, although, for all practical purposes, both sentences convey the same negative message.

1.13 Tense. Verbs show the time of an action by their tense. Speakers and writers can use six tenses to show the time of sentence action; for example:

Present tense:	I *work*; he *works*.
Past tense:	I *worked*; she *worked*.
Future tense:	I *will work*; he *will work*.
Present perfect tense:	I *have worked*; he *has worked*.
Past perfect tense:	I *had worked*; she *had worked*.
Future perfect tense:	I *will have worked*; he *will have worked*.

1.14 Guidelines for Verb Tense

a. Use present tense for statements that, although they may be introduced by past-tense verbs, continue to be true:

What did you say his name *is*? (Use the present tense *is* if his name has not changed.)

b. Avoid unnecessary shifts in verb tenses:

The manager *saw* (not *sees*) a great deal of work yet to be completed and *remained* to do it herself.

Although unnecessary shifts in verb tense are to be avoided, not all the verbs within one sentence have to be in the same tense; for example:

She *said* (past tense) that she *likes* (present tense) to work late.

1.15 Irregular Verbs. Irregular verbs cause difficulty for some writers and speakers. Unlike regular verbs, irregular verbs do not form the past tense and past participle by adding *-ed* to the present form. Here is a partial list of selected troublesome irregular verbs. Consult a dictionary if you are in doubt about a verb form.

TROUBLESOME IRREGULAR VERBS

Present	**Past**	**Past Participle** *(always use helping verbs)*
begin	began	begun
break	broke	broken
choose	chose	chosen
come	came	come
drink	drank	drunk
go	went	gone
lay (to place)	laid	laid
lie (to rest)	lay	lain
ring	rang	rung
see	saw	seen
write	wrote	written

a. Use only past-tense verbs to express past tense. Notice that no helping verbs are used to indicate simple past tense:

The auditors *went* (not *have went*) over our books carefully.

He *came* (not *come*) to see us yesterday.

b. Use past participle forms for actions completed before the present time. Notice that past participle forms require helping verbs:

Steve *had gone* (not *had went*) before we called. (The past participle *gone* is used with the helping verb *had.*)

c. Avoid inconsistent shifts in subject, voice, and mood. Pay particular attention to this problem area because undesirable shifts are often characteristic of student writing.

Inconsistent: When Mrs. Taswell read the report, the error was found. (The first clause is in the active voice; the second, passive.)

Improved: When Mrs. Taswell read the report, she found the error. (Both clauses are in the active voice.)

Inconsistent: The clerk should first conduct an inventory. Then supplies should be requisitioned. (The first sentence is in the active voice; the second, passive.)

Improved: The clerk should first conduct an inventory. Then he or she should requisition supplies. (Both sentences are in the active voice.)

Inconsistent: All workers must wear security badges, and you must also sign a daily time card. (This sentence contains an inconsistent shift in subject from *all workers* in the first clause to *you* in the second clause.)

Improved: All workers must wear security badges, and they must also sign a daily time card.

Inconsistent: Begin the transaction by opening an account; then you enter the customer's name. (This sentence contains an inconsistent shift from the imperative mood in the first clause to the indicative mood in the second clause.)

Improved: Begin the transaction by opening an account; then enter the customer's name. (Both clauses are now in the indicative mood.)

REVIEW EXERCISE C—VERBS

In the space provided for each item, write *a* or *b* to complete the statement accurately. When you finish, compare your responses with those provided. For each item on which you need review, consult the numbered principle shown in parentheses.

1. Our directory of customer names and addresses (a) *was* (b) *were* updated with e-mail addresses and cell phone numbers.

2. There (a) *is*, (b) *are* a customer service engineer and two salespeople waiting to see you.

3. Increased computer use and more complex automated systems (a) *is*, (b) *are* found in business today.

4. Crews, Meliotes, and Bove, Inc., (a) *has*, (b) *have* opened an office in Boston.

5. Yesterday Mrs. Phillips (a) *choose*, (b) *chose* a new office on the second floor.

6. The man who called said that his name (a) *is*, (b) *was* Johnson.

7. *Office Computing and Networks* (a) *is*, (b) *are* beginning a campaign to increase readership.

8. Either of the flight times (a) *appears*, (b) *appear* to fit my proposed itinerary.

9. If you had (a) *saw*, (b) *seen* the rough draft, you would better appreciate the final copy.

10. Across from our office (a) *is*, (b) *are* the parking structure and the information office.

11. Although we have (a) *began*, (b) *begun* to replace outmoded equipment, the pace is slow.

12. Specific training as well as ample experience (a) *is*, (b) *are* important for that position.

13. Inflation and increased job opportunities (a) *is*, (b) *are* resulting in increased numbers of working women.

14. Neither the organizing nor the staffing of the program (a) *has been*, (b) *have been* completed.

15. If I (a) *was*, (b) *were* you, I would ask for a raise.

16. If you had (a) *wrote*, (b) *written* last week, we could have sent a brochure.

17. The hydraulic equipment that you ordered (a) *is*, (b) *are* packed and will be shipped Friday.

18. One of the reasons that sales have declined in recent years (a) *is*, (b) *are* lack of effective advertising.

19. Either of the proposed laws (a) *is*, (b) *are* going to affect our business negatively.

20. Merger statutes (a) *requires*, (b) *require* that a failing company accept bids from several companies before merging with one.

1. a (1.10c) 3. b (1.10f) 5. b (1.15a) 7. a (1.10j) 9. b (1.15b) 11. b (1.15b) 13. b (1.10f)
15. b (1.12) 17. a (1.10a) 19. a (1.10h)

REVIEW EXERCISE D—VERBS

In the following sentence pairs, choose the one that illustrates consistency in use of subject, voice, and mood. Write *a* or *b* in the space provided. When you finish, compare your responses with those provided. For each item on which you need review, consult the numbered principle shown in parentheses.

1. (a) You need more than a knowledge of technology; one also must be able to interact well with people.

   (b) You need more than a knowledge of technology; you also must be able to interact well with people.

2. (a) Tim and Jon were eager to continue, but Bob wanted to quit.

   (b) Tim and Jon were eager to continue, but Bob wants to quit.

3. (a) The salesperson should consult the price list; then you can give an accurate quote to a customer.

   (b) The salesperson should consult the price list; then he or she can give an accurate quote to a customer.

4. (a) Read all the instructions first; then you install the printer program.

   (b) Read all the instructions first, and then install the printer program.

5. (a) She was an enthusiastic manager who always had a smile for everyone.

   (b) She was an enthusiastic manager who always has a smile for everyone.

1. b (1.15c) 3. b (1.15c) 5. a (1.14b)

CUMULATIVE EDITING QUIZ 2

Use proofreading marks (see Appendix B) to correct errors in the following sentences. All errors must be corrected to receive credit for the sentence. Check with your instructor for the answers.

1. Assets and liabilitys is what my partner and myself must investigate.

2. If I was you, I would ask whomever is in charge for their opinion.

3. The faculty agree that it's first concern is educating students.

4. The book and it's cover was printed in Japan.

5. Waiting to see you is a sales representative and a job applicant who you told to drop by.

6. Every employee could have picked up his ballot if he had went to the cafeteria.

7. Your choice of hospitals and physicians are reduced by this plan and it's restrictions.

8. My uncle and her come to visit my parents and myself last night.

9. According to both editor in chiefs, the tone and wording of all our letters needs revision.

10. The Davis'es, about who the article was written, said they were unconcerned with the up's and down's of the stock market.

ADJECTIVES AND ADVERBS (1.16–1.17)

Adjectives describe or limit nouns and pronouns. They often answer the questions *what kind? how many?* or *which one?* Adverbs describe or limit verbs, adjectives, or other adverbs. They often answer the questions *when? how? where?* or *to what extent?*

1.16 Forms. Most adjectives and adverbs have three forms, or degrees: positive, comparative, and superlative.

	Positive	**Comparative**	**Superlative**
Adjective:	clear	clearer	clearest
Adverb:	clearly	more clearly	most clearly

Some adjectives and adverbs have irregular forms.

	Positive	**Comparative**	**Superlative**
Adjective:	good	better	best
	bad	worse	worst
Adverb:	well	better	best

Adjectives and adverbs composed of two or more syllables are usually compared by the use of *more* and *most*; for example:

The Payroll Department is *more efficient* than the Shipping Department.

Payroll is the *most efficient* department in our organization.

1.17 Guidelines for Use

a. Use the comparative degree of the adjective or adverb to compare two persons or things; use the superlative degree to compare three or more:

Of the two plans, which is *better* (not *best*)?

Of all the plans, we like this one *best* (not *better*).

b. Do not create a double comparative or superlative by using *-er* with *more* or *-est* with *most*:

His explanation couldn't have been *clearer* (not *more clearer*).

c. A linking verb (*is, are, look, seem, feel, sound, appear,* and so forth) may introduce a word that describes the verb's subject. In this case be certain to use an adjective, not an adverb:

The characters on the monitor look *bright* (not *brightly*). (Use the adjective *bright* because it follows the linking verb *look* and modifies the noun *characters*.)

The company's letter made the customer feel *bad* (not *badly*). (The adjective *bad* follows the linking verb *feel* and describes the noun *customer*.)

d. Use adverbs, not adjectives, to describe or limit the action of verbs:

The business is running *smoothly* (not *smooth*). (Use the adverb *smoothly* to describe the action of the verb *is running*. *Smoothly* tells how the business is running.)

Don't take his remark *personally* (not *personal*). (The adverb *personally* describes the action of the verb *take*.)

Serena said she did *well* (not *good*) on the test. (Use the adverb *well* to tell how she did.)

e. Two or more adjectives that are joined to create a compound modifier before a noun should be hyphenated:

The *four-year-old* child was tired.

Our agency is planning a *coast-to-coast* campaign.

Hyphenate a compound modifier following a noun only if your dictionary shows the hyphen(s):

Our speaker is very *well-known*. (Include the hyphen because most dictionaries do.)

The tired child was four years old. (Omit the hyphens because the expression follows the word it describes, *child*, and because dictionaries do not indicate hyphens.)

f. Keep adjectives and adverbs close to the words they modify:

She asked for *a cup of hot coffee* (not *a hot cup of coffee*).

Patty *had only two* days of vacation left (not *only had two days*).

Students may sit in the *first five* rows (not *in five first* rows).

He *has saved almost* enough money for the trip (not *has almost saved*).

g. Don't confuse *there* with the possessive pronoun *their* or the contraction *they're*:

Put the documents *there*. (The adverb *there* means "at that place or at that point.")

There are two reasons for the change. (The pronoun *there* is used as function word to introduce a sentence or a clause.)

We already have *their* specifications. (The possessive pronoun *their* shows ownership.)

They're coming to inspect today. (The contraction *they're* is a shortened form of *they are*.)

REVIEW EXERCISE E—ADJECTIVES AND ADVERBS

In the space provided for each item, write *a, b,* or *c* to complete the statement accurately. If two sentences are shown, select *a* or *b* to indicate the one expressed more effectively. When you finish, compare your responses with those provided. For each item on which you need review, consult the numbered principle shown in parentheses.

1. After the interview, Tim looked (a) *calm*, (b) *calmly*.
2. If you had been more (a) *careful*, (b) *carefuler*, the box might not have broken.
3. Because a new manager was appointed, the advertising campaign is running very (a) *smooth*, (b) *smoothly*.
4. To avoid a (a) *face to face*, (b) *face-to-face* confrontation, she sent an e-mail.
5. Darren completed the employment test (a) *satisfactorily*, (b) *satisfactory*.
6. I felt (a) *bad*, (b) *badly* that he was not promoted.
7. Which is the (a) *more*, (b) *most* dependable of the two models?
8. Can you determine exactly what (a) *there*, (b) *their*, (c) *they're* company wants us to do?
9. Of all the copiers we tested, this one is the (a) *easier*, (b) *easiest* to operate.
10. (a) Mr. Aldron almost was ready to accept the offer.

    (b) Mr. Aldron was almost ready to accept the offer.
11. (a) We only thought that it would take two hours for the test.

    (b) We thought that it would take only two hours for the test.
12. (a) Please bring me a glass of cold water.

    (b) Please bring me a cold glass of water.
13. (a) The committee decided to retain the last ten tickets.

    (b) The committee decided to retain the ten last tickets.
14. New owners will receive a (a) *60-day*, (b) *60 day* trial period.
15. The time passed (a) *quicker*, (b) *more quickly* than we expected.

16. We offer a (a) *money back*, (b) *money-back* guarantee.

17. Today the financial news is (a) *worse*, (b) *worst* than yesterday.

18. Please don't take his comments (a) *personal*, (b) *personally*.

19. You must check the document (a) *page by page*, (b) *page-by-page*.

20. (a) We try to file only necessary paperwork.

    (b) We only try to file necessary paperwork.

---

1. a (1.17c) 3. b (1.17d) 5. a (1.17d) 7. a (1.17a) 9. b (1.17a) 11. b (1.17f) 13. a (1.17f)
15. b (1.17d) 17. a (1.17a) 19. a (1.17e)

PREPOSITIONS (1.18)

Prepositions are connecting words that join nouns or pronouns to other words in a sentence. The words *about, at, from, in*, and *to* are examples of prepositions.

1.18 Guidelines for Use

a. Include necessary prepositions:

What type *of* software do you need (not *what type software*)?

I graduated *from* high school two years ago (not *I graduated high school*).

b. Omit unnecessary prepositions:

Where is the meeting? (Not *Where is the meeting at?*)

Both printers work well. (Not *Both of the printers.*)

Where are you going? (Not *Where are you going to?*)

c. Avoid the overuse of prepositional phrases.

Weak: We have received your application for credit at our branch in the Fresno area.

Improved: We have received your Fresno credit application.

d. Repeat the preposition before the second of two related elements:

Applicants use the résumé effectively by summarizing their most important experiences and *by* relating their education to the jobs sought.

e. Include the second preposition when two prepositions modify a single object:

George's appreciation *of* and aptitude *for* computers led to a promising career.

CONJUNCTIONS (1.19)

Conjunctions connect words, phrases, and clauses. They act as signals, indicating when a thought is being added, contrasted, or altered. Coordinate conjunctions

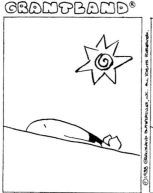

GRANTLAND®

THIS MAY SEEM LIKE FUN, BUT I'M REALLY WORKING VERY HARD.

I'M LYING HERE IN THIS HEAT JUST THINKING ABOUT ADJECTIVES, ADVERBS, PREPOSITIONS, AND CONJUNCTIONS —

DOING EVERYTHING I CAN TO BAKE THOSE CONCEPTS INTO MY BRAIN

© WWW.GRANTLAND.NET

(such as *and, or, but*) and other words that act as connectors (such as *however, therefore, when, as*) tell the reader or listener in what direction a thought is heading. They're like road signs signaling what's ahead.

1.19 Guidelines for Use

a. Use coordinating conjunctions to connect only sentence elements that are parallel or balanced.

Weak:	His report was correct and written in a concise manner.
Improved:	His report was correct and concise.

Weak:	Management has the capacity to increase fraud, or reduction can be achieved through the policies it adopts.
Improved:	Management has the capacity to increase or reduce fraud through the policies it adopts.

b. Do not use the word *like* as a conjunction:

It seems *as if* (not *like*) this day will never end.

c. Avoid using *when* or *where* inappropriately. A common writing fault occurs in sentences with clauses introduced by *is when* and *is where*. Written English ordinarily requires a noun (or a group of words functioning as a noun) following the linking verb *is*. Instead of acting as conjunctions in these constructions, the words *where* and *when* function as adverbs, creating faulty grammatical equations (adverbs cannot complete equations set up by linking verbs). To avoid the problem, revise the sentence, eliminating *is when* or *is where*.

Weak:	A bullish market is when prices are rising in the stock market.
Improved:	A bullish market is created when prices are rising in the stock market.

Weak:	A flowchart is when you make a diagram showing the step-by-step progression of a procedure.
Improved:	A flowchart is a diagram showing the step-by-step progression of a procedure.

Weak:	Word processing is where you use a computer and software to write.
Improved:	Word processing involves the use of a computer and software to write.

A similar faulty construction occurs in the expression *I hate when*. English requires nouns, noun clauses, or pronouns to act as objects of verbs, not adverbs.

Weak:	I hate when we're asked to work overtime.
Improved:	I hate it when we're asked to work overtime.
Improved:	I hate being asked to work overtime.

d. Don't confuse the adverb *then* with the conjunction *than. Then* means "at that time"; *than* indicates the second element in a comparison:

We would rather remodel *than* (not *then*) move.

First, the equipment is turned on; *then* (not *than*) the program is loaded.

REVIEW EXERCISE F—PREPOSITIONS AND CONJUNCTIONS

In the space provided for each item, write *a* or *b* to indicate the sentence that is expressed more effectively. When you finish, compare your responses with those provided. For each item on which you need review, consult the numbered principle shown in parentheses.

1. ___ (a) The chief forgot to tell everyone where today's meeting is.

   (b) The chief forgot to tell everyone where today's meeting is at.

2. ___ (a) She was not aware of nor interested in the company insurance plan.

   (b) She was not aware nor interested in the company insurance plan.

3. (a) Mr. Samuels graduated college last June.

   (b) Mr. Samuels graduated from college last June.

4. (a) "Flextime" is when employees arrive and depart at varying times.

   (b) "Flextime" is a method of scheduling worktime in which employees arrive and depart at varying times.

5. (a) Both employees enjoyed setting their own hours.

   (b) Both of the employees enjoyed setting their own hours.

6. (a) I hate when my cell loses its charge.

   (b) I hate it when my cell loses its charge.

7. (a) What style of typeface should we use?

   (b) What style typeface should we use?

8. (a) Business letters should be concise, correct, and written clearly.

   (b) Business letters should be concise, correct, and clear.

9. (a) Mediation in a labor dispute occurs when a neutral person helps union and management reach an agreement.

   (b) Mediation in a labor dispute is where a neutral person helps union and management reach an agreement.

10. (a) It looks as if the plant will open in early January.

    (b) It looks like the plant will open in early January.

11. (a) We expect to finish up the work soon.

    (b) We expect to finish the work soon.

12. (a) At the beginning of the program in the fall of the year at the central office, we experienced staffing difficulties.

    (b) When the program began last fall, the central office experienced staffing difficulties.

13. (a) Your client may respond by e-mail or a telephone call may be made.

    (b) Your client may respond by e-mail or by telephone.

14. (a) A résumé is when you make a written presentation of your education and experience for a prospective employer.

    (b) A résumé is a written presentation of your education and experience for a prospective employer.

15. (a) Stacy exhibited both an awareness of and talent for developing innovations.

    (b) Stacy exhibited both an awareness and talent for developing innovations.

16. (a) This course is harder then I expected.

    (b) This course is harder than I expected.

17. (a) An ombudsman is an individual hired by management to investigate and resolve employee complaints.

    (b) An ombudsman is when management hires an individual to investigate and resolve employee complaints.

18. (a) I'm uncertain where to take this document to.

    (b) I'm uncertain where to take this document.

19. (a) By including accurate data and by writing clearly, you will produce effective messages.

    (b) By including accurate data and writing clearly, you will produce effective messages.

20. (a) We need computer operators who can load software, monitor networks, and files must be duplicated.

  (b) We need computer operators who can load software, monitor networks, and duplicate files.

1. a (1.18b) 3. b (1.18a) 5. a (1.18b) 7. a (1.18a) 9. a (1.19c) 11. b (1.18b) 13. b (1.19a)
15. a (1.18e) 17. a (1.19c) 19. a (1.18d)

CUMULATIVE EDITING QUIZ 3

Use proofreading marks (see Appendix B) to correct errors in the following sentences. All errors must be corrected to receive credit for the sentence. Check with your instructor for the answers.

1. If Cindy works faster then her, shouldn't Cindy be hired?
2. We felt badly that Mark's home was not chose for the tour.
3. Neither the company nor the workers is pleased at how slow the talks seems to be progressing.
4. Just between you and I, it's better not to take his remarks personal.
5. After completing there floor by floor inventory, managers will deliver there reports to Mr. Quinn and I.
6. If my cell phone was working, Jean and myself could have completed our calls.
7. Powerful software and new hardware allows us to send the newsletter to whomever is currently listed in our database.
8. The eighteen year old girl and her mother was given hot cups of tea after there ordeal.
9. We begun the work two years ago, but personnel and equipment has been especially difficult to obtain.
10. Today's weather is worst then yesterday.

PUNCTUATION REVIEW

COMMAS 1 (2.01–2.04)

2.01 Series. Commas are used to separate three or more equal elements (words, phrases, or short clauses) in a series. To ensure separation of the last two elements, careful writers always use a comma before the conjunction in a series:

Business letters usually contain a dateline, address, salutation, body, and closing. (This series contains words.)

The job of an ombudsman is to examine employee complaints, resolve disagreements between management and employees, and ensure fair treatment. (This series contains phrases.)

Trainees complete basic keyboarding tasks, technicians revise complex documents, and editors proofread completed projects. (This series contains short clauses.)

2.02 Direct Address. Commas are used to set off the names of individuals being addressed:

Your inquiry, *Mrs. Johnson*, has been referred to me.

We genuinely hope that we may serve you, *Mr. Lee*.

2.03 Parenthetical Expressions. Skilled writers use parenthetical words, phrases, and clauses to guide the reader from one thought to the next. When these expressions interrupt the flow of a sentence and are unnecessary for its grammatical completeness, they should be set off with commas. Examples of commonly used parenthetical expressions follow:

all things considered	however	needless to say
as a matter of fact	in addition	nevertheless
as a result	incidentally	no doubt
as a rule	in fact	of course
at the same time	in my opinion	on the contrary
consequently	in the first place	on the other hand
for example	in the meantime	therefore
furthermore	moreover	under the circumstances

As a matter of fact, I wrote to you just yesterday. (Phrase used at the beginning of a sentence.)

We will, *in the meantime*, send you a replacement order. (Phrase used in the middle of a sentence.)

Your satisfaction is our first concern, *needless to say*. (Phrase used at the end of a sentence.)

Do not use commas if the expression is necessary for the completeness of the sentence:

Kimberly had *no doubt* that she would finish the report. (Omit commas because the expression is necessary for the completeness of the sentence.)

2.04 Dates, Addresses, and Geographical Items. When dates, addresses, and geographical items contain more than one element, the second and succeeding elements are normally set off by commas.

a. Dates:

The conference was held February 2 at our home office. (No comma is needed for one element.)

The conference was held February 2, 2006, at our home office. (Two commas set off the second element.)

The conference was held Tuesday, February 2, 2006, at our home office. (Commas set off the second and third elements.)

In February 2006 the conference was held. (This alternate style omitting commas is acceptable if only the month and year are written.)

b. Addresses:

The letter addressed to Mr. Jim W. Ellman, 600 Via Novella, Agoura, CA 91306, should be sent today. (Commas are used between all elements except the state and zip code, which in this special instance are considered a single unit.)

c. Geographical items:

She moved from Toledo, Ohio, to Champaign, Illinois. (Commas set off the state unless it appears at the end of the sentence, in which case only one comma is used.)

In separating cities from states and days from years, many writers remember the initial comma but forget the final one, as in the examples that follow:

The package from Austin, Texas {,} was lost.

We opened June 1, 2004 {,} and have grown steadily since.

REVIEW EXERCISE G—COMMAS 1

Insert necessary commas in the following sentences. In the space provided write the number of commas that you add. Write *C* if no commas are needed. When you finish, compare your responses with those provided. For each item on which you need review, consult the numbered principle shown in parentheses.

1. As a rule we do not provide complimentary tickets.
2. You may be certain Mr. Martinez that your policy will be issued immediately.
3. I have no doubt that your calculations are correct.
4. The safety hazard on the contrary can be greatly reduced if workers wear rubber gloves.
5. Every accredited TV newscaster radio broadcaster and newspaper reporter had access to the media room.
6. Deltech's main offices are located in Boulder Colorado and Seattle Washington.
7. The employees who are eligible for promotions are Terry Evelyn Vicki Rosanna and Steve.
8. During the warranty period of course you are protected from any parts or service charges.
9. Many of our customers include architects engineers attorneys and others who are interested in database management programs.
10. I wonder Mrs. Stevens if you would send my letter of recommendation as soon as possible.
11. The new book explains how to choose appropriate legal protection for ideas trade secrets copyrights patents and restrictive covenants.
12. The factory is scheduled to be moved to 2250 North Main Street Ann Arbor Michigan 48107 within two years.
13. You may however prefer to correspond directly with the manufacturer in Hong Kong.
14. Are there any alternatives in addition to those that we have already considered?
15. The rally has been scheduled for Monday January 12 in the football stadium.
16. A check for the full amount will be sent directly to your home, Mr. Jefferson.
17. Goodstone Tire & Rubber for example recalled 400,000 steelbelted radial tires because some tires failed their rigorous tests.
18. Kevin agreed to unlock the office open the mail and check all the equipment in my absence.
19. In the meantime thank you for whatever assistance you are able to furnish.
20. Research facilities were moved from Austin Texas to Santa Cruz California.

1. rule, (2.03)   3. C (2.03)   5. newscaster, radio broadcaster, (2.01)   7. Terry, Evelyn, Vicki, Rosanna, (2.01)   9. architects, engineers, attorneys, (2.01)   11. ideas, trade secrets, copyrights, patents, (2.01)   13. may, however, (2.03)   15. Monday, January 12, (2.04a)   17. Rubber, for example, (2.03)   19. meantime, (2.03)

COMMAS 2 (2.05–2.09)

2.05 Independent Clauses. An independent clause is a group of words that has a subject and a verb and that could stand as a complete sentence. When two such clauses are joined by *and, or, nor,* or *but,* use a comma before the conjunction:

We can ship your merchandise July 12, but we must have your payment first.

Net income before taxes is calculated, and this total is then combined with income from operations.

Notice that each independent clause in the preceding two examples could stand alone as a complete sentence. Do not use a comma unless each group of words is a complete thought (that is, has its own subject and verb).

Net income before taxes is calculated *and* is then combined with income from operations. (No comma is needed because no subject follows *and*.)

2.06 Dependent Clauses. Dependent clauses do not make sense by themselves; for their meaning they depend on independent clauses.

a. Introductory clauses. When a dependent clause precedes an independent clause, it is followed by a comma. Such clauses are often introduced by *when, if*, and *as*:

When your request came, we responded immediately.

As I mentioned earlier, Mrs. James is the manager.

b. Terminal clauses. If a dependent clause falls at the end of a sentence, use a comma only if the dependent clause is an afterthought:

The meeting has been rescheduled for October 23, *if this date meets with your approval*. (Comma used because dependent clause is an afterthought.)

We responded immediately *when we received your request*. (No comma is needed.)

c. Essential versus nonessential clauses. If a dependent clause provides information that is unneeded for the grammatical completeness of a sentence, use commas to set it off. In determining whether such a clause is essential or nonessential, ask yourself whether the reader needs the information contained in the clause to identify the word it explains:

Our district sales manager, *who just returned from a trip to the Southwest District*, prepared this report. (This construction assumes that there is only one district sales manager. Since the sales manager is clearly identified, the dependent clause is not essential and requires commas.)

The salesperson *who just returned from a trip to the Southwest District* prepared this report. (The dependent clause in this sentence is necessary to identify which salesperson prepared the report. Therefore, use no commas.)

The position of assistant sales manager, *which we discussed with you last week*, is still open. (Careful writers use *which* to introduce nonessential clauses. Commas are also necessary.)

The position *that we discussed with you last week* is still open. (Careful writers use *that* to introduce essential clauses. No commas are used.)

2.07 Phrases. A phrase is a group of related words that lacks both a subject and a verb. A phrase that precedes a main clause is followed by a comma if the phrase contains a verb form or has five or more words:

Beginning November 1, Worldwide Savings will offer two new combination checking/savings plans. (A comma follows this introductory phrase because the phrase contains the verb form *beginning*.)

To promote its plan, we will conduct an extensive direct mail advertising campaign. (A comma follows this introductory phrase because the phrase contains the verb form *to promote*.)

In a period of only one year, we were able to improve our market share by 30 percent. (A comma follows the introductory phrase—actually two prepositional phrases—because its total length exceeds five words.)

In 2005 our organization installed a multiuser system that could transfer programs easily. (No comma needed after the short introductory phrase.)

2.08 Two or More Adjectives. Use a comma to separate two or more adjectives that equally describe a noun. A good way to test the need for a comma is this: Mentally insert the word *and* between the adjectives. If the resulting phrase sounds natural, a comma is used to show the omission of *and*:

> We're looking for a *versatile, error-free* operating system. (Use a comma to separate *versatile* and *error-free* because they independently describe *operating system*. *And* has been omitted.)

> Our *experienced, courteous* staff is ready to serve you. (Use a comma to separate *experienced* and *courteous* because they independently describe *staff*. *And* has been omitted.)

> It was difficult to refuse the *sincere young* telephone caller. (No commas are needed between *sincere* and *young* because *and* has not been omitted.)

2.09 Appositives. Words that rename or explain preceding nouns or pronouns are called *appositives*. An appositive that provides information not essential to the identification of the word it describes should be set off by commas:

> James Wilson, *the project director for Sperling's*, worked with our architect. (The appositive, *the project director for Sperling's*, adds nonessential information. Commas set it off.)

REVIEW EXERCISE H—COMMAS 2

Insert only necessary commas in the following sentences. In the space provided, indicate the number of commas that you add for each sentence. If a sentence requires no commas, write *C*. When you finish, compare your responses with those provided. For each item on which you need review, consult the numbered principle shown in parentheses.

1. A corporation must be registered in the state in which it does business and it must operate within the laws of that state.
2. The manager made a point-by-point explanation of the distribution dilemma and then presented his plan to solve the problem.
3. If you will study the cost analysis you will see that our company offers the best system at the lowest price.
4. Molly Epperson who amassed the greatest number of sales points was awarded the bonus trip to Hawaii.
5. The salesperson who amasses the greatest number of sales points will be awarded the bonus trip to Hawaii.
6. To promote goodwill and to generate international trade we are opening offices in South Asia and in Europe.
7. On the basis of these findings I recommend that we retain Jane Rada as our counsel.
8. Scott Cook is a dedicated hardworking employee for our company.
9. The bright young student who worked for us last summer will be able to return this summer.
10. When you return the completed form we will be able to process your application.
11. We will be able to process your application when you return the completed form.
12. The employees who have been with us over ten years automatically receive additional insurance benefits.
13. Knowing that you wanted this merchandise immediately I took the liberty of sending it by Fed Ex.
14. The central processing unit requires no scheduled maintenance and has a self-test function for reliable performance.
15. A tax credit for energy-saving homes will expire at the end of the year but Congress might extend it if pressure groups prevail.

16. Stacy Wilson our newly promoted office manager has made a number of worthwhile suggestions.

17. For the benefit of employees recently hired we are offering a two-hour seminar regarding employee benefit programs.

18. Please bring your suggestions and those of Mr. Mason when you attend our meeting next month.

19. The meeting has been rescheduled for September 30 if this date meets with your approval.

20. Some of the problems that you outline in your recent memo could be rectified through more stringent purchasing procedures.

---

1. business, (2.05)   3. analysis, (2.06a)   5. C (2.06c)   7. findings, (2.07)   9. C (2.08)   11. C (2.06b)   13. immediately, (2.07)   15. year, (2.05)   17. hired, (2.07)   19. September 30, (2.06b)

COMMAS 3 (2.10–2.15)

2.10 Degrees and Abbreviations. Degrees following individuals' names are set off by commas. Abbreviations such as *Jr.* and *Sr.* are also set off by commas unless the individual referred to prefers to omit the commas:

> Anne G. Turner, *M.B.A.*, joined the firm.

> Michael Migliano, *Jr.*, and Michael Migliano, *Sr.*, work as a team.

> Anthony A. Gensler *Jr.* wrote the report. (The individual referred to prefers to omit commas.)

The abbreviations *Inc.* and *Ltd.* are set off by commas only if a company's legal name has a comma just before this kind of abbreviation. To determine a company's practice, consult its stationery or a directory listing:

> Firestone and Blythe, *Inc.*, is based in Canada. (Notice that two commas are used.)

> Computers *Inc.* is extending its franchise system. (The company's legal name does not include a comma before *Inc.*)

2.11 Omitted Words. A comma is used to show the omission of words that are understood:

> On Monday we received 15 applications; on Friday, only 3. (Comma shows the omission of *we received.*)

2.12 Contrasting Statements. Commas are used to set off contrasting or opposing expressions. These expressions are often introduced by such words as *not, never, but,* and *yet*:

> The president suggested cutbacks, **not** layoffs, to ease the crisis.

> Our budget for the year is reduced, *yet* adequate.

> The greater the effort, the greater the reward.

If increased emphasis is desired, use dashes instead of commas, as in *Only the sum of $100—not $1,000—was paid on this account.*

2.13 Clarity. Commas are used to separate words repeated for emphasis. Commas are also used to separate words that may be misread if not separated:

> The building is a long, long way from completion.

> Whatever is, is right.

> No matter what, you know we support you.

2.14 Quotations and Appended Questions

a. A comma is used to separate a short quotation from the rest of a sentence. If the quotation is divided into two parts, two commas are used:

> The manager asked, "Shouldn't the managers control the specialists?"

> "Not if the specialists," replied Tim, "have unique information."

b. A comma is used to separate a question appended (added) to a statement:

> You will confirm the shipment, won't you?

2.15 Comma Overuse. Do not use commas needlessly. For example, commas should not be inserted merely because you might drop your voice if you were speaking the sentence:

> One of the reasons for expanding our East Coast operations is {,} that we anticipate increased sales in that area. (Do not insert a needless comma before a clause.)

> I am looking for an article entitled {,} "State-of-the-Art Communications." (Do not insert a needless comma after the word *entitled*.)

> A number of food and nonfood items are carried in convenience stores *such as* {,} 7-Eleven and Stop-N-Go. (Do not insert a needless comma after *such as*.)

> We have {,} at this time {,} an adequate supply of parts. (Do not insert needless commas around prepositional phrases.)

REVIEW EXERCISE I—COMMAS 3

Insert only necessary commas in the following sentences. Remove unnecessary commas with the delete sign (✗). In the space provided, indicate the number of commas inserted or deleted in each sentence. If a sentence requires no changes, write *C*. When you finish, compare your responses with those provided. For each item on which you need review, consult the numbered principle shown in parentheses.

1. We expected Anna Cortez not Tyler Rosen to conduct the audit.
2. Brian said "We simply must have a bigger budget to start this project."
3. "We simply must have" said Brian "a bigger budget to start this project."
4. In August customers opened at least 50 new accounts; in September only about 20.
5. You returned the merchandise last month didn't you?
6. In short employees will now be expected to contribute more to their own retirement funds.
7. The better our advertising and recruiting the stronger our personnel pool will be.
8. Mrs. Delgado investigated selling her stocks not her real estate to raise the necessary cash.
9. "On the contrary" said Mr. Stevens "we will continue our present marketing strategies."
10. Our company will expand into surprising new areas such as, women's apparel and fast foods.
11. What we need is more not fewer suggestions for improvement.
12. Randall Clark Esq. and Jonathon Georges M.B.A. joined the firm.
13. "America is now entering" said President Saunders "the Age of Information."
14. One of the reasons that we are inquiring about the publisher of the software is, that we are concerned about whether that publisher will be in the market five years from now.
15. The talk by D. A. Spindler Ph.D. was particularly difficult to follow because of his technical and abstract vocabulary.

16. The month before a similar disruption occurred in distribution.

17. We are very fortunate to have, at our disposal, the services of excellent professionals.

18. No matter what you can count on us for support.

19. Mrs. Sandoval was named legislative counsel; Mr. Freeman executive advisor.

20. The data you are seeking can be found in an article entitled, "The Fastest Growing Game in Computers."

---

1. Cortez, Rosen, (2.12) 3. have," said Brian, (2.14a) 5. month, (2.14b) 7. recruiting, (2.12) 9. contrary," Stevens, (2.14a) 11. more, not fewer, (2.12) 13. entering," Saunders, (2.14a) 15. Spindler, Ph.D., (2.10) 17. have at our disposal (2.15) 19. Freeman, (2.11)

CUMULATIVE EDITING QUIZ 4

Use proofreading marks (see Appendix B) to correct errors and omissions in the following sentences. All errors must be corrected to receive credit for the sentence. Check with your instructor for the answers.

1. Business documents must be written clear, to ensure that readers comprehend the message quick.

2. Needless to say the safety of our employees have always been most important to the president and I.

3. The Small Business Administration which provide disaster loans are setting up an office in Miami Florida.

4. Many entrepreneurs who want to expand there markets, have choosen to advertise heavy.

5. Our arbitration committee have unanimously agreed on a compromise package but management have been slow to respond.

6. Although the business was founded in the 1970's its real expansion took place in the 1990s.

7. According to the printed contract either the dealer or the distributor are responsible for repair of the product.

8. Next June, Lamont and Jones, Inc., are moving their headquarters to Denton Texas.

9. Our company is looking for intelligent, articulate, young, people who has a desire to grow with an expanding organization.

10. As you are aware each member of the jury were asked to avoid talking about the case.

SEMICOLONS (2.16)

2.16 Independent Clauses, Series, Introductory Expressions

a. **Independent clauses with conjunctive adverbs.** Use a semicolon before a conjunctive adverb that separates two independent clauses. Some of the most common conjunctive adverbs are *therefore, consequently, however*, and *moreover*:

Business messages should sound conversational; *therefore*, familiar words and contractions are often used.

The bank closes its doors at 5 p.m.; *however*, the ATM is open 24 hours a day.

Notice that the word following a semicolon is *not* capitalized (unless, of course, that word is a proper noun).

b. **Independent clauses without conjunctive adverbs.** Use a semicolon to separate closely related independent clauses when no conjunctive adverb is used:

Bond interest payments are tax deductible; dividend payments are not.

Ambient lighting fills the room; task lighting illuminates each workstation.

Use a semicolon in *compound* sentences, not in *complex* sentences:

After one week the paper feeder jammed; we tried different kinds of paper. (Use a semi-colon in a compound sentence.)

After one week the paper feeder jammed, although we tried different kinds of paper. (Use a comma in a complex sentence. Do not use a semicolon after *jammed*.)

The semicolon is very effective for joining two closely related thoughts. Don't use it, however, unless the ideas are truly related.

c. **Independent clauses with other commas.** Normally, a comma precedes *and, or*, and *but* when those conjunctions join independent clauses. However, if either clause contains commas, change the comma preceding the conjunction to a semicolon to ensure correct reading:

If you arrive in time, you may be able to purchase a ticket; but ticket sales close promptly at 8 p.m.

Our primary concern is financing; and we have discovered, as you warned us, that money sources are quite scarce.

d. **Series with internal commas.** Use semicolons to separate items in a series when one or more of the items contains internal commas:

Delegates from Miami, Florida; Freeport, Mississippi; and Chatsworth, California, attended the conference.

The speakers were Kevin Lang, manager, Riko Enterprises; Henry Holtz, vice president, Trendex, Inc.; and Margaret Slater, personnel director, West Coast Productions.

e. **Introductory expressions.** Use a semicolon when an introductory expression such as *namely, for instance, that is*, or *for example* introduces a list following an independent clause:

Switching to computerized billing are several local companies; namely, Ryson Electronics, Miller Vending Services, and Black Advertising.

The author of a report should consider many sources; for example, books, periodicals, databases, and newspapers.

COLONS (2.17–2.19)

2.17 Listed Items

a. **With colon.** Use a colon after a complete thought that introduces a formal list of items. A formal list is often preceded by such words and phrases as *these, thus, the following*, and *as follows*. A colon is also used when words and phrases like these are implied but not stated:

Additional costs in selling a house involve *the following*: title examination fee, title insurance costs, and closing fee. (Use a colon when a complete thought introduces a formal list.)

Collective bargaining focuses on several key issues: cost-of-living adjustments, fringe benefits, job security, and work hours. (The introduction of the list is implied in the pre-ceding clause.)

b. **Without colons.** Do not use a colon when the list immediately follows a *to be* verb or a preposition:

The employees who should receive the preliminary plan are James Sears, Monica Spears, and Rose Lopez. (No colon is used after the verb *are*.)

We expect to consider equipment for Accounting, Legal Services, and Payroll. (No colon is used after the preposition *for*.)

2.18 Quotations. Use a colon to introduce long one-sentence quotations and quotations of two or more sentences:

Our consultant said: "This system can support up to 32 users. It can be used for decision support, computer-aided design, and software development operations at the same time."

2.19 Salutations. Use a colon after the salutation of a business letter:

Gentlemen: Dear Mrs. Seaman: Dear Jamie:

REVIEW EXERCISE J—SEMICOLONS, COLONS

In the following sentences, add semicolons, colons, and necessary commas. For each sentence indicate the number of punctuation marks that you add. If a sentence requires no punctuation, write *C*. When you finish, compare your responses with those provided. For each item on which you need review, consult the numbered principle shown in parentheses.

1. Technological advances make full-motion video viewable on small screens consequently mobile phone makers and carriers are rolling out new services and phones.

2. Our branch in Sherman Oaks specializes in industrial real estate our branch in Canoga Park concentrates on residential real estate.

3. The sedan version of the automobile is available in these colors Olympic red metallic silver and Aztec gold.

4. If I can assist the new manager please call me however I will be gone from June 10 through June 15.

5. The individuals who should receive copies of this announcement are Jeff Doogan Alicia Green and Kim Wong.

6. We would hope of course to send personal letters to all prospective buyers but we have not yet decided just how to do this.

7. Many of our potential customers are in Southern California therefore our promotional effort will be strongest in that area.

8. Since the first of the year we have received inquiries from one attorney two accountants and one information systems analyst.

9. Three dates have been reserved for initial interviews January 15 February 1 and February 12.

10. Several staff members are near the top of their salary ranges and we must reclassify their jobs.

11. Several staff members are near the top of their salary ranges we must reclassify their jobs.

12. Several staff members are near the top of their salary ranges therefore we must reclassify their jobs.

13. If you open an account within two weeks you will receive a free cookbook moreover your first 500 checks will be imprinted at no cost to you.

14. Monthly reports from the following departments are missing Legal Department Human Resources Department and Engineering Department.

15. Monthly reports are missing from the Legal Department Human Resources Department and Engineering Department.

16. Since you became director of that division sales have tripled therefore I am recommending you for a bonus.

17. The convention committee is considering Portland Oregon New Orleans Louisiana and Phoenix Arizona.

18. Several large companies allow employees access to their personnel files namely General Electric Eastman Kodak and Infodata.

19. Sherry first asked about salary next she inquired about benefits.

20. Sherry first asked about the salary and she next inquired about benefits.

---

1. screens; consequently, (2.16a)   3. colors: Olympic red, metallic silver, (2.01, 2.17a)
5. Doogan, Alicia Green, (2.01, 2.17b)   7. California; therefore, (2.16a)   9. interviews:
January 15, February 1, (2.01, 2.17a)   11. ranges; (2.16b)   13. weeks, cookbook; moreover,
(206a, 2.16a)   15. Department, Human Resources Department, (2.01, 2.17b)   17. Portland,
Oregon; New Orleans, Louisiana; Phoenix, (2.16d)   19. salary; (2.16b)

APOSTROPHES (2.20–2.22)

2.20 Basic Rule. The apostrophe is used to show ownership, origin, authorship, or measurement.

Ownership:	We are looking for *Brian's keys*.
Origin:	At the *president's suggestion*, we doubled the order.
Authorship:	The *accountant's annual report* was questioned.
Measurement:	In *two years' time* we expect to reach our goal.

a. **Ownership words not ending in *s*.** To place the apostrophe correctly, you must first determine whether the ownership word ends in an *s* sound. If it does not, add an apostrophe and an *s* to the ownership word. The following examples show ownership words that do not end in an *s* sound:

the employee's file	(the file of a single employee)
a member's address	(the address of a single member)
a year's time	(the time of a single year)
a month's notice	(notice of a single month)
the company's building	(the building of a single company)

b. **Ownership words ending in *s*.** If the ownership word does end in an *s* sound, usually add only an apostrophe:

several employees' files	(files of several employees)
ten members' addresses	(addresses of ten members)
five years' time	(time of five years)
several months' notice	(notice of several months)
many companies' buildings	(buildings of many companies)

A few singular nouns that end in *s* are pronounced with an extra syllable when they become possessive. To these words, add *'s*.

my boss's desk
the waitress's table
the actress's costume

Use no apostrophe if a noun is merely plural, not possessive:

All the sales representatives, as well as the assistants and managers, had their names and telephone numbers listed in the directory.

2.21 Names. The writer may choose either traditional or popular style in making singular names that end in an *s* sound possessive. The traditional style uses the apostrophe plus an *s*, whereas the popular style uses just the apostrophe. Note that only with singular names ending in an *s* sound does this option exist.

Traditional style	Popular style
Russ's computer	Russ' computer
Mr. Jones's car	Mr. Jones' car
Mrs. Morris's desk	Mrs. Morris' desk
Ms. Horowitz's job	Ms. Horowitz' job

The possessive form of plural names is consistent: the Joneses' car, the Horowitzes' home, the Lopezes' daughter.

2.22 Gerunds. Use *'s* to make a noun possessive when it precedes a gerund, a verb form used as a noun:

Mr. Smith's smoking prompted a new office policy. (*Mr. Smith* is possessive because it modifies the gerund *smoking*.)

It was Betsy's careful proofreading that revealed the discrepancy.

REVIEW EXERCISE K—APOSTROPHES

Insert necessary apostrophes in the following sentences. In the space provided for each sentence, write the corrected word. If none were corrected, write *C*. When you finish, compare your responses with those provided. For each item on which you need review, consult the numbered principle shown in parentheses.

1. In five years time Lisa hopes to repay all of her student loans.
2. If you go to the third floor, you will find Mr. Londons office.
3. All the employees personnel folders must be updated.
4. In a little over a years time, that firm was able to double its sales.
5. The Harrises daughter lived in Florida for two years.
6. An inventors patent protects his or her invention for 17 years.
7. Both companies headquarters will be moved within the next six months.
8. That position requires at least two years experience.
9. Some of their assets could be liquidated; therefore, a few of the creditors were satisfied.
10. All secretaries workstations were equipped with Internet access.
11. The package of electronics parts arrived safely despite two weeks delay.
12. Many nurses believe that nurses notes are not admissable evidence.
13. According to Mr. Cortez latest proposal, all employees would receive an additional holiday.
14. Many of our members names and addresses must be checked.
15. His supervisor frequently had to correct Jacks financial reports.
16. We believe that this firms service is much better than that firms.
17. Mr. Jackson estimated that he spent a years profits in reorganizing his staff.
18. After paying six months rent, we were given a receipt.
19. The contract is not valid without Mrs. Harris signature.
20. It was Mr. Smiths signing of the contract that made us happy.

---

1. years' (2.20b)　3. employees' (2.20b)　5. Harrises' (2.21)　7. companies' (2.20b)
9. C (2.20b)　11. weeks' (2.20b)　13. Cortez' or Cortez's (2.21)　15. Jack's (2.21)
17. year's (2.20a)　19. Harris' or Harris's (2.21)

CUMULATIVE EDITING QUIZ 5

Use proofreading marks (see Appendix B) to correct errors and omissions in the following sentences. All errors must be corrected to receive credit for the sentence. Check with your instructor for the answers.

1. The three C's of credit are the following character capacity and capital.
2. We hope that we will not have to sell the property however that may be our only option.
3. As soon as the supervisor and her can check this weeks sales they will place an order.
4. Any of the auditors are authorized to proceed with an independent action however only the CEO can alter the councils directives.
5. Although reluctant technicians sometimes must demonstrate there computer software skills.
6. On April 6 2004 we opened an innovative fully-equipped fitness center.
7. A list of maintenance procedures and recommendations are in the owners manual.
8. The Morrises son lived in Flint Michigan however there daughter lived in Albany New York.
9. Employment interviews were held in Dallas Texas Miami Florida and Chicago Illinois.
10. Mr. Lees determination courage and sincerity could not be denied however his methods was often questioned.

OTHER PUNCTUATION (2.23–2.29)

2.23 Periods

a. **Ends of sentences.** Use a period at the end of a statement, command, indirect question, or polite request. Although a polite request may have the same structure as a question, it ends with a period:

Corporate legal departments demand precise skills from their workforce. (End a statement with a period.)

Get the latest data by reading current periodicals. (End a command with a period.)

Mr. Rand wondered whether we had sent any follow-up literature. (End an indirect question with a period.)

Would you please reexamine my account and determine the current balance. (A polite request suggests an action rather than a verbal response.)

b. **Abbreviations and initials.** Use periods after initials and after many abbreviations.

R. M. Johnson	c.o.d.	Ms.
M.D.	a.m.	Mr.
Inc.	i.e.	Mrs.

Use just one period when an abbreviation falls at the end of a sentence:

Guests began arriving at 5:30 p.m.

2.24 Question Marks. Direct questions are followed by question marks:

Did you send your proposal to Datatronix, Inc.?

Statements with questions added are punctuated with question marks.

We have completed the proposal, haven't we?

2.25 Exclamation Points. Use an exclamation point after a word, phrase, or clause expressing strong emotion. In business writing, however, exclamation points should be used sparingly:

> Incredible! Every terminal is down.

2.26 Dashes. The dash (constructed at a keyboard by striking the hyphen key twice in succession) is a legitimate and effective mark of punctuation when used according to accepted conventions. As an emphatic punctuation mark, however, the dash loses effectiveness when overused.

a. **Parenthetical elements.** Within a sentence a parenthetical element is usually set off by commas. If, however, the parenthetical element itself contains internal commas, use dashes (or parentheses) to set it off:

> Three top salespeople—Tom Judkins, Tim Templeton, and Mary Yashimoto—received bonuses.

b. **Sentence interruptions.** Use a dash to show an interruption or abrupt change of thought:

> News of the dramatic merger—no one believed it at first—shook the financial world.

> Ship the materials Monday—no, we must have them sooner.

> Sentences with abrupt changes of thought or with appended afterthoughts can usually be improved through rewriting.

c. **Summarizing statements.** Use a dash (not a colon) to separate an introductory list from a summarizing statement:

> Sorting, merging, and computing—these are tasks that our data processing programs must perform.

2.27 Parentheses. One means of setting off nonessential sentence elements involves the use of parentheses. Nonessential sentence elements may be punctuated in one of three ways: (1) with commas, to make the lightest possible break in the normal flow of a sentence; (2) with dashes, to emphasize the enclosed material; and (3) with parentheses, to de-emphasize the enclosed material. Parentheses are frequently used to punctuate sentences with interpolated directions, explanations, questions, and references:

> The cost analysis (which appears on page 8 of the report) indicates that the copy machine should be leased.

> Units are lightweight (approximately 13 oz.) and come with a leather case and operating instructions.

> The IBM laser printer (have you heard about it?) will be demonstrated for us next week.

> A parenthetical sentence that is not embedded within another sentence should be capitalized and punctuated with end punctuation:

> The Model 20 has stronger construction. (You may order a Model 20 brochure by circling 304 on the reader service card.)

2.28 Quotation Marks

a. **Direct quotations.** Use double quotation marks to enclose the exact words of a speaker or writer:

> "Keep in mind," Mrs. Frank said, "that you'll have to justify the cost of networking our office."

> The boss said that automation was inevitable. (No quotation marks are needed because the exact words are not quoted.)

b. **Quotations within quotations.** Use single quotation marks (apostrophes on the keyboard) to enclose quoted passages within quoted passages:

> In her speech, Mrs. Deckman remarked, "I believe it was the poet Robert Frost who said, 'All the fun's in how you say a thing.'"

c. **Short expressions.** Slang, words used in a special sense, and words following *stamped* or *marked* are often enclosed within quotation marks:

Jeffrey described the damaged shipment as "gross." (Quotation marks enclose slang.)

Students often have trouble spelling the word "separate." (Quotation marks enclose words used in a special sense.)

Jobs were divided into two categories: most stressful and least stressful. The jobs in the "most stressful" list involved high risk or responsibility. (Quotation marks enclose words used in a special sense.)

The envelope marked "Confidential" was put aside. (Quotation marks enclose words following *marked*.)

In the four preceding sentences, the words enclosed within quotation marks can be set in italics, if italics are available.

d. **Definitions.** Double quotation marks are used to enclose definitions. The word or expression being defined should be underscored or set in italics:

The term *penetration pricing* is defined as "the practice of introducing a product to the market at a low price."

e. **Titles.** Use double quotation marks to enclose titles of literary and artistic works, such as magazine and newspaper articles, chapters of books, movies, television shows, poems, lectures, and songs. Names of major publications—such as books, magazines, pamphlets, and newspapers—are set in italics (underscored) or typed in capital letters.

Particularly helpful was the chapter in Smith's EFFECTIVE WRITING TECHNIQUES entitled "Right Brain, Write On!"

In the *Los Angeles Times* appeared John's article, "E-Mail Blunders"; however, we could not locate it in a local library.

f. **Additional considerations.** In this country periods and commas are always placed inside closing quotation marks. Semicolons and colons, on the other hand, are always placed outside quotation marks:

Mrs. James said, "I could not find the article entitled 'Cell Phone Etiquette.'"

The president asked for "absolute security": All written messages were to be destroyed.

Question marks and exclamation points may go inside or outside closing quotation marks, as determined by the form of the quotation:

Sales Manager Martin said, "Who placed the order?" (The quotation is a question.)

When did the sales manager say, "Who placed the order?" (Both the incorporating sentence and the quotation are questions.)

Did the sales manager say, "Ryan placed the order"? (The incorporating sentence asks a question; the quotation does not.)

"In the future," shouted Bob, "ask me first!" (The quotation is an exclamation.)

2.29 Brackets. Within quotations, brackets are used by the quoting writer to enclose his or her own inserted remarks. Such remarks may be corrective, illustrative, or explanatory:

Mrs. Cardillo said, "OSHA [Occupational Safety and Health Administration] has been one of the most widely criticized agencies of the federal government."

REVIEW EXERCISE L—OTHER PUNCTUATION

Insert necessary punctuation in the following sentences. In the space provided for each item, indicate the number of punctuation marks that you added. Count sets of parentheses, dashes, and quotation marks as two marks. Emphasis or de-emphasis will be indicated for some parenthetical elements. When you finish, compare your responses with those provided. For each item on which you need review, consult the numbered principle shown in parentheses.

1. Will you please send me your latest catalog
2. (Emphasize) Three of my friends Carmen Lopez, Stan Meyers, and Ivan Sergo were all promoted.
3. Mr Lee, Miss Evans, and Mrs Rivera have not responded.
4. We have scheduled your interview for 4 45 p m
5. (De-emphasize) The appliance comes in limited colors black, ivory, and beige , but we accept special orders.
6. The expression de facto means exercising power as if legally constituted.
7. Was it the president who said "This, too, will pass
8. Should this package be marked Fragile
9. Did you see the Newsweek article titled How Far Can Wireless Go
10. Amazing All sales reps made their targets

---

1. catalog. (2.23a) 3. Mr. Mrs. (2.23a) 5. colors (black, ivory, and beige) (2.26a)
7. said, pass"? 9. *Newsweek* "How Go?" (2.28e)

CUMULATIVE EDITING QUIZ 6

Use proofreading marks (see Appendix B) to correct errors and omissions in the following sentences. All errors must be corrected to receive credit for the sentence. Check with your instructor for the answers.

1. Although the envelope was marked Confidential the vice presidents secretary thought it should be opened.
2. Would you please send my order c.o.d?
3. To be eligible for an apartment you must pay two months rent in advance.
4. We wanted to use Russ computer, but forgot to ask for permission.
5. Wasnt it Jeff Song not Eileen Lee who requested a 14 day leave.
6. Miss. Judith L. Beam is the employee who the employees council elected as their representative.
7. The Evening Post Dispatch our local newspaper featured an article entitled The Worlds Most Expensive Memo.
8. As soon as my manager or myself can verify Ricks totals we will call you, in the meantime you must continue to disburse funds.
9. Just inside the entrance, is the receptionists desk and a complete directory of all departments'.
10. Exports from small companys has increased thereby affecting this countrys trade balance positively.

STYLE AND USAGE

CAPITALIZATION (3.01–3.16)

Capitalization is used to distinguish important words. However, writers are not free to capitalize all words they consider important. Rules or guidelines governing capitalization style have been established through custom and use. Mastering these guidelines will make your writing more readable and more comprehensible.

3.01 Proper Nouns. Capitalize proper nouns, including the *specific* names of persons, places, schools, streets, parks, buildings, religions, holidays, months, agreements, programs, services, and so forth. Do not capitalize common nouns that make only *general* references.

Proper nouns	**Common nouns**
Michael DeNiro	a salesperson in electronics
Germany, Japan	major trading partners of the United States
El Camino College	a community college
Sam Houston Park	a park in the city
Phoenix Room, Statler Inn	a meeting room in the hotel
Catholic, Presbyterian	two religions
Memorial Day, New Year's Day	two holidays
Express Mail	a special package delivery service
George Washington Bridge	a bridge
Consumer Product Safety Act	a law to protect consumers
Greater Orlando Chamber of Commerce	a chamber of commerce
Will Rogers World Airport	a municipal airport

3.02 Proper Adjectives. Capitalize most adjectives that are derived from proper nouns:

Greek symbol	British thermal unit
Roman numeral	Norwegian ship
Xerox copy	Hispanic markets

Do not capitalize the few adjectives that, although originally derived from proper nouns, have become common adjectives through usage. Consult your dictionary when in doubt:

manila folder	diesel engine
india ink	china dishes

3.03 Geographic Locations. Capitalize the names of *specific* places such as cities, states, mountains, valleys, lakes, rivers, oceans, and geographic regions:

New York City	Great Salt Lake
Allegheny Mountains	Pacific Ocean
San Fernando Valley	Delaware Bay
the East Coast	the Pacific Northwest

3.04 Organization Names. Capitalize the principal words in the names of all business, civic, educational, governmental, labor, military, philanthropic, political, professional, religious, and social organizations:

Matrix Steel Company	Board of Directors, Midwest Bank
*The Wall Street Journal***	San Antonio Museum of Art
New York Stock Exchange	Securities and Exchange Commission
United Way	National Association of Letter Carriers
Commission to Restore the Statue of Liberty	Association of Information Systems Professionals

3.05 Academic Courses and Degrees. Capitalize particular academic degrees and course titles. Do not capitalize general academic degrees and subject areas:

Professor Bernadette Ordian, *Ph.D.*, will teach *Accounting* 221 next fall.

Mrs. Snyder, who holds *bachelor's* and *master's degrees*, teaches *marketing* classes.

Jim enrolled in classes in *history, business English*, and *management*.

---

*Note: Capitalize *the* only when it is part of the official name of an organization, as printed on the organization's stationery.

3.06 Personal and Business Titles

a. Capitalize personal and business titles when they precede names:

Vice President Ames	Uncle Edward
Board Chairman Frazier	Councilman Herbert
Governor G. W. Thurmond	Sales Manager Klein
Professor McLean	Dr. Samuel Washington

b. Capitalize titles in addresses, salutations, and closing lines:

Mr. Juan deSanto	Very truly yours,
Director of Purchasing	
Space Systems, Inc.	Clara J. Smith
Boxborough, MA 01719	Supervisor, Marketing

c. Generally, do not capitalize titles of high government rank or religious office when they stand alone or follow a person's name in running text.

The president conferred with the joint chiefs of staff and many senators.

Meeting with the chief justice of the Supreme Court were the senator from Ohio and the mayor of Cleveland.

Only the cardinal from Chicago had an audience with the pope.

d. Do not capitalize most common titles following names:

The speech was delivered by Robert Lynch, *president*, Academic Publishing.

Lois Herndon, *chief executive officer*, signed the order.

e. Do not capitalize common titles appearing alone:

Please speak to the *supervisor* or to the *office manager*.

Neither the *president* nor the *vice president* was asked.

However, when the title of an official appears in that organization's minutes, bylaws, or other official document, it may be capitalized.

f. Do not capitalize titles when they are followed by appositives naming specific individuals:

We must consult our *director of research*, Ronald E. West, before responding.

g. Do not capitalize family titles used with possessive pronouns:

my mother	our aunt	your father	his cousin

h. Capitalize titles of close relatives used without pronouns:

Both *Mother* and *Father* must sign the contract.

3.07 Numbered and Lettered Items. Capitalize nouns followed by numbers or letters (except in page, paragraph, line, and verse references):

Flight 34, Gate 12	Plan No. 2
Volume I, Part 3	Warehouse 33-A
Invoice No. 55489	Figure 8.3
Model A5673	Serial No. C22865404-2
State Highway 10	page 6, line 5

3.08 Points of the Compass. Capitalize *north, south, east, west*, and their derivatives when they represent *specific* geographical regions. Do not capitalize the points of the compass when they are used in directions or in general references.

Specific regions	General references
from the South	heading north on the highway
living in the Midwest	west of the city
Easterners, Southerners	western Nevada, southern Indiana

Specific regions	**General references**
going to the Middle East	the northern part of the United States
from the East Coast	the east side of the street

3.09 Departments, Divisions, and Committees. Capitalize the names of departments, divisions, or committees within your own organization. Outside your organization capitalize only *specific* department, division, or committee names:

The inquiry was addressed to the *Legal Department* in our *Consumer Products Division*.

John was appointed to the *Employee Benefits Committee*.

Send your résumé to their *human resources division*.

A *planning committee* will be named shortly.

3.10 Governmental Terms. Do not capitalize the words *federal, government, nation,* or *state* unless they are part of a specific title:

Unless *federal* support can be secured, the *state* project will be abandoned.

The *Federal Deposit Insurance Corporation* protects depositors from bank failure.

3.11 Product Names. Capitalize product names only when they refer to trademarked items. Except in advertising, common names following manufacturers' names are not capitalized:

Magic Marker	Dell computer
Kleenex tissues	Swingline stapler
Q-tips	3M diskettes
Levi 501 jeans	Sony dictation machine
DuPont Teflon	Canon camera

3.12 Literary Titles. Capitalize the principal words in the titles of books, magazines, newspapers, articles, movies, plays, songs, poems, and reports. Do *not* capitalize articles (*a, an, the*), short conjunctions (*and, but, or, nor*), and prepositions of fewer than four letters (*in, to, by, for*) unless they begin or end the title:

Jackson's *What Job Is for You?* (Capitalize book titles.)

Gant's "Software for the Executive Suite" (Capitalize principal words in article titles.)

"Performance Standards to Go By" (Capitalize article titles.)

"The Improvement of Fuel Economy With Alternative Motors" (Capitalize report titles.)

3.13 Beginning Words. In addition to capitalizing the first word of a complete sentence, capitalize the first word in a quoted sentence, independent phrase, item in an enumerated list, and formal rule or principle following a colon:

The business manager said, "*All* purchases must have requisitions." (Capitalize first word in a quoted sentence.)

Yes, if you agree. (Capitalize an independent phrase.)

Some of the duties of the position are as follows:
1. *Editing* and formatting Word files
2. *Receiving* and routing telephone calls
3. *Verifying* records, reports, and applications (Capitalize items in an enumerated list.)

One rule has been established through the company: *No* smoking is allowed in open offices. (Capitalize a rule following a colon.)

3.14 Celestial Bodies. Capitalize the names of celestial bodies such as *Mars, Saturn,* and *Neptune.* Do not capitalize the terms *earth, sun,* or *moon* unless they appear in a context with other celestial bodies:

Where on *earth* did you find that manual typewriter?

Venus and *Mars* are the closest planets to *Earth*.

3.15 Ethnic References. Capitalize terms that refer to a particular culture, language, or race:

Asian	Hebrew
Caucasian	Indian
Latino	Japanese
Persian	Judeo-Christian

3.16 Seasons. Do not capitalize seasons:

In the *fall* it appeared that *winter* and *spring* sales would increase.

REVIEW EXERCISE M—CAPITALIZATION

In the following sentences correct any errors that you find in capitalization. Underscore any lowercase letter that should be changed to a capital letter. Draw a slash (/) through a capital letter that you wish to change to a lowercase letter. In the space provided, indicate the total number of changes you have made in each sentence. If you make no changes, write *0*. When you finish, compare your responses with those provided. For each item on which you need review, consult the numbered principle shown in parentheses.

5 _____

Example   Bill McAdams, currently /Assistant /Manager in our Personnel department, will be promoted to /Manager of the Employee Services division.

1. The social security act, passed in 1935, established the present system of social security.

2. Our company will soon be moving its operations to the west coast.

3. Marilyn Hunter, m.b.a., received her bachelor's degree from Ohio university in athens.

4. The President of Datatronics, Inc., delivered a speech entitled "Taking off into the future."

5. Please ask your Aunt and your Uncle if they will come to the Attorney's office at 5 p.m.

6. Your reservations are for flight 32 on american airlines leaving from gate 14 at 2:35 p.m.

7. Once we establish an organizing committee, arrangements can be made to rent holmby hall.

8. Bob was enrolled in history, spanish, business communications, and physical education courses.

9. Either the President or the Vice President of the company will make the decision about purchasing xerox copiers.

10. Rules for hiring and firing Employees are given on page 7, line 24, of the Contract.

11. Some individuals feel that american companies do not have the sense of loyalty to their employees that japanese companies do.

12. Where on Earth can we find better workers than Robots?

13. The secretary of state said, "we must protect our domestic economy from Foreign competition."

14. After crossing the sunshine skyway bridge, we drove to Southern Florida for our vacation.

15. All marketing representatives of our company will meet in the empire room of the red lion motor inn.

16. Richard Elkins, ph.d., has been named director of research for spaceage strategies, inc.

17. The special keyboard for the Dell Computer must contain greek symbols for Engineering equations.

18. After she received a master's degree in electrical engineering, Joanne Dudley was hired to work in our product development department.

19. In the Fall our organization will move its corporate headquarters to the franklin building in downtown los angeles.

20. Dean Amador has one cardinal rule: always be punctual.

---

1. Social Security Act (3.01) 3. M.B.A. University Athens (3.01, 3.05) 5. aunt uncle attorney's (3.06e, 3.06g) 7. Holmby Hall (3.01) 9. president vice president Xerox (3.06e, 3.11) 11. American Japanese (3.02) 13. We foreign (3.10, 3.13) 15. Empire Room Red Lion Motor Inn (3.01) 17. computer Greek engineering (3.01, 3.02, 3.11) 19. fall Franklin Building Los Angeles (3.01, 3.03, 3.16)

CUMULATIVE EDITING QUIZ 7

Use proofreading marks (see Appendix B) to correct errors and omissions in the following sentences. All errors must be corrected to receive credit for the sentence. Check with your instructor for the answers.

1. The Manager thinks that you attending the three day seminar is a good idea, however we must find a replacement.

2. We heard that professor watson invited edward peters, president of micropro, inc. to speak to our business law class.

3. Carla Jones a new systems programmer in our accounting department will start monday.

4. After year's of downsizing and restructuring the u.s. has now become one of the worlds most competitive producers.

5. When our company specialized in asian imports our main office was on the west coast.

6. Company's such as amway discovered that there unique door to door selling methods was very successful in japan.

7. If you had given your sony camera to she or I before you got on the roller coaster it might have stayed dry.

8. Tracy recently finished a bachelors degree in accounting, consequently she is submitting many résumé's to companys across the country.

9. The Lopezs moved from San Antonio Texas to Urbana Illinois when mr lopez enrolled at the university of illinois.

10. When we open our office in montréal we will need employees whom are fluent in english and french.

NUMBER STYLE (4.01–4.13)

Usage and custom determine whether numbers are expressed in the form of figures (for example, *5, 9*) or in the form of words (for example, *five, nine*). Numbers expressed as figures are shorter and more easily understood, yet numbers expressed as words are necessary in certain instances. The following guidelines are observed in expressing numbers in written sentences. Numbers that appear on business forms—such as invoices, monthly statements, and purchase orders—are always expressed as figures.

4.01 General Rules

a. The numbers *one* through *ten* are generally written as words. Numbers above *ten* are written as figures:

The bank had a total of *nine* branch offices in *three* suburbs.

All 58 employees received benefits in the *three* categories shown.

A shipment of *45,000* light bulbs was sent from *two* warehouses.

b. Numbers that begin sentences are written as words. If a number beginning a sentence involves more than two words, however, the sentence should be written so that the number does not fall at the beginning.

Fifteen different options were available in the annuity programs.

A total of 156 companies participated in the promotion (not *One hundred fifty-six companies participated in the promotion*).

4.02 Money.
Sums of money $1 or greater are expressed as figures. If a sum is a whole dollar amount, omit the decimal and zeros (whether or not the amount appears in a sentence with additional fractional dollar amounts):

We budgeted *$30* for CDs, but the actual cost was *$37.96*.

On the invoice were items for *$6.10, $8, $33.95*, and *$75*.

Sums less than $1 are written as figures that are followed by the word *cents*:

By shopping carefully, we can save *15 cents* per unit.

4.03 Dates.
In dates, numbers that appear after the name of the month are written as cardinal figures (*1, 2, 3*, etc.). Those that stand alone or appear before the name of a month are written as ordinal figures (*1st, 2nd, 3rd*, etc.):

The Personnel Practices Committee will meet *May 7*.

On the *5th* day of February and again on the *25th*, we placed orders.

In domestic business documents, dates generally take the following form: *January 4, 2007*. An alternative form, used primarily in military and foreign correspondence, begins with the day of the month and omits the comma: *4 January 2007*.

4.04 Clock Time.
Figures are used when clock time is expressed with *a.m.* or *p.m.* Omit the colon and zeros in referring to whole hours. When exact clock time is expressed with the contraction *o'clock*, either figures or words may be used:

Mail deliveries are made at *11 a.m.* and *3:30 p.m.*

At *four* (or *4*) *o'clock* employees begin to leave.

4.05 Addresses and Telephone Numbers

a. Except for the number *one*, house numbers are expressed in figures:

540 Elm Street	17802 Washington Avenue
One Colorado Boulevard	2 Highland Street

b. Street names containing numbers *ten* or lower are written entirely as words. For street names involving numbers greater than *ten*, figures are used:

330 Third Street	3440 Seventh Avenue
6945 East 32 Avenue	4903 West 103 Street

If no compass direction (*North, South, East, West*) separates a house number from a street number, the street number is expressed in ordinal form (*-st, -d, -th*).

256 42d Street	1390 11th Avenue

c. Telephone numbers are expressed with figures. When used, the area code is placed in parentheses preceding the telephone number:

Please call us at *(818) 347-0551* to place an order.

Mr. Sims asked you to call *(619) 554-8923*, Ext. 245, after 10 a.m.

4.06 Related Numbers. Numbers are related when they refer to similar items in a category within the same reference. All related numbers should be expressed as the largest number is expressed. Thus if the largest number is greater than *ten*, all the numbers should be expressed in figures:

Only *5* of the original *25* applicants completed the processing. (Related numbers require figures.)

The *two* plans affected *34* employees working in *three* sites. (Unrelated numbers use figures and words.)

Exxon Oil operated *86* rigs, of which *6* were rented. (Related numbers require figures.)

The company hired *three* accountants, *one* customer service representative, and *nine* sales representatives. (Related numbers under ten use words.)

4.07 Consecutive Numbers. When two numbers appear consecutively and both modify a following noun, generally express the first number in words and the second in figures. If, however, the first number cannot be expressed in one or two words, place it in figures also (*120 37-cent* stamps). Do not use commas to separate the figures.

Historians divided the era into *four 25-year* periods. (Use word form for the first number and figure form for the second.)

We ordered *ten 30-page* color brochures. (Use word form for the first number and figure form for the second.)

Did the manager request *150 100-watt* bulbs? (Use figure form for the first number since it would require more than two words.)

4.08 Periods of Time. Seconds, minutes, days, weeks, months, and years are treated as any other general number. Numbers above ten are written in figure form. Numbers below ten are written in word form unless they represent a business concept such as a discount rate, interest rate, or warranty period.

This business was incorporated over *50* years ago. (Use figures for a number above ten.)

It took *three* hours to write this short report. (Use words for a number under ten.)

The warranty period is limited to *2* years. (Use figures for a business term.)

4.09 Ages. Ages are generally expressed in word form unless the age appears immediately after a name or is expressed in exact years and months:

At the age of *twenty-one*, Elizabeth inherited the business.

Wanda Tharp, *37*, was named acting president.

At the age of *4 years and 7 months*, the child was adopted.

4.10 Round Numbers. Round numbers are approximations. They may be expressed in word or figure form, although figure form is shorter and easier to comprehend:

About *600* (or *six hundred*) stock options were sold.

It is estimated that *1,000* (or *one thousand*) people will attend.

For ease of reading, round numbers in the millions or billions should be expressed with a combination of figures and words:

At least *1.5 million* readers subscribe to the ten top magazines.

Deposits in money market accounts totaled more than *$115 billion*.

4.11 Weights and Measurements. Weights and measurements are expressed with figures:

The new deposit slip measures *2* by *6 inches.*

Her new suitcase weighed only *2 pounds 4 ounces.*

Toledo is *60 miles* from Detroit.

4.12 Fractions. Simple fractions are expressed as words. Complex fractions may be written either as figures or as a combination of figures and words:

Over *two thirds* of the stockholders voted.

This microcomputer will execute the command in *1 millionth* of a second. (A combination of words and numbers is easier to comprehend.)

She purchased a *one-fifth* share in the business.*

4.13 Percentages and Decimals. Percentages are expressed with figures that are followed by the word *percent.* The percent sign (%) is used only on business forms or in statistical presentations:

We had hoped for a *7 percent* interest rate, but we received a loan at *8 percent.*

Over *50 percent* of the residents supported the plan.

Decimals are expressed with figures. If a decimal expression does not contain a whole number (an integer) and does not begin with a zero, a zero should be placed before the decimal point:

The actuarial charts show that *1.74* out of 1,000 people will die in any given year.

Inspector Norris found the setting to be *.005* inch off. (Decimal begins with a zero and does not require a zero before the decimal point.)

Considerable savings will accrue if the unit production cost is reduced *0.1* percent. (A zero is placed before a decimal that neither contains a whole number nor begins with a zero.)

Quick Chart—Expression of Numbers

Use Words	Use Figures
Numbers *ten* and under	Numbers *11* and over
Numbers at beginning of sentence	Money
Ages	Dates
Fractions	Addresses and telephone numbers
	Weights and measurements
	Percentages and decimals

REVIEW EXERCISE N—NUMBER STYLE

Circle *a* or *b* to indicate the preferred number style. Assume that these numbers appear in business correspondence. When you finish, compare your responses with those provided. For each item on which you need review, consult the numbered principle shown in parentheses.

1. (a) 2 alternatives   (b) two alternatives
2. (a) Seventh Avenue   (b) 7th Avenue
3. (a) sixty sales reps   (b) 60 sales reps
4. (a) November ninth   (b) November 9

---

*Note: Fractions used as adjectives require hyphens.

5. (a) forty dollars   (b) $40
6. (a) on the 23rd of May   (b) on the twenty-third of May
7. (a) at 2:00 p.m.   (b) at 2 p.m.
8. (a) 4 two-hundred-page books   (b) four 200-page books
9. (a) at least 15 years ago   (b) at least fifteen years ago
10. (a) 1,000,000 viewers   (b) 1 million viewers
11. (a) twelve cents   (b) 12 cents
12. (a) a sixty-day warranty   (b) a 60-day warranty
13. (a) ten percent interest rate   (b) 10 percent interest rate
14. (a) 4/5 of the voters   (b) four fifths of the voters
15. (a) the rug measures four by six   (b) the rug measures 4 by 6 feet
        feet
16. (a) about five hundred people   (b) about 500 people attended
        attended
17. (a) at eight o'clock   (b) at 8 o'clock
18. (a) located at 1 Wilshire Boulevard   (b) located at One Wilshire Boulevard
19. (a) three computers for twelve people   (b) three computers for 12 people
20. (a) 4 out of every 100 licenses   (b) four out of every 100 licenses

1. b (4.01a)   3. b (4.01a)   5. b (4.02)   7. b (4.04)   9. a (4.08)   11. b (4.02)   13. b (4.13)
15. b (4.11)   17. a or b (4.04)   19. b (4.06)

CUMULATIVE EDITING QUIZ 8

Use proofreading marks (see Appendix B) to correct errors and omissions in the following sentences. All errors must be corrected to receive credit for the sentence. Check with your instructor for the answers.

1. The president of the U.S. recommended a 30 day cooling off period in the middle east peace negotiations.
2. Please meet at my attorneys office at four p.m. on May 10th to sign our papers of incorporation.
3. A Retail Store at 405 7th avenue had sales of over one million dollars last year.
4. Every new employee must receive their permit to park in lot 5-A or there car will be cited.
5. Mr thompson left three million dollars to be divided among his 4 children rachel, timothy, rebecca and kevin.
6. Most companys can boost profits almost one hundred percent by retaining only 5% more of there current customers.
7. Although the bill for coffee and doughnuts were only three dollars and forty cents Phillip and myself had trouble paying it.
8. Only six of the 19 employees, who filled out survey forms, would have went to hawaii as their vacation choice.
9. Danielles report is more easier to read then david because her's is better organized and has good headings.
10. At mcdonald's we devoured 4 big macs 3 orders of french fries and 5 coca colas for lunch.

CONFUSING WORDS

accede:	to agree or consent
exceed:	over a limit
accept:	to receive
except:	to exclude; (prep) but
adverse:	opposing; antagonistic
averse:	unwilling; reluctant
advice:	suggestion, opinion
advise:	to counsel or recommend
affect:	to influence
effect:	(n) outcome, result; (v) to bring about, to create
all ready:	prepared
already:	by this time
all right:	satisfactory
alright:	unacceptable variant spelling
altar:	structure for worship
alter:	to change
appraise:	to estimate
apprise:	to inform
ascent:	(n) rising or going up
assent:	(v) to agree or consent
assure:	to promise
ensure:	to make certain
insure:	to protect from loss
capital:	(n) city that is seat of government; wealth of an individual; (adj) chief
capitol:	building that houses state or national lawmakers
cereal:	breakfast food
serial:	arranged in sequence
cite:	to quote; to summon
site:	location
sight:	a view; to see
coarse:	rough texture
course:	a route; part of a meal; a unit of learning
complement:	that which completes
compliment:	(n) praise, flattery; (v) to praise or flatter
conscience:	regard for fairness
conscious:	aware
council:	governing body
counsel:	(n) advice, attorney; (v) to give advice
credible:	believable
creditable:	good enough for praise or esteem; reliable
desert:	arid land; to abandon
dessert:	sweet food
device:	invention or mechanism
devise:	to design or arrange
disburse:	to pay out
disperse:	to scatter widely

elicit:	to draw out
illicit:	unlawful
envelop:	(v) to wrap, surround, or conceal
envelope:	(n) a container for a written message
every day:	each single day
everyday:	ordinary
farther:	a greater distance
further:	additional
formally:	in a formal manner
formerly:	in the past
grate:	(v) to reduce to small particles; to cause irritation; (n) a frame of crossed bars blocking a passage
great:	(adj) large in size; numerous; eminent or distinguished
hole:	an opening
whole:	complete
imply:	to suggest indirectly
infer:	to reach a conclusion
lean:	(v) to rest against; (adj) not fat
lien:	(n) a legal right or claim to property
liable:	legally responsible
libel:	damaging written statement
loose:	not fastened
lose:	to misplace
miner:	person working in a mine
minor:	a lesser item; person under age
patience:	calm perseverance
patients:	people receiving medical treatment
personal:	private, individual
personnel:	employees
plaintiff:	(n) one who initiates a lawsuit
plaintive:	(adj) expressive of suffering or woe
populace:	(n) the masses; population of a place
populous:	(adj) densely populated
precede:	to go before
proceed:	to continue
precedence:	priority
precedents:	events used as an example
principal:	(n) capital sum; school official; (adj) chief
principle:	rule of action
stationary:	immovable

stationery:	writing material	*to:*	a preposition; the sign of the infinitive
than:	conjunction showing comparison	*too:*	an adverb meaning "also" or "to an excessive extent"
then:	adverb meaning "at that time"	*two:*	a number
their:	possessive form of *they*	*waiver:*	abandonment of a claim
there:	at that place or point	*waver:*	to shake or fluctuate
they're:	contraction of *they are*		

160 FREQUENTLY MISSPELLED WORDS

absence	desirable	independent	prominent
accommodate	destroy	indispensable	qualify
achieve	development	interrupt	quantity
acknowledgment	disappoint	irrelevant	questionnaire
across	dissatisfied	itinerary	receipt
adequate	division	judgment	receive
advisable	efficient	knowledge	recognize
analyze	embarrass	legitimate	recommendation
annually	emphasis	library	referred
appointment	emphasize	license	regarding
argument	employee	maintenance	remittance
automatically	envelope	manageable	representative
bankruptcy	equipped	manufacturer	restaurant
becoming	especially	mileage	schedule
beneficial	evidently	miscellaneous	secretary
budget	exaggerate	mortgage	separate
business	excellent	necessary	similar
calendar	exempt	nevertheless	sincerely
canceled	existence	ninety	software
catalog	extraordinary	ninth	succeed
changeable	familiar	noticeable	sufficient
column	fascinate	occasionally	supervisor
committee	feasible	occurred	surprise
congratulate	February	offered	tenant
conscience	fiscal	omission	therefore
conscious	foreign	omitted	thorough
consecutive	forty	opportunity	though
consensus	fourth	opposite	through
consistent	friend	ordinarily	truly
control	genuine	paid	undoubtedly
convenient	government	pamphlet	unnecessarily
correspondence	grammar	permanent	usable
courteous	grateful	permitted	usage
criticize	guarantee	pleasant	using
decision	harass	practical	usually
deductible	height	prevalent	valuable
defendant	hoping	privilege	volume
definitely	immediate	probably	weekday
dependent	incidentally	procedure	writing
describe	incredible	profited	yield

KEY TO GRAMMAR/MECHANICS CHECKUPS

CHAPTER 1

1. companies (1.05e)   2. Saturdays (1.05a)   3. cities (1.05e)
4. turkeys (1.05d)   5. inventories (1.05e)   6. Bushes (1.05b)
7. 2000s (1.05g)   8. editors in chief (1.05f)   9. complexes
(1.05b)   10. counties (1.05e)   11. Cassidys (1.05a)
12. C (1.05d)   13. liabilities (1.05e)   14. C (1.05h)
15. runners-up (1.05f)

CHAPTER 2

1. she (1.08b)   2. his (1.09b)   3. him (1.08c)   4. whom (1.08j)
5. hers (1.08d)   6. me (1.08c)   7. I (1.08a)   8. yours (1.08d)
9. whoever (1.08j)   10. me (1.08i)   11. (108f)   12. us (1.08g)
13. her (1.09c)   14. its (1.09g)   15. his or her (1.09b)

CHAPTER 3

1. *are* for *is* (1.10e)   2. *is* for *are* (1.10c)   3. *was* for *were*
(1.10d)   4. *knows* for *know* (1.10g)   5. *lose* for *loose* (1.15)
6. *are* for *is* (1.10f)   7. C (1.10g)   8. *begun* (1.15b)   9. *seen*
(1.15b)   10. *were* for *was* (1.12)   11. *gone* for *went* (1.15b)
12. b (1.15c)   13. b (1.15c)   14. a (1.15c)   15. b (1.15c)

CHAPTER 4

1. tried-and-true (1.17e)   2. seven-year-old (1.17e)
3. bright (1.17c)   4. quickly (1.17d)   5. by only 5 percent
(1.17f)   6. work-related (1.17e)   7. their (1.17g)   8. spur-of-
the-moment (1.17e)   9. C (1.17e)   10. well-thought-out (1.17e)
11. change-of-address (1.17e)   12. case-by-case (1.17e)
13. were nearer (1.17b)   14. bad (1.17c)   15. smoothly (1.17d)

CHAPTER 5

1. a (1.19d)   2. b. (1.19c)   3. b (1.19d)   4. b (1.19c)   5. b
(1.19a)   6. b (1.18a)   7. b (1.18b)   8. b (1.18c)   9. b (1.18d)
10. b (1.18e)   11. b (1.19a)   12. b (1.19b)   13. b (1.19c)
14. a (1.18b)   15. b (1.19c)

CHAPTER 6

1. (2) think, hand, (2.03)   2. (2) certain, Mr. Nosrati, (2.02)
3. (2) creative, collaborative, (2.01)   4. (0)   5. (1) say, (2.03)
6. (4) McDonough, Georgia, Grand Forks, North Dakota,
(2.04c)   7. (1) way, (2.03)   8. (2) March 23, 2005, (2.04a)

9. (2) Mr. Maslow, Mrs. Kim, (2.01)   10. (4) Industries,
6920 Main Street, Detroit, MI 48201, (2.04b)   11. (2) feels,
nevertheless, (2.03)   12. communication, fairly, (2.01)
13. (1) business, (2.02)   14. (2) Carson, however, (2.03)
14. (4) Hartford, Connecticut, to San Diego, California, (2.04c)

CHAPTER 7

1. (1) Australia (2.06a)   2. (1) world, (2.05)   3. 0 (2.05) 4. (2)
Sanchez, France, (2.06c)   5. (1) imaginative, (2.08)   6. (0)
(2.06c)   7. (2) Manning, Generation, (2.09)   8. (1) weeks,
(2.07)   9. (1) language, (2.06a)   10. successful, (2.07)
11. (2) meetings, plans, (2.01)   12. (3) hired, Monday, June 2,
(2.06a, 2.04a)   13. (1) Sunnyvale, (2.06c)   14. (3) telephone,
Thursday, March 4, (2.06a, 2.04a)   15. (I) times, (2.05)

CHAPTER 8

1. (2) optimism," Powell, (2.14a)   2. (3) Cox, Ph.D., Pam
Rankey, (2.10)   3. (1)   June 2, (2.14b)   4. (0) (2.15)
5. monitor, (2.12)   6. (3) know, work, travel, (2.06a, 2.01)
7. (2) think, however, (2.03)   8. (2) position, Creek-Lea, (2.07,
2.06c)   9. (3) considered, Vegas, Scottsdale, (2.03, 2.01)
10. (2) closely, Friday, (2.06a, 2.11)   11. (2) years, individuals,
(2.07, 2.09)   12. (2) DuBay, week, (2.06, 2.15)   13. (0) (2.06c)
14. (4) weapons, report, companies, more robots, (2.06c, 2.01)
15. (2) fact, unprotected, (2.03, 2.08)

CHAPTER 9

1. (3) less; long-term financing, on the other hand, (2.03,
2.16b)   2. (2) January; therefore, (2.16a)   3. (3) months:
October, November, (2.01, 2.17a)   4. (1) are [delete comma]
(2.17b)   5. (1) money, (2.06a, 2.16b)   6. (3) credit; resort,
however, (2.03, 2.16b)   7. (3) credit: commercial, paper,
(2.01, 2.17a)   8. (9) businesspeople: Lynne Krause,
financial manager, American International Investments;
Patrick Coughlin, comptroller, NationsBank; and Shannon
Daly, legal counsel, (2.16d, 2.17)   9. (1) largest banks, (2.05)
10. (5) charges; for example, average daily balance, adjusted
balance, two-cycle average daily balance, (2.16e. 2.01)
11. (2) rating, loan; (2.06c, 2.16c)   12. (2) Union Bank, to
[delete colon] (2.06a, 2.17b)   13. (2) high; therefore, (2.16)
14. (2) 18 percent, prohibitive; (2.06a, 2.16c)   15. (1)
resources; (2.16b)

CHAPTER 10

1. Sullivan's (2.21)   2. years' (2.20b)   3. weeks' (2.20b)
4. Miller's (2.21)   5. employees' (2.20b)   6. witness's (2.20b)
7. Lisa's (2.22)   8. money's (2.20a)   9. C (2.20a)   10. month's
(2.20a)   11. boss's (2.20b)   12. secretary's (2.20a)
13. C (2.20a)   14. company's (2.20a)   15. businesses' (2.20b)

CHAPTER 11

1. (2) recipients—Peerson—(2.26a)   2. please, Dr. Kerlin, filed
(2.02, 2.23a)   3. figures (see Appendix A) (2.27)   4. (2) "Web
site" (2.28c)   5. (4) Harvard—M.B.A. (2.23b, 2.26c) 6. (2) said,
"Why like?" (2.28f)   7. (4) *The Wall Street Journal* "Oracle's
Study"? (2.28e, 2.28f)   8. (2) states—Oregon—(2.26a)
9. (5) Mr. Francisco M. Arce, Ms. Brenda Marini, and
Dr. Patricia Franzoia? (2.23b, 2.24)   10. (3) "The Meeting"
The Etiquette Advantage in Business (2.28e)   11. (2) "task";
however, (2.16, 2.28f)   12. *speculator* "one changes." (2.28d)
13. (2) "gross." (2.28c)   14. (3) 2 p.m.? (2.23b, 2.24)   15. (3)
Wow! out, haven't you? (2.24, 2.25)

CHAPTER 12

1. (8) United plane Gate 3B Key West International Airport
(3.01, 3.02, 3.07)   2. (6) Japanese international Japanese
economics professor University (3.01, 3.02, 3.04, 3.06d)
3. (3) entrepreneur consulting firm (3.01)   4. (4) psychology
math history English (3.05)   5. (4) Harry Potter Endless Cash
(3.12)   6. (4) Dell Inspiron notebook computer (3.11)   7. (4)
federal government state county (3.10)   8. United States We
foreign (3.01, 3.06c, 3.13)   9. (8) comptroller president board
directors Securities Exchange Commission company (3.01,
3.04, 3.06e)   10. (5) father Death Valley moon stars (3.03,
3.06g, 3.14)   11. (7) marketing director manager ad campaign
wireless phone (3.01, 3.06d, 3.06e, 3.09, 3.11)   12. (7)
spring admissions director Venezuela Colombia Ecuador
students (3.01, 3.06a, 3.16)   13. (4) Park island River Bridge
(3.01, 3.03)   14. (3) Accounting Department master's (3.05,
3.07, 3.09)   15. (5) Figure Chapter Census Bureau English
(3.02, 3.04, 3.07)

CHAPTER 13

1. b (4.01a)   2. a (4.05b)   3. a (4.01a)   4. b (4.03)
5. b (4.02)   6. a (4.03)   7. b (4.04)   8. b (4.07)   9. b (4.08)
10. b (4.10)   11. b (4.02)   12. b (4.08)   13. b (4.12)   14. a
(4.06)   15. a (4.06)

CHAPTER 14

1. b (2.16a)   2. c (2.05)   3. b (2.06)   4. a (2.16a)   5. c (2.15)
6. b (2.16b)   7. b (2.17a)   8. a. (2.20)   9. c (2.16d)
10. b (2.04a)

Endnotes

CHAPTER 1

1. Michael Kinsman, "Are Poor Writing Skills Holding Back Your Career?" *California Job Journal*, 1 February 2004 <http://www.jobjournal.com/article_printer.asp?artid=1039> (Retrieved 16 February 2005); Mary L. Tucker and Anne M. McCarthy, "Presentation Self-Efficacy: Increasing Communication Skills Through Service-Learning," *Journal of Managerial Issues*, Summer 2001, 227–244; A. Cohen, "The Right Stuff," *Sales and Marketing Management* 151, 1999, 15; and Max Messmer, "Skills for a New Millennium," *Strategic Finance*, August 1999, 10–12.

2. Janette Moody, Brent Stewart, and Cynthia Bolt-Lee, "Showcasing the Skilled Business Graduate: Expanding the Tool Kit," *Business Communication Quarterly*, March 2002, 23.

3. "Wanted: Leaders Who Can Lead and Write," *Workforce*, December 1997, 21.

4. Max Messmer, "Enhancing Your Writing Skills," *Strategic Finance*, January 2001, 8. See also Brent Staples, "The Fine Art of Getting It Down on Paper, Fast," *The New York Times*, 15 May, 2005, WK13(L).

5. "Writing Skills Necessary for Employment, Says Big Business," The National Commission on Writing—Press Release, 14 September 2004 <http://www.writingcommission.org/pr/writing_employ.html> (Retrieved 10 May 2005).

6. Ibid.

7. Sam Dillon, "What Corporate America Can't Build: A Sentence," *The New York Times*, 7 December 2004, A1.

8. J. Burgoon, D. Coker, and R. Coker, "Communicative Explanations," *Human Communication Research 12*, 1986, 463–494.

9. Ray Birdwhistell, *Kinesics and Context* (Philadelphia: University of Pennsylvania Press, 1970).

10. William E. Nolen, "Reading People," *Internal Auditor*, April 1995, 48–51.

11. E. T. Hall, *The Hidden Dimension* (Garden City, NY: Doubleday, 1966), 107–122.

12. Helen Wilkie, "Professional Presence," *The Canadian Manager*, Fall 2003, 14, ABI/Inform Database (Retrieved 15 February 2005).

13. Anthony Patrick Carnevale and Susan Carol Stone, *The American Mosaic* (New York: McGraw-Hill, 1995), 160.

14. Lennie Copeland and Lewis Griggs, *Going International* (New York: Penguin Books, 1985), 1.

15. Nancy Rivera Brooks, "Exports Boom Softens Blow of Recession," *The Los Angeles Times*, 29 May 1991, DI.

16. Mitra Toossi, "Labor Force Projections to 2012: The Graying of the U.S. Workforce," *Monthly Labor Review*, February 2004 <http://www.bls.gov/opub/mlr/2004/02/art3full.pdf> (Retrieved 20 February 2005).

17. Anne Fisher, "How You Can Do Better on Diversity," *Fortune*, 15 November 2004, 60.

18. Carnevale and Stone, *The American Mosaic*, 60.

19. Joel Makower, "Managing Diversity in the Workplace," *Business and Society Review*, Winter 1995. See also Terry Lefton, "Bok in the Saddle Again," *Brandweek*, 8 February 1999, 26–31.

20. John H. Bryan, CEO, Sara Lee Corporation, speech before the Corporate Affairs Communications Conference, 21 May 1990, Chicago.

21. Bob Kerrey, reported in "Writing Skills Necessary for Employment, Says Big Business," National Commission on Writing.

22. "What's the Universal Hand Sign for 'I Goofed'?" *Santa Barbara News-Press*, 16 December 1996, D2.

23. Somporn Thapanachai, "Awareness Narrows Cross-Cultural Gap in Thai Management Training Courses," *Bangkok Post, Knight Ridder/Tribune Business News*, 6 October 2003, pITEM0327901, InfoTrac College Edition database (Retrieved 18 February 2005).

24. Makower, "Managing Diversity in the Workplace," 48–54. See also "Reebok International Ltd.," *Black Enterprise*, February 2005, 66.

CHAPTER 2

1. John Berlau, "Ebony's John H. Johnson: How He Went From a Tin-Roof Shack to the Forbes 400," *Investor's Business Daily*, 26 March, 1999, A1. See also "Medal of Freedom Recipient John H. Johnson," <http://www.medaloffreedom.com/JohnHJohnson.htm> (Retrieved 12 May 2005).

2. Berlau.

3. Hugh Hay-Roe, "The Secret of Excess," *Executive Excellence*, January 1995, 20. See also Ed Burghard, quoted in Kevin Ryan's *Write Up the Corporate Ladder* (New York: Amacom, 2003), 217.

4. Vanessa Dean Arnold, "Benjamin Franklin on Writing Well," *Personnel Journal*, August 1986, 17.

5. Mark Bacon, quoted in "Business Writing: One-on-One Speaks Best to the Masses," *Training*, April 1988, 95. See also Elizabeth Danziger, "Communicate Up," *Journal of Accountancy*, February 1998, 67.

6. Paula J. Pomerenke, "A Short Introduction to the Plain English Movement," *Issues in Writing* 10:1, 1999, 30.

CHAPTER 3

1. Max Messmer, "Enhancing Your Writing Skills," *Strategic Finance*, January 2001, 8–10.

2. Robert W. Goddard, "Communication: Use Language Effectively," *Personnel Journal*, April 1989, 32.

3. Adapted from Roger N. Conaway and Thomas L. Fernandez, "Ethical Preferences Among Business Leaders: Implications for Business Schools," *Business Communication Quarterly*, March 2000, 23–38.

CHAPTER 4

1. Kevin Ryan, *Write Up the Corporate Ladder* (New York: Amacom, 2003), 51.

2. Louise Lague, *People* Magazine editor, interview with Mary Ellen Guffey, 5 February 1992.

CHAPTER 5

1. Michael D. Eisner, "Enlightened Communication," *Vital Speeches*, 15 July 2000, 593.

2. Dianna Booher, *E-Writing* (New York: Pocket Books, 2001), 148.

3. "Market Numbers Quarterly, Update, Q1, 2005," *The Radicati Group, Inc.* <http://www.radicati.com> (Retrieved 23 April 2005).

4. American Management Association, "2003 E-Mail Rules, Policies and Practices Survey" <http://www.amanet.org/research/pdfs/Email_Policies_Practices.pdf> (Retrieved 2 May 2005).

5. Kevin Maney, "How the Big Names Tame E-Mail," *USA Today*, 24 July 2003, 1A.

6. Eisner, "Enlightened Communication."

7. "E-Mail Becoming Crime's New Smoking Gun," *USA Today Marketplace* <http://www.usatoday.com/tech/news/2002-08-15> (Retrieved 25 April 2005); and Jim Carroll, "What Evil Lurks in E-Mail?" *CA Magazine*, June/July 2003, 16.

8. Randall Smith, "Quattrone Found Guilty on 3 Counts in Big U.S. Win," *The Wall Street Journal*, 4 May 2004, A1; Stephen Baker, "A Painful Lesson: E-Mail Is Forever," *BusinessWeek*, 21 March 2005, 36.

9. Leslie Helm, "The Digital Smoking Gun," *Los Angeles Times*, 16 June 1994, EI.

10. Nicholas Varchaver, "The Perils of E-Mail," *Fortune*, 3 February 2003 <http://www.fortune.com/fortune/technology/articles/0,15114,418678,00.html> (Retrieved 1 May 2005).

11. Based on Douglas P. Shuit, "Sound the Retreat," *Workforce Management*, September 2003, 39–40.

12. HRM Guide Network, "2003 E-Mail Survey Reveals: One in Five Companies Has Fired an Employee for E-Mail Abuse,"

HRMGuide.com <http://www.harmguide.com/communication/e-mail-use.htm> (Retrieved 2 May 2005).

13. "E-Mail Abuse Takes Up More Than Employee Time," *Fair Employment Practices Guidelines*, 15 April 2003, 8. See also Sushil K. Sharma and Jatinder N. D. Gupta, "Improving Workers' Productivity and Reducing Internet Abuse," *The Journal of Computer Information Systems*, Winter 2003/2004, 74.

14. Eleena de Lisser, "One-Click Commerce: What People Do Now to Goof Off at Work," *The Wall Street Journal*, 24 September 1999, B1.

15. Michael J. McCarthy, "Virtual Morality: A New Workplace Quandary," *The Wall Street Journal*, 21 October 1999, B1, B4.

CHAPTER 6

1. Malcolm Forbes, "How to Write a Business Letter," International Paper Company, reprinted in *Strategies for Business and Technical Writing*, 4e, Kevin Harty, ed. (Boston: Allyn and Bacon, 1999), 108.

2. Marcia Mascolini, "Another Look at Teaching the External Negative Message," *The Bulletin of the Association of Business Communication*, June 1994, 46; Robert J. Aalberts and Lorraine A. Krajewski, "Claim and Adjustment Letters," *The Bulletin of the Association for Business Communication*, September 1987, 2.

3. Ameeta Patel and Lamar Reinsch, "Companies *Can* Apologize: Corporate Apologies and Legal Liability," *Business Communication Quarterly*, March 2003, 9.

4. Moshe Davidow, "Organizational Responses to Customer Complaints: What Works and What Doesn't," *Journal of Service Research*, February 2003, 225+; Elizabeth Blackburn Brockman and Kelly Belanger, "You-Attitude and Positive Emphasis: Testing Received Wisdom in Business Communication," *The Bulletin of the Association for Business Communication*, June 1993, 1–5; C. Goodwin and I. Ross, "Consumer Evaluations of Responses to Complaints: What's Fair and Why," *Journal of Consumer Marketing*, 7, 1990, 39–47; Marcia Mascolini, "Another Look at Teaching the External Negative Message," *The Bulletin of the Association for Business Communication*, June 1994, 46.

5. Bob Leduc, "Complaining Customers Are Good for Business" Small Office Home Office SOHO <http://www.soho.org/Marketing_Articles/Complaining_Customers_Are_Good.htm> (Retrieved 10 May 2005).

6. Margaret H. Caddell, "Is Letter Writing Dead?" *OfficePro*, November/December, 2003, 22.

7. Based on McDonald's Corporation "Waste Management" <http://www.mcdonalds.com/corp/values/socialrespons/enviroment/waste_management.html> (Retrieved 12 May 2005); Elizabeth Crowley, "EarthShell Saw Big Macs and Big Bucks-Got Big Woes—Environmentally Safe Sandwich Containers for McDonald's Haven't Been Easy to Make," *The Wall Street Journal*, 10 April 2001; Frank Edward Allen, "McDonald's to Reduce Waste in Plan Developed With Environmental Group," *The Wall Street Journal*, 17 April 1991, B1; Martha T. Moore, "McDonald's Trashes Sandwich Boxes," *USA Today*, 2 November 1990, 1; Michael Parrish, "McDonald's to Do Away With Foam Packages," *Los Angeles Times*, 2 November 1990, 1; and Mark Hamstra, "McD Supersizes Efforts to Cut Down on Costs," *Nation's Restaurant News*, 29 June 1998, 1, 60.

8. Based on Mark J. Scarp, "Hotel to Cease Pigeon Poisoning," *Scottsdale Tribune*, 28 October 1995.

CHAPTER 7

1. René Nourse, vice president, Investments, Prudential Securities Incorporated, interview with Mary Ellen Guffey, 16 January 1995.

2. "How to Ask For—And Get—What You Want!" *Supervision*, February 1990, 11.

3. Dean Rieck, "Great Letters and Why They Work," *Direct Marketing*, June 1998, 20–24. See also John R. Graham, "Improving Direct Mail," *Agency Sales*, January 2002, 47–50.

4. Ernest W. Nicastro, "Deadly Sales Letter Mistakes," *Agency Sales*, March 2000, 41–43.

5. Dennis Chambers, *The Agile Manager's Guide to Writing to Get Action* (Bristol, VT: Velocity Press, 1998), 86.

6. Kevin McLaughlin, "Words of Wisdom," *Entrepreneur*, October 1990, 101.

7. Based on Virginia Heffernan, "For the Age of Do-It-Yourself Finance, She Wrote the Book(s) and the Programs," *The New York Times*, 17 June 2005, p. B-29.

8. Based on "PDA-Based Software Allows Realtors to Show Homes 'Practically Anywhere'" <http://www.pdare.com/vertical/articles/article-460.xml> (Retrieved 20 June 2005); Michael Antoniak, "Buyer's Guide: PDA Software," *Realtor Magazine Online*, 1 May 2003; and Frank Nelson, "Real Estate Agents' Best Friend," *Santa Barbara News-Press*, 6 June 2004, F1.

9. Based on Debbie D. DuFrene and Carol M. Lehman, "Persuasive Appeal for Clean Language," *Business Communication Quarterly*, March 2002, 48–55. With permission from the Association for Business Communication.

CHAPTER 8

1. Cathy Dial, former manager, Consumer Affairs, Frito-Lay, interview with Mary Ellen Guffey, 26 November 1996.

2. Mohan R. Limaye, "Further Conceptualization of Explanations in Negative Messages," *Business Communication Quarterly*, June 1997, 46.

3. "Filene's Basement Bans 2 Shoppers Who Returned Too Much Stuff," *USA Today*, 14 July 2003, 7B.

4. "2004 Survey on Workplace E-Mail and IM Reveals Unmanaged Risks," *The ePolicy Institute* <http://www.epolicyinstitute.com/survey/> (Retrieved 2 July 2005).

5. Sandra Swanson, "Employers Take a Closer Look," *InformationWeek*, 15 July 2002, 40.

6. Elizabeth A. McCord, "The Business Writer, the Law, and Routine Business Communication: A Legal and Rhetorical Analysis," *Journal of Business and Technical Communication*, April 1991, 183.

7. Ibid.

8. Douglas P. Shuit, "Do It Right or Risk Getting Burned," *Workforce Management*, September 2003, 80.

9. Maryann Hammers, "Breaking (Bad) News," *Shape*, April 2004, 34.

10. "Letters to Lands' End," *February 1991 Catalog* (Dodgeville, WI: Lands' End, 1991), 100.

11. Jeff Mowatt, "Breaking Bad News to Customers," *Agency Sales*, February 2002, 30; and Elizabeth M. Dorn, "Case Method Instruction in the Business Writing Classroom," *Business Communication Quarterly*, March 1999, 51–52.

12. Malcolm Forbes, "How to Write a Business Letter," International Paper Company, reprinted in *Strategies for Business and Technical Writing*, 4th ed., Kevin Harty, ed. (Boston: Allyn and Bacon, 1999), 108.

13. Sandra O'Neal, principal, Towers Perrin (global consulting and human resources firm), as quoted in "Need to Deliver Bad News? How & Why to Tell It Like It Is," *HR Focus*, November 2003, 3.

14. Michael Granberry, "Lingerie Chain Fined $100,000 for Gift Certificates," *Los Angeles Times*, 14 November 1992, D3.

15. Elizabeth M. Dorn, "Case Method Instruction in the Business Writing Classroom," *Business Communication Quarterly*, March 1999, 51–52.

16. Based on Gene Sloan, "Under 21? Carnival Says Cruise Is Off," *USA Today*, 29 November 1996; Jill Jordan Sieder, "Full Steam Ahead: Carnival Cruise Line Makes Boatloads of Money by Selling Fun," *U.S. News & World Report*, 16 October 1995, 72; and "Fun Ship Fleet," <http://www.carnival.com/CMS/Ships/FunShips.aspx> (Retrieved 2 July 2005).

17. Andrew Ross Sorkin, "J. Crew Web Goof Results in Discount," *The New York Times*, 11 November 1999, D3.

18. Based on Oren Harari, "The POWER of Complaints," *Management Review*, July-August, 1999, 31.

19. Based on "SUV Surprise," *The Wall Street Journal*, 15 June 2004, W7.

20. Andrew Osborn, "New From McDonald's: The McAfrika Burger (Don't Tell the 12m Starving)," *The Guardian*, 24 August, 2002.

21. Tom Cahill, "Bear Stearns Tells Employees Dress Up—Dot Com Is Over," Bloomberg News Service, 17 September, 2002; "Bear Stearns Reinstates Formal Dress Code," Reuters Business Report, 21 September, 2002; "Dress Codes: 'Business Conservative' Is Making a Comeback," *HR Briefing*, 1 March 2003, 7; and Ellen Gregg, "What Do You Mean 'Business Casual'?" *Office Solutions*, March/April 2004, 42.

22. Jeanette W. Gilsdorf, "Metacommunication Effects on International Business Negotiating in China," *Business Communication Quarterly*, June 1997, 27.

23. Linda Beamer and Iris Varner, *Intercultural Communication in the Global Workplace* (New York: McGraw-Hill Irwin, 2001), 141.

CHAPTER 9

1. *Top 50 Leadership Quotes for Highly Effective Leaders* <http://www.leadership-tools.com/leadership-quotes.html> (Retrieved 29 May 2005).

CHAPTER 10

1. Douglas Harbrecht, "Google's Larry Page: Good Ideas Still Get Funded," *BusinessWeek Online*, 13 March 2001 <http://www.businessweek.com/bwdaily/dnflash/mar2001/nf20010313_831.htm> (Retrieved 10 June 2005).

2. Herman Holtz, *Proven Proposal Strategies to Win More Business* (Chicago: Upstart Publishing Company/Dearborn Publishing Group, 1998), 104–107.

3. Mary Piecewicz, Hewlett-Packard proposal manager, interview with Mary Ellen Guffey, 12 January 1999.

4. Kimberly A. Killmer and Nicole B. Koppel, "So Much Information, So Little Time: Evaluating Web Resources With Search Engines," *T.H.E. Journal (Technological Horizons in Education)*, August 2002, 21.

5. Leslie Brooks Suzukamo, "Search Engines Become Popular for Fact-Finding, Game Playing," *Knight-Ridder/Tribune News Service*, 3 July 2002, pK 6110.

6. Wikipedia, <http://en.wikipedia.org/wiki/Blog> (Retrieved 13 June 2005).

7. William M. Bulkeley, "Marketers Scan Blogs for Brand Insights," *The Wall Street Journal*, 23 June 2005, B1.

8. Benjamin Pimentel, "Writing the Codes on Blogs: Companies Figure Out What's OK, What's Not in Online Realm," *San Francisco Chronicle*, 13 June 2005, E1.

9. "A Growing Tide of Blogs," *BusinessWeek Online*, 14 April 2005 <http://www.businessweek.com/technology/tech_stats/bloggrowth050414.htm> (Retrieved 13 June 2005).

10. Stephen Baker and Heather Green, "Blogs Will Change Your Business," *BusinessWeek Online*, 2 May 2005. <http://www.businessweek.com/magazine/content/05_18/b3931001_mz001.htm> (Retrieved 13 June 2005).

11. Ibid.

12. "Philosophy," The Academy of NikeFree, <http://www.nike.com/nikefree/usa/index.jhtml#howitworks> (Retrieved 14 June 2005).

13. Jerry Large, "Jayson Blair and Jack Kelley Are Journalism's Unbelievable Problem," *The Seattle Times*, 29 March 2004, K1904; and Gabriel Snyder, "Journalists Devour Their Own in Eager Scrutiny," *Variety*, 19 January 2004, 3.

14. Writing Tutorial Services, Indiana University, "Plagiarism: What It Is and How to Recognize and Avoid It" <http://www.indiana.edu/~wts/pamphlets/plagiarism.shtml> (Retrieved 20 June 2005).

15. Gerald J. Alred, Walter E. Olin, and Charles T. Brusaw, *The Professional Writer* (New York: St. Martin's Press, 1992), 78.

16. Based on Karen S. Sterkel, "Integrating Intercultural Communication and Report Writing in the Communication Class," *The Bulletin of the Association for Business Communication*, September 1988, 14–16.

CHAPTER 11

1. Woopidoo Quotations <http://www.woopidoo.com/business_quotes/authors/alan-greenspan-quotes.htm> (Retrieved 27 June 2005).

2. Shearlean Duke, "E-Mail: Essential in Media Relations, But No Replacement for Face-to-Face Communication," *Public Relations Quarterly*, Winter, 2001, 19; Lisa M. Flaherty, Kevin J. Pearce, and Rebecca B. Rubin, "Internet and Face-to-Face Communication: Not Functional Alternatives," *Communication Quarterly*, Summer 1998, 250.

3. Aimee L. Drolet and Michael W. Morris, "Rapport in Conflict Resolution: Accounting for How Face-to-Face Contact Fosters Mutual Cooperation in Mixed-Motive Conflicts," *Journal of Experimental Social Psychology*, January 2000, 26.

4. Jean Miculka, *Speaking for Success* (Cincinnati: South-Western, 1999), 19.

5. Motivational and Inspirational Corner <http://www.motivational-inspirational-corner.com/getquote.html?startrow=11&categoryid=207> (Retrieved 27 June 2005).

6. "Dull Meeting? I'd Rather See the Dentist," International News, *Personnel Today*, 19 October 2004.

7. Kris Maher, "The Jungle: Focus on Recruitment, Pay and Getting Ahead," *The Wall Street Journal*, 13 January 2004, B6.

8. Morris Schechtman, as quoted in Hal Lancaster, "Learning Some Ways to Make Meetings Less Awful," *The Wall Street Journal*, 26 May 1998, B1.

9. ThinkExist.com <http://en.thinkexist.com/quotation/by_failing_to_prepare-you_are_preparing_to_fail/199949.html> (Retrieved 27 June 2005).

10. John C. Bruening, "There's Good News About Meetings," *Managing Office Technology*, July 1996, 24–25.

11. Christopher Marquis, "Doing Well and Doing Good," *The New York Times*, 13 July 2003, BU 2.

12. 3M Meeting Network, "Nonverbal Messages in Meetings" <http://www.3m.com/meetingnetwork/readingroom/meetingguide_nonverbal.html> (Retrieved 27 June 2005).

13. Kirsten Schabacker, "A Short, Snappy Guide to Meaningful Meetings," *Working Women*, June 1991, 73.

14. Cheryl Hamilton with Cordell Parker, *Communicating for Success*, 6e (Belmont, CA: Wadsworth, 2001), 311–312.

15. Joan Burge, "Telephone Safety Protocol for Today," *The National Public Accountant*, June 2002, 35.

16. Cellular Online, "Latest Mobile, GSM, Global, Handset, Base Station, & Regional Cellular Statistics" <http://www.cellular.co.za/stats/stats-main.htm> (Retrieved 28 June 2005).

17. Scott Lanman, "Mobile-Phone Users Become a Majority," *San Francisco Chronicle*, 9 July 2005, C1.

18. Gattine, Kara, "Don't Kill the Instant Messenger," SearchExchange.com, 2 March 2004 <http://searchexchange.techtarget.com/originalContent/0,289142,sid43_gci953145,00.html> (Retrieved 29 June 2005).

19. B. L. Ochman, "Best Business Blog Examples and Why It's High Time to Think About a Blog for Your Company," What'sNextOnline.com <http://www.whatsnextonline.com/wno/ newsletter96.cfm> (Retrieved 10 July 2005).

20. Bob Tedeschi, "Blogging While Browsing, but Not Buying," *The New York Times*, 4 July 2005.

21. Dianna Booher, "Resolving Conflict," *Executive Excellence*, May 1999, 5.

22. Gerald L. Wilson, *Groups in Context*, 4e (New York: McGraw-Hill, 1996), 299–300.

23. Deborah DeVoe, "Don't Let Conflict Get You Off Course," *InfoWorld*, 9 August 1999, 69.

24. DeVoe, "Don't Let Conflict," 70.

25. Nora Wood, "Singled Out," *Incentive*, July 1998, 20–23.

CHAPTER 12

1. Hal Lancaster, "Practice and Coaching Can Help You Improve Um, Y'Know, Speeches," *The Wall Street Journal*, 9 January 1996, B1.

2. Catherine M. Petrini, "A Survival Guide to Public Speaking," *Training & Development*, September 1990, 15.

3. Jeff Olson, *The Agile Manager's Guide to Giving Great Presentations* (Bristol, VT: Velocity Printing, 1999), 8.

4. Painless Public Speaking <http://www.publicspeaking.com.au/humour.htm> (Retrieved 6 June 2005).

5. PBS, Floor Speeches, "Vice President Al Gore Speaks at the Democratic National Convention," 28 August 1996 <http://www.pbs.org/newshour/convention96/floor_speeches/gore_8-28.html> (Retrieved 6 June 2005).

6. Wharton Applied Research Center, "A Study of the Effects of the Use of Overhead Transparencies on Business Meetings, Final Report," cited in "Short, Snappy Guide to Meaningful Presentations," *Working Woman*, June 1991, 73.

7. Stanford communications professor Clifford Nass quoted in Tad Simons, "When Was the Last Time PowerPoint Made You Sing?" *Presentations*, July 2001, 6. See also Geoffrey Nunberg, "The Trouble With PowerPoint," *Fortune*, 20 December 1999, 330–334.

8. Simons, "When Was the Last Time," 6.

9. "How to Avoid the 7 Deadly Sins of PowerPoint," *Yearbook of Experts News Release Wire*, 30 July 2004, (Retrieved 11 October 2004 from LexisNexis Academic database).

10. Becky Bergman, "Saving Time and Money With Web Conferencing," *Silicon Valley/San Jose Business Journal*, 27 December 2004, <http://www.bizjournals.com/sanjose/stories/2004/12/27/focus1.html?page=2> (Retrieved 24 July 2005).

11. John Ellwood, "Less PowerPoint, More Powerful Points," *The Times (London)*, 4 August 2004, 6.

12. Dianna Booher, *Speak With Confidence: Powerful Presentations That Inform, Inspire and Persuade* (New York: McGraw Hill, 2003).

13. Peter Schneider, "Scenes From a Marriage: Observations on the Daimler-Chrysler Merger From a German Living in America," *The New York Times Magazine*, 12 August, 2001, 47.

14. Ronald E. Dulek, John S. Fielden, and John S. Hill, "International Communication: An Executive Primer," *Business Horizons*, January/February 1991, 23. See also Susan J. Marks, "Nurturing Global Workplace Connections," *Workforce*, September 2001, 76+.

15. Dulek, Fielden, and Hill, "International Communication," 22.

16. Michael Jackson, quoted in "Garbage In, Garbage Out," *Consumer Reports*, December 1992, 755.

CHAPTER 13

1. Woopidoo Quotations <http://www.woopidoo.com/business_quotes/authors/bc-forbes-quotes.html> (Retrieved 3 August 2005).

2. Julie Jansen, "What's Keeping You From Changing Careers?" <http://www.careerjournal.com/jobhunting/change/20030225-jansen.html>

(Retrieved 26 July 2005). Article adapted from Jansen's book, *I Don't Know What I Want, But I Know It's Not This: A Step-by-Step Guide to Finding Gratifying Work* (New York: Penguin Books, 2003).

3. J. H. Boyett and D. P. Snyder, "Twenty-First Century Workplace Trends." *On the Horizon*, 1998, *6*(2), 1, 4–9 <http://horizon.unc.edu/ projects/seminars/OTH/Boyett-Snyder.html> (Retrieved 26 July 2005).

4. Brian O'Connell, *The Career Survival Guide* (New York: McGraw-Hill, 2003), 11–12.

5. Anne Kates Smith, "Charting Your Own Course," *U.S. News & World Report*, 6 November 2000, 57.

6. "The Hot List: Top Job Boards," *Workforce Management*, June 2004, 28.

7. Lorraine Farquharson, "Technology Special Report: The Best Way to Find a Job," *The Wall Street Journal*, 15 September 2003, R8.

8. Pam Nixon, "The Truth Behind Online Job Hunting," CareerJournal.com, 17 April 2002 <http://www.careerjournal.com/jobhunting/usingnet/ 20020417-needleman.html> (Retrieved 26 July 2005).

9. "HotJobs Move Seen As Threat to Paid Listings," *Workforce Management*, August 2005, 16.

10. Professor Mark Granovetter, quoted in Susan J. Wells, "Many Jobs on Web," *The New York Times*, 12 March 1998, A12.

11. George Crosby of the Human Resources Network, as quoted in Hal Lancaster, "When Taking a Tip From a Job Network, Proceed With Caution," *The Wall Street Journal*, 7 February 1995, B1.

12. "Résumé Styles: Chronological Versus Functional? Best-Selling Author Richard H. Beatty Joins in the Résumé Discussion," *Internet Wire*, 5 November 2002, p. 1008309u4205.

13. Elizabeth Blackburn-Brockman and Kelly Belanger, "One Page or Two?: A National Study of CPA Recruiters' Preferences for Résumé Length," *The Journal of Business Communication*, January 2001, 29–57.

14. Kim Isaacs, "How to Decide on Résumé Length," <http://resume .monster.com/articles/length/> (Retrieved 27 July 2005).

15. Katharine Hansen, "Should You Use a Career Objective on Your Résumé?" *Quintessential Careers* <http://www.quintcareers.co/ resume_objectives.html> (Retrieved 5 October 2004); and Robert Half, "Some Résumé Objectives Do More Harm Than Good," *CareerJournal.com* <http://www.careerjournal.com/jobhunting/ resumes/19971231-half3.html> (Retrieved 5 October 2004).

16. Katharine Hansen, "Should You Use a Career Objective on your Resume?" <http://www.quintcareers.com/resume_objectives.html> (Retrieved 27 July 2005).

17. "Build the Résumé Employers Want," <http://www.jobweb.com/ resources/library/Interviews_Resumes/Build_the_Resume_37_01 .htm> (Retrieved 27 July 2005).

18. Tom Washington, "Effective Résumés Bring Results to Life," *CareerJournal.com*, 13 September 2000 <http://www.careerjournal .com/jobhunting/resumes/20000913-washington.html> (Retrieved 26 July 2005).

19. "Getting Past the Recruiter's In-Box," <http://www.assureconsulting .com/resources/eresumes.shtml> (Retrieved 4 August 2005).

20. Roland E. Kidwell Jr., "'Small' Lies, Big Trouble: The Unfortunate Consequences of Résumé Padding From Janet Cooke to George O'Leary," *Journal of Business Ethics*, May 2004, 175.

21. Cynthia Wright, "Networking, the No. 1 Way to Find a Job," *Chattanooga Times Free Press* (Tennessee), 30 September 2004, E6.

22. "The Hot List: Top Job Boards," *Workforce Management*, 28.

CHAPTER 14

1. Joyce Lain Kennedy, *Job Interviews for Dummies* (New York: Hungry Minds, 2000), 8.

2. Nita Wilmott, "Interviewing Styles: Tips for Interview Approaches" <http://humanresources.about.com/cs/selectionstaffing/a/interviews .htm> (Retrieved 9 August 2005).

3. Ibid.

4. Job-Employment-Guide.com, "Panel Interview" <http://www .job-employment-guide.com/panel-interview.html> (Retrieved 13 August 2005).

5. J. Steven Niznik, "What's a Group Interview?" <http://jobsearchtech .about.com/od/interview/l/aa121602.htm> (Retrieved 13 August 2005).

6. Greenfield Community College Career Center, "Type of Interviews" <http://www.gcc.mass.edu/resources/career/docs/interview.pdf> (Retrieved 13 August 2005).

7. "Face to Face: Interviews With Hiring Professionals at Places You Want to Work, Gap Inc.," provided by WetFeet to *San Francisco Chronicle*, 20 October 2005.

8. Kris Maher, "Job Seekers and Recruiters Pay More Attention to Blogs," 5 October 2005 <http://www.careerjournal.com/jobhunting/ usingnet/20041005-maher .html?jobhunting_whatsnew> (Retrieved 13 August 2005).

9. Steven Richards, "How to Survive an 'Extreme Interview,'" 29 September 1999 <http://www.careerjournal.com/jobhunting/ interviewing/19990929-richards.html> (Retrieved 13 August 2005).

10. Money-Zine.com, "Situational Interview" <http://www.money- zine.com/Definitions/Career-Dictionary/Situational-Interview/> (Retrieved 13 August 2005).

11. Catherine Hansen, "Behavioral Interviewing Strategies" <http://www.quintcareers.com/behavioral_interviewing.html> (Retrieved 13 August 2005).

12. Daisy Wright, "Tell Stories, Get Hired," *OfficePro*, August/September 2004, 32–33.

13. John Kador, *How to Ace the Brain Teaser Interview* (New York: McGraw-Hill, 2005), xi.

14. Kador, 8–10.

15. Kador, 13, 18–19, 21, 53, 58, 91, 96–97.

16. YourLawyer.com, "Overview: Employment Discrimination" <http:// www .yourlawyer.com/practice/overview.htm?topic=Employment% 20Discrimination> (Retrieved 15 August 2005).

17. J. Steven Niznik, "Illegal Interview Questions" <http://jobsearchtech .about.com/od/interview/l/aa022403.htm> (Retrieved 15 August 2005).

18. CollegeGrad.com, "How to Handle Illegal Interview Questions" <http://www.collegegrad.com/ezine/23illega.shtml> (Retrieved 15 August 2005).

19. USAToday.com, "Illegal Interview Questions" <http://www.usatoday .com/careers/resources/interviewillegal.htm>; Tom Washington, "Advice on Answering Illegal Interview Questions <http://www .careerjournal.com/jobhunting/interviewing/19971231-washington .html>; FindLaw.com, "Illegal Interview Questions: Special Considerations for Women" <http://employment.findlaw.com/ articles/2446.html>; Lawyers.com, "Asking the Right Questions" <http://www.lawyers.com/legal_topics/browse_by_topic/browse_ parent/browse_child/content/show_content.php?site=537& articleid=1001412> (All retrieved 15 August 2005).

20. Kathryn Lee Bazen, "The Art of the Follow-Up After Job Interviews" <http://www.quintcareers.com/job_interview_follow-up.html> (Retrieved 15 August 2005).

21. Valerie Patterson, "Earning the Salary You Want in Today's Tough Economy," 30 March 2004 <http://www.careerjournal.com/ salaryhiring/ negotiate/20040330-patterson.html> (Retrieved 15 August 2005).

22. Karass.co.uk, "About Karrass" <http://www.karrass.co.uk/ aboutdrkarrass.htm> (Retrieved 15 August 2005).

23. J. Michael Farr, *The Very Quick Job Search* (Indianapolis: Jist Works, 1991), 177–178; Randall S. Hansen, "Job Offer Too Low? Use These Key Salary Negotiation Techniques to Write a Counter Proposal Letter" <http://www.quintcareers.com/salary_counter_proposal.html>; Randall S. Hansen, "Salary Negotiation Do's and Don'ts" <http://www .quintcareers.com/salary-dos-donts.html>; Susan Ireland, "Salary Negotiation Guide" <http://susanireland.com/ salarywork.html>; James Powell, "Salary Negotiation: The Art of the Deal" <http://www .careerbuilder.com/JobSeeker/CareerBytes/ 0201salarynegotiation .htm?cbRecursionCnt=1&cbsid=9353c1897f6448aea37f320d24e9c6a0- 177456918-rc-1>; and Lee E. Miller, "Eleven Commandments for Smart Negotiating," 24 June 2003 <http://www.careerjournal.com/ salaryhiring/negotiate/20030624-miller.html> (All retrieved 15 August 2005).

Index